SAS ITALIAN JOB

SAS ITALIAN JOB

Damien Lewis

Quercus

First published in Great Britain in 2018 by Quercus.

Quercus Editions Ltd
Carmelite House
50 Victoria Embankment
London EC4Y 0DZ

An Hachette UK company

A CIP catalogue record for this book is available
from the British Library

HB ISBN 978 1 78747 513 7
TPB ISBN 978 1 78747 512 0
Ebook ISBN 978 1 78747 514 4

PICTURE CREDITS

1. Credit/©: Imperial War Museum 2. Credit/©: National Archives and Records Administration. 3. Credit/©: James Selby Bennett 4. Credit/©: http://wio.ru/galgrnd/podryvnk.htm 5. Credit/©: UK Government 6. Credit/©: UK Government 7. Credit/©: Wikimedia 8. Credit/©: Imperial War Museum 9. Credit/©: Don North, from *Inappropriate Conduct* 10. Credit/©: Don North, from *Inappropriate Conduct* 11. Credit/©: Don North, from *Inappropriate Conduct* 12. Credit/©: Don North, from *Inappropriate Conduct* 13. Credit/©: German Federal Archive. 14. Credit/©: Imperial War Museum. 15. Credit/©: Imperial War Museum 16. Credit/©: German Federal Archive 17. Credit/©: Nikki Cartlidge 18. Credit/©: WWII SAS veteran families 19. Credit/©: Lees family 20. Credit/©: National Defence Library and Archives Canada 21. Credit/©: Lees family 22. Credit/©: WWII SAS veteran families. 23. Credit/©: WWII SAS veteran families. 24. Credit/©: Wikimedia 25. Credit/©: Luke Griffiths 26. Credit/©: Lees family 27. Credit/©: Imperial War Museum 28. Credit/©: Imperial War Museum 29. Credit/©: Wikimedia 30. Credit/©: Tara Mulvey 31. Credit/©: US Army 32. Credit/©: WWII SAS veteran families. 33. Credit/©: WWII SAS veteran families. 34. Credit/©: Imperial War Museum 35. Credit/©: Jack Mann 36. Credit/©: Blind Veterans UK

10 9 8 7 6 5 4 3 2 1

Typeset by CC Book Production
Printed and bound in Great Britain by Clays Ltd, Elcograf S.p.A.

For the fallen of the SAS and SOE as depicted in these pages

Major Neville 'Temple' Darewski DSO, SOE
Major Ross Littlejohn MC, SAS
Lieutenant James Riccomini MBE MC, SAS
Serjeant Sidney Guscott, SAS
Corporal Sammy Bolden MM, SAS
Corporal Joseph Crowley, SAS
Lance Corporal Robert Bruce (Balerdi), SAS

And for Michael Lees, SOE, who was
denied a Military Cross at war's end.

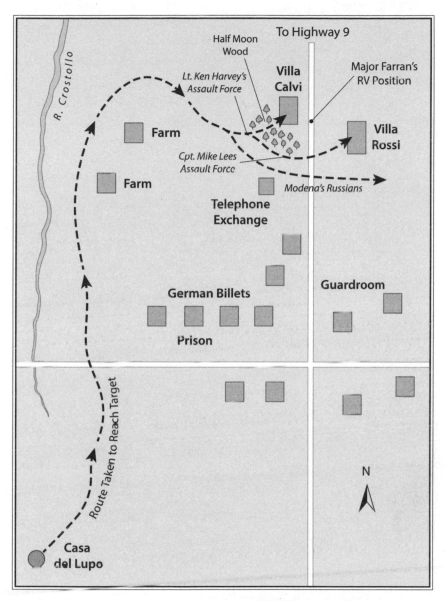

To Highway 9

Half Moon
Wood

Lt. Ken Harvey's
Assault Force

**Villa
Calvi**

Major Farran's
RV Position

R. Crostollo

Farm

**Villa
Rossi**

Cpt. Mike Lees
Assault Force

Farm

Modena's Russians

**Telephone
Exchange**

German Billets

Guardroom

Prison

Route Taken to Reach Target

N

**Casa
del Lupo**

Attack on the German 14 Army Villa Headquarters
(*Adapted from Major Farran's official report on
Operation Tombola*)

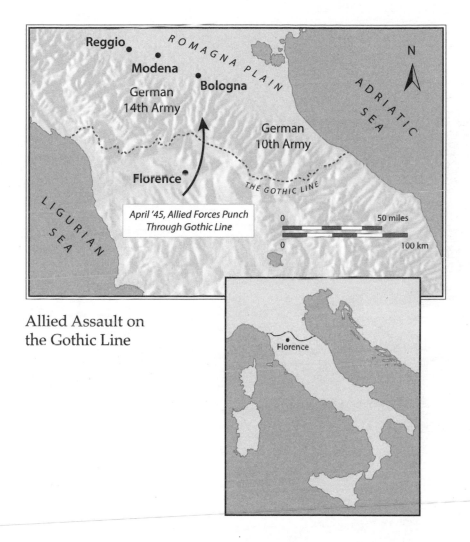

Allied Assault on
the Gothic Line

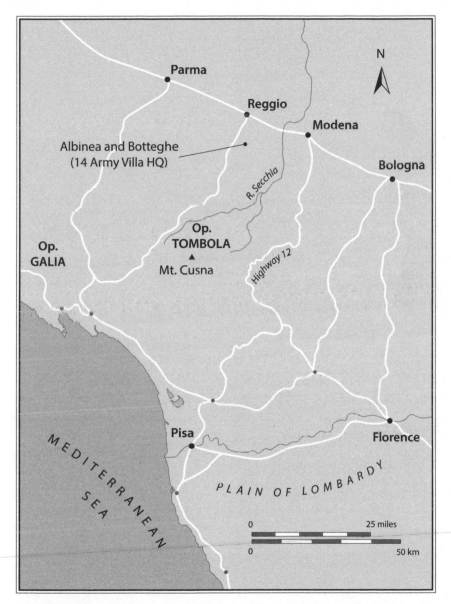

Operations Galia and Tombola – Area of Operations

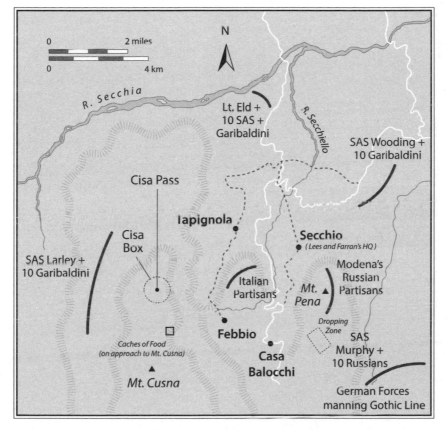

SAS and Partisans' Defence of 'Tombola Valley'

Author's Note

There are sadly few survivors from the Second World War operations depicted in these pages. Throughout the period of researching and writing this book I have endeavoured to be in contact with as many as possible, plus surviving family members of those who have passed away. If there are further witnesses to the stories told here who are inclined to come forward, please do get in touch, as I will attempt to include further recollections of the operations portrayed in this book in future editions.

The time spent by Allied servicemen and women as Special Forces volunteers was often traumatic and wreathed in layers of secrecy, and many chose to take their stories to their graves. Memories tend to differ and apparently none more so than those concerning operations behind enemy lines. The written accounts that do exist also tend to differ in their detail and timescale, and locations and chronologies are often contradictory. That being said, I have endeavoured to provide a proper sense of place, timescale and narrative to the story as depicted in these pages.

Where various accounts of a mission appear to be particularly confused, the methodology I have used to reconstruct where, when and how events took place is the 'most likely' scenario. If two or more testimonies or sources point to a particular time or place or sequence of events, I have opted to use that account as most likely. Very occasionally, I have re-created small sections of dialogue to aid the story's flow.

The above notwithstanding, any mistakes herein are entirely of my own making, and I would be happy to correct any in future editions. Likewise, while I have endeavoured to locate the copyright holders of the photos, sketches and other images and material used in this book, this has not always been straightforward or easy. Again, I would be happy to correct any mistakes in future editions.

Chapter 1

The Italian admiral was a proud man and justifiably so. Before joining the resistance he'd commanded a good proportion of the Italian fleet. Too old to operate like a partisan any more, fighting against an occupying force, his role now was to observe Allied airstrikes from this mountaintop fastness positioned well behind enemy lines, and to radio through battle damage reports to Allied headquarters.

Entirely military-like in his attitude, he had an eye for detail and for range and bearing that made him ideally suited to his task. But on this late-September evening in 1944 he'd put away his binoculars, turning his mind to entirely different and more urgent matters.

Captain Michael Lees felt the admiral's firm grip shaking him awake. He'd been drifting into sleep, hoping for a rare night uninterrupted by enemy ambushes, shellfire or raids. It was remarkable how comfortable a rickety old hayloft could prove, after so many weeks living rough behind enemy lines. It made a passable billet for himself, assorted Brits and other nationalities who'd come here to assist the Italian partisans, striking with lightning speed from the mountains.

'There's a message from Major Temple,' the admiral hissed. 'You're to get to his headquarters immediately.'

Lees fumbled for his boots, hurrying to pull them on in the

chill night air, the admiral's tone reflecting the import of the major's summons. In Major Darewski – 'Temple' was his operational cover name – Lees had discovered a fellow adventurer who hungered for action. After parachuting into the unknown and executing a tortuous and perilous route to get here, Lees was keen to lead the kind of guerrilla operations for which Major Temple was famed.

Lacing up his boots and pulling on a jacket, he set off at a run. The path ahead glistened blue-white in the moonlight, the night beautifully starlit and crystal clear. As his feet pounded upon the rough, stony ground, Lees felt the excitement rising within him. He wondered what might lie behind the major's summons. It was either a juicy sabotage mission, or perhaps the Germans were launching a sweep through the valley, in an attempt to encircle the partisans, in which case they would need to act swiftly to organise their defences.

Such efforts as this – to raise, train and arm the Italian partisans for war – were largely at the behest of Winston Churchill. The Allied invasion of Italy in the summer of 1943 had been at Churchill's urging, designed to drive a dagger into the 'soft underbelly of Europe'. By doing so, Britain's wartime leader intended to strike at Nazi Germany via Italy, so splitting the enemy's defences in the run-up to the D-Day landings. Initially the proposal had met with fierce opposition, especially from the Americans. By way of response Churchill had sketched out a picture of a crocodile, pointing out how it was just as good to strike at the belly as the snout.

Eventually the Americans had been convinced that hitting Europe's 'soft underbelly' was the right thing to do. Yet despite early successes in southern Italy, the Italian campaign had proven anything but 'soft'. Hitler had little intention of leaving the back door to Europe open. He'd rushed reinforcements into the country, the Germans fighting a series of die-hard battles, first under the command of General Erwin Rommel, and then under another of Hitler's favourites, Field Marshal Albert Kesselring.

Come the approach of winter, the Allied advance had stalled on the Gothic Line, a string of formidable defences – thousands of machine-gun bunkers, concrete gun emplacements, deep tunnels, minefields and razor wire – stretching from coast to coast across northern Italy's Apennine mountains. The forces manning the Gothic Line were some of Germany's finest. They included the 1st and 4th Parachute Divisions, arguably some of the best troops in the Reich, plus two *Panzergrenadier* – mechanised infantry – divisions equipped with heavy armour.

All of Italy south of the Gothic Line had been seized in fearsome fighting by the Allies. But territory to the north of the line remained in enemy hands, excepting pockets of remote, mountainous territory held by the Italian resistance – Major Temple's mission being one such example. At Churchill's urging, the partisans were being armed and trained to rise up in the enemy's rear, to help achieve a decisive breakthrough. Lees and Temple's operation, headquartered towards the western end of the Apennines and just to the rear of the Gothic Line, was intended to strike hard at enemy lines of supply and communications.

Whatever tonight's mission, Lees felt an immense sense of respect and camaraderie for Major Temple, who'd already won a DSO (Distinguished Service Order) in the war. Formerly an officer with airborne forces, but now serving as an agent with the Special Operations Executive (SOE) – Churchill's shadowy 'Ministry for Ungentlemanly Warfare' – Lees was second-in-command here, and in Major Temple he believed he had found a real kindred spirit.

On his earliest operations with the SOE, Lees had earned the nickname 'Mickey Mouse'. It was Yugoslav guerrillas who had coined the name, Mickey Mouse being the only 'Michael' they had ever heard of. But there had been nothing Mickey Mouse about the long months Lees had spent soldiering with them: he'd led dozens of dramatic raids on enemy railway tracks, blowing trains laden with war materiel to smithereens.

When told to cease offensive operations with the Yugoslav guerrillas, Lees had decided to interpret his orders rather literally: he'd stopped working with the resistance, launching a string of solo sabotage missions instead, ones of breathtaking – some might argue suicidal – daring. In doing so he'd earned a somewhat more apposite nickname – Michael 'Wild Man' Lees. His linking up with Major Temple promised fireworks and heroics in equal measure.

With delicious irony, Temple's mission had been codenamed Operation Flap. In truth, no one was inclined to 'get a flap on' with Temple – or Lees – in command. At thirty years of age, Major Neville Lawrence Darewski was comparatively old for an SOE operative. (By contrast, Lees was still in his early twenties.) The son of Polish-born Herman Darewski, a famous music hall musician of the time, and the English actress Madge Temple, it was from her that Darewski had coined his *nom de guerre*.

Major Temple had been operating behind the lines for months now. He'd parachuted in to link up with the partisans prior to Italy's signing the 3 September 1943 Armistice of Cassibile, in which the Italian people had renounced their deal with the devil – the alliance with Nazi Germany and Japan, forming the Axis Powers – surrendering to the Allies.

The signing of the Armistice was a watershed moment, as far as Temple was concerned. Prior to that, he'd reported to SOE headquarters on what a perilous existence he'd been forced to lead with the partisans. It was a 'cloak-and-dagger affair, only moving at night . . . minimum of smoke from fires, kit always ready for immediate move . . . I covered some one thousand miles on foot carrying my kit and arms . . . We had to cross rivers, roads and railways all held by the Germans . . . in small, very mobile parties . . .'

Come the Armistice, all that had changed. Temple had urged his partisans to seize the moment and embrace the spirit of resistance. Taking advantage of the ensuing confusion, he'd led his band of fighters to strike at a major airbase lying just to the rear of the Gothic Line, in a daring mission that had proven spectacularly successful.

'We surrounded the airfield and held it for long enough to destroy eighty-nine Italian planes on the ground, and all the hangars and buildings,' Temple had reported. Then with characteristic flair: 'We flew away one CR.42 to start the Partisan Air Force . . .'

In destroying those dozens of enemy warplanes, Temple's operation was on a par with some of the most successful raids of the war. The lone CR.42 *Falco* – Falcon – that his force had liberated was a biplane fighter widely used by the Italian air force. Despite its seemingly archaic design, it had scored an enviable kill ratio on many fronts due to its robustness and manoeuvrability.

In the aftermath of the raid, Temple's forces had been hunted remorselessly by the German military using armour, artillery and dive bombers. The lone CR.42 *Falco* that they'd 'liberated' was blown up by a tank. Temple responded in textbook fashion: 'We withdrew from direct offensive tactics and went back to guerrilla warfare.' While the enemy held the main population centres, his bands of partisans began to tighten their grip on the remoter villages and hills.

'Outside the perimeter of the towns the Germans put up notices: BEWARE, YOU ARE NOW ENTERING BANDIT TER- RITORY,' Temple reported of the time. He sent out his men at night to turn the signs around, so that 'BANDIT TERRITORY' became the German-held towns. 'The Hun got very annoyed and threatened the direst of penalties to anyone caught doing this,' Temple pointed out, which only served to encourage him.

By late September 1944, Major Temple was master of all that he surveyed. Set at an altitude of some 3,000 feet, his headquarters lay in a mountain hut nicknamed 'The Farm'. It boasted views across the plains to Turin – once Italy's capital, and a major busi- ness hub – and the Alps beyond. On a clear day the glistening peaks of Mont Blanc and the Matterhorn were visible. On a flat patch of ground several thousand feet higher Temple had estab- lished his dropping zone (DZ), into which the Allies were flying loads of kit, explosives and weaponry.

From their Apennine valley fortress Temple's 500-strong band of partisans launched daring raids, using captured vehicles to execute fast hit-and-run strikes. As Mike Lees was about to learn, Temple's night-time summons was the result of one such recent mission.

After thirty minutes dashing through the moonlit landscape, Lees arrived at The Farm. Typically, he was in standard British battledress. By contrast, Major Temple cut a very different kind of a figure. A big part of Temple's remit here was intelligence- gathering, and he'd just paid a clandestine visit to Turin disguised as a local. Such derring-do was all part of a normal day's work as far as Temple was concerned. With his dark looks plus his tanned and weather-beaten features, he could easily pass as a local.

'Dressed as he was,' Lees remarked of Temple that evening, 'he could never have been recognised as an Englishman.'

At well over six foot and with a broad, rugby-player's physique, Lees towered over most of his contemporaries. Blessed with no-nonsense, honest looks, he was a man born and bred for plain-speaking action, as opposed to subterfuge. Hailing from a family with a long history of soldiering, he had cousins and even a sister serving with elite forces in various theatres of the war.

Temple and Lees had operated together for little more than three weeks here, and for much of that time Temple had been away in Turin on clandestine business. It was precious little time to really get to know each other. Temple viewed Lees as a hard and a tough operator, but what he was about to propose would test any man's resolve. It would be the measure of Lees as to whether he accepted the mission. No man could be ordered to do as Temple intended, especially as all in SOE were volunteers.

'Sorry to drag you out at this time of night,' Temple began, 'but we've got an important decision to make.'

As he spoke, he gestured at the two – presumably Italian – civilians who were with him. Lees had never laid eyes on either of them. They were older, better dressed and somehow more distinguished looking than your average partisan. Lees closed the door firmly behind him, sensing that tonight's business was especially sensitive. Temple introduced the two strangers, using their war names only.

'Salvi' and 'Piva' hailed from Turin, he explained, and they were senior members of the Italian resistance. They had crucial intelligence that they somehow needed to get into Allied commanders' hands. 'This information from Turin is red hot . . . they also know a lot about enemy dispositions and weaknesses . . . They've volunteered to go to southern Italy if we can get them out.'

'How d'you intend to do that?' Lees queried. 'By air?'

The partisans were busy building an airstrip so Allied cargo planes could land with supplies, but Lees didn't think it was going to be ready for some time.

Temple waved a hand dismissively. 'We can't wait for that . . . They'll have to walk out through the lines.' He paused. 'Salvi and Piva are damned important, and I don't want them falling by the wayside. It's going to prove a tricky journey, especially as there are no guides who've been through before, and the front is always changing.' Temple gazed at Lees, searchingly. 'I need someone who knows the ropes to command the party.'

By now Lees realised what was afoot. 'Would you like me to go?' he ventured.

Someone had to say it, even though it would mean attempting to cross the formidable defences of the Gothic Line. It had never occurred to him that this might be the kind of mission he would be offered. Indeed, he had been looking forward to waging war with the partisans, making life a living hell for the enemy until all of Italy was liberated from Nazi control.

As if sensing what was on Lees' mind, Temple began outlining exactly what he intended, stressing just how quickly Lees could return. 'You get the party through to France – if you're with them they won't get held up by security. Beg a plane to take you all to southern Italy, report on everything we've been doing to the chaps at base and chivvy them up to send more supplies. Then come back again, dropping with the first sortie.'

8

That was more like it, as far as Lees was concerned. 'All right, I think it's an excellent idea,' he agreed, his spirits brightening.

He had another, personal reason for accepting the mission. Shortly before deploying Lees had married Gwendoline Johnson, who was serving with the First Aid Nursing Yeomanry – the FANYs – in Italy. To a large degree the FANYs provided cover for women who were serving as SOE agents. He and 'Gwen' had met during a time when Lees had been agitating to join Temple's mission and refusing to take the leave to which he was entitled, post-Yugoslavia. That had only served to fuel his 'wild man' reputation, but Gwen hadn't seemed to mind.

Indeed, as she was serving as an assistant to one of SOE's key planners in Italy, she began quietly lobbying for her sweetheart to land a mission with Temple, despite the fact that it would take him behind the lines once more. If he took up Temple's present proposal, Lees figured he could catch a few days in his wife's delightful company, before flying back to rejoin the partisans.

'Just make sure you come back as soon as you can,' Temple reminded him.

'Don't worry,' Lees replied, 'I want to be in at the kill. So, when do we start?'

'How does tomorrow morning sound?'

All being well, Lees would set out to cross the lines on 28 September 1944.

For Temple, Lees was the only man able to execute such a hazardous mission. In addition to the two Italian resistance leaders, he would be leading a group of fourteen, including escaped prisoners of war and downed US airmen. Brits, Americans, Australians, French and Italians, his was a distinctly motley escape party, many of whom had little military training of the type required to sneak through enemy territory. It would take superlative leadership skills, immense daring and real single-minded tenacity to shepherd such a disparate party to safety.

Fortunately, Lees had such attributes in abundance. Following the long months that he'd spent in Yugoslavia, none other than Major General Colin McVean Gubbins – known simply as 'M' and the head of SOE – had poured lavish praise on the young Lees, then only twenty-one years of age. 'An enthusiastic and reliable officer. Had a difficult area in southern Serbia and did all he could to carry out operations there against the Axis . . . most successfully maintained good relations between the Mission and Jugoslav forces . . . has plenty of go and initiative.'

Scion of a titled, landed family hailing from Lytchett Minster, a village in deepest rural Dorset, Lees' means of recruitment into the SOE had been highly unconventional. In 1943 he'd been kicking his heels in Cairo, lamenting the lack of action he seemed to be getting with regular forces, when he'd ended up in Shepherd's Bar, one of the city's more popular drinking dens. He'd got talking to an intriguing individual who'd let slip that he served with 'the Tweed Cap Boys'. Upon learning that this mysterious force was sending in lone operators to Europe charged to wage war no-holds-barred, Lees desperately wanted in.

He'd never for one moment imagined there might be scope for himself to operate deep inside enemy-occupied Europe. It was a tantalising proposition. He proceeded to get that 'Tweed Cap Boy' as drunk as possible, all the while pumping him for information. It turned out that the route into the SOE was somewhat convoluted. It was hardly possible to advertise for volunteers to join a secret service that was not supposed to exist: you could only be recruited at the personal behest of someone already in.

As Lees wasn't personally known to any of this exclusive club, he decided to manufacture a 'recommendation' from his new Shepherd's Bar acquaintance. Learning that he was just about to take several weeks' leave, a day or so later Lees brazenly walked into the SOE'S Cairo office, claiming to be there at the personal behest of a 'schoolboy chum' – in truth, the man he'd met in the Cairo bar. He even had a freshly-forged letter to back up his claims.

To those charged to investigate Lees' story, it appeared to have merit. He hailed from the right kind of background. He'd been educated at Ampleforth – the Roman Catholic boarding school known as the 'Catholic Eton', of which David Stirling, the founder of the SAS, was a fellow alumnus – plus the Lees family was steeped in military tradition. Grandson of Sir Elliott Lees, the First Baronet of Lytchett Minster, Michael's father, Bernard Percy Turnbull Lees, had served with distinction in the Queen's Own Dorset Yeomanry during the First World War, winning a Military Cross (MC).

Bernard Lees had died in a shooting accident when Michael was just two years old, so he had never got to know his father. After the tragic loss, Michael had grown very close to his cousin James Lees – direct heir to the baronetcy – hunting, fishing and riding together in the Dorset countryside. They'd become inseparable, to the extent that James's father had become an honorary guardian to Michael. Bereft of a father and brought up by his widowed mother and elder sister, Dolores, Lees was effectively the man of the house and felt fiercely protective over all. When he was just twelve, he caught an older boy trying to kiss his sister. He stepped forward and punched the boy firmly on the chin.

Lees hungered for more male and martial company, which was largely why at age seventeen he'd joined the Queen's Own Dorset Yeomanry, the regiment that his father and grandfather had served in, before volunteering for airborne forces at the outbreak of war and being posted to India and Egypt.

Michael's sister Dolores would serve as a nurse with both the French Army and later the French resistance (the Maquis), with whom she would earn the Croix de Guerre twice – once for walking into a minefield to rescue a wounded comrade. Michael Lees' cousin, James, was also about to start serving on special operations. At the very moment that Michael was trying to blag his way into the SOE in Cairo, James was volunteering for the Special Boat Service (SBS), the sister regiment to the SAS, which specialised in daring seaborne sorties.

The Lees family pile, the grand edifice of South Lytchett Manor, had been turned over to war use, the grounds harbouring American tanks and the house itself becoming war offices. Likewise, during the First World War the Manor had served the war effort, being transformed into a hospital for those evacuated from the battlefields of France. In short, the Lees family was steeped in the kind of special duty warfare of which Churchill would be proud, but that didn't earn anyone an automatic right to join an outfit like the Tweed Cap Boys.

With Lees' 'sponsor' away on leave, he performed a sterling act at the SOE's Cairo office. After several robust cross examinations, he'd bluffed his way in. His SOE recruitment file listed Lees' 'Hobbies and Sporting Interests: Riding, shooting, running, rugby football, fishing, skiing, driving, sailing.' His subsequent SOE training courses included: 'April '43, Para Military. May '43, "Cloak & Dagger". July '44, Lysander – Above Average.' (The

Westland Lysander – nicknamed the 'Lissie' – was a light aircraft used for inserting lone SOE agents into enemy-occupied lands.)

At grand country mansions scattered across Britain the SOE had established their Special Training Schools – teaching the dark arts of killing, sabotage, espionage, deception and more. In what became known as their 'school for mayhem and murder', at the apparently genteel Ashdon Manor, in Hertfordshire, recruits were trained to fight 'without a tremor of apprehension, to hurt, maul, injure or kill with ease.' Instructors taught killing by silent strangulation, how to disable with a powerful blow by boot or fist to key organs, and how to wield a pistol fast and deadly, shooting from the hip. In a pistol duel, the first on the draw was almost always the winner, and by firing from the hip the shooter was very likely to get the drop on his or her opponent.

One such school, in Borehamwood, was devoted entirely to the arts of camouflage and subterfuge in all its forms. Part of its remit was to furnish agents with proper clothing, documents and accoutrements, before they were dropped into occupied Europe. Whenever the genuine article wasn't available, the SOE's forgery factory would rustle up a convincing copy. At MD1, an SOE facility nicknamed 'Churchill's Toyshop', boffins and inventors worked on perfecting the most secretive and innovative forms of weaponry. These included booby-trapped rats and animal droppings, plus exploding 'coal' – the latter to be slipped into the fuel supply of an enemy train, so blowing up the steam engines.

After passing through various such training schools, Lees was ready to pursue Churchill's 1940 edict – issued during Britain's darkest hour, following Dunkirk and the surrender of France – 'to set Europe ablaze'. The formation of the SOE – after the Army, Navy and Air Force, the 'fourth armed service' – was in response to such calls. Gubbins defined the SOE's early remit as being 'paramilitary and irregular warfare, the sabotaging and subversion of our enemies by every possible means . . . a free-for-all . . . with no holds barred. Germany was engaged in total war . . . and total war is a very cruel business indeed.'

The SOE was a secret service whose very existence was deniable. The normal rules of war would not apply. In the SOE's version of total war, the unethical and illegal were to be commonplace. Agents were expected to lie, deceive, bribe, blackmail, and where necessary, assassinate and kill. If captured, an agent would be disowned by his or her government, and torture and execution would doubtless follow. Before deploying on his first mission, Lees, like all agents, had been given 'communion' – a suicide pill that he could take if he feared he was about to break under torture.

The SOE recruited from a broad church. Its early volunteers included actors, professional burglars, peers of the realm, a rubber-goods salesman, several baronets, a pimp, prostitutes, jockeys, art experts and bankers. They shared certain traits in common: robust independence of mind and contempt for regular hierarchies.

Gubbins exhorted those early recruits to execute 'sabotage, ambushes behind enemy lines, and calling out secret armies into open warfare'. By the autumn of 1944, the SOE'S Italian operations had become deeply personal for 'M'. In the spring of that year, his son Michael had been killed in Italy on SOE business. On 6 February he was hit by a German shell while operating behind the lines. Gubbins had received the news of his son's death via telegram, with its 'killed in action' message, and a hand-scribbled expression of 'deepest sympathy'. He had been consumed by grief and remorse.

All the more important, therefore, that the SOE's Italian operations were to succeed, and to be *seen* to succeed. One of the SOE's most secretive remits had become the spreading of 'black' and 'white' propaganda. The latter involved placing positive stories about the fortunes of the Allies in the press, and negative ones about the Axis powers, while the former spread disinformation among enemy ranks. There was another top-secret priority behind Michael Lees' Italian mission: it was to further the SOE's 'white propaganda' role.

When Lees had parachuted in to join Temple, in August 1944, he'd brought with him two highly unusual individuals: South African war artist Geoffrey Long, and Canadian war reporter Paul Morton. Of the two, Morton, a globetrotting newspaper man, was perhaps the more controversial. He was the first reporter ever embedded with a behind-the-lines SOE mission, and few would follow.

That summer, Churchill had decided that the Italian partisans deserved a far higher profile, both to encourage them in their operations and to spur Allied forces to train and arm them properly. A former war reporter himself, Churchill believed wholeheartedly in the need to win the 'information war'. Borrowing a phrase from Stalin, he believed that 'in wartime, the truth is so precious she should be attended by a bodyguard of lies.'

The Political Warfare Executive (PWE) was the arm of the SOE established to ensure that the information war would be won. In the summer of 1944, Paul Morton had been based in Italy, fearing the real war was passing him by. Desperate for a scoop, when the Political Warfare Executive approached him with their offer – that he should join Captain Lees to report from behind the lines – Morton jumped at the chance.

Morton's bona fides were exhaustively checked. Dated 4 July, his SOE 'Trace and Card' – his vetting form – recorded that he'd spent 'Ten Years with the Toronto Daily Star', and was a 'War Correspondent accredited to Canadian forces'. It noted that his brother, David Morton, was 'possibly in enemy hands (reported missing two months ago over North Sea)'. Morton had personal reasons to hate the enemy, and he was a seasoned reporter with one of Canada's most respected publications. On paper, he was the ideal recruit.

By 6 July Morton had been signed up as an 'attached correspondent' with 'Maryland', the codename for the SOE in Italy. Shortly thereafter he was issued with his SOE 'Operational Instruction'. It read: 'To provide the Press an account of patriot activities and sabotage exploits . . . You will be dropped to [Operation] FLAP . . . in the September moon period . . . On arrival you will ask for Major TEMPLE and will put yourself under his command.'

Morton was given the honorary rank of Captain, armed and expected to fight if the need arose. His reporting was to be syndicated – distributed – to all Allied press outlets, promising a series of global scoops. It was heady stuff. Six weeks after parachuting in with Lees, Morton had prepared a series of scintillating articles, describing in vivid tones the heroic exploits of the partisans – including one episode in which they'd surrounded enemy forces holed up in a church, and wiped them out to the last man.

He'd given his first article the dramatic headline, 'I LIVE WITH PATRIOTS IN NAZI LINES – MORTON'. In short, Morton was poised to fire a propaganda broadside, showcasing the daring and panache of the Italian resistance. Geoffrey Long, the war artist, had drawn a series of brilliant sketches to illustrate, including one of the partisans scavenging boots and explosives from the enemy dead, and portraits of the key Allied players – Morton, Temple and Lees included.

But Morton and Long's stories and images – their white propaganda – would only get to hit the press if Lees managed to shepherd them through the lines, for they were to join his escape party.

It was dawn on 29 September when the group formed up. They'd been delayed for twenty-four hours by the late arrival of some. As Lees surveyed his men, he was assailed by doubts as to whether they really could complete such an unproven route passing through such formidable defences. Temple sought to calm his fears. If it reached the stage where Lees felt it necessary, he was to drop all but the essential members.

Even so, Lees decided that he really did need a trusted pair of hands to share the load. Glaswegian William McClelland was six-foot-six tall and about as broad in the shoulder, dwarfing even Lees. His craggy, bearded features, snaggle-toothed grin and dress – shorts, ski boots, faded battledress tunic adorned with the Scots Guards insignia, and slung Sten gun – lent him a decidedly piratical air. It was absolutely fitting.

Captured by Rommel's Afrika Korps when serving in North Africa, Private McClelland had escaped from an Italian prisoner of war (POW) camp and fled into the mountains, linking up with the partisans. Over the past year he'd hijacked vehicles, kidnapped their occupants and raided Nazi cellars. His favourite occupation was ambushing German staff cars, finishing off the officers, then rifling the pockets of the dead. When one partisan band had run short of funds, he'd done the obvious thing and organised a bank robbery.

In short, McClelland was a freelance raider who owed no particular allegiance to any one partisan unit. He and Lees had hit it off immediately. 'He was a bandit, not a partisan,' Lees remarked of McClelland. 'Whatever his intentions, he was doing far more for the war effort than he could have done serving as an ordinary private . . . One William in the mountains was an incomparable asset, but thirty Williams in barracks would provide a problem with which I should hate to be faced . . .'

The other redoubtable operator Lees would have liked to join his party was Corporal Albert 'Bert' Farrimond, a dour Lancashire coal miner in civilian life, who'd proved as constant and unyielding as the moors in recent weeks. Hailing from Standish, near Wigan, Farrimond was a keen poacher who loved the wild freedom of the mountains. He and Lees had formed a special bond, but as Farrimond was Major Temple's radio operator – his vital link to SOE's Maryland headquarters – he was one man that was unable to join Lees.

His party thus assembled, it only left to bid farewell.

Temple offered a hand. 'Goodbye, old cock, and good luck. We'll expect you back in a couple of weeks.'

Little did Lees realise this was the last time he would ever see the man alive.

Lees turned away, taking a well-trodden bridleway that climbed into the hills. He'd opted to travel light, urging his party to do likewise. He was carrying only his trusty Sten gun, with the detachable wooden pistol-grip that he favoured, plus ammunition and a rolled blanket. The days were still relatively hot, so he wore shorts and a khaki shirt. The skies above were a cloudless blue and they'd rely on good weather to see them through.

At the head of the valley they paused by a goat herd, to refresh themselves with milk. Before them the path rose to a steep ridge several miles away. They were making for a pass set at some 6,000 feet, after which they'd descend to a mountain village on the far side. But as Lees gazed at the heights, they appeared to be wreathed in swirling cloud. It looked ominous: he knew how quickly the weather could turn in the mountains. He urged everyone on.

As they climbed towards the pass the sky overhead took on a dull grey hue and the first snow began to fall. The wind picked up, whipping icy flakes against Lees' bare legs, forming stiff little icicles. He cursed the fact that they had set out so ill-prepared and chiefly at his urging. It wasn't long before they had their first casualty. Long, the war artist, took a fall on the icy ground, bruising his spine. His pack and weaponry had to be passed to one of the guides, for he was in some pain.

Lees closed the column up, so they would not lose sight of each other in the gathering storm. But Long was soon at the very back, finding it difficult to keep moving. They reached a perilous section of terrain that required the use of both hands and feet to scale it. Lees had scrambled halfway up, when he heard the shrill blast of a whistle from behind, which normally signalled that someone was in trouble.

Holding onto a rocky outcrop, he craned his neck to see through the swirling snow. He counted heads: four were missing. Among their number were Long and Morton, the two press men.

Telling the guides to climb to a ledge one hundred feet above, Lees doubled back. It wasn't long before he found the errant four. They were slumped on a rock beside the path, smoking.

'What the devil are you doing here?' he demanded. 'No halt has been called.'

19

'Geoffrey's hurt,' Morton countered. 'I gave the order to stop.'

'I know,' Lees fired back, 'but you'll keep going 'til I order otherwise.'

Morton bristled. 'I'm an honorary captain, and as such I will not place myself under your command.'

Lees drew himself to his full height. 'I don't give a damn who you are or what you write. While you're with my party you'll do as you're told. So make your mind up: d'you want to continue, or go back to Temple?'

Morton glared at Lees, but the other three had already capitulated. Long and his two companions began to struggle onwards. Lees was deadly serious. On a mission such as this, he needed absolute clarity of command. If he and Morton were to pull in opposite directions, one or other party might get lost in the snows or blunder into enemy positions. Muttering darkly, Morton levered himself to his feet, before turning into the storm's icy blast. Lees felt a flood of relief. As he well knew, time was set against them now.

If they didn't reach the pass before the snow began to drift they were as good as finished.

Chapter 2

Major Roy Farran was already a legend within SAS circles, but even by his own standards this morning's mission was something of a stretch. During August and September 1944 he'd led a column of jeeps – the SAS's C Squadron – in a mission code-named Operation Wallace, breaking out from the bulge of terrain seized in the D-Day landings and pushing two hundred miles behind enemy lines.

His orders were simplicity itself: he and his men were to cause chaos and havoc behind the German front in north-eastern France, to give the impression that Allied forces had broken through and spreading panic through the enemy ranks. Hence today's daring assault on the German garrison headquarters, situated in the ancient town of Châtillon-sur-Seine, lying 250 kilometres east of Paris, a town graced with Roman-era cobbled streets and buildings.

The plans for the dawn assault had been hatched with Colonel Claude, the leader of the local Maquis – the French resistance – the previous evening, over a sumptuous dinner complemented by several bottles of fine wine. Late into the proceedings and partly inspired by Dutch courage, Farran had proposed they hit Châtillon in an all-out attack, Maquis and SAS united, and while the change of garrison was in full swing.

One hundred and fifty enemy troops were based at the

centuries-old Château du Maréchal Marmont, situated on a low hill surrounded by fine parkland. Built in the 1700s by the French General Auguste Frédéric Louis Viesse de Marmont, a native of the town, the chateau had been burned to the ground and rebuilt some seventy years earlier. Farran sensed that now was the time to have another go at wrecking the place, or at least killing its occupants.

Equipped with twenty army trucks, the German garrison housed at the chateau was about to be relieved by a unit of *Panzergrenadiers*, a mechanised infantry force riding in specialist combat vehicles, including *Sonderkraftfahrzeug* 251 half-track troop carriers. The previous day Farran and Captain Grant Hibbert – his second-in-command – had carried out a recce. After driving into town in their SAS jeep, Farran had covered Hibbert as he'd vaulted over the chateau's perimeter wall and checked out the trucks in the courtyard.

The alarm having been raised, the two SAS commanders had high tailed it out of there, but not before the recce had served its purpose. The intelligence they'd been given had proved correct: the column of trucks was laden with equipment for a garrison poised to move. One German unit was about to be replaced by another at the chateau, and amid the confusion of that change-over Farran sensed they could seize the advantage.

Colonel Claude had expressed suitable enthusiasm for Farran's plan, and toasts had been drunk long into the night. The colonel had pledged to provide five hundred local fighters, to match Farran's sixty SAS spread across a dozen-odd jeeps. The vehicles' raw firepower helped compensate for the SAS's paucity in numbers. Each Willys Jeep boasted two pivot-mounted weapons, often a heavier Browning machine gun matched with the rapid-firing Vickers K, invariably mounted in pairs. As such, they could put down a devastating field of fire.

Farran's intention was to keep it simple for this morning's attack. His men would seize the main junction on the outskirts of town, on the road leading south to the city of Dijon. Leaving some jeeps to hold that vital position – through which the German vehicles carrying the incoming garrison would have to pass – Farran would lead a party further into town, armed with mortars and Bren light machine guns. They would sneak up to the chateau on foot, the first round fired by the mortar signalling the all-out assault.

Setting out at 0630 hours from their deep woodland hideout, the column of SAS jeeps nosed through scenery typical of the region – small green fields, thick hedges and red-tiled cottages, set amid gently rolling, wooded hills. Farran kept the convoy's speed at a steady crawl. The roads were dry and earthy from the long summer months, and he needed to avoid throwing up a tell-tale dust cloud, which might reveal their position to any watching enemy.

The Châtillon road junction was taken without a shot being fired. Farran left Lieutenant 'Big' Jim Mackie – his long-standing right-hand man, who commanded his lead 'scout' vehicle – in charge of the roadblock, while he led the main force of forty men riding in nine jeeps further into town. Ominously, there was still no sign of Colonel Claude's Maquis, but Farran put that down to a delayed start due to the previous night's carousing.

At each road junction he left a jeep and a handful of men, so securing their route of retreat. They reached the main square seemingly without having been detected, cutting telephone lines as they went. Up ahead lay the chateau. It was the obvious place to billet a garrison: grandiose and thick-walled, boasting turrets, spires and parapets, it was a veritable fortress.

Of course, the beautiful grounds and approach would be guarded by enemy sentries, but that was where the mortar would come into its own. Farran intended to strike from a distance and by utter surprise, lobbing in as many rounds as possible to spread chaos among a garrison who would be in the midst of loading up in preparation for the move.

At seven sharp the mortar barrage began. By now Farran's men were experts in quick-fire shoot-n'-scoot tactics. Within minutes several dozen of the 3-inch shells had pounded into the chateau's courtyard, their high-explosive charges sending a swathe of razor-sharp shrapnel tearing through the air and ripping into the column of trucks. Hit by utter surprise, this was some awakening for the garrison. Chaos ensued as Farran ordered his Bren-gunners to open fire, raking the chateau's defenders with savage bursts.

The narrow, twisting streets of the town echoed with the deafening noise of battle – the rattle of the Brens, the rasp of the Vickers, the howl of rounds ricocheting off walls, and behind it all the deeper bass thud of the mortars, as one-by-one the high explosive shells hammered into the chateau's grounds. Towards his rear, Farran sensed the grunt of powerful diesel engines. Sure enough and bang on cue, the column of thirty vehicles was approaching from the south, bearing the *Panzergrenadier* relief column.

At this moment, Farran's sixty-strong force was outnumbered some five-to-one by the enemy, and it was high time that Colonel Claude's Maquis put in an appearance. But still there was no sign of them. Taking his jeep, Farran raced back towards the crossroads, where he'd left the redoubtable Big Jim Mackie in control. It was vital to stop that *Panzergrenadier* column from linking up with the forces presently under siege at the chateau.

As Farran neared the junction, he sensed there was little need for worry: typically, Lieutenant Mackie had it all under control. He'd positioned his own jeep to form the core of the roadblock, with a second set to one side. Those manning the guns allowed the enemy column to approach to within twenty yards, before opening up with an utterly devastating broadside. Within seconds, a whirlwind of fire had torn into the leading vehicles, two of which happened to be laden with stores. Moments later fuel and ammunition detonated in a sea of flame, exploding rounds tearing into the vehicles further along the column.

With the telephone lines cut, the *Panzergrenadiers* had been taken by total surprise. They'd driven into town unawares, presuming the SAS jeeps had to constitute some kind of a friendly checkpoint. It was an easy-enough mistake to have made: who would ever have expected to encounter an enemy roadblock this far behind their own front line?

'The first five trucks, two of which were loaded with ammunition, were brewed up and caused a great firework display,' was how the SAS operational report described the ambush. The jeeps hammered in fire, raking the column from either side. 'Those added to the fire, which the Germans returned, and for some time the fierce engagement continued . . . Fierce street fighting developed . . .'

Farran grabbed a Bren and, balancing it on a convenient wall, he began to hose down the trucks to the rear of the *Panzergrenadier* column. He watched as a German motorcycle-and-sidecar combination veered across the road and toppled over a bridge, plummeting into the river below. As Farran pumped in bursts of tracer rounds – following the red streak of the bullets to their targets – he saw figures bailing out of vehicles at the rear of the stalled column.

Machine guns opened up from the direction of the besieged convoy and mortars crashed down onto the streets. One of Farran's men collapsed, felled by a shot to the head. A brave French civilian dashed out and dragged his bloodied form into the shelter of a doorway. A pretty, dark-haired woman wearing a dashing red dress leaned out of an upper floor window, defiantly giving the 'V' for Victory sign. To Farran, that woman's smile and her poise offered the perfect riposte to the bursts of fire now tearing down the streets.

A runner approached from the direction of the chateau. He brought word that a force of Germans had broken out of the grounds and were fighting their way towards Farran's position. One SAS jeep had been hit, in a situation that was fast-moving and confused. The enemy had even begun to mortar their own side, mistaking the fire from the chateau as being that of the mystery Allied attack force.

Even so, Farran's men were going to be hard-pressed to defend their positions. He sent a jeep to reinforce those at the chateau, with orders that they should hold firm. His priority was to decimate what was left of the *Panzergrenadier* column, and to do that they had to stop the two forces uniting. At the same time his chief concern was becoming the absent Maquis. Where on earth was Colonel Claude and the five hundred fighters that he had promised?

As the battle intensified, Farran sensed his SAS squadron was in danger of becoming trapped – sandwiched between the Germans advancing from the chateau, and the *Panzergrenadiers* now mustering fierce resistance. He and his men had been embroiled in fierce combat for approaching two hours, and the Maquis were nowhere to be seen. Accordingly, he decided it was time for the 'scoot' period of the assault to be enacted.

With a gallant wave to the girl in the red frock – Farran was very much a charmer and a ladies' man – he strode into the centre of the road and fired two flares from a Very pistol. They looped a fiery arc through the sky, scorching a fierce scarlet across the battle-torn town – two red flares being the signal to withdraw.

As Farran and Captain Hibbert led the force in a helter-skelter retreat they finally ran into the vanguard of the Maquis, mustering on the outskirts of town. Two hours late and less than an eighth of the number that Colonel Claude had promised, at least they were here. The Maquis seemed desperate for a slice of that morning's action, so Farran and Hibbert decided they would lead a second push into Châtillon.

This time their numbers would be swollen to one hundred and twenty fighters, but the element of surprise was entirely gone. Even so, Farran was banking on the enemy mistaking his larger force for the vanguard of General Patton's 3rd Army, those American troops and armour that had spearhead the thrust east through France. If that happened, the entire enemy force – those at the chateau and the *Panzergrenadiers* – might break and run.

It was an audacious gamble, but hardly the first by this veteran SAS commander. Already one of the most highly decorated soldiers of the war, Farran would earn a DSO, MC and two bars (three MCs) during the war, among many other decorations. Of Irish descent, he was known to all as Major Patrick McGinty, after an irreverent and somewhat ribald Irish ballad entitled 'Paddy McGinty's Goat'.

Like many a former prisoner of war – Farran had escaped German captivity in 1941 – he'd adopted a nom de guerre, knowing that the Germans kept detailed records of all POWs. Major Patrick McGinty had become Farran's official war name, and indeed his DSO was issued in that name. The ballad about the goat gives something of a sense of Farran's nature: colourful, distinctly Irish, rebellious, unconventional, contemptuous of mindless bureaucracy and decidedly merciless towards his enemies.

Mr Patrick McGinty, an Irishman of note,
Fell into a fortune and brought himself a goat.
Says he, 'Sure, of goat's milk I'm goin' to have me fill.'
But when he bought the nanny home he found it was a bill.

The goat goes on to woo several of the young beauties in the Irish village of Killaloe, before it got shipped off to France as a mascot for the Irish Guards regiment in the Great War, whereupon it decided to fight, the enemy ranks breaking before its charge:

The Germans retreated, hurriedly they fled.
Holding their noses they tumbled over dead.
'Ach,' says the Kaiser, 'There's poison gas afloat.'
But it was only the effluvium from Paddy McGinty's goat.

Just twenty-four years of age by the time of the Châtillon attack, Major McGinty – short, sandy-haired and blue-eyed – had been born into a devout Roman Catholic family in England, but educated in India, where his father had served in the military. He'd been sent to the Bishop Cotton School, in Shimla – a province of India – the oldest boarding school in Asia, renowned for turning out judges, politicians and senior military commanders.

The alumni of the school were known as 'Old Cottonians', and its motto was 'Overcome evil with good'. Arguably, it was one that Farran had applied to the war with single-minded rigour.

In 1941 Farran – then serving in the 3rd King's Own Hussars, an armoured (cavalry) regiment – had been injured in both legs and an arm, in what became known as the battle of Cemetery Hill, in Crete. Farran was taken captive and held as a POW, but only for as long as it took for him to recover enough to walk on crutches, after which he managed to crawl under the camp's wire. Linking up with fellow escapees, he'd made a daring bid for freedom in a caique – a traditional wooden fishing boat. After an epic voyage and being marooned at sea, Farran and his fellows had finally made it to British-held Egypt.

He would win his first MC for his heroic actions on Crete and a bar – a second – for this daring escape. 'Throughout the whole of the operations this officer had shown courage, resource and initiative,' read the citation for his first award. 'He has set a very fine example of determination and leadership to the men of his command.'

Farran's physical courage and his apparent recklessness would lead him back into enemy fire, and in July 1942 he was wounded in the first battle of El Alamein. This time, his injuries were so serious as to require his medical evacuation to Britain. But via a judicious pulling of strings he managed to convince an Army medical board that he was fit to serve in a front-line role.

Not only that, but in February 1943 he'd volunteered for the

SAS. Brought into the regiment by a mutual friend, Farran was hugely impressed. He delighted in the no-nonsense, freewheeling and aggressive nature of the unit, and felt he had found his true home. In the regiment's founders he recognised true kindred spirits.

'The Stirlings did not leap over red tape; they broke right through it,' Farran would declare of David and Bill Stirling. 'Although they made many enemies by slipping round smaller fry, they always got there in the end.'

By September 1943 Farran was in action again, this time in Italy, commanding an SAS patrol on daring sabotage missions on the Adriatic coast. Within weeks he'd won a second bar to his MC. 'The success of the detachment was due to the courage, tenacity and leadership of Capt. FARRAN,' read the October 1943 citation, 'ably backed by his men, whom he has trained himself.' Arguably, there was no one better to be leading the daring and audacious Châtillon raid.

It was mid-morning by the time the combined SAS and Maquis force advanced back into town. Farran's main priority was to launch some kind of decoy action, so as to draw the enemy away from Captain Hibbert and his force of Maquis, who were moving into the narrow streets on foot. Gathering the redoubtable Jim Mackie, with his jeep as a supporting gun-platform, he led a foot patrol in a thrust east towards the far side of town, hoping to convince the enemy that they were being hit from all sides, as if by the US 3rd Army's vanguard.

As Hibbert's force pushed into the western outskirts of Châtillon, they stumbled upon an armoured car with thirty enemy soldiers in support, forming a bicycle patrol. They opened fire, gunning down four of those in the armoured car as they tried to bail out, and hitting the bicycle patrol from both the front and the rear. Savage street fighting ensued and another SAS soldier was hit. Forced to take cover in a large garden, Hibbert and the Maquis fought for their very lives as fierce bursts of gunfire echoed through the bullet-pocked terrain.

Meanwhile, Farran's force stole ahead through streets that were eerily quiet, apart from the bursts of fire echoing across from Hibbert's direction. Crouched low, he led his men past a unit of Germans positioned in the cover of some beech trees. He pushed on, crossing a canal, where his small force flitted along the towpath. Farran spotted another unit of German soldiers standing guard at the hospital, but somehow they failed to notice the SAS men.

Finally, having pushed east across two miles of terrain, they reached the road leading north to the city of Troyes. Taking cover in a narrow side street, Farran chanced a peek around the corner of the nearest building. He almost choked at what he saw. Just a few yards away were a pair of German machine-gun posts, flanking the Troyes road and covering the direction from which Farran and his men had come. Dressed in greatcoats, the machine-gun crews had their backs to the SAS party, seemingly oblivious to their presence.

Farran sank back into cover, wondering how best to proceed. From a nearby house one of his men begged some wine, cheese and bread. As they deliberated on their next move, they wolfed down the food and drink. It was approaching midday and they'd been on the go in fierce combat for six hours or more. Farran felt gripped by a leaden fatigue and he sensed that many of his men were likewise shattered. Still, this was an opportunity too good to miss.

On his word, he and his men leaned around the corner and took careful aim, opening fire on the German machine-gunners, raking their unprotected rear. A soldier on a bicycle was hit, tumbling off his machine, but the enemy were swift to respond. As more bodies fell, all hell let loose. The narrow street in which Farran and his men were hiding became a death trap, as fire from the Germans' MP40 'Schmeisser' sub-machine guns ricocheted off the walls.

Farran could see only one route of escape: to bolt through the front door of the nearest house and dash out the rear, in the hope they could scramble down to the banks of the canal. With rounds cutting around their heads, he led his men in the mad charge through.

They made it safely to the canal bank, reached a lock, scuttled across and darted further eastwards on the tow path, hoping to extricate themselves from enemy clutches. Farran felt confident that Big Jim Mackie would be following their every move, as so often he and his jeep had got them out of seemingly impossible situations.

As he led his men towards the cover of a ridge top hedgerow, one of the enemy's machine-gunners must have spotted them. Within moments, a long burst of fire from an MG42 'Spandau' was tearing into the terrain to either side. As Farran dived for the sparse cover of the hedge, a second Spandau joined in the turkey shoot. It was hellish, especially as he hadn't even realised that he and his men were visible to the enemy.

The Spandau had earned a telling nickname among Allied troops – 'Hitler's Buzzsaw', referring to the incredibly high rate of fire of the weapon and the corresponding noise it made. Capable of putting down 1,200 rounds per minute, it had twice the firepower of the British Bren, if not quite the accuracy. In spite of the terrifying effect of being pinned down by two such machine guns, Farran told himself they had to move. If they stayed where they were they were dead, yet still the veteran SAS commander felt frozen.

By this stage of the war many of those serving with the regiment had begun to view Farran as some kind of a lucky genius – the kind of commander who seemed to lead a charmed life, and who could miraculously command his men on an assault of today's daring and still somehow pull it off. But in truth, Farran feared that after four long years at war and numerous brushes with death, he was getting 'windy'.

Pinned beneath that hedge, he felt gripped by – frozen by – fear. He had never felt so scared as he did now, or so incapable of leading his own men to safety. He'd been in similar scrapes before, and he'd always managed to get him and his fellows out alive. He felt paralysed by fearful inaction, and above everything he hoped that his men hadn't sensed how he was feeling.

Over the years Farran had proved himself blessed with the most vital of attributes for an SAS commander: the instinctive ability to assess the level of danger posed by any battlefield situation, and to deliver an instant and optimum response. His spirited leadership inspired a deep loyalty in his men, not to mention the resistance fighters with whom they often operated.

But right at this moment, Farran had led his followers into what was seemingly a death trap. For every moment they remained pinned down beneath that bullet-blasted hedge, he sensed the enemy closing in for the kill. Finally, he forced himself to move. Keeping to his belly and with bursts of fire kicking up dirt on every side, he led his men in a desperate crawl, sticking to the sparse cover of the deepest furrows that lay beyond the hedgerow. As he steeled himself to press on, he realised that he had never felt so tired or dispirited. In the long years of operations stretching from the North African deserts to the shores of Italy, and from the Greek Islands to the Aegean Sea, he had rarely felt so close to being finished.

If they didn't get out of the machine-gunner's line of fire they were done for, but he couldn't get himself to move any faster. Behind him, Sergeant Roberts, another of his C Squadron veterans, was hit in the leg. Despite the wound, the man seemed to belly-crawl ahead faster than Farran, as he dragged himself along a bloody furrow. They reached a small patch of dead ground, beyond which they would need to move back into the enemy's line of fire.

Farran tried to go to the aid of his wounded sergeant, but he was so utterly exhausted that he could barely help himself. Momentarily lifting his head from the dirt, he sensed the grunt of a distant engine. He fancied it had the distinctive sound of an SAS jeep. Could it be the cavalry riding to the rescue? Had Big Jim Mackie found where they had gone to ground? If so, Farran would need to dig deep for one last burst of energy, to lead a dash for Mackie's vehicle.

He and his men might die in the process, but they were surely dead if they remained where they were.

Chapter 3

If anything, Mike Lees' descent through the Italian mountains had been even more hair-raising than the snow-bound ascent. Sometime after cresting the high pass two-feet deep in wind-driven drifts, they had linked up with a reception party from the neighbouring band of partisans. They'd brought with them a battered truck, one recently captured off the enemy. It looked close to derelict, but at least it offered the promise of mobility and shelter.

Frozen stiff, Lees and his party had clambered aboard, looking forward to arriving in the partisan village in a degree of comfort and style. Instead, the onwards journey had turned into the wildest ride any of the men had ever known. Apparently, a German garrison based beyond Pigna – the partisan village to which they were heading – had learned that their force was on the move. The enemy had fanned out in an effort to catch them – hence the need to reach the village by the fastest means possible. The journey ahead was a race against time.

That appeared to be the explanation for what happened next: the driver of the truck gripped the wheel tightly, turned off the engine, took his feet off the pedals and down they went, free-wheeling all the way. The truck just seemed to keep gaining speed, as it swung crazily from side to side, careering around hairpin bends in a death-defying fashion. Fear gripped the minds of those riding in it, until their hearts were in their very throats. Men became sick with fear. Soon the truck bed was slick with vomit.

There was little point trying to voice any objections, or of urging the driver to a greater degree of caution: the speed and the noise were so all-consuming, all they could do was hang on for dear life and mouth their prayers. Finally, miraculously, the truck gave a last series of death-defying lurches, before grinding to an uncertain halt in the village square. The driver practically fell out of the cabin door and lay on the ground, staring at the heavens.

He glanced at his sickly, pallid passengers. 'No petrol.' He shrugged, then guffawed. 'No brakes!'

Whether the story about the German hunter force was true or not, or just a smoke screen to disguise the perilous nature of their conveyance, no one was entirely certain. But of one thing they could be sure: even now that they had reached Pigna village, there seemed little hope for their onwards journey. The leader of the partisans declared that any attempt to push further south towards the Gothic Line would be akin to suicide.

He had no contact with the Allied forces positioned on the far side, the commander explained, so no way to warn them that a friendly force was coming through. The front line kept shifting as the battle ebbed and flowed, making any close reconnaissance impossible. Moreover, the ground ahead was broken, impassable country, so Lees and his men would be forced to move on well-trodden paths and roads, all which would be closely guarded by the enemy.

Behind the front ran a main road, he warned, slicing through the mountains in a knife-cut cleft. It was heavily patrolled, and if Lees and his force tried to cross it they were bound to be seen.

After much heated discussion, Lees finally managed to secure the offer of a guide who would take his party south as far as that road. After that, they would be on their own.

As Lees was painfully aware, it would be suicide to press on with his full party. As far as he could ascertain, the enemy fortifications stretched for miles either side of the Gothic Line. All of that terrain would have to be crossed by stealth and ideally under cover of darkness. He would need to lead a small, fit, fighting patrol, one able to travel fast and silently and primed to avoid contact with the enemy, or to fight ferociously should the need arise.

It was better to slip a few good men through successfully, than to get them all killed. The two Italian resistance leaders were in excellent physical shape, so would stand the march well. But the war artist, Long, was unfit to move, at least until he'd recovered from his fall. Lees and the reporter, Morton, had had their differences high on the mountain, and he reckoned Morton was best left behind. If Lees could establish an escape route, all the more chance that the both of them might make it through with their stories.

Lees decided to take two others only. The first was an escaped British POW called Fred Dobson, a fit and capable soldier who was keen as mustard to press on. The other was an Italian called Secondo Balestri, who had been serving with Temple's partisans for some time. Balestri had one of the most incredible war stories that Lees had ever heard.

A former Italian Navy wireless operator turned partisan, he had been captured by the Germans. Under Gestapo torture he'd acted as if he had broken, professing his willingness to transmit false intelligence to the Allies. Instead, Balestri, who was gifted

37

with an extraordinary mathematical memory, had altered a coded signal which read 'I am in good hands', to 'I am in German hands'. He'd also managed to insert further warnings into the radio messages the Gestapo forced him to send. Because he could do so 'live' – during the process of encoding the signal – the Gestapo had never suspected what he was up to.

Balestri had subsequently escaped from the enemy and made it back to partisan lines. He, like Fred Dobson, was keen to continue despite the dangers. That, Lees decided, would make up his escape party. He'd leave William McClelland, the Royal Scots private turned piratical raider, to shepherd the remaining men through – but only once they had received word from Lees of what was the best route, or, conversely, that he and his party had failed.

It was some twenty-four hours after reaching Pigna that Lees called his party together. Once he had outlined his intentions to split them into two groups, neither Morton nor Long appeared particularly upset. On the contrary, they could see the sense – not to mention the sheer courage – in Lees trying to forge a path for the rest to follow.

'He was twenty-one, tough, brave as the British are brave; born, as they say, to command,' Morton would write of Lees. In that there was perhaps a tacit admission that he had been wrong to rebel against Lees' orders, high on the snow-swept mountain. As for Lees, he'd realised by now that the Canadian press man had a certain grit and spirit: indeed, enough of each to place him in formal command of those left behind.

Lees eyed the reporter, searchingly. 'You, Morton, seem to think everything is a big joke . . . You fraternise too easily with the Commos; with everyone for that matter.' By 'the Commos'

Lees meant the communists, for a good proportion of the Italian partisans professed to communist leanings. 'Still, I'm putting you in charge.'

Morton, amply assisted by McClelland, would lead the second escape party, Lees explained. 'You're loaded down with money. That's better than guns or brains in a situation like this. Use the money to get the rest of this crowd through to France . . . And Morton, that's an order.'

'He never called me Paul whenever he was giving orders,' Morton reflected wryly of Lees, 'and he seemed, mostly, to be giving orders.' Morton – like Lees – had parachuted in on the present mission carrying a slush-fund provided by the SOE: cash, with which to oil the wheels of guerrilla warfare. Now, he was to use that money to buy their way out again.

Lees shook hands with all, speaking a few last words to the Canadian reporter and the South African war artist. 'Well, goodbye. We'll tell the Americans you're coming through. Perhaps they'll polish their bayonets, so you give them a good write up.'

Morton snorted. 'That'll be the day. They might be a million miles away, for all the use they are at the moment.'

'You'll get through all right,' Lees reassured him.

'Well, thank God I'm not going today,' Morton confessed. 'I couldn't walk another step.'

'That's the worst of you correspondents,' Lees needled him. 'You don't do enough PT.'

Morton laughed. 'Oh, shut up and push off, you bloody thug.'

With those final words ringing in his ears, Lees and his fellows departed Pigna, mounting up the death trap of the partisan truck for the initial stage of the journey. It would take them as far as the first major obstacle, a road bridge that the partisans had blown up to prevent the Germans from raiding their valley stronghold, not far beyond which lay the first of the massive defences of the Gothic Line.

The *Gotenstellung* – the Gothic Line – was Nazi Germany's last line of defence in northern Italy, running coast to coast in essentially an east–west direction. Positioned on the slopes of the Apennine mountains, it consisted of a series of massive fortifications strung between the natural defences of the high ridges and snowbound peaks. Concerned about whether the *Gotenstellung* would hold, Hitler had ordered 15,000 slave labourers shipped in, to extend the defences in strength and depth. Working under the Todt Organisation – Nazi Germany's forced labour ministry – they consisted of prisoners of war, concentration camp internees, plus conscripted Italian civilians.

Those slave labourers had constructed hundreds of reinforced-concrete gun pits, deep trenches, 2,376 machine-gun nests boasting interlocking arcs of fire, 479 anti-tank, mortar and artillery positions, plus observation posts with interconnecting tunnels burrowed deep beneath the ground. Miles of anti-tank barriers had been dug, plus 130,000 yards of barbed wire strung between key positions. As a result, Field Marshal Kesselring had declared himself satisfied, contemplating any Allied assault on the *Gotenstellung* 'with a certain confidence'.

Sure enough, by the autumn of 1944 Allied forces had fought themselves to a standstill on the *Gotenstellung*. With combat losses mounting and the harsh winter weather setting in, General Harold Alexander, Kesselring's opposite number, had accepted that the Allied push through Italy had hit a major stumbling block. 'The last battles in Italy were just as fierce as any we had experienced . . .' General Alexander remarked. 'I was not faced with a broken and disintegrating Army . . .' No breakthrough was going to be possible, at least not before the spring.

The partisans' decrepit truck coughed and backfired spasmodically, but after an hour's tortuous drive it made it to that first obstacle. There, Lees and his four-man party dismounted and clambered across what remained of the demolished bridge. They pushed ahead on a road cut into the sheer side of the mountain, one that had been built to service the rearmost defences of the *Gotenstellung*.

The first massive bunkers hove into view. Lees was astounded at the sheer impregnability of those fortifications. The last line of defence, they looked to be deserted at present, but once manned by German troops they would constitute a veritable mountain fortress. As the partisan leader had warned, the only possible route ahead lay along a thin ribbon of road, and they were forced to pass below the giant, gaping, eyeless sockets of those concrete bunkers.

It was an eerie, shadowed place and Lees was hugely relieved to reach the ridge that lay on the far side. It was midday by now and their partisan guide pointed out the main road that cut through the valley below. Lees gazed upon that highway: what he saw was not encouraging. To either side of the twisting ribbon of black rose grey-walled mountains, slashed through by precipitous ravines. The terrain looked utterly daunting.

Here and there tiny white puffs of smoke revealed where Allied shells were bursting amid the hidden defences. The noise of battle drifted across to them, echoing confusingly around the rocky slopes.

'It's going to be difficult,' Salvi, one of the resistance leaders, ventured.

'Very,' Lees confirmed, grimly.

Salvi found a cleft in the rock-face via which he assured Lees they could descend. The Italians led the way, Lees and Dobson following. Big, heavy and ungainly at heights, Lees found the next hour or so hellish, as he clung to the rock with aching fingertips and with his Sten slung across his shoulders. Each glance down was rewarded by a fresh surge of nausea, and by the time he reached the bottom his legs were shaking uncontrollably.

From there, they followed a faint track that led to a small patch of woodland, lying just above the road. It was late afternoon by now, and Lees reckoned dusk was no more than two hours away. Already the highway was busy with trucks motoring to and fro. Come nightfall, it would become packed with traffic, for the enemy tended to use the cloak of darkness to shield their convoys from marauding Allied warplanes.

The guide from Pigna village was still with them, but he would go no further than the road. He was dressed like a local villager and carried ID papers, which meant that he should be able to pass freely through enemy positions. Lees persuaded him to press on to the nearest village, a small place called Fanghetto, which lay just before the road.

An hour later he was back. What he reported underscored the futility of trying to make it across anywhere hereabouts. The village was full of enemy troops whose job it was to patrol the road. Even if Lees and his men did sneak through undetected, on the far side lay a fierce mountain river. It was fast, deep and treacherous, and only one bridge spanned its breadth, which was under permanent guard. Beyond that lay a road snaking into the high-ground, but it was a heavily used supply route for German front-line troops.

In short, there was no way through.

With heavy hearts Lees and his men retraced their steps, arriving back at the cliff-face that they had descended earlier. Too exhausted to attempt the ascent, they found a deserted shepherd's hut in which to spend the night. At dawn the following morning, the climb up the sheer rock-face proved even more terrifying than the descent had done.

Once at the top, an exhausted Lees and Salvi took stock. They were all out of water and running low on food. They questioned the guide, but he had few viable suggestions. As Lees gazed out over the enemy-infested terrain, he felt utterly spent and close to beaten. His eyes drifted further south, to the beguiling shimmer of the Mediterranean. It was little more than a couple of miles away.

A British warship was steaming up the coast, shelling what had to be the *Gotenstellung*'s defences. A thought suddenly struck Lees: *the sea*. Why not use the sea? The sea was owned by the Allies, British warships keeping up a steady barrage of fire against the enemy. Surely, crossing the lines would be far easier if attempted by sea. In essence, if they rowed across they could outflank the enemy's defences. Surely, there lay the answer?

Lees turned to the guide. Did he know any fishermen, he demanded, ones who were friendly to the partisan cause? He did, the guide replied, but the Germans had confiscated all of their oars. Could any be found, Lees asked. The guide thought they could, with the right kind of incentive. A plan was hatched. The guide would get a letter through to his fisherman friend, offering a bundle of cash if he could get a boat ready and meet with Lees and his men that afternoon. The letter would have to be bicycled through to the fisherman, to make it into his hands in time.

'What if he fails to show or gives us away?' Salvi asked Lees.

43

Lees shrugged. 'We'll have to take our chances . . . If he fails to make it, we can't wait another night. We'll just have to risk trying to get across near the coast.'

The plan set, Lees felt a surge of renewed energy. They set off, keeping to the cover of woodland and descending by a gentler slope. By midday, they were in sight of the fisherman's village. With little food remaining, they gorged on bunches of juicy black grapes plucked from a nearby vineyard.

The meeting point was a small quarry, set in a patch of woodland about two miles from the beckoning sea. They approached it with caution. As luck would have it, the place was occupied. A gypsy family were using it as a site for making charcoal. Typically no friends to the enemy – along with the Jews, Slavic peoples, the disabled and others, gypsies were also classed as *Untermensch* (subhuman) by the Nazis – they proved decidedly welcoming, once they understood who Lees and his party were.

They offered food and wine, but Lees was more interested in what intelligence they might furnish. The elder of the family led Lees to a small knoll on the fringes of the woodland. He pointed out two steep-sided hills that lay before them, each like a mini-volcano and covered in dense scrub. Each was fortified by hidden German positions, he explained.

Beneath their vantage point the road was busy with horse-drawn carts, laden with artillery shells: to one side of the woodland lay a camouflaged gun battery. Every now and then Lees heard the whine of a passing shell, followed shortly by the crack of the gun firing. He realised then that some of the enemy artillery was positioned behind them, lobbing shells high into the air at the Allied lines. Somehow, unwittingly, Lees and his men must have slipped through the rearmost enemy defences that morning.

Lees sketched out all the positions the gypsy could identify. If they did make it across the lines this would constitute priceless intelligence for planning bombing raids with pinpoint accuracy. They returned to the quarry. By four o'clock there was still no sign of the fisherman, and Lees was getting worried. With the approach of dusk no one doubted that he wasn't coming. Something had gone wrong. Maybe the message hadn't even reached him.

Lees turned to the gypsy. Was he able to guide them at all, he demanded? The man said that he could, but only as far as the road. Beyond that, he knew little if anything of the terrain. Lees figured if they could reach the scrub that cloaked the first of the two fortified hillocks, from there they might spy a route ahead and try to sneak onwards in the gathering darkness.

'Our objective after that?' Salvi queried.

Good question. Lees eyed the distant wall of mountains. Somewhere among those towering peaks lay the Allied front line. Even via his binoculars, it was impossible to make out any obvious route through. Lees chose a particular peak, unmistakeable due to its pyramidal shape, and picked it out on the map.

'We'll make for Mount Grammondo. There's a full moon tonight, and we can't miss it.'

They'd set out as soon as it got dark, knowing they had to make safe territory by daybreak. Before departure, Lees penned a short letter to Morton. He outlined the route they planned to take, but advised the press man to explore the sea-borne option, if a suitable boat could be found. That done, he sent someone to carry the note back to Pigna village.

Lees and his men prepared for the off, checking kit and weaponry to ensure nothing was loose or clanked as they moved.

Apart from Lees' Sten, Salvi and Piva also carried sub-machine guns, and Balestri had a rifle, while Dobson hefted two grenades. It was scant weaponry if they ran into any trouble. Just then the gypsy man's wife emerged from their tent, pressing a hip flask of cognac into Lees' hands, with murmurs of good luck.

Lees thanked her, before turning to his men. 'No talk,' he warned them. 'We get through without a fight if possible. No one fires unless I give the order. Keep closed-up all the way. We are few enough to avoid being seen and we can't afford to get separated.'

They set out. The moon was not due to rise until nine, and Lees wanted to get as far as possible under the cloak of night. Below, he could just make out the phosphorescent shimmer of the river. Their gypsy-guide led them forwards until he dared go no further. Lees pressed a bundle of Lire gratefully into his hands. That done, they flitted onwards, hugging a hedge until the road melted out of the darkness.

Lees signalled a halt. From up ahead came the tread of boots on tarmac. Lees crept on a few paces, until he spied a sentry. He paced slowly past, so close that Lees could almost reach out and touch his boots. Fifty yards further on the sentry stopped to exchange a few words in German, before turning and pacing slowly back again. It looked as if there was a guard in place for every hundred yards or so.

From his right Lees heard a new noise, cutting the still night air. The thud of hooves and the rumble of wagons, bearing a heavy load. He signalled to his party. 'Dash across just as soon as the wagon column has passed,' he hissed.

The noise grew to a deafening roar, as the line of wooden carts thundered closer, the horses' manes flowing and their harnesses jingling rhythmically. Just as soon as the last was past, Lees dashed across, keeping as low as he could. Four figures flitted after him. They made the open field on the far side without any cries of alarm, and sprinted across it in pairs. Moments later they scrambled down the riverbank and were lost from view.

Just as Lees had intended, the column of passing carts had masked any noise that they had made. The river was wide but mercifully shallow. They waded across one at a time and pressed onwards into a maize field. To their right the clank of steel on steel revealed the location of an artillery position. Moments later, the roar of a gun firing split the night, the flash of the muzzle throwing all into momentary stark relief.

Monte Pozzo, the first of the wooded hillocks, was revealed in that harsh pulse of light, just a few hundred yards ahead. Keeping to the shadowed edge of the maize crop, Lees led his men on. Every now and then the guns fired a further salvo, and with each Monte Pozzo drew noticeably closer. Finally, Lees slipped in among the trees that fringed its lower slopes.

It seemed as if only a few scant minutes had passed, but in reality they'd been on the move for two hours. In another hour the moon would rise, and before them lay a second river that they had to cross. Lees hurried on. A road snaked this way and that up the side of Monte Pozzo. As Lees tried to steer a straight course, their route kept crossing it.

All of a sudden there was a clatter in the darkness. A pair of German soldiers had been freewheeling down the road on bicycles. Spotting Lees and his party, they'd jumped off, the bikes falling to the ground. As Lees dashed ahead shots rang out in the darkness. Thankfully, the German troopers were armed only with rifles, but those shots had doubtless raised the alarm. From behind, Lees heard the soldiers remount their bicycles to pedal frantically onwards.

Lees was hyper-alert for any watchers now. They reached a vantage point, looking outwards across the valley. Before them nestled the town of Torri, cradled at the foot of a steep ravine. That precipitous crevice offered the only obvious route via which to scale the mountains beyond. To reach it Lees would have to lead his men across the river, which lay just this side of the town, via a bridge. There was no other way.

As Lees scrutinised the road, he detected several glowing pin-pricks of light, rhythmically pulsing in the darkness: sentries enjoying a smoke. The moon rose, large and bright, bathing the river in its light. The main question in Lees' mind was whether Torri was occupied by the enemy. In the moonlight, it looked like a mass of shattered, shell-blasted ruins. It was just possible that the ferocity of Allied bombardments had caused the town to be evacuated.

Lees pulled his men in close. 'We've got to cross the bridge. If we try to wade the river they'll see us. We'll have to march openly, hoping they mistake us for one of their own patrols.'

There were silent nods in the darkness.

With Lees leading, five figures stole down the hillside, before stepping brazenly into the open. They formed up as a column, turned right and began to march towards the bridge. From behind Lees could hear figures talking and laughing in German. He tensed for a cry of challenge, but none came. After three minutes of utter spine-chilling tension, they made it across the bridge without a shot being fired or even a cry of alarm.

The war-blasted streets of Torri seemed utterly deserted. Once or twice a stray chicken or pig started at their presence, sending five pairs of hands to their weapons, but they reached the far side of the ghost town without facing a single challenge. Ahead rose the lower slopes of the mountain, terraced into vineyards like a gigantic ladder. They began to scramble up, scaling one terrace after another and tripping and stumbling over the wires which held up the vines. They were reluctant to seek out any paths in case they were mined.

Directly ahead lay the bulky form of Monte Grammondo, its peak grey and forbidding. A salvo of shells burst between them and the heights, setting a copse of pines ablaze. The fire scorched and crackled, throwing ghostly shadows across the dark heights. Now and again a machine gun rasped out a long burst of fire, but it was impossible to tell exactly who was shooting at whom, or if nervous German gunners were simply unleashing upon ghosts.

Finally, the vineyards came to an end. The slopes were more precipitous now, forcing Lees to take a path that snaked ever more steeply. It was around 0200 hours when Salvi tapped him on the shoulder. He sank to the path, doubled over and in pain.

'I can't go on,' the resistance leader murmured.

'What's wrong?' Lees hissed.

'My stomach. I have an ulcer. The walking must have aggravated it.'

Lees considered their predicament. He reckoned they had climbed about halfway to the heights, beyond which he figured lay the Allied front line. It would get light at six and they had to make it across by then. He allowed the resistance leader half an hour to rest, before telling him they had to press on.

Reluctantly, Salvi clambered to his feet. Lees dropped the pace a little, as they recommenced the climb. They entered a knife-cut ravine, following a faint path strewn with mule droppings. As

49

Lees led them through, Dobson, the escaped British POW, drew level with him.

'There's someone following us,' he whispered, hoarsely.

Lees turned and listened. Sure enough he could detect the faint murmur of voices from further down the narrow cleft. He had no option but to up their pace. If their mystery pursuers cornered Lees and his small party in that ravine, it would be the end of them.

A few minutes later, panting hard as he climbed, Lees stumbled over a wire strung along the track. It looked like a communications cable and it had to lead to a field telephone. As Lees stared at it, trying to catch his breath, Salvi pointed excitedly. 'That's no German wire! Theirs is always black.'

He was right: the strand of cable was a bright red. Still, Lees remained doubtful. 'The Americans can't be this far advanced,' he objected. 'We've only recently passed through the enemy's artillery. Ahead must lie their infantry.'

No matter how long they stared at that wire, glowing a faint red in the moonlight, there was no way of knowing. Lees ordered them on. The cable seemed to dog their every step. Twice they turned off the main path, only to run into that red strand of wire once more. Lees sensed they were about to stumble into trouble. They neared the crest of a ridge and crept into the cover of a small copse. The wire was there, running dead ahead. They followed it, rounded a bend and came upon a heap of equipment lying by the path.

Lees spied a pile of blankets, a distinctive metal helmet, a leather ammo belt and a Mauser rifle: *German stuff*. He bent to finger the nearest blanket: *still warm*. The enemy had to be close. As quietly as he could, Lees handed the ammo belt and rifle to

Dobson. They paused as he checked and readied the weapon. Fortuitous. One more of them was now a little better armed.

Lees signalled them on – five figures creeping silently as wraiths through the trees. They reached an area where the cover thinned out, and all five of them seemed to spy the enemy at the same instant. Barely ten paces ahead stood half a dozen German soldiers, gazing further across the mountainside. To one side knelt a signaller, speaking quietly into a field telephone. It was obviously some kind of forward observation position.

Lees and his men sank into cover. The standing figures stared ahead at shells bursting on a ridgeline some distance away. They were checking and correcting the artillerymen's fire, seemingly oblivious to the presence of Lees and his men. Their weapons and helmets lay beside them on the ground, their eyes fixed on the distant explosions.

Lees figured he'd seen enough. He stole to his feet, Sten levelled at the enemy. Four figures rose with him, their weapons likewise readied. As if warned by some sixth sense, one of the Germans turned towards them. Lees pressed his trigger. Half the figures fell in a matter of seconds, cut down by long bursts of fire unleashed at close range. As the survivors tried to flee, Dobson hurled a grenade in among them.

With the route ahead now clear Lees burst through, vaulting over the fallen enemy figures. The others followed. They tore out of the woodland, racing along a path snaking along the ground. The terrain here was open, the track leading to a final line of low, rocky cliffs, which delineated the high point.

As they sprinted for that escarpment, a machine gun opened up from behind. Bullets tore past, as Lees and his fellows slithered and dived into cover, then darted onwards. Salvi seemed to be fully recovered by now. A born mountaineer, he made a desperate dash for a crevice in the rock-face, one that seemed to offer a final route through. As they sprinted for its uncertain embrace, fierce bursts of machine-gun fire cut the night to all sides.

Salvi led the climb, shinning up the near-vertical cliff, with Lees and the others right behind. They were some fifty feet up when the first shell whistled out of the night and tore into the rocks below. Several more followed, splinters of steel cutting through the air on all sides. With zero shelter and a precipitous drop below, there was little option but to keep climbing.

The shells kept coming. Probing with his finger tips, Salvi steered them to the very top, before darting into the shelter of some rocks. Moments later, Lees had crawled in beside him, and shortly the others followed. They wormed their way further into cover, lying there in utter exhaustion. No one could believe that they had made it through thus far, and unscathed.

From behind, they could spy the baleful red flashes of the German artillery. Ahead, silhouetted against the moonlight glimmering off the sea, lay the ancient port town of Menton, which was held by the Allies. Lees reasoned it would be far safer to press on towards 'friendly' lines come daybreak. They rested for an hour, until the stars faded in the lightening sky.

All seemed eerily quiet as Lees led the small party off, moving cautiously through the dawn light. A path ran along the ridge, perpendicular to the way they needed to go. They crossed it, pushing due south, reaching a strand of wire running along the ground. Lees stepped towards it, mouthing silent prayers: if mines had been laid on this stretch of front, he figured the wire would delimit the borders of the safe ground.

He stepped gingerly across. No shattering explosion met his

footfall. They made one hundred, two hundred, then three hundred yards without mishap, when finally a burst of fire tore apart the silence. Directly ahead a machine-gunner had opened up, unleashing a burst of warning shots above their heads.

Lees threw himself flat on the earth. 'Don't shoot! Don't shoot! We're British!'

The voice that responded was the sweetest that he had ever heard.

'Put that gun down,' came a hard-edged, American-accented cry. 'Advance one and be recognised.'

Chapter 4

From the shelter of the rutted field beyond the bullet-torn hedgerow, Major Farran saw the distinctive form of an SAS jeep nose into view, with the redoubtable Big Jim Mackie at the wheel. It was the most welcome sight that he had ever seen. They now had its vehicle-mounted machine guns to counter the Germans' fire.

Under the cover of their smoking barrels, Farran and his men rushed the wounded Sergeant Roberts to the vehicle and bundled him aboard. Figures jumped on wherever there was space. The heavily laden jeep moved out, engine howling, its thick mud-eater tyres making short work of the ploughed field. Once they'd reached the nearby lane, the priority had to be to get as far away as possible from the hornet's nest that they had kicked – and kicked hard – in Châtillon, and to get Roberts some medical treatment.

They headed for the nearest friendly farmstead. There, Farran himself proceeded to dress Roberts' wounds, while he lay on the kitchen table and a bevy of farm-maids bustled about with hot water and towels. Once the SAS sergeant was stabilised, he was loaded aboard a vehicle and despatched to the nearest location where the Maquis were known to keep an operational field hospital. There, he'd be in good hands.

That done, Farran led his jeep column back through isolated

country to their remote, deep-woodland base. Reports filtered in from Châtillon of one hundred German dead and many more injured, plus scores of trucks, cars and motorcycle combinations destroyed. Almost of more importance, the entire German force occupying the town was said to be preparing to withdraw from what it believed was advancing US troops.

Farran had lost one SAS soldier killed and several wounded. By anyone's reckoning, the battle for Châtillon-sur-Seine had been a spectacular victory. The SAS's official report – marked 'SENSITIVE' – would declare that 'this must rank as one of the most successful sorties ever carried out by a small harassing force behind enemy lines.'

But Farran's greatest fear now was reprisals. The Gestapo and SS were bound to learn of the attack, and they were known to wreak terrible vengeance on the locals, as 'punishment' for the role the Maquis may have played. He decided to make himself scarce. If his entire force melted away, it would lessen any chance of any such savagery. If no SAS could be found, who was to say it wasn't forward elements of the US 3rd Army that had attacked the town?

He sent out a signal for his entire squadron to return to their woodland base: other elements had been out hitting a variety of targets. They gathered as one unit, boasting eighteen jeeps in all, before moving out to establish three separate bases, from where to plot further mischief and mayhem. They left behind them the one casualty, Parachutist Holland, who'd been killed in the initial stages of the battle. Unbeknown to Farran the enemy had found his body, which served to dissuade them from executing the fifty-odd locals they had taken hostage. As it was clearly a British-led raid, such reprisals against 'the Maquis' were deemed unjustified.

Farran led his patrol 150 kilometres east, to a patch of wood-land not far from the town of Grandrupt-de-Bains. En route they reconnoitred key targets, radioing through coordinates for Allied airstrikes. 'Urgent. Recced today railway station at 14H/373305 . . .' read one such message. 'Petrol train on track being used as refuelling point . . . Impossible attack from ground as 200 enemy with heavy weapons dug in . . . bomb whole area immediately to prevent escaping convoys from refuelling.' There were many such messages.

Grandrupt-de-Bains lay on the western border of the Vosges region of France, an area of thick woodland and rain-washed mountains that straddles the Franco-German border. Hitler had vowed that on the western wall of the Vosges his Panzer divisions and infantry would make a heroic last stand, hurling the Allies back into France and preventing them from marching into the Fatherland. It seemed a fitting area in which Farran and his SAS might cause trouble, but things weren't quite to turn out as he had planned.

It was the second week of September 1944 when Farran linked up with a new resistance group at Grandrupt. This one – some-what implausibly – was based around a Boy Scout troop. The members of the Grandrupt Maquis struck Farran as being a little young to go to war, although those in command were seasoned resistance fighters. They'd set up base in a cluster of white canvas bell-tents pitched beside a mountain stream, and the whole scene struck Farran as being reminiscent of a scout camp in peacetime.

It was somehow so incongruous, yet their spirit to fight appeared to be unmatched. Farran delivered a stirring speech in his best schoolboy French and was mobbed by a crowd of young would-be warriors. He decided to arrange an air-drop of much-needed arms and supplies onto the boy scouts' drop zone, which if nothing else would give them some direct experience of a '*lancée*', as the Maquis tended to call such an event.

The DZ was a large flat field fringed by trees, so well screened from any watchers. There was a cold wind blowing, as September ushered in the autumn and winter storms so typical of the Vosges. Farran explained in detail the configuration of signal lights and fires that were required to guide the aircraft in, but he doubted if the scouts had completely grasped it. He was just giving up hope of any aircraft appearing, when, at around 0200 hours, the distant drone of a Handley Page Halifax's four Rolls-Royce Vulture engines cut the skies.

The Halifax was designed for use as a heavy bomber, but specialised versions had also been built for parachute and cargo operations. It had become the work-horse of special forces resupply missions. As the pair of aircraft homed in on the DZ, Farran figured they were making their approach at too high an altitude. Sure enough, when they released their loads the wind blew a good proportion of the parachutes off course, which plummeted into the trees.

By now, Farran and his men were shivering with the night's cold, but there was urgent work to be done. Three human parachutists had also dropped in, alongside the supplies. Lieutenant Hugh Gurney, Lance Corporal Challenor and Parachutist Fyffe had gone missing weeks earlier, shortly after Farran's column had crossed the lines. Somehow, they'd made it back to friendly forces and were now parachuting in to rejoin their unit. Unfortunately, the wind had driven Fyffe into a stand of tall pine trees. It was three long hours before Farran and his men finally got him safely to the ground.

The resupply containers were so widely scattered that by day-break several were still to be found. A somewhat disgruntled Farran took a break for some much-needed breakfast, leaving the boy-scout Maquis in charge. It was around 0900 hours when a youth of no more than ten came tearing over to Farran in something of a panic. He'd been sent with an urgent message: some 600 German soldiers, supported by armoured cars plus *Sonderkraftfahrzeug* half-tracks – troop-carriers fitted with machine guns – were converging on the DZ.

There was, as Farran well knew, a crack SS battalion based at Grandrupt-de-Bains. They must have learned of the resupply drop and set out early intending to spoil Farran's day. Equipped as they were, the enemy were going to heavily outnumber his force, not to mention outgun it.

Farran ordered his men to mount up their jeeps. As he scanned their surroundings, searching for an escape route, the DZ seemed to be completely enclosed in thick, impenetrable woodland. There would be no slipping away via jeep through any of that. One rutted track led out of the clearing, but that was the direction in which the SS battalion were fast approaching.

Opting to stand and fight would be suicide. The half-tracks – known as 'Hanomags' to Allied troops – boasted half-inch-thick armour and pairs of pivot-mounted machine guns, and each could carry ten soldiers in full combat gear. Advising the boy-scout Maquis to disperse into the woodland, Farran set about trying to find some means for his jeep-borne force to escape. As if to underscore the dire nature of their predicament the first bursts of fire erupted from the eastern fringes of the DZ, from where the enemy were making their approach.

Farran led his column of jeeps in a desperate dash around the perimeter of the DZ, searching for an elusive means to make their getaway. Here and there expanses of white parachute silk still cloaked the odd tree top, if ever the enemy needed a marker to guide them to their prey. As they gunned the jeeps' engines, figures came charging out of the woodland – young Maquis, fleeing from the approaching convoy.

To the north of the DZ Farran spied a river cutting through the trees: it would be impossible to ford that in the jeeps. East lay only the enemy, and south and west rose dark walls of pine-woods. Giving up any hope of escape, Farran ordered his men to place their jeeps in the 'hull-down' position – so with their body-work sheltered behind a low ridge, but with the vehicle-mounted machine guns able to menace the line of approach of the enemy.

As they waited, Farran wondered whether they might be better off doing a Last Charge of the Light Brigade, as opposed to something more akin to the heroic stand of the 300 Spartans at Thermopylae. It was then that he noticed what appeared to be a small break in the wall of trees, in the far south-western corner. As the grunt of powerful engines rose to a crescendo to the east, Farran led his column in a mad dash for that tantalising promise of escape.

With bursts of fire chasing after them, the jeeps crashed through a wire fence and careered onwards through a copse of young sap-lings, mowing them down like a herd of crazed elephants put to flight in the jungle. Farran led the column across a small field, the jeeps bucking over the rough ground, before they made the better going of a small lane on the far side.

A mile or so later, they emerged onto a tarmacked road. Far-ran's thoughts now were all for the fate of the young Maquis. Facing an SS battalion was some baptism of fire. He ordered

Lieutenant Gurney, freshly parachuted into theatre, to take two jeeps to hit the enemy's rear, by motoring up the Grandrupt road. More jeeps were placed in ambush positions along the highway, intent on catching the SS as they withdrew from the DZ.

Lieutenant Gurney was the first to draw blood. Taking the enemy by complete surprise, he was able to strafe a group of officers positioned on a hillock, knocking out their command vehicle. Meanwhile, one of Farran's jeeps lying in ambush got lucky. Two staff cars were motoring for the DZ, intent on witnessing the success of the operation. Instead, they drove into a withering hail of fire.

Not a man riding in those vehicles was allowed to get out alive. As luck would have it, they were carrying the top commanders of the SS assault force – their colonel and his officers. While the SS had succeeded in seizing the drop-zone and some of the remnant supplies, Farran and his SAS had definitely cut the head off the snake. Having done so, his fear, once again, was of the reprisals.

He ordered his column to move out. They probed south, seeking a new patch of forest in which to hide. Over several days they covered just eighty kilometres, the enemy were so thick on the ground. Retreating from the advancing Allied forces, the Germans were converging on the western wall of the Vosges, being funnelled into the very area where Farran had chosen to operate. In short, at every turn the ground was thick with their forces.

Farran's patrols left more burning vehicles and dead Germans – as often as not, officers – in their wake. Their war diary gave the flavour of one such bloody confrontation. 'Two jeeps met an enemy six-wheeled car, which halted; two officers got out, one armed with a Schmeisser. Dvr. Beckett, expecting them to be Americans, walked towards them. One officer with a Luger pointed it . . . and said "Haende Hoch". Beckett pushed the gun away and fell into the ditch to escape the tracer fired from the jeep . . . The remaining officers in the car tried to get out. Two succeeded and attempted to climb over a wall, but were killed against it. The others perished in the car, which caught fire.'

But as the war diary reflected, the hue and cry was up for Farran's patrol. 'Truck loads of Germans had been inquiring at all villages to the south of the forest about British parachutists, and there were rumours that the maquis at Grandrupt had been betrayed by one of their own officers. The squadron felt a little uneasy.' To all sides the search intensified, and villages were put to the torch by a vengeful enemy.

Somewhere to the north of the town of Vesoul, Farran was forced to go to ground in a tiny patch of woodland no more than two miles square. It was mid-September by now and to all sides lay the enemy. It was last light by the time Farran had sorted his encampment, and he was gripped by a sense of unease. To left and right he could hear the sound of grunting engines – hostile forces on the move.

He ordered Lieutenant Gurney to take a jeep and push to the western fringe of the woods. Might it offer an avenue of escape, should there be trouble? Gurney was under firm orders not to 'brew up' any traffic on that side, but he'd been gone barely five minutes when the distinctive rasp of the jeep's Vickers machine-guns tore apart the dusk. As the war diary recorded, he'd 'brewed up a staff car containing five brass hats. The death of those senior officers, including a general, was confirmed . . .'

In short, the target had proved just too tempting. Farran had got his signaller to break out their wireless set, to send that evening's scheduled radio report to London, but he sensed that

Gurney's action spelled trouble. The lone jeep came charging back and Gurney had disturbing news. The vehicle he'd shot up was at the vanguard of a large enemy column, which had followed their jeep. As if to reinforce his warning, a sudden burst of fire tore through the woodland. 'The cover was thin . . .' the war diary recorded. 'More firing came through the trees, the bullets cutting the branches overhead.'

Any doubts that Farran had entertained vanished: the Germans knew the SAS were there and were coming in to get them. Worse still, with such a small patch of cover to hide in there would be little means to escape or evade the enemy. Farran yelled orders at his men to start up their engines and move out, as jeeps began to hammer out return fire, the smog of cordite fumes drifting thick beneath the trees.

The incoming fire intensified, as Farran kept yelling orders. It was then that he noticed Corporal Cunningham, his radio operator, calmly rolling up his W/T cable, a look of cool determination on his features: *just another night's work in the SAS*. Cunningham's steely calm was like a bucket of cold water in the SAS commander's face. As at Châtillon, when they'd been pinned under that hedge by ferocious machine-gun fire, it was time for Farran to get a grip.

He steeled himself to lead the column of jeeps onto the lone track that cut through the trees – the same one that the enemy were advancing along. He turned right, pushing ahead at top speed, the jeeps bucking over the rough ground as they raced away from the enemy. They reached the far end of the phalanx of woodland, turned right again onto a rutted farm track, finding their way into some thick bushes. Farran had just managed to steer them into cover, when the lead vehicles got bogged in deep mud. Now they were well and truly for it.

He ordered the engines cut. Frantically, desperately, men tore down branches and vegetation and threw it over the jeeps to camouflage them, while others hurried along the track to obliterate their tyre tracks, using the foldable spades that each of the vehicles carried. If they were discovered here they would fight, but there was little hope of getting mobile any time soon. There was nothing for it but to lie low and wait.

Noises drifted across to them. Cries in the night-dark woodland. The odd burst of gunfire. The sound of figures crashing about among the trees. The SAS men were afraid even to cough, let alone to drop a tin of food. One tell-tale sound might give them away. It began to rain – a cold, hard rain frosted by the high ground of the Vosges. There was no option but to sit in those jeeps mired in the mud, shivering, as the rain soaked everyone to the skin.

A long column of enemy vehicles began to move down the nearby road, less than a hundred yards away. They could hear a German military policeman directing the traffic, and yelling out warnings to each passing vehicle to be wary of 'terrorists'. It proved to be a night of knife-edge tension, deep discomfort and very little sleep and by first light the enemy half-tracks and trucks were still thundering past.

'It was the most unpleasant night ever spent,' Farran recorded in the war diary. 'The party was faced with a situation which almost seemed hopeless; if they were attacked at dawn as seemed probable, they would have lost their mobility, as three jeeps were completely stuck and the remainder behind in the bottle neck.'

But at eleven o'clock that morning the woods finally fell silent. Farran reckoned almost 2,000 vehicles had passed in the night, but now the highway was deserted. He ordered his men – sodden, fatigued and chilled to the bone – to wrestle the jeeps free of the mud. That done, they had to push them by hand down the track, as he dared not risk starting their engines. It was back-breaking work. Only when they had finally reached the road and could make a dash for uncertain safety, did he order his men to fire up the jeep's straight-four 'Go Devil' petrol engines.

The squadron took to the highway, racing further east, following the enemy's line of retreat. They'd motored for some thirty-five kilometres, when, on the approach to the town of Luxeuil-les-Bains, they encountered a sizeable patch of woodland. It appeared to be deserted, and Farran seized on it as their new base of operations. By luck, they managed to link up with a new band of Maquis, commanded by a surgeon called Docteur Topsent. With his help and guidance, Farran selected a slew of targets for the coming night's operations. He 'was determined to make the Germans pay for the miserable night he had just passed', the war diary recorded.

Lieutenant Gurney was despatched to Velorcey village, about ten kilometres south of their hideout, where a column of enemy were said to be holed up. Gurney had one of Docteur Topsent's Maquis riding with him, as guide. Farran sent Lieutenant Burtwhistle, another officer newly arrived with the squadron, to Fontaine-lès-Luxeuil, ten kilometres in the opposite direction, where a German horse-drawn artillery column had recently set up camp. And Big Jim Mackie led an attack towards Luxeuil-les-Bains itself.

Gurney's team were the first into action, but they were dogged by bad luck. As fate would have it, their jeeps rounded a bend and came face-to-face with the enemy column at a range of no more than ten yards. Gurney got the drop on the enemy, but his initial burst of fire cut through a truck loaded with explosives. It detonated in an almighty explosion, both the enemy troops and the SAS jeeps being caught in the blast.

Both sides in the confrontation – SAS and Germans – were ripped to pieces. Gurney managed to extricate himself from the carnage, but he was cut down by a burst of fire as he dashed up the village street. 'Lieut. Gurney was hit in the back and fell; he died shortly afterwards,' the war diary recorded. 'The French . . . described how the Germans kicked the body of the "English terrorist", but eventually they were able to bury him in the village cemetery.'

Lieutenant Burtwhistle's patrol fared little better in Fontaine-lès-Luxeuil. Opening fire on the horse-drawn column, his guns tore into the enemy ranks and set a line of carts ablaze. But in the process, three of his men were wounded, and one jeep totally destroyed. They were lucky to make it out of there alive.

Typically, Jim Mackie's attack at Luxeuil-les-Bains went better, but after that night's losses Farran didn't doubt that luck was turning against them. By now, he could hear the thunder of American artillery somewhere to the west, and the roads were bumper-to-bumper with retreating enemy vehicles. There was little question of mounting any further offensive operations. Instead, they needed to shrink further into the depths of the forest and hide. 'The German resistance had stiffened,' the war diary recorded, 'and the situation . . . had become very precarious.'

No sooner had Farran's squadron camouflaged their vehicles, than a German artillery column drew into the cover of some nearby trees. It consisted of a unit of *Panzerabwehrkanone* 43 anti-tank guns, which had earned a fearsome reputation among

Allied troops. The 88mm cannon could penetrate the armour of any British, American or Russian tank and it was accurate up to a thousand yards. It would make mincemeat out of the SAS's unarmoured jeeps, especially as the nearest guns were no more than a hundred yards away.

For three days Farran and his men hunkered down, listening to the voices of the 88mm crews filtering through the trees. Other than sending out the odd patrol on foot, to try to make contact with US forces, there was little they could do but keep silent, hide and wait. In the war diary Farran described this time as 'absolute hell. No one dared talk above a whisper, and every time somebody dropped something they expected a German to appear.'

At one juncture a tin of bacon spontaneously exploded. It must have been damaged during a drop and the contents gone off, the pressure of the gas caused by decomposition building up inside the tin. It sent everyone into a panic, diving for their weapons. If the German gunners heard it, they didn't seem inclined to respond. US artillery was hurling forward a constant barrage of fire, so what was a tin of exploding bacon between enemies?

On the morning of their fourth day in hiding, the Maquis led a group of figures into Farran's position. Overnight, the 88mm gunners had collapsed their camp and melted away. Docteur Topsent had brought with him the crew of an American armoured car, who were riding at the vanguard of the advancing US forces. Farran and his men were so overjoyed at seeing them that they danced a highland jig on the spot.

During a month of such operations deep behind the lines, the SAS commander and his men had been under enormous nervous strain. It wasn't a moment too soon to have been relieved. So began the squadron's long drive back through liberated France, during which Farran was able to observe the burned-out skeletons of staff cars and trucks that they had destroyed, as they'd wrought carnage among the enemy across northern France.

Farran would be awarded a DSO for his actions, the citation for which speaks volumes: 'Confirmed damage, inflicted upon the enemy by the small force under Major Farran, amounted to approximately 500 killed or wounded, 23 staff cars destroyed, 6 motorcycles, and 36 vehicles including trucks, troop-carriers and a petrol wagon. In addition a dump of 100,000 gallons of petrol was destroyed, a goods train taken out, and . . . much essential information and bombing targets passed back by W/T.'

'W/T' stood for wireless transmission – reflecting the ability of Farran's signallers to radio back target coordinates.

Of the Châtillon attack in particular, Farran's citation stated: 'at least 100 Germans killed and a considerable number wounded, while SAS casualties were 1 killed and 2 wounded. This well-conceived and brilliantly-executed operation caused the enemy to mistake Major Farran's squadron for the advance elements of the US 3rd Army and therefore to withdraw from Châtillon sooner than necessary. His personal courage, initiative and tactical sense, enabled him to direct his small force with minimum loss.'

A week or so after linking up with those advance US troops, Farran and his men arrived back in the UK. They were looking forward to some much-needed leave, before the next behind-the-line mission, most likely northern Europe again – possibly the Netherlands or Norway.

But for Major Roy Farran an entirely different future beckoned, on a mission of untold sacrifice and daring.

Chapter 5

Unsurprisingly, Mike Lees emerged from his epic crossing-the-line mission to a hero's welcome. His verbal briefings and the sketches he carried of enemy positions electrified Allied high command, while the two Italian resistance leaders – Salvi and Piva – also yielded priceless intelligence. Lees' record from October 1944 reflected what a star performer he had become in the eyes of the SOE.

'He is energetic, courageous, fit and willing to undergo physical hardships, and has a good knowledge of Para Military activities for which he is ideally suited,' concluded Lt.Col. R. T. 'Dick' Hewitt, one of SOE Maryland's senior commanders. 'An excellent paramilitary officer,' added none other than Major General William Stawell, head of special operations across the Mediterranean region. 'He has a most attractive personality.'

Lees seemed destined for higher things. Hewitt and Stawell's Special Confidential Report on Lees was rushed to SOE's headquarters, in London. His record from autumn 1944 reflected the fact that Lees was being shaped for a new role – namely to join the Secret Intelligence Services (SIS, also known as MI6). MI5 – the UK's domestic intelligence agency – began running deep background checks on Lees, with a view to clearing such a role.

Oddly, MI5 picked up an issue of possible concern. 'During 1939 and 1940 a titled lady with identical surname, of Lytchett

Minster, Dorset, came to our notice as a pacifist propagandist. Her pacifism was based upon religious principles . . .' MI5 were referring to Lady Madeleine Lees, Michael Lees' aunt, known as 'Auntie Maddie' to all. Thankfully, the domestic intelligence agency was able to conclude there were 'no grounds for believing her activities intended to be subversive'.

That October a formal application for Lees to transfer to SIS was got underway. Lees duly signed the Official Secrets Act, declaring: 'I undertake not to divulge any official information gained by me as a result of my employment either in press or book form . . .'

Perhaps unsurprisingly, those at the helm of SOE were less than keen to let Lees go, or at the very least not until the war was won. SOE wrote to the Secret Intelligence Service, agreeing only to 'submit this officer's name and qualifications . . . at the termination of hostilities in Europe . . . His name will not be submitted now, as it is felt that his release from S.O.E. at this stage . . . is undesirable.' A few days later a reply on 54 Broadway headed paper – for two decades 54 Broadway was the central London headquarters of the Secret Intelligence Service – read: 'Let us leave it that when the time comes that you have no further employment for him, you will let us know.'

While the tug-of-war over Michael Lees was underway, what the man himself hungered for most was getting a flight over the Gothic Line to rejoin Major Temple and his Italian partisans. That autumn Lees found himself in the SOE's forward base in the city of Florence, which lay just to the south of the Gothic Line. Florence had recently been liberated and was fully under Allied control, and Lees was desperate to find a way to return to war.

His other chief concern, of course, was whether Morton, Long, McClelland and the rest of his original party would make it safely through the lines. The news, when it reached him, was most edifying. It came by telegram in November 1944: 'Morton and Long with four others arrived by boat at Mentone this morning.' Mentone was the same ancient port town that Lees and his party had first been taken to, after crossing the lines on foot.

War reporter Morton had commanded a reduced party of just six, including the giant piratical raider, McClelland, plus Sergeant Bob La Rouche, a USAAF air gunner who had been shot down on operations. Forced to leave Pigna village when it had come under enemy assault, they had disguised themselves as Italian country-folk, opting to follow Lees' advice and seek a sea-borne means of escape.

En route to the coast they'd stumbled upon a piece of priceless intelligence. A partisan leader had passed on captured German documents, including maps showing all the minefields for that section of the Gothic Line. Morton, Long and party had pro-ceeded to sneak through German checkpoints carrying those documents, and disguised in the traditional dress for locals shel-tering from the rain – potato sacks.

'We were able to wear sacks over our heads in the approved peasant fashion, which added to our disguise,' recorded Morton and Long in their post escape report, penned for the SOE. It was a real dash of ingenuity.

Thus disguised, they'd made it to a friendly fisherman's house, intending to row across the lines themselves. Instead, he'd offered the assistance of his two strapping sons – sea-soned seafarers. Their addition made what had been a daunting voyage something of a pleasure cruise. 'Once out of mortar,

88mm and machine-gun range we turned broadside to the coast,' Morton recorded. 'I unlimbered the bottle of Cognac and passed it around. We started to sing patriotic songs. Fair stood our boat for France!'

Upon reaching Allied lines, Morton, Long and La Rouche personally briefed Colonel Blythe, of the American 7th Army, on their escape. La Rouche and Morton went on to report to Major General Curtis LeMay, a senior USAAF commander in Europe, on all that they had learned. LeMay was keenly interested in their accounts of operations with the resistance. He wanted to build airstrips across territory held by the partisans, to greatly increase the Allies' reach.

Subsequently Long and Morton appeared on *Italia Combatte* (Italy Fights), a radio station based in southern Italy, and operated by the Political Warfare Executive, transmitting direct to the Italian resistance. They had emerged from their daring sojourn with a huge respect for the partisans, and this was reflected in their *Italia Combatte* broadcasts.

In his official SOE report Lees made clear he shared their enthusiasm. 'The Partisans are always ready to take advice and grateful for encouragement or acknowledgement of their work . . . The morale of the Partisans is excellent. The Italians are particularly suited to this flamboyant type of work. They have great ingenuity and are very keen. They do not need encouragement to carry out demolitions.'

Lees urged greater 'propaganda' support for the partisans, and for the message of their successes to be more widely heard. 'The Partisans should be encouraged by broadcast to mine all roads and attack German convoys and troops on the move. There are tremendous possibilities in this type of work.' Such efforts to arm and support the partisans could significantly aid the breaking of the Gothic Line, he argued.

Long was interviewed on BBC radio, where he spoke in glowing terms about how the partisans 'make the Germans' life a hell. They snipe [at] them in the street. They ambush them wherever they move in small numbers . . . I don't suppose the partisans kill more than ten Germans a week. They make for a constant nerve-racking hell for thousands every day though.'

Tellingly, Long concluded: 'There is a faith in one thing, an indefinable fineness in human nature, a quality they believe will live again in this their country, given one condition – that not one man of the enemy's [forces] will remain.' Such a message must have been music to the partisans' ears.

Morton echoed Long's sentiments, speaking on CBC (Canadian Broadcasting Corporation) radio. 'Patriot guns are roaming all northern Italy. They are hitting the Germans and Fascists wherever they find them. They are controlling villages and towns, helping the poor and depressed, feeding the starving. And when the opposition against them grows too tough they creep back into their mountain strongholds, fighting as they go.'

In so speaking out, Morton and Long were fulfilling Churchill's edict to win the information war by lauding the achievements of the resistance. They were also fulfilling their SOE brief, to 'provide the Press an account of patriot activities and sabotage exploits'. Their daring escape and the intelligence – and white propaganda – they had furnished was another feather in Michael Lees' cap, or so it should have been.

But it was now that a shadow began to cast its malevolent presence over the SOE's Italian operations, one that would dog Mike Lees' return to behind-the-lines operations. As Morton set about preparing a series of scintillating newspaper reports – which the British Army censor declared to be the most exciting that he had ever read on the Italian campaign – the winds of fortune were rapidly turning against him.

By the time Morton had polished off his stories, which were to be syndicated worldwide, he was called to Rome, to appear before the senior commanders of Canadian Army Public Relations. Having led a daring escape across the lines, bringing with him priceless intelligence and an American airman, plus the 'white propaganda' that he and Long had prepared, Morton was more than a little surprised at the reception he received.

With little ceremony, he was told that due to 'inappropriate conduct' and other 'unspecified offences', his accreditation as a Canadian war correspondent was being revoked. Further disciplinary action was pending. On the night before deploying to the field it was SOE tradition – long-standing, irrevocable – that agents would have a few stiff drinks. Indeed, a redoubtable SOE veteran, one Sergeant Carter, ran a bar beside the flight line for just such purposes.

Likewise, Lees and his party had enjoyed a good booze-up before they deployed on Operation Flap. Someone had challenged Morton's martial credentials, for he was a reporter and no soldier. Morton had responded by pulling his pistol and shooting some holes in the bar. Fairly tame stuff, by the standards of SOE pre-departure high jinks. Supposedly, that was the 'inappropriate conduct' being cited as the reason for Morton's accreditation being cancelled.

Far worse was to follow. When Morton contacted his employer, the *Toronto Daily Star*, he learned that only one of his reports – the first, 'I live with patriots in Nazi lines' – was to be published.

It was too late to stop that. But all the rest – Morton's eight sub-sequent stories, all of which had been cleared by the British Army censor – were to be cancelled.

Stubborn, dogged, undeterred, Morton sought other outlets for his stories, but after initial enthusiastic reactions doors kept slamming in his face. In short, he could find no publisher for those further articles, and the original plans for worldwide syndication withered and died. That this should all be due to some drunken high spirits immediately prior to mission departure made little sense.

In truth, the dark machinations now being orchestrated against the hapless reporter went far deeper. Morton had earned a reputation among the SOE as being a brave and talented reporter and a capable leader of men, so who had slid in the proverbial knife? Why the stab in the back for a man who should have won fulsome praise?

That autumn, the Political Warfare Executive had been transferred to the Foreign Office, the arm of the British state overseeing foreign affairs. Subsequently, it had been amalgamated with the equivalent American body, the new organisation being renamed the Psychological Warfare Division (PWD). PWD was to specialise in many forms of psychological operations. One of its favourite tactics was scattering 'black propaganda' leaflets over enemy lines from the air, or assaulting the enemy ranks with loud-speaker-born propaganda.

In the autumn and winter of 1944 the message emanating from the PWD – the mouthpiece of the secret British and American states – began to change markedly over Italy. At first, there were intimations that the role of the resistance should be given a little less prominence. Suggestions were made that the partisans, many of whom had avowedly communist leanings, should no longer receive such widespread Allied support, with a view to the new war that was coming – the Cold War.

By November 1944 this had crystallised into a specific set of directives, by which the Foreign Office sought to redefine Allied objectives. They identified the first and overriding policy in Italy as being the need to halt the spread of communism. Second was the need to create a stable nation following liberation, which would look to the Allies – and not Soviet Russia – in the post-war world. The third – *and last* – priority was to mobilise the partisans to aid in the defeat of Nazi Germany.

'I am very much afraid that, if we are not careful, we shall be building up in northern Italy with arms and money a rival Italian government,' the Foreign Office (FO) warned. The FO criticised the cageiness of Allied commanders to 'make use of this Resistance Movement', worrying that communist partisans would seize control. In November PWD issued a clear directive ordering the 'playing down' of the role of the partisans by all concerned.

Those at the helm of SOE Maryland railed against this *volte face*. They lobbied for the support of the partisans to continue. Time and again they argued that the communist partisans would come peacefully into line once the war in Italy was won. That same month General Alexander himself – Allied commander-in-chief in Italy – issued his 'Winter Directive', in which he continued to laud the achievements of the Italian resistance, working hand in glove with the SOE.

'What do the partisans do?' he asked, rhetorically. 'The toll of bridges blown, locomotives derailed ... small garrisons liquidated, factories demolished, mounts week by week, and the German nerves are so strained, their unenviable administrative situation taxed so much further, that large bodies of . . . troops are constantly tied down . . . Almost any frontline troops could tell stories of Partisan assistance . . . Their fighting qualities and local knowledge are constantly proved invaluable.'

An increasingly bitter power struggle was in train over the fate of the Italian resistance. On one side was the military and the SOE; on the other, the Foreign Office and the PWD. It was no secret who wielded the darker power: the Psychological Warfare Division were past-masters. In the dying months of 1944 war reporter Paul Morton's message – that the Italian partisans, communists included, were embroiled in a noble and heroic struggle deserving full Allied support – ran contrary to what they intended.

There was a rift developing between those determined to further military support for the partisans, in order to help vanquish the enemy, and those who believed the need to combat communism should take priority. That fault line had sucked in an unwitting victim: Paul Morton. That was why he – and his stories – had to be disavowed and, if necessary, destroyed.

Of course, Michael Lees was privy to little if any of this. His reports made clear that he had few concerns regarding the partisans' political leanings. Pragmatically, he concluded: 'At present, the political situation is not dangerous. There is ill-feeling amongst the two main Parties, but as yet no action. With firm Allied control there is no reason why any dissention should arise . . .'

Unaware that moves were afoot to sideline – betray – the Italian resistance, Lees continued to lobby for a return to 'his' partisans, as he saw it, rejoining Major Temple's mission. But in late November 1944 his hopes were to be utterly dashed. Lees received a shattering message: surrounded by enemy forces determined to finish off his partisan forces, Major Temple had been killed. News of his tragic loss had reached SOE headquarters via radio, from Bert Farrimond, Temple's dour Lancastrian coal miner turned W/T operator.

'The area was under considerable enemy mortar fire,' Farrimond telegraphed, 'and Major DAREWSKI decided we should leave on a truck loaded with stores . . . Before he was able to climb on the truck the driver let in the clutch and the truck seemed to skid and crush Major DAREWSKI against the wall. I was told that he had fractured both arms and probably his pelvis.'

Major Temple had been evacuating his headquarters, as the enemy executed a fierce sweep of the valley. Never one for hyperbole, Farrimond reported that 'everything went wrong, catastrophe overtook us, the Major receiving fatal injuries in the accident.' Within forty-eight hours Farrimond had been pulled out by air. 'With the Major gone the mission was finished, so to this end . . . I came out with eleven others in a bomber . . .'

Lees mourned the loss of such an iconic figure and good friend, not to mention the collapse of the entire Flap mission. A few days after being pulled out, Farrimond met up with him in Florence. They had much to discuss. In the days prior to his death Temple had taken his mission to new and unprecedented heights. Via the landing strip that they'd just finished constructing, he'd requested a drop of fifty million Lire, to fund ongoing partisan operations. He'd also asked for twenty-five cargo aircraft to fly in, with weaponry and arms.

Temple's 12 November shopping list reflected the scale of combat that he feared was coming: '25 81mm mortars (English), petrol 500 gallons, clothing and 3,000 blankets, 2,500 rifles and Stens and heavy automatic weapons. What about Breda 20mm or even 40mm [heavy cannons]. Is it possible to land? If so both the landing ground and the whole area could be held against all-comers.'

He reported on a recent raid by his partisans, one that had been so successful that Il Duce – Mussolini, the Italian Fascist dictator – himself had decreed that Temple's partisans were to be destroyed 'at all costs'. In response, some 3,000 German and Italian troops backed by armoured cars and tanks had thundered into the region, to wipe out Temple's 500-odd partisans.

It was mostly to resist this offensive that Temple had sent his 12 November shopping list of arms and equipment. Though its tone was somewhat desperate, little had reached him in terms of the supplies that he'd requested, and six days later Temple was dead, his surviving partisans scattered into the mountains. As for Farrimond, he'd got out by the skin of his teeth: he'd been lifted out from the airstrip just before enemy forces overran it.

Had Major Temple received the supplies that he'd requested, his forces might have held firm. The failure to provide them arguably cost him his life and signalled an end to the Flap mission. By the winter of 1944, supply flights to the partisans had dropped off to critically low levels. SOE agents in the field were complaining bitterly that they and their partisans were being thrown to the dogs.

Having lamented the loss of their dear friend, Lees turned to the other business that was foremost in his mind. He had a sense that an alternative mission was about to come his way, and he wanted to know if the long-experienced radio operator might join him. Married to local Lancashire girl Jane Glover, Farrimond was an utterly reliable salt-of-the-earth type. Now approaching his 34th birthday, he was a hugely-experienced pair of hands, hence Lees' hunger to recruit him.

At outbreak of war Farrimond had signed up to the 2nd Fife and Forfar Yeomanry, an armoured regiment more commonly known as the 'Knife and Forkers' – motto, 'For Hearth and Home'. But in August 1943 he'd been sought out by SOE. On paper Farrimond was an odd recruit: it was his wireless abilities that would draw him into the cloak-and-dagger world. In October 1943 he'd duly signed the Official Secrets Act, pledging to preserve 'any sketch, plan, model, article, note, document or information which relates to munitions of war,' or 'any secret official code word, or pass word . . .'

In November 1943 the former coal miner was posted to India, to complete a short course at SOE's Eastern Warfare School, before being sent for wireless training at their specialist radio school, codenamed ME9, situated near Meerut, a city in northern India near the foothills of the Himalayas. In a sense, there was no better training ground for behind-the-lines operations in the Italian mountains. For his subsequent services on Operation Flap, Farrimond was recommended for a Mention in Despatches. But the gritty former collier didn't much hanker after gongs: what he wanted most was to return to the mountains.

Lees asked what he had been up to since his evacuation. 'I'm just waiting around for orders,' Farrimond replied.

'D'you want to get back into North Italy?' Lees probed.

Farrimond paused before answering. 'It all depends on what I'd have to do.'

Lees had already been assigned a radio operator, but he'd far prefer to take a man of Farrimond's pedigree, one with whom he'd built up such a close rapport. 'Would you like to come in again with me, Bert?'

Farrimond was silent for a moment. 'I'd go with you, sir, if I went with anyone . . .' he ventured. 'When are you going?'

Lees replied that he didn't know for sure, but no sooner than a week's time, at the very earliest. He asked Farrimond to think it over. That evening Farrimond returned to see Lees. He told him that he wanted in: if Captain Michael Lees was deploying, so would Corporal Albert Edward Farrimond. It now only remained for the SOE's Maryland office to clarify the nature of their coming operation.

SOE'S Italian mission had been codenamed Maryland by its chief, Commander Gerald 'Gerry' Holdsworth, for a very specific reason. A still-waters-run-deep type, Holdsworth – a seasoned mariner and a former rubber planter from Malaya (now Malaysia) – nursed a deep passion for the things he cared about, plus an occasionally explosive temper. He'd been described variously as being 'as brave as they come', 'half hero, half pirate', and an 'expert in clandestine warfare in all its aspects'.

A former film-maker, Holdsworth had been recruited into SOE by the traditional 'tap on the shoulder' method. He'd played a key role organising and commanding the 'Helford Flotilla', a collection of small boats that ferried the earliest SOE recruits to and from occupied France. Its base was a farmhouse called Ridifarne, on the secluded Helford River, in Cornwall, from where the flotilla set sail. The Ridifarne HQ had been run by Holdsworth's wife, Mary, herself a top expert in the use of explosives for demolition and sabotage work.

Fittingly, Holdsworth had named SOE'S Italian mission after her, and he cared about it as passionately as he did its namesake. He was backed to the hilt by Major General Gubbins, SOE's chief.

'It is desperately important to encourage resistance in northern Italy by every means possible,' Gubbins had urged. Likewise, General Alexander had exhorted SOE to unleash maximum efforts against the enemy, and he had gone as far as speaking to the Italian resistance leaders directly, urging 'violent and sustained' attacks.

That their work had borne fruit was perhaps best gauged by the reaction of the enemy. By the summer of 1944, German intelligence had reported some 20,000 dead, wounded or missing at the hands of the partisans. None other than Field Marshal Kesselring – Hitler's chosen commander in Italy – had started to refer to the Italian resistance in the following haunting terms: 'Our Wehrmacht [unified armed forces] is being stopped by a shadow.'

By October Kesselring had become so concerned that he decreed 'a week of anti-partisan war'. He'd ordered his best forces, equipped with tanks, flame-throwers and artillery, to take the fight to the hills. When such measures failed to secure a definitive victory, Kesselring – with Hitler's encouragement – ordered his men to resort to widespread brutality.

'It is the duty of all troops and police in my command to adopt the severest measures,' he announced. 'Every act of violence committed by the partisans must be punished immediately.' He ordered 'a proportion of the male population' to be shot, while pledging to 'protect any commander who exceeds the usual restraints'. Hitler added fuel to the fire, ordering ten partisans killed for every German casualty.

Winston Churchill – a key proponent of irregular warfare across occupied Europe – was privy to Kesselring's orders. Codebreakers working at Bletchley Park had decrypted the German commander's messages, sending them directly to the British prime minister. They made for grim reading. In August 1944, in the village of Sant'Anna di Stazzema, SS troops had machine-gunned 560 men, women and children, as reprisals for partisan operations. Then, in late September, at Marzabotto, they had perpetrated one of the single greatest massacres of the war, wiping out over 700 villagers, including the priest.

These were far from isolated examples, and the level of bestial horror visited on remote Italian populations was terrifying. It reflected the growing desperation of Kesselring. For many this was seen as being out of character for a commander of his long experience. A decorated First World War veteran who had masterminded the rebuilding of the Luftwaffe, Kesselring had commanded the Condor Legion in the Spanish Civil War, the forces of Nazi Germany that had fought alongside the Fascist armies of General Franco.

At the outbreak of hostilities in 1939 he had orchestrated the invasion of Poland, Holland and France. From there he'd gone on to oversee the invasion of the Soviet Union, earning Hitler's very highest regard. Kesselring had vowed to the Führer to fight for every inch of Italian soil. He was a diehard believer in the Nazi cause and had recently adopted a policy of hanging any would-be German deserters. Allied commanders respected, if not feared, his military acumen.

Come the winter of 1944, Kesselring worried about the partisan threat more than ever. It was a phenomenon that he absolutely hated and reviled – irregular, unpredictable guerrilla operations by forces that could melt into the mountains. He branded Italian resistance activities 'a degenerate form of war', deserving 'the utmost severity'. In short, Kesselring was rattled.

A high-level Allied report, written from the enemy's perspective, spelled out the 'Reasons Why the Germans Stay in Italy'. It read: 'If we wish to defend the Reich it is better to defend the frontier as far south as possible and do the fighting on someone else's soil . . . The important industrial output of North Italy contributes to our war effort . . . Italy is one of the Axis partners and nearly our only Ally left. It would be a serious blow to the political morale of our own people to abandon Fascist Italy.'

Aware of all this, SOE Maryland's chief, Holdsworth, fought tooth and nail to counter any directives that might pour cold water on the work of the Italian resistance. He had few doubts what the 150,000-odd partisans positioned north of the Gothic Line could achieve, if properly armed and trained. Crucially, they could 'harass German lines of communication by sabotage and guerrilla warfare and . . . impede the withdrawal of German forces from Italy, in order that the Allied armies might be able to get at them and destroy them.'

Heaven forbid that they should be stopped, and by what amounted to outright abandonment by the Allies. This was doubly so, for in the winter of 1944 Allied forces were under-strength, compared to those of the enemy. In December, the Allies had nineteen divisions facing Kesselring's twenty-seven, and while the Allies enjoyed air and sea superiority, the terrain, the weather and the Gothic Line itself favoured the enemy.

Allied commanders reckoned that Kesselring's attempts to crush the partisans were tying down eleven divisions. Militarily, their role was utterly critical, and so far Holdsworth and his ilk had succeeded in beating off the naysayers. Mike Lees had been promised his new mission courtesy of such efforts, but for how much longer the believers could persevere was anyone's guess.

In early December Lees was briefed on his coming deployment by Major Charles Macintosh, head of the SOE's Florence headquarters. Lees mission was critical: he was to parachute to join the partisans positioned to the rear of the Gothic Line, at the exact point at which the Allies planned to achieve their vital breakthrough.

The cold, snow-bound months of winter 1944 had become known as the 'winter of disappointment in Italy'. Churchill had been promised that the war there would be over by Christmas. Instead, the Gothic Line had held. The fighting had been relentless and the few territorial gains had been won at enormous cost. Troops were exhausted, morale was low and the weather bitter. If Lees could foment havoc in the enemy's rear, Allied forces might achieve the elusive breakthrough.

Lees' mission – codenamed Envelope – came with one or two unfortunate caveats. As Macintosh was at pains to point out, Lees was being sent in to join another SOE agent, a Major Wilcockson. Wilcockson was of an age and rank that fully justified his posting, whereas Lees, a twenty-three-year-old captain, apparently was not.

Once in the field, Lees would be under the orders either of Wilcockson, or another SOE agent, Major Jim Davies, who ran a neighbouring mission. Davies had served in the Burma jungle, before deploying to Greece with the SOE and working closely with the resistance. On the upside, he was a die-hard believer in the potential of partisan warfare. On the downside, Lees didn't particularly relish the idea of being under anyone's direct control.

Still, a mission was a mission – and this one was not to be sniffed at.

Lees and Farrimond were to be dropped during daytime to a point just a few miles behind the enemy front. They would do so during broad daylight, and Lees could only imagine that the partisans were in real strength and must hold considerable territory. Inserting that close to the Gothic Line, they were bound to see serious action and would need to liaise closely with Allied forces on the opposite side of the lines.

As Lees studied his maps, his enthusiasm grew: the terrain was high, broken and mountainous, so ideal for guerrilla operations. To Lees' mind, the potential to wage war here appeared unlimited. But while he thrilled to the prospect, he didn't feel that he'd exactly hit it off with Macintosh. The man had a somewhat effeminate manner, Lees decided, and a 'limp and clammy hand'.

Macintosh had seen action, before becoming chained to his desk at SOE's Florence headquarters. In August 1944 he'd driven into enemy-held Florence in an armoured car borrowed from the Americans, with a large white Angolan rabbit called Poggibonsi perched on top of the Vickers machine gun. It was vintage SOE. The 27-year-old Macintosh was of New Zealand extraction, and was tall, broad-shouldered and charming. Women, apparently, went wild about him. On paper, he and Lees should have hit it off, but it hadn't exactly felt that way.

A few days after his mission briefing Lees was woken at five o'clock in the morning. He dressed quickly, pulling on underclothes and battledress, plus the plethora of kit vital to such a mission: binoculars, compass, fighting knife, revolver, water bottle and medical gear. Over it all went a thick woollen flying jacket, which in turn was zipped inside a set of overalls, fashioned without any buttons or tags that might snag in a parachute harness. Lees knew that he would be thankful for all the layers: outside it was bitterly cold and it would be especially so at altitude.

For today's deployment – as with his previous SOE missions –

Lees was laden down with an extra burden: money. In addition to the several million Lire he was carrying, he'd been given a bag of gold sovereigns. That he'd tied in a handkerchief and stuffed into an ammo pouch on his belt, while thick wads of Lire were jammed into his every pocket.

It struck Lees how ludicrous the situation was: his pay, all thirty pounds a month, would be dribbling into his bank account, yet he here he was entrusted with a king's ransom in cash and gold. If he cared to steal it, no one could possibly prove that he had done so. But how else was SOE supposed to fund such operations?

The previous night he and Farrimond had transferred to Rosignano Airfield, located a few dozen kilometres south of the SOE's Florence HQ, which was situated in a villa on the outskirts of the city. At Rosignano, the US 64th Troop Carrier Group had established a flight of Douglas C-47 Skytrains – the DC-3 in civilian parlance; dubbed the 'Dakota' in British military service – the classic twin-engine transport aircraft of the Second World War. From Rosignano the 64th's mission was to service the needs of special operations across all northern Italy.

Alongside the ranks of Dakotas there were one or two other, more curious airframes. One was a distinctive Nardi FN.305, a sleek Italian two-seater trainer and liaison aircraft, which in 1939 had achieved a world speed record. The other was even more instantly recognisable: it was a spindly, long-legged Fieseler Fi 156 *Storch* – Stork – a single-engine German spotter plane with an unrivalled short take-off and landing capability.

Both aircraft had seen service with the Italian air force against the Allies. Now, they'd been repainted in friendly colours to meet the SOE's needs. They were perfect for executing ultra-clandestine flights behind the Gothic Line, and especially as they boasted a pilot of untold renown. Lieutenant Furio Lauri was an Italian fighter ace credited with twelve Allied kills, including one Lancaster bomber. He'd been shot down twice, once by a Hurricane and once by anti-aircraft fire. Both times he'd survived.

By the time of the Italian surrender he'd been awarded the War Cross for Military Valour and the Italian Crown, plus the Order of the German Eagle, among other decorations. Regardless, he'd signed up with the Italian resistance and it wasn't long before the clandestine operators had come calling. Lauri had been approached by both the SOE and the US equivalent, the Office of Strategic Services (OSS). He'd decided to work with the British, hence his installation at the Rosignano airbase on SOE business.

As he strode out to the waiting Dakotas, Lees paid those former-enemy aircraft small heed, little realising what a crucial role they would play on his coming mission. He clutched the flying suit closer to his six-foot-two frame. The sky was grey, the weather bitingly cold. Three aircraft were being readied: one was already packed with Lees and Farrimond's weaponry and kit, while the others were stuffed full of arms, ammo and supplies to drop to the partisans.

As Lees clambered aboard the American transport aircraft he was struck by how different this deployment was from those that had gone before. When heading into Yugoslavia, and later to join Major Temple, there had been rich theatre and drama in the moment. He remembered his 1943 departure, flying out to join the Yugoslavian Chetniks. The dark, gaping bomb-bay of the Halifax – the route via which agents had had to exit the aircraft – had been somehow so symbolic: a gateway into another world, one wherein all the normal rules of warfare were to be torn up and burned to a cinder. They'd dropped into a world where anything goes.

By contrast, there was something curiously flat and unemotional about climbing aboard a purpose-built aircraft like the Dakota and settling into a relatively comfortable seat. As the aircraft roared into the skies, Lees had to remind himself just what he was flying into here: he was going in to wage total war. Their destination lay less than 200 kilometres north, and he had to focus and get into the zone.

With a flight of powerful P-51 Mustang fighters as escort, the Dakotas crossed the coast before turning north. Faint flashes from a coastal hill battery revealed that they had crossed into enemy territory. The shells burst harmlessly far below their 20,000 feet cruise altitude. In perfect arrow-shaped formation the three-aircraft rumbled on towards the high mountains, as a pair of Mustangs broke off and dived to strafe the enemy gunners.

Lees studied the terrain below. He could see tiny puffs of white smoke: the opposing sides, hurling artillery barrages at each other's lines. He had crossed this war-blasted landscape barely three months earlier, executing his daring mission on foot, yet Allied and enemy positions hardly seemed to have changed at all in the interim. The stranglehold had to be broken, and Lees hungered to play his part.

The aircraft began to bank this way and that, threading a path between the highest, snowbound peaks. Beyond, the vast plain of the mighty River Po – the longest river in all of Italy – opened out before them. If Allied forces could break through to that, they could steamroller across it with their armour.

Lees thoughts were pulled back to the present by a cry that echoed through the Dakota's hold. 'There it is! There it is!'

He glanced through the aircraft's open doorway. A distinctive pattern of red dots was visible on a high snowfield. The Dakotas began to circle in line astern, spiralling down towards that point. The distinctive red dots resolved themselves to be salvaged parachutes. Figures dashed among them, now and then stopping to wave at the approaching aircraft.

The Dakota's aircrew clipped their safety straps to the hold, to prevent themselves from being thrown out accidentally. They began to stack Lees and Farrimond's kit beside the gaping doorway. Lees clambered to his feet, making one last check of his parachute harness and the kitbag strapped to his leg. It contained all his personal equipment, and was fitted with a quick-release mechanism, which would enable him to lower it on a twenty-foot rope, so it would hit the ground first, taking the impact of its own weight.

Three runs were executed over the DZ, during which the despatchers hurled out the supply containers. On the approach to the fourth, Lees struggled to the open doorway, hampered by the heavy kitbag. He took up position, glancing behind. The redoubtable Farrimond was right on his shoulder. He looked up, to check his parachute line was firmly attached to the cable running along the roof of the hold. It would trigger his chute automatically just seconds after he jumped.

He turned back to the howling void, as the floor tilted, then gently righted itself. Moments later he sensed a distinctive flutter, as the pilot throttled back the engines and the red light flashed on: prepare to jump.

The red switched to green.

With both hands gripping the side of the doorway Lees catapulted himself forwards, the fuselage of the aircraft flashing past in a blur.

An instant later he was tumbling into the thin and icy blue.

Chapter 6

A few weeks after his return to Britain, Major Farran was given a completely new operational area and command. He was to take charge of a recently formed SAS unit, No. 3 Squadron, and to deploy with them to Italy. There, they were to be placed under a highly unorthodox chain of command.

In Italy Farran was to report directly to the Special Operations Executive, but for its battle orders, Farran's squadron was to fall under the direct command of US General Mark Clark, the comparatively youthful and hard-charging commander of the Allies' 15th Army Group, whose forces were tasked with the liberation of northern Italy.

It was a most unusual proposition – that a full SAS squadron, some sixty-strong, would be placed under the orders of the American high command. But with Allied forces outnumbered and very possibly outgunned along the Gothic Line, nothing that might help break that bloody impasse was being ruled out, no matter how unorthodox or irregular.

Farran viewed his new mission with great enthusiasm. While he would miss his old squadron – Big Jim Mackie, among many other unique and irreplaceable characters – his new command had great promise. Raised from fresh – mostly airborne – volunteers, the men of No. 3 Squadron had been trained by one of the best, Major Oswald 'Mike' Rooney. Major Rooney was one of the longest-served veterans of British Commando and special forces operations, having raided targets from as far apart as Norway, the Channel Islands, France and Italy.

Rooney had been forced to surrender his command of No. 3 Squadron, due to injury. He'd parachuted into France on post D-Day operations, but had broken his back in the process. His loss was very much Farran's gain. Rooney's men were young, fit, well-disciplined and raring to go. Mostly in their early twenties, many had yet to see action and were keen to prove themselves. In Farran, they sensed they had a commander who would enable them to do so.

Anyone with a view to getting down and dirty on – or behind – the *Gotenstellung* had to be in Florence, the jumping-off point for combat missions. In its sumptuous villa, set within the Fiesole suburb of Florence, the SOE had established their forward operating base, and the US 15th Army Group had likewise established a headquarters in the city.

Farran would report to two equally distinctive individuals. One, Colonel John Held Riepe, was the square-jawed US Army officer in charge of all special and irregular warfare along the Gothic Line. Colonel Riepe – US Military Academy West Point graduate of the class of 1924, and a cavalry officer – was forty-three years of age, so only five years junior to his commanding general, Mark Clark. He was cut from similar cloth: rigorously professional, driven and unrelenting, Riepe was prepared to pull out all the stops to out-think and outfight the enemy.

Of course, the reputation of the British Special Air Service went before it and Colonel Riepe was a self-confessed aficionado. In Major Farran and his No. 3 Squadron SAS, he sensed he'd been sent a commander and a body of men that could truly deliver, if only the right kind of deployment could be found for them. Colonel Riepe was determined to furnish just such a mission, Florence being the springboard for all Allied special operations and partisan missions north of the Gothic Line.

The other figure who would decide Farran's fate was Major Charles Macintosh. Macintosh had been with SOE since the first Allied landings in Italy, and he'd forged a reputation as being the daring agent who had penetrated war-torn Florence in the US armoured car that he'd borrowed, proving that a telephone cable could provide communications links to the partisans in the northern half of the besieged and starving city.

Superficially, Macintosh and Farran shared many traits. It was odd, then, how the two seemed to rub each other up the wrong way. At first, Macintosh declared himself delighted to have the tough and daring special forces unit at his disposal, and with the potential to link up with SOE agents and partisans. But he soon got wise to Farran's distinctive temperament: the SAS commander was impulsive, dismissive of orders of which he didn't particularly approve and hungry for action, and Macintosh began to worry that Farran's arrival might prove something of a poisoned chalice.

'I was somewhat concerned,' Macintosh concluded of the SAS major. His worries were chiefly for the SOE's behind-the-lines intelligence-gathering networks, something that he viewed as almost of more importance than offensive operations. 'Our Intelligence networks . . . were in a very delicate security situation, and security was not one of the SAS['s] strongpoints,' Macintosh remarked.

According to him, the very nature of the SAS and Farran's own character meant that 'codes, safe houses, agents and such things would weigh lightly in their plans, which, in any case, were very short term.' Macintosh saw himself and his SOE agents as playing the long game, while Farran was intent on causing maximum havoc and mayhem as quickly as possible.

One night in Florence, Farran dragged a reluctant Macintosh away from his desk on a trawl of the city bars. After a good few drinks the SAS major got into 'a couple of scraps' and Macintosh began to take an even dimmer view of the man. As Farran would be the first to recognise, the years of back-to-back missions had left him somewhat on the edge. He drank too much. He had developed a dark side. His recklessness was coupled with a growing merciless-ness for his enemies that some found disturbing. But as his actions across France had proved – and especially at Châtillon – this was a commander who very much got the job done.

Here in Italy Farran hungered for a mission that might enable his No. 3 Squadron SAS to strike a decisive blow. Farran was convinced that his men could play a seminal role, enabling Allied troops to punch through the *Gotenstellung*'s defences and precip-itating the enemy's rout. He knew that no such behind-the-lines operation would be possible without the help, guidance and firepower of the local partisans. He also knew that the Italian resistance was riven with rivalries, but where was that not the case? From Norway to Greece and from France to Yugoslavia, it pretty much came with the territory.

As far as he understood it, about two-thirds of the partisans were nominally communist, while the remainder were right-wing 'democrats'. Tensions often ran high between the two, especially over Allied weapons drops. But Farran didn't particularly give a damn. He'd have done a deal with the Devil himself, if it enabled him to fight the reviled enemy.

He didn't doubt that the Italian resistance – armed, trained and led by SAS soldiers – would prove just as capable as the French Maquis had done. All he needed was to secure a mission that would enable him and his men to link up with a suitable band of fighters. Farran longed for that mission; he burned for it, and for a very specific reason.

Several times throughout the war – most recently in France – Farran believed he'd been gifted a second life, so miraculous were his escapes and his survival. He was determined to make maximum use of it. Throughout late November and early December 1944, he lobbied tirelessly; repeatedly made his case; trod the corridors of the SOE and US Army offices in Florence without let-up. Sooner or later he felt certain he would land the kind of deployment he sought.

A previous mission, codenamed Operation Galia, had more than demonstrated how a crack SAS unit, when married up with the SOE agent on the ground, could wreak havoc in the enemy's rear. That mission had come about almost by chance, and largely due to the extraordinary exploits of one individual.

British Major Gordon Lett had escaped from an Italian prisoner of war camp in 1943, headed into the mountains and raised his own force of partisans, completely independent of any Allied support. Before the war Lett had been an accomplished mountaineer, and he was a natural at this kind of work. Incredibly, he was recruited into the SOE in July 1944 while still commanding his band of partisans and having never returned to Britain.

In November 1944, Kesselring ordered a daring counter-attack to strike the Allies where he perceived them to be at their weakest, on the far western end of their offensive line. The Allied high command learned of the threat, and turned to the SOE for a solution. It just so happened that Major Lett had established his partisan operation – codenamed Mission Blundell Violet – in exactly the area of interest to the enemy.

A troop of SAS under the command of Captain Robert 'Bob' Walker-Brown prepared to parachute into Lett's area of operations. This was no small undertaking: it would be the largest single drop of men and supplies undertaken by the SOE to date. Walker-Brown was charged to hit the enemy's lines of communication and supply, stirring up a hornet's nest in their rear. That in turn should scupper Kesselring's planned counter-attack, by tying up swathes of his troops.

No better commander could have been allocated to such a mission: Walker-Brown was himself an escaped POW, and he'd been recruited into the SAS on the strength of his own spirited getaway. Serving with the Highland Light Infantry he'd been wounded in the June 1942 Battle of the Cauldron, in the North African desert, and taken captive. He'd ended up in the Campo Prigionieri di Guerra 21, situated at Chieti, in the foothills of the Apennine mountains.

An ingenious and masterful set of tunnels were excavated, through which Walker-Brown and fellow POWs planned to slip beneath the perimeter of the camp. Amid the confusion of the signing of the Italian armistice, he and six others managed to hide there and break out. On 5 October 1943 Walker-Brown finally reached Allied lines. Subsequently recruited into the SAS, he had parachuted in to join Major Farran in France, just before his audacious assault on the German garrison at Châtillon.

There, Walker-Brown had accounted for himself admirably: so well, in fact, that just a month later he was tasked to command a mission of Operation Galia's import. Galia had proved a spectacular success. Walker-Brown and Lett led a combined SAS-partisan force through deep snows, rugged terrain and freezing, ice-bound conditions. Fording treacherous mountain streams and scaling peaks up to seven thousand feet in height, they'd marched for days on end to strike the enemy at a time and from a direction he believed impossible.

Repeatedly they'd ambushed German transport convoys, mortared enemy positions, mined roads and machine-gunned infantry columns. They executed a perfect series of butcher-and-bolt raids, of which Churchill would have been inordinately proud. The Germans reacted by launching a massive *rastrellamento* – raking through – committing 10,000 troops to surrounding the joint SAS-partisan force and annihilating it.

Walker-Brown and his SAS managed to slip the noose. They went on to capture a German officer, forcing him at gunpoint to act as their guide. They made it back to Allied lines having lost very few men, and having scuppered Kesselring's much-vaunted counter-offensive. Walker-Brown won a DSO for his achievements, the citation for which stressed his 'unparalleled guerrilla skills and personal courage'.

In short, he was driven, unconventional, impatient of political correctness, occasionally prone to cussedness and blessed with a devilish wit. Following Galia, he had a very high view of the Italian partisans, whom he found to be possessed of 'quite remarkable courage, bravery and endurance . . . after all it takes a very brave man to decide that a very small force of British parachutists is a wise thing to back, when his home and his family are surrounded . . .'

In many ways Walker-Brown and Farran were cut from similar cloth. In Italy, they would form the dream team, joining forces on a mission of untold audacity and daring. But all of that lay some-time in the future. For now, Farran was struggling to convince someone – anyone – that his No. 3 Squadron had a vital role to play. They were here, fresh into theatre, armed to the teeth and raring to go.

All they needed was someone to champion them.

Chapter 7

It was 2 January 1945 when Michael Lees, drifting beneath his parachute and blown somewhat off course, landed in an icy mountain stream. His radio operator, Bert Farrimond, ended up snagged in a nearby tree, its branches frosted with snow. With help from Lees and the partisans, Farrimond was brought down from the treetops uninjured.

They'd landed on the flank of a wide, open valley. Beyond the high peaks to the south, the crash of artillery fire echoed noisily. It struck Lees as being unbelievable that they could have parachuted so brazenly, this close to the front line. As far as he could tell, this was a heavily populated region; paths led off to left and right, and they were thick with locals leading mule trains, ready to load up the newly arrived supplies. Half a mile further down the valley the SOE agent – or British Liaison Officer (BLO) as they were known in the field – had his headquarters.

That all this could be taking place in broad daylight and in plain sight of the enemy unsettled Lees, but he reassured himself the BLO had to know what he was doing. With an escort of heavily armed partisans, he and Farrimond set off, making for his base. They'd not been walking long when they rounded a bend and came face-to-face with a tall man wearing thick glasses. The iconic tommy gun slung over his shoulder marked him out as being British, as did his bearing.

The figure gestured apologetically. 'How do you do?' he called. 'I'm Wilcockson. So sorry I wasn't there to meet you chaps in person, but no one told me you were coming.'

It was true. No one had thought to warn Wilcockson to expect Lees and Farrimond. He'd been awaiting a resupply drop only, and he'd entertained few hopes that even that would materialise. Since his deployment in September 1944, Wilcockson had succeeded in calling in just one air-drop of twelve containers, so little more than a single plane-load. He and his local fighters had survived months of terrible winter privations, after which, he reported angrily, 'the Partisans' morale was nil'.

They had been left bereft of boots, ammunition, winter clothing and rations. By Wilcockson's own admission, they saw themselves as being 'handicapped by a British Mission and alleged supply officer whose record to date was . . . a pitiful show.' It was hardly Wilcockson's fault. A former artillery officer, Major Ernest Hulton Wilcockson had carried out small-arms and explosives instruction at one of SOE's training schools, before going on to smuggle agents into enemy-occupied Crete. He was committed, experienced and capable.

But here in northern Italy he had fallen foul of the same malaise which had struck down Canadian war reporter Paul Morton – the growing rift over whether to back the Italian resistance to wage war against the enemy. During the winter months air-drops had dried up. So few and far between were they that Colin Gubbins had railed against the failures, and Gerry Holdsworth had resorted to almighty shouting matches with those in power, declaring it 'a bloody poor show'.

The statistics spoke for themselves. In June 1944, 221 tonnes of supplies had been dropped to the partisans, with even more in July. But come the autumn, resupply missions had fallen off a cliff-edge. By October they were down to a third of the summer numbers, and worse followed. It was a situation in which it was 'impossible to supply even . . . minimal needs', the SOE complained, 'and this has meant disaster to many an excellent group'.

Finally, Roundell Cecil Palmer, the 3rd Earl of Selborne and Britain's Minister for Economic Warfare – so the political chief of the SOE – raised the issue directly with Churchill. 'When you have called out a Maquis into open warfare,' he wrote of the Italian resistance, 'it is not fair to let it drop like a hot potato. These men have burned their boats and have no retreat. If we fail them with ammunition, death by torture awaits.'

This was no hyperbole. Across the eighteen SOE missions presently in place north of the Gothic Line, there was a feeling close to open rebellion. One BLO wrote: 'If Command has no intention of being interested, it should not have promised arms and materials or have sent Allied Missions to give false hopes . . .' Others spoke angrily of being 'abandoned, and that therefore the only thing to do was to hide'.

Wilcockson's autumn and winter reports echoed this sense of hopeless neglect. Lack of air-drops had made the 'prestige of the British Mission reach rock bottom and all-out efforts come to [a] virtual standstill . . . The position of the Partisans' supplies . . . [is] now extremely critical and any offensive operations against the enemy [are] impossible.'

This was the dire situation into which Lees – and Farrimond – had unwittingly parachuted. Regardless, they made their way to Wilcockson's headquarters, situated in the small mountain village of Gova. Before the war Gova had been a popular winter sports resort, boasting two fine hotels. Wilcockson had chosen to base himself in one, and Farrimond was delighted to learn that it still had electricity with which he could power up his radio.

As Farrimond went about establishing communications with Macintosh, at SOE's Florence headquarters, Wilcockson proceeded to brief Lees. The partisans that he was scheduled to join were called the Reggiani, after the town of Reggio Emilia, some thirty kilometres away. They'd not seen action for months, their morale was at rock bottom and their supplies and kit were in a pitiful state. It wasn't the rosiest of pictures.

'So where are the nearest enemy?' Lees asked.

'The plains are thick with them and they have garrisons strung along the main roads,' Wilcockson explained. 'The nearest is about two hours' march away.'

'But surely they must know you're here,' Lees objected. 'I'm surprised they allow you to exist so close to them.'

'Don't worry,' Wilcockson reassured him, 'they've not got the troops to spare for a full-scale attack. We've had no trouble for months now.'

Lees remained sceptical. The weather was still relatively fine for winter in these parts, but sooner or later it would break and then the real test would come. With only a few inches of snow on the ground, the partisans were still able to move relatively freely. Thick drifts and freezing conditions would change all of that. He didn't doubt that the enemy lacked the troops to man the Gothic Line and to clear out the pockets of resistance permanently, but they could launch swift, stabbing attacks to disrupt operations.

'Well, make sure your patrols are watchful tonight,' Lees warned Wilcockson. 'I'm allergic to Germans. Wherever I land they always seem to cause trouble in a day or so.'

While it had been said with a smile, Lees wasn't joking. Within forty-eight hours of deploying on his first mission, in Yugoslavia, the enemy had swooped. Lees had escaped by the skin of his teeth, but three of his party of fellow Brits were left dead or mortally wounded. Likewise, upon parachuting in to join Major Temple's mission north of the Gothic Line, Lees, Morton and Long had been under fire and fighting a series of desperate battles within hours of their arrival.

Of course, such fierce actions would have made for great newspaper copy, if only Morton had been allowed to publish his stories. As it was he had been silenced and Lees had a new and pressing mission to execute.

Wilcockson outlined the strength of the partisan forces. There were four separate brigades, of which three were communist and one hailed from the right-wing Christian Democrats – known as the *Fiamme Verdi*, or the Green Flames. When serving with Major Temple, Lees had grown accustomed to how Italians of apparently opposing political views seemed to operate happily together, so he wasn't unduly concerned. The overall commander of the partisans was a former Italian Army officer, Colonel Augusto Monti, who Wilcockson described as being pleasant enough, but hardly a live wire.

That evening Lees, Farrimond and Wilcockson dined in the hotel, waited on by a servant in formal dress and with a table laid for several courses. The food was first class: spaghetti steeped in wine with grated cheese, omelettes made with real butter, and each course accompanied by a fine vintage. The aperitif was a Marsala – similar to sherry – followed by a sparkling red, and to finish an excellent bottle of Sassolino, a strong aniseed liqueur made locally.

They had eaten far better than in so-called 'liberated' territory. Lees was amazed, especially as they were surrounded by the enemy. It was somehow so unreal, and he was determined to get down to some real war-fighting as soon as possible. The very next morning he planned to set out for Colonel Monti's HQ, to get a better sense of the lie of the land, not to mention the fighting calibre of the partisans.

But Lees awoke to find that the weather had turned. A thick blizzard was howling outside. Dressed in every item of warm clothing that he could muster, Lees headed for the hotel's front door. It was jammed solid with snow. He found an alternative exit on the lee side and stepped into the icy blast. His exposed skin was assaulted by freezing, stinging gusts, his boots sinking into the thicker drifts.

Wilcockson suggested they postpone the trip, at least until the storm blew itself out. Lees remained adamant that a start should be made. With a guide leading the way, they set forth into the tempest. The snow was falling so fast it was impossible to see from one side of the street to the other. They'd been struggling through thigh-deep drifts for half an hour or so, when the guide confessed that he couldn't find the way.

Lees wasn't entirely surprised. If they didn't retrace their steps they would be obliterated by the storm, and they mightn't even find the hotel again. By the time they reached it, their clothes were stiff with ice and all were frozen to the bone. They gathered by a crackling fire to thaw out, after which Farrimond went about raising Florence headquarters. He was in excellent spirits, despite the abortive trek, and declared that this was just the kind of mission that he'd been hoping for.

Unfortunately, his good spirits were to be short-lived.

A signal came back from Macintosh at Florence headquarters, which Farrimond duly decoded. It was addressed to Wilcockson, and it suggested that Lees had overstepped his orders. He had not been sent in to take over control of the Reggiani partisans. Any suggestion he'd made to that effect was wrong. While the message fell short of ordering Lees to withdraw – just – he'd had the rug pulled out from under his feet in spectacular fashion, and barely twenty-four hours after his arrival.

Lees sent back a typically robust missive. 'I should like to point out that this message was received by Major Wilcockson and my wireless operator, and has been the cause of considerable embarrassment . . . If it is considered that I have come into the field to pursue a position not recorded, I should be delighted to return and account for my actions . . .'

Of course, Lees had only just got his boots on the ground and he sensed an opportunity for real action here; to achieve great things. The last thing he wanted was to somehow attempt a return to Florence, to face some kind of dressing down for whatever obscure reasons. Indeed, both he and Wilcockson were left dumbfounded. The source of the growing tension – and confusion – from headquarters eluded them.

In an effort to head off the enemy at the pass, Lees telegraphed: 'Have placed myself under orders of Major Wilcockson.' He added, with emphasis, that this message 'has been read by Major Wilcockson' – so in other words, the two SOE officers were in full agreement. Lees made clear that the entire exchange should also be copied to London, as he sought some top cover from senior SOE figures.

Unbeknown to Lees, there were hidden reasons behind SOE Florence's apparent antagonism. Their hands were becoming increasingly tied. In recent weeks, none other than General Alexander himself had issued a series of orders, which on the face of it telegraphed that the military, too, was turning its back on the Italian resistance.

Alexander's directive – broadcast direct to the senior partisan leadership – had told them to 'stand-down' for the winter months. Not only that, they were to go home and conserve their ammunition and abandon all offensive action. Even more shocking, the broadcast had been made without consulting the SOE. The fear that drove Alexander's proclamation – of the Italian partisans being 'Reds' and being poised to seize power – emanated from the Foreign Office, but the orders, coming from General Alexander himself, caused utter consternation.

'Despair and confusion filled the minds of Partisans and Liaison Missions . . .' SOE Maryland bemoaned. Key partisan leaders expressed disgust at such an order. 'The battle continues and must continue,' declared one. 'There must not be a weakening of the Partisan effort, but an intensification . . .'

Faced with a growing backlash, Alexander made a telling admission. His 'go-slow' order was not of his – not of the military's – making. 'You have to realise,' he told one foremost resistance leader, who raised bitter objections, 'I am a soldier, not a politician.' It was all entirely political, and the naysayers – those who were arguing for the Italian resistance to be abandoned – were gaining the upper hand.

On 8 January 1945 a two-page memo marked 'SECRET' was circulated to the British military's Chiefs of Staff. Signed simply 'A Cadogan', its author was the Foreign Office luminary Sir Alexander Montagu George Cadogan, one of the central figures driving British policy. Scion of a titled and wealthy aristocratic family, Cadogan cited in his memo Anthony Eden, the Foreign Secretary, and one of Churchill's key deputies.

Cadogan's memo pulled no punches. He wrote: '[F]rom the political perspective the situation was potentially dangerous . . . we could not overlook the danger that the Communists who, by all accounts, are by far the best-organised of the anti-Fascist parties . . . would make a view to capturing so useful and powerful a machine, with a view to building it up as a rival of the Italian government in Rome.' That 'useful and powerful machine' was the Italian resistance, armed and organised by the SOE.

The memo went on to warn of the dangers of 'creating the essential elements for a civil war . . . While not wishing to dispute the value which . . . may be attached to the services which the Italian guerrillas in the North have rendered . . . the Secretary of State feels bound to take into consideration the possible political repercussions which may result if these guerrillas are built up beyond a certain point. He feels, therefore, that the Chiefs of Staff ought to watch the situation . . . with the utmost care.'

Increasingly, the British military's hands were tied by their political taskmasters in London. The Chiefs of Staff responded to Cadogan's directive by issuing their own orders, marked 'TOP SECRET', directing the BLOs to take the partisans in hand. 15 Army Group declared that 'future policy regarding the resistance movement in northern Italy will be to . . . concentrate on the supply of food, clothing, boots and money, rather than arms and ammunition . . .'

By January 1945, the Chiefs of Staff were referring to the 'serious problem' of the 'resistance question' in Italy, which needed to be 'thrashed out'. The focus was rapidly shifting towards a perceived need for 'the rapid disarmament and absorption into civil life . . . of all Italian Patriots,' and the 'prevention of fighting between

Patriots and Fascist forces . . . when the Germans withdraw from those parts of Italy they at present occupy.'

Michael Lees had parachuted in to join a band of partisans who, along with their BLO, had been subjected to the miseries of such directives. A wild man of action, it stood to reason that Lees wouldn't accept the status quo. As he had on previous occasions, he would find a way to fight. After all, this was a man who, when ordered to abandon offensive operations with the guerrillas in Yugoslavia, had resorted to solo sabotage missions.

Those at headquarters were getting cold feet at Lees being dropped into theatre. Charles Macintosh, chief of SOE's Florence mission, felt bound by such orders, much that he might abhor them. 'No new orders were forthcoming and the proclamation was to serve as our official guide to the Partisans throughout the winter,' he remarked. In other words, go-slow it was, at least until someone decreed otherwise.

Of course, Lees – and Wilcockson – were privy to little if any of this bigger picture stuff. Marooned in a largely deserted and snowbound hotel, and with the enemy to all sides, little of what was happening made any sense to them. In which case, they decided, they would simply bash on regardless. There was, after all, a war to be fought.

The morning after the snowstorm Lees awoke to a wonderfully still and sunlit dawn. It was just what he needed to lift his spirits. After wolfing down a breakfast of fresh eggs and bacon, he set out following the tracks villagers had beaten through the snow. The scenery was bewitchingly beautiful, but the going proved tough, and it was evening before they reached Colonel Monti's head-quarters. The journey had taken fully eight hours, demonstrating the extent to which winter conditions would hamper operations.

Colonel Monti had established his HQ in the priest's house in Febbio, a village set high in a cleft in the mountains. Only one track led into Febbio, while a narrow twisting path crawled towards a high mountain pass on the far side, now rendered impassable by the snows. It was a veritable fortress, and the colonel's headquarters was seemingly a hive of activity.

A large stone building set on the village outskirts, the priest's house turned out to be a warren of rooms. As Lees entered, he could hear the clack-clack of typewriters to all sides and the chatter of women's voices, as orderlies darted to and fro with stacks of papers. To Lees, it was doubly incongruous. He might have expected this in safe, liberated territory, but a mobile guerrilla headquarters this most definitely was not.

Colonel Monti was a man in his early fifties, tall and distinguished-looking, with a clipped cavalry officer's moustache and swept-back greying hair. Charming and well-mannered, he didn't strike Lees as being the forceful and dynamic character that a leader of irregular forces needed to be. Over dinner, the colonel briefed Lees on the forces under his command, which supposedly amounted to some 2,000 men-at-arms.

'What about defences?' Lees queried. Again, he'd been struck by how dismissive all seemed to be of the enemy threat.

'Oh, that's all taken care of,' the colonel replied. Where their positions were not shielded by the mountains, they had partisan units holding key paths and roads. But of course, if the British could drop in better weapons – mortars and heavy machine guns, for example – they could be rendered doubly secure, the colonel argued.

'What about sabotage operations?' Lees probed. 'What kind of things have your men been up to?'

It was now that the colonel became evasive. He kept trying to change the subject, waxing lyrical about the intelligence they had gathered and propaganda leaflets distributed around the towns. Lees kept pressing him, and finally the colonel admitted that over recent months offensive action had been woefully thin on the ground.

He offered excuses, some of which – such as their lack of ammunition – were entirely valid, but still Lees suspected that much was not as it should be with the Reggiani partisans. They were living in the mountains but not *fighting* in them. He worried about how he might catalyse them into action. Getting proper supply drops was key, but so too would be reigniting the partisans' belief in themselves and their ability to wage war against the enemy.

Lees sensed that the partisans needed a jolt into action. A kick up the proverbial backside. As luck would have it, they were about to receive it, but not from him. It would come from the enemy, and much sooner than even he had imagined.

Early the following morning Lees set out to return to Wilcockson's hotel base, in Gova. It was another glorious day and he had an unusual escort – a village priest turned guerrilla fighter. The warrior-priest's real name was Domenico Orlandini, but everyone knew him by his nom de guerre, Don Carlo. Don Carlo had founded the local right-wing partisans, the *Fiamme Verdi*, and he'd earned something of a reputation for fearlessness.

The priests tended to constitute the backbone of the Italian resistance. Like many, Don Carlo was a stickler for the weekly mass. One Sunday he'd been officiating with a pistol tucked under his cassock, when a messenger arrived to say that the enemy was approaching. With a remarkable coolness Don Carlo had detailed a patrol to break off from the service and take on the enemy, while he finished mass, after which he'd joined them in battle.

From the path's vantage point Don Carlo proceeded to point out the key features. To their backs lay Monte Cusna, the second highest in the Apennines at 7,000 feet, its humped expanse thick with snow. To their left reared Mount Prampa, a little over 5,500 feet, with one of the few roads that cut through the region snaking around its lower slopes. To their front lay the village of Villa Minozzo, which had been twice burned by German troops in reprisals for partisan actions. Beyond that lay the Secchia river, one of the Po's main tributaries, and beyond that again lay the nearest German garrison.

'What's the strength of the garrison?' Lees asked, as he eyed their position through binoculars.

'About three hundred, normally,' the priest answered. 'But I hear a battalion of *Brigate Nere* arrived last night.'

The *Brigate Nere* – Black Brigades – were more formally known as the Auxiliary Corps of the Black Shirts' Action Squads, a Fascist militia loyal to Mussolini. Equipped with standard Italian Army uniforms, they tended to favour items of German military dress. They wore a distinctive badge: a death's head skull with a dagger gripped between its teeth, very similar in design to the SS's own *Totenkopf*. Raised to fight the Allies and the partisans, they'd proved ill-disciplined and ineffective, earning a reputation for brutality, especially against civilians.

But Lees' chief concern was what the arrival of this battalion, some three hundred-strong, might signify. 'Any idea why they've been brought in now?'

Don Carlo shrugged. 'Who knows? Maybe to reinforce the

front line, though *Brigate Nere* don't normally serve a front-line role.'

They set off again. The route before them had been well trodden, and it carved a path between deep banks of snow that glittered in the fine January light. It was mid-morning when, without any kind of warning, they rounded a bend and came face-to-face with Wilcockson. Behind him stretched a long mule train, and Lees could see that his wireless set, weaponry and other kit was loaded aboard one of the heavily laden pack animals.

'Hello, moving house or something?' he called.

Wilcockson stopped and stared. 'Good God, haven't you heard? The Jerries put in an attack last night . . . They captured Gova this morning and we only just managed to get out in time. You're a bloody Jonah, you are! Your arrival's broken our luck.'

Wilcockson's 'Jonah' reference was to the biblical figure popularised in the story of Jonah and the whale – more commonly referring to a person who brings bad luck. It struck Lees as being a little unfair. After all, he'd warned Wilcockson to be doubly vigilant. It also struck him that despite Colonel Monti's expansive set up, they'd received zero warning of the enemy attack.

Clearly, whatever kind of bush telegraph the partisans relied upon to spirit warnings around these hills, it wasn't working very well. As Lees garnered a hurried briefing from Wilcockson, what news there was appeared worrying. Resistance by the partisans was piecemeal and chaotic, Colonel Monti's so-called leadership seeming non-existent. There was an air of panic, as enemy forces closed what looked to be a carefully set trap.

They'd sent in a full division of German troops – some 10,000-plus soldiers – on a massive sweep of the territory. Organising such a push must have taken weeks, so it was sheer coincidence

Where it all began. In 1940 Winston Churchill called for Special Duty Volunteers to 'set the lands of the enemy ablaze'. Cue David Stirling and his Special Air Service (SAS), the butcher and bolt raiders *par excellence*.

More secretive than the SAS, the Special Operations Executive was Churchill's shadowy 'Ministry for Ungentlemanly Warfare'. The SOE taught assassination, sabotage and all the dark arts of war.

SOE agent Captain Michael Lees, pictured with his wife Gwendoline (also SOE), was charged to make this dirty war a reality. Parachuted into Yugoslavia, he linked up with resistance fighters, blowing up and derailing enemy trains. Often working alone, he would earn the nickname Mike 'Wild Man' Lees.

Severely wounded and taken captive in 1941, Major Roy Farran (seated, in jeep) executed a daring and epic escape. Already an SAS legend, in the autumn of 1944 he took his SAS squadron deep behind enemy lines in northern France on a daring mission codenamed Operation Wallace.

Farran led the spectacularly successful attack on the German garrison at Châtillon, housed in a grand chateau. Hunted remorselessly by the enemy, Farran and his men had to go to ground in woodland, jeeps becoming bogged in autumn mud. They survived by the skin of their teeth.

In preparation for D-Day, Churchill charged Allied forces to launch a thrust into the 'soft underbelly of Europe' – Italy – to force the enemy to fight on many fronts. But by autumn 1944 the advance had stalled on the fearsome defences of the Gothic Line, a stretch of high terrain across Northern Italy's Apennine Mountains honeycombed with trenches, tunnels and bunkers. Below, Churchill (in pith helmet) surveys Italian lines.

In September '44 SOE's Mike Lees was parachuted behind the Gothic Line to link up with the Italian resistance and foment havoc in the enemy's rear.

Lees led a highly unusual force, including war artist Geoffrey Long (who drew these images and is pictured in the sketch above), plus war reporter Paul Morton (right). Long and Morton were charged to file stories about how the partisans were raising merry hell. Armed by air-drops from SOE, they ambushed German forces, before driving hell-for-leather for the safety of the mountains, providing Long and Morton with gripping stories.

After weeks in the field Lees was tasked to cross the Gothic Line, spiriting vital intelligence to the Allies. Moving on foot, he would have to pass through many kilometres of gun-emplacements, machinegun nests, bunkers and minefields, plus towns blasted apart by fighting.

In autumn '44 SAS Major Roy Farran (front right of photo, with captured German weapon) deployed to Italy. With Allied forces bogged down on the Gothic Line, the dash and daring of the SAS was in high demand. Farran was placed under joint command of SOE plus those American forces charged to break the Gothic Line.

Supreme German commander in Italy, Field Marshal Albert Kesselring (with staff), vowed to give no quarter. One of his greatest problems was the Italian resistance, who'd accounted for some 20,000 German casualties. Backed by Hitler, he ordered savage reprisals against villages he accused of harbouring the partisans.

Farran launched his first mission, Operation Cold Comfort, a daring sortie to block the Brenner Pass, the key resupply route for the Gothic Line. It proved disastrous. Despite linking up with partisans, his SAS force – pictured above – was harried across snow-swept mountains.

After Cold Comfort, Farran was plagued by guilt. Banned by high command from deploying, he vowed to do so anyway, leading a force of volunteers including 'Churchill's Spaniards' – war-bitten Spanish fighters. Raphael Ramos, kneeling second right, Juan Abadia, on his immediate left, and Francisco Jeronimo (not pictured) were Spanish Civil War and French Foreign Legion veterans.

that it had happened a day or so after Lees' arrival. Enemy commanders had clearly been awaiting the first heavy snowfalls, in the hope of trapping the partisans and wiping them out.

Advancing from the east, they had overrun the key defences on that flank of the valley. Simultaneously, the *Brigate Nere* – the same force that Don Carlo had identified – had advanced from the north, crossing the Secchia river and thrusting deep into the valley. Even the high mountains to the south had proved no block to the enemy: a battalion of Austrian alpine troops equipped with skis were even now assaulting Febbio, site of Colonel Monti's HQ.

In short, Lees and the warrior-priest had escaped by a combination of sheer luck and good timing. But only so far. Panic seemed to be the order of the day, and partisans were donning civilian clothes in an effort to escape. Worst of all, little reliable information was available about the exact whereabouts of the enemy. In short, the legions of the resistance had buckled, broken and run.

Blind to enemy gains, the only option open to Lees and Wilcockson was to avoid every track and path, no matter how little used. Only by so doing might they evade the enemy. So began a nightmare march, as long bursts of gunfire echoed across the terrain. Struggling through the deep snow they dropped towards the valley floor, beyond which lay the uncertain refuge of the high ground. To reach it they would need to push north across the Secchia and the main road, which hugged the river's course.

It was dusk by the time their exhausted party reached the nearside river bank. The scene was utterly bleak: a deep carpet of white fringed the roaring waters, which snaked through flat, open, windswept terrain, with flanking mountains to either side.

The small village of Costabona lay just ahead of them, a satellite of the larger Villa Minozzo. If the enemy were watching, now was the time when Lees and his party would be hit, out in the open and devoid of cover as they were.

To make matters worse, one of the mules refused to enter the water. Nothing would persuade the pig-headed animal to move. As daylight faded and the moon rose eerily from behind the hills, that lone mule remained stubbornly immobile. In desperation, Lees, who'd spent much of his youth riding on his family's Dorset estate, climbed into its rough wooden saddle, but even he couldn't budge it. There was no option but to unload the obdurate beast and pile the extra kit onto aching shoulders.

Thus doubly encumbered, Lees waded into the raging, waist-deep waters. Inching ever further and with feet struggling for purchase on the boulder-strewn river bed, he staggered through the icy torrent. He reached the far side, throwing an evil glance in the mule's direction. It stood resolute, seemingly laughing at their predicament.

They began to climb towards the road, which ran along the spine of a low ridge. The approach was steep, the snow sculpted into wind-driven drifts, the moonlight glistening off their surface. Dressed in their dark clothing, the long column of men – and the mules – stood out for many miles around. If the enemy were smart, they'd have placed sentries along the road to guard the back door to their trap. Lees couldn't imagine that they hadn't done.

Struggling through the thick drifts and bowed under their loads, the column of figures moved at a snail's pace. Lees felt utterly exposed. It struck him that a pair of German machine-gunners sited on the road could mow them down with ease. Unbelievably, they reached the ribbon of tarmac only to discover that it was unguarded. For some inexplicable reason the enemy commanders had failed to lock and bolt the exit.

It was twelve hours' solid marching before they reached Ranzano village, higher up the mountainside and a place of relative safety. They'd slipped through the noose, but few felt any sense of triumph. As they collapsed exhaustedly, they noticed a ragged line of fighters emerging from the moonlight. It turned out to be Colonel Monti with his headquarters staff, who had likewise fled before the enemy onslaught.

They stumbled past in disarray. Figures trudged forward, their weapons strapped to the mules, their feet painful from frostbite. But as Lees watched them shuffle past, he felt a curious upsurge of hope. Perversely, a part of him felt glad that this rout had come so quickly. No longer could Colonel Monti and his deputies pretend to be leading a potent and effective guerrilla force. The Reggiani partisans needed rebuilding from scratch, and Lees felt confident that he had the ability and the experience to do just that. By demolishing any semblance of battle-worthiness, the enemy had done him a favour. Sometimes, you had to destroy to start anew.

Over the next forty-eight hours Lees went about putting flesh on his plans. He called a meeting with Colonel Monti, explaining just what he intended: they would rebuild the guerrilla movement, armed, trained and fully equipped to take the fight to the enemy. As delicately as he could, he explained how dissatisfied he was with the colonel's leadership, and how he would need to take over command.

To his credit, the colonel was in enthusiastic agreement. If he could remain the nominal figurehead, he would happily give Lees the lead. If nothing else, this would prevent the communists from seizing control, which they had been agitating to do for some time. That was the last thing that anyone wanted. The Reggiani partisans had to remain resolutely apolitical and to concentrate totally on taking the fight to the enemy.

In this regard, the British captain and the Italian colonel could make common cause. Of course, by seizing command Lees didn't doubt that he would be seen as going against orders, but he really didn't give a damn. He was here to wage war, and right now the partisans weren't capable of doing so. Only by taking control could he turn that around.

It would be days before the Germans departed the Reggiani valley. While Lees couldn't know it, they were here on Kesselring's personal orders, charged with exterminating the Reggiani partisans. Exhibiting what Lees observed was a typical Teutonic lack of lateral thinking, they combed the partisans' known hideouts, burning villages and looting, but never thinking to widen the net or to leave ambush parties in wait.

Lees was likewise busy, but utilising a somewhat more outside-the-box mentality. He got Farrimond to radio through a shopping list of kit and supplies, chief among which was explosives, while he set about raising an elite sabotage squad. He chose as its head one Glauco Monducci – war name 'Gordon' – formerly an Italian alpine trooper, so a man well versed in mountain warfare. Monducci was tall, strong and confident, not to mention striking-looking with his long dark hair. Armed with a letter of authority from Lees, he was despatched on a tour of the surviving partisan bands to recruit forty of the best fighters.

Lees told Gordon not to return until he had those men. In exchange, he would ensure that they would be fully equipped with arms and ammunition from the first air resupply, presuming that he could persuade Florence to send flights. They would be trained in all forms of sabotage, something in which Lees himself was an expert. That done, they would be sent out to train the various partisan bands, after which they would be unleashed upon the enemy.

That done, Lees sought to organise an intelligence-gathering apparatus. There were to be no more surprise attacks by the enemy. He wanted to be forewarned and forearmed of everything the Germans might be up to. Lees appointed Giulio Davidi as the head of his intelligence service. Davidi had adopted the nom de guerre 'Kiss', which was inordinately peculiar, even among a band of fighters who seemed to affect the oddest war names.

Kiss was no Romeo. In an otherwise unremarkable face, his one arresting feature was a pair of huge, icy, penetrating grey eyes. He had a slow and very deliberate way of speaking, and a strangely secretive manner, which made him an obvious choice as spy-master. Lees explained that he didn't just want information brought in. He wanted a body of agents who could be sent out with urgent messages, or on bespoke spying missions. Kiss was adamant that it was the female partisan members who would be best suited to such tasks.

Lees agreed. From what he'd seen, the women had courage and front in abundance, and they were clearly not averse to using their not-inconsiderable feminine charms to hoodwink the enemy. Equally important, a pretty woman 'innocently' pedalling a bicycle through a German position could pass without suspicion, where any number of men might fail. Lees and Kiss decided to christen the female recruits their *Stafettas* – 'couriers' in English.

Twelve days after having been despatched, Gordon returned.

He'd managed to garner twenty recruits for his elite sabotage force, and somehow he'd managed to arm them, including acquiring two Bren light machine guns. Though half the number that Lees had asked for, they were a first-class band of toughs, and he certainly favoured quality over quantity. Arming them had been a touch of genius, especially as Lees had been warned that he would receive no air-drops until he had returned to his base of operations.

Two of the recruits struck Lees as being particularly promising. One, called Reubens, was a wiry little hard-case who'd worked for years as a doorman at a shady Paris nightclub. The other, a Sicilian, had a particularly stirring story. Captured by the enemy, he'd been taken to their base to be beaten and tortured. He'd managed to break free and leap through a second-floor window. Miraculously, he'd escaped unharmed, but the brutality he'd suffered had left its mark and he hungered to exact revenge.

Lees and Gordon christened their elite force the *Gufo Nero* Brigade – the Black Owls. In Lees' mind he wanted them to operate along SAS lines, executing highly mobile hit-and-run attacks, melting into the hills before the enemy had a chance to retaliate. That was the kind of tactics that he figured the target-rich Reggiani valley was crying out for.

Two weeks had passed by the time Lees' Stafettas reported that the enemy were in the process of withdrawing. He formed up his column to march back into the Secchia valley, putting Gordon and his Black Owls in the vanguard. They proceeded as a fighting patrol, with the mules carrying their all-important radio in the midst of the column. Upon nearing the main road, Gordon sent his Bren-gunners ahead to secure the crossing.

As Lees flitted across, he felt a thrill of excitement. He was returning 'home', to a region from which he fully intended to unleash merry hell. But first, he was to make an unexpected acquaintance . . . The column was nosing its way into the heart of the valley, when they came across a bunch of partisans wearing the red star of the communists. Lees had just begun to question them in his pidgin Italian, when a quite extraordinary figure stepped forwards.

Round-shouldered, portly, and leaning on a heavy alpenstock – a primitive, long-handled ice-axe – he was instantly recognisable as being non-Italian. Something of a cross between a hobbit and a mountain troll, a pair of bulging blue eyes peered through jam-jar glasses, above a bearded red face, which came complete with a permanently open mouth and drip on the end of a hooked nose. Lees couldn't help but be intrigued.

'How do you do, sir,' the mystery figure announced, in somewhat archaic but crisp English. 'I am Fritz Snapper, Reserve Lieutenant of the Royal Dutch Army.'

Lees could barely contain his laughter. While he'd stumbled upon any number of nationalities in the Italian mountains, he couldn't for the life of him conceive of how a Dutch soldier had ended up with this ragged band of communist partisans.

'How the devil did you get here?' he asked.

Snapper endeavoured to draw himself to his full height. 'I have the honour, sir, to have been attached to the Reggiani partisans for some months now, in an honorary capacity.'

That, plus the Shakespearian English, was just too much for Lees. He sat down in the snow and practically wept with laughter. As Snapper remained remarkably unperturbed, Lees felt he'd better recruit him.

He waved an arm at his column of fighters. 'You're such a tonic, you'd better stick around. Will you do me the honour of joining us . . . in an honorary capacity, of course?'

Snapper looked almost tearful. 'That, sir, is a compliment which it gives me the greatest pleasure to accept.'

With that, Fritz Snapper – alpenstock in hand – formed up next to Lees, and they marched onwards. Lees was keen to hear the man's story. It didn't disappoint, and from just about anyone else Lees would have found it utterly unbelievable. In May 1940, as the German blitzkrieg had steamrollered across Holland, Snapper, a Dutch Army lieutenant, joined the Dutch resistance, before deciding to make his way to Britain and the real war.

For some reason, he'd reckoned the best way to get there was via neutral Switzerland, where he'd sought in vain for a flight. The odd aircraft did of course leave for England, but seats were reserved for far more important personages than Lt. Snapper. After a year's wait he decided he'd cross the Alps, find his way into Italy and from there to Tunisia, to join up with British forces in North Africa. The plan fell through on a small oversight: Fritz Snapper spoke barely a word of Italian. He was picked up by the Italian Fascist police and charged with being an Allied spy. Taken to court, the case fell apart when the Italian judge ruled that even the British wouldn't be stupid enough to send a man to spy on a country whose language he didn't speak. Saved from execution, Snapper was sent to a POW camp. There he managed to convince the camp commander, a German, of his love for all things German. He was duly released, and promptly made his way into the mountains to join the partisans, fully intending to show the Germans what he really thought of them.

Lees sensed that Snapper was 'quite mad', but who wasn't among this ragtag band? More importantly, he'd carved out for himself a unique niche with the partisans. Snapper had taken charge of running a courier network via which messages were spirited across the lines. Incredibly, this service – often employing young boys who could slip through undetected – proved highly effective. In time it would enable Lees to write a missive to Florence headquarters, with the confidence that it would be delivered in three to four days.

For his part, Snapper saw in Lees the salvation of the Reggiani partisans. After months of non-existent supply drops, near-starvation and in-fighting, they were desperate for a figure behind whom to unite. Lees was it. He was the unifying force that the partisans were crying out for. Snapper would write of his arrival that the 'new BLO for Reggio Emilia saved the situation . . . Capt Lees completely understood Partisan mentality.'

Love him or loathe him, Lees was the man for the job.

Chapter 8

Inspired by Operation Galia's achievements, Farran tried to go one better by striking at a prime target – the Brenner Pass, which cuts through the Alps, providing the vital rail links from Austria into northern Italy. Appropriately codenamed Cold Comfort, the mission's objective was to blow up the high mountainside, causing a massive landslide that would block the railway lines, significantly disrupting supplies to the Gothic Line.

But sadly, Cold Comfort was to prove as cheerless as its name suggested. Led by the fearless Major Ross Robertson Littlejohn MC, operation Cold Comfort employed a similar troop-sized – twelve-man – force as had Galia. But there the similarities ended. Widely scattered in the drop, the men found themselves among unfriendly locals of essentially German extraction. For days Littlejohn and his team fought against inhuman conditions, hunger and exposure, as the atrocious weather prevented any resupply drops.

Littlejohn was no stranger to such hardships. He'd won his MC in June 1944, having stormed Sword Beach in the D-Day landings with No. 4 Commando, a unit that suffered fifty per cent casualties. Not content with surviving that, Littlejohn – then a captain – went on to launch a solo assault on a German bunker, attacking it with grenades, becoming injured and isolated in the process. Playing dead, he'd avoided capture by German troops, who prodded him with bayonets, eventually crawling 2,000 yards to reach friendly lines.

By September 1944 he'd made a full recovery and had volunteered for the SAS, which led him to Cold Comfort. Eventually, Littlejohn – just twenty-three years of age – and one other patrol member, Corporal Joseph Crowley, were captured by an elite German ski unit. The two men, last seen engaged in fierce combat with the enemy, would be executed under Hitler's notorious 'Commando Order', which stipulated that 'all enemy troops encountered ... during so-called commando operations ... armed or unarmed, are to be exterminated to the last man ...'

The order – issued in October 1942 and personally signed by Hitler – reflected how enraged the Führer had become at the successes of Churchill's butcher-and-bolt raiders. It ended with a chilling warning to any who might dare oppose it. 'I will summon before the tribunal of war, all leaders and officers who fail to carry out these instructions ...' Each copy was stamped: 'This order is intended for commanders only, and must not under any circumstances fall into enemy hands.' It was classified 'MOST SECRET' and was to be committed to memory, after which all printed copies were to be destroyed.

With Littlejohn's capture Cold Comfort imploded – the Brenner Pass remaining resolutely open. One of those who did miraculously survive the mission was SAS Private Robert 'Bob' Sharpe. Upon parachuting into Cold Comfort, Sharpe had had his kitbag torn away, leaving him bereft of much of his equipment. He'd been forced to bivouac wrapped in his chute, in a snow-hole excavated at the base of a tree. Sharpe and others had been dogged by kit failures: issued with no specialist alpine equipment, their boots had proved next to useless. They'd ended the mission dressed largely in scavenged German Army gear.

Sharpe and others returned to Allied lines angry and disillusioned at such failures. Farran hadn't escaped their ire. He felt plagued by guilt at the loss of such brave men as Major Littlejohn, plus the horrendous trials and tribulations suffered by the others. He hungered to make good; to score a signal success in Italy, fearing that he'd ordered Littlejohn to undertake a mission of which he himself would have fought shy. It was the old terror coming back to haunt him – that after the long years at war he'd become 'windy'.

Major Littlejohn's mission had failed for one crucial reason, as far as Farran was concerned, apart from the appalling weather: lack of local support on the ground. He vowed the same mistake would not be made again. He approached SOE's Charles Macintosh, in Florence, asking who among his SOE agents could best accommodate an entire SAS squadron, one that would be embraced wholeheartedly by the partisans.

Oddly, Macintosh seemed somewhat less than enthusiastic at the proposition. Privately, he doubted whether his men in the field – his British Liaison Officers – would welcome Farran's squadron, whose arrival would doubtless disturb the status quo. The news of several dozen SAS parachutists dropping in would be inflated by enemy spies until reports cited hundreds, risking savage German reprisals, which was the last thing anyone needed right now. Or at least, so Macintosh reasoned.

Some BLOs, certainly, had no need of such potent support as Farran and his SAS offered. Many, like the SOE's Major William McKenna, had been given predominantly non-offensive roles. Embedded with partisans to the far western end of the Gothic

Line, at Val d'Aosta, McKenna's Clarinda Mission was charged with 'anti-scorch' work, which was intended to prevent the enemy from sabotaging key targets as they withdrew, a tactic known as 'scorched earth'.

The Allies had drawn-up a list of vital installations that were to be safeguarded at all costs, chief among them being hydro-electric plants, and BLOs like McKenna had been tasked with their protection. As the weather was atrocious and parachuting wasn't an option, McKenna had been forced to trek in over the Alps, using skis wherever possible. That alone was an incredible feat, and all to stop the Germans from blowing up key dams – something that would have a catastrophic impact on the Italian people.

McKenna – formerly of the Royal Berkshire Regiment and SAS – had been mentioned in despatches for service with the SOE in Sicily, back in 1944. Long-serving and battle-hardened, he mastered his defensive anti-scorch role with aplomb, recruiting thousands of partisans. He trained them in anti-aircraft drills, using Bren guns to shoot down aircraft, just in case the enemy came at them from the skies. When a group of German soldiers did attempt to sabotage a power station they were summarily caught and shot.

Charles Macintosh reached out to the agents he had serving in the area where Farran was keenest to deploy – to the rear of the central section of the Gothic Line. Two, Major Jim Davies and Major Charles Holland, demurred. Long-experienced at SOE work, they expressed reservations that Macintosh could well appreciate. For his part, Farran reacted with incredulity. To his mind, their lack of hunger to take the fight to the enemy was unconscionable.

But the third individual seemed to be of an entirely different mind set and came back with an altogether more enthusiastic response. Lower in rank, younger and arguably less worldly-wise, Captain Michael Lees had only recently inserted into his area of operations. Via Bert Farrimond, his radio operator, Lees sent back a crystal-clear response to Farran's offer of SAS troops: 'Send as many as you can!'

Macintosh had already formed his own opinion of Lees. He believed him to be the 'most impatient and headstrong of the BLOs'. Considering there were over a dozen such agents spread across northern Italy, those were harsh words indeed. There was little love lost between Macintosh and Farran, either. Once Lees had sent his message of unqualified welcome, Macintosh feared that this – *Farran plus Lees* – would turn out to be a marriage made in hell.

Once in the field, Farran would outrank Lees. He was also several years his senior and a legendary figure in his own right. 'Together, they would be a bloody menace,' Macintosh concluded, somewhat churlishly. 'I consoled myself with the thought that it was the Hun who should be worried.' There was one other complicating factor, as far as Macintosh was concerned. Major Farran was banned from deploying with his troops, yet he felt convinced that the SAS commander would find some way to join them, regardless.

'It was clear that contrary to orders, he was thinking of jumping with the squadron,' Macintosh would write of Farran. 'It was also clear that once in enemy territory he would act as he pleased . . .'

In one respect Macintosh was right: Farran had been forbidden from deploying, and by none other than London headquarters. In part, the ban resulted from his previous injuries, which rendered him unfit for front-line duties, at least in the eyes of some. In part, it reflected the acute lack of availability of experienced SAS officers, and the pressing need to keep some at headquarters, to oversee wider strategy and command.

Armed with Lees' unqualified message of welcome, Farran went about clearing the forthcoming mission, codenamed Operation Tombola, with Colonel Riepe, the American commander in charge of special operations. In the process he quietly slipped in a request that he be allowed to lead his men in the field. While the colonel gave his blessing to Tombola, he categorically refused Farran's entreaty.

Painfully short of experienced officers, he needed Farran in Florence, Riepe explained. Farran acted as if he had accepted the colonel's strictures with good grace. But in truth, he knew in his heart that very shortly only a slender thread would be hanging between himself and a court martial.

Of course, Farran had heard the rumours about Michael Lees. He knew of his 'wild man' reputation. But that simply reflected that he was a man of 'sterner calibre', as far as Farran was concerned, and his positive attitude spoke volumes. Lees had been awaiting just such an opportunity, and he was convinced that the arrival of an SAS squadron would boost partisan morale hugely. He promised to recce potential targets immediately.

If Lees' actions were as good as his words, Farran felt certain that he'd found his kindred spirit. In time, he would go on to judge Michael Lees as being 'the best partisan Liaison Officer in the whole of Italy'. High praise indeed from a man of Farran's standing.

His deployment set, Farran went about selecting the force to join him on the ground. No. 3 Squadron SAS had deployed from England under-strength, and especially with regard to the senior ranks. Farran would need to beg, borrow and steal officers from wherever he could find them.

With no Big Jim Mackie to serve as his bulletproof right-hand man, Farran sought out another of the old and bold – Captain James 'Jock' Easton, a grizzled, battle-worn Scot with a heart of gold and guts of steel. By rights, Easton should not even have been available. Just returned from two years as a POW, he was supposed to be enjoying a safe desk job in Florence. But typically, when Farran suggested a bit of fun and games behind enemy lines, Easton jumped at the chance.

Farran's main challenge was one of comprehension: a rough diamond hailing from the tough streets of Falkirk, Easton was blessed with a thick accent. When issuing orders in pidgin Italian garbled by his broad Scots, it was a wonder any of the locals got the barest gist, especially as his every utterance tended to be laced with a good dose of ribald cussing. But Easton had the pedigree that a mission such as this – challenging, ambitious, unprecedented – called for.

One of SAS founder David Stirling's 1941 originals, Easton had soldiered across the scorching deserts of North Africa, raiding scores of enemy bases and airfields. Wounded and taken prisoner, he'd escaped in Italy and made his way to neutral Switzerland, and from there to the French resistance. He'd subsequently fought his way through France, making it back to England. In short, Easton constituted Farran's safe pair of hands to backstop the coming mission.

With Easton thus purloined from his desk job, it made perfect sense to recruit another SAS officer who by rights also shouldn't have been available. One look at Lieutenant James Arthur 'Ricky' Riccomini's résumé accounted for why Farran held him in such high esteem, and why he hungered to have him join the Tombola team. Tall, sandy-haired and always with a ready smile, Lieutenant Riccomini had had some kind of war.

One of five brothers hailing from Kent, Riccomini had volunteered for 'The Snowballers', a Scots Guards battalion formed to help the Finns fight the Russians, in what had become known as the Winter War. It was early 1940 and Russia was allied to Nazi Germany, under a 1939 Non-Aggression Pact. The Snowballers were formed to soldier in Finland's cause, to deter Russian aggression. With Finland being largely snowbound, Riccomini was trained in alpine warfare, but the battle proved short-lived, and in March 1940 Finland signed a peace treaty.

Posted to Egypt, Riccomini was captured while on a reconnaissance mission and sent to an Italian prison camp. After repeated escape attempts he was sent to Italy's equivalent of Colditz, for the real 'bad boys' – Campo PG 5, at Gavi, in mountainous north-west Italy. Then in September 1943 he was one of a group of POWs being moved north by train to Austria. He and others sawed a hole in the side wall of the cattle truck in which they were travelling and jumped for it. Having made his getaway, Riccomini – half Italian, and fluent in the language – headed for the hills, along with fellow escapee Lieutenant 'Pete' Peterson.

Using forged papers the two soldiered with the partisans for many months. In his most memorable operation, Riccomini led a guerrilla unit disguised as Fascist troops to sabotage a railway bridge. Setting explosives stolen off the enemy, they waited for a troop train before detonating the charges. In his diary Riccomini wrote: 'There was an almighty explosion, a whooping crescendo of sound, followed by a screaming of metal and indescribable splintering crashes. The world was flooded with scarlet followed by a pall of thick blackness.'

Riccomini was finally betrayed by a Red Cross representative, who'd promised to get a Christmas letter to his wife, Joyce, in England. They'd married in October 1939, spending precious little time together over the war years. That Red Cross agent doubled as a Nazi spy, and a truck load of German troops arrived. Riccomini and Peterson escaped by jumping from a second-floor window, after which they scaled an Alpine pass and made it to Switzerland. There, Riccomini was duly recruited by the SOE as an 'agent in the field'.

In August 1944 he crossed into France, linked up with the French resistance and attacked the German's 90th *Panzergrenadier* Division. Finally making it back across the lines, the SOE recommended that Riccomini should be 'SOS wef' – struck off strength, with effect from . . . 26 September 1944. They suggested that he take permanent sick leave for the remainder of the war, such was the toll the behind-the-lines missions had taken upon him.

Instead, Riccomini penned a report very much to the contrary. 'I would welcome an opportunity for further work of this nature . . . I speak and write both German and Italian . . . May I request an interview with Lt.Col. William Stirling, SAS. I was with his brother, Lt. Col. David Stirling, in PG 5 Gavi, Italy, and was recommended by him for appointment to the SAS Regiment.'

Taken into the SAS, he quickly won renown for his unbreakable good spirits: 'Nothing ever got him down and his great sense of humour was a real tonic in hard times.' Not long after joining the SAS he was flown to Italy. Being a former POW and very probably known to the Germans, he'd taken on the somewhat facetious cover name of Lieutenant Richard Hood.

Riccomini deployed with Captain Walker-Brown on Operation Galia, for which he earned a Military Cross. The citation read: 'He was a personal source of inspiration and encouragement to his men. His conduct could not have been excelled in any way, being far above the normal call of duty.' Having only recently returned from Galia, Riccomini was supposed to be on leave and he had every reason to reject Farran's approach. Instead, he agreed at once to the SAS major's invitation to join the Tombola party.

Still short of officers, Farran went hunting. In a nearby infantry depot he delivered a recruitment speech of Churchillian proportions, calling for volunteers for special duties and offering little but 'sweat, blisters and frostbite and the probability of being shot as spies'. One of the first to step forward was the smallish, quietly spoken, pipe-smoking Lieutenant Arthur David Eyton-Jones. A member of the Royal Sussex Regiment, Eyton-Jones had deployed to Italy fresh out of training, and he'd yet to get his boots dirty.

When war broke out, Eyton-Jones – hailing from Brighton, on the south coast of England – had been at Jesus College, Cambridge. He was a keen rower and had indulged his dreams of forging a career in agriculture. Coming from a long line of clergymen, he was breaking the mould by looking to a future working the land. Now, some five years later, he found himself in Italy stepping forward to volunteer for the famed SAS, along with a dozen other would-be recruits.

Apart from his infantry training, Eyton-Jones' war experience was restricted to a stint in the Home Guard. He'd been stationed around Bath, on a hillock watching out for German invaders. For several nights a bird had stubbornly sung from its place of hiding, keeping Eyton-Jones awake. Finally, he'd cracked, unleashing a shot from his .303 Lee Enfield rifle. The bird flew off unharmed, but the rifle shot triggered an invasion alert, for which Eyton-Jones was severely reprimanded.

In the summer of 1944 he'd embarked for Italy on the troopship *The Empress of Scotland*. He was commanding thirty infantrymen, and they were supposed to link up with their parent regiment, the Royal Sussex. Instead, the ship had been forced to zig zag to avoid U-boat attacks, and the soldiers were plagued by sea-sickness and delayed by the heavy seas. They reached Italy too late to join their regiment, which had already deployed to Greece.

Eyton-Jones was understandably frustrated. His family had titled roots, there being a baronetcy and a Buckinghamshire mansion in the lineage. It was there, waited on by twenty staff, that the teenage Eyton-Jones had listened to Neville Chamberlain announcing the declaration of war on Germany. The housekeeper had been summoned and ordered to introduce rationing based upon First World War lines. His great aunt, the Honourable Gertrude Aird, had donated £5,000 to fund a Spitfire, which had been named 'Gerty' in her honour.

Lieutenant David Eyton-Jones, still just twenty-one years of age, longed to play his part. Farran weeded down the volunteers to just two: fortunately, Eyton-Jones was one of them. The other, Lieutenant Kenneth 'Ken' Harvey, hailed from Rhodesia (now Zimbabwe), in southern Africa. If anything, Harvey had even less war experience than Eyton-Jones. He was just nineteen years of age, so barely out of his school uniform.

As Farran's No. 3 Squadron was just days away from deploying, there would be precious little time for any specialist training.

Indeed, Eyton-Jones and Harvey would have to parachute behind the lines with no practice, on their first ever jump from an aircraft. Farran told them not to worry. In the SAS they found the best way to learn was live, on the job as it were.

But in truth, No. 3 Squadron was a relatively newly raised unit, and Farran craved experienced operators. The ranks were also plagued by malaria, contracted during previous operations. Farran figured as many as seventy-five per cent of the men had been hit by the debilitating disease, and he'd ordered those affected to take mepacrine, an anti-malarial drug. He needed experienced recruits, and much of the kind of irregular warfare skills he sought were vested in the regiment's 'international brigade'. Fittingly, perhaps, as Field Marshal Kesselring had once commanded the Condor Legion fighting on the side of Franco's Fascists in the Spanish Civil War, Farran sought out veterans who'd fought on the other side – men who'd been soldiering in one form or another for approaching ten years.

About a dozen Spaniards were serving with the SAS, and two were immediately available. They had the most incredible stories. Lance Corporal Robert Bruce – real name, Justo Balerdi – and Parachutist Frank Williams – real name Francisco Jeronimo – had fought for the Republicans, the democratic left-leaning forces in Spain's 1936–39 civil war. Upon the Fascist victory they'd escaped to France, where they were interned by the French authorities. They were given a stark choice: join the French Foreign Legion, or rot – and starve – in the internment camps.

Hailing from Sestao, a town lying on the outskirts of Spain's northern port city of Bilbao, Justo 'José' Balerdi had worked as a telephonist prior to the outbreak of the conflict. Francisco Jeronimo came from the opposite end of the country, Málaga, on

Spain's southern coast, where he'd been an apprentice electrician. They bonded in surviving the harsh privations of the French internment camps, in contrast to which the rigours of the French Foreign Legion looked immensely preferable. Posted to Syria – then a part of French North Africa – they hungered to join the fight against the powers of Nazism then sweeping Europe.

Following Germany's lightning victory over France, fate turned against them. All Spanish members of the French Foreign Legion were ordered to be sent to German-held soil. Knowing they faced execution or the concentration camps, the officers turned a blind eye as many deserted. Francisco Jeronimo and Justo Balerdi joined a sixty-strong force of Spaniards determined to make it to British territory. They 'deserted' en masse, taking their weapons with them and headed for British-held Palestine in a convoy of army trucks.

Having reached the first British checkpoint, a sentry tried to bar their way: with no papers they couldn't be allowed through, he argued. A figure jumped down from the rear of one of the vehicles and knocked the man unconscious, after which the trucks thundered past. Two maverick British officers, Colonel George Young and Lt.Col. Stephen Rose, happened to be in Palestine at the time, recruiting for the newly raised Middle East Commando. Making a virtue out of necessity, the Spaniards were taken en masse into No. 50 ME Commando. War-bitten guerrilla fighters and experienced Legionnaires, they made for ideal recruits.

They first saw action in Operation Abstention in February 1941, a raid on Castelorizzo, an island in the eastern Mediterranean. A suspected Italian sea-plane base, the commandos struck by total surprise, Italian resistance crumbling. They'd seized the key objective, Paleocastro Fort, perched atop an 800-foot cliff that dominated the harbour, its garrison surrendering. But failure to land reinforcements left the two hundred men of 50 Commando under siege from air and the sea, hounded by warplanes and motor-torpedo boats.

With ammunition, water and food running low and casualties mounting, the survivors were lifted off the beaches under cover of darkness, in a daring evacuation by Royal Navy warships. Three months later 50 Commando were back in action, in the battle for the Mediterranean island of Crete. Under ferocious assault by German paratroopers, Crete fell, with Francisco Jeronimo and others being taken prisoner.

With his shock of unruly black hair and dark, good-humoured eyes, Justo Balerdi – Robert Bruce – could easily have passed for a local Cretan, but as luck would have it he'd just been pulled off the island, so he missed the fate that befell so many of his comrades. Realising their Spanish backgrounds would spell a death sentence, the Spanish commandos decided to claim that they were Gibraltarians, a plausible tale given their accents.

Francisco Jeronimo, similarly dark-haired and intense of gaze, had no intention of being held captive for long. He broke out of the Cretan POW camp and spent long months hiding out in the mountains, along with other escapees. One was a British colonel whom Jeronimo befriended, helping him fend for himself in the hills. When they were finally rescued by a British warship, the colonel invited Jeronimo to join his regiment as his personal batman. The Spaniard's response was typically emphatic: 'I polish the shoes of no man.'

Hospitalised with malaria after their stint in Crete, it wasn't until late 1943 that Jeronimo (and Balerdi) were able to volunteer for the SAS. There they linked up with a third Spaniard, a former policeman and comparatively grizzled veteran called Juan Torrents Abadia. Realising he was too old for parachute training, Abadia had lied about his age, reducing it by four years to blag his way into the SAS. None other than the commanding officer of 2nd SAS, Lt.Col. Brian Franks, would write of him: 'An excellent soldier. Reliable, willing and respectful. Was an Officer in the Spanish Republican Army. First class individual.'

Abadia 'fathered' the younger Spanish recruits through their earliest months in the regiment, during which they were asked to change their identities. Over drinks in a bar, they were advised that taking British war-names might be advisable. There was a cloak-and-dagger justification: former Spanish freedom fighters could expect no mercy from the enemy, if caught. But it was also as much for the sake of convenience: the British found it hard to pronounce – let alone remember – their real names.

Juan Torrents Abadia – the elder of 'Churchill's Spaniards' as they were known – chose the surname Colman, for he was the spitting image of Ronald Colman, the iconic 1930s actor who'd starred in such classic movies as *Beau Geste* and *A Double Life*. Jeronimo and Balerdi favoured the names of famous British warriors – Francis Drake, Walter Raleigh or Robert the Bruce. Robert Bruce was allowed: it fell to Balerdi. But Drake and Raleigh were seen as being just a little too obvious. Francisco Jeronimo had to settle for the typically English – and somewhat un-warrior-like – Frank Williams.

On Francisco Jeronimo's remarkably brief signing-up papers, where it asked for the parish, town and county of his birth, two brief words were inscribed: 'NO – SPANISH'. With his change of name, 'GERONIMO, FRANCISCO' was struck out by hand, the words 'WILLIAMS, FRANK' replacing them (Jeronimo's last name had been misspelled by the military). His army number was duly altered to 1304867, and that was it – ID change complete. A similarly brief exercise switched 'Justo Balerdi' to 'Robert Bruce'.

After SAS training in Scotland, Balerdi – Robert Bruce – was first into action, being dropped on 5 August 1944, as Major Mick Rooney's signaller for Operation Rupert. Rooney's forces shot up a troop train and linked up with the French resistance to launch a series of harassing attacks, before finally withdrawing on 10 September.

Jeronimo (now Frank Williams) also saw action that August with the SAS. He was deployed on Operation Trueform, with orders to 'harass the enemy with a priority on the destruction of petrol tankers, petrol dumps etc'. Linking up with the French resistance, the thirty-seven-strong SAS patrol was guided to a German ammunition dump. There, Jeronimo – Frank Williams – shot dead the sentries with a Bren gun. 'The explosion was terrific,' the official report concluded of blowing up the dump.

Trueform was a great success: in addition to the enemy killed, seventy-eight Germans were taken prisoner, five ammo and fuel dumps destroyed, scores of trucks, half-tracks and field guns put out of action, and only three men lost. In operations in France Colman had also distinguished himself, saving the lives of three fellow SAS operators – Arthur Huntbach, Taffy Rogers and Jock Sinclair. In short, Churchill's Spaniards had earned for themselves a sterling reputation.

Those long-serving Spanish veterans had just the kind of experience that Roy Farran craved, for Operation Tombola. Abadia – Colman – was off serving in pastures far from Italy, so he was ruled out. But Robert Bruce and Frank Williams – fluent Italian speakers to boot – were available to deploy as part of Farran's team. Whether they were fit and ready for such a behind-the-lines mission was another matter entirely, though.

On a previous operation Frank Williams had been faced with the worst of all dilemmas. Even as they'd been ordered into action, an eighteen-year-old partisan had turned and bolted. They had a phrase for losing one's nerve in the SAS: it was called 'crapping out'. Though Williams had tried to forgive the boy, it had been a moment of intense fear and risk, as the lad's flight could have alerted the enemy, and 'we would all have been dead', he reflected.

Williams had been asked by one of the partisan commanders what they should do with the errant fighter. 'He's only eighteen,' the partisan leader had pointed out.

Williams face had hardened. 'Shoot him.'

The partisans refused, a decision for which Williams would be eternally grateful. Reflecting on this dark moment, he realised that he had been waging war behind the lines, dodging bullets, captivity and worse for too long. The blood, the brutality and savagery had seeped into him. Normally a bright, light-hearted fellow, Williams feared it had become a dark stain on his soul. But surely, he figured, the war must come to an end soon. Williams reckoned he could weather one more mission, and he and Bruce signed up for Tombola.

To round off his international brigade, Farran chose to take Lieutenant 'T. G. Stephens' – his anglicised nom de guerre – an Austrian Jew and long-serving SAS member, who was fluent in German, which should prove useful where they were heading. Plus he approached another Operation Galia veteran, a grizzled Italian sailor called Luigi 'Pippo' Siboldi. In spite of his sixty years of age, Siboldi had guided Walker-Brown through the mountains as they'd harassed the enemy on Operation Galia. Having done so, he'd been quietly recruited into the SOE.

Farran felt sure that Siboldi's skills and experience, not to mention his ready smile, would prove useful for Tombola. Team sorted, he didn't believe that a man among those recruited was a 'passenger'. Each promised his own worth. 'It was a collection of old toughs,' Farran would write of his team, the newbies Eyton-Jones and Harvey included. 'I loved every one of their cracked, leathery faces.'

Prior to departure for the mission, he led his entire No. 3 Squadron on a fifty-mile trek across the Apennine mountains. Not all would deploy. Some would be weeded out during this final trial. Sixty-odd men returned aching, footsore and weary. They knew now what those lucky enough to be chosen should expect. The heady scent of methylated spirits – alcohol, with a foul-tasting colouring added, to render it undrinkable – filled the barracks, as desperate attempts were made to harden the soles of battered, blistered feet. Rucksacks were packed and repacked, in an effort to refine loads. Non-essential items of kit were binned, to cut weight. Above all, an atmosphere of fevered excitement filled the air.

The DZ that Farran's advance party would drop into for Operation Tombola had been codenamed Swell Crimson. Fittingly, Tombola had originated in southern Italy, being similar to the British game of bingo or a raffle. It was a form of gambling, and Farran didn't doubt that the coming operation was a gamble of the highest order.

But not a man among his 'collection of old toughs' could wait to get started.

Chapter 9

Michael Lees chose as his headquarters the small hamlet of Secchio, set equidistant between Colonel Monti's HQ – which he re-established at Febbio – and the warrior-priest Don Carlo's base, from where he commanded the Green Flames. Secchio consisted of a clutch of houses perched in a valley formed by a tributary of the main Secchia river. At the head of the valley lay a flat, open area where Lees would establish his DZ.

Don Carlo introduced Lees to Don Pietro Rivi, the Secchio village priest known to all as 'Don Pedro'. Don Pedro volunteered his home as a base for Lees' mission, despite the dangers this brought him and his family. The priest was thin and seemingly retiring, but appearances can be deceptive: he was in truth a heartfelt Italian patriot. The previous summer he'd raised a group of partisans, and with weapons they'd managed to beg, borrow and steal they'd ambushed an enemy patrol (not entirely successfully, but at least they'd tried).

Don Pedro's elderly mother, who lived with him, would treat Lees and his team as if they were her own flesh and blood. This sense of kindred spirits was accentuated by the faith Lees shared with the priest, his family and the wider village. Brought up a strict Catholic by his eccentric and devout mother, Lees had been made to wear red for the first eight years of his life, signifying 'the blood of Christ' as his mother had told him. His sister, Dodo, had worn bright blue, to signify 'Mary the Queen of Heaven'. Any issues Lees had were to be dealt with by prayer, his mother advised. It was not the easiest of boyhoods.

But here in the Secchia valley, Lees found his Catholic faith helped build bridges with those that he had come to lead to war. There was no better way to break the ice than sharing Sunday mass. Secchio had a fine defensive layout, and Lees intended it to be a permanent base of operations. Gordon chose to billet his Black Owls in Secchio's former school, while Kiss placed his Stafettas in a farmhouse on the outskirts of the village, where he could better guard their moral fortitude.

It was early February 1945 by the time Lees had got his plan-of-action agreed with all parties. The Reggiani partisans would fortify the Secchia valley, from where they would sally forth on hit-and-run operations. Each of the four partisan brigades was allocated a section of the valley perimeter that it was to hold at all costs, and a segment of enemy territory where its job was to wreak havoc and mayhem.

In the face of bitter opposition from Colonel Monti, Lees slashed his HQ staff by half. Responsibility for provisioning the partisans was devolved to brigade level. The plains were rich in food and wine and when they fought – and vanquished – the enemy, the partisans were to seize provisions. Conversely, if they didn't fight they would go hungry. In return, Lees promised to provide weaponry, including heavy machine guns, to hold the valley, and to clothe and supply the partisans for war.

In the past, 'theft' from the drop zones had been a serious cause of bitterness and resentment. Rival bands had been in the habit of seizing everything. To put a stop to this, Lees recruited a wonderful old ruffian called Ettore Scalabrini – known as 'Scalabrino' to all. Scalabrino boasted a thick, tangled white beard and carried an ancient-looking shotgun. He was the type who would have been a mountain bandit in another age, and indeed he'd spent years in America working the remote and lawless frontier minefields.

Lees could barely understand a word of Scalabrino's English, which was peppered with colourful American curses, but somehow they made each other understood. Prior to the much-heralded receipt of their first resupply drop, Lees warned Scalabrino that if one container went missing then he would have him shot. Scalabrino countered that if one pair of socks went missing, a lot of other people were going to get shot before him.

As it turned out, Scalabrino was far from joking.

It was the second week of February 1945 by the time Lees had persuaded Florence headquarters of their urgent need for a resupply. On 7 February he penned a long and notably conciliatory letter to Major Macintosh, to be taken by courier across the lines.

'Just a line to wish you all the best, and say that everything is going well,' Lees began. 'At the moment things are getting almost beyond us . . . As you know we're handling a lot of W/T traffic, about ten messages most days . . . Then there's intelligence . . . dropping grounds, and God knows what . . . Personally, I'm far more interested [in] and better at the more active side of the job . . . but we're very satisfied really.'

By sounding a mollifying note, Lees hoped to secure delivery of the first major resupply drop for many months. As good fortune would have it, the sheer scale and muscularity of the American cargo fleet now assembled at Rosignano Airfield meant that requests for arms and supplies could hardly be stymied much longer. The Dakotas would be lying idle, their American aircrews frustrated, their commanders perplexed beyond reason.

Early on the morning that the drop was scheduled, Lees was heading to the DZ when he heard a wild outbreak of fire. The rattle of rifles, sub-machine guns and heavier weapons echoed alarmingly across the valley, as the first of the Dakotas swooped low over the valley. Fearing that a perfectly timed enemy attack had been launched, Lees broke into a run.

He reached a vantage point, only to hear the sharp blast of a whistle, at which point the firing abruptly ceased. The unmistakable figure of Scalabrino strode into the middle of the DZ, where containers and parachutes lay thick on the ground. It turned out that he'd posted men to all sides, with orders to open fire without warning to dissuade any would-be thieves. Under the cover of their guns Scalabrino checked that each and every package was present and correct. Though a little draconian, his methods ensured that Lees was never to lose a single container.

Resupplied with ammo and explosives, Gordon's Black Owls sallied forth with sabotage in mind. Shortly, they were pouncing on enemy convoys, striking under cover of darkness and always at a different location. This was butcher-and-bolt at its best. At the same time Kiss's Stafettas were out and about, hoovering up the intelligence. Lees found himself inundated with details of enemy positions and movements, and he was often awake into the early hours, collating all.

Condensed into summaries, most could be telegraphed by Farrimond to their Florence headquarters. In no time the W/T specialist was working fourteen-hour days, encoding and transmitting those urgent missives. With any that were too long to be sent by radio, Lees summoned the Tolkien figure of Fritz

Snapper, alpenstock in hand, to organise a courier to sneak across the lines.

In short, by the third week of February 1945, Lees had taken control absolutely – despite Florence warning him not to – and his forces were well and truly going on the offensive. But still he wasn't satisfied. Still he hungered to do more. As luck would have it he was about to receive a highly unusual visitor, one who would give him a sense of how he might expand the scope of his operations in unforeseen ways.

Captain Neil Oughtred parachuted in on a top-secret mission, codenamed Cisco Red II. Like Lees, Oughtred – formerly of the Lincolnshire Regiment – had served in Yugoslavia, and he dropped in with his own radio operator, Sergeant Ted Fry. Upon arrival Oughtred explained they were an advance party charged to set up a discreet SOE intelligence cell. They were doing so with one aim in mind: to receive Major Bernard James Barton, an SOE agent with a long history of assassination missions.

Targeted assassinations were a rare, but necessary, weapon in the SOE's arsenal of ungentlemanly warfare. In 1942, SOE had masterminded Operation Anthropoid, the assassination of SS Obergruppenführer Reinhard Heydrich, a favourite of Hitler and a main architect of the Holocaust. Then, in early 1944, they'd orchestrated 'Rat Week', a coordinated series of assassinations against senior Nazi figures across Europe. In recent months, much planning had gone into an assassination attempt on Hitler himself.

Barton – just twenty-four years old and formerly of the Buffs (Royal East Kent Regiment) – was known either as 'Lucky' or 'Killer' to his comrades. He'd first demonstrated his penchant for assassinations during a raid in February 1944 on the German-held island of Brač, in the Adriatic Sea. As the citation for the DSO he'd earned made clear, he'd deployed with the intention of 'finding the German commander of the troops there and killing him'. He'd linked up with local partisans, who'd smuggled his Sten gun into the target's location hidden in a bundle of sticks and strapped to a donkey.

Barton followed, sneaking his way past the German checkpoints disguised as a local shepherd. He'd entered the commander's house at dusk, searched it and located the dining room, 'where he saw a German officer. He at once opened fire and killed him with two bursts from his silenced Sten gun.' The man he'd killed was indeed the Brač garrison commander. Barton slipped away and hid in caves for several days, before he could be taken off the island.

For that mission he was granted an immediate DSO, though the write-up is marked: 'NO PUBLICITY TO BE GIVEN TO THIS CITATION'. Even in war, assassinations were a risky and highly controversial business. In November 1944 Barton had been parachuted north of the Gothic Line, on a mission to assassinate General Heinrich von Vietinghoff, a Hitler lookalike who had taken over command from Kesselring in Italy, while the latter recovered from injuries received in a car crash.

Barton's citation for his bar to his DSO (second DSO) takes up the story. Though deserted by his guide and interpreter, Barton 'continued alone to search for his objective . . . his journey took him into the towns of Reggio and Modena, where German patrols, Fascist checks and house-to-house searches were made at every stage . . . Major Barton spent over a month in the area moving short distances at night and living by day in barns, stables and holes in the ground.' During one period he spent ten days hiding in such a hole, and gave up only when he had absolute proof that General von Vietinghoff had moved his HQ out of the area.

Now, in mid-February 1945 Barton was scheduled to return for a second assassination attempt, only this time hosted by Michael Lees. Lees thrilled to the proposition. More to the point, it opened his mind to other tantalising possibilities. He called a meeting with Kiss, and ordered him to use his Stafettas to locate, identify and document the enemy's key headquarters, those housing senior German commanders. As far as Lees was concerned, they would offer the juiciest targets.

The more he considered such a possibility – the concept of targeted assassinations – the more one area intrigued him. On the fringes of the plain around the town of Reggio Emilia, Lees had heard reports of a foremost enemy headquarters, but every piece of fresh intelligence seemed to contradict that which had come before it. It was frustrating and alluring in equal measure.

As chance would have it, Gordon had just recruited two unusual new figures to the Black Owls. Both were German soldiers who had deserted, due to their disillusionment at the Nazi cause. Not only were they well trained and disciplined, but they proved extremely useful when called upon to confuse the enemy. A few shouted orders in German at exactly the right moment seemed to work wonders on sentries.

During the third week of February one of the Germans brought in a fellow deserter, who turned out to be Austrian. Due to the priceless intelligence he brought with him, this young Wehrmacht sergeant was henceforth known only as 'Hans'. Hans had served with the elite German 4th Parachute Division, but he came to Lees' attention when it transpired that he had intelligence concerning the elusive target that he sought.

Hans knew of a headquarters located near Reggio Emilia, which commanded an artillery regiment. But of far greater significance, he argued, was another HQ, which orchestrated command and control for a huge stretch of the Gothic Line. Hans knew only of its rough whereabouts, for the enemy guarded such secrets fiercely. It was staffed by senior generals, and Field Marshal Kesselring himself was said to put in regular appearances.

Feeling his pulse quicken, Lees briefed Kiss. Even if it meant dropping all other work, he wanted that elusive headquarters found. The SOE and SAS favoured two types of behind-the-lines missions: sabotage operations, and those designed to target senior officers, so cutting the head off the snake. As missions to decapitate the Nazi serpent went there would be none better, though the mystery HQ was bound to be extremely heavily guarded.

If Lees could find and hit that headquarters and kill the senior commanders based there, he would have out-Bartoned 'Killer' Barton, the SOE's chief assassin. But to do so he would need more than just his partisans, he reasoned. This called for a unit of British commandos or similar, to stiffen their punch and their resolve.

Lees set about finding out all he could about Hans the deserter – a typically blond and athletic Aryan type. Why had he deserted? What was his motive? Was there any chance he was feeding disinformation to Lees, as some kind of a trap? It turned out that Hans had a very compelling set of reasons to turn his back on the German military and unleash his ire on his former comrades. In short, he had been wounded deep in his heart.

It took all of Lees' powers of persuasion to get the deserter – often morose and brooding – to talk. He hailed from Vienna, Hans explained, where he still had a wife, but he never wanted to see her again. He had been away fighting in Stalingrad on the Eastern Front, when he'd received a letter from his mother, telling him that his wife was due to give birth to a child. Only trouble was, Hans had not been home to Vienna for two long years.

Hans asked his commanding officer for leave on compassionate grounds. That man, an ardent Nazi, had laughed in his face. He'd chided Hans for being selfish and possessive over his wife. She had done her duty to the Fatherland and to Hitler by making another soldier happy, he argued, and in conceiving a child for the Reich. In fact, if Hans were a good Nazi he should celebrate the fact.

'That is why I fight my countrymen,' Hans had concluded, a line of argument that Lees – only recently wed – could relate to.

A few days later, Lees found himself at their Secchio base watching Farrimond decode a message from Florence. 'Please report on possibilities of dropping a force . . .' his W/T operator scribbled on a cypher pad, as a fine spring sunshine streamed through the windows.

There was a knock at the door. Kiss walked in, glancing from Farrimond to Lees with those big, bulbous grey eyes of his. 'Excuse me, sir,' he began, in his slow, ponderous way, 'but I've got the information you requested.'

Lees was amazed. 'Well done, but how the devil did you manage it and so quickly?'

Kiss allowed himself the rare hint of a smile. 'Well, one of the Stafettas is a very . . . beautiful young lady. She is not . . . averse to love. Last night she returned from Castelnovo, where she paid a visit to the officer commanding the garrison.' Kiss reached out with a slip of paper for Lees. 'She . . . obtained this information in the course of her duties.'

Lees grabbed the paper and ran his eyes across it. 'There is an important German headquarters at Villa Rossi, in Botteghe,' he read. 'It is the HQ of 5 Corps and serves as headquarters of the 14th Army. General Feuerstein is living in the villa. Last week Marshal Graziani visited him there.'

Lees stared, dumbfounded. He could hardly believe it. By chance, his area of operations happened to include territory that housed what had to be one of the enemy's most important head-quarters for the whole of the Gothic Line. It was incredible, but seemingly true, unless of course the Stafetta had erred in her amorous endeavours.

A 'Corps' would amount to some 25,000–50,000 men; an 'Army' 100,000–150,000. In short, this was the HQ for fully four of the enemy divisions manning the Gothic Line. More importantly, those four divisions held the key section where Allied commanders planned to launch their spring offensive. If Lees could hit it, and comprehensively, he could decimate enemy command and control at exactly the point Allied commanders intended to punch through.

The enemy commanders mentioned in the message were well-known. Marshal Rodolfo Graziani, the First Marquis of Neghelli, was a die-hard Fascist fiercely loyal to Mussolini. His position – that of Marshal – outranked a general, so he was about as senior as one could get in the Italian military. For his part, General Valentin Feuerstein was an Austrian commander in charge of the 2nd Mountain Division, a unit of elite alpine troops. One of Kesselring's trusted deputies, Feuerstein had played a key role in the Battle of Monte Cassino in the spring of 1944, wherein fear-some German defence had cost the Allies dear. He was a holder of the Knight's Cross of the Iron Cross, one of the highest military awards in Nazi Germany.

In all his operations to date, Lees had never once taken on any target anything as remotely ambitious as this. He would need to scrutinise the information. He'd need to gather further intel on the HQ's defences. He'd need absolute certainty. But if the Stafetta's note turned out to be anything like accurate, this was a chance too good to be missed. It was an incredibly tempting target. Irresistible, in his mind. At one fell stroke Lees and his partisans might strike a blow to change the course of the war.

By the time Farrimond had finished decoding the incoming message from Florence, it seemed serendipitous in the extreme. 'Please report on possibilities of dropping a force of British SAS parachutists in your area to carry out attacks against enemy lines of communication.'

Never mind *lines of communication*, Lees told himself, he had a far better target in mind. He grabbed a message pad and scribbled out a short reply. 'Excellent idea. Send as many as you can!'

He turned to Farrimond. 'Get that one off soon as, Bert, will you?'

In a sense Lees was chancing his arm here. He had only the Stafetta's word for it about the target. But hell, faint heart never won fair lady.

Once the message was sent, Lees had one priority foremost in his mind: to prove that target once and for all. To do so he reckoned he needed to get sight of it himself. Not averse to sneaking about the Yugoslav mountains dressed as a peasant, Lees didn't doubt he could infiltrate the plains around Reggio similarly disguised. But before he could do so, the enemy would prove to have very different ideas in mind.

By now Kesselring himself was alert to the ferocity of partisan attacks emanating from the Secchia valley region, which had 'spread like lightning in the past ten days'. That February, the toll of bridges blown, convoys ambushed and trains derailed exceeded the total efforts of the Reggiani partisans for the preceding six months. In railing against this, Kesselring pointed to the 'more commanding leadership' at the helm of the resistance. Something would have to be done, he declared.

The day after Lees had received those two momentous messages – one from his amorous Stafetta, the other from Florence headquarters – the enemy arrived in force. Soon after dawn Lees heard fierce gunfire echoing up the valley. Reports came in that Don Carlo's Green Flames were in action, and Lees set out to help. He'd not gone far when a messenger arrived, carrying a missive from the warrior-priest himself. Two companies of Fascist *Brigate Nere* – Black Brigades – were attempting to push into the valley, but the Green Flames had it all under control.

Lees was doubtful. In any case, he sensed an opportunity to inflict a crushing defeat on the enemy, massively boosting partisan morale. Instead of heading back to his headquarters, he turned down a little side valley, making for one of the communist brigades. Upon arrival, he told Giovanni 'Gianni' Farri, its commander, to take his men and outflank the Fascist forces, so as to cut off any route of escape. Then they were to be annihilated.

Gianni was a short, squat, battle-hardened commander with a rough grip and ready smile. Lees had every faith in his abilities. Once he'd set out, Lees hurried off to stiffen Don Carlo's resolve. He arrived to discover the battle had reached stalemate. The enemy were hunkered down on the far bank of the Secchia, from where they were unleashing mortar and machine-gun barrages. Don Carlo's Green Flames were holding the nearside bank, and each time the enemy tried to advance they were cut down in the water.

Bearing in mind the Green Flames' spirited resistance, Lees' main worry was that Gianni's partisans might not get into position before the enemy decided to retreat. He told Don Carlo to stage a mock withdrawal. From each of his positions half a dozen fighters ran backwards, making sure they were seen doing so. Heartened, the *Brigate Nere* increased their fire. Just as they broke cover to advance, Lees heard the sound that he'd been longing for – the eruption of fire from the direction of the enemy's rear.

The trap had been sprung, the *Brigate Nere* surrounded. Knowing that the partisans would take no prisoners, they fought for their lives. It was two hours before a final grenade charge by Gianni's communists silenced them. Of the two-hundred-strong *Brigate Nere* force, less than fifty had escaped with their lives. It was a crushing defeat for the enemy and it sent exactly the kind of message Lees had intended: enter the Secchia valley at your peril.

With the enemy so chastened, Lees could return to his main focus: executing a reconnaissance of the newly discovered German headquarters. Several days had passed since Florence had mooted – and Lees had accepted – the offer of SAS paratroopers. There had been no further word of them, and Lees' Plan B was to hit the German headquarters, or at least the key commanders, with the forces he could muster here in the valley.

If they could log General Feuerstein's movements, there was no reason why Lees' Black Owls shouldn't ambush him. They were hitting road convoys nightly now, and Lees could see no argument why General Feuerstein's staff car shouldn't likewise end up riddled with bullets. They could always mount a full-scale attack on the HQ at a later date.

Lees had a new companion to accompany him on his

reconnaissance journey. Lance Corporal Phil Butler had only recently parachuted in to join his mission. Butler had been working locally as a schoolmaster before the war, learning to speak Italian while wandering about these mountains. Quiet, charming and with considerable intelligence-savvy, his other key attribute was his ability to march across the hills at a stiff pace. That was just to Lees' liking, for he hated being slowed down by anyone.

Leaving the ever-capable Farrimond in charge at Secchio, Lees and Butler prepared for the off. As they would be slipping into the heart of enemy territory, the key thing they needed was a convincing disguise. Due to his imposing physical presence, Lees had always found getting local civilian dress something of a challenge. In Yugoslavia, they'd been forced to search the mountains high and low for the tallest man around. Eventually one had presented himself approximating to Lees' height and girth.

He was persuaded to exchange his rough and much-patched trousers for Lees' combat pants, plus his gaily knitted stockings, fur coat and black woollen cap. Lees' feet were wrapped in the skin of a freshly slain calf, so forming the traditional footwear of the region, akin to a lightweight pair of moccasins. Thus adorned, he'd taken on the guise of a local. He'd faced one major problem: within minutes of his transformation he'd started itching horribly. He'd been forced to conclude that when he swapped his clothes back again, his uniform would be similarly riddled with lice.

Here in the Secchia valley, Lees settled for a less onerous form of a compromise. A pair of moth-eaten trousers were conjured from somewhere, plus a voluminous cloak. With that thrown over his battledress tunic and with his Sten gun – fitted with silencer – hidden beneath, he figured he could pass muster. Butler was similarly disguised.

They set out early, sticking to faint paths and tracks. It was a thirty-mile trek to their first port of call, Viano village, perched on the very edge of the hills. They reached it about midnight, creeping along the main street cautiously, for German patrols were known to billet themselves there. Their guide took them to a house standing a little apart, where one of Kiss's contacts lived. No lights were showing and all was silent within. The guide used the pre-arranged signal – a sequence of rings on the back-door bell – to alert those inside.

A voice answered from an upstairs window. 'Who's there?'

'Partisans,' the guide answered.

'Go away at once,' the voice hissed. 'I have nothing to do with partisans ... The Germans were in the village today. They may come back at any moment.'

Lees stepped out of the shadows. 'I'm an English captain. Open up, please.'

As far as he was concerned, it was his Lire that were paying the man for the intelligence he supplied, so he had every right to demand a bed for the night. The window slammed shut. Moments later the back door opened and Lees and party were ushered inside.

After being served a meal, Lees and Butler were shown to a room they could share for the night. Lees decided to open the window, to let in some air. He detected movement in the bushes below. He hissed to Butler to call out a challenge, while he readied his Sten, releasing the bolt of his weapon with a sharp steel-on-steel rasp.

'Answer at once!' Butler cried.

'It is I, your host,' came back the fearful reply from the bushes.

Lees ordered the man into the open, and demanded to know what the devil he was up to.

'I am afraid to sleep in the house in case the enemy return at dawn.'

'So where are you going?' Lees demanded. 'If you inform on us, don't you know you will be shot!'

The man seemed genuinely distraught at the suggestion he might betray them. 'No, no, no. Never! I was just going to a farm close by.'

Lees was convinced the man was telling the truth, and he eased his finger off the trigger.

Early the following morning they made contact with Gordon, who was holed up in a patch of nearby woodland. The previous night he and his Black Owls had ambushed an enemy convoy, after an armoured car had driven over one of their mines. They'd destroyed two trucks, left the armoured car a smoking wreck, and had one man lightly wounded in the exchange of fire. All in all, it had been a good night's work.

From the shelter of the woods, Gordon sent out word for the leaders of the local underground movement to come. They arrived around midday, whereupon Lees proceeded to ask about the enemy HQ. It was situated in a hamlet called Botteghe, they explained, lying on the outskirts of the village of Albinea, some ten kilometres south-west of Reggio Emilia. They were able to furnish several more fascinating details, plus they offered a guide who could take Lees and Butler to within sight of the place.

Lees chose Gordon and 'Giorgio', one of the German deserters, to accompany them. After three hours' march through the darkness following a difficult and convoluted route, they reached an isolated farmhouse lying on a small hillock overlooking the plain. While Lees and Butler held back, Gordon went ahead to deal with the farmer. Issuing fearful threats, he informed the man that he needed use of the farmstead for twenty-four hours. No one was allowed to leave or enter on pain of death during that time.

As Gordon and Giorgio took turns standing sentry, Lees and Butler crawled into a hayloft and dropped to sleep. The following morning dawned bright and clear. The sun burned off the mist that clung to the low-ground, as Lees gazed out over a vast plain that stretched unbroken to the banks of the River Po. Directly to the north some ten miles away, Reggio Emilia shimmered in the early morning heat. A convoy of trucks crawled along a road.

Using his binoculars and map Lees began to identify the smaller, closer landmarks. A village here marked as 'Sundiano'. A large building there with a bright red-tiled roof – a farmstead marked as the 'Villa Spandoni'. Closer and to Lees' left, a clutch of homesteads, seemingly nothing more than a few cottages clustered around a crossroads. But just beyond those lay two large and imposing buildings, one constructed in rich red brick, the other in fine white stone. That had to be it – Villa Rossi; Red Villa – as identified in the Stafetta's note, plus a sister HQ building, Villa Calvi.

He pointed to the place. 'Is that Botteghe?' he asked the guide, feigning a passing interest.

'Si, Signor.' He pointed at the large red-brick building. 'And that is Villa Rossi. They say a general lives there.'

Lees drew a detailed sketch of the place, including the two grand villas, one of which came complete with its own chapel. Via his binoculars he studied Villa Rossi: it was a multi-storeyed fortress, graced by square-walled towers and arched windows, and surrounded by fancy, wrought-iron gates and railings with imposing pillared entryways. It had clearly been a wealthy country residence, before the enemy seized it. The neighbouring building,

Villa Calvi, appeared like a towering, white-walled mansion, and was equally impressive.

Before the two villas lay a small patch of woodland. If they were to attempt an approach unseen and undetected, that might offer good cover. At eight o'clock sharp, the roads, which had been thronged with traffic, suddenly became empty. The reason why shortly became clear: a flight of Thunderbolts roared into the airspace, searching for targets. The Germans clearly knew the hour the Allies sent over their first air patrols, and they timed their convoys accordingly.

All that day Lees and Butler hid in the hayloft, gazing through their binoculars. From all that Lees had learned, ambushing General Feuerstein's car was looking like a non-starter: the German commander varied his movements. He came and left at different times of day and night. His driver took different routes, and sometimes the general never left Villa Rossi for days.

Without a regular schedule, shooting up his staff car was going to be nigh-on impossible. Bar the SAS getting parachuted in, and launching a full-frontal assault on the two buildings, Lees didn't know how exactly they would execute the hit. Still, the recce had gone well and he felt buoyed. Something would shake out of it, of that he felt certain.

Come nightfall he and Butler left, paying the farmer handsomely for his pains. But they arrived back at their Secchio base to disappointing news. The insertion of the SAS parachutists was looking doubtful. Florence worried that sending such a high-profile force might prove counter-productive, by drawing the enemy's ire. Lees was enraged. He was the best judge of the situation on the ground.

He sent a very strongly worded message back to headquarters

to that effect. His anger was fuelled by what else he was to learn, following his return to his Secchio base. By chance, a German prisoner had been brought in by one of the communist brigades. A nondescript private, Lees left him to Fritz Snapper's questioning, alpenstock in hand. That evening, over dinner, Lees asked if the prisoner had had anything to say.

Snapper waved a hand, dismissively. 'Nothing much. He was in the Signals Corps, stationed at some place called Botteghe.'

Apart from Kiss, none of Lees' men knew anything about his intentions regarding the 14th Army's headquarters.

'Where is he now?' Lees demanded.

'I sent him to Febbio, to the POW pens.'

Lees eyed the Dutch Army lieutenant. 'I'm afraid you'll have to fetch him back at once. Go yourself, and for God's sake don't let him escape.'

Snapper, ever willing, set out right away, bringing the prisoner back directly. Lees proceeded to question him into the early hours. He could be a hard man when he had need, and he was ready to do whatever it took to make the man talk. Fortunately, the captive spoke relatively freely and knew the Botteghe headquarters intimately. A German private, he'd served as General Feuerstein's personal telephonist at Villa Rossi, so in his private residence. It was sheer good fortune that he'd fallen into Lees' clutches. He'd been out for a stroll when he'd stumbled into a unit of partisans who were returning from an ambush mission. Not being particularly warlike, he'd surrendered pretty much right away.

He knew everything. He knew the exact strength of the guard forces and where they were stationed. There were some five hundred at the two villas, with hundreds more in reserve, billeted at a barracks just a short drive away and with armoured cars and tanks in support. He knew the layout and role of the two buildings. He confirmed that the HQ oversaw command of German forces manning the Gothic Line from Reggio Emilia to the western coast, so for over a hundred kilometres, or around half of its total length.

From Villa Calvi there was said to be a hotline running direct to Berlin. Field Marshal Kesselring was known to visit the place twice a week, and he was very likely speaking to the Führer himself. While Villa Rossi – two centuries old, and formerly the properly of an Italian lawyer – provided accommodation for senior staff, Villa Calvi housed the 14th Army's communications, command and control set-up. In other words, it was the absolute nerve centre for four German divisions.

The prisoner had one other key piece of intelligence to depart. General Feuerstein had just been replaced, one General Friedrich-Wilhelm Hauk taking over. The blond, blue-eyed Hauk was a highly decorated veteran who had led the invasions of Poland and France in the early stages of the war. He'd won the Knight's Cross of the Iron Cross, in June 1944, for extreme battlefield bravery and leadership, before being posted to Italy that autumn. As assassination targets went, General Hauk was preferable in many ways to his predecessor, but the news of his arrival placed Lees in something of a quandary.

A few days earlier Kiss had presented him with an alternative plan to do away with General Feuerstein, as the SAS seemed to be so long in the coming. One of his Stafettas had just discovered that the general was a devout Catholic and a regular at Sunday morning mass. As Kiss knew the priest local to the area, he'd proposed that he hide himself in the priest's house on a Saturday night, overlooking the steps of the church. From there he'd proceed to shoot the general when he arrived for Sunday worship, with a silenced pistol.

The key to Kiss's plan had been slipping into the priest's house unremarked. They'd decided to disguise him as a holy man, which would provide the perfect cover. Lees had approached Don Pedro, his host, who had provided Kiss with a set of his own cleric's robes.

Kiss had already departed on his devilish assassination mission, not knowing that General Feuerstein had flown the nest. Unless General Hauk was likewise a devout Catholic, Kiss was going to return empty-handed, at which stage Lees would need those SAS parachutists as never before. He signalled as much to Charles Macintosh, at Florence headquarters.

'LEES to MACINTOSH. Have here German who is private telephonist to Lt-Gen HAUK of . . . Staff Corps HQ of 14 Army. Subject is intelligent and willing to talk and am sure he is genuine . . . Am absolutely set for attacking this HQ; can I go ahead either with SAS or partisans, using subject as guide? We have tremendous chance of success and this HQ is vitally important.'

The reply Lees received was surprisingly enthusiastic: '15 Army Group sanction attack . . . Submit plan of attack for possible coordination air support . . . Will SAS be involved?'

Lees replied confirming all points, and strongly requesting that the SAS parachutists be sent in. He received confirmation that an advance force would be despatched the very next day, under the command of an SAS captain. Lees had no idea what lay behind this apparent change of heart at headquarters. In truth, he'd had assistance from several key figures behind the scenes in Florence.

One was Captain Walker-Brown, the brilliant commander of

Operation Galia. Walker-Brown had been lobbying in the background and working his magic on the Americans. Appointed as No. 3 Squadron SAS's liaison officer in Florence, he'd been arguing forcefully for the squadron to be sent in. Upon hearing of Lees' discovery of the Botteghe HQ, he'd recognised that here was a mission ready-made for the special forces raiders.

'It was planned,' he wrote of the Botteghe raid, '. . . in the hope that destruction caused in a major headquarters would result in some loss of control, however momentary . . .' In that moment, Allied forces massing to the south of the Gothic Line could seize the advantage.

Major Jim Davies, one of Macintosh's favourite BLOs, who commanded a neighbouring band of partisans, had also reported back most positively on Lees, saying that he had totally resurrected the fortunes of the Reggiani partisans. Davies wrote: 'I am sure they would be most effective, even decisive, in attacks on the trans-Apennine communications.' Of Lees' HQ assault plan, he noted: 'LEES . . . doing very well. I have discussed SAS question . . . He wants them for the Corps HQ and will get everything teed up first.'

In Secchio, Lees remained oblivious to such behind-the-scenes manoeuvres. Hardly a politician or diplomat, he didn't particularly give a damn about such things.

All he cared about was getting the mission of a lifetime done.

Chapter 10

It was dawn on 4 March 1945 when Major Farran clambered aboard the lead flight of six Dakotas bound for the Secchia valley. Some forty minutes later, he found himself at the open doorway of the aircraft, buffeted by icy blasts. As they swooped low over a mountain pass, Farran could see tiny black figures outlined against the sparkling, sunlit expanse of the snowfields.

Behind him, five fellow parachutists were bunched up close, each weighed down with heavy kit. As one, they staggered when the aircraft hit a patch of fierce turbulence. Farran noticed their nervous glances, as they stared down at the barren terrain flashing past, and at the pair of P47 Thunderbolts flying escort, close on their wingtips. He could well appreciate their nerves.

It had been three days since their last contact with Mike Lees, the SOE's man on the ground. As the area was crawling with enemy, a lot could have happened in the interim. And even if the pilots did find the DZ and it was in friendly hands, the partisans might have failed to leave the proper designation of markers. If that happened, should they leap regardless? The weather was bound to break soon, so there was no knowing when they might get another chance.

Farran held the US aircrews who flew the Dakotas in very high regard. During Operation Galia, Colonel Hardt, their squadron leader, had personally flown a mission of untold import. Harried through the ice-bound mountains, Walker-Brown's men were sick to death with dysentery and scabies – a horrible infection caused by mites that burrow beneath the skin. Hardt had piloted a lone, unarmed Dakota through deep, fog-bound valleys, dropping Captain John 'Jock' Milne, an SAS doctor, into their isolated location, saving many lives.

Likewise, Farran had every confidence in today's aircrew. He'd been jammed in the Dakota's doorway buffeted by the freezing slipstream for a good ten minutes, when he felt the aircraft lose altitude and start to circle. Sure enough, the point below was marked by a distinctive arrangement of coloured parachutes showing red and yellow in the snow. Tiny figures darted about, busy with last minute preparations. The DZ lay at the head of a long, narrow valley, above which towered the unmistakable form of Monte Cusna.

Smoke drifted lazily from one or two villages scattered across the terrain. Farran studied them closely, trying to ascertain if they had been burned out in a recent *rastrellamento* – raking through. The red light flashed on, marking the ten-minutes-to-jump point. Farran turned to the six men behind him: each forced an uncertain smile.

Jock Easton, Farran's second-in-command, seemed the calmest. Hardly surprising, as he was one of the genuine old and bold. Behind him, Kershaw, a British Olympic bobsleigh competitor before the war, gave a thumbs-up and shouted something, but his words were torn away on the wind. It was Kershaw's first parachute jump, but no doubt he would be very much at home once in the snowfields. After Kershaw came the two war-bitten Spaniards, Robert Bruce and Frank Williams, arguably the most experienced of the lot in irregular warfare. But even they looked nervous.

The men's disquiet underscored one of the main reasons that Farran had decided that he *would* be joining them today, regardless of orders to the contrary. He needed to lead from the front, to set an example. But even so his guts were knotted tight with nerves. For a moment he wondered if he could back out. God knows, he had every excuse – not least of which, he would be jumping against orders. But if he bottled it, his men would know the real reason and it might deter them from making the leap themselves.

More to the point, Farran would be judged by his peers. He'd not been too windy to send Captain Littlejohn and team into the freezing darkness above the snow-bound Brenner Pass, on operation Cold Comfort, but he would have been too windy to jump now. At the end of the day it was neither duty nor patriotism that stiffened Farran's resolve: it was his relationship with his men and that age-old desire to stand high in their regard, and to lead from the front.

He braced himself at the doorway, feeling the cold burn of the air against his fingers. He leaned further forwards, the slipstream tearing at his face. He tried to remember how to do this: *feet and knees together as you jumped*. He consoled himself with the thought that in many ways it was easier to go first. That way, you didn't see the man before you dive into the howling void, something that was so utterly unnatural that it went against your every instinct.

As he peered at the ground flashing past, Farran sensed they were too low. The gleaming white flank of Monte Cusna towered above them. He turned to speak to the despatcher, but the words froze in his throat. The man thumped Farran on the shoulder, and indicated that the light had switched to green. After a moment's hesitation, he threw himself forward.

There was a second's gut-wrenching panic, before the para-chute snapped like a yacht's mainsail catching the wind and it blossomed above his head. Farran found himself drifting towards earth, the white folds of the valley rising to great heights on either side. He reached for the pin that held his kitbag fastened to his leg, and ripped it out, letting it fall on its retaining rope. As he did so, a voice yelled beside him, exultantly.

'Whoa Mahomet! Whoa Mahomet!'

It was the curious war-cry of the British 1st Airborne Division, something that the paratroopers had picked up from the locals – and no doubt bastardised – during the 1942 Operation Torch landings in North Africa. Farran laughed. It was Kershaw who was yelling, and to Farran it signalled that his men were with him in spirit, as well as in body.

As the ground drifted up to meet them, he spared a thought for the predicament he was in, although there was no getting back into that aircraft now. He'd told the American aircrew an utterly fanciful story, one that he'd begged them to deliver to headquar-ters as straight-faced and sober as they possibly could. They were to report the sad tale that Major Farran had unexpectedly fallen from the aircraft, even as the others had jumped.

He wondered how long the ruse would hold. Once it was dis-covered that he'd 'fallen' with a parachute strapped to his back and his kit and weaponry slung on his person, he figured the game would be up. He would be in grave danger of ending a distinguished wartime career with a court martial. The one thing that might mitigate his disgrace was the success of the coming mission, for which so much depended on the man on the ground here, Michael Lees.

Farran had heard much about Lees and his reputation as a

force of nature. He was 'the best and yet the wildest, most difficult to tame and the most domineering mission commander in northern Italy', as Farran understood it. He couldn't wait to see Lees in action.

Farran's kitbag had barely reached the end of its rope, before he felt it thump down with a hollow plop. Moments later he hit the snowy ground, which proved to be deceptively hard. He rolled twice, coming to rest with the breath knocked out of him and lying on his back. He reached up and tried to get his parachute under control, which was billowing wildly and threatening to drag him away.

Fortunately, a figure appeared to help. Cloaked in baggy battledress, he looked barely out of his teens.

'Buongiorno,' he cried, as he helped Farran wrestle with the chute. 'I am Bruno.'

Moments later, Bruno had hoisted Farran's kitbag onto his shoulders and was climbing up the slope towards the DZ, which was set a little way above them.

Farran struggled to his feet. 'Come back, you little brute!' he yelled, before promptly falling over again in the snow.

Over the past few days the surface had repeatedly thawed and frozen, making it as slippery as an ice rink, hence Farran's problems.

Bruno returned, dropped the kitbag, and helped the struggling SAS major to his feet. All around them freshly released supply containers drifted to earth. Some broke free from their parachutes and came screaming down like bombs. Farran thanked his lucky stars he wasn't under one of those.

By a combination of crawling and sliding he reached the DZ, only to find that not one of his men was in sight. A tall fellow with a giant white beard seemed in charge. Upon spying Farran he saluted smartly, and introduced himself as 'Scalabrino', but that did little to dispel his Robin Hood air. Still, he struck Farran as being the most soldierly of any present. The remainder – presumably, Mike Lee's finest – were as long-haired and bearded a bunch of ruffians as ever he'd laid eyes on.

They were a distinctly motley crew, sporting items of uniform from just about every nation that had fought in this war: British, American, Italian and German. The one unifying feature appeared to be the lengths of colourful parachute silk each had wrapped around his neck, as a makeshift scarf. That, plus the fact that every single one of them was armed to the teeth bristling with knifes, daggers, grenades, pistols and tommy guns.

As initial impressions went it left something to be desired. Only Scalabrino impressed. The efficiency with which he had mule trains and oxen sleds collecting up the supplies was striking. Farran asked if he'd seen any others from his stick. 'Yessir,' Scalabrino replied, indicating a nearby village. Farran spied Kershaw wandering up the track. He was hatless, his uniform was torn and he was a little dazed-looking, but he managed a broad smile.

Kershaw reported that they'd been dropped over the village itself, landing among the roofs and hard, icy streets. In the process, Jock Easton had injured his shoulder. Kershaw himself was only saved when he landed on a snowy roof, slid off and a comely Italian woman happened to break his fall. Bruce, the Spaniard and former Foreign Legionnaire, had smashed his carbine upon landing, but otherwise he was in relatively good shape, as was his fellow Spaniard, Williams.

Farran spotted Jock Easton stumbling up the track, looking white as a sheet. He was in the company of a second figure, a

Lieutenant Smith. Farran had met Smith in Florence several weeks earlier and he'd warmed to the man. A Scot, he seemed either to be talking non-stop or to lapse into long silences. Wholly at home in the mountains, Smith was acutely shy and prone to fits of depression. He had been dropped in recently to assist Lees, and Farran wondered how he was faring under the command of such a man, serving in his not-inconsiderable shadow.

Easton was in great pain, and he collapsed and vomited into the snow. Farran, Smith and Kershaw carried him to the nearby village, a tiny place called Casa Belocchi. There, Bruno the teenage partisan volunteered to fetch the nearest doctor, which might take some time. While they waited they put Easton to bed, and Smith led them to a nearby café for breakfast.

A wizened old crone blew twigs into crackling flames, and lit oil lanterns. Shortly, she'd rustled up a fine breakfast of chestnut bread, fried eggs and red wine. This was Farran's first introduction to chestnuts, a staple of the poverty-stricken villagers. Their coarse mountain bread was studded with chestnuts, to help bulk it out.

Houses lined the village square, linked by steep cobbled paths slippery with ice. From the outside, they looked like hovels. Inside they were spotless, each boasting an open charcoal fire and dancing oil lanterns. In a way, they reminded Farran of the neat little white-painted cottages you'd find all over County Tyrone and South Down – the part of Northern Ireland that his family hailed from.

As he sipped his wine, Farran marvelled that such a place and such a life could exist, so close to the German lines. Everywhere he looked figures were busy hauling supplies through the streets. The place was alive with partisans and their local helpers, while a

168

force of newly arrived parachutists breakfasted in the village café, yet the enemy were but a short march away. It was all so utterly brazen, with the main front just the far side of the mountain.

They'd never have got away with this in France, Farran reasoned. Smith, in garrulous mood, explained how things worked around here. The partisans held the mountains, the enemy the plains. If the partisans caused too much trouble, the Germans tended to mount a *rastrellamento*, but they were only ever short-lived. The enemy just didn't have the forces to man the front line and to drive the partisans out of their mountain redoubt.

'Are they all Reds?' Farran queried, remembering his Florence briefings.

'Most of them call themselves communists, but . . . they don't really know what communism means.'

'Are they holding on to seize power when the war's over?' Farran asked. Again, it was something he'd heard talk about in Florence.

Smith shrugged. 'That may be partly it.'

A sudden burst of gunfire echoed through the streets, cutting their conversation short. As Farran and his men reached for their weapons, Smith told them not to worry. It was just a bout of high spirits. Overjoyed with the drop – fully five plane-loads – the partisans were celebrating as only they knew how.

Of course, the spirit of resistance would run deep in these mountains, Farran reflected. The locals were the descendants of Garibaldi's originals, those brave Italian souls who had fought centuries back to liberate and unify the Italian nation. In 1860 the famed Italian commander General Giuseppe Garibaldi had raised a volunteer army, to march on southern Italy, in the celebrated Expedition of the Thousand.

With a thousand volunteers he had defeated a much larger regular army, leading to the unification of a hitherto divided nation. General Garibaldi was a fierce advocate of democracy, tolerance and liberty, and he'd won international renown particularly in Britain and the USA. His volunteer fighters had worn red shirts, as their one distinguishing feature, and they had named themselves the Garibaldini. The general's present-day descendants, the communist partisans, referred to themselves by the same name.

At last the doctor arrived. A tall moustachioed individual, he appeared somewhat servile and frightened. Farran did his best to put the man at ease, before stiffening Jock Easton's spirits with a good draft of red wine. That done, the doctor seized his injured arm and twisted it behind his back. There was a sharp crack and the dislocated shoulder was forced back into place. Agonising though it doubtless was, Easton appeared instantly happier. With his arm bound up in a sling, he should be good to move.

Farran noticed the crowds thronging the streets seeming to part ways spontaneously. A tall figure mounted on a fine brown mare rode forwards, making a beeline for the café. Farran didn't doubt for one moment that this was the illustrious Mike Lees, the man upon whom everything now depended. Swinging with ease from his saddle – he used to hunt regularly with the South Dorset Hounds – Lees towered over the locals. They cheered his arrival, like a football star at a big match.

Lees was wearing a stylish, sand-coloured American windbreaker jacket, topped off by a dashing black beret. No doubt about it, he looked the part. He strode forward and grabbed Farran's hand, pumping it so enthusiastically that he wondered whether his soldiering days were over.

'Delighted to see you,' Lees began. 'I didn't think they'd ever get around to sending British troops. No one warned me you were coming, but it's just as well if the other chap is hurt.' By that he meant Easton.

'Didn't you get a message from Florence?' Farran asked.

'Got a message. Said there was going to be a drop, so I sent Smith. Didn't say you were coming. Don't believe half of what they say, anyway. Sometimes they say there's going to be a drop and nothing turns up. Didn't know you were coming yourself.'

Farran's blue eyes twinkled mischievously. 'No one knew. In fact, my chief refused permission, but I thought I'd come in the plane and see the chaps jump. Well, you know how it is . . . I thought I'd wear a parachute, just in case we had trouble. I was standing by the door and someone tripped over me, and bless my soul there I was in the air. And a man on a parachute can hardly go upwards, can he?'

Lees saw Farran's left eye droop momentarily, in the vaguest suggestion of a wink. 'Of course, there's no way I could get out again, is there?' Farran ventured. 'I'm supposed to be doing a desk job in Florence – chairborne!'

'Well, there's a courier service that regularly crosses the lines,' Lees replied. 'But it's very dangerous,' he added, with emphasis. '*Very dangerous indeed.*'

'And we'll be liberated soon?' Farran prompted.

Lees nodded vigorously. 'Oh yes, I expect so. Very soon, I expect.'

Both men burst out laughing.

'In that case I think I'll have to stay,' Farran declared. 'Now, tell me about this place you want to beat up. I'm itching to get at it.'

'Good show!' Lees enthused. 'Lots of targets for you, actually. The Army HQ's a sitting duck. At last we can get cracking. These farts are bloody useless. You lot will shake 'em up. Farts is what we call 'em – you know, bastardisation of "partisans". No strength and gone with the wind.' He laughed. 'I've arranged for Colonel Monti to come over tonight. He's supposed to be the CO around here. Let's get moving. My base is at Secchio, three hours from here.'

Farran explained that Jock Easton was walking wounded, and Lees immediately offered his horse. He turned to Scalabrino to outline what was required.

'See this old scoundrel,' Lees continued, once he was done explaining, 'he's the only fart I trust in the whole valley. He'll account for everything, down to the last pair of bootlaces.'

'So what are the plans now?' Farran asked.

'*Andiamo.*' – Let's go. 'We walk to Secchio. It'll take three hours. Do myself pretty well there. Lodge with the priest. You'll see.'

Secchio village was pointed out to Farran – he could see it perched on the far side of the valley. It looked about five miles away. How could it take three hours to get there? he asked.

Lees' shoulders shook with laughter. It took three hours or more to cross the valley, no matter where you tried, he explained. With that Lees was off, heading up the narrow, rocky path that led out of Casa Belocchi. As he strode ahead, he started to sing in a stentorian voice:

> *The cow kicked Nellie in the belly in the barn,*
> *And the old man said it wouldn't do her any harm . . .*

Caught up in his enthusiasm, Farran grabbed his heavy kit, wondering how on earth he was going to keep up with the almighty great strides of this giant of a mountain man.

That evening, Farran and his men were shown to their billets scattered across Secchio. In the priest's house, the SAS major was led to his room by Don Pedro's elderly mother. He threw open the window and gazed over the scene. It was captivating. Beyond the goats and chickens in the back yard rose the flanks of a mountain, its slopes tinged purple in the evening haze. Oil lanterns flickered in cottages to left and right.

As Farran marvelled at the apparent peace here, a chill crept in to the room. This was far from what he was used to as a soldier's billet: the flowery wallpaper and crucifix adorning the wall; the crisp white sheets on the bed. Next door, a hot bath was running. Dinner was to follow. He lay back and laughed at the ceiling. This was the oddest way to begin operations behind the lines that he had ever known.

He wondered if Lees had somehow grown soft; if the SOE's man-on-the-ground here had somehow got it all wrong. Gung-ho, larger-than-life and battle-hungry, Lees didn't strike Farran as being the type to mess up. Regardless, he resolved to carry a carbine with him at all times, just in case.

But for now, more pressing matters beckoned. Farran needed to count a massive pile of cash. His rucksack was stuffed full of Lire – operational funds. As he flicked through the thick wads, he reflected upon how unlikely he was ever to be this wealthy again. Trusted implicitly with such a vast sum, little if any book-keeping was going to be possible. But he was too bound up in the spirit of the moment to wonder how a small portion of those funds might benefit his life in the future.

Downstairs, Lees was waiting over a dinner of ravioli. He offered Farran a choice of grappa – a strong, grape-based brandy – or Sassolino, the locally-made aniseed liqueur. Farran chose grappa, having acquired a taste for it on previous behind-the-lines operations. Fittingly, the priest's dining room had a giant portrait of the original General Garibaldi gracing one wall. Don Pedro looked on, bemusedly, as the two men got down to business.

The partisan leadership would be wary of Farran, Lees warned, as they'd been of him upon his arrival. The key was to allow individuals like Colonel Monti to appear as if still fully in command, while leading quietly from the shadows. The enemy were likely to know soon enough that Farran and his advance party had dropped in, which led around to the main point of interest for Lees.

'How big a force do you plan to bring?' he asked.

'Around fifty, with everything up to heavy mortars. That's a lot for us. We may even get jeeps and a howitzer dropped in before we're done.'

Farran had discussed such possibilities with Walker-Brown. He believed the US Willys jeep the 'greatest invention of the war'. Getting jeeps parachuted in would lend them the vital mobility upon which fast, hit-and-run guerrilla operations thrived. Getting a big 75mm howitzer dropped in would open up a whole new world of possibilities in terms of targets.

Lees leaned forward eagerly. 'Look,' he whispered, 'let's have a go at the German headquarters ... Ever since arriving I've wanted to attack it. That's why I pleaded for British troops, never dreaming they'd send some. I know all about the place ... Are you game for a really big show like that?'

'If you think we can do it, we'll take it on,' Farran replied.

Even as he'd said it, Farran had felt a flutter of nerves. For years now he'd grown accustomed to brewing up enemy convoys, blowing bridges, wrecking trains and shooting up aircraft on the ground. But taking on a heavily guarded army headquarters was a different matter entirely. The nearest Farran had ever got to anything like this was his wildly successful autumn '44 assault on the German garrison at Châtillon – but even that was small fry compared to what Lees was proposing. The headquarters of the German 14th Army was in a whole different league, and as far as he was aware the SAS had never attempted anything as remotely ambitious as this.

As Lees outlined its fearsome defences – several hundred German troops, boasting armour and anti-aircraft guns – Farran felt ever more daunted. When Lees explained its exact location, situated out on the plain of the Po and surrounded by enemy garrisons, he was doubly unsettled. But faced by Lees' unbridled enthusiasm, and benefiting from several refills of grappa, all Farran could do was live up to his fearsome reputation as a highly decorated and fearless SAS commander, drinking toast after toast to the coming mission.

Lees summoned Gordon, the Black Owls' chief, to join them with his accordion. Farran was struck by the man's appearance. His battledress displayed a black owl badge stitched onto one pocket – the newly minted emblem of their elite unit – and in his belt was tucked a pair of daggers and a matching pair of pistols. With his fingers flashing over the accordion's keys, Gordon began to sing in a rich, ringing tenor, belting out revolutionary songs, some of which dated back to the days of the original Garibaldini.

Gordon sang romantically and passionately, Italian style, and Farran found himself caught up in the spirit of the moment. Shortly, he was doing his best to croon along. The carousing was brought to a halt with the arrival of Colonel Monti, who had ridden from Febbio to make the SAS major's acquaintance. At first the colonel seemed guarded, as Lees had warned he might be, when introduced to 'Major McGinty', Farran's nom de guerre.

Farran offered up a bottle of whisky to break the ice, Lees producing some fine German cigars. He proceeded to regale his audience with the tale of how he'd come by them. There was a German Army deserter called Hans, Lees explained, who hated his former comrades with a vengeance. He'd taken to standing on the main highway seeking a lift, dressed in full German uniform. A truck would stop and Hans would hold it up at gun-point. The cigars had been purloined from one of his hijacked rides.

With the Scotch whisky flowing and German cigars glowing, the three commanders got down to business. Colonel Monti's foremost concern, it became clear, was that his prestige as chief of the Reggiani partisans was under threat. Lees handled the situation with remarkable skill, briefing Farran on the nature of the various partisan brigades, and translating everything for the colonel. Now and again he threw in a witty aside, which served to put Colonel Monti increasingly at ease.

There were four partisan brigades, Lees explained, amounting to some five hundred men-at-arms. In his view, the communist Garibaldini were the finer units, for they were led by commanders of more level temperament than the Green Flames. Gianni, Rames and Zito, the Garibaldini commanders, were rock-solid and dependable. Their fighting spirit was stiffened by Eros, the political commissar or chief of the Garibaldini brigades. A driven, fiercely ideological and somewhat difficult individual, nevertheless Eros had fought the Nazi enemy with enormous grit and courage over the years.

Lees moved on to outline the debilitating effect of the 'go-slow' and 'stand-down' orders issued by Allied high command, not to mention the winter shutdown in resupply drops. It had caused a sense of abandonment and betrayal, resulting in a complete loss of offensive spirit. What Lees had tried to focus on was turning all of that around.

As Lees talked, translating for the colonel's benefit, Farran could see the Italian commander fingering the stem of his glass uncomfortably. The colonel was impressed by the depth of Lees' understanding, if not a little discomfited by how completely he had seen through their façade. But he appeared far more discomfited to learn that a full squadron of SAS was scheduled to follow Farran, dropping in to join them.

'Whose command will they be under?' Colonel Monti ventured, addressing his question to Lees.

Farran jumped in. As the Italian colonel outranked him, he explained, he, Major Farran, would be under Colonel Monti's command. But as he had to take his orders from Florence, Monti's orders to Farran would have to originate in Florence headquarters. Convoluted and unworkable though this might be – Farran would obviously be taking his orders direct from headquarters – it was as fine a piece of weasel wording as he could muster.

'Then this is my understanding,' Colonel Monti ventured. 'You are under my command, but receive your orders from Florence.'

'Your orders to us originate in Florence,' Farran corrected him. 'And no one in the valley need know the details of this arrangement, of course.'

The colonel nodded. The peculiar arrangement seemed to pass muster. 'Very good. So, what now will you need?'

Farran explained that the first priority was a base for his SAS field headquarters, suitable for accommodating fifty men-at-arms. Easton and the rest would move in right away, preparing for the others to follow. Plus they'd need rations and some runners, to carry messages to and from Colonel Monti's HQ and to Lees' mission here in Secchio.

The colonel began to speak more freely now. The delicate negotiations done, he seemed far more comfortable. There was a disused church at Tapignola, he explained, just across the valley from Secchio. It was ideal for housing that size of force. The priest, Don Pasquino Borghi, had been a foremost resistance figure, until the enemy had arrested him. That had been in January 1944, when the priest had been officiating at a religious ceremony, the Festival of Saint Agnes.

A show trial followed, designed to demonstrate that even the clergy were not immune to the harshest of punishments for consorting with the resistance. On 30 January Don Pasquino Borghi had been executed by a shot in the back. Deprived of its priest, the church at Tapignola had fallen into disuse. In a sense, there was no more suitable a place to house those who would drop in, seeking vengeance. Farran couldn't agree more. His No. 3 Squadron SAS would be based in a church, whose priest had been executed by the Nazis. It was somehow so devilishly fitting.

Colonel Monti promised that supplies of food staples – spaghetti and flour – would be delivered there. He also offered six mules, to carry the SAS's kit and armaments. It was generous, for nearly all such beasts of burden had been commandeered by the Germans. Farran suggested they could also use the church as a base to train the partisans in the use of heavier weapons.

'Does that mean we are to receive more and heavier arms?' Colonel Monti queried.

'Of course,' Farran replied.

Florence recognised that the Reggiani partisans were of

unusually high calibre, he explained, which was why the SAS were being sent in. This was mostly hot air, of course, and Farran was chancing his arm by promising more and heavier weaponry. For all he knew, he might make contact with Florence only to be ordered out again, under threat of court martial. But it was a case of nothing ventured, nothing gained.

It was now that Lees aired an entirely new proposition. With the SAS's arrival, why not form a bespoke partisan brigade, one benefiting from top training and weaponry? It could be christened the 'Allied Battalion' and be permanently attached to the SAS. If it combined right-wing elements and communists, it would be truly apolitical. Barba Nera, a commander whom Lees held in high regard, could be appointed its chief, so directly under Farran.

As Colonel Monti seemed to favour the idea, Lees followed through with a further suggestion. 'What about the Russians? Surely, Modena's Russians would be far better under Major McGinty? That way, three companies would form the battalion: one British, one Italian and one Russian.'

Who on earth were the Russians, Farran wondered? But Lees was on a roll, and the good spirits and good liquor seemed to be doing the trick with Colonel Monti. He wasn't about to object. The colonel seemed to like the idea of adding the mysterious Russians into the mix. Swelled with the hundred men they could muster, Major McGinty's Allied Battalion would amount to some three hundred men-at-arms, SAS included.

Farran's head swirled. Given the time to train and arm them properly, this would truly be a force to be reckoned with. It wasn't the usual way the SAS went about doing things: small-scale, shoot-and-scoot raids didn't require a unit of that size and strength. But there was the 14th Army's Botteghe headquarters to be reckoned with.

Colonel Monti raised a glass to toast the *Battaglione Alleato* – the Allied Battalion. Lees winked at Farran and clapped his hands, summoning Gordon for a round of revolutionary songs. Farran was impressed by the skilful and adept way in which he had handled the delicate negotiations. There were clearly hidden depths to Mike Lees, to which his wild-man reputation didn't fully do justice. With Walker-Brown at base, to orchestrate air-drops, and Lees here on the ground, it struck Farran that this was a marriage made in heaven.

But only if headquarters swallowed the story of his miraculous survival – his accidental fall from the skies.

Chapter 11

Having slept well Farran was called for breakfast, where the question of the mysterious Russians was answered most emphatically. He was met by Lees and a stranger – a tall, dashing figure dressed in calf-high German Army boots, with a blue sailor's cap atop his close-cropped fair hair, and a strip of matching blue parachute silk knotted around his neck. He had a guileless, open face, and a surprisingly boyish air.

Farran warmed to the man's firm handshake and easy smile. This, it turned out, was Victor Pirogov, the commander of the Russian brigade of partisans, whose chosen nom de guerre was 'Modena'. Farran was struck by something else: a tall, dark and intriguingly silent woman was seated in one corner of the dining room, seemingly oblivious to her arresting beauty. It turned out that this was Modena's Italian mistress whom he took everywhere, even into battle.

Their arrival at Secchio was purely by chance: they had been riding through, heading to Febbio to plead for more and better arms with Colonel Monti. En route, and serendipitously, they'd dropped in for a chat.

Modena had a remarkable story. A former lieutenant in the Red Army, he'd been taken captive during fighting on the Eastern Front and sent to a POW camp in Austria. He'd escaped, crossed the border into Italy and proceeded to raise his own band of partisans. Mostly, they were former Russian POWs, though some had slipped away from the Todt Organisation, the Nazi forced-labour ministry which had thousands working to stiffen the Gothic Lines defences.

The Garibaldini had huge regard for Modena, presuming him to be an ardent communist. In truth, he was far more interested in leading his men in battle, or being seen with his pretty girl on his arm. Indeed, he struck Farran as being the ultimate swash-buckling adventurer, and if the rest of his partisans were cut from the same cloth, he could understand why Lees was so keen to have the Russians join the Allied Battalion. If they were to hit the 14th Army headquarters, they were just the kind of fighters he'd need.

Lees wasted no time in laying out their proposition to Modena, whose blue eyes shone with excitement. He expressed delight that 'proper soldiers' – the SAS – were dropping into the Secchio valley. He was confident of raising a force of a hundred of the finest Russian warriors, he declared. Indeed, he could recruit far more, for Russians were deserting daily from the 162nd Turkoman Division, a German Army unit formed mostly from Russian and Caucasus POWs. Given the choice between the concentration camps or fighting for the Reich, many had chosen the latter, but only for as long as it took to find a way out. Right now, they were flocking to the hills.

Farran told Modena to cap his unit at one hundred, to keep the Russian company in similar strength to the Italian one. Modena offered to contribute twelve mules as well, for his partisans were better equipped with the pack animals, which were crucial for mountain-based guerrilla operations. That agreed, Lees and Farran watched Modena mount up his big mare, his weapon slung upon his back, his mistress jumping onto the saddle in front of him.

As they waved farewell, setting off towards Febbio, Lees began to regale Farran with stories about the Russian's exploits. In the early days Modena had served with the Garibaldi brigades, when their fighters numbered in the few dozen only, earning a fearsome reputation. Upon forming his Russian brigade, he'd appointed Nikolai, a former Red Army sergeant, as his second-in-command. Apparently, Nikolai ruled the brigade as a British sergeant major would tend to – with a loud voice and a rod of iron.

Modena received sporadic liaison visits from another young Russian officer, who was Mike Lees' opposite number in Moscow. But since that man had little means to contact Moscow, some 3,000 kilometres away, and had such a vast area of territory to cover, his influence was minimal. On the ground it was the Western Allies – chiefly Britain and the US – who were pumping in the hard cash and the weaponry.

While Modena's enthusiastic embracing of the Allied Battalion was unlikely to go unnoticed in Moscow, he and his men had every reason to seek a closer alliance with the British and Americans. The Russians were known to look askance at any of their countrymen who had fought alongside Western 'capitalist' forces. By signing up to the Allied Battalion, Modena doubtless hoped that he and his men would be better shielded by Britain and the US, come war's end.

With the Russians on-board, Farran was struck by the linguistic challenges commanding the Allied Battalion might entail. Modena's Italian seemed about as good as his own, so pretty much non-existent. Apart from Russian, he also spoke German, which was of little help. It was all the more reason for Farran to speed the delivery of Lieutenant Stephens, their Austrian Jew, into the Casa Balocchi DZ. Fluent in German, Stephens could serve as the linguistic bridge to Modena and his men.

But Farran sensed that a Russian-speaker would also prove invaluable, especially if that person understood the Russian mentality. As it happened, he had just such a figure in mind. Karl Nurk was as colourful a character as ever there was, and while not strictly Russian, he was fluent in the tongue. He hailed from the republic of Estonia, sandwiched between Finland and Russia. Born in 1904, he'd served in the Estonian military, before deciding to attempt to cross the Sahara along with a fellow Estonian adventurer.

In 1925 they'd done just that, ending up completing the epic journey on foot when their camels died. Finding himself in East Africa, Nurk became variously a farmer and a big game hunter. He'd travelled to Britain at the outbreak of hostilities and volunteered to fight against the Russians in the Winter War, joining the British Volunteers, also known as the Snowballers (along with James Riccomini, who was already a stalwart of Farran's Tombola force).

Commanded by Orde Wingate, a passionate advocate of irregular warfare, the British Volunteers were backed enthusiastically by Churchill. As Nurk was a fluent Finnish speaker, he became invaluable to Wingate and served as his aide throughout the campaign. The spirited defence of Finland proved ultimately abortive, but Wingate was undeterred. His irregulars set out for Ethiopia to fight the Italians, with Nurk foremost among them.

There, Nurk had trained local Ethiopians in guerrilla warfare, scoring a series of daring victories. He was promoted to captain and won a Military Cross, being praised for 'conspicuous gallantry and devotion to duty'. Despite the terrible terrain and lack of water, his irregulars had surrounded and routed the Italians, taking 150 prisoners. 'This officer's determination and will to succeed are beyond all praise,' his MC citation had concluded.

By then, Nurk was in his late thirties, so an 'old man' compared to the likes of Farran and Lees. But he was far from done. Recruited into the SAS, he was wounded on operations in Yugoslavia, before parachuting into France in June 1944 and winning a DSO. In short, Nurk was just the kind of figure who would work well with the Russians, as they prepared to hit the 14th Army headquarters, which was exactly the kind of operation that Nurk would thrill to.

Farran was determined to get him dropped into theatre. The only trouble was, that would entail making contact with Florence headquarters, and getting Walker-Brown to pull some strings, putting up a request to London. And that in turn meant Farran raising his head above the parapet. He was worried he was going to get it summarily shot off, once those in command realised he was alive and well and doing exactly as they'd forbidden.

But first, there was another surprise visitor in Secchio. Word of the raising of the Allied Battalion was spreading fast, and Annibale Alpi – nom de guerre Barba Nera (black beard) – turned up. Short, portly, and seemingly dwarfed by a massive spade-shaped beard, he wore smart Italian battledress and a peaked Italian Army forage cap. A former sergeant in the Italian military, he had a certain presence and bearing. He'd served as the Reggiani partisans' quartermaster for an age now, furnishing their supplies and stores.

With the ground thick with enemy, it was far from easy soliciting food and other provisions. By all accounts, Barba Nera had done a fine job. Farran sensed that here was a man who could prove difficult, if crossed, but he was just the kind of skilled and resourceful organiser that the Allied Battalion would need. After some discussion Barba Nera agreed to serve as Farran's second-in-command, with key responsibility for providing rations and kit.

Farran sensed that Barba Nera was swayed in part by the money. From his pile of cash Farran had offered 75,000 Lire, to be paid on a weekly basis, to cover all provisioning and other non-weaponry requirements. In truth, this wasn't overly generous. Much had to be purchased at extortionate prices on the black market, and Barba Nera would also have to find fodder for their mules. But on the plus side of the equation, each resupply drop furnished highly valuable parachute silk, which he could barter in exchange for supplies.

They rounded off their negotiations with Farran demanding that all elements of the Allied Battalion – Russians, Garibaldini, Green Flames and Barba Nera's quartermaster corps, plus the SAS, of course – be ready to muster by 9 March, so just a few days hence.

'Arrivederci' – until we meet again – Barba Nera replied. Then he came stiffly to attention, placed his cap on his head and saluted crisply. The SAS tended not to go in for such formality, but as Farran told himself, wryly, they were all in the Italian Army now . . .

With Modena and Barba Nera squared away, Farran decided a visit to his new base at Tapignola church was in order. It lay due west across the valley and he decided to cross it 'as the crow flies'. He set out heading directly downhill, forcing a path through thick bush, clambering over huge grey boulders and slipping down vast expanses of scree. In places the snow lay waist deep, especially in the deepest gullies where the sun's warmth rarely reached.

The lower Farran plunged, the less sunlight there was, until he reached a narrow defile shrouded in permanent shadow. It was a place of bare rock, confusing echoes and little birdsong. He began to feel lonely and almost afraid. After what seemed like an age, he felt the icy waters of the Secchiello, a tributary of the Secchia, lapping at his boots. He waded across and began to climb the far side; away from the frozen depths; towards life; to light.

Farran sweated on the hard climb under a fierce afternoon sun. He scrambled up steep meadows cropped close by goats and sheep, pausing to gaze back at Secchio village. Tiny figures crawled like ants through the streets. It seemed so close he could barely believe the two hours it had taken him thus far. He turned back to the climb and stumbled onto a road. Gravelled and wide, it was navigable by jeep, which got his mind thinking along fast, mobile-raiding lines.

Farran paused to light his pipe. He could only imagine the road had been built by the Germans, in an effort to control – vanquish – the partisans. It was too fine for any common mountain track, but it was perfect for Farran's purposes if only he could get some jeeps dropped in. No doubt about it, he needed to break his silence and make contact with headquarters.

A short while later he reached the church. It sat on the outskirts of the village overlooking a quaint little meadow cut into the hillside. Constructed of grey stone, it had clearly seen better days. There was a gaping hole in the roof, and one corner was in danger of collapse. More importantly, Farran could hear voices echoing from the far side and shouts and laughter – exactly the kind of life that he sought.

He stole through the gate, to spy Jock Easton sitting on the grass with two striking-looking locals. Raven-haired beauties, they seemed to have made themselves well at home, as if they were already an integral part of the Allied Battalion. For his part, Easton seemed to have forgotten his recent injuries and to be in remarkably high spirits.

'Hello, Roy,' he cried. 'Plenty to tell you about, how we're getting this bloody dump into shape!'

Farran glanced at the two women. One had the most arresting look in her deep grey-blue eyes, offset by her very business-like battledress tunic with a pistol tucked into her belt. Her feet were bare, but her head was adorned with one of the SAS berets.

'And who the devil are *they*?' he asked.

'They're on establishment,' said Jock with a grin. 'They belong to Mike Lees, and they're called Stafettas. Eytie for "messenger". Whenever they want to find out what's going on, they send the girls for a look-see. They cycle through, flirt with Jerry, then come back and report. Intelligence squad, that's what they are. Believe it or not, they're under command of a fellow called Kiss.'

'How many are there?' Farran asked incredulously. He'd used such young women on missions in France, but never so blatantly.

'Three here,' Easton replied. 'They double-up by helping fetch water, clean and cook.' The grey-eyed Stafetta was called Norice, he explained. 'Smith says she's got all the devils of the world in her eyes.' Farran had to agree.

He told Easton he was a little concerned that all the pretty company and home cooking might make the men slack and lazy, and the enemy might take them by surprise. Easton told him not to be so silly. They were keeping a proper lookout. He showed Farran their quarters, which were in a barn attached to the church, the men billeted in sleeping bags laid out on a thick bed of straw.

Easton led Farran into a side-room, what had once been the church vestry. A bare-armed girl was bent at a giant cauldron, stirring spaghetti over an open fire. Smoke rose through a hole in the roof and drifted through the room. She smiled at Farran and waved her spoon gaily.

Easton led Farran on into the church itself. It was in a sorry state. Apart from the jagged hole in the roof, plaster peeled and sagged from the lime-washed walls. Easton motioned to a black stallion, which was tethered to a stone in the centre of the church, calmly munching hay. It was around fourteen hands, so some sixty inches tall, making it more like a Welsh hill pony in size, but still lovely in Farran's eyes.

'That's yours,' he announced. 'You'll need it with that gammy leg of yours.' Farran had never fully recovered from the injuries he'd sustained on Crete. 'I commandeered it from a war widow in Coriano, the next village. She wasn't too happy, but it was the only mount free in the whole of the valley, the rest having been taken by the Germans.'

'Gosh, Jock,' Farran declared, gratefully, 'but I'd rather walk than ride bare back.'

Easton grinned. 'Oh, we've fixed that. You'll be trotting across the valley like the Scots Greys in no time.'

He gestured at a figure in the shadows. It was Kershaw, and he emerged laden down with what had once been parachutist gear, but from which they'd fashioned a makeshift saddle. As he watched them fit it to the pony, Farran felt humbled. These were not the men that he had led through France, and he'd never trained or fought with the most of them, yet he felt as if he'd served with them for a lifetime.

The make-do tack was rounded off with a red and white rosette, courtesy of one of the Stafettas. His men had christened the steed Whoa Mahomet. Farran was overwhelmed. He rode Whoa Mahomet up and down outside the church to cheers from all, especially when he kicked him into a canter.

Easton wasn't done yet. He blew a sharp blast on a whistle, and four boys appeared from nowhere, lining up smartly. They wore battledress on the pockets of which were embroidered in black silk the motif of an arrow, with 'McGinty' stitched beneath it. On their shoulders in red thread were spelled the words, *'Chi osera vincera'*, a rough translation of the SAS motto, 'Who dares wins'.

Farran eased back his beret and scratched his head in amazement.

'These are the Arrows,' Jock announced, proudly. 'They're our runners. They go anywhere, even across the lines. All you have to do is whistle!'

Jock Easton was one of the old and the bold all right, and this was exactly what Farran had brought him here for. As well he knew, any fool could be uncomfortable in the field of battle. It took a genuine old soldier to achieve what Jock Easton had here in a matter of days. To top it all, he'd got Farran's signaller set up in a separate house nearby, where he could decode and encode his messages in relative peace.

After a hearty supper of spaghetti and red wine, Farran mounted Whoa Mahomet and rode off to the signaller's place. It was time to grasp the proverbial nettle and make contact with Florence. Fired by what he'd seen, Farran had all sorts of ideas running through his head. The Italians loved show and colour. He wanted distinctive berets, belts and even hackles – traditional feathered plumes – dropped in for his Allied Battalion. He wanted jeeps, plus he wanted a piper complete with tartan kilt and bagpipes, to pipe the partisans into battle.

He needed Stephens and Nurk, so he could communicate with German deserters and Russian partisans alike. He wanted heavy mortars, at least one howitzer, and scores of heavy machine guns. Normally, such requests – pipers, colourful hackles, British uniforms for Italian guerrillas – would have been rejected out of hand. Most hidebound staff officers would have refused point-blank. But Farran had Walker-Brown fighting his corner, and he felt certain that the former Op Galia commander would understand.

Farran's radio man was an old hand: it was Corporal Cunningham, the cool-headed operator who'd carefully rolled up his wireless aerial, despite the hail of bullets that had cut through the French woodland, during their September 1944 operations. Farran drafted out a signal, listing all that he could imagine Walker-Brown might conjure, and handed it to Cunningham.

Radio contact was established. At first there was utter con-sternation at Florence headquarters. SAS Major Farran had been reported dead, having fallen from a Dakota during the initial insertion, so how on earth could he be making contact from the field now? Had a man who'd fallen from an aircraft somehow survived? If so, how? Nothing made any sense.

Charles Macintosh, the SOE chief there, wasn't fooled for long. The initial report on Farran's 'air-accident' had noted that the SAS major had been 'helping despatch the men from the door of one of the Dakotas, overbalanced and fell'. All had presumed Major

Farran dead. Serendipitously, it now appeared, he'd had a para-chute strapped to his back when he tumbled out, which was 'most unusual for an assistant despatcher', Macintosh observed, tartly.

By playing up Jock Easton's injuries suffered during the parachute drop – he had been slated to command the SAS party – Farran was able to argue that following his miraculous survival, it made sense for him to remain on the ground. He was needed here, and Florence headquarters – Charles Macintosh and US Colonel Riepe – should make a virtue out of necessity, not to mention Farran's extraordinary powers of survival.

By the time Farran took to Whoa Mahomet again, for the dusk ride back to Secchio, he figured the dust was beginning to settle over his seemingly miraculous resurrection. A distinctive figure trotted at his side, guiding the way. It was one of the McGinty's Arrows. By the time they'd reached Secchio, Farran had failed to acknowledge the boy, who seemed rather hurt. Didn't he recog-nise Bruno, he demanded, the first Italian ever to receive him in these hills?

Farran placed an arm around his young shoulders. The SAS commander apologised for his lapse of memory: it had been a busy few days. Bruno's spirits brightened, and he pledged undying allegiance to 'Il commandante Inglesi'. Farran responded by appointing Bruno as his official personal messenger and the keeper of Whoa Mahomet, to which Bruno appeared overjoyed.

As he led the horse away, the young partisan paused, then turned back. Could he possibly have a gun, he asked. Of course, said Farran. After all, Bruno was a soldier now. Bruno Gimpel was just sixteen years old, but he'd been born in London and spoke decent English. Farran felt inordinately proud of his motley force of many nationalities. Between these tall, shadowed mountains, everything as far as he could see was McGinty's – and Mike Lees' – kingdom. They were the chieftains of the valley, just as General Garibaldi had been in days of yore.

During Farran's absence, Lees had been busy. Kiss had returned from Albinea and his putative assassination mission. He'd turned up at Don Pedro's place still dressed in the cassock that the Secchio priest had loaned him – his cunning disguise. But the cloak was covered in mud, his dog collar was awry, and he didn't look in a particularly good mood.

'The bastard never showed up!' Kiss announced, angrily. He'd been awaiting General Feuerstein's arrival at Sunday mass, pistol in hand, unaware that he'd been replaced by General Hauk.

Don Pedro dissolved into fits of laughter. Lees had to admit, Kiss's discomfiture was somewhat amusing. 'General Hauk must be a bad Catholic,' he observed. 'Thus he was saved.'

'Oh no,' Don Pedro countered, 'it is because General Feuerstein is a good Catholic that *he* was saved. It is true General Hauk did not go to church.' He turned and gestured at a couple of the SAS men cleaning their weapons outside. 'But perhaps his life will not be spared, after all.'

That evening, Farran and Lees talked through their plans. Lees was keen to have Hans, the German deserter, ease their way into the 14th Army HQ, speaking German if there were any challenges. Farran suggested that if Walker-Brown succeeded in rustling him up a piper, the skirl of the bagpipes would leave an indelible British mark on the operation. That in turn might lessen the severity of any German reprisals, for the piper would signify that it was a British-led operation.

The one potential bugbear remained the Germans, and how they would react once they heard about the British parachutists' arrival. Lees – always the lateral thinker – had a suggestion. In recent months the SAS had been forced to dispense with their traditional beige berets, which they'd worn throughout the war. Instead, high command – somewhat pernickety and resentful of the elite unit's freewheeling ways – had insisted they wear the standard red beret of airborne forces.

Right now Lees figured they could make a virtue out of that necessity. What if the red berets signified that the parachutists were a team of British leftists – 'reds' – sent in to stiffen the Garibaldini's political backbone. Farran thought it a wickedly clever deception. Lees summoned Fritz Snapper, whom he trusted on such things, asking him to spread the word that the new arrivals had been sent by the British Labour Party, to liaise with the communist partisans.

Snapper, too, thought it a wonderful wheeze. Lees decided they should seal the deal with a bottle of grappa, and by the time Snapper departed on his black propaganda mission he was fired up with high spirits. So effective was he in spreading the word, that two ardent communists approached Farran shortly after to ask if it were true that he was the famous British Labour politician Sir Stafford Cripps.

Whether the enemy would swallow the story that the SAS were actually leftist emissaries was a moot point. But first, it was to be their own command who would try to scupper Lees and Farran's best laid plans.

While it was key to have a strong presence of partisans on the raid, so they would feel ownership of it and raise their fighting spirits, Lees and Farran were in no doubt that it would be the SAS who would be in the vanguard. That made it vital that the remainder of the squadron be parachuted in, along with all necessary weaponry.

But worryingly, SOE's Florence headquarters had been nig-gling Lees of late, warning him against 'making trouble'. He feared opinion at headquarters was turning against the planned raid, which certainly would cause huge amounts of 'trouble', if suc-cessful. Convinced he needed to nip such sentiments in the bud, on 6 March Lees penned a strongly-worded letter to Charles Macintosh, to be rushed across the lines by one of Fritz Snapper's couriers.

'Don't please think this is directed AT you, Charles,' he wrote, 'it is directed TO you, imploring you to get the powers that be to give us a break. I am terribly embittered to this sort of treatment, the same thing happened in Yugoslavia . . .' There, Lees had been ordered to drop his support of the Chetnik resistance fighters, which was the trigger that had prompted him to launch his solo sabotage operations.

'I have lost everything by joining this firm,' Lees continued. (The SOE was often referred to simply as 'The Firm'.) 'But I don't mind provided somebody will help me to fight the Ger-mans, but when one is told in a signal "not advisable to make the fur fly" well, that is tantamount to making a pact with the enemy . . .' Even with Farran and his advance SAS party on hand, Lees found himself having to beg to be allowed to take the fight to the enemy.

Fortunately, his entreaties were endorsed by Major Jim Davies, the BLO operating with the neighbouring partisans. Davies had dropped over to Secchio for a chat. 'RORY is enjoying himself,' Davies messaged Florence. (Rory was one of Farran's nicknames.) 'He is growing his long hair and Jesus Christ beard, but his saintly appearance does not deceive the village maidens . . . Says he's going to make this his last fling . . .' he wrote of the 14th Army

HQ raid. 'I am all for it, so long as it is not let loose prematurely and goes off at half-cock.'

But despite such support on the ground, trouble was brewing. Wilcockson had been pulled out of the Secchia valley on compassionate grounds, and to all intents and purposes Lees had taken over his SOE command lock, stock and barrel. This rankled, and behind the scenes Florence was agitating to get Lees removed from the field. On 10 March 1944 Macintosh penned a note to Lt.Col. Hewitt, the newly-appointed chief of the SOE in Italy, Gerry Holdsworth having moved on. Macintosh's memo bemoaned Lees' 'usurping' of Wilcockson's command.

'Capt. M. LEES told me he is not going to be under command of Major WILCOCKSON ...' Macintosh wrote. 'I had understood from signals from Base that Major WILCOCKSON was to command Capt. M. LEES.' With Wilcockson gone, such niceties of the chain of command were surely an irrelevance. Love him or loathe him, Lees was the man on the ground. But even so, pressure kept growing to somehow have him removed.

Hewitt, the new chief of SOE Italy, had penned the glowing October 1944 report on Lees, concluding that he was 'energetic, courageous' and 'ideally suited' to paramilitary operations. It seemed to cut little ice now, as Lees found himself battling against his own headquarters as much as the enemy. Matters broke out into open hostility, with Lees being 'invited' to leave the Secchia valley. He refused, penning an angry letter to Macintosh bemoaning the 'armchair crushers', who were intent on wasting 'the glorious possibilities of this show'.

Not mincing his words, Lees implored Macintosh – Florence headquarters – to back him. 'Dear Charles, I am sorry we have declared war on each other, but over this recent affair the way we have been treated is bloody . . . I realise and admit that by not accepting your invitation to come out I gave you a moral victory, but I did not accept because I realise that the firm would have jumped at the opportunity of putting in some BLO type who would sit here doing fuckall and give them a peaceful job with FANYs on their knees . . .'

By 'FANYs' Lees was referring to the First Aid Nursing Yeomanry – cover for women serving with the SOE. The spat might seem somewhat rancorous and small-minded, and it was doubly so from the position of the Secchia valley, where Lees and Farran were poised to unleash merry hell, if only they could get the kind of support they required. Frustration levels were reaching boiling point, as Lees sensed the fates turning against them.

Indeed, the Lees family were about to suffer the first of several terrible misfortunes to befall them during the war. James Lees, Michael Lees' cousin, had been serving with the Special Boat Service, executing raids off Italy's Adriatic coastline, so not so very far from Mike Lees' domain. James was just a year older and the two cousins had been brought up almost as brothers, after the death of Mike Lees' father.

In early March 1945 James Lees had set out leading a small, canoe-born raiding force, to strike at an enemy-held island. They'd attacked, but the battle had turned into 'complete murder, absolute hell', reported one of his patrol members. 'Bullets firing all over the place and grenades going off . . . bodies lying on the floor.' Someone had cried out 'Tansy's down!' – Tansy being Captain James Lees' nickname. Mortally injured and taken captive, he'd died of his wounds.

James Lees had been revered by those he commanded. 'A smashing chap he was,' remarked one. 'A real gentleman. I couldn't speak too highly of him.' Likewise, Mike Lees was loved by those he led in the Secchia valley.

It was only the high-ups that seemed to have a problem with his cussed, plain-speaking ways.

Chapter 12

By his own admission, Roy Farran had developed a 'profound contempt for the staff' – those desk officers who stood in the way of getting the job done. Fortunately, he had connections in high places. Apart from the rock-solid backstop of Bob Walker-Brown, 'chairborne' in Florence, Farran had powerful top-cover in the form of Lt.Col. John 'Jackie' Profumo. The 5th Baron Profumo was then the youngest serving MP, and he'd been a vocal opponent of appeasing Hitler, becoming closely aligned with Churchill.

Having fought in the D-Day landings, Profumo had been transferred to Italy to serve on Field Marshal Alexander's staff, winning an OBE 'in recognition of gallant and distinguished service'. Farran was acquainted with Profumo – whose career had yet to be sullied by the sexual and political scandal that became known as the Profumo Affair – and knew him to be wholly supportive of special forces operations. Fortuitously, Profumo's role was to liaise with the Americans overseeing air-missions, which would be all to Farran's benefit.

By the second week of March 1945 the logjam appeared to be breaking. Among the first to be parachuted into the Secchia valley were several officers whom Farran desperately needed to boost the training of his Allied Battalion. Just days into his service with the SAS, virgin parachutist Lieutenant David Eyton-

Jones plummeted towards the night-dark terrain, hopeful that he might survive the landing, and that his pre-war agricultural studies at Cambridge might help with the handling of stubborn mules in these hills.

Captain John 'Jock' Milne also jumped, a man who had last parachuted into these mountains to tend to the desperately sick on Walker-Brown's Operation Galia mission. Milne was a battle-hardened war surgeon who'd served with Montgomery's Eighth Army in North Africa, after which he'd experienced the bloody horrors of the Allied advance up the spine of Italy. The scion of a foremost farming clan from Angus, on Scotland's eastern coast, the larger-than-life Milne was a gifted physician. Serving with the Royal Army Medical Corps, he'd been seconded to the SAS, where his ebullient good humour helped him operate under terrible conditions.

Both men would prove huge assets to the Allied Battalion, and both landed well on the moon-washed snows. Less fortunate was a second Galia veteran – the grizzled Italian sailor, Luigi 'Pippo' Siboldi, who'd been Walker-Brown's guide. A gust of wind caught his chute and he was dragged along the frozen ground, ending up dislocating his shoulder. Fortunately, Jock Milne was on hand to tend to him.

A massive quantity of supplies was delivered that night, as a squadron of Dakotas thundered overhead, threading long strings of parachutes across the dark skies. The scale and grunt of the drop sent a powerful message to the partisans, telegraphing that SAS Major Farran at least was blessed with the full backing of the Allies.

It was approaching midnight by the time the new arrivals had furled their parachutes and gathered up their kit for the trek to Tapignola. As they marched into the early hours, the young Eyton-Jones confessed that today was his birthday. Upon arrival at Tapignola they proceeded to toast Eyton-Jones with shots of grappa, celebrating the fact that he was all of twenty-two years old. High spirits were boosted when the 'comfort containers' arrived. Stuffed full of whisky, cigarettes and the all-important mail from home, they'd been parachuted into the DZ along with the weaponry needed to train a force of three hundred to wage war.

As Farran had known he would, Walker-Brown had worked wonders. One resupply container was packed full of battledress for the Allied Battalion recruits, plus hackles that had been originally earmarked for the Transvaal Scottish, a South African infantry regiment, but somehow syphoned off for Operation Tombola. Green and yellow were prominent in the Transvaal Scottish insignia, and the feathered hackles were reminiscent of the white and green of the Italian flag. Showy, colourful and symbolic, Farran was hugely satisfied.

Blessed with an innate understanding of human nature, its tendency towards tribalism and the need to belong, Farran was convinced that such tokens would help weld together his multinational force. With the Italians especially, much was about appearances. The fine uniforms and hackles would give them pride in their identity, and Farran saw no reason why the Italian brigades shouldn't follow the example of McGinty's Arrows, and adopt the '*Chi osera vincera*' motto. They too would have it sewn onto their battledress tunics.

Following that resupply drop it was as if the floodgates opened. During the third and fourth weeks of March scores more flights thundered into the Secchia valley, as Farran exploited his direct line of communication via Walker-Brown and Profumo to US General Mark Clark himself. While the British might vacillate, the Americans were proving typically bullish. They showed few qualms about arming and training the partisans to rise up in the enemy's rear, and in Farran they sensed they had a commander who meant business.

Over a forty-eight-hour period twenty-six SAS were dropped in, including Lieutenant Ken Harvey, another of those recruited in Farran's speech offering nothing but 'sweat, blisters and frostbite and the probability of being shot as spies'. At just nineteen, Harvey had been serving with the Seaforth Highlanders, and he was blessed with that 'baby-faced beauty that is so typically English', Farran observed. He had no combat record to speak of, but Farran had high hopes. He'd gambled upon the nineteen-year-old being fresh into battle and desperate to prove himself.

Harvey was inexperienced, but sometimes a good dose of youthful recklessness was exactly what was required. With almost biblical eloquence he would write of his arrival at the Tapignola church base: 'It was a long and tiring march . . . particularly after all the excitement of an early morning operational jump . . . It was late that night when the last sleigh drawn by mules was unloaded and the supplies broken down. I crept into my sleeping bag having gathered some straw in the stable and, with the others, was soon sound asleep.'

Stephens the Austrian Jew was parachuted in, which meant that Farran and Lees could communicate more easily with their German deserter-recruits. Lieutenant Mike Eld was dropped in, one of the most experienced and capable officers in No. 3 Squadron and a man Farran felt he could rely on to hold the front line. Once they hit the 14th Army HQ, he didn't doubt that the

Germans would come seeking vengeance, and it would be crucial to defend their valley against all-comers. Lieutenant Eld was the man for the job.

Lieutenant James Riccomini was dropped in, following the largest single drop of Operation Tombola, which delivered twenty-four SAS operators in one go. Half-Italian, half-English and with a wife waiting for him back in Kent, Riccomini had not been home since his capture in 1941, his subsequent escape and joining the Italian resistance. Another Galia veteran, Riccomini was the one operator that Farran had sought with a vengeance. Brave and fearless to a fault, he would be perfect for spearheading the 14th Army HQ assault.

Corporal Stanley 'Sammy' Bolden, a Glaswegian originally with the Cameron Highlanders, was part of that twenty-four-man drop. Bolden, a Military Medal winner, had a wartime record almost to rival that of Riccomini. In March 1941 he'd volunteered for the Commandos, winning his MM during the ironically-named Operation Cartoon, a daring raid on an iron pyrite mine on the Norwegian island of Stord. Bolden had been wounded on the operation – which wrecked the mine and sank enemy shipping – but he'd continued fighting regardless of his injuries, for which he was awarded the MM.

Following recovery from his injuries, Bolden had married Sergeant Andre Chapman, who served with the Auxiliary Territorial Service (ATS), the women's branch of the British Army. Shortly thereafter he'd volunteered for the SAS. In training, Bolden was assessed as being an 'outstanding performer, keen and confident. Very good NCO. Morale A1.' Post D-Day, he'd joined Major Rooney's squadron on Operation Rupert, the raid on the ammo dumps in north-eastern France. One of Bolden's fellows concluded of him: 'He certainly was a tough egg!' In short, Corporal Sammy Bolden was just the kind of operator that Tombola called for.

One of the last in was Serjeant Sidney Elliott Guscott, a fellow Galia veteran who had made the most extraordinary efforts to join Team Tombola. Known as 'Gus' to his men, Guscott hailed from Pennymoor in rural Devon, where his parents owned the village store. He'd met Doreen, his future wife, at a local knees-up, both being keen ballroom dancers. They'd married and soon had a son, Ken, and daughter, Pauline, to care for, but the war had cut short their hopes of becoming ballroom dancing professionals, Guscott signing up for the Devonshire Regiment instead.

Guscott volunteered for an airborne unit, being subsequently recruited into the SAS. A 'good performer, cheerful and hard-working', he too parachuted on Operation Rupert as part of Major Rooney's squadron. Promoted to sergeant, the open-faced and guileless Guscott had commanded a troop of parachutists, but they got isolated from the main force. They resorted to living with the French partisans, surviving off what little supplies they had and the land.

By January 1945 Guscott was back in action, this time in northern Italy on Operation Brake, commanding a party of three – including Spanish Civil War and French Foreign Legion veteran, Private Raphael Luis Mansens Ramos. Born in 1919, Ramos was adopted at an early age, never knowing his real parents. He'd found his way into the SAS via a similar route to Francisco Jeronimo (aka Frank Williams) and Justo Balerdi (Robert Bruce). But in contrast to them, he'd refused to change his name for anyone, not even the Gestapo. Come what may, he'd stick doggedly to Ramos.

A native of Barcelona, Ramos's adoptive father had run a successful publishing business. Educated at a Jesuit – strongly Catholic – boarding school, Ramos had been brought up in a martial tradition and with a sense of service to the cause of global justice. In the battle of the Ebro, Ramos had been captured by Franco's forces, but he'd managed to escape. Fleeing to France, he'd found his way into the French Foreign Legion and from there to the British Army.

It was early December 1943 when Ramos volunteered for the SAS. Young, battle-hardened, hot-headed and hungry for action, he was a perfect recruit. He earned the reputation that when all others might be diving for cover, Ramos would be unloading with his machine gun. In his military references, Ramos was described thus: 'Character – very good. A fine war record . . .'

In Ramos, Serjeant Guscott was blessed with an ideal behind-the-lines guerrilla fighter. Guscott had led his Operation Brake team into a region adjacent to where Bob Walker-Brown's Operation Galia force had been operating. Via their wireless set, Guscott and his men had radioed back vital intelligence about enemy troop movements and targets, before linking up with the Galia party.

Ordered to assist Galia in every way they could, Guscott and his team remained in the field when Walker-Brown and his force withdrew. After promised reinforcements failed to materialise, Guscott opted to trek east through the mountains in an effort to link up with Farran. The SAS major viewed Guscott as 'the best sergeant in my Squadron . . . We had formed a battalion of Russians, Italians and British,' he remarked, 'and I wanted a good NCO to act as RSM so I ordered Sergt. Guscott to join me.'

'RSM' stood for regimental sergeant major, the man Farran

wanted to enforce order and discipline on his motley crew of fighters. He got a radio message through to Guscott, never imagining that he would be able to make it. But on 17 March, almost two months after he had deployed across the lines, Guscott arrived at Farran's Secchio headquarters. 'He walked across the mountains and covered sixty miles in . . . in awful country,' Farran remarked. Not only that but he had brought with him Raphael Ramos, another major bonus.

By now, over forty SAS had dropped into the Secchia valley or marched across the mountains, which left only one man outstanding, as far as Farran was concerned – his much-vaunted bagpiper. But finding a 'piper' at such short notice to parachute behind the lines was proving something of a challenge.

Finally, an approach was made to a young man serving in the 2nd Highland Light Infantry. As his nickname suggested, David 'The Mad Piper' Kirkpatrick had earned something of a sterling wartime reputation, which was all the more extraordinary considering his youth. But as far as he was concerned his job was to pipe the troops into battle no matter where they might be – on the front line or even behind enemy lines, for that matter.

'You're at the front with all the company behind you,' the plain-speaking Kirkpatrick would remark. 'That's why you're made the company piper.'

Something of a wild, troubled character in his teens – he'd earned a reputation for drinking and insubordination – Kirkpatrick had recently piped ashore a unit of commandos, as they'd stormed the beaches in Albania on a daylight raid from landing craft. Resting after the mission and assigned to a job in the stores, Kirkpatrick had been approached by the commander of his regiment.

'I'm looking for a piper to do a wee job,' he'd announced, enigmatically. 'I know you're more or less qualified for these things.'

'Aye,' Kirkpatrick had agreed, simply, 'I'm way fed up in the stores.' That was how he'd volunteered to be Major Farran's piper on Operation Tombola.

When Kirkpatrick's father found out that his son had taken on a mysterious 'wee job', he wasn't overly happy, but the die was cast. As soon as he could be made ready, 'The Mad Piper' was to be parachuted into the Secchia valley.

The British high command's attitude to the Italian resistance remained painfully schizophrenic. At the SOE's Florence headquarters they had often discussed plans to capture or kill Field Marshal Kesselring, yet at the same time they fought shy of their BLOs causing too much trouble. By the time Lees and Farran were readying the Allied Battalion to strike the 14th Army HQ, there was little chance of catching the German Field Marshal there.

On the night of 10 March 1945 Kesselring had been quietly removed from the Italian theatre and transferred to the Western Front. Hitler was anxious that Kesselring's withdrawal should remain secret, but maps discovered on the body of a dead German officer and smuggled out by the SOE confirmed that he was gone. Whichever high-level German officers Lees and Farran might hit, Kesselring would not be among their number.

Undeterred, they set a date for the 14th Army HQ assault: it was to take place on the night of 26/27 March 1945, so less than ten days away. Training at the church intensified, especially in the use of mortars, which would be key for the coming battle. The partisans forming the Allied Battalion – especially Modena's

Russians – proved remarkably quick learners. The Ordnance ML '3-inch' mortar was actually 3.209 inches – or 81.5mm – in calibre, and in the right hands it was a reliable and hugely effective weapon.

Now, at their Tapignola church base, the SAS gunners set out to ensure that it *was* in the right hands, no matter if it were former Italian farmers or Russian POWs. The Russians were particularly adept: they could lay out the constituent parts of the mortar on a ground sheet in exactly the same order as the instructor, after only one demonstration. It was all the more impressive considering that most lessons were being rendered in a colourful mixture of sign language, pidgin English and execrable Italian.

Within no time partisans of all nationalities were able to dismantle and assemble the mortars almost as well as their instructors. The one drawback was the limit that had to be placed on live firing. There was a shortage of ammunition, dictated by the simple logistics of flying in heavy crates of shells, plus there was the ever-present risk of the enemy hearing the loud explosions echoing across from the far side of the mountains.

Still, it wasn't exactly uncommon to detect the rattle of a distant Bren gun or the thud of a 3-inch mortar ringing out from Tapignola. Farran never stopped being jumpy about it. The enemy were positioned within a few miles in practically every direction. He feared a surprise attack. Yet still there was no response, let alone any attempt to interfere with the training.

As morale soared, so too did the opportunities for entertainment and fun. Gordon was a dab hand at the accordion, which always got the ladies on their feet. There were nightly knees-ups, especially at Secchio, where most of the Stafettas were based. The Black Owls boasted several fine fiddlers among their number, and the British soldiers soon found they were having the time of their lives, dancing to fine Italian ballads. They in turn tried to teach the locals the joys of Scottish reels and jigs.

In a sense there was little point trying to hide what they were about here. The red-berets-equals-communists-deception wasn't going to last for ever. On one level it was better to shout it from the rooftops, for the partisans tended to fight best 'when in the mood and not when ordered', as any number of BLOs had observed. Of course, that had to be balanced against the need not to betray to 'enemy Intelligence the true strength of one's forces', but getting the message heard was key to boosting morale.

To that end, the *Italia Combatte* (Italy Fights) radio broadcasts orchestrated by the SOE played a vital role. Partisans liked nothing more than to hear reports of themselves in action, ambushing the enemy. As the BLOs were at pains to point out: 'Resistance Movement Bulletins giving accounts of actions were listened to avidly, and did much to raise morale and make one Brigade vie with its neighbour in performing feats of arms.'

Still, Farran and Lees weren't entirely surprised when the first reports of suspicious enemy action filtered through to them. Two German battalions were advancing towards the mouth of the Secchia valley. It was worrying news, especially since the training of the Allied Battalion was still not complete. What Lees and Farran needed was stability, so as to round off their preparations for the coming assault, and that meant holding the valley.

Although it went against all doctrines of guerrilla warfare, they decided to defend their positions at all costs. If they lost the valley, the attack on the HQ would be all but finished. If the pressure became too great, they would retreat through well-prepared lines deep into the mountains, where it would be hard for the enemy to follow. Whatever else, they would do everything to keep the Allied Battalion together and primed to strike.

Fighting from fixed lines of defence wasn't the chosen form of warfare of either the SAS or the SOE. Still, extraordinary times called for extraordinary measures. With Colonel Monti's assistance, they set the valley's defences. At key outposts they sited one SAS soldier with detachments of partisans. Their role was to delay any German advance for long enough to get a warning to the Allied Battalion's Tapignola base, so that reinforcements could be rushed in.

To the far south-eastern boundary, in the shadow of Monte Pena, they sent Parachutist (the SAS equivalent rank of private) Murphy, with ten Russians, equipped with a Browning .50-calibre heavy machine gun and a pair of Brens. Murphy established himself in Civago village, just this side of the Gothic Line and the jumping-off point for Fritz Snapper's couriers.

Corporal Larley, who had been among the first dozen SAS dropped in, was despatched to the far western fringes of the valley, with ten Garibaldini and a 37mm anti-aircraft cannon, which was equally devastating in a ground defence role. From his vantage point Larley had a direct line of sight – and fire – to the nearest German garrison, situated on the main road.

Parachutist Wooding, one of those inserted in the mass, twenty-four-man drop, was another soldier who had impressed Farran. He was despatched north, posted alongside Don Carlo's Green Flames, to boost the forces guarding the main crossing points of the Secchia river. Wooding took with him a Browning machine gun and ten of the finest Garibaldini.

To Lieutenant Mike Eld fell the most important position of all. He was sent north of the river to guard the main road leading into the valley – the route by which any mechanised forces would attempt to punch through. Eld took with him ten SAS Parachutists, and he would link up with Gianni's Garibaldini partisans, whom Farran viewed as the most capable.

Eld's position was vital to the entire defensive plan, and Farran ordered him and Gianni to dig in. They were to hold that line until ordered otherwise. To Eld's unit fell the heaviest responsibility and likewise the heaviest weaponry: they had a 3-inch mortar, a heavy .50 Vickers water-cooled machine gun and a Bren. If Eld's line broke, they were to fall back towards Monte Cusna and the 3,000-foot Cisa Pass. There on the high-ground Farran tasked his men to construct a final defensive position, which they nicknamed the 'Cisa Box'.

The Cisa Box would be heavily entrenched, with the Allied Battalion's prized weapon, their M116 75mm pack howitzer dug in as the centrepiece. Walker-Brown had worked miracles getting that weapon dismantled, packed into parachute-ready parcels and dropped into the Swell Crimson DZ. Designed to be semi-portable – hence the 'pack howitzer' designation – the M116 could be broken down into pieces to be moved by pack animals, but as far as Farran knew this was the first time one had ever been parachuted behind the lines.

Farran placed young Lieutenant Harvey in command of the Cisa Box. His position was reinforced with 37mm cannons, heavy machine guns, ten Brens and mortars. As far as the partisans were concerned, it was at the Cisa Box that the Allied Battalion would mount a glorious stand and drive the enemy out of the valley. But in secret, Farran and Lees decided to explore a final, last-ditch line of retreat. If all else failed, the SAS and SOE would attempt to break out over the supposedly impassable heights of Monte Cusna.

Harvey was charged to get enough food buried in the deep snows on Cusna's slopes, so as to provision their force for up to three weeks on the run. 'The time was spent in perfecting our positions and laying caches along the escape route,' Harvey recalled. '"K" rations, biscuits, bully beef, 24-hour packs and Oleomarge were buried and the positions recorded. We also hid sacks of maps that would be most useful if . . . the Germans put in an all-out effort to clear out our small British force.'

'K rations' were US military 24-hour combat rations, while 'Oleomarge' referred to tubs of margarine. Lieutenant Harvey described his local fighters as 'Red Star partisans, communists to a man . . . The force at Cisa was now forty-eight and was, I considered, a strong one which I was proud to command.' They were equally proud of their howitzer, which had been nicknamed *Molto Stanco* – 'very tired' – due to the Herculean effort involved in manhandling it into such an elevated position.

With the Cisa Box sorted, it left one massive unknown. Was there a route over Monte Cusna, as a last-ditch means of escape? No one seemed to know, which meant that someone was going to have to attempt to prove it, one way or the other.

Farran sought two men to make the attempt. The first choice was obvious: Kershaw, the former Olympic bobsleigh man, was a dab hand in the snow. The other, David Eyton-Jones, was a some-what less enthusiastic recruit. His only apparent qualification was that he had enjoyed a little skiing in Switzerland during his youth. When Farran ordered the two men to seek out a route over Monte Cusna, Eyton-Jones feared it was a true mission impossible.

Kershaw and Eyton-Jones sought out a local guide. Apparently, all thought them stir-crazy. There was no way across Cusna's snowbound heights, they argued. Even the Germans' alpine troops never attempted it, properly equipped as they were. Finally, at Casa Belocchi, the village adjacent to the Swell Crimson DZ, they managed via a combination of cajoling and liberal doses of red wine to get a local man to agree to act as guide.

He came fully equipped with skis, ski poles and snow goggles. Kershaw and Eyton-Jones had none of those things, and they refused the man's offer to provide any, knowing that it would be impossible to equip a force of fifty with such kit. If there was a route over Cusna's peak, it would have to be proved by trudging through the drifts in British Army footwear.

They set out. The snow was a clogging three-foot-thick layer that dragged at their every footfall. After several hours they reached the avalanche line, where fifty-degree slopes reared to the heights. It was there that the guide made it clear that he believed Kershaw and Eyton-Jones were stir-crazy, if they opted to continue.

'I advise you to turn back,' he announced, darkly. 'You won't make it.'

He made a quick sign of the cross before heading back the way they'd come, convinced that the two British soldiers were going to their deaths. In truth, Kershaw and Eyton-Jones didn't feel entirely confident that they weren't. It hadn't escaped their notice that Monte Cusna was known locally as *Uomo Morto* – Dead Man.

It took the entire day to reach Dead Man's summit. At times they were struggling through waist-deep snow, when the entire slope would suddenly begin to peel away in a thunderous roar, leaving the two figures clinging to bare and treacherous scree. It was almost dark when they reached the very peak. There, at some 7,000 feet of altitude, they would surely die if they didn't find shelter.

They began searching for a *rifugio*, a tiny mountain hut that they'd been told was somewhere thereabouts, but everything was covered in a thick blanket of snow. Trees, bushes, boulders – all had been subsumed by the snowfall. A handful of such refuges had been built by the Italian Alpine Club, but it was like searching for the proverbial needle in a haystack. Finally, they stumbled upon what they first mistook for a giant snowdrift, but which turned out to be the *rifugio*, snow piled to the eaves.

With frozen hands they began to shovel, in an effort to clear the door. It opened inwards but proved near-impossible to budge. There were several feet of wind-driven snow *inside* the hut. It had blown in via a grating set in the eastern wall. With sinking hearts the two surveyed the interior. It was as cold as a deep freezer, the fireplace was blocked with snow and there were no logs or anything that could be burned. Both men were utterly exhausted, and there was no way they could summon the energy to forage for firewood.

They unrolled their sleeping bags and laid them on the snow, before wolfing down some tins of Heinz self-heating soup. It came in oxtail, pea, tomato and mock turtle flavours, and a hollow tube down the centre of the tin contained a self-heating element, which boiled the contents in thirty seconds flat. Soup eaten, they crawled into their sleeping bags without bothering to remove their boots, and promptly fell asleep.

Sometime later Eyton-Jones awoke to a bizarre spectacle. Though dawn light filtered in through the side-grating, it appeared ethereal and muted, and he seemed to have been thrown into a grave of shadows. For several seconds he wondered if he had died and gone to heaven. It turned out that overnight he had sunk in his sleeping bag through the several feet of snow, coming to rest on the hut floor.

Faced with a long descent of the mountain, Kershaw and Eyton-Jones were desperate: they broke out the Benzedrine pills they'd been issued with. Known colloquially as 'bennies', they were issued as part of the standard SAS escape kit. A powerful amphetamine popular in London's glitzier nightclubs, with its euphoric stimulant effect Benzedrine could keep a man alert for days. The benefits were obvious, but it was only possible to fuel a man with amphetamines for so long: eventually the body would simply burn out.

Having taken two each, Kershaw and Eyton-Jones stumbled outside. In every direction the fierce spring sunlight glittered off the snowfields. Within moments, Eyton-Jones found that he was suffering from 'snow blindness'. He was assailed by intense pain and a stabbing headache. His vision clouded, and he felt as if he'd had a handful of sand thrown into his eyes.

It was glaringly obvious by now that Monte Cusna offered no easy escape route. Indeed, this had become a desperate survival mission. Kershaw, the former Olympic bobsleigher, decided their only option was to descend as quickly as possible. They should attempt to toboggan down the slopes, sliding on their backsides. He led the way, guiding Eyton-Jones, his feet spread wide and using his heels to steer a route around the occasional boulder.

Hours later the two men reached more familiar terrain, heralding their return to the Secchia valley. They were bruised, battered and sore and Kershaw had injured his leg when he caught it on a protrusion. Their boots had frozen solid, but they stumbled onwards, every step being sheer agony. By the time they reached Secchio, they were convinced they had frostbite. When they leveraged off their footwear, sure enough their toes were horribly blackened, the toenails swollen and cracked.

That, if nothing else, convinced Farran that relying on any escape via Monte Cusna would be ill-advised. It might provide a last-ditch route to safety, but how many of his men might survive such a crossing? If his forces were driven back from their defence of the valley, the Cisa Box would have to hold.

By the end of the third week in March, Lees and Farran believed they had done everything possible to prepare their defensive lines. At the same time, the Stafettas had been feeding back daily intelligence reports on the 14th Army HQ, allowing Lees to build up an incredibly detailed picture of the target. The two villas lay to the north of the Botteghe crossroads, which formed the epicentre of the headquarters' defences. To wolf whistles and catcalls, the Stafettas were daily cycling through there, taking note of all. Norice in particular was not averse to stopping and apparently flirting outrageously with the sentries.

As a result, Lees knew the names of most of the officers who served there and much personal information. Locations of anti-aircraft guns, machine-gun posts and sentries had been minutely plotted. Florence headquarters, alert to the intended target, had flown in up-to-date maps and aerial photos, which were dropped to their Secchio base by fighter pilots leaning out of their cockpit windows.

As the picture of the target continued to build, Lees and Farran's greatest worry was that the Germans would relocate it before they could strike. 'A damaging attack on a main headquarters would certainly be a big contribution to the Allied cause,' Farran would write, 'especially if it coincided with the main offensive.' But no strike could succeed if the Germans decided to move the location of their headquarters.

In the final plan of attack the Allied Battalion – SAS included –

would be divided in two. While a force 100 strong would hit the HQ, the remainder – some 200 troops – would remain in their positions to hold the valley, for without a refuge to retreat to theirs was basically a suicide mission.

The one-hundred-strong assault force would be made up of thirty Russians, forty Italians and twenty-four SAS, with Lees' Black Owls making up the remainder. They would muster at the extreme border of partisan territory, and from there advance to a vantage point overlooking the plain of the Po. Come nightfall, the force would split into three for the approach to the target. The Russians, under Modena, would form a protective screen, isolating the two villas from any reinforcements that might try to reach them.

Each of the other two columns would be led by ten SAS, men who had been selected for their raw aggression and spirit. They would force an entry into the villas, to be followed by the Italians, guns blazing. Mike Lees was to lead the assault on Villa Rossi, where the senior officers were billeted, while young Lieutenant Harvey would spearhead the hit on Villa Calvi. Farran, meanwhile, would establish a base between the two villas from where he could orchestrate operations.

The orders Farran issued to his Allied Batallion were uncompromising and stark: cause maximum death and destruction. The priority was to kill high-ranking German officers – General Hauk and his Chief of Staff, one Colonel Lemelsen, being the prime targets. No prisoners were to be taken, for that would only serve to hamper their helter-skelter retreat.

Farran's chief worry remained the enemy's reaction, which he feared would be swift and determined. Accordingly, he allowed just twenty minutes for the parties to execute the raid, during all of which time Modena was to have his Russians spray the roads leading to the villas with machine-gun fire. Like that, he hoped to keep the German heads down and prevent them from bringing up reinforcements.

After wreaking havoc and ruin, the raiders would enter the 'run' phase of the attack – so fleeing for the mountains, wherein two-thirds of the Allied Battalion would shield them from pursuit. But once they had started to withdraw the real battle for survival would begin. They would be faced with a twenty-four-hour forced march over terrain crawling with the enemy, and with only a few hours of darkness in which to disappear. That alone was a chilling proposition, but there was no way around it.

On 20 March Lees and Farran sent a short radio message to Florence, seeking final clearance for the attack. 'Staff HQ of 14 Army – FARRAN agrees to use SAS to lead the attack . . .' In response, 15 Army Group radioed back a green light, while cautioning that the exact timing should be coordinated with their own plans. 'Confirm we attack . . .' Farran cabled a reply. 'First wave 20 British, second wave 30 Russians, third wave 40 Italians. All on foot. Plans irrevocable now.'

But it was at this very moment that the enemy decided to strike.

A German patrol crossed the river to the north-east, which marked the border of the Secchia valley. As a long line of grey-uniformed troops snaked into the partisans' territory, Farran fretted. The inevitable day of reckoning had come, but were the forces that he and Lees had armed, trained and encouraged up for the fight?

Now would prove it, one way or the other.

Chapter 13

Worryingly, the initial resistance proved hopelessly short-lived. The Green Flames positioned at the valley's entranceway fled, leaving the route of advance wide open. Mounted upon their two highly contrasting steeds – one large and powerful, the other doing a fine impression of a Welsh hill pony – Lees and Farran rode out to meet the enemy onslaught.

The heavily armed German troops advanced up the road, confident that the partisans would fall back before them. Instead, they stumbled into the murderous fire of a well dug-in Browning heavy machine gun. While Don Carlo's Green Flames may have taken to their heels, Parachutist Wooding and his ten-man Garibaldini unit had not. They'd been charged to hold the northern gateway to the valley, and hold it they would.

In a vicious day-long exchange of fire the Germans quickly learned there was no easy way through. The road, at least, was closed to them. When they tried to outflank Wooding's position, they ran into pockets of Green Flames, dug-in on the high ground. Upon witnessing how Wooding and his Garibaldini had stood firm, the Green Flames' backbone had been miraculously stiffened.

The ferocity of the resistance seemed to convince the German commander that this route of advance would prove too costly. By nightfall, the enemy patrol had withdrawn across the Secchia river, making for the safety of the plains beyond. Lees and Farran didn't doubt that they would be back, and in greater numbers, which made it all the more critical to proceed with the HQ assault. Any delay could scupper their plans utterly.

Florence headquarters had also got word of the enemy action. BLO Jim Davies had radioed through an alert about a *rastrellamento*. Lees and Farran received warnings, coupled with pleas that they not make life 'too difficult' for the neighbouring missions. Lees replied that their positions in the Secchia valley would hold, and anyway there was a war to be fought.

When Florence kept on repeating their *rastrellamento* warnings, the two commanders finally cracked. Farran and Lees drafted a terse, two-word reply: 'Rastrellamento balls'. Farrimond encoded it and sent it via the radio, knowing that it would not make them any the more popular at headquarters.

Farran's presence at Secchio had unchained Lees from the control of SOE Florence, just as Charles Macintosh had feared it would, and the SAS major's hotline to senior US and British commanders was deeply resented. 'Florence hated that,' Lees remarked, recognising that it made both him and Farran 'very unpopular'. But they were there to fight and sod the consequences.

In March 1945 US General Mark Clark had broadcast a special message to the partisans, making it crystal clear what he expected of them. 'Your bands, which contain only the finest examples of Italian soldiers, proved by their ability to resist the enemy through the hard winter, should now be . . . ready at a moment's notice to undertake the tasks which are ahead. Quality is what is necessary . . . compact highly disciplined and trained groups for efficient action . . .' In the Allied Battalion, Lees and Farran had honed just such an elite fighting group and they were poised to strike a killer blow.

On the night of 23/24 March David 'The Mad Piper' Kirkpatrick was the final figure to plummet into the darkness above the Secchia valley, to join Tombola. As with so many who had dropped before him, he'd never parachuted into action. With his safe arrival that made forty-two SAS and attached deployed on Tombola, Major Farran included.

No fading violet, Kirkpatrick had jumped in full piper's regalia, bagpipes and kilt included. Those on the ground – the Italians at least – thought that a woman was being sent in to join them. Fortunately, Farran was on hand to explain why a young man dressed in a 'skirt' had dropped from the sky. As part of that explanation, he got Kirkpatrick to pipe 'Highland Laddie' – the then-marching song for all British highland regiments – over the Swell Crimson DZ.

As the haunting, lyrical tones echoed across the snows, Farran felt a chill run up his spine. Silhouetted by the burning light of the marker flares flickering across the slopes to either side, the erect form of the piper, wreathed in smoke, appeared like some ghostly figure of ancient myth or legend. Farran was doubly excited by the partisans' reaction. They clapped and yelled for joy, keeping time to the lilting tune. They were still singing patriotic songs at the tops of their voices, as Farran led Kirkpatrick off to their church base.

Upon arrival at Tapignola, he asked the obvious question, it being early morning. 'Are you hungry, piper?'

'Aye, sir, I'm very hungry,' Kirkpatrick replied.

'What about some fried bacon and eggs?'

'Yes, sir, I'd like that very much.' Fresh bacon and eggs were a rare wartime treat.

Farran's grand flourish – getting a piper dropped in – proved a massive hit. Those gathered at the church decided to dance an Eightsome, a lively Scottish reel for eight dancers, as Kirkpatrick struck up the tune. He wanted to donate his parachute to the elderly lady who made him welcome in her Tapignola home. She had her eye on it, to make a silk wedding dress for her grand-daughter.

'Sir, is it all right for me to give her my parachute for looking after us?' he asked.

Farran said he could. It was the least they could do.

That evening back in Secchio, Farran gazed across the valley as the unmistakeable tones of 'The Retreat' echoed across from the church. Kirkpatrick had played it without any prompting, for it was the job of a piper to do so at the end of each day. Farran and Mike Lees marvelled as the stirring notes of the pipes rolled up and down the hills. It had to be audible for miles around on a still evening such as this, including to the enemy.

It was somehow both thrilling and daunting. The two com-manders signalled back with their torches, acknowledging that they had heard Kirkpatrick, and that all was good with the world. But as they prepared to set forth from the Secchia valley, disaster struck. Mike Lees, always a whirlwind of action and a veritable human dynamo, was struck down. The iconic figurehead of the Reggiani partisans was hit by a debilitating bout of malaria, something he'd first contracted when on operations in Yugoslavia.

It was the summer of 1943 when Lees had been tasked with an urgent mission – the destruction of a railway that the Ger-mans were using to resupply their forces lying to the south of Yugoslavia, in Greece. In the final stages of executing a recce of the target, Lees had been hit by heavy fever. Racked by nausea, pain and hallucinations, he'd stubbornly completed the days-long march, only to collapse at the end. Diagnosed with malaria, he was treated by an old crone, or a 'wise woman of the mountains' as the locals called her.

That 'wise woman' readied a mixture of herbs, roots, animal entrails and spices, laced with the strongest rakia (a locally-brewed fruit brandy). Lees was ordered to drink the concoction. It was dark green, thick and heady, with a bitter aftertaste. Having done so, he'd fallen into a deep sleep. The following morning he'd awoken with his body aching all over, but with a clear head. The fever had passed, and Lees put it down to a combination of natural remedies and powerful witchcraft.

But now, almost eighteen months later, the malaria had come back with a vengeance. Lees felt the first worrying symptoms as he, Farran, Gordon, Kiss and fellow commanders toasted their imminent departure for the raid. Farran had called for Kirkpatrick, telling him: 'Use this night, piper, as if it's a night you play to your officers in your own battalion.' It was a tradition in the Highland Light Infantry that every Friday, the piper would play tunes of his choice in the officers' mess, over dinner.

But as Kirkpatrick proceeded to play, Lees had felt increasingly weak and feverish. Taking a leaf out of the old crone's book, he'd dosed himself with a mixture of grappa and quinine, an extract of tree bark used to treat malaria. Even so, by the time the attack force was readying itself for departure the following morning, he was looking distinctly unwell. Attempts were made to persuade him against going, but to no avail.

'I tried to stop Mike,' remarked Gordon, his Black Owls commander, 'but he was a very proud man and very courageous.'

Farran had little more success. 'I was worried about Lees, for

223

all my pleasure at his company. He had developed a fever . . . but refused to be left behind. He dosed himself frequently with quinine, but I did not like the unnatural drops of sweat on his forehead . . . His face was grave and pallid beneath the sweat. And he was unusually quiet.'

If anything, Bert Farrimond, Lees' radio operator, was even more concerned. As Lees bade a fond farewell to his Secchio crew – Farrimond and Lieutenant Smith would remain behind, manning the headquarters – the tough Lancastrian shook him gravely by the hand.

'Good luck, sir,' he told Lees. 'Don't stick your neck out too much, will you.'

Lees feigned good spirits. 'Don't worry, I've too much to live for.'

Lees turned to leave, but Farrimond reached out a hand to stop him. 'Can't I come with you, sir?'

Lees was surprised. Farrimond was a solid, pragmatic, salt-of-the-earth type and this was very out of character. 'Of course not, you've got to stay here to work the set.'

'I know that,' Farrimond countered, 'but I've had a feeling all morning that something's going to happen and I'd like to come.'

Lees forced laughter. 'Don't be a bloody fool. You'll be seeing ghosts next.'

With that he joined Farran and the advance party, and set off for Tapignola. Lees led a core of Black Owls, who would help spearhead the assault. Norice and Argentina, two of the finest Stafettas, marched alongside them, as did their commander, Kiss. The sun beat down as Farran moved abreast of Lees, the latter mopping the sweat from his brow. Strictly speaking, Lees was an SOE agent sent to liaise with the partisans, and Farran could have insisted he remain behind. But ever since he'd dropped in, Lees had hungered to hit the Botteghe HQ. He'd fought tooth and nail to make it happen, and in truth this was Mike Lees' mission. It was right and fitting to have him along, fevered though he was.

They descended the valley and climbed to Tapignola, where Farran spoke a few last words to those disappointed fighters who were being left behind. Jock Easton was among them, but someone had to command the defences – for no one doubted the blowback that would come. Here in the Secchia valley they would truly reap the whirlwind, of that they felt certain.

Having formed up with the twenty-four SAS, twenty Garibaldini and a similar number of Black Owls, Farran set a route north, heading for the rendezvous with Modena and his Russians. But even as they moved off, trouble was brewing once more at their Florence headquarters – as unforeseen and unsuspected as it would prove utterly infuriating.

Charles Macintosh held a meeting with US Colonel Riepe. The date for the Allied spring offensive to punch through the Gothic Line had been set: it would be unleashed between 1 and 5 April 1945. In light of this, a decision was made at high level to postpone Lees and Farran's operation, so it could coincide with that date – something that was easy enough to declare at headquarters, but perhaps a little harder to effect in the field

'An isolated attack on a Corps HQ would alert the Germans to security needs of all HQs near partisan areas,' Macintosh reasoned, 'and, at the worst, might give them some idea of our future plans.' The fear was that the Germans would be forewarned of Allied intentions and thus forearmed.

Upon learning of this change of timescale, if not of heart, Walker-Brown interceded with General Clark himself, pleading that the raid be allowed to continue as planned. 'I forcibly put over that partisan morale, having been wound up to fever pitch could only be unwound at substantial risk to the success of the operation,' he remarked. For once, General Clark was not swayed by such sentiments.

A decision was taken to stand down the HQ raid and a message to that effect was radioed through to Farrimond. 'Signal No. 141 . . . to ENVELOPE . . . For ROY and MIKE . . . You will destroy this signal and ciphers after reading and guarantee security. News stolen from Colonel's desk means that you have only to wait one week after target date . . . and your plan is on with six jeeps. Your scheme will then be correctly timed for maximum effort . . . Will give you exact dates and details soonest.'

The signal embodied a carrot and stick approach. The carrot was the offer of 'six jeeps' to be dropped into the Secchia valley, which would mean that the HQ raid could be a quick in-and-out, vehicle-mounted affair. The stick was the need to coordinate the attack with the coming Gothic Line offensive, although the exact start date couldn't be radioed through, for fear of it leaking to the enemy. The 'news stolen from Colonel's desk' referred to intelligence that SOE had acquired regarding movements of senior German officers.

At Secchio, the message was received and decoded by a morose Farrimond. He sent a plainly worded reply: he was unable to deliver the missive because 'the party had started down towards the foothills'. Macintosh responded by *ordering* a postponement of the attack, and by copying his orders to Major Jim Davies, the neighbouring BLO.

'Please confirm you have proof subject received our orders to postpone attack,' he telegraphed, his suspicions of Lees and

Farran deepening. 'If not can you still send STAFETTA stating that these are 15 Army orders.'

Major Davies decided to take personal responsibility for getting the message into Lees and Farran's hands. He set off for Secchio himself, alternately bicycling and marching on foot as the terrain allowed. But of course, by the time he reached there Lees and Farran were long gone. Only one option remained. He'd have to send a courier dashing after the two commanders, in the hope of catching them before they slipped out of the hills.

Lees and Farran, meanwhile, were forging ahead. They approached the Secchia river, and the bridge that Wooding and his Garibaldini had defended so assiduously just a few days before. As they crossed it, Farran gave the order to Kirkpatrick: he was to play his pipes as the men stomped onwards through the dust and the spring sunshine. Lees, silent and sweat-soaked, strode ahead, as the ranks of fighters broke into song. Rendered to the notes of a rousing German marching tune, the words had been composed by the SAS themselves, capturing the dark humour of the time.

> *We're reckless parachutists,*
> *At least that's what we're told,*
> *But when action station's sounded,*
> *Then we don't feel quite so bold.*
> *We're the boys who ride the slip stream,*
> *We're the heroes of the sky,*
> *But we all know deep inside us,*
> *It's an awful way to die.*
> *Stand to the door, stand to the door,*
> *And my poor old knees are trembling,*
> *Up off the floor, up off the floor,*

And I'm seeing scores of gremlins.
Red light on! Green light on!
Out through the door we go,
F-f-fighting for breath, b-b-battered near to death,
Drifting down to earth below.
We're the boys who ride the slip stream,
We're the boys who jump for fame.
If our parachutes don't open,
Then we get there just the same.
There's a big court of inquiry,
And the packer gets the sack,
But all the juries in creation,
Can't fetch that poor chap back.

A hard climb from the river took the party to Valestra, the village rendezvous with Modena and his Russians. With former ballroom dancer Serjeant Guscott arranging clean straw to be laid in a barn as a billet for the men, Farran and Lees took stock. Resting on the village green, and with the evening sun illuminating the scene, they wondered vaguely at the line of villagers trudging up the main street, with bundles piled high on their shoulders. Their steps appeared hurried – harried almost – as they moved back the way the raiders had come.

It struck Farran that they looked almost like *refugees*. He sat up, suddenly more alert and ordered Riccomini to investigate. He was back within minutes. The news was not good. The Germans had launched another sweep towards the Secchia valley and were but a few miles distant, hence the fleeing villagers. Partisans had taken up positions in the northern limits of Valestra village, in preparation for what they feared was coming.

Wearily, Farran followed Riccomini to a high point, where figures were scattered among the rocks. Occasionally, one fired a burst into the distance, but the enemy were hopelessly out of range. Farran ordered the shooting to stop. He surveyed the far terrain through binoculars. A thin line of grey troops was advancing with purpose towards a small village set atop a ridge-line. Occasionally, he heard the distinctive *tack-pung* of a Mauser rifle firing.

Farran ordered more sentries set. This was the last thing they needed – to tire some among their force of raiders just prior to the HQ attack. But worse would be the enemy surprising them here, under cover of darkness. He returned to the village and was just in time to spy Modena's Russians arriving. Modena had marched them at a furious pace to get here, so they would need at least a full night's rest to recover.

The best chance of slipping through the line of advancing enemy troops would be to march that very night, before they closed in. But with so many among their force so fatigued, no such thing was going to be possible. With sentries set, Farran bedded down as best he could in the open on the village green.

'There were so many restless nights like that behind the lines,' Farran remarked of the moment. 'The strain on the nerves caused by constant watchfulness was the most tiring thing of all.'

With dawn there was both good news and bad. The Germans had advanced no further. Indeed, their chief aim seemed to be rounding up villagers for forced labour. That was the good news. The bad was that Lees' malaria had worsened. As Norice brought Farran a breakfast of a fried egg sandwich and a steaming mug of tea, Lees seemed to have little appetite at all.

Farran munched away, surveying his 'motley crew of ruffians'.

A group of SAS leaned against a nearby wall, trading war stories with the Garibaldini and wisecracks with the Stafettas. The Garibaldini were as tough a bunch of pirates as Farran had ever laid eyes on. Their uniforms were torn and stained, their boots similarly cracked, their faces pinched and weather-beaten. The red stars on their caps complemented the sprinkling of SAS red berets, intermingled with the colourful splash of the dresses worn by the girls.

But what struck Farran most were the smiles and grins and thumbs-ups he received from all who caught his eye. Their morale was peaking, as they sensed that this was their moment; that soon they would strike a daring and decisive blow. As Farran well appreciated, you couldn't order such an irregular force into action: you had to inspire and move them to fight. It was all about carefully timed theatre, leadership and inspiration, and right now he reckoned they'd got it spot on.

A figure approached him, a little nervously. It was one of the political commissar Eros's deputies. Should they proceed with the raid? he ventured. Or was now not the time to join the defence of the valley, as a major *rastrellamento* seemed to be in the offing? Farran knew that any such change of plan would be disastrous. For one thing, they were never going to alight upon such a fateful or determined moment as this again. For another, it was vital to prove that the partisans could carry out a plan of action regardless of counter moves by the enemy.

He decided to answer the man's query by making a general address. He called in the sentries. All gathered at the village green, straw from night quarters clinging to their clothing, the British unshaven and unkempt after days living rough in oxen stables. Modena's Russians kept to themselves, forming a phalanx of Slavic solidity. For sure, they were a force to be reckoned with. The SAS and the Italians milled about freely, mixing easily. The vibes were good. Very good. Now was not the moment to delay.

With a sweating Lees at his side, Farran laid out his plan of action, explaining why no delay could be countenanced. Each sentence was translated into Italian, plus German for Modena, and for Hans and the handful of other deserters from the Wehrmacht. Stage one of the operation would commence at dusk. It involved Hans ferrying the entire force north, using the one navigable road. He would do so in relays, using a truck he'd recently hijacked from the enemy.

Once the truck-leg was done, they would press ahead on foot, sticking to minor tracks and skirting enemy positions. Farran would lead the way, accompanied by a pair of SAS scouts and an Italian guide. Behind would come the rest of the force, divided into three columns. One would be led by the young Lieutenant Harvey, and consist of ten SAS plus their Garibaldini. The second would be led by Lieutenant Riccomini and Mike Lees, with ten SAS and twenty Black Owls. The third would be led by Major Modena, and would consist entirely of his Russians.

There would be no smoking or talking allowed, and the march would need to be executed double quick, if they were to reach their planned lying-up point by daybreak. If the lead figures stumbled into any trouble they would throw themselves flat on the deck, at which all behind would follow suit. Battle would only be joined if those at the head of the column opened fire on the enemy. The absolute priority was to slip through undetected.

Upon reaching their isolated farmstead destination they would lie low all day and move off after sunset, aiming to hit the Botteghe

HQ an hour before midnight. They'd creep in to the patch of woodland adjacent to the target, whereupon each column would move off – the Russians to block the road, Harvey's column to hit Villa Calvi, and Lees and Riccomini's to assault Villa Rossi. They'd withdraw on Farran's signal and scramble for the mountains.

In view of the momentous nature of their target, the objections of Eros's deputy seemed to evaporate. Who could not be caught up in the spirit of the moment? Seizing the initiative, Kirkpatrick broke out his pipes and began to play an Eightsome. As young men grabbed girls and twirled around excitedly, Farran knew now was the time. If he could only keep them in such a mood for a further forty-eight hours, nothing in the world could stop them.

As the dancing and clapping continued a diminutive figure elbowed his way through the crowd, making a beeline for Farran and Lees. It was a courier, and he had a slip of paper clutched in his young hand. Farran read it with a growing sense of shock and bewilderment. It was a curt message from Florence headquarters, which had been forwarded via a runner from Jim Davies. He read it three times over in utter disbelief: in essence, their mission had been cancelled. They were to stand their force down.

Countless times on previous missions Farran had found himself cursing distant staff officers, who had 'not the remotest idea of what was involved in a guerrilla attack . . . These people seemed unable to realise that assault by irregulars cannot be coordinated to a definite time table . . . they can only be carried out successfully by seizing opportunities when the time is ripe.'

Quietly fuming, he handed the slip of paper to Lees with a suitable disparaging remark. The big SOE officer seemed almost too fevered to pay it any heed. He glanced at the message, grunted, but Farran couldn't be sure if it had really even registered. Whatever

232

action they chose to take it would be at Farran's bidding, the decision lying on his shoulders.

He pondered what they should do. The Stafettas had confirmed that there appeared to be little suspicion at the Botteghe HQ that an attack might be imminent. No extra or unusual defences had been set. But how long would that last? Once the enemy had learned that a sizeable raiding force had reached as far as the fringes of the plains, they were bound to be suspicious. What were its intentions, they'd ask themselves? What was the intended target?

As for the partisans, they would surely lose faith in the intent of Farran, Lees et al., if ordered to stand down. They would conclude that the British commanders, similar to their own, liked to talk the talk, but that was as far as it went. Having worked the partisans up into the kind of fighting frenzy that was required, Farran doubted if he could do so again, and certainly not following such a signal let-down.

By rights, he shouldn't even be here, leading this force of magnificent desperadoes. He'd jumped from the Dakota against orders. Yet he sensed he was going to have to do something similar again now. Far less physically daunting, the ramifications were incalculably more serious. It was one thing leaping from an aircraft when told not to; quite another laying waste to an entire German Army HQ entirely against orders.

Even so, Farran made his decision: he would act as if the message had never been received. As he knew well, a postponement was only one step away from a cancellation, and surely any attack was better than no attack at all. He shared his thoughts with Lees, while making one thing crystal clear: the responsibility for this sleight of hand – this necessary subterfuge – would be his, and his alone. Lees – dosed up and battling his fever – seemed almost beyond caring.

All that day they lay low in Valestra village. Now and again sporadic rifle fire echoed from the valley beyond, where German troops were in action. That was the very terrain they would have to slip through, come nightfall. With dusk, a battered ten-tonne former German Army truck rolled into the village. It was an incongruous sight, especially with blond, blue-eyed Hans at the wheel.

Lees had sworn that the deserter was utterly reliable. As the first contingent of raiders piled aboard the truck, Farran guessed he was about to find out. For the next hour or so Hans plied the route back and forth, his furthest reach limited by a road bridge that had been demolished by the partisans in an earlier action. Each trip proceeded without incident, Hans proving Lees' faith in him entirely justified. It was late evening on 26 March 1945 when the last fighters were ferried to the point of no return, where they would have to ford the river on foot.

There was one eventuality that Farran hadn't foreseen: Major Davies had asked for confirmation from his runner that the message had been delivered; this he had now received and had radioed back same to headquarters. In Florence there was a disquieting disconnect. On the one hand, Davies had guaranteed their order to cancel the raid had been delivered. On the other, there was a wall of silence emanating from the two maverick commanders, Farran and Lees.

Farrimond was bombarded with further messages, demanding confirmation that the attack had been cancelled. He argued that he could do nothing more. Tempers in Florence seemed close to breaking point. Finally, an extraordinary order was telegraphed to Farrimond, relieving Lees of his command. In a bizarre irony,

Mike Lees' replacement, who was already being made ready, was SOE Captain John W. Lees (no relation), formerly of the Manchester Regiment, a regular infantry unit.

But again Farrimond was unable to deliver the message, for by now Mike Lees and Roy Farran were beyond all reach. Of course, Farrimond was trying to shield his CO from such bothersome meddling, as he saw it. Lees would later write of his radio operator that he was 'Tough, unswervingly loyal and, like his Boss, outspokenly intolerant and contemptuous of poseurs. He never once let me down.' Farrimond, Lees and Farran were birds of a feather. They had little time for the 'pen-pushing map boys in Florence', as they disparagingly called them.

Yet in truth, right at that moment Lees would almost have welcomed a stand-down. 'Had I received an order delaying the operation I would have been mightily relieved, because I was very ill at the time and in no shape to march or to fight,' he would write. 'I strongly believed . . . that I was set up by . . . HQ in Florence. At the very least I was being used as a scapegoat . . . I was too aggressive for them by half.'

At their Secchio base, another key figure was being drawn into the furore over the stand-down order – Fritz Snapper, Reserve Lieutenant of the Royal Dutch Army and chief of the partisans' courier service. He was of a mind with Farrimond. 'Postponement would not only have been detrimental to the prestige of the BLO and SAS officers, but also to partisan morale which was very sensitive,' he reported of the incident. 'Major FARRAN and Capt LEES decided they must proceed with the attack even if it was against orders.'

Thus the dividing lines were drawn: between those chairborne at headquarters, and those soldiering at the hard end of operations.

Chapter 14

It was 0100 hours by the time most of the raiding party had forded the river. One of the last to do so was Lieutenant Harvey, marching at the head of the third column. They had navigated 'extremely rugged country, up mountains of considerable height and across rivers . . . flooded from the thawing snows.'

In an amusing if tricky moment, young Harvey's braces broke just as he was part way across the icy waters. 'This small occurrence caused me considerable discomfort, which I had to endure for some 24 hours, before I could make some makeshift arrangement to see me through.' No one wanted their trousers falling down in the midst of what was coming.

Once over the river, the column formed up as one. With Farran at its head the raiders moved off into the darkness. Before them, constantly quartering the ground back and forth, went the SAS scouts and their Italian guide. The noise they were all making seemed dangerously loud. Weapons clattered against kit; rocks set loose by footfalls tumbled into the river below; boots crunched on loose, friable earth.

Farran paused, glancing back at the dark line of men snaking south, the last figures silhouetted on a ridge against the moonlight. He had never once commanded a force as large as this – one hundred raiders – heading deep into enemy territory. It seemed impossible that they wouldn't be detected. He sent a whispered order to be passed from man to man, urging greater silence. The quiet of that still night seemed to magnify any sound.

'Marching at night through enemy country is an eerie experience at the best of times,' Farran remarked. 'But when it is with a long line of one hundred men, all completely silent apart from involuntary noise, the strain on one's nerves is indescribable . . . causing us to pause in dread of discovery.'

The column marched across a valley, fording another tributary of the Secchia. A narrow track wound ahead, its path washed by the silvery-blue of the moon, twisting and turning around a series of high rocky outcrops before reaching an isolated farmstead. As Farran approached, a dog started barking. A figure came to the door, swinging a lamp this way and that. Farran froze, the long line of men behind doing likewise.

Finally, cursing the dog for awakening him, the farmer slammed shut the door. Beyond the farmhouse lay the first major choke-point, where Farran feared they might hit trouble. They had to cross the main Carpineti to Valestra road, which threaded east–west through the foothills. The highway barred their route: the target, the Botteghe HQ, lay some fifteen kilometres beyond it, across equally rugged country.

A small village, Casa de' Pazzi, lay astride the road and it was known to be garrisoned by German troops. Farran's plan was to make a detour around it, so avoiding any danger. But after two hours' punishing march, it became clear that their best laid plans had gone awry. One of his scouts, darting backwards and forwards in his canvas-soled shoes, encountered some kind of a settlement. It seemed they'd stumbled into the edge of the village. Farran dropped flat to the earth, crawling in close with Lees and the others. It wasn't long before the guide admitted that in the thick darkness he had miscalculated the way. They were already among the outskirts of Casa de' Pazzi.

Two choices lay open to Farran. One – to retrace their steps, which would entail a major detour. It was approaching four o'clock in the morning, with just two more hours until first light. There just wasn't the time. They'd have to plump for option two, deeply unattractive though it might be: to press on through the enemy position. Amid angry stage-whispers a second guide took over, berating his colleague for leading them into such danger.

He steered the men towards a scree slope that stretched beyond the southern limits of the village, which itself was carved into a dramatic hillside. With the black, blocky silhouettes of the nearest buildings just above them, the column of raiders began to creep along the precipitous drop. As Farran and Lees inched across the treacherous bed of loose rocks, they could hear voices drifting down to them. It stood to reason that only sentries – or insomniacs – would be awake at this hour.

No matter how one tiptoed, it was impossible to move without dislodging the odd stone, which careered down the slope in an ear-splitting clatter. A dog barked. Another and another took up the hue and cry. The column of raiders pressed on, at every step fearing discovery – at which moment their much-vaunted mission would become a debacle, SAS and partisans fighting a battle for a village that was of little strategic value.

As Farran was painfully aware, to disobey orders and succeed was one thing, but to do so and fail would be quite another. He figured they were about halfway across when the lead scout hissed a warning. He'd heard the distinctive *clatch-clatch* of steel on steel, as from somewhere a rifle bolt was rammed home and a weapon primed. Farran dropped flat, those behind following suit, as they clung to the loose, rocky terrain, struggling to anchor themselves and to keep still.

For ten minutes they remained motionless, ears straining for any further sounds. None came. Eventually, Farran signalled them on. They reached the far side and climbed towards the road itself. There Farran called a halt, as the scouts checked the way across. They indicated the coast was clear, and Farran and Lees flitted over, figures scurrying after them like so many frightened rabbits.

Farran urged everyone on, scrambling ever upwards through jumbled rocks and moving further away from the danger. Finally, the lead scouts slipped between a pair of giant boulders, into the shelter of a wide bowl of grassy land. There, Farran called the first halt of the night. They'd been on the move for eight hours, for the most part of which they'd been assailed by fear and tension. It was both nerve-racking and hugely wearying.

SAS and partisans alike threw themselves onto the long grass. One of the guides found a source of water. One by one they drank their fill. That done, Farran lay back on the soft turf and stared at the sky, resplendent above them in all its starlit radiance. He felt a nudge at his elbow. He glanced over, to find Norice the grey-eyed-Stafetta sitting cross-legged beside him.

Wordlessly, she handed him a hard-boiled egg, freshly peeled, together with a slice of bread. Farran smiled his thanks. He couldn't help but admire her in the fine light thrown off by stars and moon. With a tumble of thick dark hair fringing her features, she looked mysterious; magical; bewitching. Her muscled brown legs were complimented by white ski socks and ski boots, perfect kit for trekking through the mountains. She seemed barely touched by fatigue after the long night's march, whereas Farran felt whacked.

He forced himself to his feet. '*Andiamo*,' he signalled, the whisper being passed around from figure to figure: let's go.

All around tired men and women lumbered to their feet. Farran's eyes searched out the distinctive figure of Lees. The big SOE officer had barely spoken a word. For hours he'd stumbled along in a grim-faced silence, gripped by fever. Farran was worried if he'd even finish the march, let alone be able to play any part in the coming assault.

Twice he'd urged Lees to turn back, but both times he'd uttered a refusal, stubborn until the last. Instead, he'd somehow forced his legs to keep powering him forwards. Farran hoped to persuade Lees to remain at the farmstead, which was their intended lying-up point prior to the attack, but he wasn't exactly hopeful.

The way ahead led through hard, rocky terrain, scattered with thick clumps of trees clinging to wherever their roots could gain a grip. The mountain path wound up and down endlessly, taking them ever closer to the plains. There was less danger here in the foothills; less chance of discovery. Accordingly, the scouts ranged further ahead, alert to any threat, while the column of raiders straggled out for a good mile or so.

Farran could barely believe it when the first blush of dawn lightened the sky to the east. They were behind schedule, being a good few miles short of the farmstead. As good fortune would have it, a thick blanket of mist cloaked the surrounding terrain. They were winding their way into more open, flat meadowlands, which were mostly devoid of any cover, making the dawn mists a total life-saver.

Thankfully, the mist proved persistent, stubbornly refusing to burn off in the early morning sun. It hovered some three feet above the ground, shrouding his force from view. For once Farran indulged the hope that the gods were smiling upon them.

He glanced behind. The wisps of thick, wet mist conveniently distorted the shapes of those who followed. It was a godsend, for they were too tired to indulge in any great cunning or deception.

As the sun rose higher and the heat intensified the mist started to clear. With huge relief Farran climbed a slight rise, to spy the form of a brick-built farmstead perched atop a ridgeline, protruding from the mist like an island in the sky. That, he knew, was the aptly-named Casa del Lupo – House of the Wolf – their lying-up point for the hours of daylight. Their target lay just three miles beyond it as the crow flies.

He drove himself on, summoning hidden reserves of energy. When he judged they were close enough, he passed word down the line for Lieutenant Riccomini to come forward, along with ten SAS. He was ordered to push ahead and recce the House of the Wolf, while the rest of the column lay flat in the grass, shrouded by the last lingering wisps of mist. Riccomini was to move cautiously and to take his time, Farran cautioned. On no account was anyone to be allowed to escape from the farmstead – German or Italian.

Farran watched intently as the SAS flitted forwards, throwing a cordon around the place. That done, figures slipped through the front gateway and stole inside. Farran tensed for the sound of gunshots, but none came. After a minute or so he was waved forwards. It turned out that the only people present were the old farmer and his wife.

Mike Lees knew this place well: he'd visited it before, when carrying out his original recce of the Botteghe HQ. But none of them had ever been to this place attired as they were now – in full British battledress and bedecked with all the accoutrements of war, including a distinctive M1 bazooka, complete with rockets.

The bazooka – a man-portable, recoilless anti-tank rocket-launcher – had been included in one of the last air-drops. According to press reports, the American-made M1 'packed the wallop of a 155mm cannon'. It was a gross exaggeration, and early versions proved highly unreliable. More recent models were supposedly much improved, and Farran didn't doubt that it would make mincemeat out of the front doors of the villa targets, as they blasted an initial entry-way.

As the raiders filed silently in, Farran surveyed the farmstead. It was ideal for their purposes. The buildings formed four sides of a square, arranged around a central courtyard. The one narrow entrance faced south, so away from the direction of their target. The walls were thick and fortress-like, and indeed the place had very likely been designed to defend against mountain bandits in times gone by.

Farran allotted each of the three columns a stretch of the barns as a billet, and a flank of the farmstead to defend, in the event of trouble. Sleep was permitted, but sentries were to be posted, peeping cautiously from the upper windows, so as to keep out of sight. If anyone was seen coming to the farm, they were to be allowed to enter, after which the exit would be sealed shut. Whether German or Italian, they would be held captive until the mission was over.

Farran and Lees set up base in the kitchen. At first the farmer and his wife appeared terrified at the sudden arrival of so many rough-looking men-at-arms. But once they realised this was no raid, they become fawning and friendly. As the woman of the house rustled up breakfast, the farmer produced a bottle of grappa. He poured a round of shots, relating how German soldiers often paid them visits in search of eggs. Farran sent out word to double the watchfulness of the sentries.

The farmer seemed unable to comprehend that they were British. He insisted they had to be Germans, proudly relating how his son had served in North Africa and was now an officer in a Black Brigade unit. He produced photographs of a young man in Italian Army uniform, standing before a row of light tanks. A simple, rural type, the farmer seemed incapable of grasping that the force now billeted at his farmstead was fighting for the other side.

Fearing that one of the Garibaldini would overhear his pro-Fascist boasts and cut his throat, Farran told the farmer to put away his photos. Though puzzled and confused, the old man had let the grappa get the better of him. He insisted on relating a final story of how the dashing young man in the Italian Army uniform was actually the son of the village priest and not his at all, after which he roared with laughter, slapping Farran conspiratorially on the back.

Lees, meanwhile, seemed oblivious to all. He sat at the kitchen table head in hands, looking desperately sick. As the morning progressed and he swigged grappa and downed quinine pills, he seemed barely able to keep conscious. But still he refused to lie down, arguing that it would only make him feel worse. 'I dared not rest,' Lees remarked of this moment. 'I knew that if I lay down now I should not be fit to go on again.'

Finally, Farran broached the subject that was foremost on his mind – that Lees was clearly too ill to continue.

'I'll be all right,' Lees mumbled. 'I'll be all right.' Meanwhile beads of perspiration pricked his forehead and trickled down his temples.

At midday Farran despatched Norice and Argentina on a final recce of the target. Their mission was to make doubly certain that the movement of the Allied Battalion hadn't been detected and the enemy's defences strengthened. Pulling off their battledress tunics and discarding their pistols, the young women set out as if they didn't have a care in the world, cracking jokes about how they would arrange dates with the German soldiers. Farran was hugely impressed. They had as much courage as any of their male counterparts.

Shortly after they'd left, two cowering Italians were herded into the kitchen. They came from a neighbouring farm, and while denying they knew of the presence of Farran and his men, in the same breath they claimed to have come here to warn of an approaching German patrol. They reported that the enemy were searching all neighbouring farms for partisans. Farran was used to such widely exaggerated rumour. While he didn't entirely believe them, he did warn Riccomini to alert his sentries to be on the lookout.

Farran ordered that the new arrivals be placed under guard in the shade of the courtyard. They would need to remain there all day and all night, he explained, but were free to depart come morning. They objected that they would be missed and that they had livestock to feed, but Farran couldn't help that. A little later three more farmers drifted in to Casa del Lupo, with similar stories – that German patrols were on the search.

It was worrying and Farran asked Lees what he made of the reports. After all, he had far more experience in these parts. Lees muttered something about the unreliability of the locals and that it was far safer to remain hidden. Farran agreed. If they sent out teams to search for the enemy, they'd risk blundering into those enemy patrols.

Farran's main concern was becoming the Stafettas. They'd been gone for a worryingly long time, and if they'd been captured that would blow the mission wide open. As a local BLO had recently reported, the fate of a Stafetta captured by the 'fiendish S.D.' – the *Sicherheitsdienst*, or the intelligence service of the SS – had been both horrific and hugely damaging. 'One of the girls [was] caught . . . [and] interrogated 26 times in 14 days. Given electric shocks and arrived back in a frightfully bruised state. Of course she spilt all she knew.'

As the sun set in a blaze of golden light, Farran became increasingly unsettled. He gazed out of the farmstead, searching for signs of the two missing women. To the south snow-capped peaks glowed red in the sun's last rays. A thousand feet lower the snow petered out, the mountains being fringed with a dark necklace of trees interspersed with isolated farmsteads. Lower still were villages, vineyards and olive groves, reaching out into the plains. In each of the cowsheds near him rough men were sleeping, their weapons and ammo piled in the mangers, the air thick with the scent of warm dung. But no mission could be launched from here, if Norice and Argentina failed to return.

Finally, a pair of figures sauntered out of the gathering dark. They had been delayed by over-attentive Germans, Norice explained, her grey eyes sparkling mischievously. She had wandered right through the enemy HQ, and produced a German cigarette from the bosom of her blouse, as evidence. She poured out information in a flood of Italian, punctuated by peals of laughter. The only significant new development was that a unit of anti-aircraft guns had been set up, to the east of the crossroads. That was hardly of any great significance.

Having congratulated the two women, Farran delivered his bombshell. They were not to be allowed to accompany the raiders, but would remain at the farmstead. Norice and Argentina were furious. They turned their wrath on Lees, berating him in wild outbursts of Italian. Though Lees understood, he was too far gone to care much. As they screamed and stamped and wept, Lees told Gordon to take them outside to cool off. His face was noticeably flushed and he appeared close to delirious.

Farran made one last attempt to persuade Lees to remain behind. The big man shook his head in wordless refusal. He knew fully well that the 'Malaria germ contracted in Yugoslavia . . . was active again, raising my temperature and sapping the strength that I would need . . .' Regardless, he steeled himself to continue, setting aside any thoughts of the long march back again: 'Sufficient only to see this attack a success and I should be content.'

With nightfall the mist returned. Farran had managed to grab a short sleep in the farmer's bed and he felt reasonably rested. It was time to issue final orders, over the fine meal that the farmer's wife had prepared – salami, spaghetti and bread, plus wine. As a fire roared in the hearth and Farran briefed the key figures – SAS, SOE and partisans alike – there was a distinctly last supper feel to the gathering.

'We move off at ten-thirty,' he announced, with his back to the blazing fireplace. 'We should reach Botteghe around midnight. We march in three parallel columns: the Russians, the Garibaldini and the *Gufo Nero*. You all know your roles when we get there. Any questions?'

Farran glanced around the gathering – Russians, Italians, Spanish, Germans and British united in one cause. He could just imagine how, three miles away, the German general and senior commanders would be sitting down to supper in Villa Rossi's magnificent dining hall. In Villa Calvi, staff would be locking

246

away files and sending a last flurry of messages, believing a good supper and rest beckoned. Little did any of them know . . . Outside, guards would pace the perimeter, stamping their feet to drive out the chill. Stamping as the Nazis had done all over Europe, treading on the citizens of so many countries until even their friends, the Italians, rose up against them.

Racked with fever though he was, Lees likewise felt a surge of pride – pride that tonight would be the moment when 'Italy found her soul'; pride that tonight the spirit of resistance would rise up and strike a decisive blow.

Farran felt moved to make a final exhortation. 'Remember, the Corps HQ controls the whole of the front from Bologna to the coast. Its destruction will save thousands of Allied lives . . .' He glanced at the distinctive figure of Hans, dressed in full German uniform. 'If we are challenged, Hans will answer in German, and if we meet a patrol or the alarm is given, move straight in and attack. Is that understood?'

'*Capito*' – understood – the chorus of replies came back in Italian.

The raiders were ordered to muster in the darkness outside. The night was as black as pitch. Farran executed a last-minute inspection, just to ensure all had sufficiently darkened their faces, smearing them with soot. That done, Lees – seeming to have summoned hidden reserves of energy – did a final round of checks.

'Gordon, *pronto*?' he asked his *Gufo Nero* leader.

'*Pronto, Capitano.*' Ready, captain.

'Modena, *vy gotovi*?' Are you ready, in Russian.

'*Da, Gospodine Kapitan.*' Yes, dear captain.

'*Êtes-vous prêt*, Roberto?' French – for after years in the French

Foreign Legion, French was a second language for the Spaniard, Lance Corporal Robert Bruce.

'*Oui, monsieur le capitaine.*' Yes, captain.

With that, the long column of raiders marched out of the House of the Wolf, to war.

Chapter 15

With one of the local farmers acting as their guide they passed over some meadowland, there being little sound but the brush of boots through wet grass. The moon had risen and it glowed an eerie blueish-white through the low-lying banks of mist. They pressed on, crested a rise and suddenly the plains stretched before them as far as the eye could see.

Farran was amazed. The foothills stopped so abruptly, terminating in a vast and dark flatland, which seemed broken only by the moonlight glinting off the mighty River Po – a sliver of twisting silver snaking through the blackness. As Farran's eyes adjusted to the scene he spotted the odd pinprick of light – presumably a farmstead or home too remote for Italy's wartime blackout to have been fully enforced.

He glanced in the direction where he knew the Botteghe HQ had to lie: all there was dark and enveloped in a thick, brooding silence. It seemed impossible that soon it was to be torn asunder by the thunder of battle. Treading softly, Farran began to descend, slipping carefully into the black abyss. Once he glanced back: the last figures were stark on the skyline, seemingly elongated into giants by the weird distorting effect of mist and moonlight. Bizarrely, it reminded him of bushes warped by the intense heat of the Sahara, from his earliest missions in the war.

They neared the one major road that they had to cross, and the guide whispered a farewell, hurrying back the way they had come. The SAS scouts crept onwards. Bent double they scurried back and forth, checking that the route ahead was clear. At their signal, Farran led his men to the cover of a ditch, which ran along the nearside of the highway, ordering them to fan out on either side. On his word they broke cover and dashed across, but blundered into a thick hedge on the far side.

As men dived beneath it and wriggled through, weapons and kit banged and clanked alarmingly. To Farran if sounded as if a herd of elephants was on the rampage. He lay in the thick grass on the far side of the hedge, taking a moment to catch his breath. Beside him was Kirkpatrick, the piper, and his faithful 'aide' Bruno, the boy-partisan. Word filtered back that all one hundred of his fighters had made it across safely.

Ahead a farmhouse gleamed white in the moonlight. Farran recognised it from the aerial photos: it was his marker point from which to navigate the last few hundred yards to target. From now on that responsibility would be his, and his alone. He would steer a route across the night-dark terrain using a process known as 'pacing and bearing' – a simple technique that was the bread and butter of SAS operations. Taking a north bearing and setting his sights on a distinctive landmark lying due north, he would move off, counting his right footfalls.

From long experience he knew that ten such footfalls under a heavy pack amounted to some nine yards of terrain covered. By keeping to that northerly bearing, he'd need only to count out the paces and distance covered to know when to swing due east, for the target would then lie on their eastern flank. It sounded simple enough, but the mental effort involved in such pinpoint-accurate navigation, while remaining silent and alert for the enemy, was hugely draining.

He closed up the column, so no more than an arm's length separated each man. He couldn't afford to lose any now. They set forth, Farran moving stealthily at the very head of the snake. He tested his every footfall before putting down his full weight, his ears alert for the slightest noise or hint of danger. His heart leapt as a dog barked in a farm ahead and to his right. He crept onwards, making a slight detour around that and another farmstead, neither of which he could remember from the aerial photos.

There was the grunt of a heavy engine from the direction of the road they'd just crossed. Farran threw himself onto the dewy grass. Behind him a long line of figures did likewise. They lay still for several minutes, until the noise of the truck faded into silence. Moving with its headlamps blacked out, its progress was all but invisible to the naked eye. Farran clambered to his feet and signalled the off once more.

Shortly, they reached a ploughed field. The going worsened, thick loamy soil clinging to boots as one hundred heavily-armed raiders endeavoured to move silently across the rough, uneven ground. From pacing and bearing, Farran calculated they were close now – no more than a few hundred yards from the nearest enemy positions. He was terrified lest those on watch might hear the racket they were making, as they struggled across the rutted terrain.

All of a sudden he felt the ground give out beneath him. Moments later he'd stumbled face-first into a ditch. Most likely an irrigation channel, it had been invisible in the half-light. Passing a warning back down the line, he scrambled out and inched ahead, moving with ever more caution. Even so, when a second ditch yawned before him he was too late to prevent it from bringing him to his knees.

As he froze among the dank, muddy wetness of that second ditch, he heard a challenge ring out in German. For several seconds he tensed for the snarl of Mauser shots ringing past their heads in the darkness. Thankfully, none came. But it had taken more than an hour to cover a few hundred yards and they were falling behind schedule.

Farran felt a desperate urge to rush onwards, but he fought against the temptation. He crept resolutely on, moving with infinite care. His parachute smock snagged on a length of barbed wire. Carefully, silently, he untangled it and clambered over the fence, those behind whispering a warning to those who followed.

After his detailed studies of the aerial photos, the terrain here was etched in Farran's memory. He reckoned now was the time to swing east, to cover the final three hundred yards. If he'd got his sums right, they would reach the cover of the crescent-shaped woodland – which they'd nicknamed 'Half Moon Wood' – lying on the western flank of Villa Calvi. At that moment they'd be within spitting distance of the nerve-centre of the German 14th Army HQ.

Farran turned east and stole ahead more stealthily. A faint breath of wind seemed to part the mists for an instant, a beam of moonlight illuminating an utterly arresting sight. The distinctive form of Villa Calvi lay before them, no more than two hundred yards away, a ghostly white-walled mansion perched on a low hill and surrounded by a fringe of trees, and all seeming to float upon a sea of low-lying mist.

Not a light showed in any of the villa's windows, and Farran began to doubt if this really was their target. Were there any Germans present here at all? he wondered. The place looked utterly deserted. He felt a presence at his side. It was Lees, still somehow managing to master his fever.

'There it is, Roy,' he whispered, pointing out Villa Calvi, plus Villa Rossi beyond. There wasn't the vaguest hint of any light from that direction either.

Farran's eyes swung right, following Lees' outstretched arm as he indicated further landmarks: the telephone exchange, just to the south, with beyond that the guardrooms and the ranks of billets for the troops charged to protect the headquarters. Further south again lay the prison, plus the Spandau nests they had been warned about, but not a light was visible anywhere.

It was 0050 hours by now and all seemed so peaceful, so devoid of life. Both men found it distinctly unsettling. Had the enemy moved on? For days now that had been their greatest fear. Maybe all the delays and the insane flip-flopping in orders meant that they had reached the target, only for their prey to have flown?

'Doubts started to beset me now: could this be the right place . . . ?' Lees wondered. 'If this was the Botteghe headquarters, surely one of the many guards would have spotted us and opened fire?'

They had no choice but to continue, for that would prove it one way or the other. Farran gestured the column back into motion. Shortly, the first trees loomed stark and menacing before them. Moments later they'd slipped into the dark embrace of Half Moon Wood, Farran's navigation proving spot-on. Incredible as it might seem, he'd led his force of raiders to the heart of this German headquarters, seemingly undetected.

Under the cover of those trees Farran mustered his men. The

tension and adrenalin had been building for hours now. 'Fear, nerves, excitement, apprehension, worry, plans – all jumbled together to make me start at any noise,' he remarked. 'It would all be all right once we got going.'

Farran tried to speak, but the words froze in his throat. Finally, he managed to talk, but what he needed to say came out in a series of hoarse, barely-audible whispers. Were all present and correct? he asked. Somehow, it looked as if Modena and his Russians had disappeared. Lieutenant Harvey was there, with his SAS and Garibaldini, and Lieutenant Riccomini was there with his SAS and Black Owls, but the thirty Russian partisans were gone.

Farran felt a stab of alarm. The night was utterly still. The air itself seemed heavy and oppressive. He didn't for one moment doubt Modena's loyalty or his good intentions, but somehow they had lost a third of their force. He sent Kirkpatrick, the piper, to find them, with orders that they should form up their blocking group just to the south of the villas, from where they were to hose down any enemy movement.

The remaining figures bunched closer around Farran, tense and expectant, awaiting the final off. Kirkpatrick reappeared. There was no sign of Modena, he reported. Farran had to presume the battle-hardened Russian commander had split from the main force when it made sense to, making direct for their agreed position. It was a huge assumption to make and a massive risk to take, but time was against them now. They could afford no delay.

Farran grabbed Riccomini. 'Start time,' he hissed. 'You've got three minutes to get to Villa Rossi, so move fast. I'm sending in Harvey's force three minutes from now. Remember, the main German strength lies to the south, so it's from there you'll likely take fire. You've got twenty minutes on target, no more. If I fire the red flare before that, you're to withdraw. Understood?'

'Understood,' Riccomini confirmed.

Beside him stood Lees, massive and silent in the darkness. For an instant Farran wondered how he was coping, but it was too late for any such worries now. He signalled them to move. Riccomini led off, Lees lumbering after, with behind them ten SAS and Gordon with his Black Owls forming up the rear. They pushed ahead, weapons at the ready.

Most carried the Thompson sub-machine gun. Two decades old, it remained a favourite with irregular forces for a variety of reasons, many of which were reflected in the gun's nicknames: the 'Trench Sweeper', 'Trench Broom' or 'The Chopper'. The Thompson was of rugged design, had a high rate of fire, and its heavy .45-calibre cartridge delivered real punch. When fitted with a 30-round stick magazine, it was possible to sweep an entire enemy trench with bullets . . . or likewise the bedroom of an Italian villa.

As Farran watched that first raiding party leave, he wondered if Riccomini had noticed his very obvious fear – fear that had frozen his words in his throat. Farran had to hope that Ricky wasn't unduly affected by his CO's windiness. He counted out the seconds in his head, as the darkness and silence crowded close, as deep and still as the grave. He shivered, whether from the growing chill or from fear, he wasn't quite certain.

Farran cocked his carbine, trying to shake off the malaise that had gripped him. He signalled for young Lieutenant Harvey and they eased their way further into the woodland, following a narrow path that pointed the way to the perimeter of Villa Calvi. A short distance along it a thin strand of wire barred their way. It seemed to serve no defensive purpose, for it was easily stepped over. Farran was about to do just that when one of the Garibaldini stopped him.

He pointed to a sign nailed to a tree above the wire. Etched in red were the words: 'ACHTUNG. MINEN'.

Farran froze. The wire marked the border of a minefield, but there was no time to detour around it, for the three minutes were running. Without a word being spoken young Lieutenant Harvey stepped over the wire and pushed up the path, the SAS swarming after. The Garibaldini hesitated for a moment, before Farran urged them to follow, especially as there had been no explosions. Unbeknown to Farran, Harvey hadn't even seen the warning.

'A last "Good luck" from Roy Farran . . .' Harvey remarked of this moment, 'and we stepped over a low wire, crossed a largish patch, and then over another low fence. I thought this a peculiar arrangement, but then the penny dropped . . . Good heavens, surely I had not led my men over a minefield! . . . Then to my horror I saw the words . . . "Beware Mines." Well, we'd crossed it without mishap; the problem of how we'd get back could be solved later. There was going to be a lot of action in the next hour and a hard and fast plan would be doomed to failure.'

With Harvey and his men creeping ever closer to Villa Calvi, Farran forced himself to move, making for the road, with Kirkpatrick at his side. As they emerged from the cover of the trees, Farran tumbled into a dark slit trench. It was his third fall of the night, and it proved the most debilitating. In the process of trying to clamber out he lost his grip on his carbine. Kirkpatrick jumped in to retrieve it, handing it back to the SAS major, who had more than enough on his mind right now.

They pushed on, reaching the road leading to the villas, setting up temporary camp in the cover of some bushes. It was from there, sandwiched between the two targets, that Farran would orchestrate the battle. This was also the rendezvous (RV) point at which all would gather to execute their escape. He prepared his Very pistol and its flares, and nodded at Kirkpatrick to ready his bagpipes. He counted down the seconds in his head to the three-minute mark. Now was almost time . . .

Lieutenant Harvey, meanwhile, led his column of men towards the ornate, pillared gateway of Villa Calvi, keeping off the gravel drive as much as possible, which scrunched alarmingly underfoot. They slipped through as silently as wraiths and Harvey set his outer cordon, leaving his Bren-gunners within the fringes of the woods, their barrels menacing the building from all sides. He whispered final instructions: they were to shoot dead anyone who appeared at the windows or tried to use any of the doors.

There was to be one exception: the front door should be left unmolested. Harvey intended to blast it open with the bazooka, as the sleeping villa's rude awakening. Bren-gunners set, he led his men onto the wide expanse of manicured lawns that stretched up to the villa itself. It was incredible, but they had yet to encounter any resistance.

He gathered his force of men-at-arms – ten SAS, plus twenty Garibaldini – in a tight knot on the lawn. They were set a few dozen yards back from the massive wooden doorway and poised to storm through. Still there had been no cry of alarm or sign of discovery. Acting on instinct, Harvey darted across the close-cropped grass to try the door. He reached out to the massive iron-handle, but sure enough it was securely locked and bolted.

He hurried back to his men and readied the bazooka. It had a maximum effective range of a little more than a hundred yards –

but that was more than enough for its shaped rocket charge to tear across the lawn and rip the door into blasted wooden splinters, at which moment Harvey would lead his men forward at the charge.

They levelled the tube, held their breath and prepared to let rip. But there was a soft thud from the bazooka's firing mechanism and nothing more. The M1's rocket rounds were notoriously unreliable, and sure enough it had misfired. Hurriedly, fumbling in the dim moonlight, they armed it with a second round and again tried to fire. Again, it was a dud.

'No result – damn, now bad luck was with us ...' Harvey recorded of the moment. 'We gathered around to try to determine the cause of the failure. Then I heard the unmistakeable crunching of boots on gravel ... and then the deep guttural voices. Germans!'

They were in danger of getting caught in the open of the villa's grounds. Ordering his men to lie flat and motionless, Harvey dashed back the few yards to the gateway, taking cover behind one of its massive stone pillars. He spied the enemy patrol almost immediately. Four Germans were marching up the road towards where he was concealed, looking purposeful and determined. This was no mundane sentry duty, that was for certain.

Harvey waited until they were barely a dozen yards away. He needed to kill them all outright, so that none might escape. Then he stepped out of cover, Bren levelled at the hip, and pressed the trigger, unleashing a whirlwind of rounds. The sudden noise of that long and deafening blast tore apart the stillness of the night, like a clap of thunder and lightning.

'It was essential that this was all done at point blank range,' Harvey reported, 'to ensure that they were killed immediately, for those shots would set the whole area off . . . I could not afford to have wounded Germans on the road while I engaged myself in getting into the house.'

Breaking into the villa would require busting through that massive wooden doorway, and there was no time to get the bazooka working. Leaving four bloodied figures sprawled on the gravel, Harvey turned on his heel and ran, sprinting across the lawn and yelling for the others to follow. As they neared the cover of the villa's grand porch, the first yells of alarm were heard from a window high above, followed almost instantly by a long burst of fire.

It was answered by the rasping of a Bren, as above them glass shattered and voices screamed in shock and agony. Even as Harvey levelled his weapon at the door-lock and pulled the trigger, the fire from above intensified. One of his men – SAS Parachutist Mulvey – tumbled over, hit in the knee. From the shadows at the lawn's edge muzzles spat fire, as Harvey's Bren-gunners tore into the enemy figures now crowding the villa's windows, .303-inch rounds blasting splinters out of masonry and shattering wooden frames.

Directly below, Harvey was desperate to break into the building. 'I gave the lock a final burst,' he reported, 'pushed in the door, threw in a few hand grenades and ran into the dark interior.'

Those grenades had detonated inside Villa Calvi's fine entranceway, the deafening explosions echoing throughout the building and telegraphing that the impossible was seemingly happening – a hostile force had broken into the 14th Army's headquarters, apparently all but undetected.

Harvey dashed further inside, the Villa's hallway shrouded in darkness and wreathed in grenade smoke. 'There were scuffling

259

noises and bullets started to fly,' he reported. 'The din was deafening in the enclosed space. I must see the lie of the room, so, holding my torch at arm's-length so as not to attract fire to myself, I switched it on and had a quick look around. The firing increased. They could see me, so I dived under a table . . . My sergeant opened up as I went to ground and killed the chief offender.'

SAS Sergeant Godwin let rip over Harvey's shoulder with his Thompson sub-machine gun, cutting the enemy fighter down. An instant later Harvey was back on his feet, sprinting for the staircase just ahead. Outside, someone must have got the bazooka working. There was the roar of the weapon firing, and moments later the rocket charge tore through an upper floor window and detonated, devastating fire and shrapnel punching through the rooms like a whirlwind.

Back at his roadside position, Farran had heard Harvey's first sustained burst of Bren fire with mixed emotions. Coming from the direction of Villa Calvi, it had sounded as if an entire magazine had been unleashed, the operator keeping his finger on the trigger without pause. Farran could only imagine that Harvey and his men were in action, and he felt a stab of excitement that the first fire had been British, as he had dearly hoped it would be.

But at the same time there was silence from the direction of Villa Rossi. Where were Riccomini, Lees and their men and why hadn't battle there also been joined? Villa Rossi's defenders would be waking up to the assault, and within seconds they would be at their defensive positions.

Harvey's burst was like a signal for all hell to let loose. A deafening barrage erupted from the ground just a hundred yards to the south of Farran's position, where the roadway ran past the

HQ's telephone exchange. From the muzzles sparking in the darkness, Farran knew that it had to be Modena and his Russians, as his line of thirty fighters let rip. True to form, Modena wasn't holding back: Farran could see streams of red tracer ricocheting off the walls of the telephone building and beyond that a cluster of guardrooms and billets.

Taken by utter surprise in the heart of their fortress, and hit hard in the depths of night, the enemy had to be wondering what on earth was happening. Which reminded Farran – his piper needed to play. He needed to stamp an indelible British signature on the battle, to deter against reprisals, plus he needed to stiffen the resolve of those charged to fight their way into the headquarters buildings, intent on wreaking bloody mayhem and murder.

Farran turned to Kirkpatrick, ordering him to play the marching song for all British highland regiments. All of a sudden the haunting tones of 'Highland Laddie' cut the night, the defiant skirl of the pipes rising above the snarl of battle. It was utterly spine-tingling. By way of answer, a ragged cheer went up from the Bren-gunners at Villa Calvi, but the enemy seemed equally keen to respond.

A burst of fire tore apart the air above Farran and Kirkpatrick's heads, targeting the unmistakeable tones of the pipes. It came uncomfortably close and it had the distinctive snarl of a Spandau. As further rounds ripped into their position, Farran grabbed his piper and bundled him into the nearby ditch.

'Keep playing,' he cried above the roar of battle. 'You're my secret weapon!'

Chapter 16

Kirkpatrick resumed his piping from a sitting position in the bottom of the trench, seemingly unfazed by the rounds that were snarling past. The bold notes of the pipes drew the enemy fire like nothing else. One round even nicked his bass drone, the longest pipe that creates the harmonising bass tone, and which protruded above both his head and the level of the ditch.

For a second or so Farran wondered whether he should move up to join Lieutenant Harvey at Villa Calvi, but someone had to man the RV point and signal their withdrawal. Instead, he dived into the trench to join his piper, cursing himself for not having held Harvey back for a few moments longer, to allow the Villa Rossi assault force time to reach their attack positions.

As if to underscore Farran's worries, the eerie wail of an air-raid siren started up. Low and barely audible at first, it wound up in pitch and volume, until the high-pitched scream echoed across the battlefield for a full dozen seconds, before dropping off to a low wail, and cranking up again. On and on it went, blaring out its oscillating warning. By now General Hauk and his senior staff would be fully awake, and preparing to fight back. The alarm had been well and truly raised at Villa Rossi, and Farran wondered what on earth could have delayed Riccomini and Lees.

In truth, Lieutenant Riccomini and Lees' approach had been somewhat more measured and stealthy than that of Lieutenant

Harvey at Villa Calvi. They'd crouched in a roadside ditch surveying Villa Rossi's boundary railings and the best route of approach, when Harvey's long burst of Sten fire had ripped the night apart. In response there had been a guttural yell, followed by a single shot ringing through the darkness, as a nearby sentry raised the alarm.

Riccomini reacted instantly. With Thompson sub-machine gun levelled at the shoulder, he unleashed a long series of bursts through the railings, blasting down the sentries one after the other. With four cut down, he was on his feet, yelling for his men to follow as he rushed the villa's gateway. The time for stealth was long past: this had become a full-frontal assault, guns-blazing, and the enemy knew it.

As Lees, Gordon and his Black Owls joined 'Ricky' and his SAS brethren sprinting for the gateway, so the first bursts of answering fire licked out of Villa Rossi's windows and the ghostly howl of the air-raid siren wound up to an ear-splitting crescendo. But as if to answer it, the wild skirl of the bagpipes rose up from behind them, spurring the raiders on. A wild cheer swept the ranks of the charging figures, SAS and partisans alike.

Lees – his fever momentarily forgotten – pounded through the gateway, as rounds cut around his head, ricocheting angrily off the massive stone pillars. On the left hand was inscribed the word 'VILLA' and on the right 'ROSSI', with each word surrounded by ornate stone carvings. Lees swerved left, and there, ten yards before him, was the expanse of Villa Rossi itself, rising four storeys to the highest towers.

A figure lunged out of the bushes to his right, barely an arm's length away. He saw a Mauser rifle raised, club-like, to strike. Before the sentry could swing it around to bludgeon his skull open, Lees fired, the muzzle of his Sten practically jabbing into the German's ribs. The blast forced the man backwards. He collapsed onto the lawn, face contorted in agony. Lees charged on, Gordon close at his heels and the Black Owls racing after.

Up ahead Riccomini scanned the target, desperately seeking a way in, while avoiding the line of fire from the upper windows. The high-arched front entrance was barred by a massive wooden door, strengthened with a cross-hatching of thick beams. Instead, Riccomini headed for a ground-floor window at which the slatted wooden shutters seemed to have been left mercifully open. Tommy gun spitting fire, he blasted in the glass and dived through, landing in a heap and rolling to his feet again.

Further figures vaulted in after, the SAS raiders dashing ahead and raking the ground floor with savage volleys of .45-calibre fire. Lees, meanwhile, made a beeline for the villa's front doorway. Using his bulk and his strength to force a way in, he barged it open, only to find himself momentarily blinded. Behind the closed doors and barred wooden shutters, the stone-flagged hallway proved surprisingly bright-lit. That he hadn't been expecting.

'Alarm was given by a hooter on the roof,' the official SAS report recorded, 'and all the lights were switched on. The British ran through machine-gun fire, through the main gate . . . After fierce fighting the ground floor was taken, but the Germans resisted furiously from the upper floors . . .' How 'furious' that resistance would prove Lees was about to discover.

To left and right he could hear the crash of breaking furniture and the tearing rasp of gunfire. A pair of German soldiers, caught by surprise, surrendered instantly. But Lees had thoughts only for one thing: finding his way to the upper floor and dealing with a sleep-befuddled General Friedrich-Wilhelm Hauk and his senior staff. He dashed through the hallway, yelling for Gordon and the others to follow.

The hall opened onto a vast downstairs lounge, scattered with ornate furniture. There was still no sign of the staircase. Racking his brains for what the Stafettas and German deserter plus the POW had told him of the villa's layout, he took a sharp turn left, twisted left again, and suddenly found himself at the foot of a wide staircase, with a deep stairwell reaching into the shadowed depths below. It stretched above in a switchback fashion, the stone steps flanked with intricately carved wooden balustrades.

With barely a second's pause Lees began to pound his way up the steps, his Sten levelled at the hip. He powered onwards, all symptoms of his fever subsumed by the rush of adrenalin that had flooded his system. The landing above was ill-lit, so it was hard for Lees to make out who might be lurking there. Even so he sensed movement and the first hints of an enemy primed to meet fire with fire. He let rip with his Sten, as he raced up the staircase towards his quarry.

Back at Farran's roadside trench position Kirkpatrick piped on. High above them a blinding light suddenly blazed through the darkness. Farran recognised it instantly as a star shell – an artillery round that bursts to release a flare, which floats to earth beneath a parachute. It hung in the dark heavens, transforming the ground below into a harsh fluorescent-blue, the illumination creating a near-approximation of daylight.

Via the blinding light Farran could see how Modena's Russians were holding firm, pouring intense fire into the enemy positions beyond. 'The Russians returned fire very accurately and their ring was never broken . . .' the official SAS report recorded. 'Several enemy machine guns were silenced and heavy casualties were inflicted, especially in the area of the telephone exchange.'

Even so, Farran reckoned that a half-dozen or more MG42 Spandaus – Hitler's Buzzsaw – were now in action, the same weapon as had pinned him down during their exfiltration from the Châtillon garrison attack, months earlier, in France. As then, the German gunners were spraying the area with a fearsome volume of fire, which seemed to sweep right up to the villas' very walls.

At Villa Calvi, Lieutenant Harvey made a dash for the staircase, with Sergeant Godwin at his shoulder, both men hell-bent on winning the high-ground. 'We rushed the staircase, but the Germans were firing over the balustrade from above,' Harvey reported. Repeated attempts were made to reach the landing, but each was driven back in a rain of fire. 'It would be impossible to get past the hail of bullets,' Harvey concluded. 'We had just not enough men for that sort of thing.'

As if to underscore his worries, one of the villa's defenders tossed a grenade down the stairs. It came to rest between Harvey, Sergeant Godwin and one other SAS man, a Corporal Layburn. It was the latter who was closest to the blast. The explosion blew him off his feet, and he ended up lying on the flagstone floor in a pool of his own blood. Layburn was seriously wounded, and Harvey ordered him carried outside, to join the other casualties. Hopefully, their superlative medic, the Operation Galia veteran Jock Milne, would be able to stabilise him.

Harvey resolved to consolidate their hold on the ground floor and the stairs, so as to keep the enemy bottled in above. Via the Brens and the bazooka firing through the windows, they could still wreak havoc up there, while making sure the all-important ground floor remained theirs. One by one the key stations of the 14th Army's nerve centre fell to the attackers, as SAS and Garibaldini fought side by side, and Harvey and Sergeant Godwin held back the enemy at the staircase.

The 14th Army's map room, the registry and the W/T room were overrun in savage hand-to-hand combat, as figures fought and died amid the bloody chaos and confusion. Chilling screams rent the air. Some, from the floors above, had a distinctly female ring to them, but there was little time to worry about that now. Finally, the operations room itself was taken, and with it a distinctive figure fell victim to the assaulters.

'There was furious fighting,' the SAS report recorded of this moment, 'during which Colonel Lemelsen, the Chief of Staff, was killed.' Lemelsen, General Hauk's right-hand man, had been cornered in the ops room and gunned down.

It was now that the nineteen-year-old Lieutenant Harvey took a momentous decision. Time was running out and they needed a means to finish the job. 'No enemy remained alive on this floor,' he reported; 'outside our Bren gunners were continuing their good work, and many Germans were killed when they tried to shoot from the windows or run out the back door.'

But it was impossible to take the entire villa in the twenty minutes allotted. Instead, he decided to raze it, using fire. Harvey gave the order. Working frantically, his men grabbed heaps of 14th Army papers, maps, cypher and code books, piling them up in the map room, the registry and the operations room itself. They threw on broken furniture and added explosives, just to make sure the bonfires would go with a real bang and truly take hold.

As a final flourish, Harvey sent one of his men to search the villa outhouses for some petrol. He was back shortly brandishing a can. They sloshed it liberally over the piles of combustibles, as gunfire echoed from the upper floor, the surviving Germans fighting to prevent what they feared was coming, and the Brens hammered answering fire through shattered windows. Harvey and his men beat back several attempts to storm down the staircase, as the mountains of combustibles were set afire. Flames danced up the curtains and flashed across the debris-strewn floors, a thick pall of smoke rolling through the villa, billowing up the staircase and choking all.

Even as the fire at Villa Calvi took hold, Lees charged higher up Villa Rossi's spiral staircase, intent on reaching General Hauk's sleeping quarters. But as he dashed across a lower landing and climbed towards a second, he heard a cry of warning from behind. Before he could react a flash cut through the shadows above, and instantaneously a bolt of agony pulsed through his chest. Moments later he tumbled backwards, feeling his head crack against the floor.

Lees had rolled partly down the staircase before coming to a halt. It seemed as if something inordinately heavy lay across his legs, pinning him down. He felt along his body, realising there was someone lying across him, unmoving. His hand came away grasping a red beret, but it was drenched in blood. Lees tried to remember who had been with him on the staircase and could only think that it was Gordon, the commander of his Black Owls.

He started yelling now, urging those below to redouble their efforts to storm the upper floors. He pushed the body off his legs, as the roar of tommy guns from below grew into a deafening crescendo. Over all, he fancied he could hear the evocative tones of Kirkpatrick's bagpipes. They seemed to be saying: 'Get up, get up, why are you lying there,' Lees recalled. 'Why was I lying there? I felt no pain. There seemed nothing wrong.'

He clambered to his feet but collapsed again almost as quickly. His left leg was dangling limp and unresponsive. No matter how he tried to focus, the leg would not respond to anything that his mind told it to do. Savage fire was traded back and forth, as heavy boots thundered up the stairs once more. The distinctive form of Lieutenant Riccomini led the charge, with Serjeant Guscott close behind.

They dashed past Lees, racing for the upper landing. Riccomini had all but made it, tommy gun blazing, when a round caught him in the head, felling him instantly. It was obvious by the way that he had fallen that he'd been killed outright. Serjeant Guscott bent to drag his body clear, but then, enraged at the SAS lieutenant's loss, he turned and charged back up the staircase once more.

Guscott reached the landing beside the fallen Lees, yelling for others to follow. But as he turned back to the charge a burst from above tore into him, and a second Operation Galia veteran was cut down, dying where he fell. Both men had volunteered for this mission, though their Galia heroics had by rights earned them well-deserved leave. For their dedication and their courage on the Villa Rossi staircase, Lieutenant Riccomini and Serjeant Guscott had paid the ultimate price.

As for Mike Lees, his very life hung in the balance. Heavily wounded and unable to move, he was trapped between the guns of his own side and those of the enemy. The German defenders seemed emboldened by their kills. It was their turn to attempt to rush the staircase. As jackboots thundered down the polished stone steps, their charge was met by a hail of fire from below. Three of their number were cut down, falling in a torn and bloodied heap beside the bodies of Riccomini and Guscott, and with that their counter-attack faltered and died.

It was clear to all now – attackers and defenders – that the battle for the staircase had reached a stalemate. With all three of their commanders cut down – SAS, SOE and Black Owls – the Villa Rossi raiding force had been left bereft of a leader. Their half of the mission, at least, was turning into something of a disaster.

At Villa Calvi, the flames crackled and roared deafeningly and a series of explosions rocked the ground floor. Moments later, Harvey gave the order to withdraw. As they raced for the exit, his thirty-odd fighters little realised what awaited outside. They crowded through the blasted entranceway, which was billowing thick smoke, only to find themselves under attack from several directions.

'Despite our determined and accurate gunfire,' Harvey reported, of his Bren-gunners, 'grenades from above were being thrown onto the lawn and we had to run the gauntlet. Germans were now in the road where I had killed the sentries and they were firing towards the house. Our exit fully silhouetted against the fire was not easy and how we managed to get out without further casualties I do not know.'

Suffering only the two wounded, Harvey ordered his force to turn their guns on the villa. Figures were trying to drop from upper windows or dash out of the doors, as the fire and smoke took savage hold. 'We kept up our fire outside as more and more of the trapped enemy in the house tried to get out,' Harvey reported. Finally, having checked his watch and realising they had run well over their allotted time, he ordered his men to fall back. Having hit and hit hard, it was time to run.

At his position by the roadside, Farran was growing anxious. He kept fingering his Very pistol, wondering whether to fire the signal to end the attack. The twenty minutes was long past, but by the ferocity of the firing the battle for the villas was still underway. It was then that he noticed the red glow of flames licking high around the roof of Villa Calvi, lighting up the night sky. There at least the raiders seemed to have done their work.

Beside him, Kirkpatrick's bagpipes wailed, but they were in danger of being drowned out by the cacophony of enemy fire. A barrage of mortars tore into Half Moon Wood, crashing into the southern fringes of Villa Calvi's grounds and sending shrapnel winging through the trees. That was the terrain over which Harvey and his men were scheduled to withdraw. It was one thing launching such an attack against orders, and getting away with few losses. It would be quite another if his force was devastated, most being captured or killed.

One or two figures hurried through the trees, making for Farran's position. They were Russian and Italian stragglers – the first of those starting a spontaneous retreat. Soon, German reinforcements would break through Modena's cordon, Farran reasoned, for the battle-hardened Russians had to be running seriously short of ammo. If he and his men were to stand any chance of escape, now was the time to sound the retreat.

Farran raised his Very pistol and fired three red flares in rapid succession – the signal to withdraw. The first reaction was a spray of Spandau fire, as the ever-alert German gunners targeted his position. No doubt about it – it was time to get the hell out of there.

*

At Villa Rossi, Mike Lees began to crawl. While his leg was incapable of supporting his weight, it seemed to work as far as the knee, which meant he could inch along on all fours. Apart from the dead, he found himself alone on the bloodied staircase. Now, with his strength ebbing with every effort, he made a desperate bid to drag himself down, with the aim of making for the villa's exit. It would take a truly Herculean effort to get there, and then what? But he wasn't dead yet and God knows he wasn't the type to give in. He made the ground floor of the villa and, gritting his teeth, forced himself to keep crawling.

Kershaw, the former Olympic bobsleigher, had taken charge here on the ground floor. He remembered the final words that Farran had spoken to him, back at the Casa del Lupo: *If we cannot force a way in . . . surround them, burn them down and see that no one escapes.* While Private Raphael Ramos, the fearless Spanish Civil War veteran and French Foreign Legionnaire, kept the Germans bottled in upstairs, he and a group of fellow SAS tore down curtains, grabbed soft furnishings and wooden chairs and piled them in a heap in the kitchen.

It was centrally located, and it looked as if it would burn ferociously, once the mountain of combustibles had been ignited. They had been here, fighting for their very lives for well over thirty minutes now. As Kershaw set a match to the pile, fanning it into a roaring furnace of flame, he yelled to the others to prepare to evacuate. If they could burn General Hauk and his surviving fellow officers to death, that would be fitting revenge for the three commanders they had lost on the Villa Rossi staircase – Riccomini, Gordon and Mike Lees.

On duty at the stairs, Ramos reckoned he'd accounted for

'Wild Man' Lees – arm around horse – was already in the field, along with his radio operator, Bert Farrimond, (standing on his left), priest and partisan commander Don Carlo (astride horse), and fellow SOE agent Major Ernest Wilcockson (on Lees' right). Lees welcomed Farran and his SAS with open arms.

Having parachuted in against orders on a mission codenamed Operation Tombola, Farran linked up with Lees, billeting his forty-strong SAS at a derelict church. The enemy had executed the priest for supporting the partisans, so there was no more fitting place from which to plot revenge.

Lees had established his base at the remote village of Secchio, just a few kilometres to the rear of the Gothic Line. From there he called in weapons drops to arm the partisans, and raised a force of female agents – his 'Stafettas' – to spy out choice German targets.

Spanish SAS veteran Franscisco Jeronimo with female recruits. The 'Stafettas' were armed and would fight if necessary, but their real power lay in using their seduction skills to lure enemy troops into giving away crucial secrets.

Lees and Farran trained the partisans to use heavy machine guns and mortars, which were parachuted in by fleets of American DC3 'Dakota' cargo aircraft.

Some partisan bands, like this one led by Major Ian Mckenna, were charged to safeguard key targets like hydro-electric dams from cnemy sabotage.

SOE Major Bernard 'John' Barton was scheduled to join Lees and Farran, charged to hunt down a top German general, inspiring Lees and Farran to target senior enemy commanders.

Lees sought intelligence on an enemy HQ that Field Marshal Kesselring was known to frequent. Dressed in local garb to recce the target, he discovered that the HQ – seat of the German 14th Army and situated in two fortress-like villas – controlled a vast stretch of the Gothic Line, commanding some 100,000 enemy troops.

Farran and Lees raised a force to hit the German HQ. It consisted of SAS, Italian partisans, Russian fighters who had fled enemy captivity and a smattering of German deserters. They rode in captured vehicles, Union Jacks roped over the roofs to safeguard them from marauding Allied warplanes.

On 26 March 1945 the raiders set out to destroy the HQ and kill the senior officers. Farran and Lees decided to ignore last-minute orders to stand down: it was impossible to command such guerrilla forces to a strict timescale, and they would never get another chance.

The raiders struck at night, having penetrated fearsome defences. Taking the enemy by surprise they torched the HQ villas, killing some sixty enemy and wreaking havoc on the 14 Army's command and communications.

Francis William Mulvey, an SAS veteran, was one of those wounded in action during the 14 Army HQ raid.

Days later, the Allied assault on the Gothic Line was launched, but the fighting proved ferocious with the enemy giving no quarter.

With Lees badly wounded, Farran's SAS launched all-out warfare, striking hard and fast from their mountain bases. During one such daring raid SAS Spaniard Justo Balerdi – battle name Robert Bruce – (centre photo, with cigarette), was shot in the head and killed.

Using mortars and a 75mm Howitzer nicknamed Molto Stanco – 'very tired', seen here in a photo with the Italian SAS detachment – the SAS shelled enemy lines, convincing German commanders that Allied forces had broken through and forcing them to abandon their positions.

By the third week of April 1945 the Gothic Line was broken. As northern Italy fell, the SAS staged victory parades with their partisan brothers-in-arms.

Post-war Roy Farran (in SAS beret) and Mike Lees paid regular visits to commemorate the partisan actions. WWII SAS veteran Jack Mann (in glasses) stands on Farran's immediate right.

Lest we forget. A reunion at Villa Rossi, former sight of the 14th Army HQ, with SAS veteran Lt. David Eyton-Jones far right. The plaque behind lists those SAS and others who died in the raid.

six German officers, as they'd made repeated attempts to storm their way down and reclaim the villa's ground floor. With thick smoke billowing through the rooms he finally turned to leave, firing one last burst up the bullet-pocked stairway. As he went to depart he all but tumbled over a figure on the floor. It was Mike Lees, doggedly crawling on his bullet-torn legs and making for the villa's entrance.

Ramos reached to help the wounded SOE officer, as a third figure joined them. It was Siciliano, one of Lees' Black Owls, who began yelling excitedly above the din of battle.

'*Capitano! Capitano!* Come away!' he told Lees. 'We could not get up the stairs. We are going to burn the place down.'

'Who's that?' Lees croaked a reply.

'Siciliano. We are going to burn the place down!'

'Plus it's Ramos,' the Spaniard added. 'We've got to get you out of here.'

Ramos and Siciliano draped Lees around their shoulders, hauled the wounded captain to his feet and hustled him towards the villa's smoke-enshrouded doorway. As waves of pain and nausea swept over him, Lees began alternately to hop and to be half-carried outside. They emerged from the burning villa to be met by 'heavy machine gun fire', enemy soldiers crowding the windows above them.

Leaving Lees in cover, Ramos dashed back inside to deter any who might attempt to shoot them down. Only once the flames and smoke took irrevocable hold, making any attempt to reach the ground floor impossible, did Ramos leave. With Siciliano's help he took up the thirteen-stone form of Lees, and the trio made a dash for the cover of the nearby woodland. It was the thick smoke billowing from the windows that saved them. As they stumbled for the trees, heavy bursts of fire ricocheted around their ears, but the shots went wide of the mark.

They limped into cover, miraculously dodging enemy fire and laden down with the injured Lees. The area remained 'alive with angry Germans', and behind them a lone figure was cut down. Typically one of the last to break fire, SAS Corporal Sammy Bolden was caught in a furious fusillade of bullets and grenades unleashed from the villa's upper floor as the enemy fought to the bitter end. Veteran of Operation Cartoon, the daring Commando raid off Norway's coast, Bolden was another to fall victim to the lack of time allotted to the Villa Rossi assault.

With Lees in tow, Ramos and Siciliano retraced their steps towards the rendezvous point, as behind them the firing at last died down to sporadic bursts. The three paused so they could catch their breath. Siciliano turned back towards the two villas. 'Look, look, they are burning!' he exclaimed, excitedly.

Lees glanced where the man indicated: a halo of angry red lit up a wide swathe of sky. Villa Calvi appeared like a raging inferno; Villa Rossi too was wreathed in thick smoke and flames. In spite of his injuries, Lees felt a flood of relief. Against all odds it seemed that they had accomplished what they had come here to do.

'We must hurry, *Capitano*,' Siciliano urged.

He was right: the time to flee was now. But Lees felt overcome by a crushing sense of hopelessness. 'I'll never crawl thirty miles back to the mountains and they can't drag me that far,' he told himself. He felt so weak and faint he didn't particularly care what happened to him any more.

He turned to Siciliano and Ramos. 'Leave me here, my friends . . . I must stay and take my chances with the Germans.'

The men shook their heads, emphatically. 'To be tortured? Never!'

Siciliano and Ramos managed to attract the attention of another SAS man, a giant of a red-headed Irishman called Patrick 'Pat' Burke. Together the three began to hurry Lees' bloodied form through the last of the trees, as they sought out Farran and the rest of the party.

But by the time they reached the RV point, the SAS commander and his raiders were nowhere to be seen.

Chapter 17

At Villa Calvi Lieutenant Harvey had decided to do the unexpected and dispense with the immediate RV. 'As our troops got thinner on the ground the Germans would soon be rushing about unhindered and here we were, still in the middle of the hornet's nest . . . I decided to head in the opposite direction . . . this would probably deceive the enemy, who would try to cut us off on the direct route back to the mountains. We were extremely tired and the extra miles I was inflicting on my men was not an easy decision . . .'

Harvey pushed north through the darkness, before turning west, giving the burning HQ as wide a berth as possible. 'We walked straight through an enemy post unchallenged and cut the telephone wires,' he reported. 'I got a severe shock while cutting the wires strung along a hedge. One was a power line!' By severing lines of communication, they would spread more confusion among the enemy, which could only boost their chances of escape.

But Harvey's task was far from easy. His thirty-odd battle-worn men were laden down with injured – Parachutist Mulvey, shot in the knee, and Corporal Layburn, suffering from his grenade wounds. Harvey decided the 'risk to the remainder of us was too great', if they attempted to flee with both men. Mulvey, whose knee had been shattered, was the least mobile. It made sense to leave him. 'Having explained this to my men, a couple of them volunteered to stay . . .' Harvey recorded, '[in order that] this small party could hide up and make its way back more easily . . .'

Harvey's report, written sometime after the raids, makes it all sound so simple and straightforward. In truth, this must have been one of the most fraught decisions for a commander to have to make – to leave three of his men behind, one severely wounded – let alone for an inexperienced lieutenant of just nineteen years, engaged on his first combat mission.

Harvey advised the three stay-behinds to hide up during daylight, to move only at night and to live off the land as they edged their way towards the safety of the mountains. With that agreed, the main force departed, heading for the fallback RV point – Casa del Lupo, the House of the Wolf – the wounded Parachutist Mulvey being left in the care of his two fellows.

At his roadside position just south of the burning villas, Farran had waited and waited. He'd delayed for as long as he dared, but there had been no sign of either the wounded Lees or those who were supposedly helping him to safety. Lees had been strapped to a discarded ladder to form a makeshift stretcher, or so Farran had been told, but he and his bearers failed to materialise. Finally, as the sky blazed an angry crimson, Farran gave the signal for the off.

Lieutenant Harvey and the Villa Calvi raiding party were nowhere to be seen, but it made sense they were making their own way to the fall-back RV. Likewise Modena and his Russians. It was the badly wounded Lees who worried Farran. Regardless, he took up position at the head of what remained of his raiding party and set a course due west, making for the Crostollo river, a tributary of the Po. They'd trekked in moving up the Crostollo's eastern bank. To execute their escape, he planned to cross the river, before turning south towards Casa del Lupo.

It was 0225 hours on 27 March 1945 when they hurried away from the 14th Army HQ. A raid scheduled to last twenty minutes had morphed into a ninety-minute epic. As Farran well knew, time was set against them now – they had precious few remaining hours of darkness in which to execute their flight into the safety of the hills.

Behind them, star shells burst like a firework display across the night sky, illuminating a scene of utter devastation. 'It was a satisfying sight,' Farran wrote. 'If only we could regain the safety of the mountains, the raid could be marked up as at least a partial success.'

Indeed, Farran had received reports that General Hauk himself had died during the fighting at Villa Rossi. That, plus the utter inferno of devastation wreaked at Villa Calvi – the 14th Army's operational HQ – was approaching the knock-out blow that he and Lees had hungered for.

The withdrawal turned into something of a helter-skelter dash. Parties split up into smaller groups as they raced for the river. By something close to a miracle they managed to link up at the crossing point, after which Farran formed up his column. Though they were plagued by a crushing fatigue, he couldn't countenance the slightest pause. Already the sky to the east was lightening, and convoys of German trucks could be heard racing along the road ahead of them – reinforcements, making for the headquarters.

Sporadic bursts of fire echoed from the direction of the burning villas. Either there were remnants of Modena's Russians still in action, or the Germans were shooting at ghosts. The progress of Farran's weary column proved frustrating slow, and he was desperate to cross the road before first light. From that direction came the steely clatter of tank tracks, forcing the ragged line of men to go to ground. They lay low for several minutes, as the rattle faded into silence.

Farran drove his men onwards. In his haste, he made an error of navigation. It was only the eagle-eyed gaze of one of his men that saved them. He pointed out a warning sign – they'd almost stumbled into an anti-aircraft battery. To skirt around it, they were forced to execute another exhausting detour. Finally, they reached the road. Choosing a moment when it seemed deserted of traffic, Farran urged his men across. Figures flitted over in the half-light, dirtied and bent double like so many scurrying rats.

Moments later, they hit the slope that ascended to the first ridgeline, upon which perched the fall back RV – Casa del Lupo. The farmer hardly seemed overjoyed at the raiders' return. After the night's dramatic pyrotechnics, he'd finally grasped that the mystery force weren't Germans, after all. He was scared stiff at their reappearance and begged them to leave as soon as possible. Farran needed little urging – they couldn't afford to tarry.

Lieutenant Harvey's force straggled into the RV, and together the surviving commanders got a quick heads-up as to the cost of the battle and the fate of the missing. While the British losses – two dead, three wounded – were extraordinarily light, con-sidering the carnage they had wrought, Farran took the news particularly badly. It was the death of Lieutenant Riccomini that hit him hardest, 'one of the bravest chaps that ever lived.'

'It was his second operation in three months,' Farran would write of Riccomini's loss, 'and by rights he should have been resting in safety . . . Another grave loss was Serjeant Guscott, who marched across the mountains . . . to join me.' Guscott had made the epic sixty-mile journey on foot through 'awful country' to join the SAS raiders. 'It is strange how the best men are always the first to die. Perhaps we others are not good enough.'

But for now, there were several dozen of those 'others' whom Farran somehow had to spirit to safety. Modena's Russians arrived, minus half a dozen of their number. Those six had been captured in fierce fighting, and few doubted what dark fate now awaited them. Along with the absent Mike Lees, Gordon, the Black Owls commander, was also missing. But the news on Gordon at least seemed somewhat promising: wounded on the Villa Rossi staircase alongside Lees, he'd been dragged out and carried away from the burning villa by his Black Owls.

Farran had no idea where those two wounded commanders might be. Lees and Gordon – plus their stretcher-bearers – were missing, fate unknown. They would have to fend for themselves. He was incapable of offering any kind of assistance, not least until he made the safety of the Secchia valley, which lay over forty kilometres due south of their present position. It would be a far greater distance, of course, using the convoluted series of paths and tracks that Farran intended to follow.

The sun rose, flooding the expanse of rumpled foothills before them with a fierce light, and making their onward journey an even more daunting proposition. Near by, the byres in which the men had slept the previous day beckoned enticingly, but Farran was having none of it. Within a matter of minutes he had formed up his ragged band for the off.

'The strain of the fighting and the carrying of the wounded men was telling on us all,' reported Lieutenant Harvey, 'but we had to keep going. It was daylight now and we had to get as many miles between us and the scene of the action in the shortest possible time. The odds against us in the attack on the Headquarters had been great . . . and the enemy would surely send a very large force after us . . . We could ill-afford in our present state to fight them. We had lost one-third of our force killed and wounded . . .' And missing, of course.

Harvey found a decrepit old mule in one of the barns. That would have to do for the wounded Corporal Layburn. After Farran had dressed Layburn's wounds with bandages, they roped him tightly to the saddle. He was far more badly injured than most had imagined, when he'd stumbled doggedly from the scene of the attack. Caught in the grenade blast at the foot of the Villa Calvi staircase, Layburn's legs had been peppered with shrapnel.

Once strapped into the saddle they hung limply down. Despite the bandaging, they oozed blood. But the most amazing thing was that the wounded corporal had yet to cry out, despite the agony of his injuries. Farran ordered the off, making it clear there could be no more halts.

At first spirits were remarkably high. A soft mist cloaked the ground, which should aid in their escape. Stories were whispered back and forth down the line of march, as men recounted the wildest of tales of the night's action. The best seemed to be that of a certain German officer who had been chased onto the lawn of the Villa Rossi, dressed only in his pyjamas. Thin cotton had done little to stop bullets.

But as the day progressed the sky clouded over and a thin rain began to fall. It made the path underfoot muddy and treacherous. Here and there villagers hurried past, looking distinctly harried. They all spoke of the same thing – the countryside thereabouts was crawling with vengeful Germans. Their patrols were everywhere, the locals reported, and all roads were blocked. This time Farran didn't doubt their word. It was exactly as he had expected.

'We were too short of ammunition and our weapons had fallen too often in the mud for us to look for a fight,' he remarked. Their only hope of escape lay in slipping through undetected. As the raiders trudged onwards, voices charged with the thrill of battle fell silent. Farran kept them marching through the rain, and they straggled out on the path behind. Like the others, he began to swallow Benzedrine tablets as if they were boiled sweets.

Before long, the old mule carrying Layburn had to be abandoned. Half-blind, it kept stumbling in the mud, causing the wounded man to slip sideways. Eventually it collapsed, trapping Layburn. Men whose limbs were leaden with fatigue fashioned a makeshift stretcher from cut branches strung with parachute blouses. With one man on each corner they hoisted the injured Layburn and began to carry him, stretcher poles balanced on their shoulders.

The stretcher-bearers were so tired they repeatedly collapsed to their knees in the mud. Despite his old injuries, Farran took his turn at this exhausting task. Eventually, Layburn asked to be left behind. None would hear of it. They marched blindly, reeling forwards as if on a drunken sally home from the pub. Farran was painfully aware of their predicament: if they met a German patrol of any strength they were virtually incapable of resistance.

Bearing weapons caked thick with mud from repeated falls, they dispensed with scouts even. No one had the energy to dash from ridgetop to ridgetop ahead of the party. Farran led them over a main highway without a pause, not even bothering to check if it was clear of the enemy. Somehow they made it across. They trudged through the centre of a village, making no attempt at any kind of concealment. Locals stared at their harrowed, muddied faces in open astonishment.

Meanwhile, a few dozen kilometres to their rear two other parties of desperate fugitives slipped into precarious hiding. One was made up of the two men from Lieutenant Harvey's force, bearing the injured SAS Parachutist Mulvey between them. An Irishman, an underage Mulvey had actually falsified his date of birth, so as to qualify for recruitment into the British military. Now, as a baleful sun rose high over the plains of the Po, he and his escorts darted into an isolated farmstead, begging shelter and aid.

They were blessed with good fortune. As luck would have it, the family were resolute supporters of the resistance. On the kitchen table Mulvey had his shattered knee bathed and dressed, whereupon the three men were shown to a place of hiding. Wads of cash were thrust into the farmer's hands, as a token of their gratitude. He seemed grateful, though money would do little to save him and his family, should the Germans come calling.

A patrol of German soldiers had arrived at the Albinea church that morning, bearing three bodies – those of Licutenant Riccomini, Serjeant Guscott and Corporal Bolden. The priest was ordered to organise a grave-digging party. He chose a spot in the north-eastern corner of the ccmetery, which overlooked the direction of the two villas, which even now were wreathed in thick smoke. That the dead were 'Commandos' was seen as being proof that this had been a British-led raid, which was good for the locals, for it militated against reprisals.

If anything, Mike Lees found himself in the most perilous situation of all of the raid's survivors. His journey that morning had been an utter nightmare. Strapped on the ladder, Siciliano,

Ramos and Burke had hurried him through open terrain, desperately seeking refuge. With the enemy headquarters just two miles behind them they had collapsed exhaustedly at a farmstead. There Lees learned that the wounded Gordon – his Black Owls commander – was with them. Gordon's leg was broken, so both he and Lees were stretcher cases, and there seemed little hope that they might escape a vengeful enemy.

The party pressed on, the inferno of the burning villas red and angry at their backs. Three hours later the stretcher-bearers stumbled into a barn. It formed part of a farm that was owned by 'friends', Lees was told; rock-solid allies of the resistance. As Ramos and Burke went to close the massive barn doors, Lees raised himself weakly on one elbow. In the distance the sky was burnished red where the 14th Army HQ blazed. How on earth could they stay here, he wondered, in plain sight of the target they had so audaciously attacked?

Lees didn't have long to ponder the question. He and Gordon were carried to a bed of straw and laid down to rest. Their escorts built a pile of bales around their place of hiding, until it would appear from the outside to be a solid stack of hay. At least, that was their intention. An old farmer woman lived there alone, and only she would know where they were hidden. She had been sworn to absolute secrecy.

Ramos, Burke and Siciliano, plus the other stretcher-bearers, prepared to depart. They had to try to make it back to the Secchia valley, and they were leaving Lees and Gordon in the hands of the very capable local resistance. One of the partisans reassured Lees that his sister, who lived in a nearby town, would come to visit within the next few hours. She was a nurse and she would be able to tend to his, and Gordon's, wounds.

Lees had one last request, before the three departed. He got Burke to scribble down a note to Farran, dictating what he wanted to say. Riddled with gunshot wounds, incapable of movement, bereft of proper medical attention, and marooned in the heart of enemy territory, he knew his chances were slim. Now, he figured, was the time to tell it like it was.

'Dear Old Roy – I think we pulled it off fairly well,' Lees began. 'I got my dose with Gordon and Sgt. Guscott being slap-happy and trying to get upstairs in Villa Rossi. Wounded in . . . left leg and right shoulder. Gordon got a smashed leg. Guscott dead. These two English boys carried me away, with the help of the Garibaldini.' By 'these two English boys' he meant Burke and Ramos, an Irishman and a Spaniard – both honorary Brits in the SAS.

'I hope the show was a success,' he continued. 'I am at Rivalta near Canali, hiding up and hoping not to be caught . . . Look after the show for me as I will be laid up for a long time . . . and tell Charles Macintosh to fuck himself.' The sentiments directed at Macintosh reflected the level of Lees' anger at Florence head-quarters. Though not privy to all of their machinations, he was convinced they had had it in for him. In effect, this was his death's-bed revenge.

Lees ended the missive asking Farran to get a letter through to his wife, Gwen, 'saying I am OK.' The letter was signed '(Written as dictated for Capt Lees) (Pat Burke)'.

Burke folded the sheet of paper into his pocket, and with that he, Ramos, Siciliano and the others hurried out of the barn, swinging the doors shut behind them, and leaving the stricken forms of Mike Lees and Glauco Monducci – Gordon – in pitch darkness. As exhaustion, trauma and blood loss got the better of them – not to mention Lees' malaria – the two men drifted into an exhausted sleep.

Their last waking thoughts were whether anyone would ever come to find them.

Chapter 18

By the time they stumbled into the final approach to Valestra, the village from which they'd set out, Farran and his party's endurance was at its very end. They had been marching for over twenty hours with barely a break, but even so Farran decided a little show was in order, to mark their muddied, bloodied return. That they had evaded capture was little short of a miracle, for which he could only think to give thanks.

He ordered his ragged line to form up into columns, three abreast, with those carrying the injured Layburn taking up the lead. As they approached the village, Farran told his piper to play. Though he was utterly wrecked, Kirkpatrick summoned the strength to blow life into his bagpipes. Women came to their doorways, drawn by the music, and they cheered. Crowds of excited children began to scamper along, marking the column's progress.

To left and right, exhausted men did their best to pick up sore and leaden feet and march in time to the piping. Shoulders were thrust higher and backs straightened, as the men realised they had made it through the enemy lines to the Secchia valley, their place of refuge. Farran hoped that the pursuing Germans might hear the notes of the bagpipes, and take them for defiant proof that the British raiders had reached a point beyond their easy reach.

After leading the Valestra victory parade, Farran's legs gave up on him completely. From somewhere a horse was found to carry him the last few miles. It was midnight by the time the raiders marched into Tapignola, making their way to their church quarters. They were met with a tumultuous reception, but most were far too gone to care.

'The men bedded down in the cattle shed and the wounded were given attention,' Lieutenant Harvey reported. 'I too snatched a couple of hours sleep, my first since the few we had had . . . before setting out . . .' While there were few medical facilities at Tapignola, SAS doctor Jock Milne transformed the church's hallowed grounds into a makeshift hospital. So professional was the care the injured were to receive there, that when eventually they had the bullets and shrapnel removed from their wounds, there were to be few if any complications.

Utterly spent, Farran was put to bed in the house of a local schoolmistress, who happened to be away. All in all, they had marched for twenty-two hours to escape the enemy dragnet, and, bar the halt at Casa del Lupo, they'd been on the go for fully two days. Counting the cost of the raid, the losses were incredibly light . . . so far: two British dead, two missing presumed dead, three wounded (two of whom – Mulvey and Mike Lees – were missing); three Italians wounded (one missing) and six Russians captured (and presumably summarily executed), plus two wounded. At first Farran believed General Hauk himself had been killed, but recent reports were equivocal. Even so, Colonel Lemelsen, his Chief of Staff, was dead, as were countless others of his officers and men.

They'd turned Villa Calvi into a gutted ruin, and Villa Rossi was also badly fire-damaged. More importantly, the entire nerve centre of the 14th Army – maps, registry and operations room – had been eviscerated. As Farran would report, 'Villa Calvi was completely destroyed along with the greatest part of the Headquarters' papers, files and maps.' The enemy must have realised they were far from safe anywhere. Incredibly, the convoys of trucks arriving at Botteghe the morning after the assault weren't just bringing in reinforcements: they were also there to evacuate whatever remained of the headquarters.

Farran fully expected a reaction of utmost savagery, to answer the daring and audacity of the raid. But first, back on the plains of the Po, Mike Lees and Gordon had visitors.

Even as Farran had fallen into an exhausted sleep in the schoolmistress's bed, so Lees had heard the creak of midnight hinges, as the door to their barn was swung ajar. Voices whispered softly in Italian, as bales of hay were prised aside. By the light of a lantern Lees spied the farmer woman with two pretty young Italian ladies at her side. The taller of the two stepped forwards.

'I am Gianni's sister,' she introduced herself, Gianni being the partisan leader whom Lees held in such high esteem. 'My friend and I have come to stay with you . . . You will have more visitors tonight. Antonio is bringing a doctor.'

Lees asked the obvious question: 'Who's Antonio?'

'He's the leader of the resistance in this area.'

She turned to ask for hot water. Minutes later the old farmer lady was back, hefting a huge and smoke-blackened kettle. Together, the two young women set about readying Lees and Gordon for the doctor. Lees heard the Black Owls commander groaning in agony, as they cut his trousers off him. He had been shot on the staircase at the same time as Lees, a bullet shattering his leg.

One of the women turned to Lees. 'Where are you wounded?'

'I don't know; I can't feel or move my leg below the knee,' he explained.

Having ripped up his trousers – they were stiff with congealed blood – she still couldn't find any injury. Eventually, she discovered a bullet hole in Lees' hip, and another in the back of his leg, just above the knee. He wondered what that might mean. Another round had passed clean through his chest, with a fourth hitting his left arm and a final one passing through the calf of his right leg.

'As they worked tenderly and efficiently cleansing and bandaging the wounds, I reflected how lucky I was still to be alive,' Lees observed, with signature understatement. The doctor arrived. He'd clearly been brought there against his will, and he kept muttering darkly as he inspected the two men's wounds. With the help of the young women he managed to improvise a rough wooden splint for Gordon's leg.

But after studying Lees' injuries, the doctor confirmed what he had most been fearing. 'The nerve has been hit.'

'How long until it gets better?' Lees asked. He needed to be well enough to walk and to escape.

The doctor shrugged. 'Who knows? I can do nothing. You should be in hospital.'

Lees hardly needed a medical doctor to tell him that. He felt his hand tighten around the revolver hidden beneath his blanket. The nearest Allied lines were over fifty miles away and the plains were crawling with the enemy, so where exactly did the doctor suggest he find a hospital? His mind flipped to thoughts of Gwen, the woman he'd only recently married. Thank God she didn't know of his plight. Most likely, she would be asleep right now, dreaming of their future together, but that future had never felt so far away.

The doctor left. He was right: Lees did need to get to hospital. The question was, how? It was then that Antonio, the local resistance leader, showed himself. He'd not wanted the doctor to see him, or at least not in his present role. He was small and wiry and dressed in a thick leather coat, but the most remarkable thing about him was his weapon: he had a big German Spandau slung across his chest, which quite simply dwarfed him.

Having introduced himself, he gave it to Lees straight. 'The Germans are searching everywhere for you. You must move tomorrow. It's not safe to stay here.'

'But how can we do that?' Lees asked.

Antonio shrugged, unconcernedly. 'Ah, we will find a way. We can do nothing at night. There is a curfew and patrols everywhere following your attack.'

'So how did it go?' Lees couldn't help but be curious.

Antonio's face creased into a smile. Ambulances had been buzzing to and fro for twenty-four hours, he explained, ferrying the wounded to the hospital in Reggio. At the town's cemetery, ranks of fresh graves had been dug. Villa Calvi was a gutted wreck, and Villa Rossi was fire-scorched and deserted. As for the Germans, they seemed both terrified and furious in equal measure.

Antonio pulled out a cutting from a local Fascist paper and handed it to Lees. 'Last night a strong force of bandits attacked the garrison stationed at Botteghe,' the report said. 'After fierce fighting they withdrew, having suffered heavy losses. It is believed these brigands were British and some damage was done.'

Apart from the disinformation it contained, one other thing did make Lees smile: Farran's piping of 'Highland Laddie' had clearly done the trick. A British signature had been stamped indelibly on the 14th Army HQ raid, and there had been no mention in the article of any reprisals.

'Did we kill the general?' Lees asked, popping the question foremost in his mind.

'I don't know,' Antonio answered. 'Many officers were killed, and he has not been seen since.'

With that Antonio left, promising to return later with a plan for how they might move the two wounded men. Instinctively, Lees liked the resistance leader. He seemed a straight-talker and remarkably unfazed by their present predicament. Once Antonio was gone, the young women injected Lees and Gordon with morphine, to help ease the pain. That done they closed the bales of hay around them, leaving them to sleep.

Sometime later Lees was shaken awake. A hand closed around his mouth, as a voice hissed close on his ear: 'Don't make a sound.' It was one of the nurses.

Beside him, Gordon had his back propped against some bales and his pistol gripped in hand. Outside, Lees could hear a woman wailing in distress.

'Fascists,' the nurse murmured. '*Brigate Nere.* They are searching everywhere.'

The *Brigate Nere* were known for their bloodthirsty brutality. If they were discovered, he and Gordon would have no choice but to go down fighting. Lees struggled onto his one good knee, readying his pistol. Neither man would want to be taken alive.

He gestured to the rear of the barn, eyeing the nurses worriedly. 'For God's sake, slip away now, while you still have a chance.'

The nearest one smiled. 'We are partisans too, and you are in *my* charge,' she said with emphasis, revealing the tiny revolver she had hidden in the palm of her hand. 'Lie down,' she added, 'and keep quiet and still.'

The old woman's voice sounded nearer now. 'There is nothing there, I swear! It is only a barn.'

Then the sound of a blow and the wailing started again. The door crashed open, light flooding in. For several long seconds there was silence, as the Black Brigade militiamen scrutinised the barn's interior. Then the door crashed closed and the voices died away.

The nurse beside Lees was crying softly. 'Thank God,' she muttered, 'but we must get you away today.'

It was early on the morning of 28 March when the *Brigate Nere* had searched Lees and Gordon's place of hiding. In the Secchia valley, Roy Farran had just woken from the mother of all sleeps. Following a hurried breakfast he had a first, urgent task to perform: he needed to break cover. Heaven only knew what would happen, once he broadcast news of the past forty-eight hours, but delaying could only make matters worse for all, especially Mike Lees.

He penned a short, succinct message, stripped of any of the high emotion of the moment, and had his radio operator send it. '51 Corps HQ attacked night of 26/27. Fair success. Heavy casualties. Fierce resistance. 40 German dead, one villa blown up, other partially destroyed. LEES wounded.'

Lord only knew what would result. Had Farran done enough to avoid the repercussions that the message might provoke? He just didn't know. More to the point, he had bigger things to worry about just now. His friend and fellow commander was wounded and at the mercy of the enemy, plus shortly the Secchia valley was bound to have visitors. Unwelcome ones.

'I expected the German reaction to our impudence would not be long delayed,' Farran wrote. 'And I was right.'

Farran's first priority was to muster the valley's defenders. That morning, he despatched Lieutenant Harvey back to the all-important Cisa Box, their final redoubt, boasting their 75mm howitzer, Molto Stanco. Runners were sent to the defensive positions scattered around the perimeter, carrying the same warning: they were to expect the enemy to come in strength and driven on by anger at the success of the Botteghe raid.

That morning Farran received the first worrying reports. Four columns of German troops were pushing towards the mouth of the Secchia valley, boasting some four hundred troops. They came equipped with mortars, two field guns and horse-drawn transport, which was not such an unusual form of carriage for German infantry moving through such terrain.

Facing them Farran had Lieutenant Mike Eld, a man hand-picked to hold this position. But Eld commanded a perilously thin line. Dug in on high ground overlooking the Secchia river, he had ten fellow SAS, armed with one mortar, one Vickers heavy machine gun and several Brens. On paper, it was something of a David versus Goliath confrontation, but thankfully Eld's tiny force was stiffened by the brigade of Garibaldini led by Gianni, the finest partisans in the entire valley, Farran believed.

As with Eld and his SAS, the Garibaldini had dug trenches along the ridgeline. So long as the river was in spring flood – swollen by meltwaters – their positions should hold against a full-frontal attack. The Germans advanced to the river's northern bank, from where savage battle was joined. Mortar barrages and machine-gun volleys scorched back and forth across the Secchia's boiling waters, as Eld targeted the enemy's chief point of vulnerability – their horse-drawn transport.

Lieutenant Eld had been busy while his commander was away, raiding the Botteghe headquarters. Repeatedly, he'd crossed the Secchia and paced out the distances to key targets, noting them down for future reference. As a result, as soon as a horse-drawn gun-carriage was spotted, Eld could call out distance and bearing to his mortar team and the shells would rain down. It must have been utterly unnerving for the enemy, who were blessed with no such foresight.

Typically, Eld had set upon some highly imaginative means to wrong-foot the enemy, and to make his tiny force seem far more numerous than it was. He got his men to open up with the Vickers machine gun, via pre-established lines. The Vickers was peculiarly suited to being fired in a parabolic trajectory, so effectively lobbing rounds over long range and from behind cover. In that way enemy troops were hit by savage bursts of highly-accurate fire, with little idea whence it came. It left the impression that multiple such weapons were in action.

Eld had signs posted along the riverbank warning of minefields. To give substance to such – imaginary – barriers, he had his men detonate charges of dynamite along the river, using timer-pencils (time-delay fuses). By such means, they had charges going off at all times of the day and night. Eld got the better of the first bruising exchanges of fire, but Farran remained concerned. His chief fear was that his front-line forces would run out of mortar and machine-gun rounds, for resupply by air was always an issue.

Accordingly, he mounted up his diminutive pony – the black stallion Jock Easton had procured for him – and rode out to the front-line. There he linked up with Gianni, the Garibaldini commander, who offered to guide him onwards, cautioning that they should continue on foot. Leaving his horse behind, Farran pushed ahead, as the rattle of machine-gun fire and the boom of exploding mortars grew ever louder. With Gianni warning him to keep his head down, they clambered into a trench, which led to the ridge top position.

Eld seemed delighted to have visitors. Having given Farran a quick tour of his positions, he asked for news of the raid and especially any casualties. Farran told him what he knew. Jock Milne, the medic, was working wonders at his Tapignola church-cum-hospital. That morning, the wounded Mulvey had arrived, after a hair-raising flight through enemy-held terrain and a miraculous escape. Jock Milne had already got to work stabilising his injuries. Mike Lees and Gordon were badly hurt, and they had been hidden under the very noses of the enemy. Farran was working on a plan to try to pluck them to safety.

Though saddened at the news of the loss of Riccomini and Guscott, who were hugely popular members of the SAS, Eld and his men were boosted by the success of the raid. As Farran scanned the enemy positions through his field glasses, Eld explained that he feared the Germans were there to stay. He'd landed a barrage of mortar bombs in the midst of a horse-drawn column and machine-gunned groups of infantry, but the grey-uniformed troops kept coming.

Eld reckoned they were establishing some kind of a forward base, in preparation for the big push. From what he observed, Farran had to agree. He ordered a show of strength, directing a pin point accurate mortar barrage that blasted into one of the enemy's positions, scattering their troops. But the Germans answered quickly and in kind, their field guns belching smoke and flame, 88mm shells tearing into the ridgeline and sending the defenders diving for cover.

Faced with such firepower Eld's force were outgunned, and as the enemy built its strength, they were heavily outnumbered. But whatever it might take, the enemy had to be prevented from crossing the Secchia, for the river was the Allied Battalion's crucial defensive line. If that was breached, the forces of the enemy could sweep into the valley all but unhindered.

With the Germans' initial build-up 'the position was becoming serious,' Farran concluded, 'and I was even more worried when I received reports of the arrival of enemy reinforcements.' He didn't doubt that more and fierce action was coming.

Sure enough, on 1 April – Easter Sunday – 1945, the German battalions would launch their drive across the river, aiming to tear deep into the valley, and they would catch its defenders by surprise. Farran had twice disobeyed orders to poke a stick into the hornet's nest deeper and harder than any special forces had ever done before.

The enemy would come seeking vengeance at a fittingly ominous juncture – April Fool's Day.

Chapter 19

At Florence headquarters, Farran's radio message had landed like a bombshell. Upon learning that the raid on the 14th Army HQ had gone ahead regardless, there was utter consternation from all quarters bar one – veteran Operation Galia commander, Bob Walker-Brown.

'My reaction was at first one of absolute admiration,' Walker-Brown declared, upon learning of the news, 'but I was prepared for . . . a fairly sizeable rocket from Headquarters . . . In the event I found little difficulty in presenting the senior staff officers with the facts of life at the Partisan sharp end.'

Walker-Brown hailed the raid as being one of the SAS's 'most heroic actions and brave and effective attacks'. He made it clear that it would never have happened had they been forced to stand down. 'There's no doubt in my mind that had Roy Farran accepted a go-slow order, that operation would . . . have disintegrated.' But his was sadly a lonely voice in the wilderness.

Senior Allied commanders bemoaned the growing tendency of partisan leaders all along the front to take matters into their own hands, stressing that they had absolutely 'no authority to defy the central command'. In their eyes the raid on the 14th Army headquarters was even worse, for in this case, it was Allied commanders who had chosen to disobey orders. It hardly set the kind of example they sought.

Of the Botteghe raid, SOE's Charles Macintosh would conclude: 'It was all a great pity since, had it been ten days later, the attack on the Corps HQ would have brought a major contribution to the all-out effort, and the brave men who participated would have received greater recognition.'

Far from receiving 'great recognition', the top brass proposed that Farran be court-martialled for his flagrant breach of orders. It was only when US Colonel Riepe pointed out that the SAS commander had to be given free rein to defend the Secchia valley, that such sentiments were shelved. Shelved but not forgotten. Retribution for his insubordination could wait – that was if he survived the coming showdown.

As for the badly wounded Lees, his punishment was already being meted out. Even as he'd suffered his terrible injuries, so his replacement BLO, his namesake, John Lees, was being readied to parachute into the Secchia valley. While Mike Lees lay trapped on the plains of the Po, fighting for his life and surrounded by the enemy, John Lees was taking over his field of command – just as war red in tooth and claw was coming to the valley.

After his visit to Lieutenant Eld's front-line positions, Farran was back at his Secchio base by 31 March, where he got busy hatching a plot to rescue Mike Lees. It was to be as audacious and daring as anything that he had ever conceived. During the weeks that he'd spent in Florence agitating for a mission, Farran had stumbled across some highly unusual characters in the shadowy employ of the SOE. One was the Italian fighter ace Flight Lieutenant Furio Lauri, recently installed at Florence's Rosignano Airbase.

The tales of Furio Lauri's exploits were legion – most notably a series of breathtaking rescues of downed Allied airmen from behind enemy lines. In the most recent, in February 1945 Lieutenant James of the 12th (US) Air Force had been forced to eject from his stricken fighter plane. As he'd bailed out he'd collided with the tail of his own aircraft, further smashing up his leg upon landing.

He'd ejected over the plain of the Po, near the city of Parma, some fifty kilometres north-west of the Secchia valley. Rescued by the resistance, it was arranged via radio to lift him out for urgent medical attention. The mission would be flown by Lauri in his Fieseler Storch, the spotter aircraft that he could practically land on a sixpence.

From Rosignano Lauri had taken off in the long-legged ungainly-looking plane and flown across the Gothic Line. He'd reached the tiny airstrip only to find it menaced by strong crosswinds. He'd landed anyway, but in the process had damaged the Storch's spindly landing gear and its single propeller. The aircraft was stranded, as was Lauri and the wounded American pilot. Worse still, the Storch made a hugely visible target.

Lauri ordered the aircraft to be wheeled behind a barn and covered in brushwood, so as to conceal it. The village carpenter and blacksmith began to fashion replacement landing gear, using the parts of an old bicycle, the bodged-together repairs being bolted to the airframe. But attempts to craft a replacement propeller from wood proved beyond them. Instead, Charles Macintosh, back at the SOE's Florence headquarters, managed to persuade a senior Allied commander to loan him the propeller from his own Storch, which was used to fly air-liaison missions.

The propeller was carefully wrapped and loaded into a Mitchell B-25's bomb bay. It was parachuted into the stranded pilot, whereupon it was bolted onto the Storch. Furio Lauri duly took to the air, the wounded Lieutenant James riding shotgun. At Rosignano Airbase a team of press reporters and senior US commanders awaited the heroes' return. Upon touchdown, Lieutenant James gave his first interview to US Armed Forces Radio as he was being stretchered to a waiting ambulance, a proud Furio Lauri walking beside him.

Farran concluded that what Lauri had done for Lieutenant James he could also do for Mike Lees. But there were enormous challenges. First, they'd need somehow to spirit Lees out of the hornet's nest of enemy forces now crawling over the plains. Second, they'd need to get him – and possibly Gordon, depending on the extent of his injuries – to a usable airstrip. And third, Farran would need to persuade the SOE top brass to pull out all the stops, for without them no such mission was going to be possible.

SOE headquarters already had an inkling as to how serious were Mike Lees' injuries. On 31 March they'd received the first official casualty report telegraphed from the field. It read: 'Capt. Michael Lees. Wounded on 26 March 1945. 3 Bullets left thigh.' Highly inaccurate, it did nevertheless record that Lees had been shot multiple times, while doing little to reflect how truly desperate was his predicament.

Aware of Lees' recent, distinctly 'undiplomatic' letters and missives, Farran sent a short radio message to Macintosh, in an effort to build bridges. 'From ROY to CHARLES. Sorry to hear LEES in disgrace owing to his rude signals . . .' It was followed by Farran's desperate plea for help. 'MIKE's condition critical. Operation essential. Carrying to PALANZANO . . . Warn HOLLAND and lay on Torch pick up . . . Ack when laid on.'

Major Charles Holland was one of the neighbouring BLOs.

His territory lay closest to Lees' hideout, and he was known to possess a tiny but usable airstrip situated near the village of Palanzano. 'Torch' was code for the Storch – Furio Lauri's distinctive, do-anything aircraft, with its unrivalled short take-off and landing capabilities.

Farran sent that plea for help early on the morning of 1 April 1945, the very day that he was to learn of the enemy's potentially catastrophic breakthrough in the Secchia valley. But first, Mike Lees was to have unexpected visitors.

At his hideout Lees was oblivious to all but his and Gordon's dire fate. Right now, their very survival hung by the slenderest of threads. Thankfully, in Spandau-toting Antonio they had an ally beyond compare. It was dawn when a horse-drawn cart turned up at the old woman's farmstead, piled high with manure. Nothing so remarkable about that. But this cart contained a false bottom – a compartment constructed beneath the thick and oozing load.

Lees and Gordon were helped aboard, dark liquid seeping from the dung above and soaking into their bandages and hair. Despite the extreme discomfort – not to mention the deleterious effect a good dousing in manure-juice might have on their wounds – the carriage proved a stroke of genius. For twelve agonising kilometres they jolted along tracks thick with enemy forces, but no one seemed particularly keen to search the cart and its pungent cargo too thoroughly.

In this way they were brought to a safe house on the outskirts of Reggio Emilia – well out of the dragnet cast by an enraged enemy. By now Lees' leg appeared to be paralysed, and he was so weak from his injuries that he could barely move. But at the safe house Antonio had worked miracles. Resistance fighters armed with machine guns stood watch in neighbouring buildings, forming a cordon around their place of hiding. There the nurses were installed on permanent duty, and a motor car made ready in the courtyard, in case they had to make a rapid getaway.

Fresh dressings, medicines and morphine had been readied, all stolen from a local hospital. Their host, a short and sturdy farmer very much in Antonio's mould, seemed utterly unperturbed at their presence and the untold dangers it brought. He busied himself preparing fine meals, washed down with choice bottles of wine. Gordon's father, who lived locally, even paid a visit, bearing gifts of soap, toothbrushes and shaving gear.

A second doctor came to inspect the wounded men. Gordon's leg was troubling him, and it turned out not to have been set properly. When that doctor, a Dr Chiesi, had finished dealing with it, he turned his attentions to Lees. He proved to be a very different kettle of fish to his predecessor: he cared passionately for the cause of the resistance and showed little fear of the enemy.

By the time he had finished inspecting Lees' wounds, Dr Chiesi's expression was grim. 'The nerve in your leg is severed,' he announced, gravely. 'If it is not repaired within ten days it will die completely.'

'What exactly does that mean?' Lees pressed.

'That unless you have an operation, you may never again be able to work that leg properly. You might walk about in irons, but it would never again be normal.'

Lees blanched. 'Well, I can't get to a hospital, as you know. Can you operate on me here?'

The doctor gestured at their surroundings. 'It would be impossible. There is no proper light, no equipment, and you would need to lie absolutely still. No, I could not do it. Here, it is impossible, I am afraid.'

Once the doctor was gone, Lees reflected upon his predicament: ten days to save his leg. Even if he were able to walk, it was impossible. Two days to the Secchia valley, maybe more; from there, a four-day trek to cross the Gothic Line and from there the march to Florence. Paralysed and unable even to stand, it was beyond hopeless. Much that Lees might rack his brains, he could think of no alternatives.

Shortly after the doctor's visit a courier arrived. It was a Stafetta, but due to Antonio's intense security she had had the devil of a time tracking down their place of hiding. She brought Lees' mail from home – delivered in a recent resupply drop – plus a note from Roy Farran. Lees ran his eager eyes over the letters from his sweetheart, Gwen. New spirit and determination ebbed into him as he read those words. He had to get out of there, for her as much as anything. Then he tore open the letter from Farran.

Dear Mike . . . You don't know how sorry we all are about your rotten luck and will do everything we can to help you escape. Gianni has volunteered to take his whole Garibaldini brigade to bring you back from the plains . . . The couriers have also volunteered to take you through the lines if you could stand the journey. Alternatively, base have wirelessed to say that if we can prepare a landing ground they will send a light aircraft to fly you out. We can do nothing, however, 'til we know where you are and if you are fit to move.

Lees crunched some numbers. If he sent the courier back today, she would take two days to reach Secchio. One day for Gianni to prepare his partisans and they could be here in forty-eight hours.

304

Possibly. Moving slowly on a stretcher, Lees' ten days to save his leg would be up almost before he'd been spirited back to Secchio. More to the point, if the Garibaldini came in force and in the open on the plains, the enemy – roused to wrath by the Botteghe raid – would pounce. It wasn't even worth contemplating.

But a light aircraft putting down at an airstrip . . . Lees had heard the tales of Furio Lauri's exploits. The nearest safe strip was in BLO Holland's territory, which neighboured their own. He grabbed a map. Ten miles across the plains then twenty over the foothills – there lay the strip. But how on earth was he to complete such a journey?

Farran signed off his note, stressing that the Botteghe raid had been 'a good night's work and we are preparing for plenty more. The Partisans are in fine fettle. I only wish you were here to lead them. Bert is prostrated; he wanders around Secchio murmuring, "I knew it would happen, I warned the silly bastard!"' This was a reference to Bert Farrimond, Lees' radio operator, whose premonition that something bad would happen had seemingly come to pass.

That evening Antonio came to visit. Lees explained his predicament and asked if there was anything he could suggest. Antonio thought for a moment, before a wicked gleam came into his eye.

'I can't promise, but I have an idea,' he ventured.

'What is it?' Lees pushed, eagerly.

Antonio smiled, enigmatically. 'I will say nothing more. But tomorrow, I will return.' With that he was gone.

As Lees' longed-for escape seemed just a little more tangible, so Roy Farran was about to embark upon a ferocious battle for survival himself – and for all in the Secchia valley.

The runner woke him at three o'clock on the morning of 1 April 1945, bearing alarming news. German troops had launched a surprise attack, advancing in force at night and crossing the all-important River Secchia. They'd opted to bypass Lieutenant Eld's positions, striking instead at the line supposedly held by Don Carlo and his Green Flames. Resistance had crumbled, especially since Don Carlo's brother had been killed in the fighting, which resulted in the warrior-priest himself losing heart.

'If the reports were correct,' Farran concluded, 'the Germans were already deep into our valley,' and Lieutenant Eld's forces were 'threatened with encirclement'. Knowing how fragile the partisans' morale tended to be, he worried that 'the slightest pressure would put them to flight'. He was hardly surprised when the first reports filtered in of partisan units taking to the hills.

The move by the enemy was unexpected, swift and astute. They'd struck by the Secchia valley's weakest point, and the 'only solution that might save our base was to drive the Germans back across the river', Farran reasoned. He sent a runner to Eld, with orders to hold his positions at all costs. A second runner was despatched to Tapignola, to warn those based at the church to ready themselves for immediate battle. Jock Easton was told to take the Allied Battalion and march north to reinforce Eld's positions, in an effort to stabilise the front-line.

Meanwhile, Farran would meet the enemy head-on, in an effort to 'halt the German advance before our entire position in the valley crumbled'. A third runner was sent to Modena, to muster his Russians. Farran desperately needed their help spearheading the full-frontal counter-attack that he was contemplating. Orders given and plan of battle sorted, he set out on his tiny black steed, Whoa Mahomet, to lead his men into battle.

As the dawn sky brightened, Farran spied the disturbing evidence of how far the enemy had broken through: hundreds of refugees were on the move, driving herds of cattle and sheep deeper into the hills. The entire valley was awash with figures like swarms of ants, which was so unusual at such an hour. Here and there he spied the distinctive forms of groups of armed fighters, as bands of partisans headed for whatever refuge they could find. The German drive was in danger of becoming an out-and-out rout.

Shortly, Farran ran into the first group of Green Flames fleeing in the opposite direction – away from the advancing enemy. They told alarming stories of their commander being inconsolable at the loss of his brother, and of the Germans advancing in unassailable strength. The shock and surprise of the night attack had served only to fuel such fears.

Farran pressed on, dispensing with his trusty steed as the noise of battle drew closer. Finally, he reached a low ridge where the Green Flames' rearguard were in contact with the enemy. Twenty-odd veterans lay behind the cover of a hillock, facing the enemy's foremost units – German machine-gunners positioned on a hill about two hundred yards away. These men had been fighting for hours now, in a desperate effort to stabilise a chaotic retreat and with no effective command: they were overjoyed to see the familiar figure of the SAS major.

Farran belly-crawled the last few yards to join them. Via his field glasses he studied the enemy lines for a few long moments, before rolling over to question one of the partisans. An instant later a fierce burst of fire tore into the terrain where he'd just been lying, spattering Farran in grit. Had Farran needed a reminder of how desperate the present situation was, he'd just got it. He estimated the enemy had pushed three hundred troops across the river, facing which he presently had some twenty men.

'The situation was extremely dangerous,' he concluded, but if they could halt the enemy here until dark, or until the Russians arrived, 'we still had a chance of saving the valley.' Those chances were about to get a boost from an entirely unexpected quarter.

Farran had been on the ridge for about an hour, trading fire with the enemy, when John Lees – Mike Lees' replacement BLO – arrived. Tall, dark and powerfully built, John Lees struck Farran as looking very much like the Black Owl fighters that he had inherited from his predecessor. He had brought twenty of those elite warriors with him, and as bullets tore around their heads Farran pointed out the nearest enemy positions.

John Lees appeared to be 'no man to run at the first whistle of bullets,' Farran concluded. He spread the Black Owls along the ridgeline, lending the valley's defenders a total force of forty. Equally important, he'd managed to bring two Bren guns and a good quantity of ammunition. Farran explained the key priority was to somehow make the enemy believe they were facing a far stronger force than they really were.

As the sun rose higher, signal flares continued to arc into the sky. Worryingly, they seemed to be aimed to the rear of Farran's line now, suggesting that the enemy were moving behind his position, executing an encirclement. From the north-west he could hear the echo of battle, indicating that Lieutenant's Eld's forces were in action. All across a wide front the enemy seemed to be advancing, and Farran could only hope that Jock Easton had reached Eld's positions in time.

It became roasting-hot on the ridgeline, but Farran could afford no retreat to any place promising shade. At the slightest sign of weakness he felt certain the enemy would be up and at them. Their positions here simply had to hold. For three hours they sweated in the heat, as machine-gun fire whipped along the ridgeline, bullets whining as they ricocheted off the hard, sun-baked earth. Farran could only hope that the enemy didn't mount a full-frontal charge, for his line was bound to crumble and break.

He kept loosing off shots with his carbine, aiming at the distinctive grey helmets of the German gunners. It seemed to take an age before he detected the pounding of approaching feet – boots thumping upon the rough track behind. The voices confirmed it: it was Modena and his Russians. Heedless of the bullets that whipped after him, Farran raced down the slope to meet them.

It turned out that the Russian commander had been one step ahead of Farran: as soon as he'd heard the sounds of fighting, he had got his men on the move. After a good amount of back-slapping, Farran explained the plan to Modena, using Lieutenant Stephens, his Austrian Jewish SAS man, as interpreter. Surprisingly, Modena seemed eager for what Farran suggested – a full frontal charge to drive the Germans out of their positions, after which they'd chase them back across the Secchia river. Dramatic and near-suicidal, it seemed to appeal to the Russian commander no end.

Modena suggested one refinement to the plan. His men had completed the forced march laden down with a three-inch mortar and rounds. They would begin the assault with a softening-up barrage. That agreed, Modena broke out a bottle of grappa, took a large swig, passed the bottle on and kissed his Italian girlfriend, before yelling out orders. His men listened intently, and almost before he'd finished they doubled up the hillside to join the ridge-line's defenders.

As Modena took charge of the mortar team, Farran paused to shake hands and wish him luck, before returning to his position in the centre of the line. After a few false starts, the Russian mortar crew seemed to find their range and began to scatter high-explosive shells among the German positions. As the mortar barrage grew to a crescendo, so the combined force of partisans and SAS began to pour fire into the enemy, scores of Brens, Stens and tommy guns hammering in the rounds, long tongues of burning tracer licking across the terrain.

With the Germans' heads well down, Farran clambered to his feet atop the ridge. Raising an arm above his head he gestured first to the right side and then to the left, urging all to rise up and follow. He was about to set off when he realised that not a soul had stirred from their positions, and as bullets cut the air to either side of him he dived back into cover. It was late-afternoon by now and if they didn't seize the initiative shortly, darkness would fall and it would be too late.

A few moments later Farran steeled himself once more, this time yelling for all to follow and dashing forwards several paces, so as to set an example. A handful of Russians got to their feet, but no more, and sustained bursts of enemy fire soon drove them scurrying back again. Farran lay in cover gasping for breath, wondering what to do. Maybe it might be a case of third time lucky. Or maybe the third time he raised his head from cover, he would get it blown off.

Shouting, yelling and berating all to find their courage, Farran sprang to his feet once more and began to dash down the slope. One by one the Russians rose behind him, cheering wildly. A ragged line formed up and began to sweep downhill, chaotically at first but gaining in shape and energy as more and more joined the surge. Farran sensed that this time he would carry the partisans with him. Sure enough the wild mob thickened, as scores of screaming fighters began to thunder towards the nearest enemy positions.

On Farran's right he could see Stephens in the vanguard, leading the surge. To his left, fittingly, was the distinctive figure of Modena, driving his men on. Once, twice, Farran stumbled on the rough ground, but the momentum was well and truly unstoppable by now. Incredibly, the Italians – moved by the dramatic spectacle and the stirring war-cries – began to outpace the more solidly built Russians. Soon, they were in the very vanguard of the charge. The line of bearded, unwashed wild-men, yelling curses in a colourful mixture of languages, swept towards the enemy, the Italians firing long bursts from the hip as they went.

As they closed on the enemy their line began to break before the barbarian horde. Along a broad front Farran saw red Very lights arc into the sky – presumably the signal for retreat. He was now lagging well behind the vanguard, but he witnessed one of the enemy's more-dramatic attempts to make a stand. Taking cover in a white-walled farmhouse, a group of German troops were overwhelmed as crazed partisans seemed to charge right through their bullets, unleashing long bursts of tracer as they ran.

An Italian partisan wielding a Bren led the final assault, the Russians close on his heels. He unleashed a torrent of fire at point-blank range through the windows, as moments later grey-uniformed figures stumbled out with their hands held high. The partisans took few prisoners – gunning down most of the enemy. The frenzied bloodlust that Farran had unleashed was beyond anyone's control, the Germans throwing down their weapons and fleeing.

Farran struggled on, trying his best to keep up. A wild young partisan, long dark hair flowing in the breeze, came up to him and pumped his hand enthusiastically. He had sweat pouring down his features. 'Maggiore McGinty,' he exclaimed, 'what a wonderful *Festa di Pasqua*' – Easter Festival. Good point, Farran thought: it was after all Easter Sunday.

With that the partisan ran off to join the melee, leaving Farran alone in the fading light. The enemy advance the previous night had been ordered and seemingly unstoppable; their retreat the following evening was a rout. As they tried to cross piecemeal back over the swollen Secchia they were gunned down by their pursuers, or they strayed unwittingly into the range of Lieutenant Eld's and Jock Easton's guns.

'By nightfall not a single enemy soldier remained alive on our side . . .' Farran remarked. 'It was an accomplishment that surprised me no less than the enemy . . . For the first time the Reggio partisans had outfought a German Battalion, completely defeating it.'

The Secchia would run red that night.

Chapter 20

As evening faded to darkness Farran found himself alone. The sporadic sounds of fighting drifted across to him – the final mopping-up operations. It was a starlit night and he was cold and beyond exhausted. He was forced to trudge his weary way back to Secchio, his horse being nowhere to be found. Now and again he stopped to drink from a muddy puddle, so desperate was he to quench his thirst.

As he stumbled along in the dark Farran ran into a familiar figure: it was Colonel Monti, the 'commander-in-chief' of the Reggio partisans. Immaculate as ever, he sat astride his big brown mare, wearing riding jodhpurs and with a smart crop in hand. Farran saluted, and Colonel Monti informed him that he was riding out to join the battle.

'*Mon colonel*, the Germans are utterly defeated,' Farran informed him, in his best schoolboy French, the only language that he and the colonel shared. 'We have driven them back across the river.'

Colonel Monti looked incredulous. He asked Farran to repeat himself, as if unable to grasp that it might be true, or perhaps fearing that he had misunderstood Farran's French.

'The Germans are beaten,' Farran told him, by way of the simplest explanation he could muster. 'It is a great victory.'

The colonel stared, wide-eyed with amazement, before whipping his steed around and cantering off towards the front. Farran could appreciate the colonel's consternation. The victory was unprecedented. It just went to show what irregular forces could achieve when given the right leadership and the self-belief that was so crucial to any battle.

Following the dramatic turn-around, Farran – together with John Lees – decided it was time to shout it from the rooftops. If the partisans could hear of their exploits earning widespread renown, it would stiffen their spirit for future sorties. And as Farran well knew, with Allied forces poised to punch through the Gothic Line, soon the partisans would be called upon to hit the enemy hard. Boosting their morale right now was critical.

John Lees sent a plea to Macintosh to that effect: 'Please ask PWB to broadcast on ITALIA COMBATTE a programme praising the REGGIO . . . formations. A mention of the counter-attack on Easter day when three coys of Germans were chased back over the R. SECCHIA . . . leaving 20 dead and 30 prisoners would do. I really want this as the MODENA AND PARMA DIVS have been mentioned, but never my lads.'

'PWB' was the Psychological Warfare Bureau, the Psychological Warfare Division by another name. The Modena and Parma divisions were neighbouring bands of partisans. Notably, while stressing the challenges of replacing such a towering figure as Mike Lees – 'It was difficult taking over without anybody who really understood the form' – John Lees was already referring to the partisans as 'my lads'. He'd got his feet well and truly under the table at Secchio and he'd led the spirited counter-attack from the front.

As for Mike Lees, he was about to begin a journey of epic proportions, one that would determine whether he would live or die.

*

The maverick SOE agent and his resistance leader guardian, Antonio, had set upon a plan of unprecedented audacity to spirit him away to the hills. Recognising that Mike Lees couldn't survive such a back-breaking journey hidden under a heap of manure, they'd decided to resort to a spot of inspired thievery and bluff.

Desperate times called for desperate measures, and in that spirit Antonio had got his men to hijack a German field ambulance. The first Lees knew of this was a visit by Antonio, shortly after dusk on 3 April. One glance at the man's face told Lees that he was bringing good news.

'You must be ready at dawn tomorrow morning,' Antonio announced. 'An ambulance will take you into the mountains, speeding you through the checkpoints.'

Lees was overjoyed. By his reckoning he had six days left to save his leg. If they could get the Storch in to the landing zone to rendezvous with the ambulance, he might just make it. To that effect he scribbled two notes for Antonio to deliver via courier. One was to Farran explaining their plans, and asking him to contact Florence and request the aircraft. The other was to Charles Holland, asking him to make ready the airstrip.

It was the early hours of the following morning when Lees awoke to footsteps on the stairs outside his room. As his hand went to his weapon, the door opened softly. A candle spluttered by his bedside, throwing the mystery visitor into faint light and shadow: to Lees, it looked suspiciously like a man dressed in the full grey of a German army uniform.

'Who is it?' Lees barked a challenge.

By way of answer there was a short, throaty laugh, as the figure pushed the peaked forage cap up from his forehead. 'Sir, your ambulance awaits!' he announced. It was Antonio.

Under the cover of darkness Lees and Gordon were loaded aboard the waiting vehicle – a square-bodied truck, iconic red cross symbols as tall as a man emblazoned across its roof and side. This was only stage one of the journey, Antonio warned. If they made it across the plains, blagging their way through the German checkpoints, they could get only so far into the hills. Eventually, Lees and Gordon would have to transfer into a bullock cart, for the going would be too difficult for the truck. Even so, as they set forth into the pre-dawn darkness Lees felt buoyed by a spirit of hope.

But even as that hijacked ambulance rumbled through the dark streets of Reggio Emilia, so an urgent cypher message was winging its way to London from SOE Florence headquarters. It made clear that even should Lees survive the coming journey and escape, he was about to face a witch-hunt . . . regardless.

'In a recent engagement Capt Michael LEES rpt LEES wounded in leg as a result of an attack made by him contrary to orders. It is thought possible he may have acted under orders issued by Major FARRAN of SAS, but matter will be fully investigated on his return. As LEES' condition said to be critical am attempting exfiltration by special Op on 5th, rpt 5th.'

Even if Lees' life and his leg could be saved, he was seemingly being rescued in part so that he could face the music. Farran, likewise, was far from exonerated, despite having rallied the defenders of the Secchia valley. There were others of Lees' brothers-in-arms who were facing dark troubles the likes of which none might have reasonably foreseen.

As Lees settled back in the ambulance for the ride of his life, so Paul Morton, the Canadian reporter with whom he had shared the Operation Flap mission, was also in the line of fire.

In early April 1945 a query arrived in London from SOE's New York office, which used the cover name of the Inter Services Research Bureau (ISRB). 'A newspaper correspondent called Paul Morton has been writing articles and making broadcasts . . . describing his experiences after being dropped in occupied territory in Northern Italy. If he has in fact been employed as an agent, some of his statements are indiscreet . . .'

A flurry of further messages arrived at the SOE's London headquarters, questioning Morton's 'indiscretions' and his credentials. 'I note from our records MORTON was employed in July, 1944, as an attached correspondent with MARYLAND. Will you kindly advise . . . if he was, in fact, dropped in Italy and whether he was given any authority to write articles and make broadcasts . . .'

Morton's problem was that he was now peddling an 'inconvenient truth' as many saw it – that the Italian partisans, communists included, were taking the fight to the enemy with spirit and panache. Even as the Italian resistance was being called upon to rise up and help sever the Gothic Line, fear of 'Reds' taking over meant that such exploits were to be downplayed. The schizophrenic flip-flopping of Allied policy – both to simultaneously support and subvert the Italian resistance – continued. Indeed, in April 1945 BLOs were still telegraphing from the field berating the lack of weaponry drops, due to the 'political winds of change' turning against them.

Those trying to garner support for the partisans were to be subjected to a witch-hunt. For Morton, it was to be of a signal savagery. Not content with spiking his stories, his ten-year stint as a reporter with the *Toronto Daily Star* came to a sudden end. Morton was sacked, with no credible explanation as to why. Quietly, secretly, a report had been written accusing Morton of making up his tales of operations behind the lines, branding him a liar and rendering him utterly unemployable. By April 1945 his reputation had been comprehensively mauled and lay in tatters.

Fortunately for Roy Farran, the fact that he was needed by Allied commanders, the Americans first and foremost, rendered him immune to such predations – for now. He was about to be called upon to rouse his Allied Battalion to spearhead an assault on Highway Twelve, one of the key resupply routes feeding the Gothic Line. In short, Farran, despite his rather flexible interpretation of orders, was seen as being indispensable. By contrast Mike Lees, badly wounded and out of action, was fair game.

Even as he fought for his very life, considerable efforts were being devoted to nailing him. A flurry of messages sought to prove that he had received the signal to stand down the Botteghe raid, and that it had been deliberately ignored. One read: 'A personal message was sent to Major FARRAN and Capt LEES advising them that the attack should be postponed ... Confirmation that Capt LEES and Major FARRAN received this signal [to stand down] was given ... 26 Mr 45.'

Another provided London with a searing indictment of Lees' supposed record in the field. 'This officer gave considerable trouble from the time he was first infiltrated. He was resentful of all orders ... and his attitude towards these is typified by the extracts from letters written by him in the Field (attached as Appendix "B").'

Some of Lees' more colourful and forthright messages were appended to that report and they made for damaging reading. In short, the knives were out for him. Farran, meanwhile, received Lees' hand written message about his escape by hijacked German ambulance with a surge of hope: maybe his friend was about to be plucked to safety, after all?

At the same time – 5 April 1945 – Farran received urgent orders in the field. He was warned that the main Allied offensive to breech the Gothic Line had begun, but that it had run into ferocious resistance. He was urged to take his Allied Battalion and make all efforts to hit and harass enemy traffic on Highway Twelve, the main supply route for two German divisions manning the key section of the Gothic Line. There was no time to delay.

Thankfully, a fresh pair of hands had just been parachuted in to boost Farran's command. On 4 April 1945 Colonel Hardt's DC3s had flown yet another resupply mission over the Secchia valley. Along with the crates of mortars, heavy machine-gun rounds, grenades and ammunition, they'd parachuted in a distinctive figure – Karl Nurk, the Estonian big game hunter, irregular warfare veteran and fluent Russian speaker.

In recent months Nurk had been serving with the Special Boat Service, operating across the Aegean, the stretch of sea sandwiched between Greece and Turkey. But Farran's summons – that he needed Nurk as his bridge to the Russian partisans – had duly plucked him out of the Aegean and parachuted him into the skies over Secchio.

Farran was overjoyed. 'No longer would I have to rely on Lieutenant Stephens' interpretation of Modena's German.' Nurk 'had all the likeable qualities of the Russian émigré – recklessness, a taste for wine, women and song and a perpetual sense of drama . . . He immediately made great friends with Modena and on the first night I heard them singing Russian songs together at a very late hour.' Nurk wasn't a Russian émigré, of course. He was

Estonian and had fought *against* the Russians in the Winter War. But he was the bridge that Farran longed for.

There was another key reason that Farran had agitated to have a man like Nurk – a fellow major – join him, as he prepared to launch an all-out offensive against the enemy. Tellingly, with Mike Lees gone, command of the Allied Battalion had become something of a lonely occupation. Not any more. 'A born adventurer,' Farran wrote of Nurk, 'he was as gay as his reputation and equally fearless. I felt I had found a kindred spirit.'

Striking Highway Twelve was a daunting proposition, even as a classic hit-and-run exercise. But Farran had been called upon to do so much more. He was tasked with moving the Allied Battalion lock, stock and barrel onto the plains, to savage the enemy's supply lines. It was a herculean task, breaking down all of their defensive positions and mobilising their heaviest weaponry. Even Lieutenant Harvey's 75mm howitzer, Molto Stanco, was to be brought to join the hotchpotch convoy that was being assembled – led by Hans the German deserter's captured truck and scores of lumbering ox-carts.

By 7 April Farran intended to move to within striking distance of Highway Twelve, and to somehow hide by day and attack at night, when the road tended to be chock-full with German military traffic. But to get there, the column would have to cross 'appallingly rugged country, and would, therefore, be in no condition for an immediate attack. They had to be fresh for the actual raids,' Farran cautioned, 'because utmost care would be needed for the final approach . . .' Highway Twelve ran along the top of an exposed ridge and there were no convenient gullies or defiles from which to mount ambushes.

By removing the Allied Battalion Farran knew that he was

leaving the Secchia valley vulnerable. He was warned of such by Colonel Monti, who felt as if he were deserting them. In part to deflect any reprisals, Farran charged Kirkpatrick, his piper, to execute a last-minute tour of the villages, playing at every opportunity, so as to stamp the indelible signature of 'Britishness' on all that had transpired. Kirkpatrick's was to be a whistle-stop tour, and Farran was just about to have delivered the means to make it happen.

On the night of 5/6 April 1945, Farran invited the key resistance figures – Colonel Monti, Gianni, Don Carlo, Barba Nera, Eros – to watch a truly awesome display of Allied military might in action, all orchestrated by Scalabrino, his veteran drop-zone enforcer. In part, it was to reinforce in their minds that for Italy, the hour of liberation was now at hand. Now was the moment to rise up and seize back their country.

It was well past midnight by the time the drop zone – a round-topped hill, whose sides fell away to sharp gullies – was ready. Next to the Casa Balocchi DZ, this was the next-best field, and it lay close to the exit of the valley – the route by which Farran's Victory Column would head, to hit Highway Twelve. But that also put it well within sight of the nearest enemy positions.

As Farran and the resistance leaders stood waiting, wrapped up against the night chill, his veteran W/T operator, Corporal Cunningham, employed a radio-homing set to guide the incoming planes. Known as the 'Rebecca/Eureka transponding radar', it consisted of an airborne receiver and antenna system fitted to an aircraft, to detect a radio signal transmitting from the ground-based 'Eureka' unit. The Rebecca calculated the range and position of the Eureka, based upon the timings and direction of the signal.

Bang on schedule the faint throb of straining aero-engines

echoed through the dark skies. Farran yelled for the flares to be triggered and the signal fires lit. The ghostly silhouette of an aircraft roared overhead, but it wasn't the kind of warplane that Farran was expecting. For an instant he wondered whether to douse the signals, in case it was a marauding enemy night-fighter. But just as quickly it was gone again, the heavens reverting to a starlit stillness and silence.

For Farran the wait became nerve-racking. Was this crucial piece of theatre to end in an embarrassing no-show? Some fifteen minutes behind schedule the distinctive laboured throb of heavily laden aircraft filled the skies, as a flight swept in at a lower and more purposeful altitude. Farran ordered the flares lit again. Steering a path between the high peaks, the flight of aircraft emerged from the darkness carrying their highly unusual payloads.

As the first plane thundered in, the underside of its fuselage was illuminated in the flares' harsh glare. It was a Halifax heavy bomber, but crammed into its bomb-bay was the square bulk of a Willys MB jeep, the bomb doors held open to accommodate the bulky cargo. The Halifax turned sharply and came in for its drop-run, making a beeline for the hilltop DZ. Moments later the black silhouette plummeted from the aircraft and parachutes blossomed in the air above it, one suspended from each corner.

But one of the chutes failed to open properly. It bunched up like a sack of damp washing, crushed by the jeep's slipstream. The vehicle flipped crazily, the other chutes became entangled, and moments later there were a series of harsh ripping sounds as the parachute silk was torn asunder, leaving the jeep plummeting towards earth like some kind of giant demented bomb. Screeching like a banshee the vehicle streaked towards the watchers, careering into the centre of the DZ right in the midst of the signal fires.

Thankfully, no one was hurt, but when Farran turned to reassure his distinguished guests he found that they had fled. He managed to round them up again, and in short order a second jeep was dropped, this one behaving impeccably. It swung to earth gently, suspended on its four chutes, landing with a faint crash on its sprung carriage – a bespoke steel pan fitted with springs. Within moments the DZ crew had freed the jeep from the pan, fired it up and were roaring away to clear the ground for the next load.

Four jeeps were dropped, not including the first that had broken free and torn itself to smithereens. The last was released in broad daylight in full sight of the nearest German garrisons. The drop had done wonders to stiffen the nerves of the partisan leaders and it must have been morale-sapping in the extreme for the enemy. Masses of ammo accompanied the jeeps – chiefly mortar and howitzer rounds. With the vehicles to hand, Farran had a sense that they could mount the kind of fast, mobile shoot-and-scoot warfare a target like Highway Twelve called for. It hadn't escaped his notice that with such mobility and grunt they could tow Molto Stanco into battle, pretty much at will.

Farran's Victory Column began to take shape, as those commanding the valley's perimeter defences were called in. Parachutist Murphy was dragged back from his position in the shadow of Monte Pena; Parachutist Wooding and Corporal Larley returned from their frontier outposts; and finally, Lieutenant Eld was pulled back from his front-line defences. Modena's Russians marched into the muster point, as did the choicest Garibaldini and Green Flames units. The guns on the jeeps were cleaned and they were fuelled for action. Molto Stanco was delivered by Lieutenant Harvey, who had collapsed the Cisa Box, breaking the big gun down into its constituent parts. It was reassembled and hitched to a jeep.

A trailer was parachuted in, to be towed behind a jeep piled with howitzer shells. Scores of ox-carts were requisitioned by Barba Nera, and heaped high with provisions, kit and weaponry. Likewise, mules grumbled under heavy burdens. By his deadline – 7 April – Farran's Victory Column was all but ready, one jeep remaining to be dropped in. He left David Eyton-Jones – whose feet had still not fully recovered from his frost-bitten ascent of Monte Cusna – to take charge of the last jeep.

As Farran set out at the head of his Victory Column, it was to be Eyton-Jones who was to see the first action. Shortly after his jeep was parachuted in, a US warplane plummeted from the sky with its starboard engine on fire, crashing in sight of their position. In its wake three parachutists drifted to earth, landing in an open field in clear sight of both Eyton-Jones and the enemy.

The young SAS lieutenant didn't hesitate: he mounted up the newly arrived jeep to ride to their rescue. Even as he set out, a German Kubelwagen – a Volkswagen light military vehicle and the Germans' nearest equivalent to the jeep – raced towards the downed airmen from the opposite side. Knowing that his jeep boasted some serious firepower – a Browning and a pair of Vickers K machine guns – Eyton-Jones didn't baulk. Understandably, the US airmen found it hard to believe that either force racing towards them could be friendly. This far behind the lines surely they had to be Germans.

As Eyton-Jones slammed his jeep to a halt, three figures came out of hiding with their hands held high. Even as his jeep-mounted weapons menaced the Kubelwagen, Eyton-Jones urged them to climb aboard. 'I called over that I was British,' he recalled, 'and would they get into the jeep, as I could see a German car with troops heading towards them.' The American pilot seemed confused: 'Aw, gee, my navigator must have got it all wrong.' Eyton-Jones told him otherwise. 'I assured him his navigator was quite correct, they were in German-occupied territory.'

With all aboard, Eyton-Jones ferried the bewildered US airmen back to comparative safety. After celebrating their miraculous salvation, Eyton-Jones charged Fritz Snapper to smuggle the airmen back through the lines, with an escort of McGinty's Arrows to speed them on their way. That done, he formed up at the head of the supply column of bullock carts, and on Barba Nera's orders they got under way, heading for the plains.

Hours later they were reunited with Farran's advance party. The SAS major formed his forces up into four distinct units. The first, Sun Column, consisted of five SAS plus Modena's Russians – now swelled to one hundred fighting men. Sun Column was a potent outfit, and it was assigned to hit the section of Highway Twelve where it linked up with the Gothic Line and where battle was likely to be at its fiercest. Accordingly, it was the most heavily armed, boasting Molto Stanco, three mortars, a heavy Browning machine gun, plus fifteen Brens.

The second unit, Moon Column, was commanded by Jock Easton, and consisted of twenty-five SAS plus thirty of the finest Garibaldini. Equipped with two Vickers machine guns, three mortars and ten Brens, its job was to raid the mid-section of the highway, where it cut across the plains. Star Column came next, consisting of five SAS plus sixty mixed Italian partisans, armed with three mortars, one Browning and fifteen Brens. In Farran's mind, Star Column was the weakest of the three. It was tasked with striking Highway Twelve at its most vulnerable point, where the roadway ran out of the foothills.

Finally, there was Farran's own command, Eclipse Column, which consisted of four jeeps and ten SAS. It was configured as a fast, hit-and-run force, which would strike at the kind of heavily defended targets that would put the fear of God into the enemy. With Eclipse Column in particular Farran had one aim foremost in his mind: if he could strike fast enough and with suitable potency, he hoped to convince enemy commanders that Allied forces had broken through the Gothic Line, so prompting a hell-for-leather retreat.

As the Victory Column wound its way out of the foothills, Farran ran his eye along its length: it straggled for many miles. Whoa Mahommet had been found again, and he trotted his diminutive steed this way and that, feeling an immense sense of pride. What they had achieved here, seemingly from nothing, was little short of a miracle. Just weeks back the partisans had been demoralised and in disarray. Now, they were setting forth to drive out the enemy invaders.

The SAS members of the Victory Column seemed in particularly high spirits. Even though he lacked a horse, Major Karl Nurk seemed happy to stick close to the Stafettas. The men sang as they marched, and Kirkpatrick gave the occasional blast on his bagpipes, though he was apparently lacking in treacle with which to lubricate the bag (treacle preserves the skin, while allowing moisture to wick through). Farran's men, dusty, unshaven and wearing mud-spattered and ripped uniforms, gave a cheer from beneath their faded red berets.

'They were the cream of this rag-tag army,' Farran remarked, 'and

I loved every one of them . . . there were no finer troops than these.'
After weeks of training with and fighting alongside the SAS, the
Italian partisans were also in fine fettle, as were the Russians. Just
how fine his motley force might prove Farran was about to discover,
as they crossed the Secchia and moved deeper into bandit country.

It was evening by the time Barba Nera's entire one-hundred-
strong bullock cart convoy had managed to ford the river, with
Eyton-Jones and his jeep to the fore. Farran formed the force
up as one defensive unit and they set up camp for the night.
But having made contact with headquarters, there was worrying
news. Cunningham delivered a long message, which had taken
an age to decode. In essence they had been ordered to strike at
Highway Twelve with no delay.

'Our orders were clear for once,' Farran remarked, 'and, having
contravened instructions over the [HQ] attack . . . and my very
presence on the wrong side of the lines, I did not dare delay our
advance . . .' He called his commanders together, to deliver the
unwelcome news. Tired as they were, they would have to push on
through the gathering darkness, moving far beyond the territory
they had covered when striking at the Botteghe HQ.

Though they faced a gruelling night march through uncharted
terrain, spirits remained high. 'As we moved into unknown
country, I felt the same excitement as I knew the men felt,' Farran
remarked, 'and began to watch from every vantage point for signs
of the enemy.'

From his own vantage point, Farran's fellow Botteghe raid
commander was also watching anxiously. In his mountain-top
position, Mike Lees searched the skies for a tiny, fragile-seeming
aircraft, which might pluck him to safety.

Tantalisingly, the impossible promise of salvation beckoned.

Chapter 21

Just as he had hoped, Antonio's ruse with the German ambulance had worked wonders, spiriting Mike Lees – and Gordon – through checkpoint after checkpoint. Time and again they'd slowed at the approach to an enemy roadblock set up for the very purpose of trapping them, only for the German sentries to gesture in greeting and to wave them through. Never before had Lees so appreciated the advantages of making like the enemy.

An agonising journey three days by bullock cart had followed, as they'd crawled ever higher into the mountains. Over time it had become a blurred kaleidoscope of heat, pain, agony and semi-oblivion, as he and Gordon had lain on a bed of straw, groaning and crying out at every lurch and jolt. Pitched this way and that, Lees' pain-racked, fevered imagination had relived the last few months of operations, which had been 'some of the happiest of my life'.

He remembered his arrival in January 1945 and 'running like rabbits frightened by a stoat', as the partisans had broken before the German *rastrellamento*. The long weeks of preparation that had followed, 'building an army from a rabble'. The day in late February when those same partisans had driven the Black Brigade battalion across the Secchia, trapping them and leaving very few alive, 'confirming that my work had been worthwhile'.

Then there was the questioning of Hans, the German deserter, and the first intimations of the kind of target offered by the Botteghe headquarters. Following that, 'on the crest of a wave, the advent of the parachutists and our attack on Botteghe', and all that had transpired in the aftermath of the raid. 'I thought back over . . . the wild music of those pipes and the terrible moment when I could not walk, then those anxious days hiding out in the plains, for the first time in my life helpless and relying on others . . .'

Beginning with his mission with Major Temple and ending with his terrible injuries, it had been 'A long trail, always moving, always alert, attacking, escaping, but always preparing for that day . . . when, guided by a few British officers, the partisans all over Europe would rise against the enemy.' Any day now, Lees reflected, 'the partisans, strong and united, will advance from their strongholds to drive the Germans out.' He lamented how, 'on the eve of that day, crippled and useless, I had to withdraw from the game. Hard justice indeed . . . but the mountains are cruel though fair and a wounded man is no use to them.' Still he longed to be a part of this final uprising, 'praising, cursing and encouraging' to the last.

As it was, that was never going to happen. Instead, on the morning of 6 April 1945 Mike Lees lay on a stretcher on the edge of a tiny field seemingly sliced from the very side of the mountain above the village of Ranzano. Strung along either side of the tiny, postage-stamp-sized 'airstrip' was a line of silk parachutes – markers for the incoming pilot. The strip was no more than a hundred yards long by thirty broad, so not a great deal wider than the wingspan of the inbound aircraft.

Beside Lees squatted a familiar figure – the former schoolmaster, Corporal Phil Butler, who'd served as Lees' right-hand man in Secchio. Butler had trekked across the hills to aid in Lees' evacuation, as had Kiss, the commander of his Stafettas. Lees turned to the pair of them, as all eyes scanned the sky to the south, ears straining for the noise of a light aircraft at altitude.

'Any sign?' he queried.

Butler shrugged. 'No, but it can't be long. They're due soon after ten. Not long now and you'll be in liberated territory. How're you feeling?'

'The leg hurts like hell,' Lees replied, honestly. 'Otherwise, not too bad. If all goes well that'll be fixed by tonight. Give me a hand to sit up, will you?'

Butler put his arms around Lees' broad shoulders and helped him into a sitting position. It was a magnificent morning. All around them spring growth, verdant green, sparkled with dew. Further north the valley carved around towards the plains, which were thick with a heat haze. South lay the humped folds of Monte Cusna – *Uomo Morto*; Dead Man – rising to the glistening white snow-cap where Eyton-Jones and Kershaw had almost met their end.

To every side woodland echoed with birdsong, and here and there blazed a riot of colour – wild primrose and crocus patches breaking into bloom. Over the months that he had soldiered here, Lees had grown to love these mountains and their people. The clear air, the open spaces, the freedom and adventure – all would soon be a thing of the past, should the aircraft reach him and pluck him to safety. But at least he should survive, and keep his health.

A cry from Butler brought Lees' mind back to the moment. 'There it is,' he yelled.

Sure enough, seemingly impossibly high above Cusna, a tiny

black speck hung in the heavens, sunlight glinting off its wings beguilingly. So slowly it seemed hardly to be moving, that speck gained shape and substance. To either side Lees could make out the dart-like forms of two further aircraft – Mustangs, circling protectively around the tiny form of the Storch.

In broad daylight, at times dropping to tree top height to avoid enemy gun batteries, at others braving high passes close to the aircraft's service ceiling, Furio Lauri had nursed the aircraft thus far, and was now beginning his approach to what appeared to be an impossible landing. Gradually, the noise of the aircraft became audible, its single engine put-puttering like a lawnmower on a hot summer's day.

The fuselage appeared impossibly spindly and improbably fragile, sandwiched between two ridiculously large, oddly curved wings. It seemed more butterfly than warplane. It circled over the tiny strip, the pilot sizing up what lay below. Would he even risk a landing, Lees wondered. He could see the pilot's face gazing out of the cockpit, as he studied the approach and the terrain, a thick frown creasing his brow.

He passed over, wingtip practically kissing the grass as he banked and dipped below the height of the field, dropping from view. Lees wondered if he had decided it was not worth the risk. The ground was rough and the strip small, plus unpredictable cross winds sheered across these mountains. The Storch made several more approaches, but each was aborted as the pilot must have figured he couldn't quite land.

Finally, Lees heard the engine note change: from a murmur, it had become almost a roar, the noise echoing up from below and rebounding across the valley. Moments later the Storch reappeared, rearing up just a few feet above the end of the strip, where it seemed to hover motionless for a second, before touching down like a great bird. It rumbled to a bumpy halt in less than a fifth of the length of the strip, in an incredible feat of airmanship.

Eager hands lifted Lees up and rushed him to the waiting aircraft. Lauri sat at the controls, engine still running, as Lees was manhandled into the seat directly behind him. The cockpit was cramped and Lauri had to struggle to get the parachute strapped to Lees' body. Figures crowded the doorway – partisans wishing good luck and godspeed. Lees shouted a few words of farewell through the door.

'Bye-bye, Phil. My love to all and a kiss for Don Pedro's mother. And tell Bert not to bust himself.' By 'Bert' he meant Bert Farrimond, his ever-faithful radio operator.

Then, as the partisans took hold of the wings and lifted the tail, Lauri brought the engine up to full power, dropped his hand to signal release and the Storch began bumping across the strip. All too soon the aircraft dipped over the edge of the field and plummeted into the abyss. For a long moment Lees feared they were done for, before the wings began to gain lift and the nose lurched violently upwards, throwing Lees back into his seat.

Having averted disaster, the pilot set a course for Cusna and, beyond that, Florence. Major Charles Holland, the BLO who had organised this daring evacuation on the ground, would refer to that airstrip as Mike Lees' 'tennis lawn . . . The pick-up to evacuate Capt. Michael Lees took place on a flat 100 yd spur with a sheer drop on three sides. The STORCH had great difficulty landing but the take-off was perfect . . . LAURI deserves a medal for his landing . . . He made 5 attempts . . . each one more dangerous than the last.'

It was eleven o'clock in the morning on 6 April 1945, when the

Storch began the long climb to overfly the snow-bound heights of Cusna, the Mustangs buzzing and swooping protectively around it. As the aircraft droned ever onwards Lees settled back into his seat, trying to ignore the pain in his leg, and little realising the trouble that he was flying into.

Upon arrival at the Rosignano airbase, he was met by a junior SOE officer whom he didn't particularly recognise. Oddly, the man seemed acutely embarrassed and Lees didn't have a clue as to why. 'At that stage I had no knowledge that they were claiming that I had ignored orders,' he remarked. 'Indeed, at no stage was I ever told this directly to my face, although my subsequent treatment reflected their displeasure very clearly. They just handed me over to the medical services and left, washing their hands of me.'

Lees was admitted to a general military hospital, in Florence, before being transferred to a similar facility in Rome. His admission records noted the following: 'He was not admitted to any medical unit or formation during the period 26 March 45 – 6 Apr 45.' Of course, that was the time that he had languished, injured, hiding and running from the enemy on the plains of the Po. That amounted to eleven days, so longer than the ten that Dr Chiesi had given him to repair his severed nerves.

Still, Lees reached hospital hopeful that his leg might be saved. Unfortunately, he was placed in a general ward, with no one to agitate and lobby for the urgent and specialist treatment that his injuries required. Utterly exhausted from his back-breaking journey, plagued by multiple gunshot wounds that hadn't been properly treated and ailing from the recent bout of malaria, Lees was hardly in a fit state to fight for the kind of treatment that he so desperately required.

'So much for the ten days and the risks taken by the partisans to get me . . . promptly out,' Lees concluded. Indeed, it wouldn't be for many weeks, and only due to his family pulling strings at the very highest level, that Lees would finally get the specialist treatment that his damaged nerves required. By then much of the damage was irreparable.

'The war came while I was still young and inexperienced in human nature,' Lees would write of this time. 'I was dumb enough to believe that everybody else was motivated by a simple and straightforward desire to get on with the war. I learned about the perfidy of men and organisations the hard way . . . I was a tough guerrilla leader, but stupid to a degree in dealing with staff at Base; perhaps we didn't tick the same way.'

To what degree Lees and the staff didn't 'tick' was shortly to be demonstrated, as the witch-hunt gathered pace. But for now, he was languishing in a military hospital, largely forgotten, as 'his' partisans, commanded by Roy Farran, embarked upon their last great hurrah.

In the memory of Mike Lees, the Reggio partisans were to spread chaos and havoc behind the enemy's front, helping break the spirit of the Gothic Line defenders.

Chapter 22

From his ridgetop position Farran observed the helter-skelter of enemy traffic, which crammed Highway Twelve in a riot of disarray. For two weeks now he and his Victory Column had played their part in fomenting a collapse of the German defences across a wide swathe of the Gothic Line. Their actions had commenced in a mass battle against an entire German *panzerjäger* – tank-hunter – battalion.

Surprised in a village on the approaches to Highway Twelve, the Victory Column had won that ferocious firefight more by good luck than judgement. Karl Nurk had scored a lucky hit with an early shot on the howitzer. The commanders of the *panzerjäger* unit had set up headquarters in a farmhouse, but Nurk had spotted them and duly slotted a 75mm shell through the window. Meanwhile Lieutenant Harvey had used the Vickers machine guns from the high-ground to cut the enemy's ranks to shreds.

The German force – some 400 strong – had suffered a minimum of sixty dead, with many more injured. So enraged were the survivors that they had torched the village of Marinello during their retreat. It turned out that the *panzerjägers* had been endeavouring to open a new supply route to their front-line positions that would cut through the mountains, as the open expanse of Highway Twelve was proving too vulnerable to Allied airstrikes. Farran's Victory Column had stopped them in their tracks.

The battle had taken place on 10 April 1945 and many more had followed. With Lieutenant David Eyton-Jones' feet having mostly recovered from their frostbite, Farran had placed him in command of Star Column – the sixty Italian partisans, stiffened by five SAS. By 16 April all four columns – Sun, Moon, Star and Eclipse – were harassing and ambushing enemy traffic the length and breadth of Highway Twelve, but still there was no Allied breakthrough of the *Gotenstellung*.

Indeed, an 8 April assessment of enemy forces manning the Gothic Line, authored by Allied Forces Headquarters, concluded: 'They represent an as yet unbroken and coherent element of the Wehrmacht with a fine defensive record behind them. They . . . are in strong heavily defended positions which may cost the Anglo-Americans heavy losses to breach . . . Even if breached, they may be capable of sufficient power of recovery to confront the Allies with a series of delaying actions on successive river lines . . . They represent a considerable source of manpower should some form of desperate last stand materialise in the Austrian Alps.'

Eleven days into the assault on the Gothic Line, German units were still holding firm, in response to which Farran redoubled his efforts to fool the enemy into thinking that their front was crumbling. Rather than concentrating on sneaking close to Highway Twelve to launch ambushes, he ordered his columns to hold back in cover, mounting mortar, howitzer and heavy machine-gun attacks, targeting the enemy's garrisons and vehicle parks. In so doing he intended to give the impression that the Allies' heavy artillery and armour had broken through. If they could spread enough fear and panic, the lines should crumble.

In the first such exploit Farran himself took the jeep convoy –

Eclipse Column – deep into hostile terrain, with the howitzer in tow. From a high point they unleashed seventy 75mm shells onto the enemy garrison based in the town of Sassuolo. So carried away did Farran become that he even ordered the shelling of the town's military hospital. For once, the SAS commander was overruled by his men, who refused to do it. There was no need: the streets were awash with German army trucks and troops, fleeing this way and that in panic.

After the attack, Farran sent the Staffetas on their bicycles into town to check. Sure enough, they returned with news that the German commander had ordered an evacuation, fearing that the Allies had broken through. This, Farran realised, was the answer. It was hardly classic SAS tactics – which were up close and personal ambushes and raids – but it was exactly what the present circumstances called for. Fear of an Allied breakthrough was a weapon that they could wield to good effect, decimating enemy morale and causing them to flee. It was perfect.

Lieutenant Eld scored the next success, mortaring German positions from the foothills with similarly spectacular results. As more and more such attacks were executed, the only challenge for Farran was to keep his columns supplied with enough mortar, machine-gun and howitzer rounds. The Dakotas resorted to flying deep into enemy territory, dropping supplies to fields only recently secured by Farran and his men. With the jeeps to hand they could load up and motor out of there, before the enemy could cause any trouble.

Farran empowered his commanders – Eld, Harvey and Eyton-Jones first and foremost – to make nowhere safe for the enemy. 'The partisans captured a German soldier as he visited a farmhouse to buy eggs,' Eyton-Jones recounted of his next attack.

Under questioning, the captive revealed that there was a major German garrison in the nearby village of Montebonello, with a key sentry position atop the church tower. Eyton-Jones took a compass bearing on the tower, and that night they launched their attack, using a Browning heavy machine gun.

'We'd loaded belts of ammunition with tracer bullets and incendiary,' Eyton-Jones recounted. They opened fire, streams of tracer 'burning across the sky and swinging in arcs from the church tower to the village square. There must have been vehicles parked in the square, for very soon it was rocked with explosions. The barrel of the Browning was red hot when we loaded it back onto the mule . . .' The following morning the Stafettas reported German forces evacuating Montebonello.

Not to be outdone, Lieutenant Harvey launched a ferocious attack on Highway Twelve, leading the Moon Column with the unbridled aggression of youth. Harvey chose to ambush a convoy at night, where it was forced to navigate a U-shaped bend in the road. Opening fire from three sides, his forces tore apart trucks and horse-drawn carts, causing scores of casualties. Somewhat wild at heart, Harvey decided to stay to witness the bloody aftermath, as enemy troops turned on each other in the darkness and confusion.

'The enemy from each side of the U fired at each other,' he reported. 'When this started I ordered our withdrawal. I stayed on for fifteen minutes myself, fascinated by the mischief that I had started and which now had developed into quite a battle, each side thinking the other to be the ambushers.' Come morning, so shattered was their morale that 150 enemy soldiers sought to surrender to him – almost three times the number of fighters Harvey had in his Moon Column.

With Lieutenant Eld leading a series of jeep-mounted raids, Farran, an astute and driven commander, used the British successes to berate Modena and his Russians, urging them to greater efforts. Modena duly led an all-out assault on the German garrison at Lama Mocogno, a town that straddled Highway Twelve itself. In ferocious fighting they seized five hundred prisoners – five times the number of troops that Modena had in his command.

On 21 April Farran deployed Molto Stanco to unleash a barrage of 75mm shells onto Reggio Emilia itself, where an injured Lees had only recently been sheltered. The German commander reacted by ordering his entire force to evacuate that major garrison town, even sanctioning the blowing up and demolition of key positions as they pulled out.

'Within two hours of our attack, the enemy blew up the Post Office,' Farran reported. 'Various other demolitions were heard and it was reported that Fascists were levelling the town. We only realised later . . . that the timing of this attack had been so opportune.' What made it so timely was revealed the very next day, when Farran received reports that the German front was crumbling, their divisions falling into a mass retreat.

'There were only two crossings over the river Secchia left open to three German divisions (the 232, the 114 and the 334), which were withdrawing north-west towards the Po,' Farran reported. 'At midday we noticed an enormous column of lorries and carts and a few tanks head-to-tail crossing the ford . . . Our whole force, with the guns, took up position on the last foothills overlooking the plains . . .'

Farran ordered every available man, gun and vehicle into action. 'My plan was to throw everything at the Germans . . . For this was no time for caution; if we delayed, the opportunity would be lost forever.' Leaving the jeeps and guns parked in the lee of the ridge, Farran crept forward with Karl Nurk, keeping to hands and knees as they crested the high ground. An incredible sight met their gaze: as far as the eye could see columns of German troops and vehicles stretched northwards across the plain.

While the congestion was terrible everywhere, it was worst at the two chokepoints directly below – a bridge and a ford that crossed the Secchia. A dense column of troops, trucks and armour crawled towards those two crossings. Even closer, maybe a hundred feet below their position, a German infantry battalion lolled in the shade of some trees surrounding a farmhouse. They looked utterly spent. No sentries had been posted and no defensive positions set.

'The signs were unmistakable,' Farran remarked. 'This was a picture of a rout, of an army in full retreat. The Gothic Line was broken.'

Farran and Nurk crawled back to their men unnoticed by the enemy. Jock Easton was busy sighting the howitzer, drawing up ox-carts laden with shells. Leaving ten men to screen the gun from attack, Farran arranged the jeeps with their water-cooled Vickers heavy machine guns along the line of the ridge. The plan of attack was simple. Upon Farran's word Easton was to open fire with Molto Stanco, shelling the two crossing points, which were jam-packed with military vehicles.

The Vickers were to join the fray, pouring in fire, as were the mortars. The range was less than four hundred yards, making the densely packed convoys sitting targets. Positions set, Farran crawled back and slid into a convenient slit-trench that someone had dug into the forward slope of the ridge. He checked with

340

Easton, via his walkie-talkie radio-telephone, that he was ready with the howitzer.

That confirmed, Farran grabbed his binoculars and studied the sweep of the targets. Enemy forces crawled across the plain like a giant and restless colony of ants. Still he hesitated to give the order to open fire. The retreating forces were so numerous and so apparently well-armed, it seemed suicidal to give the word to attack. The Victory Column was outnumbered over a thousand to one, not to mention seriously outgunned.

'Almost any serious reaction by the enemy might mean annihilation of my force,' Farran reasoned, 'for the hills behind us were so open and so bare that escape would be impossible. This action we contemplated was far different from our customary guerrilla tactics of hit-and-run.'

Farran sensed the eyes of his men upon him, silently pleading for him to give the word. Not for the first time, he wondered if he had lost his nerve. It was then that he felt a figure wriggle into the trench beside him. It was Karl Nurk. Nurk shook Farran's elbow and pointed at the jumbled mass of German transport trying to negotiate the river crossings.

He grinned. 'Come on, let's go.'

By way of answer, Farran spoke into the radio handset. 'Jock, you ready?'

'Ready,' he replied, curtly.

Farran passed him the bearing off the map, telling him to fire one round at the river, range fifteen hundred yards. The crash of the gun split the air, the shell whistling over Farran and Nurk's heads, over those of the German infantry gathered at the farmhouse, and exploding on the river bank just to the north of the ford. Instantaneously, the Vickers opened fire, spraying the road

341

directly below with long bursts of fire. A truck was hit, bursting into flames and slewing sideways, completely blocking the route.

The Brens and mortars joined in, tracer and incendiary rounds tearing into the enemy columns with devastating effect, mortar shells crumping among hordes of fleeing figures. Farran told Easton to drop his aim one hundred yards and a little east. His second shell burst just short in the river. Farran adjusted again, and the third shell was bang on. A truck towing a gun was blown onto its side in the middle of the river crossing. Further vehicles caught fire, throwing up thick and roiling clouds of smoke.

From below, the German infantry began to return fire, Mausers raking Farran's ridgetop position. His men answered with long bursts of Sten fire, which tore into the open terrain. At the river crossing carts were hit by the shellfire, their horses panicking horribly. A terrified horse-team dragged its cart off the road. Others were hit in the water. As those coming from behind tried to find a way past, they in turn became bogged in deep mud. The confusion and chaos were indescribable.

In no time a dozen trucks were aflame in the river, surrounded by overturned carts and struggling horses. Five were burning fiercely on the riverbank, with another six on the road below. The odd ping of a rifle shot kicked up dust on the rim of the trench, indicating to Farran that the enemy were still returning fire, but it was as nothing compared to the carnage being wrought. Eventually, a Spandau gunner began to plaster rounds all over Farran's trench position. No one had been hit yet, but it needed to be silenced.

Farran ordered some of the Garibaldini into the fray. These were very different men from those Farran had set out to train, at the start of Operation Tombola. Now, in a repeat of the wild dash that had driven the Germans out of the Secchia valley, they raced down the slope, no longer needing the SAS major to take the lead. After short-lived and sporadic resistance, the Germans threw down their arms.

Only with nightfall did Farran's ridgetop guns fall silent. They had fired 150 shells via the howitzer, but it was now too dark to aim and to shoot effectively. Across the terrain a pall of thick oily smoke testified to the utter devastation wrought. In the final hours, pathetic figures whose vehicles were on fire had scrambled up the slope, brandishing white handkerchiefs and with their hands raised. They sought someone, anyone, to whom to surrender. That night, Farran's camp was overwhelmed with would-be prisoners.

At dawn the flood of enemy vehicles had become a trickle. Farran took his jeep and motored down to Highway Twelve, to check out the lie of the land, barely daring to believe that the battle might be over. On the approach to Sassuolo he ran into Ken Harvey's Moon Column, battle wearied and dust-covered, but likewise jubilant. They handed Farran something of a novelty right then – packets of American chewing gum.

Up ahead the US 1st Armoured Division was advancing and the Germans were reported to be in retreat everywhere. Farran ordered his forces to regroup in Modena, the city that dominates the south side of the plains of the Po. There, his Sun, Moon, Star and Eclipse columns were reunited. The Americans had bypassed the city, their armoured legions racing after the retreating Germans. The streets echoed to the occasional gunshot, as liberating forces celebrated and chased away the last Fascist diehards.

Yet even here victory was to be bitter sweet. There was to be a sting in the tail for Farran and his Allied Battalion. A formal victory parade was to take place in the city, immediately after which Farran and his men were ordered to disarm the Russians. Once that was done, they were to be loaded aboard transport so they could be 'repatriated' to the Soviet Union. Few doubted what fate would await the likes of Modena, if that order were carried out. Most were horrified at the very thought of it.

'I had not the moral courage for what seemed to us at the time to be such a cruel, unfair and premature act,' Farran remarked of the order. 'Those clever people in Florence could never understand the mutual trust between comrades-in-arms. We had fought together, some had died together, and now in the hour of our victory we were asked to take away their arms.' Worse still would be sending them back to the USSR to almost certain death.

'The Russians, I was sure, would feel themselves disgraced,' Farran remarked of the order, 'would feel that the British trusted them less than they trusted the Italians.' Farran couldn't contemplate openly defying his orders. There had been quite enough of that of late and he was fearful that he was going face a court martial. Still, there were ways and means to evade such impossible, inhuman instructions as these.

Someone got a warning to Modena. Along with his beautiful Italian mistress he disappeared. Eyton-Jones was one of those charged to load the Russians aboard waiting transport. He, like the others, had a simple means of 'obeying' his orders, while ensuring they proved utterly ineffectual. He opened the door on one side of the train carriage to load the Russians aboard, then unlocked the door on the opposite side to ensure they could escape.

'Few of them turned up,' he remarked happily, of his Russian comrades-in-arms, 'and their leader never came. A lot of them got onto one side of the train and got out of the other . . . for they knew if they were going back to Russia, Stalin was going to kill them.'

The victory parade and the wild partying gave the SAS the perfect way to bid farewell to their partisan brothers-in-arms. The following day the main body of No. 3 Squadron formed up in convoy for the drive back to Florence. They left a rear party, commanded by Eyton-Jones, to ensure the squadron's fallen were properly buried in the graveyard at Albinea, close to their infamous raid at Botteghe. Riccomini, Guscott and Bolden were already there. Sadly, Lance Corporal Robert Bruce – Justo Balerdi, the Spanish Civil War veteran and French Foreign Legionnaire – had been killed in the final days of operations.

On the night of 20/21 April two SAS jeeps had ambushed a German position in what Farran described as a 'daring attack'. They'd targeted a German supply dump, racing in with machine guns blazing. Long bursts of tracer from the jeep's weapons had torn into a large truck and ammunition trailer, destroying them completely, and detonating a heap of anti-aircraft shells. An enemy vehicle was seized intact, and scores of prisoners taken, but at the height of the raid Balerdi had been hit in the head by a bullet and killed outright.

Eyton-Jones' final mission was to bury Balerdi alongside his fallen comrades Bolden, Guscott and Riccomini. Balerdi's Spanish SAS comrade, Private Raphael Ramos, asked if he might accompany Eyton-Jones, to help lay his 'brother' to rest. No one was sure if they were directly related, or just 'brothers-in-arms', but it was only fitting that a fellow Spaniard should help to bury him. So it was that Ramos joined Eyton-Jones for the journey back to the site of the bloody and portentous headquarters raid.

But first, they had to inter Balerdi's corpse. Locals had buried the Spaniard in a field, his body shrouded in a tarpaulin. Eyton-Jones and Ramos unearthed his remains from the shallow grave. 'His face was still locked in grim determination,' Eyton-Jones remarked of the fallen Spaniard, 'with eyes open and teeth barred.' Upon reaching the Albinea graveyard, Balerdi was laid to rest alongside his SAS comrades. The priest seemed nervous, for German troops were still roaming the area, but Eyton-Jones and Ramos were undeterred. They arranged for a stonemason to erect crosses over the graves, in part so Balerdi's family could locate their fallen son once the war was over.

Lieutenant Harvey sought permission from Farran to return to the Secchia valley, ostensibly to shut down their headquarters, but in truth to bid a last farewell. It was granted. 'With Jock Easton we went in a jeep and . . . returned to our old haunts . . .' Harvey recounted. 'Everywhere we were feted – the war was virtually over and the peasants, with whom we had lived for so long and had done so much for the cause of liberating their country, were free.'

The main body of the SAS force prepared to depart Modena. Jeeps were loaded with the wounded. Norice, the grey-eyed Stafetta, refused to leave them, while Farran lacked the heart to order her to stay. She rode on one of the jeeps, together with the two civilian cars, captured German Army trucks, and a German Army ambulance, which rounded off the bizarre convoy. The chief stress faced by Farran and his men had been the nervous strain of long weeks operating behind enemy lines. Consequently, they were in unusually high spirits, and they draped a captured Nazi swastika over the gun carriage that held Molto Stanco.

The odd, hotchpotch cavalcade must have made an astonishing sight, as it made its way back through the advancing Allied forces. Dusty, dirty, bearded, blood-stained and in many cases long-haired after months in the mountains, Farran's SAS stood in sharp contrast to the smart, gleaming, well-ordered columns of military might.

'They must have wondered who on earth we could be,' Farran remarked. 'We were the *"Battaglione Alleato"* ... otherwise known as the *"Battaglione McGinty"*, whose motto was *"Chi osera vincera"* – Who dares wins.'

As the convoy wound its way into the highlands, passing through the Gothic Line defences, the devastation was clear: massive bomb craters pitted the blasted, denuded landscape, which in many places resembled the surface of the moon. This ghostly terrain – this valley of the shadow of death – was a testament to the ferocity of the main battle, and Farran's party fell quiet as they passed through.

During the journey the SAS major had time to contemplate all they had achieved and what troubles might now lie ahead. Over the past few weeks his Victory Column had shelled, machine-gunned and mortared nineteen towns and villages, targeting the German garrisons stationed there. At a conservative estimate Farran reckoned they'd accounted for some 300 enemy killed, with many more wounded, and hundreds taken prisoner. Scores of enemy vehicles had been destroyed.

But by far the greatest impact was the chaos, panic and insecurity such actions had caused among the enemy. Farran cited this in his official report, lauding 'the morale effect of so formidable and enterprising a force in the immediate rear of the enemy ... There is little doubt that the actions fought considerably accelerated the panic and rout of some three to four German divisions.' That equated to as many as 100,000 men-at-arms.

Farran's casualty list was stunningly light. It included four SAS 'Killed', or 'Missing – believed killed' – Lieutenant Riccomini, Serjeant Guscott, Lance Corporal Bruce (the Spaniard, Justo Balerdi) and Corporal Bolden, plus six wounded. Then there were the nine Russians killed or missing in action, plus a handful of Italian casualties. It was a tiny toll, considering the damage caused to the enemy.

Of particular note, Farran stated, was the raid on the 14th Army headquarters: 'the success of this attack . . . had a great effect on the outcome of the final battle in Italy.' In its official regimental report on Tombola, the SAS would echo Farran's sentiments: 'A Staff Colonel and sixty other Germans were killed in fighting which resulted in the destruction of the main Headquarters . . .' That same report lauded 'Major McGinty, who by threats and persuasion was able to achieve cohesion and efficiency from so heterogenous a force.'

The real impact of the Botteghe raid would only become clear in the months that followed. During that long drive to Florence, Farran's mind was mostly occupied with thoughts of what fate might now hold in store for him. Once he reached Allied headquarters, was he to be thrown into a military gaol, facing charges and a court martial? That was his overriding fear.

'Fortunately, I did not receive a trial by court martial as I expected,' Farran would note, of his arrival back in liberated territory. Certainly, there were those in British high command who were determined to try him on two counts: parachuting behind the lines against orders and attacking the Botteghe HQ when ordered not to. But their intentions were frustrated, and largely due to the efforts of US Colonel Riepe, the commander of Allied special forces operations in Florence, plus a handful of other senior American figures.

Upon reaching Florence, Farran learned that the Americans were putting him forward for the US Legion of Merit – a high valour medal given for exceptional conduct in battle. It was to recognise the service that he and his SAS had provided in raising the Allied Battalion and wreaking havoc behind the lines, which had contributed greatly to the final Allied breakthrough. It was, as Farran pointed out, his 'ace in the hole', for 'I could hardly be court-martialled for something for which I had been decorated.'

The citation for his Legion of Merit recorded that Farran's operations on Tombola had 'materially assisted' the attacks of the United States military forces and contributed significantly to the success of Fifteenth Army Group and its breaking of the German defences in Italy.

But sadly, there was to be no eleventh-hour reprieve – or glory – for the chief architect of the Botteghe HQ raid, Mike Lees.

Epilogue

Lees, Farran and their ilk had played a crucial part in bringing victory and liberation to Italy. On 26 April the city of Milan was liberated by Italian partisans and on the 29th the entire 6,000-strong German 232nd Division was captured. Allied forces marched into Milan the same day, as Hitler committed suicide in his Berlin bunker. At noon on 2 May 1945 – so less than a week after Farran and his men had withdrawn from the field – hostilities ceased in Italy, almost a million German troops surrendering complete with their equipment. That same day the Red Army took Berlin. On 7 May the Germans' unconditional surrender had been signed and the war was over.

In *Daggers Drawn*, Mike Morgan's excellent history of the SAS in the Second World War, he rightly concludes of Operation Tombola: 'The exploits of this brave, motley band . . . during the final weeks of the war were to go down in [SAS] regimental history.' No less than Lieutenant-Colonel Brian Franks, DSO, MC, commander of 2 SAS during the war years, would echo such sentiments, writing that 'the detachment of this Regiment played a big part towards bringing about the final surrender of the German armies in Italy.'

The fears expressed that the 'Reds' would somehow execute a violent and bloody communist takeover in Italy proved unfounded: with very few exceptions, in towns and villages across the country Committees of National Liberation were formed, which combined all political factions in a nationwide effort to bring the rule of law and good governance to the nation. They enjoyed widespread support and the backing of the populace.

In the run-up to the German surrender, SOE Florence had kept headquarters in London closely informed of the break-neck pace of developments. Codenamed 'Freeborn', their series of reports summarised the messages that had come flooding in from missions all across the front. One, despatched on 25 April, dealt with Macintosh's central area of operations. It read:

> Owing rapid progress in Apennine Battle Zone, all missions controlled by Macintosh at 5th Special Force Unit now overrun after making solid contribution to Allied advance and having considerable success in anti-scorch measures. Following reported from sets (a) Carrara, no repeat no excesses by partisans and no evidence of purge or blood-bath (b) Bologna no repeat no disorder. Partisans being [?] used [?] as guards, electricity and water functioning 24 hours after fall.

Despite the odd, disjointed language, it revealed the spirit with which the partisans had seized back control of their country, belying the fears of those in Allied high command who worried there would be a communist-instigated 'purge or bloodbath'. Of course, hindsight is a fine thing and perhaps one could argue this wasn't to be known at the time. However, a simple listening to the BLOs – those on the ground embedded deep within partisan command and control – would have reflected how little they credited such fears.

Ironically, a telegraph sent by Sir Noel Charles, the British ambassador in Rome, to the Foreign Office, sums up the situation admirably. 'After successful patriot insurrections in Milan, Turin, Genoa and other northern towns and withdrawal of German and Fascist troops, law and order were preserved to a remarkable degree.' It was, of course, the Foreign Office that had stoked the fears of communist-leaning partisans – the dreaded 'reds' – seizing control in a violent, post-liberation overthrow.

Subsequently, the achievements of the Italian partisans were to be lauded by many. Colin McVean Gubbins, Chief of the SOE – who had lost his son on behind-the-lines operations in Italy – heaped praise upon their efforts. His words are worth quoting in full:

> The final effort of the Italian partisans, who numbered thousands, was timed to coincide with Alexander's attack on the vaunted Gothic Line in Northern Italy. They had been harrowing Kesselring's communications all winter, and now the time for the coup de grâce had come. They fought like demons, many British officers and NCOs alongside them, parachuted in to train and organise them and to provide arms and ammunition. Some 65,000 strong they seized Genoa, Milan, Turin and other towns as the Allies advanced, opening the way for the lightning thrust of Alexander's forces to the Alps and cutting off the ignominious surrender of Kesselring's entire Armies – total victory.

In his book *Echoes of Resistance: British Involvement with the Italian Partisans*, author Lawrence Lewis echoes such sentiments, while making special mention of the 14th Army HQ raid. He concludes: 'The [resistance] movement was far more important in the disruption it caused to German activities . . . For instance, the upset caused to the German communications by an attack such as that which wiped out the Albinea headquarters – possibly the most significant single action involving Partisans in the entire history of the Partisan movement . . . cannot be quantified by pure statistics.'

Indeed, documents retrieved from German archives suggest that following the Botteghe (Albinea) raid, the 14th Army headquarters was bereft of all communications for fifteen days – constituting the vital period when Allied forces launched their final assault on the Gothic Line. When the 14th Army eventually re-established its headquarters, the Germans chose to site it in an Italian village where it was vulnerable to, and was subsequently hit by, Allied warplanes, so speeding its final demise.

Foremost SOE assassin Major Barton did parachute into the region, on his Cisco Red II mission, charged with assassinating General Heinrich von Vietinghoff, but by the time of his arrival Lees was caught up in the Botteghe HQ raid. Barton went on to call in air-drops and to build up a fresh band of partisans, with a view to the coming offensive. His citation for his mission records that at one stage, 'Major Barton and his WT operator were surprised . . . in a house by a Fascist officer who . . . held them up at the point of an automatic. Major Barton, regardless of his own safety immediately leaped on the officer and succeeded in killing him. While retrieving his automatic . . . he found the house surrounded by Fascists, but with the aid of his wireless operator he succeeded in shooting his way out.' Barton and his partisans went on to play their own role in the liberation of northern Italy. After the war he moved to Africa, became a farmer and raised a family.

*

In having to try to balance the conflicting demands from London over support for the Italian resistance, SOE Florence's Major Charles Macintosh doubtless had been handed something of a poisoned chalice. He was a smallish cog in a far larger machine. However, that does not explain the antipathy he apparently felt and extended towards Mike Lees, nor the relentless witch-hunt that would follow Lees' evacuation from Italy.

In his official report on Tombola, Farran would explain his decision to proceed with the 14th Army HQ raid as follows: 'Unfortunately, I had already left on the long march to the plains when the cancellation was received on my wireless set in the mountains. In any case, having once committed a partisan force to such an attack an alteration in plan would have been disastrous to guerrilla morale in the whole area.'

Farran must have known he was treading on thin ice: the report is very carefully worded. Fortunately his American Legion of Merit served to exonerate him of all blame. The citation reads: 'After he himself had parachuted behind enemy lines, he assumed command of his nearest operational party and led it on many raids which inflicted casualties and damage on the hostile forces . . . Major Farran's effective leadership of both his special unit and Italian partisans contributed significantly to the success of the 15th Army Group.'

Making no mention of disobeying orders, the honour effectively quashed any arguments that Major Roy Farran, DSO, MC and two bars, should face any kind of disciplinary action. Farran, to his immense credit, was one of the few in command who chose to stand by Mike Lees.

*

Long after victory had been declared in Italy, Lees was finally flown to Britain, to a military hospital in Chester. On 25 May 1945, seven weeks after Lees had been rescued via pilot Furio Lauri's dramatic air mission, a letter arrived at SOE headquarters concerning his injuries. Lees had arrived back in the UK just a week before, to be treated for 'wounds received while a BLO in Northern Italy'. The letter noted the 'gravity of Capt. Lees' condition', and concerns that he might be hospitalised for some considerable time, during which the issue of his rank was playing on his mind.

Lees had been promised promotion to the rank of major in the field, which would have fitted his role and position as Secchio BLO, or so he claimed. In the letter, an appeal was raised to 'Col. Hewitt, Commander No. 1 Special Force', latterly the official name of the SOE mission in Florence. 'It is strongly urged that everything possible be done to regularise this officer's position,' the letter noted, 'and above all to remove the cause of his present anxiety, as it is feared that this may impede his recovery.'

Lees' appeal to Hewitt was perhaps understandable. After all, this was the man who, as one of SOE Maryland's senior commanders, had issued the glowing report following Lees' crossing of the lines in September 1944, bringing with him the two Italian resistance leaders. But his response to Lees' 25 May 1945 appeal from his Chester hospital bed utterly belied such sentiments. Lees' hopes for promotion were to prove naïve and misguided. Dated 12 June 1945, Hewitt's letter pulled no punches. 'At no time, either before his departure or during his time in the field, was the question of his promotion raised with me by him or anybody else,' he wrote of Lees. There was worse to come.

'From the day he was infiltrated until the day he was exfiltrated,'

Hewitt's letter continued, 'Captain Lees was troublesome, insubordinate, unreasonable, tactless, irresponsible, and highhanded. His activities culminated in an action against the enemy which, in spite of its gallantry, he had been expressly forbidden ... to undertake. In view of the wounds he received disciplinary action against Captain Lees was not taken.' Hewitt attached a report to his letter outlining 'this officer's conduct in the field.'

Hewitt's *volte face* was all the more surprising bearing in mind that Roy Farran, who had overseen any contravention of orders and in any case outranked a malaria-racked Lees, had been decorated for commanding the 'forbidden' Botteghe raid. Regardless, Lees, hospitalised and ailing, was about to be hung out to dry. By 15 June – three days after Hewitt's damning letter – the betrayal of Mike Lees was all but complete.

The issue had been raised to a higher level. In a letter marked 'Confidential – BY BAG', the following was written of Lees: 'From the day that Capt. Lees was infiltrated into Northern Italy until the day he was exfiltrated, he has been most unsatisfactory.' Lees' conduct was described as 'troublesome, insubordinate and irresponsible,' especially in his 'action against the enemy'. After stressing that there was 'no question of this officer being promoted', the letter concluded that Lees was 'not recommended for re-employment within this organisation'.

In short, by mid-June 1945 Lees had been refused promotion, his reputation had been traduced and he had been thrown out of SOE. There was worse to follow. Ten days later, a note marked 'PERSONAL AND CONFIDENTIAL' was circulated concerning Mike Lees, landing on the desk of the Queen's Own Dorset Yeomanry – Lees' parent regiment, in which the Lees family had long served – as well as that of other interested parties.

It read: 'You will, by now, have seen the various signals and reports that have been passed between this HQ and LONDON on the subject of Capt. M. LEES; and you will appreciate that much of his report is biased and, I am afraid, untruthful.' By 25 June 1945, Lees was being accused of being 'biased' and 'untruthful' – a liar – regarding his record in the field. The note continued: 'It would be a comfort to know that his case is now fully closed. He is lucky that we should remember his gallantry without taking official note of his shortcomings.'

Actually, to the contrary, official 'note of his shortcomings' was about to be made most emphatically.

Roy Farran, to his credit, fought against this bitter tide. On 25 June, the same date that the above note was authored – it is incidentally signed anonymously 'AM 2' Farran authored a glowing citation for Mike Lees, in which he recommended him for the award of the Military Cross. It encapsulated with great eloquence Farran's view of the SOE officer and his achievements during the months that he served in the Secchia valley.

He organised his partisan division into an efficient guerrilla force and by his courageous example inspired the Italians to attacks on the enemy which they would not otherwise have performed. On March 4th he conceived a plan for attacking the German Corps H.Q. which controlled the whole . . . front from BOLOGNA to the sea. With great skill and courage he carried out a preliminary reconnaissance which revealed all the details of the H.Q.

The H.Q. was attacked with great success by a mixed force of British parachutists and partisans. Capt. Lees led his own band of partisans into the Corps Commander's villa with such dash that the ground floor and first landing on a spiral staircase were taken ... in spite of intense fire from the enemy. When his men hesitated in the face of such intense fire, with complete disregard for his own safety he stood on the staircase and waved them on, inspiring them to further efforts. Eventually he was seriously wounded, but continued to shout inspiring orders to his men ...

The citation went on to outline the convoluted and ingenious means by which Lees was evacuated from the field, before stressing the huge strategic value of the Botteghe HQ raid for 'the outcome of the final battle in Italy'. The raid's success was 'largely due to the gallantry, initiative and unequalled courage of Captain Lees', Farran concluded.

The MC recommendation was subsequently stamped 'Citation passed and approved by SOE.' After that, it was sent to 15 Army Group – the Allied command charged with the liberation of Italy – for final approval. There it apparently hit a brick wall. The official response came in a 25 July 1945 letter, marked 'Honours And Awards – CONFIDENTIAL'. It argued that in effect Roy Farran had no right to propose such an award.

'Captain LEES was not under command of 2 S.A.S. Regiment at the time nor was he working in support of that unit,' the letter stated. While admitting to the heroism and gallantry involved in the Botteghe raid, the letter continued: 'In the opinion of 15th Army Group the value of this operation depended on its timing, and Captain LEES with the SAS ... carried it out prematurely and recklessly in spite of the express orders.'

In short, it was case closed. Farran's best efforts had failed. Mike Lees was denied an MC.

In his excellent book, *Mission Accomplished: SOE and Italy 1943–1945*, David Stafford concludes: 'Given Lees' injuries, no disciplinary action was taken against him . . . although it was clear he had made himself unpopular with his superiors.' Just how unpopular is evidenced in the above correspondence, penned as Lees languished in a Chester hospital without proper treatment. Arguably, it was Farran's spirited and high-profile support that saved Lees from any greater degree of approbation.

It wasn't until the end of July – well after his MC had been proposed and denied – that Lees was finally moved to the kind of specialist unit that was required to treat his injuries. Through family connections an appeal had been made to Field Marshal Alanbrooke, who was Chief of the Imperial General Staff and a foremost adviser to Winston Churchill. Moved to a hospital near Oxford, Lees finally received the attention and treatment denied to him for approaching four months.

It's perhaps worth pausing at this juncture to revisit some of the extraordinary accusations levelled against Lees. For his service in Italy, he had been accused of being all of the following: insubordinate, unreasonable, tactless, irresponsible, highhanded, biased, reckless and untruthful. Although by the summer of 1945 Lees was yet to learn of most of these allegations – and indeed would not do so during his lifetime – his wartime record had been traduced among his peers.

What on earth had he done to attract such vile approbation and, frankly, distortions of the truth? By his own admission Lees could be tactless and he wasn't always smart and savvy in the handling of his superiors. But does that alone – the fact that he had put some of his superiors' noses out of joint – account for his treatment? Was it all down to a petty quest for revenge; for spite to have its day? If that is the case it seems utterly extraordinary, not to mention unconscionable.

Or was he so vilified simply for his alleged betrayal of orders? The SOE by its own admission sought mavericks, free-thinkers and self-starters, individuals happy to work alone and largely to their own drive and initiative. Lees was absolutely of that ilk and he demonstrated those attributes in his raising of the Secchia partisans and the attack on the Botteghe HQ. In Lees, SOE had got exactly what they had bargained for. If he had, as he was accused, disobeyed orders, what did they expect of such a man in such a position?

More to the point, if you adhere to the belief that the proof is very much in the pudding, the pudding served up at the Botteghe HQ on the night of 26/27 March 1945 proved well worth the eating. The raid, executed to the timing chosen by Lees and Farran, fully delivered. In light of which, and in view of the enormous challenges of mustering such an irregular, multinational force, surely a blind eye should have been turned to a stand-down order that was in any case a little late in reaching the field. At best, those who commanded such a raid should have received fitting recognition and praise.

Instead, Lees – wounded, hospitalised and unable to defend himself – had been utterly denigrated and pilloried. Moreover, there was a foil to his lack of tact with his superiors. The flip side was that Lees was blessed with an instinctive feel for the common man; an extraordinary gift to inspire the warrior spirit in those who were neither trained as regular soldiers, and, in the case of northern Italy in the spring of 1945, might have been forgiven for thinking the risks to themselves and their families too great.

That was an uncommon gift and a remarkable one, yet by war's end it went utterly unremarked and unrewarded. Is there perhaps another, deeper and darker explanation for how Lees was treated? Did Michael Lees – like Canadian war reporter Paul Morton – fall victim to those powers who were determined that the actions of the Italian partisans – the dreaded 'reds' – should be sidelined and consigned to the dustbin of history?

Veteran Canadian journalist Don North believes so. In his book *Inappropriate Conduct*, which tells the full story of Paul Morton's wartime career and subsequent betrayal, he argues that Morton and Lees alike were savaged due to their wholehearted support for the partisan cause. 'Lees would suffer the same fate as Paul Morton,' North concluded, 'who was also abandoned by the Canadian Army and the *Toronto Daily Star* . . .'

The darlings of Winston Churchill, the special duty volunteers – the maverick irregulars of the SOE and SAS – never proved popular with the British establishment. By January 1946 the SOE had been officially disbanded, and the SAS itself had ceased to exist three months before (though it would be reformed in the 1950s). With SOE's demise, some eighty-five per cent of the organisation's documents were lost or destroyed, with only fragments being saved for posterity, mostly at the British National Archives, at Kew.

With the case of Mike Lees, the record is patchy. As Lees died before many of the documents cited in this book were released for public perusal, much of the controversy surrounding his treatment at the end of the war comes as something of a shock, even to his immediate family. One thing is for certain: his treatment was unjustified and unwarranted.

Another thing is clear: the history of the Allied treatment of the Italian and Yugoslav partisans remains a controversial subject and is still cloaked in secrecy, more than seventy years after the events. Some British government files on the subject remain closed, even today. I have had one opened, under a Freedom of Information request. It deals with one of the Spanish SAS who served on Operation Tombola and is stamped 'CLOSED UNTIL 2050'. Another I have had opened is entitled 'ITALY: OPER-ATIONS'. The file deals with British government policy towards Italian – and Yugoslav – partisans. Even in the version that I have had opened, large sections of text have been redacted – blacked out.

Part of the file concerns a March 1945 proposal put to the Chief of Staff, to make contact with the Italian nobleman Prince Borghese, 'with the intention of encouraging anti-scorch meas-ures and assisting in the maintenance of law and order'. Don Junio Valerio Borghese – nicknamed 'The Black Prince' – hailed from a titled Italian family with close ties to the Vatican. He'd served as a Naval Commander under Mussolini and was a hard-line Fascist. Upon the Italian surrender to the Allies in September 1943, Borghese had signed a treaty with the *Kriegsmarine* – Nazi Germany's navy – raising an 18,000-strong force that would remain loyal to Hitler until the bitter end.

In the final weeks of the war, Borghese's *Decima Flottiglia* – Tenth Flotilla – as he'd named them, spent much of their time and manpower fighting against the Yugoslav communist par-tisans. At the end of the war Borghese was tried on charges of collaboration with the Nazi invaders of Italy and sentenced to twelve years in prison. He was not perhaps an ideal ally for the British to seek in the closing stages of the war. The March 1945 proposal was ruled out: 'Political considerations . . . make such an attempt to contact this Fascist officer in any way entirely out of the question.' Proposed collaborations with unsavoury individuals plus the freezing out of the Italian partisans and their special forces comrades – certainly, the closing stages of the war in Italy was a time of dark and murky intrigues. Old enmities were being laid aside, in preparation for the new war that was coming – the Cold War.

One intriguing motive for Lees' vilification has been posited – that he was thrown to the dogs due to his spirited support for the Chetniks, the right-wing Yugoslav partisans. There is evidence to suggest that elements of the SOE had been infiltrated by those who have since been revealed to have been spies for the Russians. Their influence, and their misreporting and manipulating of intelligence, are said to have convinced Churchill to drop his support for the Chetniks, and embrace Tito's communist partisans. Was Lees discredited to prevent him from sounding a credible voice in support of Tito's rivals? It seems a distinct possibility.

Whatever the case, in the autumn of 1944 Mike Lees – then seen as a high flier in SOE circles – had been lined up for a post-war role in British intelligence, most likely with the Secret Intelligence Service (MI6). After his vilification at the hands of senior figures in SOE and the Army, Lees' military career was at an end, as were any hopes of a career in the intelligence community. When he finally emerged from hospital, Lees was, according to his family, 'lost'. All that he had lived for had been taken from him.

The exception was family and friends, and of course, Gwendoline, his bride of less than a year. Through Gwen's family connections Lees eventually established a career in the world of business, where he would become the managing director of a multinational company. In later years he took up farming in southern Ireland, while still keeping a home in Dorset. He and Gwen would have two daughters. Typically, he was said to hold few grudges against those who had spoken ill of him during the war, and neither did he ever wish that he had done things differently in Italy. He was proud of what he had achieved.

Lees was dogged by his wartime injuries, being hospitalised repeatedly. He was plagued by debilitating pain – especially in his leg – for the rest of his life. At times it drove him to distraction. He would demand for the leg to be amputated, only to be told by the doctors that it would not necessarily stop the pain, for the nerves had suffered such irreparable damage. At times the pain drove him to the verge of suicide, but as a lifelong Catholic he knew he could not take his own life.

In 1949, Lees was given fitting recognition by the Italian people and nation, being made a Freeman of the City of Reggio Emilia, the conurbation in which he had been hidden by resistance leader Antonio when so badly wounded. He attended ceremonies there and at Villa Rossi, where plaques were unveiled honouring those who had died in the Botteghe assault. In 1989 Lees was also, fittingly, made an honorary member of the SAS Association.

Following a return trip to Italy in 1949, Lees was again hospitalised due to his wartime injuries. It was then that he found the time to pen a book telling the story of his wartime adventures, never intending to publish it. In it he described himself as a 'young adventurer caught up in the world of politics and intrigue'. Decades later Lees was approached by a member of the Special Forces Club, in London, which was set up to honour the memory and preserve the wartime legacy of the SOE and SAS. He asked if Lees might consider publishing his story, which Lees had sent to the Club for their archives.

Lees' book, entitled *Special Operations Executed*, was duly published in 1986. He dedicated it thus: 'To the memory of the late Corporal Bert Farrimond, miner, poacher, entrepreneur and dedicated radio operator . . . Also to those many Italians in the ranks of the Resistance and to those civilians, to whom I owe my escape and my life.'

There seems little better note on which to end the remarkable story of Mike Lees, who died of a heart attack at the age of 72, marching up a steep hill in Milton Abbas, Dorset.

What of the others involved in the battles for northern Italy recounted in these pages? Major Roy Farran went on to forge for himself a successful, colourful and sometimes controversial career, first in the British military, and then in civilian life in Canada, as a newspaperman and politician. His post-war career has been widely written about and requires no further explication here. Notably, he and Lees remained close friends and acquaintances and visited each other often.

Farran fought for decorations to be awarded to any number of the key resistance figures with whom he had soldiered in Italy. One of the many was Barba Nera, the resourceful and tough quartermaster of his Allied Battalion. In most cases, Barba Nera's included, Farran's efforts proved fruitless.

Glauco Monducci – Gordon, the Black Owls commander – was evacuated from the field shortly after Lees. Hospitalised in Florence, he recovered and spent time with the SAS as an informal liaison. After the war he built a fine career in the wine trade and the containerisation business.

Of Modena, the dashing Russian partisan commander, the news was mostly positive. Having married his Italian mistress they emigrated to South America, where they had a long, happy and adventurous life. Any number of Modena's fellow Russians also settled down with local Italian girls, and never once set foot in the mother country again. For those who did return to Russia, as ordered, it proved mostly damaging to health and longevity: Stalin had them sent to the gulags or executed.

Similarly, there had been a brief post-war attempt to hand the 'Spanish SAS' – Raphael Ramos and Francisco Jeronimo included – back to Spain, and into the clutches of Franco's pro-Fascist regime. Thanks to a press outcry in Britain that idea was quietly shelved and most went on to live long and happy lives as British citizens, retaining their anglicised war names.

In the case of Raphael Ramos, Farran played a hand in this. In August 1945 he put forward the Spaniard for a Military Medal in recognition of his actions on the Botteghe HQ raid, stressing the vital role that he'd played saving Mike Lees' life. 'Ramos showed remarkable courage both during and after the attack. His intelligence and initiative in a strange country thirty miles behind the enemy lines showed a devotion to duty worthy of the highest praise and resulted in preserving the life of a valuable British officer.'

In October 1945 Ramos married a Czechoslovakian, Libusa Kodesova, and they settled in the UK. In his naturalisation papers he was described as being 'of no nationality ... DEPOSED BY CIVIL WAR.' He found employment in the newspaper business, working on the *Express & Echo* newspaper in Exeter, in the south west of England. He was a kind man blessed with a warm sense of humour. He died in 1961 aged just forty-two, after a short illness.

Juan Torrents Abadia – John Colman – the father figure of the Spanish SAS, knew Farran well and admired him greatly. A 'gentle man and a gentleman', according to his son, Cliff Colman,

John Colman was with the SAS unit that liberated the Nazi concentration camp at Bergen-Belsen, in April 1945. After the war he married, settled in the UK and raised a family.

Francisco Jeronimo settled in the UK under his war name, Frank Williams. After demobilisation from the Army in 1946, he reportedly met Anthony Eden, then Deputy Leader of the Conservative Party. Williams and other former Spanish SAS asked Eden if the Allies intended to march on Spain, Europe's last bastion of Fascism, to liberate it from General Franco's rule. Eden reportedly said they did. Instead, old enemies rapidly became the newest of friends, as former Fascists and Nazis were recast as the bulwarks against the march of Soviet communism. When Frank Williams realised that Spain was not to be liberated, he reportedly threw away his war medals in disgust.

Williams settled in Carshalton, in Surrey, before moving to Wales in 1948. He married and raised a family in Cardiff, finding work as a pipe-fitter. In Wales he earned the unlikely nickname of 'Blod', short for Blodwin. This was so that in his local pub, whenever a friend shouted out, 'Blod, what're you drinking?' the reply would be issued in a thick Spanish accent. It never failed to bring the house down, as all the locals wondered what valley he might be from. Williams died in 1981 of asbestosis, contracted while fitting asbestos piping.

After the war Karl Nurk likewise became a naturalised British citizen. He went on to serve with the British military in Greece, on peacekeeping operations, attaining the rank of colonel, and he served on various British diplomatic missions overseas. Having retired from the military he had a brief acting career, before heading to South Africa where he lived the last years of his life, being survived by his wife and son.

After the war Canadian reporter Paul Morton – vilified, disgraced, and with his character and credentials in ruins – moved to the far north of Canada and gained employment of sorts in a remote logging camp. There he stayed for several years, drinking heavily. He eventually returned to his native Toronto, married and founded a successful public relations business. It all fell apart in the 1960s when he was accused at the Toronto Press Club by a fellow reporter of fabricating his entire story of behind the lines operations in Italy.

Upon learning the full truth – that he had been branded a fantasist and a liar – Morton spiralled into depression and alcoholism. He spent the final years of his life fixated on trying to clear his name, writing to all and sundry who might vouchsafe for the time he'd spent with Mike Lees and Geoffrey Long on Operation Flap. Towards the end of his life Morton published his story, entitled *The Partisans: Mission Inside*, but only in Italian. Morton's final days were ones of sadness, ruin and regret for what might have been. He died in 1992.

By contrast, the war artist Geoffrey Long – who deployed with Lees and Morton on Operation Flap – continued to serve with Allied forces, recording with pen and brush the devastation of many German cities at the end of the war. Later he returned to South Africa and became a lecturer at Natal University, subsequently moving to London to teach at the Central School of Theatre Design. His war art is still displayed in several museums around the world, including scenes from Operation Flap.

David 'The Mad Piper' Kirkpatrick returned to his native Ayrshire after the war, and chose not to talk about his exploits on Tombola. It wasn't until 2010 when the Italian resistance author and expert Matteo Incerti tracked him down, that

Kirkpatrick finally felt able to break his silence. He did so upon learning that in northern Italy he was viewed as a war hero, his piping the night of the Botteghe raid having saved countless Italians from what would have been savage German reprisals. Kirkpatrick died aged 91 at Girvan Community Hospital in South Ayrshire.

David Eyton-Jones rejoined his parent regiment, the Royal Sussex, after the war, served in the then-Palestine and was demobilised in 1947. He married a former WAAF and they moved to Assam, in India, where Eyton-Jones managed a 1,500-acre tea estate. He oversaw some 750 employees, starting a crèche, school and medical centre for the locals. He and his wife had four children. They returned to the UK, settled in Chidham, a village near Chichester, in a charming riverbank cottage, where his day pipes were arranged on one side of the fireplace and his evening pipes on the other (ten in all). He earned the nickname the 'Baccy Laureate'.

In later years his sight deteriorated, possibly due to the snow blindness that he had suffered on Monte Cusna. After his wife pre-deceased him he was assisted greatly by the then St Dunstan's charity – now Blind Veterans UK (BVUK) – to attend SAS and other military reunions and remembrance parades and to get on with his life generally. He last joined the BVUK contingent on Remembrance Sunday 2010, on London's Horse Guards Parade, along with a handful of fellow surviving Second World War veterans. He died in 2012.

After the war Jock Easton joined the reformed SAS, deploying to Malaya (Malaysia) in 1951, to counter a Chinese-backed communist insurgency. The Malaya missions involved deep jungle penetrations to strike at insurgents' bases and deny them territory. After leaving the military he forged a career as a stuntman of international repute, appearing in such classic films as *The Guns of Navarone* and *Where Eagles Dare*, and working alongside such stars of the screen as Clint Eastwood and Richard Burton. He died aged sixty-eight of cancer after a long illness.

Bob Walker-Brown pursued a post-war career in British special forces, going on to serve as second-in-command of 22 SAS before commanding 23 SAS – the territorial regiment – after which he joined the Defence Intelligence Staff. Married twice, he retired in Wiltshire where he was a keen angler. He had no children. He died in 2009 aged ninety.

Like many of those depicted in this book, Walker-Brown never forgot the Italian partisans with whom he had served. 'I feel an undying sense of gratitude for the very brave assistance of the Italian Partisans and numerous ordinary Italian people,' he would write. 'I think one takes a certain amount of pride in a small operation concluded with a reasonable degree of success and lack of casualties.'

Following the war Bert Farrimond left the military and returned to his home in Lancashire, in the north of England. An accident while riding his motorcycle badly affected his health and led to his early death – hence Lees' posthumous dedication of his book to Farrimond.

For their service with the Secchio partisans, several SAS received decorations (apart from Private Raphael Ramos, mentioned above). Lieutenant Harvey was awarded the DSO for his actions leading the raid on Villa Calvi, and Parachutist Patrick Burke was awarded the Military Medal (MM), for his actions spiriting a wounded Michael Lees to safety on the ladder they'd used as an improvised stretcher. SAS Corporal Ford was also awarded a MM, for his actions leading Farran's Star Column in ambushes on Highway Twelve.

Neither Justo Balerdi – Robert Bruce – nor Sidney Guscott or Stanley Bolden were to receive decorations for their actions in Italy, and despite making the ultimate sacrifice. After the war, Farran wrote to Guscott's family: 'I had great regards for Sergt. Guscott . . . He was a fine, brave boy, and I know he is in good company. One day, when I am considered good enough, I hope to see him in the place to which only the best soldiers go.'

Of those who died on the 14th Army HQ assault, Lieutenant Riccomini's loss deserves special mention. After the war, Bob Walker-Brown wrote to Riccomini's widow that her husband 'died a rare and gallant death at the head of his men during one of the most dangerous and effective attacks ever undertaken by this Regiment against the enemy. Ricci was a very great friend of mine having both been a POW and as an officer was the best in the Squadron. The men would have done anything for him . . .' That was high praise indeed, both for the man himself and for the Botteghe HQ raid.

Riccomini, along with Guscott and Bolden, was buried in Albinea church yard, but they were later moved to Milan Commonwealth War Graves Cemetery, where Riccomini's grave-stone bears an extraordinarily poignant inscription in light of the way he distinguished himself during the HQ raid: 'Bitter and brief would I have my end: it were better that way, Lord'.

Flight Lieutenant Furio Lauri became a lawyer after the war. In 1995 he was reunited with the Fieseler Storch in which he had rescued Mike Lees and other wounded Allied servicemen. Sometime after the war it had been purchased by a British air enthusiast, who had begun the work of restoring it to its wartime glory. It is presently on display at the Italian Air Force Museum, in Vigna di Valle, just to the north of Rome.

German General Friedrich-Wilhelm Hauk survived the attack on the Botteghe HQ, but by 2 May 1945 he had in any case been captured by the Allies. He spent three years in a POW camp, before retiring to his home city of Stuttgart. He died of old age at eighty-two.

Field Marshal Albert Kesselring – author of so many of the atrocities against civilians in Italy – was captured on 15 May 1945. Subsequently tried for war crimes committed in Italy, he was sentenced to death. That was commuted to life, and a media and publicity campaign led to his release in 1952, supposedly on the grounds of ill-health. He remained resolutely unrepentant until his death, describing the Marzabotto massacre – the worst in Italy during the war – as a 'normal military operation', suggesting that he had 'saved Italy' and that the Italian people should accordingly build for him 'a monument'.

He died in 1960 following a massive heart attack at the age of seventy-four.

Afterword

Although only briefly mentioned in this book, Major William McKenna requires a special note on behalf of his surviving relatives. In 1950 McKenna became a policeman in Tingewick, Bucks, having served four years in Germany immediately after the war and he remained a regular visitor to the Special Forces Club in London. After his death, his son, Ian, sought to find out more about his wartime record, as his father had rarely if ever talked about the war years. Despite making extensive inquiries, he was unable to discover any record of his father serving with the SAS, although a thin file of papers concerning his SOE service is held in the National Archives. If any reader has any information or recollections concerning Major William McKenna's wartime career, please do contact me and I will ensure the information reaches Ian McKenna.

It would be nice to clear up what is something of a mystery.

Nikki Cartlidge, the granddaughter of SAS Private Robert 'Bob' Sharpe, is likewise involved in trying to trace the records and recollections of any who may be able to shed light on her grandfather's operations during the war years. A veteran of Operation Cold Comfort, little is known about Private Sharpe's service apart from that one ill-fated mission. Nikki Cartlidge is determined that the bravery of those who served in the SAS should be documented and never forgotten. If any reader has any information or recollections concerning Private Sharpe's wartime career, please do contact me and I will ensure the information reaches Nikki Cartlidge, or email her direct on: wwiisasresearch@gmail.com.

Likewise, of course, if any reader is able to shed any further light on the treatment of Mike Lees at the end of the war, or other aspects of his wartime career that are germane, please do get in contact. His surviving family members would be keen to learn of any insights.

In particular, the denial to Mike Lees of his Military Cross stands out as a signal injustice in this story. As an author I've taken the unusual step of starting a campaign calling for Captain Michael Lees to be awarded the Military Cross that was, I believe, wrongly denied him at war's end, or for an equivalent civilian honour to be granted posthumously, and I am grateful for the assistance of surviving family members in furthering this.

To remind you of the story behind the denial of Lees wartime decoration, here it is again in summary:

Captain Michael Lees of SOE commanded the spring '45 mission to destroy the key German Army HQ in Italy, with the aim of shortening the war and saving countless Allied lives. Leading from the front he was shot five times but miraculously escaped and survived, though he was plagued for the rest of his life by his injuries. Written up for a Military Cross at war's end, it was denied.

Fellow commander on the raid, SAS Major Roy Farran, wrote the MC citation for Michael Lees, hailing his "gallantry, initiative and unequalled courage." While both commanders may have disobeyed orders in proceeding with the raid, they did so – Nelson-like turning a blind eye to orders - believing it was the right decision on the ground. Farran was duly awarded the Legion of Merit for the raid and foremost SAS commander Bob Walker-Brown hailed it as, "One of the most dangerous and effective ever undertaken by this Regiment."

You can find out more about this, or contact me with information about Mike Lees (or indeed any of the other heroes of this book) on my Facebook page (facebook.com/damienlewisauthor); my website (damienlewis.com); plus follow me on twitter for updates (@authordlewis).

Acknowledgements

In researching this book I was able to meet, speak to and receive assistance from many individuals who were exceptionally generous with their time. My special thanks and gratitude are extended to all, and my apologies to those that I may have inadvertently forgotten to mention.

First and foremost I'd like to thank the family members of those depicted in these pages, who helped me to tell their stories: Christine and Tony Bueno, for inviting me into your Dorset home and for sharing with me your memories and stories of the late Michael and Gwendoline Lees; James Selby Bennet, for inviting me into your Dorset home and for sharing your recollections and memorabilia of your late uncle, Michael Lees; Mrs J. M. Brian, for corresponding with me over your cousin, Michael Lees; Sir Christopher Lees, for corresponding with me over your second cousin, Michael Lees; Gerald & Nichola Eyton-Jones, for inviting me into your home and for sharing your recollections of the late David Eyton-Jones; Nikki Cartlidge, for sharing with me recollections of your late grandfather, Robert 'Bob' Sharpe's war years; David Farran, for corresponding with me and finding the time to talk about your late father, Major Roy Farran DSO, MC and two bars; Phil Williams, for inviting me into your home and sharing with me your grandfather, Frank Williams's (Francisco Jeronimo) story of the war years; Cliff Colman, for sharing with me your father, John Colman's (Juan Torrents Abadia) story from the war years; Ian McKenna, for inviting me into your home and sharing with me your father, Major William McKenna's story from the war years; Christopher George, for sharing with me the story of your grandfather, Lt. Col. John Douglas George, from the war years; Steven Furneaux, for meeting up and corresponding with me over your grandfather, SAS Trooper Louis Baker's, war years; and Luke Griffiths, for corresponding with me about your grandfather, Major Barton's, war years.

My very special thanks are extended to Jack Mann, Second World War veteran of the SBS, SAS and LRDG, for reading an early draft of this book and for your invaluable insights and recollections from the war years, plus the documents and photographs you were able to share with me. My gratitude is also extended to Ted Ross, wartime radio operator, for sharing with me your recollections of serving with the partisans in Yugoslavia and your photographs of those extraordinary operations.

In no particular order I also wish to thank the following, who assisted in many ways: research, proofreading and subject matter expertise. Tean Roberts, for your hard work and diligence, as always. Simon Fowler, for your expertise and inspiration, gleaned from the various archives. Paul and Anne Sherratt, for your perceptive comments and guidance. Thanks also to Ben Doyle-Cox, CEO of Platatac, for the very useful introductions you made: they were hugely appreciated. Thanks to Will Ward, Auxiliary Units researcher, for your excellent contacts, and to John Pidgeon, for same. Thanks in particular to Catherine Goodier, archivist at Blind Veterans UK, for all your help and assistance. Thanks also to Sally Allcard, for your expert advice and your translations from Italian and German.

Thanks also to Matteo Incerti, author, journalist and expert on the Italian partisans of the Second World War and the SAS and SOE operators who served alongside them (his books are referenced in the Bibliography). A very special thanks to Don North, the veteran Canadian journalist, who helped in my research of the wartime story and subsequent fate of Canadian journalist Paul Morton (told at great length in his book, *Inappropriate Conduct*). Many thanks also to Rob Hann for the correspondence, advice and for the insight provided in his book, *SAS Operation Galia*, which alerted me to the importance of that mission.

The staff at several archives and museums also deserve special mention, including those at the British National Archives; the Imperial War Museum; and the Churchill Archive Centre at Churchill College, Cambridge. Some files from the National Archives were made available to me as a result of Freedom of Information requests, and I am grateful to the individuals at the Archives who made the decision that those files should be opened.

My gratitude also to my literary agent, Gordon Wise, and film agent, Luke Speed, both of Curtis Brown, for helping bring this project to fruition, and to all at my publishers, Quercus, for same, including, but not limited to: Charlotte Fry, Ben Brock and Fiona Murphy. My editor, Richard Milner, deserves very special mention, as does John English, for his excellent copyediting.

I am also indebted to those authors who have previously written about some of the topics dealt with in this book and whose work has helped inform my writing. I have included a full bibliography.

Thanks are due also to Eva and the ever-patient David, Damien Jr and Sianna, for not resenting Dad spending too much of his time locked away . . . again . . . writing . . . again.

APPENDIX ONE

Roll of Personnel Engaged on Operation Tombola (taken from the SAS post-operational report)

Drop One: 4 March
Major R. A. Farran
Lieutenant J. Easton
Corporal K. Fitzgerald
Lance Corporal R. Bruce (Balerdi)
Parachutist P. Green
Parachutist F. Williams (Jeronimo)
Parachutist T. Kershaw

Drop Two: 7 March
Captain J. Milne
Lieutenant D. Eyton-Jones
Lieutenant T. G. Stephens
Lieutenant A. R. Tysoe
Corporal Larley

Drop Three: 9 March
Lieutenant M. F. N. Eld
Lieutenant K. G. Harvey
Sergeant R. Godwin
Sergeant F. Hughes
Corporal S. Bolden
Lance Corporal R. Ford

Lance Corporal K. Bjorklund
Lance Corporal J. Longburn
Lance Corporal J. Meager
Parachutist J. Brosnahan
Parachutist P. Burke
Parachutist W. J. Gallier
Parachutist W. H. Giles
Parachutist A. Harman
Parachutist C. Manners
Parachutist F. Mulvey
Parachutist C. McConnell
Parachutist J. Morbin
Parachutist J. Murphy
Parachutist E. Pernell
Parachutist A. Tate
Parachutist F. Taylor
Parachutist W. Whittaker
Parachutist G. Wooding

Drop Four: 10 March
Lieutenant J. Riccomini
Corporal W. Cunningham
Parachutist S. Carlisle

Drop 5: 24 March
Trooper D. Kirkpatrick

By Foot: 17 March
Serjeant S. Guscott
Parachutist R. Ramos

APPENDIX TWO

Casualties (SAS) on Operation Tombola (taken from the SAS post-operational report)

2nd SAS Regiment
Killed
Serjeant S. Guscott
Lance Corporal R. Bruce (Balerdi)

Missing – believed killed
Lieutenant J. Riccomini
Corporal S. Bolden

Wounded
Sergeant F. Hughes
Lance Corporal J. Layburn
Parachutist F. Mulvey
Parachutist S. Carlisle

Injured in parachute drop
Lieutenant J. Easton

Russians	Italians
Killed: 3	*Wounded:* 3
Wounded: 3	
Missing: 6	

Bibliography

J. G. Beever, *SOE Recollections and Reflections 1940–45*, The Bodley Head, 1981

Rudolf Bohmler, *Monte Cassino A German View*, Pen & Sword, 1965

Basil Davidson, *Special Operations Europe*, Victor Gollancz, 1980

Roy Farran, *Operation Tombola* (1960), Arms and Armour Press, 1986

Roy Farran, *Winged Dagger: Adventures on Special Service* (1950), Cassell, 1998

Tony Geraghty, *This is the SAS*, Arms and Armour Press, 1982

Matteo Incerti, *Il bracciale di sterline*, Aliberti editore, 2012

Matteo Incerti, *Il paradiso dei folli*, Imprimatur srl, 2017

Matteo Incerti, *Il suonatore matto*, Imprimatur srl, 2014

Michael Lees, *Special Operations Executed*, William Kimber & Co., 1986

Brian Lett, *SAS in Tuscany 1943–1945*, Pen & Sword, 2011

Brian Lett, *SOE's Mastermind*, Pen & Sword, 2016

Gordon Lett, *Rossano: An Adventure of the Italian Resistance*, Hodder and Stoughton, 1955

Laurence Lewis, *Echoes of Resistance: British Involvement with the Italian Partisans*, D. J. Costello, 1985

Charles Macintosh, *From Cloak to Dagger*, William Kimber & Co., 1982

Mike Morgan, *Daggers Drawn*, Sutton Publishing, 2000

Don North, *Inappropriate Conduct*, iUniverse, 2013

Patrick K. O'Donnell, *The Brenner Assignment*, Da Capo Press, 2008

David Stafford, *Mission Accomplished: SOE and Italy 1943–45*, The Bodley Head, 2011

Maurizio Di Terlizzi, *Fieseler Fi-156 Storch in Italian Service* (Aviolibri Special 12), IBN, 2009

Ex-Lance Corporal X, *The SAS and LRDG Roll of Honour 1941–47*, SAS-LRDG-RoH.com, 2016

Maurice Yacowar, *Roy & Me*, AU Press, 2010

Index

Holland, Major Charles 125, 301–2, 315, 332
Holland, Parachutist 55
Holocaust 144
Home Guard 131–2
howitzer 'Molto Stanco',Allied 211, 294, 320, 323, 325, 335, 339, 340–1

I
'information war', Churchill's 15, 72
Inter Services Research Bureau (ISRB) 317
Italia Combatte radio 71, 209, 314

J
James, Lieutenant 300–1
jeep air drop, Allied 322–3
Jeronimo, Francisco *see* Williams (aka Francisco Jeronimo), Parachutist Frank

K
Kershaw 163, 165, 167, 168, 189, 212–15, 272, 320
Kesselring, Field Marshal Albert 3, 40, 81–3, 95–6, 97, 116, 133, 145, 147, 150–1, 159, 207, 352, 372
Kirkpatrick, David 'The Mad Piper' 206–7, 221–2, 223, 227–8, 232, 250, 254, 256, 261–2, 287, 291–2, 321, 326, 368–9
Kiss (Stafetta partisan leader) 117, 141, 146, 147, 148, 159–60, 188, 193, 223, 224, 330
Kriegsmarine - Nazi German navy 362

L
La Rouche, Sergeant Bob 70–1
Lama Mocogno garrison, Russian partisan attack 339

Larley, Corporal 210, 323
Lauri, Flight Lieutenant Furio 87, 299–301, 305, 331–2, 371
Layburn, Corporal 266, 276, 281, 282, 287
Lees, Bernard Percy Turnball 11
Lees, Captain John W. 235, 299, 308, 314
Lees, Captain Michael 1–2, 3–4, 6–10, 76–8, 165–6, 363–5, 368, 374
 attack on Villa Rossi, Botteghe HQ 262–5, 268–70, 272–4, 285, 357–8, 360
 at Casa del Lupo farmstead 241, 242, 243, 244, 246, 247
 correspondence with Farran 285, 304, 315, 318
 crossing-the-Gothic Line mission 18–20, 35–7, 38–40, 41–53
 defending Secchia valley 209–12, 218, 219–20, 225
 Envelope mission 84–90, 99–100, 102–5, 108–21, 140–4, 146–9, 157–8
 escape in stolen German ambulance 315–16, 318–19, 328–9
 evacuation by air 329–33
 first meeting with Roy Farran 170–80
 guerrilla warfare in Yugoslavia 4, 10, 87, 103, 108, 153, 195
 hidden and cared for by Italian partisans 284–6, 289–93, 299, 302–4
 hospital treatment 333–4, 355, 359, 364
 journey to Botteghe HQ 223–5, 227, 228, 229, 240, 243, 244, 246, 253, 255
 malaria 222–4, 235, 243, 246, 286

money for partisan war effort 39, 86, 173, 186, 283

Monte Cusna escape route, search for 211, 212–16, 330

Monte Pozzo, Italy 47

Montebonello garrison, SAS/partisan attack on 338

Monti, Colonel Augusto 103, 104, 109–10, 113, 115–16, 140, 141, 174, 175–6, 177–80, 181, 210, 313–14, 316, 321

Moon Column (SAS/partisan force) 325, 336, 338, 343
  see also Highway Twelve operations

Morgan, Mike 350

mortar training, Allied Battalion 207–8

Morton, Paul 15–17, 19–20, 37, 38–9, 45, 70–1, 72–4, 76, 103, 316–18, 361, 368

Mulvey, Parachutist 259, 276–7, 283

Murphy, Parachutist 210, 323

Mussolini, Benito 'Il Duce' 78, 111, 149, 362

N

Nardi FN.305 86–7

Nikolai (Russian partisan) 183

Non-Aggression Pact (1939) 129

Norice (Stafetta) 188, 216, 224, 229, 239, 243–6, 346

North Africa 17, 29, 128, 165, 200, 243

North, Don 361

Nurk, Karl 184–5, 191, 319–20, 326, 335, 340, 341, 367

O

Office of Strategic Services (OSS) 87

Official Secrets Acts 69, 79

Operation Abstention 134–5

Operation Anthropoid 144

Operation Brake 204, 205

Operation Cartoon 203

Operation Flap 4, 73, 77–8, 79, 368

Operation Galia 95–7, 131, 139–40, 162–3, 200, 205, 269

Operation Rupert 137, 203, 204

Operation Tombola 127–8, 131, 132–3, 137–9, 201, 203–4, 221, 348, 350
  see also Botteghe, German 14th Army HQ; Farran, Major Roy; Highway Twelve operations; Special Air Service (SAS)

Operation Torch 165

Operation Trueform 137

Operation Wallace 21

Orlandini, Domenico 'Don Carlo' see Don Carlo (Green Flames partisan leader)

Oughtred, Captain Neil 144

P

P-51 Mustang fighters 88

Paleocastro Fort, Castelorizzo, Greece 134–5

Palmer, Roundell Cecil 101

Panzerabwehrkanone - anti-tank guns 65–6

Panzergrenadier divisions 3, 22, 24–7, 56, 130

Parma partisans 314

partisan forces, Italian 17–18, 36, 38–9, 41, 81–4, 87, 94–7, 124–5, 129, 138, 209, 311–12, 314, 350, 351–2, 353, 361–2, 370
  Allied attitude towards 15, 71–2, 74–6, 100–1, 105–8, 176–7, 207, 298, 317, 351–2, 361–2
  Major Temple and Operation Flap 1, 2, 3, 4–6, 7–8, 69

Reggiani partisans 102, 105, 110, 115–21, 127, 140, 141, 150–1, 166–7, 174, 176, 178–9, 200, 327, 348, 365
  Arrows 190, 192, 201, 325
  Black Owls 118, 141, 143, 146, 151, 152, 155, 175, 208, 217, 224, 225, 246, 254, 255, 263, 264, 268, 270, 273, 280, 284, 308
  British uniforms 191, 201
  entertainment 208–9, 221, 222
  Garibaldini 170, 176, 182, 183, 194, 210, 219, 225, 230, 243, 246, 254, 256, 257, 267, 285, 294–6, 304–5, 323, 325, 342–3
  Green Flames 103, 110, 140, 151–2, 176, 210, 219, 306, 307, 323
  Stafettas 117, 118, 141, 143, 146, 148, 188–9, 208, 216, 224, 233, 243–6, 304, 326, 337
  rescue Mike Lees 284–6, 289–93, 299, 302–4, 315–16, 318–19, 328–9
  see also Allied Battalion; Barba Nera; Eros; Gianni; Gordon; Kiss; Monti, Colonel Augusto; Don Carlo; Russian partisans
Peterson, Lieutenant 'Pete' 129–30
Pigna, Italy 35, 36, 38–9
piper, Operation Tombola *see* Kirkpatrick, David 'The Mad Piper'
Pirogov, Victor 'Modena' *see* Modena (Russian partisan leader)
Piva (Italian partisan leader) 7–8, 46, 69
Poland, invasion of 82, 159

Political Warfare Executive (PWE) 15, 71, 74
POWs 40, 96, 120, 129, 135, 181–2, 372
Profumo, Lieutenant Colonel John 'Jackie' 199, 202
propaganda 15, 17–18, 72–3, 194
Psychological Warfare Division (PWD) 74–5, 76, 314

Q
Queen's Own Dorset Yeomanry 11, 12, 356

R
Ramos, Private Raphael Luis Mansens 204–5, 206, 272–5, 284, 345–6, 366–7, 370
Rebecca/Eureka transponding radar 321
Red Army 350
Reggiani partisans *see under* partisan forces, Italian
Reggio Emilia garrison evacuated, German 339
resistance (Maquis), French 12, 21, 22–3, 26–7, 30–1, 54–61, 64, 66, 130, 137, 204
resistance, Italian *see* partisan forces, Italian
Reubens (Regianni partisan) 118
Riccomini, Lieutenant James Arthur 'Ricky' 128 31, 184, 203, 228–9, 231, 232, 241, 254–5, 260, 262–3, 264, 269, 283, 296, 345, 348, 371
Riepe, Colonel John Held 92–3, 127, 192, 225, 299, 349
Rivi, Don Pietro 'Don Pedro' 140, 160, 173, 174, 193
Roberts, Sergeant 34, 54
Rommel, General Erwin 3

BLIND VETERANS UK

Blind Veterans UK is the national charity for blind and vision-impaired ex-Service men and women. They believe that no one who has served our country should have to battle blindness alone.

Founded in 1915, the charity's initial purpose was to help and support soldiers blinded in the First World War. But the organisation has gone on to support more than 35,000 blind veterans and their families, spanning the Second World War to recent conflicts including Iraq and Afghanistan.

The charity was established by Sir Arthur Pearson, founder of the Daily Express and President of the Royal National Institute of Blind People, in response to blinded soldiers returning from the Front during the First World War.

Pearson had lost his own sight through glaucoma, but was determined to continue his life actively. He was determined to ensure that the blind veterans of the First World War would receive the training and support they needed to live fulfilling, independent lives.

This same work continues today and while they initially cared for veterans blinded in active Service, today they will help veterans no matter what caused their sight loss.

No matter how long they served or how they lost their sight, Blind Veterans UK are here to support ex-Service men and women experiencing severe sight loss. The veterans range from those suffering from macular degeneration and age-related conditions, to veterans injured in Iraq, Afghanistan and other military conflicts.

The charity has two training and rehabilitation centres, in Brighton and Llandudno, which provide training, respite and residential care as well as recreational facilities. They also provide services and support across the UK via a network of nineteen community teams.

Services offered by Blind Veterans UK include rehabilitation programs, art and craft classes, sports and recreation, clubs and societies, information technology and independent living training, care and welfare.

Blind Veterans UK currently supports over 4,700 veterans, more than ever before in the charity's history. Visit blindveterans.org.uk/support to learn more about the charity and how you can support its vital work today.

*Les
grandes
découvertes
de la
psychanalyse*

© Tchou, éditeur, 1979, pour le choix des textes
I. S. B. N. 2 – 89149 – 098 – 3
Imprimé aux Etats~Unis, 1981

LES NÉVROSES

UNE ÉDITION SPÉCIALE DE LAFFONT CANADA LTÉE

LES NÉVROSES
l'homme
et ses conflits

LAFFONT
TCHOU

Widlöcher
Freud
Breuer
F. Deutsch
H. Deutsch
Fenichel
Klein

Les
grandes
découvertes
de la
psychanalyse
Collection
dirigée par
Bela Grunberger
et Janine
Chasseguet-Smirgel
avec le concours
de Claire Parenti

SOMMAIRE

DEUXIÈME PARTIE
Les névroses et leur classification

Préface

Le terme de névrose est ancien. Créé au XVIIIᵉ siècle par l'Anglais Cullen. il fut utilisé jusqu'à la fin du XIXᵉ siècle pour définir une catégorie fort large de troubles que n'expliquait pas une lésion d'organe et qui, de ce fait, étaient imputés à un dérèglement fonctionnel des nerfs censés régler le fonctionnement des viscères. Dans ce cadre très vaste et évidemment imprécis, ont été rangées des maladies qui devaient, par la suite, être rattachées à une anomalie organique précise (le goitre exophtalmique ou la paralysie agitante, par exemple). Bien entendu, ce cadre nosologique appartenait à la pathologie interne et n'avait aucun rapport avec la folie et les troubles mentaux que décrivaient les traités des aliénistes. A mesure que progressaient les connaissances médicales, il céda la place à des reclassements nosologiques différents et subit le destin de *La Peau de chagrin* d'Honoré de Balzac. L'hystérie, toutefois, bien décrite par Briquet puis par Charcot, devait demeurer le paradigme d'un tel type de trouble. Certes, Charcot avait longtemps pensé que la « grande névrose » pouvait à son tour laisser découvrir la lésion cérébrale qui en aurait expliqué la nature. La méthode anatomo-clinique lui avait permis de jeter un regard neuf et précis sur la neuropathologie dans laquelle l'hystérie aurait dû trouver sa place. Ce fut son mérite, clairement reconnu par Freud et pourtant bien sous-estimé par la suite, de reconnaître que la névrose hystérique était bien d'une autre nature, maladie psychologique et non organique.

UNE LEÇON DE CHARCOT SUR L'HYSTÉRIE

Dans sa leçon du mardi 17 janvier 1888, Charcot compare les effets de la suggestion hypnotique et l'hystérie pour en dégager l'identité de mécanisme :

« Je vous rappellerai en deux mots quels sont les caractères de l'état

◀ *« Chez le somnambule, l'idée de l'impuissance motrice d'un membre déterminera réellement la paralysie de ce membre » (« La somnambule », gravure allemande, fin XIXᵉ siècle, Bibliothèque des Arts Décoratifs).*

mental dans le somnambulisme artificiel : absence de spontanéité, toute idée introduite dans l'esprit du sujet par l'expérimentateur soit à l'aide de la parole, soit d'une autre manière, y est reçue et s'y installe à la manière d'un corps étranger, sans subir de critique sérieuse de la part du Moi qui reste en quelque sorte plus ou moins profondément endormi. Or, les idées imposées dans ces conditions-là, privées du contrôle de cet agrégat d'idées qu'on appelle le Moi, peuvent, au gré de celui qui les a fait naître, acquérir une intensité extrême, une puissance presque sans limite, comme cela a lieu d'ailleurs souvent dans nos rêves. Vous savez que, comme l'enseignent Spencer, Bain, Ribot, dans des conditions psychologiques normales, l'idée du mouvement d'un membre, c'est déjà le mouvement de ce membre en voie de s'accomplir ; ainsi nous pensons fortement au mouvement d'extension d'une main, et nous esquissons, par ce fait, automatiquement, le mouvement en question de cette main ; si l'idée est poussée au plus haut degré d'intensité, le mouvement s'exécutera réellement, *a fortiori* dans l'état de somnambulisme où les puissances d'arrêt sont annihilées. Cette réalisation de l'idée suggérée se produira dans les conditions les plus favorables et, s'il en est ainsi, vous comprendrez aisément comment, chez le somnambule, l'idée de l'impuissance motrice d'un membre déterminera réellement la paralysie de ce membre. La connaissance de ces paralysies dites psychiques, chez les sujets placés en état de somnambulisme, est devenue d'ailleurs chose vulgaire. Et l'on sait en particulier qu'il est possible d'obtenir qu'elles persistent telles après le réveil, pendant un temps plus ou moins long.

« Je vous demanderai maintenant de me concéder immédiatement la réalité de cette analogie que je disais exister tout à l'heure entre l'état psychique de la somnambule et celui qui se développe chez une hystérique sous l'influence d'une vive émotion... »

LES NÉVROSES DE TRANSFERT : UN APPORT CAPITAL DE FREUD

Freud a joué un rôle capital dans la réorganisation du cadre des névroses. A peu près en même temps que Janet, il procède à un reclassement nosologique, en rapprochant de la névrose hystérique des troubles mentaux identifiés depuis longtemps sous le terme de folie du doute. Rapprochement étonnant, puisqu'il associe à des troubles « nerveux » des troubles mentaux, troubles qui appartenaient respectivement à la pathologie interne et à la pathologie mentale. Sans doute l'idée était dans l'air et la notion de maladie psychologique avancée par Charcot a joué un rôle important dans le reclassement. Toutefois, hystérie, phobie et obsessions ne sont pas isolables sur une base purement descriptive. La névrose d'angoisse, la neurasthénie, l'hypocondrie constituent des troubles qui ne semblent pas de nature très différente. Le cadre des névroses ou psychonévroses (ce qui implique au départ l'idée de névroses de nature psychologique, laissant ainsi place à d'éventuelles névroses d'origine organique) demeure vaste et fait d'entités morbides qui ne sont pas toujours faciles à distinguer les unes des autres. Le mérite de Freud est d'avoir su trouver un instrument d'analyse qui lui permette de dégager du cadre confus des névroses un système cohérent qu'il appela « névroses de transfert ». Mais ce mérite, il le doit à l'influence d'aînés particulièrement clairvoyants et à la manière exceptionnelle dont il a su tirer parti de ces influences. Charcot, nous l'avons vu, démontre que l'hystérie est une conduite patholo-

Scène d'hypnotisme médical au XIXᵉ siècle, sous la direction du Dʳ Vlavianos, avec, au centre, le Dʳ Bérillon, directeur de la revue de l'Hypnotisme (Musée d'Histoire de la Médecine, Paris).

13

gique en rapport avec un refus actif du patient à se représenter le fonctionnement normal de l'activité motrice, sensorielle ou perceptive altérée. Breuer observe que cette conduite est en rapport direct avec une expérience traumatique antérieure et que, si cette expérience a été éprouvée dans un état mental particulier — l'état hypnoïde —, elle ne peut se dissiper dans les formations naturelles de l'élaboration psychique et de l'oubli ; elle demeure sous la forme déguisée, convertie, de l'action hystérique. Freud tire parti de ces deux observations cruciales mais il en dégage une perspective nouvelle — si nouvelle qu'elle peut encore paraître, près de cent ans plus tard, révolutionnaire — que j'appellerai une vue « transformationnelle ».

UNE FORMULATION RÉVOLUTIONNAIRE DÈS 1893

Forçant quelque peu Breuer, il la décrit dans une communication signée en commun et datant de 1893 : le refoulement, l'oubli de l'expérience traumatique conduit à la conversion somatique et, preuve de cette hypothèse, la remémoration de l'expérience entraîne la résolution du symptôme de conversion. On n'a pas assez souligné le caractère original de cette formulation. Pour la première fois, c'est en terme de mutation des formations psychiques que se formule une théorie explicative d'un processus morbide. Jusqu'alors, la classification des troubles mentaux reposait sur des études descriptives fondées sur la ressemblance des traits et sur des études prédictives fondées sur l'évolution naturelle des maladies mentales. La « communication préliminaire » de 1893 ouvre la voie à un nouveau système d'analyse dont nous n'avons pas encore mesuré toute la fécondité : c'est en termes de transformations qu'y sont étudiés le phénomène pathologique et sa guérison. Ce qui, en effet, vient donner sens au « geste » hystérique, c'est ce que laisse voir sa transformation en remémoration, permettant du même coup de poser l'hypothèse d'un mécanisme inverse dans la genèse du symptôme. Bien entendu, Freud se sert ici des observations de Charcot et de Breuer : Charcot reproduit le symptôme hystérique sous hypnose, mais aussi vérifie son hypothèse lorsqu'il fait disparaître le symptôme en forçant le malade à se représenter la fonction « oubliée » ; Breuer découvre la fonction thérapeutique de la remémoration. Toutefois, ce qui, chez les deux précurseurs, demeure une expérimentation et une thérapeutique propres à la « grande névrose », devient chez Freud, sans jeu de mots, un instrument d'analyse qui va lui permettre de discriminer parmi les « névroses » celles qui sont aptes à subir le même mode de transformation et à se « décomposer » en conflit pulsionnel, en fantasmes et en formation de substitut. C'est donc le processus thérapeutique qui fonde pour Freud l'unicité des névroses ; du moins celles qu'il appellera d'abord psychonévroses de défense puis névroses de transfert.

DÉGAGER LE CONFLIT SOUS-JACENT À LA NEVROSE

La méthode d'investigation liée à la cure psychanalytique permet donc de voir le conflit défensif qui sous-tend les signes cliniques des névroses. Il le permet d'autant plus clairement que ce conflit se déplace dans l'organisation du transfert. Celui-ci n'est pas simple répétition dans la relation avec le psychanalyste de traits comportementaux, d'attitudes et de sentiments qui, d'habitude, s'adressent à l'entourage. Le terme de névrose de transfert sert à décrire une véritable cristallisation, dans la situation psychanalytique, d'un système de fantasmes, de conflits et de défenses qui entretiennent la névrose. On peut d'ailleurs au cours d'une cure vérifier ce déplacement quand, à mesure que la cristallisation transférentielle s'organise, les symptômes névrotiques diminuent d'intensité et perdent de leur importance dans la vie mentale du patient. Il s'agit alors d'aider le sujet à se dégager de cette nouvelle expression de l'organisation névrotique en lui permettant de faire face avec sérénité, et sans crainte excessive des affects négatifs (honte, culpabilité, angoisse), à la nature conflictuelle des pulsions qui sont engagées dans le conflit. Or, dans l'enfance, la domination de ces affects négatifs et la mise en place de défenses invalidantes face au conflit ont créé les fondements de la névrose. Freud parle donc d'une révision du procès : c'est le dégagement des solutions infantiles qui permet la résolution de la névrose de transfert. Ainsi se trouve constitué le système triangulaire qui relie la névrose infantile, la névrose clinique et la névrose de transfert. Récemment, S. Lebovici[1] a bien montré que la névrose infantile, ainsi définie, ne coïncide pas avec les symptômes névrotiques que l'on observe chez l'enfant. Ceux-ci sont multiples, évolutifs et résultent de conflits ou de fixations partielles qui jalonnent le développement de l'enfant, son histoire réelle. La névrose infantile, telle qu'elle se dégage de l'analyse de transfert, constitue au contraire un modèle, une reconstruction qui réorganise dans un système intemporel les multiples conflits et fixations ayant marqué le développement.

1. S. Lebovici : *l'Expérience du psychanalyste chez l'enfant et chez l'adulte devant le modèle de la névrose infantile de transfert*. Presses Universitaires de France, Paris.

UNE SOURCE DE SOUFFRANCE
MAIS AUSSI UNE JOUISSANCE SECRÈTE
DONT LE NÉVROSÉ DOIT SE DÉTACHER

Ce système triangulaire demeure un modèle conceptuel extrêmement utile. Il explique pourquoi, dans la cure des névroses, nous ne pouvons nous contenter de décoder les symptômes névrotiques en fonction des événements de l'enfance. Une telle reconstruction historique n'a qu'une portée thérapeutique limitée, car il existe dans la névrose un attachement au symptôme et aux fantasmes inconscients qui le sous-tendent. En effet, si la névrose est une source de souffrance, celle-ci dissimule une jouissance inconsciente. Pour que le patient y renonce, il faut qu'il en déplace le mouvement vers le psychanalyste et que, se détachant de la jouissance secrète, il accepte de désirer et d'exprimer son désir. Dans le jeu des demandes transférentielles, il s'expose à la crainte du jugement, à l'humiliation du refus, au déplaisir du renoncement. Le transfert constitue donc bien le système de transformation qui permet de reconstruire la névrose infantile.

Inversement, nous ne pouvons faire l'économie de l'analyse de la névrose infantile, car pour se dégager du transfert, le patient doit prendre la mesure des expériences infantiles, réelles ou fantasmatiques, qui l'ont jusqu'à présent fixé à ce système défensif de jouissance inconsciente.

On voit donc bien que la psychopathologie psychanalytique des névroses n'est pas descriptive. Elle repose sur une observation des transformations qui se réalisent au cours d'une cure, et une telle étude doit évidemment prendre en considération les facteurs qui entravent ou facilitent ces processus de transformation : ceux qui limitent ou favorisent le déplacement transférentiel, ceux qui rendent possible ou empêchent la révision du procès. La névrose, comme toute autre entité psychopathologique, n'est pas un état stable mais un état dont la stabilité résulte du jeu des forces complexes que l'approche psychanalytique permet d'apprécier chez chaque patient.

UNE MANIÈRE D'ÊTRE ET DE VIVRE
QUI S'IMPOSE AU MALADE

Ce que nous appelons névrose n'est pas une entité mystérieuse venant infiltrer la personnalité, mais une manière d'être, une manière de vivre qui s'impose au malade. Bien sûr, il en perçoit surtout les modes de penser et d'agir qui le font souffrir : les symptômes. Mais il ne voit pas que ceux-ci constituent la seule solution, ou du moins la plus acceptable, pour vivre avec un ensemble de pensées conscientes et inconscientes (souvenirs, fantasmes, perceptions de l'entourage) qui sont prises dans un système conflictuel. La question en fin de compte la plus passionnante n'est peut-être pas : comment devient-on « névrotique », mais : pourquoi le reste-t-on ou pourquoi change-t-on ? Car d'autres pensées, d'autres désirs, d'autres expériences du passé et la vie elle-même, les expériences nouvelles qu'elle offre, sont autant de forces qui poussent l'être humain à se renouveler. La psychanalyse, sa pratique et sa théorie nous ont apporté, avec ces questions nouvelles et les réponses que tentent d'y donner patients et analystes, une conception des névroses dont on ne peut plus se passer.

Mais, en mettant l'accent sur le contexte qui donne sens au symptôme, on risque de confondre la névrose et le conflit. En effet, si nous nous attachons moins aux symptômes qu'aux formations inconscientes sous-jacentes, nous pouvons mettre en évidence chez tous des ébauches d'organisation névrotique. La conception freudienne supprime la barrière entre névrose et formes de pensée que nous tenons pour normales. Seules des différences quantitatives expliqueraient que, chez beaucoup, les fixations pulsionnelles et défensives ne causent que des particularités mineures du caractère, tandis que chez d'autres elles seraient à l'origine d'une névrose proprement dite. Sans doute, Freud a bien montré que le système avait une fonction d'« ersatz », la jouissance fantasmatique inconsciente, refoulée, se déchargeant dans l'activité substitutive. Mais on s'explique mal pourquoi des conduites aussi singulières que la conversion somatique de l'hystérie, la phobie et l'obsession sont les expressions privilégiées de cette décharge. C'est peut-être seulement la singularité de ces symptômes qui nous a fait les individualiser sur le plan clinique et leur accorder cette fonction particulière. Il faudrait peut-être placer sur le même plan de nombreuses actions ou opérations de pensée (acte manqué, trait de comportement, attitude, jugement, activité de rêverie diurne, etc.) qui ont aussi une valeur de décharge substitutive. Toutefois, ces actes symptomatiques et ces formes de pensée s'observent surtout dans les formes mineures. C'est chez les sujets dits normaux que les conflits névrotiques trouvent des modes d'expression extrêmement polymorphes. En revanche, quand le conflit névrotique occupe une place dominante dans l'économie mentale, ce sont les symptômes « classiques » qui deviennent son mode d'expression caractéristique. En d'autres termes, on n'a pas individualisé d'autres modalités cliniques d'organisation névrotique qui puissent compléter les trois formes rassemblées par Freud sous le terme de psychonévroses de défense. La plupart des formations de substitut qui s'observent dans la psychopathologie de la vie quotidienne, c'est-à-dire dans les conflits qui s'inscrivent dans les variables de la normale, ne peuvent réaliser des organisations stables et prédominantes comparables.

Inversement, certaines formations symptomatiques ressemblent, d'un point de vue purement descriptif, aux psychonévroses de défense, sans relever du même mécanisme. Angoisse flottante, hypocondrie, asthénie psychique, dépression névrotique peuvent, par certains traits, en être rapprochées : même conscience de l'état morbide, même continuité entre le trouble et la personnalité pré-morbide, même *continuum* entre le normal et le pathologique. Toutefois, ce n'est pas sans raison que Freud a consacré une partie importante de ses travaux à établir une différence entre les psychonévroses de défense et les névroses actuelles, et plus tard les névroses dites narcissiques. En effet l'investigation psychanalytique et le processus de transfert montrent que les symptômes que nous venons de citer, et bien d'autres, ne remplissent pas la même fonction que les symptômes névrotiques proprement dits. Ils obéissent à des finalités diverses ; certains constituent en effet l'expression directe de la tension conflictuelle (angoisse), d'autres la contrepartie économique des investissements et des contre-investissements névrotiques (asthénie), d'autres une fixation narcissique sur le corps (hypocondrie).

QUE SIGNIFIE LE FAIT D'AGIR EN HYSTÉRIQUE, EN OBSÉDÉ OU EN PHOBIQUE ?

Cela nous ramène à la question cruciale : pourquoi hystérie, phobie et obsessions occupent-elles une place à part dans la symptomatologie névrotique en général ? Pour tenter d'y répondre, il convient de bien s'entendre sur cette place. Elle tient, répétons-le, au transfert. Ce qui entretient le symptôme est susceptible de se reconvertir dans le système de pensées et d'interactions qui s'établit entre le patient et le psychanalyste. Un double mouvement pulsionnel (ou ensemble de paires ambivalentes de pulsions) et un double système défensif organisent un système d'investissements et de contre-investissements qui trouvent à se décharger dans la voie finale commune que réalise le symptôme. Or, les conduites hystériques, phobiques et obsessionnelles constituent des activités qui réalisent au mieux cette voie finale commune. L'obsession convertit une opération de pensée en une action. Normalement, une opération de pensée, quelle que soit sa nature, constitue une activité d'essai sans efficacité pratique immédiate. Mais, l'obsédé confère à ses pensées, ou du moins à certaines d'entre elles, la valeur d'une action

*« Le terme de névrose est ancien. Il fut utilisé pour
définir une catégorie fort large de troubles que
n'expliquait pas une lésion organique »*
(tiré de La grande Névrose, 1889).

irréversible, aux conséquences inévitables et donc redoutables. L'hystérique accorde à une activité corporelle une valeur symbolique nouvelle, il se sent possédé, dans cette fonction, par une force qui dépasse sa volonté consciente. Pour que cette conversion se réalise, il oublie la fonction « normale » de cette activité corporelle qui se prête ainsi aux significations symboliques. Quant au phobique, si c'est dans un espace déterminé (clos ou illimité) ou face à un objet précis (foule, animal,

19

etc.) que se déclenche l'angoisse qui met en mouvement l'attitude d'évitement, la source de l'angoisse tient à une activité du corps (crises nerveuses, sensation d'une force interne insurmontable, imminence d'un état d'agitation) ou à une pensée obsédante (peur d'accomplir un geste dangereux ou absurde). En d'autres termes, le phobique met en place un dispositif d'évitement vis-à-vis d'une conduite qui s'apparente plus ou moins à l'hystérie et à l'obsession. Si nous parlons ici d'obsessionnel, d'hystérique ou de phobique, ce n'est nullement pour identifier la conduite névrotique au sujet qui la réalise. La névrose, sauf dans ses formes invalidantes extrêmes, n'occupe qu'une place limitée dans le champ des activités du sujet. Qualifier ce dernier d'hystérique ou d'obsessionnel n'a qu'une faible et bien trompeuse valeur classificatoire. Il s'agit plutôt de qualifier le type d'action qui occupe une certaine place dans le champ d'activité. Agir sur un mode hystérique, c'est user d'un système de pensées et d'actions dont l'expression la plus visible est l'acte de conversion par lequel une activité corporelle est déviée de sa fonction normale pour réaliser un geste investi de finalités inconscientes. Agir en obsessionnel, et se sentir obsédé, c'est user d'un système de pensées et d'actions dont l'expression la plus visible est l'acte de pensée qui, dévié de sa fonction opératoire normale, réalise un geste investi de finalités inconscientes. Agir en phobique, c'est fixer dans une situation donnée cet acte-symptôme et mettre en place un dispositif d'évitement vis-à-vis de cette situation.

Or, ces dispositifs ne sont pas propres à la névrose. Si celle-ci les utilise à ses propres fins, ils appartiennent au lot des conduites humaines habituelles. L'acte obsessionnel prolonge la pensée magique, l'acte hystérique amplifie la dramatisation gestuelle, l'évitement phobique trouve ses origines dans la fuite.

LE SENS INTIME DU SYMPTÔME NÉVROTIQUE : LA CONVERSION

Après un détour, nous retrouvons la question du choix du symptôme. Toutefois, l'analyse phénoménologique et structurelle nous a permis de mieux comprendre le sens intime du symptôme névrotique. Car c'est toujours d'une conversion qu'il s'agit : conversion d'un système fantasmatique inconscient dans un acte gestuel ou de pensée. Demeure évidemment la question du choix individuel de la névrose, c'est-à-dire des facteurs qui déterminent pour un individu donné la nature de la conversion dans les trois registres où elle peut s'accomplir : le corps, la pensée ou l'espace. Question à laquelle l'investigation psychanalytique n'a pas encore permis d'apporter une réponse satisfaisante. C'est sans doute la raison pour laquelle de nombreux psychanalystes se sont désintéressés des symptômes névrotiques pour ne plus accorder d'attention qu'au conflit névrotique et à la personnalité dans laquelle il s'inscrit. En donnant ainsi priorité au caractère névrotique, ils ont cru privilégier la structure causale, reléguant les symptômes névrotiques à un statut d'épiphénomène. Ils ont obéi à un modèle médical opposant processus morbide et signes apparents. En réalité, ils ont simplement déplacé leur investigation d'une pathologie à une autre, des névroses « symptomatiques » aux caractères névrotiques. Or, l'étude du caractère et son investigation au cours d'une psychanalyse n'expliquent pas pour autant la névrose « symptomatique ». Dans cette dernière, le symptôme n'est pas le signe apparent d'une réalité latente. Il constitue un système d'activités dont la place est prépondérante dans l'organisation de la névrose, lieu des investissements et des contre-investissements engagés dans le conflit défensif. La structure névrotique, c'est autant celle du symptôme que du caractère.

À QUOI TIENT L'OPPOSITION NÉVROSE-PSYCHOSE ?

Une autre conséquence de la priorité accordée au caractère sur le symptôme est la dichotomie qui tend à prévaloir entre névrose et psychose. Certes, on peut — de bien des manières — souligner les traits distinctifs entre le mode de pensée névrotique et celui du psychotique. Mais ces oppositions s'appliquent à des traits de nature différente (formation du symptôme, rapport entre le symptôme et la réalité extérieure, jeu entre processus secondaires et processus primaires de pensée, organisation du Moi, etc.). Souvent, l'opposition névrotique-psychotique reflète un simple choix binaire qui tient à la présence ou à l'absence de traits psychotiques, dans la mesure où la présence de traits névrotiques ne permet pas d'établir une discrimination entre névrose et « normalité ». On peut se demander si pareille classification ne serait pas susceptible de s'appliquer à d'autres formes d'organisation mentale (opposition entre névrose et perversion, entre névrose et pathologie du caractère, etc.). Il serait peut-être plus sage d'admettre qu'il existe de nombreuses formes d'organisations mentales dites pathologiques et que les névroses n'en constituent qu'une parmi d'autres. Par ailleurs, seul un souci classificatoire (des « malades », non des systèmes de pensée et d'action) nous conduit à opposer selon un principe d'incompatibilité ces différents syndromes alors qu'ils impliquent vraisemblablement des attitudes mentales qui ne se situent pas sur le même plan. Nous observons des systèmes névrotiques associés à des traits psychotiques (états limites), narcissiques, pervers ou psycho-pathiques. Certaines névroses hystériques graves témoignent d'une organisation narcissique importante. Certains systèmes phobiques sont révélateurs d'une structure psychotique. Plutôt que de procéder à des reclassements nosographiques incessants, ne conviendrait-il pas d'admettre une pluralité d'organisations mentales susceptibles de s'articuler les unes avec les autres ?

LES NÉVROSES SONT-ELLES UNIVERSELLEMENT RÉPANDUES ?

L'universalité des névroses demeure une question toujours débattue. On a souvent prétendu que la névrose constituait une formation conflictuelle propre à certaines conditions sociales et la répression de la sexualité a été tenue pour une condition historique déterminante. On peut, certes, admettre que les contraintes sociales jouent un rôle dans la formation des personnalités. Peut-on imaginer une structure sociale qui n'exerce aucune répression, de nature sexuelle ou agressive, sur la personne ? Sans doute, on en discutera encore longtemps, mais ce débat n'a que peu de rapport avec la névrose. Car lorsque nous parlons de conflit névrotique, nous envisageons une structure conflictuelle beaucoup plus étendue que les simples effets de la répression sociale de la sexualité. Ce serait là confondre une fois de plus la sexualité génitale et la sexualité infantile. Cette dernière se développe chez l'enfant avec des buts et des objets qui changent d'un stade à l'autre du développe-ment. Certes, à chaque étape une nouvelle dialectique s'instaure entre les demandes de l'enfant et les réponses de l'entourage. On peut concevoir que selon les événements et la personnalité des proches, les échanges affectifs, à un moment donné ou tout au long de l'évolution, se prêtent à des conflits externes qui laisseront une trace dans l'organi-sation mentale de l'enfant. Ces conflits dépendent en partie d'organisa-tions sociales qui peuvent varier dans le temps et dans l'espace. Mais on doit admettre que cette évolution est également la source de conflits internes. L'enfant, en développant de nouveaux buts et en recherchant de nouvelles jouissances, doit renoncer aux buts et aux plaisirs de l'étape précédente. Ce renoncement n'est que partiel, et l'enseignement le plus profond de la psychanalyse a peut-être été de nous montrer le poids des fixations dans l'organisation des fantasmes. Ce sont les pul-sions partielles de la sexualité infantile qui composent la pulsion sexuelle de l'adulte. Elles sont par nature conflictuelles dans la mesure où le développement a été marqué par leur succession et les avatars de cette succession.

LA NÉVROSE : UN PRIX À PAYER
PAR L'HOMME POUR ASSUMER SON HISTOIRE

Si le conflit pulsionnel intra-psychique est avant tout la conséquence du développement et des fixations infantiles, on comprend mieux son universalité et le fait que la prédisposition à la névrose affecte tout être humain. Mais cette prédisposition n'exclut pas l'influence des facteurs liés à l'environnement qui modulent le poids respectif des fixations infantiles, les particularités de l'organisation œdipienne, la manière dont s'instaure la sexualité génitale lors de l'adolescence, et enfin les expressions symptomatiques des névroses. A condition de renoncer aux clichés moralisateurs (tenir par exemple les névroses pour une pathologie « fin de siècle » ou la conséquence de la répression capitaliste), un champ pour les comparaisons transculturelles demeure largement ouvert. Ceux, d'ailleurs, qui dénoncent dans la névrose l'expression d'une maladie de la société, sont en fait prisonniers d'un préjugé qui pose la névrose comme une entité morbide dont il s'agit de définir la cause. En revanche, si l'on admet l'universalité du conflit pulsionnel qui est, certes, à l'origine des névroses, mais aussi présent dans le développement de tout être humain, on reconnaît que les névroses ne constituent qu'une forme particulière de la réponse au conflit. Cette réponse est doublement gênante, en raison des symptômes qu'elle crée et à cause de la pauvreté des investissements qui demeurent disponibles en dehors de ceux qui sont engagés dans le conflit ; mais, si l'on ne tient pas compte de son retentissement subjectif et des valeurs de santé mentale, elle représente une modalité parmi d'autres réponses possibles. La survenue d'une névrose tient sans doute à l'amplitude des potentialités évolutives qui marquent le destin des pulsions partielles infantiles. Etre de mémoire, l'homme a une histoire. Le conflit pulsionnel est là pour en garder les traces. La névrose constitue le prix que nous courons le risque de payer pour assumer cette condition.

PROFESSEUR DANIEL WIDLÖCHER

PREMIÈRE PARTIE

A la découverte des névroses

Chapitre I

Le cas d'Anna O.

Le cas princeps *de névrose sur lequel se sont édifiées la théorie et la technique psychanalytiques est celui d'Anna O., jeune fille de vingt et un ans. En fait, le thérapeute d'Anna ne fut pas Freud, mais Joseph Breuer, un médecin viennois dont Freud avait fait la connaissance vers 1880 à l'Institut de physiologie, et qui était très vite devenu son ami.*

De décembre 1880 à juin 1882, Breuer avait soigné la jeune fille. Fasciné par le déroulement de cette cure, dont Breuer lui avait fait part à l'automne 1882, Freud convainquit Breuer d'insérer l'observation du cas dans leurs Études sur l'hystérie, *publiées en 1895, et de rédiger avec lui une « Communication préliminaire[1] » consacrée au « Mécanisme psychique des phénomènes hystériques », sur laquelle s'ouvrent les* Études. *Les deux auteurs y déclarent qu'à « leur très grande surprise », ils avaient découvert que* chacun des symptômes hystériques disparaissait immédiatement et sans retour quand on réussissait à mettre en pleine lumière le souvenir de l'incident déclenchant, à éveiller l'affect lié à ce dernier et quand, ensuite, le malade décrivait ce qui lui était arrivé de façon fort détaillée et en donnant à son émotion une expression verbale[2]. *Plus loin, ils ajoutent que* c'est de réminiscences surtout que souffre l'hystérique[3].

Or, de cette constatation découlent deux conséquences majeures ; elles pèseront sur le destin de la science qui ne s'appelait pas encore la psychanalyse[4] : les symptômes ont un sens et ils sont les substituts d'un souvenir refoulé. De plus, cette phase résume la méthode thérapeutique mise au point par Breuer ; celle-ci s'écarte sensiblement de la

---

1. Reproduite dans notre anthologie intitulée *Refoulement, défenses et interdits.*
2. et 3. Souligné par les auteurs.
4. Freud emploiera pour la première fois ce terme en mars 1896.

◀ *Ernst von Brücke, directeur de l'Institut de Physiologie à l'Université de Vienne de 1849 à 1890 (Catalogue de la Maison de S. Freud à Vienne).*

suggestion hypnotique couramment pratiquée à cette époque, et à laquelle Freud s'intéressera au point d'aller rendre visite, durant l'été 1889, à Hippolyte Bernheim, dans sa clinique de Nancy[5].

La suggestion hypnotique combattait le symptôme et les idées morbides des patients en leur opposant une affirmation contraire : Bernheim, par exemple, aurait sans doute traité la phobie du verre d'eau d'Anna O. en implantant dans son esprit la conviction de l'innocuité de l'eau et de sa capacité à surmonter sa répulsion. En revanche, Breuer, usant également de l'hypnose, permit à sa patiente de recouvrer le souvenir qui se dissimulait et s'exprimait en même temps derrière son hydrophobie. Il avait appelé son traitement « méthode cathartique », le mot grec catharsis *signifiant, rappelons-le, « purgation des passions ». Aristote l'emploie pour désigner l'effet produit par la tragédie sur le spectateur, ainsi purifié de ses passions.*

*A la méthode cathartique sont liées les idées d'*abréaction *et d'*événement traumatique*. L'abréaction implique une décharge d'émotion qui libère le patient des affects attachés au souvenir pathogène de l'événement traumatique. Elle peut survenir spontanément ou sous hypnose et représente une réaction différée au traumatisme initial. Lorsqu'il n'y a pas abréaction, « les représentations devenues pathogènes conservent leur activité » et demeurent en outre isolées du cours de la pensée dans son ensemble. L'absence d'abréaction provient de ce que le traumatisme psychique est de nature à empêcher toute réaction, par exemple, disent Freud et Breuer, « lors de la perte d'un être aimé paraissant irremplaçable, ou en raison de circonstances sociales rendant cette réaction impossible ». Nous avons aussi vu, en étudiant le refoulement[6], que les deux auteurs mettent sur le même plan le fait que le patient refoule « intentionnellement ». De plus, l'état psychique du sujet lorsque se produit le traumatisme entre également en cause pour faire obstacle à l'abréaction. Selon Breuer, des états hypnoïdes se trouveraient à l'origine de l'hystérie ; ils correspondraient aux états psychiques artificiellement provoqués par l'hypnose mais, à leur différence, seraient naturels : il s'agirait donc d'une « auto-hypnose », déclenchée par un affect survenu dans un état de rêverie ou encore dans un état dit crépusculaire.*

Dans un article rédigé en 1894 et intitulé « les Psychonévroses de défense[7] », Freud s'accorde avec Breuer pour penser que cet état hyp-

---

5. Il traduira même en allemand les deux importants ouvrages de Bernheim, *la Suggestion* et *Hypnotisme, suggestion et hypnothérapie*.

6. Cf. *Refoulement, défenses et interdits*, chap. I.

7. Reproduit dans *Refoulement, défenses et interdits*, chap. II. Cf. aussi *Névrose, psychose et perversion* (P.U.F.).

noïde conditionne effectivement l'apparition de l'hystérie, car cette conception lui paraît pouvoir rendre compte du « clivage de la conscience » chez l'hystérique et de l'existence de « groupes psychiques séparés ». Le « clivage de la conscience », poussé à l'extrême, aboutissait au dédoublement de la personnalité, voire même aux personnalités multiples, assez fréquents chez les hystériques à cette époque ; pour certaines raisons culturelles et éducatives difficiles à définir, ces phénomènes sont devenus extrêmement rares de nos jours (on peut invoquer, par exemple, une moindre tolérance de l'entourage dans nos sociétés de plus en plus urbanisées et industrialisées). D'une façon générale, les grandes hystériques de conversion[8] que présentait Charcot à ses célèbres séances de la Salpêtrière offraient un tableau clinique qui semble avoir en grande partie disparu à l'heure actuelle. Nous verrons dans la suite de cet ouvrage que Freud abandonnera très rapidement l'idée d'hystérie hypnoïde (c'est-à-dire survenue dans un état hypnoïde), ainsi que la pratique de l'hypnose. Dans l'extrait de Ma vie et la psychanalyse *(1925), que nous découvrirons en premier lieu dans ce chapitre, il précisera lui-même qu'il a renoncé à cette notion pour celle de* névrose de défense *et, donc, pour celle de* conflit. *De plus, la théorie du symptôme vu comme substitut du souvenir refoulé se trouvera singulièrement enrichie et modifiée lorsque Freud dégagera précisément le conflit qui sous-tend toute névrose.*

Enfin, deux concepts fondamentaux concernant les névroses échappèrent à Breuer et furent à l'origine de la rupture précipitée du traitement. Dans sa biographie de Freud[9], Ernest Jones rapporte que Mme Breuer avait conçu de la jalousie envers Anna O., qui préoccupait tant son mari. Aussi Breuer mit-il brutalement fin à la cure ayant noté une importante amélioration dans l'état de sa patiente. Mais, le soir même, elle présentait tous les signes d'un accouchement hystérique, « fin logique, commente Jones, d'une grossesse imaginaire passée inaperçue et qui s'était produite en réponse aux soins donnés par Breuer ». Interrogée par Breuer sur ses symptômes abdominaux, Anna répondit : « Maintenant, le bébé du docteur Breuer arrive. » Selon Jones, Breuer l'aurait calmée sous hypnose et serait parti le lendemain avec sa femme pour Venise « afin d'y passer une seconde lune de miel ».

---

8. L'hystérie de conversion désigne la maladie hystérique telle qu'on la connaissait du temps de Charcot. Elle se caractérise par la présence de symptômes apparemment somatiques (paralysie, diminution du champ visuel, sensation de « boule » dans la gorge, vomissements, anesthésies, etc.), sans que l'on puisse pour autant déceler de lésion organique susceptible d'être à l'origine des troubles. Après Breuer, Freud va progressivement s'attacher à découvrir le sens symbolique de ces symptômes, véritable langage de l'hystérie ; mais il ne parvint cependant jamais totalement à expliquer le « saut mystérieux du psychique dans le soma » que représentent les phénomènes de conversion.

9. Ernest Jones, *la Vie et l'œuvre de Sigmund Freud* (P.U.F.).

Breuer, qui considérait que chez Anna O. « l'élément sexuel était étonnamment peu marqué », prit donc la fuite devant cette éclatante réfutation de son opinion. En revanche, Freud découvrit, à partir de cette observation et dans les réactions des deux protagonistes, le transfert et l'étiologie sexuelle des névroses : c'est ce qu'il précisera dans le dernier texte présenté dans le chapitre, extrait de Contribution à l'histoire du mouvement psychanalytique, *qu'il écrivit en 1914.*

La personnalité d'Anna O. (pseudonyme de Berthe Pappenheim) se révèle déjà exceptionnelle à travers le récit de la cure. Cette jeune fille a en effet découvert, en quelque sorte « d'elle-même », certains principes qui deviendront essentiels pour la psychanalyse, parmi lesquels la talking cure *(la cure par la parole), montrant ainsi sa profonde compréhension de l'importance de la verbalisation. D'autres expressions, employées pour la première fois par elle, sont devenues célèbres : le* chimney sweeping *(le ramonage), par exemple, qui désignait en fait la fameuse « purgation cathartique », ou bien le « théâtre privé », nom qu'elle donnait à ses rêveries.*

Après la fin de sa cure, elle devint morphinomane, mais parvint à s'en désaccoutumer. Accompagnée de sa mère, elle quitta Vienne pour s'installer à Francfort où elle dirigea un orphelinat. Gagnée aux idées féministes, elle écrivit entre autres une pièce sous le nom de Paul Berthold, puis fonda en Allemagne la Fédération des femmes juives et un foyer d'accueil pour les mères célibataires, les délinquantes et les arriérées. Elle joua également un rôle dans le mouvement sioniste. Convoquée au siège de la Gestapo en 1936, elle mourut peu de temps après, à l'âge de soixante-dix-sept ans.

L'un des membres du conseil d'administration du foyer qu'elle avait fondé avait un jour suggéré de consulter un psychanalyste pour l'une des pensionnaires. Berthe Pappenheim se leva et dit fermement : « Jamais ! Pas de mon vivant[10]... »

Quand j'étais encore au laboratoire de Brücke[11], j'avais fait la connaissance du docteur Joseph Breuer, l'un des médecins praticiens les plus en vue de Vienne, mais ayant aussi un passé scientifique, plusieurs travaux d'une valeur durable lui étant dus sur la physiologie de la respiration et sur l'organe de l'équilibre. C'était un homme d'une intelligence hors de ligne, de quatorze ans plus âgé que moi ; nos relations se firent bientôt plus intimes, il devint mon ami et soutien dans

10. Rapporté par Lucy Freeman dans *l'Histoire d'Anna O.* (coll. « Perspectives critiques », dirigée par Roland Jaccard, P.U.F.).

11. Ernst von Brücke (1819-1892), célèbre physiologiste allemand et directeur, à Vienne, d'un institut dans lequel Freud, de 1876 à 1882, effectua certaines recherches, notamment sur l'histologie de la cellule nerveuse. (N.d.E.)

les conditions de vie difficiles où je me trouvais. Nous nous étions accoutumés à mettre en commun tous nos intérêts scientifiques. Naturellement, dans ces rapports, c'était moi la partie gagnante. Le développement de la psychanalyse m'a coûté son amitié. Il ne me fut pas facile de le payer de ce prix, mais c'était inévitable.

Breuer m'avait communiqué, avant même que je n'allasse à Paris, ses observations sur un cas d'hystérie, qu'il avait traité de 1880 à 1882 par un procédé spécial, ce qui lui avait permis d'acquérir des aperçus profonds sur l'étiologie et sur la signification des symptômes hystériques. Ceci avait lieu en un temps où les travaux de Janet appartenaient encore à l'avenir. Il me lut à diverses reprises des fragments de l'histoire de sa malade, et j'en reçus l'impression que jamais n'avait été

L'Université de Vienne à la fin du XIXe *siècle*
(Bibliothèque des Arts Décoratifs).

encore accompli un tel pas dans la compréhension de la névrose. Je résolus de faire part à Charcot de ces résultats quand j'irais à Paris, ce qu'en effet je fis. Mais le maître, dès mes premières allusions, ne manifesta aucun intérêt, ce qui fit que je n'y revins pas et ne m'occupai moi-même plus de la chose.

JOSEPH BREUER ET SA PATIENTE : ANNA O.

Rentré à Vienne, je portai à nouveau mon attention sur l'observation de Breuer et je m'en fis conter plus de détails. La patiente qu'avait eue Breuer était une jeune fille douée d'une culture et d'aptitudes peu communes, tombée malade pendant qu'elle soignait un père tendrement aimé. Quand Breuer entreprit de s'occuper de son cas, elle présentait un tableau clinique bigarré de paralysie avec contractures, d'inhibitions et d'états de confusion mentale. Une observation fortuite permit au médecin de s'apercevoir qu'on pouvait la délivrer de l'un de ces troubles de la conscience quand on la mettait à même d'exprimer verbalement le fantasme affectif qui la dominait à ce moment. Une méthode thérapeutique résulta pour Breuer de cette observation. Il plongeait sa malade en une hypnose profonde et la laissait chaque fois raconter ce qui oppressait son âme. Après que les états de confusion dépressive eurent ainsi disparu, Breuer employa la même méthode afin de lever les inhibitions et de délivrer la malade de ses troubles corporels. A l'état de veille, la jeune fille n'aurait pu dire — en ceci semblable aux autres malades — comment ses symptômes avaient pris naissance et ne trouvait aucun lien entre eux et une impression quelconque de sa vie. En état d'hypnose, elle découvrait aussitôt les rapports cherchés. Il se révéla que tous ces symptômes remontaient à des événements l'ayant impressionnée vivement, survenus au temps où elle soignait son père malade ; ces symptômes avaient donc un sens et correspondaient à des reliquats ou réminiscences de ces situations affectives. D'ordinaire les choses s'étaient passées ainsi : elle avait dû réprimer, au chevet de son père, une pensée ou une impulsion à la place de laquelle, comme son représentant, était plus tard apparu le symptôme. En règle générale, le symptôme n'était pas le précipité d'une seule de ces scènes « traumatiques », mais le résultat de la sommation d'un grand nombre de situations analogues. Quand la malade se souvenait hallucinatoirement pendant l'hypnose d'une telle situation et réussissait à accomplir ainsi après coup l'acte psychique autrefois réprimé en extériorisant librement l'affect, le symptôme était balayé et ne reparaissait plus. C'est par cette méthode que Breuer réussit, après un long et pénible travail, à délivrer sa malade de tous ses symptômes.

La malade avait guéri et était restée bien portante, était même devenue capable d'une réelle et importante activité dans la vie. Mais sur l'issue du traitement hypnotique régnait une obscurité que Breuer ne dissipa jamais ; je ne pouvais pas non plus comprendre pourquoi il avait tenu si longtemps secrète une connaissance qui me semblait inappréciable, au lieu d'en enrichir la science. La question qui se posait ensuite était de savoir si l'on était justifié à généraliser ce qu'il avait trouvé à propos d'un seul cas. Les relations découvertes par lui me semblaient d'une nature si fondamentale que je ne pouvais croire qu'elles fissent défaut dans un cas quelconque d'hystérie, du moment qu'elles avaient été démontrées comme existant déjà dans un cas. Cependant, l'expérience seule pouvait trancher la question. Je commençai donc à reproduire les recherches de Breuer sur mes malades, et je ne fis d'ailleurs plus rien d'autre, surtout après que la visite chez Bernheim, en 1889, m'eut montré les limites d'efficacité de la suggestion hypnotique. Après n'avoir trouvé, durant plusieurs années, que des confirmations, et disposant d'un imposant ensemble d'observations analogues aux siennes, je lui proposai une publication faite en commun, idée contre laquelle il commença par se défendre violemment. Il finit par céder, après qu'entre-temps les travaux de Janet eurent anticipé sur une partie de ses résultats : le rattachement des symptômes hystériques à des impressions de la vie et leur levée de par leur reproduction sous hypnose *in statu nascendi.* Nous fîmes paraître en 1893 une étude préalable : « Du mécanisme psychique des phénomènes hystériques » *(Über den psychischen Mechanismus hysterischer Phänomene).* En 1895 suivit notre livre : « Études sur l'hystérie » *(Studien über Hysterie).*

LA MÉTHODE CATHARTIQUE : EFFICACE, MAIS SOMMAIRE

Si l'exposé que j'ai fait jusqu'ici a éveillé chez le lecteur l'idée que les « Études sur l'hystérie » fussent, en tout ce qu'elles contiennent d'essentiel par rapport à leur contenu matériel, la propriété intellectuelle de Breuer, voilà qui est précisément ce que j'ai toujours prétendu moi-même et que je voulais ici déclarer. Quant à la théorie que le livre tente d'édifier, j'y ai collaboré dans une mesure qu'il n'est plus possible aujourd'hui de définir. Celle-ci est modeste, elle ne dépasse pas de beaucoup l'expression immédiate des observations. Elle ne cherche pas à approfondir la nature de l'hystérie, mais simplement à éclairer la genèse de ses symptômes. Elle souligne ce faisant la signification de la vie affective, l'importance qu'il y a à distinguer entre actes psychiques

6

À Monsieur J. M. Charcot
souvenir d'un élève et son père
Dr Freud

STUDIEN

ÜBER

HYSTERIE

VON

Dr. JOS. BREUER und Dr. SIGM. FREUD

IN WIEN.

LEIPZIG UND WIEN.
FRANZ DEUTICKE.
1895.

Verlags-Nr. 445.

Freud dédicaça cet exemplaire des Études sur l'hystérie *au fils de son professeur, Charcot (Bibliothèque Charcot, la Salpêtrière).*

inconscients et conscients (ou plutôt : capables de parvenir à la conscience) ; elle introduit un facteur dynamique en faisant naître le symptôme de par l'accumulation d'un affect — et un facteur économique, en considérant ce même symptôme comme le résultat du déplacement d'une masse énergétique d'ordinaire autrement employée (ceci est la *conversion*). Breuer appela notre méthode la *catharsis* ; nous lui donnions pour but thérapeutique de ramener dans les chemins normaux, afin qu'elle puisse s'y écouler (être *abréagie*), la charge affective engagée dans des voies fausses et qui y était pour ainsi dire demeurée coincée. Le succès pratique de la méthode cathartique était excellent. Les défauts qui s'y révélèrent plus tard étaient ceux de tout traitement par l'hypnose. Il est encore aujourd'hui un certain nombre de psychothérapeutes qui en sont restés à la *catharsis* telle que l'entendait Breuer et trouvent à s'en louer. Dans le traitement des névroses de guerre de l'armée allemande pendant la guerre mondiale, elle a de nouveau fait ses preuves comme procédé thérapeutique succinct, ceci entre les mains de E. Simmel[12]. Il n'est pas beaucoup question de sexualité dans la théorie de la catharsis. Dans les histoires de malades qui furent ma contribution aux « Études », des facteurs de la vie sexuelle jouent un certain rôle, mais il leur est à peine attribué une valeur différente de celle d'autres émois affectifs. De sa première patiente, devenue si célèbre, Breuer rapporte que le sexuel chez elle était étonnamment peu développé. On n'aurait pu aisément deviner, d'après « Études sur l'hystérie », quelle importance a la sexualité dans l'étiologie des névroses.

LA PART DE LA SEXUALITÉ DANS LA NÉVROSE : UNE DÉCOUVERTE CAPITALE

Ce qui s'ensuivit alors, le passage de la catharsis à la psychanalyse proprement dite, je l'ai déjà tant de fois décrit en détail qu'il me sera difficile de dire ici quelque chose de nouveau. L'événement qui inaugura cette période fut le retrait de Breuer de notre communauté de travail, ce qui me laissa seul à gérer son héritage. De bonne heure, des divergences d'opinion s'étaient manifestées entre nous, mais incapables d'amener notre séparation. A la question : quand un courant affectif devient-il pathogène, c'est-à-dire quand est-il exclu d'une résolution normale, Breuer préférait répondre par une théorie pour ainsi dire phy-

12. Publié au début de l'année 1918, le livre de Simmel consacré au traitement par l'hypnose des névroses de guerre avait à tel point séduit les médecins militaires qu'il était question de créer des cliniques psychanalytiques dans divers centres de traitement des névroses de guerre : la défaite allemande allait mettre fin à ce projet (d'après E. Jones, *la Vie et l'œuvre de Sigmund Freud*, t. II, p. 211). (N.d.É.)

siologique ; il pensait que les processus ayant pris naissance dans certains états psychiques inaccoutumés — hypnoïdes — étaient ceux qui étaient soustraits à un destin normal. Une nouvelle question se posait alors : quelle était l'origine de ces états hypnoïdes ? Je croyais pour ma part plutôt à un jeu de forces, à l'action d'intentions et de tendances, telles qu'on les peut observer dans la vie normale. Ainsi la « théorie hypnoïde » s'opposait à la « névrose de défense ». Mais ceci et des oppositions de cet ordre n'auraient pas détourné Breuer de notre travail, si d'autres facteurs ne s'y étaient adjoints. L'un d'eux était certes qu'en tant que médecin praticien très recherché par les familles il était très pris et ne pouvait pas comme moi consacrer toutes ses forces au travail cathartique. En outre, il se laissa influencer par l'accueil que notre livre rencontra à Vienne et en Allemagne. Sa foi en lui-même et sa capacité de résistance n'étaient pas à la hauteur de son organisation intellectuelle. Les « Études » ayant par exemple été durement traitées par Strümpell, tandis qu'il me fut possible de rire de cette critique incompréhensive, lui se sentit blessé et découragé. Mais ce qui contribua le plus à sa résolution fut que mes propres travaux prirent alors une direction avec laquelle il tenta vainement de se familiariser.

Le théorie que nous avions tenté d'édifier dans les « Études » était restée encore très incomplète ; en particulier le problème de l'étiologie, la question de savoir sur quel terrain le processus pathogène prend naissance, avait été à peine touché par nous. Des expériences qui s'accumulaient rapidement me montraient maintenant que, derrière les phénomènes de la névrose, ce n'était pas n'importe quels émois affectifs qui agissaient, mais régulièrement des émois de nature sexuelle, soit des conflits actuels sexuels, soit des contrecoups d'événements sexuels précoces.

SIGMUND FREUD[13]

LE CAS D'ANNA O.

Fräulein Anna O..., âgée de vingt et un ans à l'époque de sa maladie (1880), semble avoir une hérédité névrotique assez chargée. On trouve, en effet, dans sa nombreuse famille, quelques cas de psychoses ; ses parents sont des nerveux bien portants. Elle-même s'est jusqu'alors fort bien portée, n'a jamais présenté de phénomènes névrotiques pendant tout son développement. Elle est remarquablement intelligente, éton-

13. *Ma vie et la psychanalyse*, p. 25 à 31.

namment ingénieuse et très intuitive. Étant donné ses belles qualités mentales, elle aurait pu et dû assimiler une riche nourriture intellectuelle qu'on ne lui donna pas au sortir de l'école. On remarquait en elle de grands dons poétiques, une grande imagination contrôlée par un sens aiguisé qui, d'ailleurs, la rendait totalement inaccessible à la suggestion ; les arguments seuls pouvaient agir sur elle, jamais de simples affirmations. Elle est énergique, opiniâtre, persévérante. Sa volonté se mue parfois en entêtement et elle ne se laisse détourner de son but que par égard pour autrui.

Parmi les traits essentiels de son caractère, on notait une bonté compatissante. Elle prodiguait ses soins aux malades et aux pauvres gens, ce qui lui était à elle-même d'un grand secours dans sa maladie parce qu'elle pouvait, de cette façon, satisfaire un besoin profond. On observait encore chez elle une légère tendance aux sautes d'humeur. Elle pouvait passer d'une gaieté exubérante à une tristesse exagérée. L'élément sexuel était étonnamment peu marqué. Je ne tardai pas à connaître tous les détails de son existence et cela à un degré rarement atteint dans les relations humaines. La malade n'avait jamais eu de relations amoureuses et, parmi ses multiples hallucinations, jamais cet élément de la vie psychique ne se manifestait

Cette jeune fille d'une activité mentale débordante menait, dans sa puritaine famille, une existence des plus monotones et elle aggravait encore cette monotonie d'une façon sans doute à la mesure de sa maladie. Elle se livrait systématiquement à des rêveries qu'elle appelait « théâtre privé ». Alors que tout le monde la croyait présente, elle vivait mentalement des contes de fées, mais lorsqu'on l'interpellait, elle répondait normalement, ce qui fait que nul ne soupçonnait ses absences. Parallèlement aux soins ménagers qu'elle accomplissait à la perfection, cette activité mentale se poursuivait presque sans arrêt. J'aurai plus tard à raconter comment ces rêveries, habituelles chez les gens normaux, prirent, sans transition, un caractère pathologique.

DES SYMPTÔMES SURVENUS PENDANT LA MALADIE D'UN PÈRE PASSIONNÉMENT AIMÉ

Le cours de la maladie se divise en plusieurs phases bien distinctes :
A) L'incubation latente : à partir de la mi-juillet 1880 jusqu'au 10 décembre environ. Nous ignorons la plus grande partie de ce qui d'ordinaire se produit dans cette phase, mais le caractère particulier de ce cas nous permet de le comprendre si parfaitement que nous en apprécions beaucoup l'intérêt au point de vue pathologique. J'exposerai plus tard cette partie de l'observation ;

B) La maladie manifeste : une psychose singulière avec paraphasie[14], strabisme convergent, troubles graves de la vue, contracture parésique[15] totale dans le membre supérieur droit et les deux membres inférieurs, et partielle dans le membre supérieur gauche, parésie des muscles du cou. Réduction progressive de la contracture dans les membres droits. Une certaine amélioration se trouva interrompue par un grave traumatisme psychique en avril (décès du père) ; à cette amélioration succéda :

C) Une période de durable somnambulisme alternant, par la suite, avec des états plus normaux ; persistance d'une série de symptômes jusqu'en décembre 1881 ;

D) Suppression progressive des troubles et des phénomènes jusqu'en juin 1882.

En juillet 1880, le père de la malade, qu'elle aimait passionnément, fut atteint d'un abcès péripleuritique qui ne put guérir et dont il devait mourir en avril 1881. Pendant les premiers mois de cette maladie, Anna consacra toute son énergie à son rôle d'infirmière et personne ne put s'étonner de la voir progressivement décliner beaucoup. Pas plus que les autres, sans doute, la malade ne se rendait compte de ce qui se passait en elle-même, mais, peu à peu, son état de faiblesse, d'anémie, de dégoût des aliments, devint si inquiétant qu'à son immense chagrin on l'obligea à abandonner son rôle d'infirmière. De terribles quintes de toux fournirent d'abord le motif de cette interdiction et ce fut à cause d'elles que j'eus, pour la première fois, l'occasion d'examiner la jeune fille. Il s'agissait d'une toux nerveuse typique. Bientôt, Anna ressentit un besoin marqué de se reposer l'après-midi, repos auquel succédaient, dans la soirée, un état de somnolence, puis une grande agitation.

Un strabisme convergent apparut au début de décembre. Un oculiste attribua (faussement) ce symptôme à une parésie du nerf abducens. A partir du 11 décembre, la patiente dut s'aliter pour ne se relever que le 1er avril.

Des troubles graves, en apparence nouveaux, se succédèrent alors rapidement. Douleurs du côté gauche de l'occiput ; strabisme convergent (diplopie) plus prononcé à chaque contrariété ; peur d'un écroulement des murs (affection du muscle oblique), troubles de la vue difficilement analysables, parésie des muscles antérieurs du cou, de telle sorte que la patiente finissait par ne plus pouvoir remuer la tête qu'en la resserrant entre ses épaules soulevées et en faisant mouvoir son dos, contracture et anesthésie du bras droit, puis, au bout de quelques temps, de la jambe droite, ce membre étant raidi et recroquevillé vers le dedans ; plus tard, les mêmes troubles affectent la jambe et enfin le

14 Trouble du langage consistant en une altération des mots. (N.d.E.)
15 Paralysie légère se traduisant par une diminution de la force musculaire. (N.d.E.)

bras gauches, les doigts conservant pourtant une certaine mobilité. Les articulations des deux épaules ne sont pas non plus tout à fait rigides. La contracture affecte surtout les muscles du bras puis, plus tard, lorsque l'anesthésie put être mieux étudiée, la région du coude qui s'avéra la plus insensible. Au début de la maladie, l'examen de l'anesthésie ne fut pas suffisamment poussé, à cause de la résistance qu'y opposait la malade apeurée.

DEUX ÉTATS DE CONSCIENCE ALTERNÉS

C'est dans ces circonstances que j'entrepris le traitement de la malade et je pus tout aussitôt me rendre compte de la profonde altération de son psychisme. On notait chez elle deux états tout à fait distincts qui, très souvent et de façon imprévisible, alternaient et qui, au cours de la maladie, se différencièrent toujours davantage l'un de l'autre. Dans l'un de ces états, elle reconnaissait son entourage, se montrait triste, anxieuse, mais relativement normale ; dans l'autre, en proie à des hallucinations, elle devenait « méchante », c'est-à-dire qu'elle vociférait, jetait des coussins à la tête des gens et, dans la mesure où sa contracture le lui permettait, arrachait avec ses doigts restés mobiles, les boutons de ses couvertures, de son linge, etc. ; si, pendant cette phase, l'on modifiait quelque chose dans la pièce, si quelqu'un venait à entrer ou à sortir, elle se plaignait de ne pas avoir de temps à elle et remarquait les lacunes de ses propres représentations conscientes. Dans la mesure du possible, on la contredisait et on cherchait à la rassurer, quand elle se plaignait de devenir folle, mais alors, chaque fois qu'elle avait jeté au loin ses coussins, etc., elle gémissait de l'abandon, du désordre où on la laissait et ainsi de suite.

Dès avant qu'elle s'alitât, on avait déjà noté chez elle de semblables absences. Elle s'arrêtait au milieu d'une phrase, en répétant les derniers mots pour la poursuivre quelques instants plus tard. Peu à peu ces troubles prirent l'acuité que nous avons décrite et, au point culminant de la maladie, quand la contracture affecta aussi le côté gauche, elle ne se montra à moitié normale que pendant de très courts instants de la journée. Toutefois, même pendant les périodes de conscience relativement claire, les troubles réapparaissaient : saute d'humeur des plus rapides et des plus prononcées, gaieté très passagère en général, vifs sentiments d'anxiété, refus tenace de toute mesure thérapeutique, hallucinations angoissantes où cheveux, lacets, etc., lui semblaient être des serpents noirs. En même temps, elle s'adjurait de n'être pas aussi stupide puisqu'il ne s'agissait que de ses propres cheveux et ainsi de suite. Dans ses moments de pleine lucidité, elle se plaignait de ténèbres dans son cerveau, disant qu'elle n'arrivait plus à penser, qu'elle devenait aveugle et sourde, qu'elle avait deux « Moi », l'un qui était le vrai et l'autre, le mauvais, qui la poussait à mal agir, etc.

L'après-midi, elle tombait dans un état de somnolence qui se prolongeait jusqu'au coucher du soleil. Ensuite, réveillée, elle se plaignait d'être tourmentée ou plutôt ne cessait de répéter l'infinitif : tourmenter, tourmenter.

LA MALADE NE S'EXPRIME PLUS QU'EN ANGLAIS

Un grave trouble fonctionnel du langage était apparu en même temps que les contractures. On observa d'abord qu'elle ne trouvait plus ses mots, phénomène qui s'accentua peu à peu. Puis grammaire et syntaxe disparurent de son langage, elle finit par faire un usage incorrect des conjugaisons de verbes, n'utilisant plus que certains infinitifs formés à l'aide de prétérits de verbes faibles et omettant les articles. Plus tard, les mots eux-mêmes vinrent à lui manquer presque totalement, elle les empruntait péniblement à quatre ou cinq langues et n'arrivait plus guère à se faire comprendre. En essayant d'écrire, elle se servait du même jargon (au début, car ensuite la contracture l'en empêcha tout à fait). Deux semaines durant, elle garda un mutisme total et, en s'efforçant de parler, n'émettait aucun son. C'est alors seulement que le mécanisme psychique de la perturbation put s'expliquer. Je savais qu'une chose qu'elle avait décidé de taire l'avait beaucoup tourmentée. Lorsque j'appris cela et que je la contraignis à en parler, l'inhibition, qui avait rendu impossible toute autre expression de pensées, disparut.

Cette amélioration coïncida, en mars 1881, avec la mobilité récupérée des membres gauches ; la paraphasie disparut, mais elle ne s'exprimait plus qu'en anglais, en apparence sans s'en rendre compte ; elle querellait son infirmière qui, naturellement, ne la comprenait pas ; quelques mois plus tard seulement, j'arrivai à lui faire admettre qu'elle utilisait l'anglais. Toutefois, elle n'avait pas cessé de comprendre son entourage qui s'exprimait en allemand. Dans les moments d'angoisse intense seulement, elle perdait entièrement l'usage de la parole ou bien elle mêlait les idiomes les plus différents. A ses meilleurs moments, quand elle se sentait mieux disposée, elle parlait français ou italien. Entre ces périodes et celles où elle s'exprimait en anglais, on constatait une amnésie totale. Le strabisme également s'atténua pour ne plus apparaître que dans des moments de grande agitation. La malade pouvait maintenant redresser la tête et quitta son lit, pour la première fois, le 1er avril.

Mais le 5 avril, son père adoré, qu'elle n'avait que rarement entrevu au cours de sa propre maladie, vint à mourir. C'était là le choc le plus grave qui pût l'atteindre. A une agitation intense succéda, pendant deux jours, un état de prostration profonde dont Anna sortit très changée. Au début, elle se montra bien plus calme avec une forte atténuation de son sentiment d'angoisse. Les contractures de la jambe et du bras droits persistaient, ainsi qu'une anesthésie peu marquée de ces membres. Le champ visuel se trouvait extrêmement rétréci. En contemplant une gerbe de fleurs qui lui avait fait grand plaisir, elle ne voyait qu'une seule fleur à la fois. Elle se plaignait de ne pas reconnaître les gens. Autrefois elle les reconnaissait sans effort volontaire, maintenant elle se voyait obligée, en se livrant à un très fatiguant *recognising work*, de se dire que le nez était comme ci, les cheveux comme ça, donc qu'il s'agissait bien d'un tel. Les gens lui apparaissaient comme des figures en cire, sans rapport avec elle-même. La présence de certains proches parents lui était pénible et « cet instinct négatif » ne faisait que croître. Si quelqu'un, dont la visite lui faisait généralement plaisir, pénétrait dans la pièce, elle le reconnaissait, demeurait quelques instants présente pour retomber dans sa rêverie et, pour elle, la personne avait disparu. J'étais la seule personne qu'elle reconnût toujours. Elle demeurait présente et bien disposée tant que je lui parlais jusqu'au moment où, tout à fait à l'improviste, survenaient ses absences hallucinatoires.

Elle ne s'exprimait maintenant qu'en anglais, sans plus comprendre ce qu'on lui disait en allemand. Son entourage se voyait forcé de lui parler en anglais et l'infirmière elle-même apprit à se faire à peu près comprendre. Mais la malade lisait des livres français et italiens ; lorsqu'on lui demandait de lire à haute voix, elle traduisait les textes avec une surprenante rapidité et dans un anglais parfaitement correct.

Elle recommença à écrire, mais d'une façon bizarre, en se servant de l'articulation de sa main gauche et en traçant des lettres d'imprimerie dont elle s'était fait un alphabet copié dans son Shakespeare.

Elle n'avait jamais été grosse mangeuse, mais maintenant elle refusait toute nourriture, en dehors pourtant de celle qu'elle m'autorisait à lui faire ingurgiter, de sorte qu'elle put rapidement reprendre des forces. Toutefois, elle refusait toujours de manger du pain et ne manquait jamais, une fois le repas terminé, d'aller se rincer la bouche, ce qu'elle faisait aussi quand, sous un prétexte quelconque, elle n'avait rien voulu avaler — un indice du fait qu'elle était alors absente.

Les somnolences de l'après-midi, le profond assoupissement au coucher du soleil persistaient. Mais quand elle avait pu « se raconter » elle-même, elle se montrait calme, tranquille et enjouée. (Je reviendrai ultérieurement, d'une façon plus explicite, sur ce point.)

Cet état relativement supportable ne se maintint pas longtemps. Dix jours environ après la mort de son père, un consultant fut appelé. Comme toujours quand il s'agissait de personnes étrangères, elle ignora absolument sa présence.

ANGOISSES ET HALLUCINATIONS MACABRES APRÈS LA MORT DU PÈRE

J'informai le médecin de tout ce qui caractérisait ma malade et, lorsque je fis traduire à celle-ci un texte en français, *That is like an examination*, dit-elle en souriant. Le médecin étranger lui parla, essaya de se faire remarquer d'elle, mais en vain. Il s'agissait, en l'occurrence, de cette « hallucination négative », si souvent expérimentalement établie depuis. Le praticien réussit enfin à marquer sa présence en lui lançant au visage la fumée de sa cigarette. Elle aperçut soudain cet étranger, se précipita vers la porte pour en enlever la clé et s'écroula inanimée. Après quoi, elle eut un court accès de colère auquel succéda une crise aiguë d'angoisse que j'eus beaucoup de mal à calmer. Le malheur voulut que je fusse obligé, ce soir-là, de partir en voyage et quand, plusieurs jours après, je revins, je trouvai que l'état de ma malade s'était bien aggravé. Elle avait, pendant mon absence, refusé tout aliment, était en proie à des sentiments d'angoisse. Ses absences hallucinatoires étaient remplies de figures terrifiantes, de têtes de mort et de squelettes. Comme elle racontait une partie de ces scènes tout en les vivant, son entourage prenait généralement connaissance du contenu des hallucinations. L'après-midi : somnolence, vers le soir : hypnose profonde à laquelle elle avait donné le nom technique de *clouds* (nuages). Si elle pouvait ensuite raconter ses hallucinations de la journée, elle se réveillait lucide, calme, gaie, se mettait au travail et passait la nuit à dessiner et à écrire, se montrait tout à fait raisonnable et se recouchait vers 4 heures. Les mêmes scènes que les jours précédents se reproduisaient le matin. Le contraste que présentait la malade irresponsable, poursuivie par ses hallucinations dans la journée, et la jeune fille parfaitement lucide qu'elle était pendant la nuit semblait des plus frappants.

En dépit de cette euphorie nocturne, l'état psychique ne cessait d'empirer. D'intenses compulsions au suicide apparurent ; c'est pourquoi nous trouvâmes qu'il ne convenait pas de la laisser plus longtemps loger au troisième étage de sa demeure. La malade, bien contre son gré, fut conduite dans une villa à proximité de Vienne (le 7 juin 1881). Il n'avait jamais été question entre nous de l'éloigner de sa maison car elle s'y serait opposée, mais elle prévoyait cette décision et la craignait en silence. A cette occasion, on put, une fois de plus, consta-

Joseph Breuer, coauteur des Études sur l'hystérie, *dans lesquelles il rapporte la célèbre « talking cure » d'Anna O. (Catalogue de la maison de S. Freud à Vienne).*

ter à quel point l'affect d'angoisse dominait le trouble psychique. Comme après la mort de son père, elle traversait, maintenant que le fait redouté s'était accompli, une période d'accalmie non point, à vrai dire, sans que le changement de demeure n'eût été immédiatement suivi de trois jours et de trois nuits d'insomnie, de jeûne complet et d'une tentative de suicide (heureusement sans danger) dans le jardin, ainsi que de bris de vitres, etc. Elle avait des hallucinations sans absences qu'elle distinguait fort bien des autres. Elle finit par se calmer, accepta que l'infirmière la fit manger et prit même le soir son chloral.

(Joseph Breuer établit ensuite un rapport entre la lucidité nocturne de sa patiente et son rôle d'infirmière, la nuit, auprès de son père. Il précise également que, durant les « absences » de la jeune fille, celle-ci racontait — en état second — des histoires se rapportant le plus souvent à une « jeune fille angoissée au chevet de son père ». Raconter à haute voix et à son médecin ces histoires lui était nécessaire : lorsqu'elle en était un jour empêchée, il lui fallait, le lendemain, en rapporter deux au lieu d'une seule.) (N.d.E.)

LA DÉCOUVERTE DE LA « CURE PAR LA PAROLE »

Pendant les dix-huit mois que dura cette observation, jamais les manifestations essentielles de la maladie ne manquèrent, à savoir : accumulation et condensation des absences allant, le soir, jusqu'à l'autohypnose, action excitante des productions fantasmatiques, soulagement et suppression de l'excitation par expression verbale sous hypnose.

Après la mort du père, les récits de la malade prirent naturellement un tour plus tragique encore, mais ce ne fut qu'après l'aggravation de l'état psychique provoquée par la brutale irruption du somnambulisme dont nous avons parlé que les narrations du soir perdirent leur caractère plus ou moins libre et poétique pour se transformer en séries d'hallucinations horribles et terrifiantes. Le comportement de la malade pendant les heures précédentes permettait d'ailleurs de prévoir celles-ci. Mais j'ai déjà dit comment elle parvenait à libérer complètement son psychisme après que, toute tremblante d'épouvante et d'horreur, elle avait revécu et décrit ces images terrifiantes.

A la campagne où il ne me fut pas possible d'aller voir quotidiennement la malade, les choses se passèrent de la façon suivante : j'arrivais le soir, au moment où je la savais plongée dans son état d'hypnose et la débarrassais de toutes les réserves de fantasmes accumulées depuis ma dernière visite. Pour s'assurer le succès, il fallait que ce fût fait à fond.

Alors, tout à fait tranquillisée, elle se montrait le jour suivant aimable, docile, laborieuse, voire même enjouée. Le deuxième jour, et surtout le troisième, son humeur devenait toujours moins bonne, elle était revêche, désagréable. En cet état, il devenait parfois difficile, même sous hypnose, de la faire parler. Elle avait donné à ce procédé le nom bien approprié et sérieux de *talking cure* (cure par la parole) et le nom humoristique de *chimney sweeping* (ramonage). Elle savait qu'après avoir parlé, elle aurait perdu tout son entêtement et toute son « énergie ». Lorsque son humeur redevenait maussade (après un intervalle prolongé) et qu'elle refusait de parler, je devais l'y contraindre en insistant, suppliant et aussi en me servant de certains artifices, en prononçant, par exemple, une formule stéréotypée du début de ses récits.

Le somnambulisme permanent disparut, mais ce qui persista fut l'alternance de deux états de la conscience. Au beau milieu d'une conversation, certaines hallucinations pouvaient survenir, la malade s'enfuyait, essayait de grimper sur un arbre, etc. Lorsqu'on la retenait, elle reprenait presque immédiatement le fil de son discours comme si rien ne s'était produit entre-temps. Mais ensuite, elle décrivait sous hypnose toutes ces hallucinations.

Dans l'ensemble son état s'améliora. Il devint possible de l'alimenter et elle laissait l'infirmière lui introduire la nourriture dans la bouche ; toutefois, après avoir réclamé du pain, elle le refusait dès qu'il était en contact avec ses lèvres. La contracture parésique de la jambe s'atténua notablement. Elle put porter un jugement exact sur le médecin qui venait la voir, mon ami le docteur B..., et s'attacha beaucoup à lui. Un terre neuve dont on lui fit présent et qu'elle aimait passionnément nous fut aussi d'un grand secours. Ce fut un spectacle magnifique que de voir, un jour où cet animal avait attaqué un chat, notre frêle jeune fille saisir un fouet et en fustiger l'énorme chien, pour lui faire lâcher sa proie. Plus tard, elle s'occupa de quelques malades indigents, ce qui lui fut très utile.

C'est en rentrant de voyage, après plusieurs semaines de vacances, que j'obtins la preuve la plus évidente de l'action pathogène, excitante, des complexes de représentations produits au cours de ses états d'absence, dans sa « condition seconde », la preuve aussi de leur liquidation par un récit fait sous hypnose. Pendant mon voyage, aucune *talking cure* n'avait été entreprise, puisqu'il était impossible d'amener la malade à parler devant qui que ce soit d'autre que moi, fût-ce même devant le docteur B... qu'elle aimait pourtant beaucoup. Je la retrouvai dans un triste état moral, paresseuse, indocile, d'humeur changeante, méchante même. Dans les récits du soir, je constatai que sa veine poético-imaginative était en train de s'épuiser ; elle donnait toujours plus de comptes rendus de ses hallucinations et de ce qui, les jours précédents, l'avait contrariée, tout cela enjolivé de fantasmes, mais plutôt traduit en formules stéréotypées qu'en poèmes.

LES DEUX ÉTATS DE CONSCIENCE SE SYSTÉMATISENT ET LA MALADE REVIT JOUR PAR JOUR L'HIVER PRÉCÉDENT

Un an s'était écoulé depuis que, séparée de son père, elle s'était alitée. A dater de cet anniversaire son état s'organisa et se systématisa de façon très particulière. Les deux états de la conscience alternaient de la manière suivante : à partir de la matinée et à mesure que la journée s'avançait, les absences (c'est-à-dire les états seconds) devenaient plus fréquentes et, le soir, seule la condition seconde demeurait. Les deux états ne différaient plus seulement par le fait que dans l'un, le premier, la patiente se montrait normale et dans l'autre, aliénée, mais surtout parce que, dans le premier état, elle se trouvait, comme nous tous en l'hiver de 1881-1882, tandis que, dans sa condition seconde, elle revivait l'hiver de 1880-1881 et tout ce qui était arrivé depuis était oublié. Malgré tout, elle semblait généralement se souvenir de la perte de son père. Toutefois la rétrogression vers l'année précédente était si marquée que, dans son nouvel appartement [16], elle se croyait encore dans son ancienne chambre et quand elle voulait aller vers la porte, elle se dirigeait vers la cheminée qui, par rapport à la fenêtre, se trouvait située comme l'était la porte dans l'ancienne demeure. Le passage d'un état dans l'autre s'effectuait spontanément, mais pouvait aussi, avec une facilité extrême, être provoqué par une quelconque impression sensorielle rappelant un fait de l'année précédente. Il suffisait de lui montrer une orange (son principal aliment pendant les premiers temps de sa maladie) pour la faire rétrograder de l'année 1882 en l'année 1881. Ce retour en arrière dans le temps ne s'effectuait pourtant pas n'importe comment, d'une façon indéterminée, et elle revivait jour après jour l'hiver précédent. Je n'aurais pu que soupçonner ce fait si, chaque soir, dans son hypnose, elle ne racontait ce qui l'avait émue le jour correspondant de 1881 et si, un carnet intime tenu par sa mère, en cette même année, ne venait confirmer l'exactitude indéniable des incidents racontés. Cette reviviscence de l'an précédent persista jusqu'à la fin définitive de la maladie, en juin 1882.

Il était également fort intéressant d'observer comment ces excitations psychiques ressuscitées passaient du second état au premier, plus normal. Parfois la malade me disait, le matin, en riant, qu'elle ne savait

16. A l'automne, la malade avait emménagé dans un autre appartement que celui dans lequel elle était tombée malade. (N.d.E.)

pas pourquoi elle m'en voulait ; grâce au journal intime, j'apprenais de quoi il s'agissait et ce qui se produirait le soir au cours de l'hypnose. En 1881, j'avais, à cette même date, violemment irrité ma malade. Ou bien elle disait que ses yeux étaient malades, qu'elle voyait faussement les couleurs : sa robe était marron, elle le savait mais la voyait bleue. On découvrit bientôt qu'elle distinguait exactement et parfaitement les couleurs d'un papier d'essai et que l'erreur ne s'appliquait qu'à l'étoffe de la robe. Le motif en était qu'en 1881, aux dates correspondantes, elle s'était beaucoup occupée d'une robe de chambre destinée à son père et faite dans le même tissu que sa robe à elle, mais bleu. En outre, on pouvait prévoir l'effet de ces souvenirs resurgis car la perturbation de l'état normal les précédait et ils ne s'éveillaient que progressivement dans la condition seconde.

LA MISE AU JOUR DES INCIDENTS TRAUMATIQUES PROVOQUE LA DISPARITION DES SYMPTÔMES

L'hypnose vespérale était très compliquée parce que la malade devait révéler non seulement les fantasmes récents, mais aussi les incidents et les « vexations » de 1881 (heureusement, j'avais déjà pu éliminer les fantasmes de 1881). Mais la tâche du médecin et de sa patiente se trouva encore énormément accrue par une troisième série de troubles particuliers qu'il fallut supprimer de la même manière : je veux parler des incidents psychiques survenus pendant la période d'incubation, de juillet à décembre 1880, incidents qui avaient créé l'ensemble des phénomènes hystériques et dont la mise au jour provoqua la disparition des symptômes.

Ma surprise fut très grande la première fois que je vis disparaître un trouble déjà ancien. Nous traversions cet été-là une période caniculaire et la patiente souffrait beaucoup de la chaleur ; tout à coup, sans qu'elle put en donner d'explication, il lui fut impossible de boire. Elle prit dans la main le verre d'eau dont elle avait envie, mais, dès qu'il toucha ses lèvres, elle le repoussa, à la manière d'une hydrophobique. Elle se trouvait évidemment, pendant ces quelques secondes, dans un état d'absence. Pour calmer sa soif ardente, elle ne prenait que des fruits, des melons, etc. Au bout de six semaines environ, elle se mit un beau jour à me parler, pendant l'hypnose, de sa dame de compagnie anglaise qu'elle n'aimait pas et raconta avec tous les signes du dégoût qu'étant entrée dans la chambre de cette personne, elle la vit faisant boire son petit chien, une sale bête, dans un verre. Par politesse, Anna n'avait rien dit. Après m'avoir énergiquement exprimé sa colère rentrée, elle demanda à boire, avala sans peine une grande quantité d'eau et sortit de son état hypnotique, le verre aux lèvres ; après quoi le symptôme ne se manifesta jamais plus. Certaines marottes étranges et tenaces disparurent de la même manière après le récit de l'incident qui les avait provoquées. Mais nous fîmes un grand pas en avant le jour où, de la même façon, un des symptômes chroniques, la contracture de la jambe droite qui, à vrai dire s'était déjà bien atténuée, fut supprimé. En observant que chez cette malade les symptômes disparaissaient dès que les incidents qui les avaient provoqués se trouvaient reproduits, nous en tirâmes une thérapeutique à laquelle il était impossible de rien reprocher au point de vue des conclusions logiques et de la réalisation systématique. Chacun des symptômes de ce tableau clinique compliqué fut isolément traité ; tous les incidents motivants se trouvèrent mis à jour dans l'ordre inverse de leur production, à partir des jours ayant précédé l'alitement de la malade et en remontant jusqu'à la cause de la première apparition des symptômes. Une fois cette cause révélée, les symptômes disparaissaient pour toujours.

C'est ainsi que furent éliminés, grâce à cette « narration dépuratoire », les contractures parésiques et les anesthésies, les troubles de la vision, de l'audition, les névralgies, la toux, les tremblements, etc., et finalement aussi les troubles de l'élocution. En ce qui concerne les troubles de la vue, par exemple, nous supprimâmes tour à tour le strabisme convergent avec diplopie, la déviation des deux yeux vers la droite obligeant la main à se porter trop à droite de l'objet qu'elle devait saisir, le rétrécissement du champ visuel, l'amblyopie centrale, la macropsie, la vision d'une tête de mort à là place du père et l'incapacité de lire. Seuls quelques phénomènes isolés survenus au cours de son séjour au lit échappèrent à cette analyse, telle par exemple l'extension au côté gauche de la contracture parésique qui ne devait d'ailleurs pas avoir vraiment une origine psychique directe.

Nous pûmes constater qu'il n'était nullement profitable de raccourcir, pour cette malade, la durée du traitement, en cherchant directement à provoquer le retour dans le psychisme de la malade de la première motivation du symptôme. Elle n'arrivait pas à la retrouver, était déconcertée, et tout allait plus lentement que lorsqu'on la laissait tranquillement et sûrement dévider l'écheveau de son souvenir en remontant vers le passé.

(Mais il arrivait à la patiente de ne pas réagir lorsqu'on l'interpellait : cette « surdité psychique » est relevée par Breuer à de nombreuses reprises. Le médecin met également au point pour sa malade, une méthode lui permettant de retrouver ses souvenirs — même les plus

insignifiants — dont on peut dire qu'elle constitue l'amorce de la technique des associations libres.) (N.d.E.)

PREMIÈRES HALLUCINATIONS
AU CHEVET DU PÈRE MALADE

Il arriva ici ce qui s'observait chaque fois qu'un symptôme se trouvait éliminé au moyen de la parole : son intensité s'accroissait pendant le récit. C'est ainsi que, pendant l'analyse de sa surdité, elle devenait si sourde que j'étais obligé de me faire, en partie, comprendre d'elle par écrit. Ce qui avait provoqué le symptôme considéré était toujours une frayeur ressentie pendant qu'elle soignait son père, un oubli de sa part, etc.

Le souvenir ne surgissait pas toujours rapidement et la malade était parfois obligée de faire de grands efforts. Une fois, même, le traitement se trouva quelque temps arrêté parce qu'un certain souvenir n'arrivait pas à resurgir : il s'agissait d'une hallucination qui terrifiait la malade : elle avait vu son père, qu'elle soignait, avec une tête de mort.

Nous avons eu maintes occasions de constater que la peur d'un souvenir — et c'est le cas ici — gêne sa survenue, et qu'en pareil cas, la patiente ou le médecin doivent à toute force en provoquer l'apparition.

Comme cette difficile analyse des symptômes était consacrée à l'été de 1880, au cours duquel s'était préparée la maladie, j'arrivai à connaître parfaitement l'incubation et la pathogenèse de cette hystérie. J'en donnerai ici un bref exposé.

En juillet 1880, un abcès subpleural rendit son père gravement malade. Anna et sa mère se partagèrent les soins à donner. La jeune fille se réveilla une nuit dans un état de grande angoisse et d'attente anxieuse : le malade était très fiévreux et l'on attendait de Vienne l'arrivée du chirurgien qui devait procéder à l'opération. La mère s'était éloignée pour quelques moments et Anna, assise auprès du lit, avait le bras droit appuyé sur le dossier de sa chaise. Elle tomba dans un état de rêverie et aperçut, comme sortant du mur, un serpent noir qui s'avançait vers le malade pour le mordre. Il est très vraisemblable que dans la prairie située derrière la maison se trouvaient réellement des reptiles qui avaient en d'autres occasions effrayé la jeune fille et qui maintenant formaient l'objet de l'hallucination. Elle voulut mettre en fuite l'animal, mais resta comme paralysée, le bras droit « endormi », insensible et devenu parésique, pendant sur le dossier de la chaise. En regardant ce bras, elle vit ses doigts se transformer en petits serpents à tête de mort (les ongles). Sans doute avait-elle tenté de chasser les serpents à l'aide de sa main droite engourdie, d'où l'insensibilité et la paralysie de celle-ci, ainsi associées à l'hallucination des serpents. Lorsque ceux-ci eurent disparu, dans sa terreur, elle voulut prier mais les mots lui manquèrent, elle ne put s'exprimer en aucune langue jusqu'au moment où elle trouva enfin un vers enfantin anglais, et qu'elle put, en cette langue, continuer à penser et à prier.

Le sifflet de la locomotive qui amenait le médecin attendu vint chasser ces fantômes. Quand, un autre jour, elle voulut enlever du buisson où il avait été lancé pendant un jeu, un certain anneau, une branche tordue ramena l'hallucination du serpent et de nouveau le bras droit se trouva raidi. Et le fait se renouvelait chaque fois qu'un objet pouvant plus ou moins rappeler un serpent provoquait l'hallucination. Mais celle-ci, comme la contracture, ne survenait que pendant de courts moments d'absence qui, depuis cette nuit-là, ne cessaient de gagner en fréquence (la contracture ne devint permanente qu'en décembre, lorsque la patiente, totalement épuisée, ne put plus quitter son lit). Lors d'un incident que j'omis de noter et dont je ne me souviens plus, une contracture de la jambe droite vint s'ajouter à celle du bras.

DES SYMPTÔMES HYSTÉRIQUES CONSÉCUTIFS À CERTAINES ÉMOTIONS

C'est ainsi que se trouva créée la tendance aux absences autohypnotiques. Au cours de la journée qui succéda à la nuit en question, son état d'absence pendant l'attente du chirurgien fut tel que lorsque, enfin, celui-ci pénétra dans la pièce, elle ne l'entendit pas entrer. Son sentiment d'angoisse l'empêchait de manger et aboutit à la longue à un dégoût intense. En dehors de cela, chacun des symptômes hystériques était apparu à l'occasion de quelques émotions. Nous ne savons pas très bien s'il y avait toujours, en pareil cas, absence momentanée totale, mais la chose paraît vraisemblable puisque, à l'état de veille, la malade n'en savait plus rien.

Néanmoins, certains symptômes provoqués par quelque émotion semblent être apparus, non pendant les états d'absence, mais bien à l'état de veille. C'est ainsi que les troubles de la vue purent être attribués à des motivations plus ou moins clairement déterminées. Donnons-en des exemples : la patiente, les larmes aux yeux, est assise auprès du lit de son père qui lui demande tout à coup l'heure qu'il est. Elle, voyant mal, fait des efforts, approche la montre de ses yeux, et alors, les chiffres du cadran lui paraissent énormes (macroscopie et strabisme convergent), ou bien elle s'efforce de refouler ses larmes afin que le malade ne s'en aperçoive pas.

Une querelle dans laquelle elle fut obligée de ne pas répondre provoqua un spasme de la glotte, lequel se répéta à chaque occasion analogue.

La parole lui manquait : *a)* par angoisse, depuis sa première hallucination nocturne ; *b)* depuis qu'elle avait étouffé, une fois de plus, une réflexion (inhibition active) ; *c)* depuis un jour où elle avait été injustement grondée ; *d)* dans toutes les circonstances analogues (offenses). La toux avait fait son apparition le jour où, veillant au chevet du malade, les sons d'une musique de danse venus d'une maison voisine, parvinrent à ses oreilles et qu'un désir d'être là-bas éveilla en elle des remords. Dès lors, pendant sa maladie, elle réagit à toute musique bien rythmée par une toux nerveuse.

Je ne regrette pas trop que le caractère incomplet de mes notes m'empêche de ramener tous les symptômes hystériques à leurs motivations. La patiente les avait retrouvées, à une exception près, comme nous l'avons dit, et chacun des symptômes disparaissait, une fois que la première cause déclenchante avait été racontée.

C'est de cette même façon que s'acheva toute l'hystérie. La malade elle-même était fermement décidée à ce que sa maladie fût liquidée le jour anniversaire de son transfert à la campagne. C'est dans cette intention qu'elle déploya, au début de juin, une grande énergie à pratiquer sa *talking cure*. Le dernier jour, après avoir arrangé sa chambre comme l'avait été celle de son père (ce qui contribua à la solution), elle me fit le récit de l'angoissante hallucination que nous avons rapportée, qui avait déterminé toute la maladie et à partir de laquelle elle n'avait plus été capable de penser ou de prier, qu'en anglais. Immédiatement après ce récit elle s'exprima en allemand et se trouva, dès lors, débarrassée des innombrables troubles qui l'avaient affectée auparavant. Elle partit ensuite en voyage mais un temps assez long s'écoula encore avant qu'elle pût trouver un équilibre psychique total. Depuis, elle jouit d'une parfaite santé.

UN CAS DÉCISIF POUR LE DESTIN ULTÉRIEUR DE LA PSYCHANALYSE

Dans sa conclusion Joseph Breuer relève deux caractéristiques dans le cas d'Anna O. :

— l'énergie psychique de cette jeune fille — très intelligente, mais « privée d'un travail intellectuel approprié » — trouvait à s'employer dans ses fantasmes ;

— la dissociation pathologique de la personnalité (la « double conscience ») avait été, selon l'auteur, favorisée par le goût de la

patiente pour la rêverie, qu'elle appelait son « théâtre privé ». Cette habitude qu'elle avait prise devait, à en croire l'auteur, avoir « préparé le terrain sur lequel s'établit... l'affect d'angoisse et d'attente anxieuse ».

De plus, tous les symptômes sont présents dès le début de la maladie : les absences passagères, qui se systématiseront pour donner la « double conscience » ; les troubles du langage ; la paraphasie et l'emploi de l'anglais à la place de la langue maternelle ; la paralysie par compression du bras droit, enfin, dont Breuer précise que « le mécanisme de formation correspond entièrement à la théorie de Charcot relative à l'hystérie traumatique : état hypnotique où se produit un léger traumatisme ».

Grâce à l'hypnose, note Breuer, et grâce à la faculté de la malade de raconter ensuite ce qu'elle s'était rappelé, le médecin — et sa malade — put retracer de bout en bout l'évolution des troubles. (N.d.E.)

Pendant toute la maladie, les deux états du conscient ont subsisté parallèlement : l'état primaire, celui où le psychisme de la malade se montrait tout à fait normal, et l'état « second » comparable au rêve à cause de sa richesse en fantasmes et en hallucinations, de ses grandes lacunes mnémoniques, de l'absence de frein et de contrôle dans les idées. Dans ce second état, la patiente était aliénée. L'intrusion de cet état anormal dans l'état normal, dont dépendait l'état physique de la malade, offre, à mon avis, une bonne occasion de connaître la nature d'au moins une forme de psychose hystérique. Chacune des hypnoses du soir apportait la preuve du fait que la malade restait parfaitement lucide, gardait sa clarté d'esprit, se montrait normale au point de vue sensibilité et volonté, tant qu'aucun produit de l'état second n'agissait, « dans l'inconscient », comme facteur incitant. La psychose qui éclatait chaque fois qu'il survenait un intervalle prolongé dans ce processus de décharge révélait justement le degré d'action de ces produits sur le psychisme « normal ». On se voit presque obligé de dire que la malade était partagée en deux personnes, l'une psychiquement normale, l'autre mentalement malade. Je pense que, chez notre patiente, la nette disjonction des deux états ne faisait qu'éclairer un comportement qui, chez bien d'autres hystériques, pose toujours un problème. Chez Anna, on s'étonnait de constater à quel point les productions de son « mauvais Moi », comme elle le qualifiait elle-même, pouvaient agir sur sa tenue morale. Si ces productions n'avaient pas été perpétuellement éliminées, nous aurions eu affaire à une hystérique du type malfaisant, récalcitrante, paresseuse, désagréable, méchante ; loin de là, après suppression des excitations, son véritable caractère, tout à fait contraire à celui que nous venons de décrire, reprenait le dessus.

Mais, bien que les deux états fussent nettement distincts, il ne s'agissait pas seulement d'une irruption du second état dans le premier, mais, comme le disait la patiente, d'un observateur pénétrant et tranquille, spectateur de toutes ces extravagances et qui restait, même pendant les plus mauvais moments, tapi dans un coin de son cerveau. Cette persistance d'une pensée claire pendant les manifestations psychotiques se traduisait d'une très curieuse façon : lorsque la patiente, une fois les phénomènes hystériques terminés, se trouvait dans un état passager de dépression, elle ne manifestait pas seulement certaines craintes enfantines, ne se contentait pas de s'adresser à elle-même des reproches, mais déclarait aussi n'être nullement malade. Tout cela, disait-elle, avait été simulé. C'est là, on le sait, un fait assez courant.

Après la maladie, lorsque les deux états de la conscience ont retrouvé leur unité, les patients, en jetant un regard en arrière, se considèrent chacun comme une personne non partagée, qui a toujours eu la notion de cette extravagance. Ils croient qu'ils auraient pu la faire cesser s'ils l'avaient voulu, ainsi, ce serait intentionnellement qu'ils auraient provoqué pareil désordre. — Cette persistance de la pensée normale pendant l'état second devrait d'ailleurs subir d'énormes variations quantitatives, voire disparaître en grande partie.

J'ai déjà décrit le fait surprenant de la suppression durable des excitations émanées du deuxième état et de leurs conséquences, toutes les fois qu'au cours de la maladie, la malade put en faire le récit. Il ne me reste rien à ajouter, mais j'affirme cependant que je n'ai nullement cherché à suggérer ma découverte à la patiente ; au contraire, ma stupéfaction a été immense et ce n'est qu'après toute une série de liquidations spontanées que je pus en tirer une technique thérapeutique.

Quelques mots encore à propos de la guérison définitive de l'hystérie. Elle survint, chez notre malade, de la façon que nous avons décrite, après une période d'agitation marquée et une aggravation de son état. On avait tout à fait l'impression de voir la masse des productions de l'état second, jusque-là assoupies, envahir le conscient et resurgir dans le souvenir, encore que ce fût d'abord dans la « condition seconde ». Reste à savoir si, dans d'autres cas encore, la psychose à laquelle aboutissent certaines hystéries chroniques n'aurait pas la même origine.

JOSEPH BREUER[17]

---

17. *Études sur l'hystérie*, p. 14 à 30, 33-35.

Eugénie. — dis donc t'y Paul, lequel des deux qu'est le monsieur?
Paul. — on peut pas savoir y sont pas habillés...

Une naïveté qui ressemble à un déni... (Musée Carnavalet).

LA QUESTION DE L'ORIGINE SEXUELLE
DES NÉVROSES DIVISE BREUER ET FREUD

La première divergence de vues entre Breuer et moi se manifesta à propos d'une question liée au mécanisme psychique intime de l'hystérie. Ses préférences allaient vers une théorie encore physiologique, pour ainsi dire, d'après laquelle la dissociation psychique de l'hystérique aurait pour cause l'absence de communication entre divers états psychiques (ou, comme nous disions alors, entre « divers états de la conscience ») ; il formula ainsi l'hypothèse des « états hypnoïdes », dont les produits feraient irruption dans la « conscience éveillée » où ils se comporteraient comme des corps étrangers. Moins rigoriste au point de vue scientifique, soupçonnant qu'il s'agit de tendances et de penchants analogues à ceux de la vie quotidienne, je voyais dans la dissociation psychique elle-même l'effet d'un processus d'élimination, auquel j'avais alors donné le nom de processus de « défense » ou de « refoulement ». J'avais bien essayé de laisser subsister ces deux mécanismes l'un à côté de l'autre, mais comme l'expérience me révélait toujours la même chose, je ne tardai pas à opposer ma théorie de la défense à celle des états hypnoïdes.

Je suis cependant certain que cette opposition n'était pour rien dans la séparation qui devait bientôt se produire entre nous. Celle-ci avait des raisons plus profondes, mais elle s'est produite d'une façon telle que je ne m'en étais pas rendu compte tout d'abord et ne l'ai comprise que plus tard d'après des indices certains. On se rappelle que Breuer disait de sa fameuse première malade que l'élément sexuel présentait chez elle un degré de développement étonnamment insuffisant et n'avait jamais contribué en quoi que ce soit à la richesse si remarquable de son tableau morbide. J'ai toujours trouvé étonnant que les critiques n'aient pas songé à opposer plus souvent qu'ils ne l'ont fait cette déclaration de Breuer à ma propre conception de l'étiologie sexuelle des névroses, et j'ignore encore aujourd'hui si cette omission leur a été dictée par la discrétion ou si elle s'explique par un manque d'attention. En relisant l'observation de Breuer à la lumière des expériences acquises au cours de ces vingt dernières années, on trouve que tout ce symbolisme représenté par les serpents, par les accès de rigidité, par la paralysie du bras est d'une transparence qui ne laisse rien à désirer et qu'en rattachant à la situation le lit dans lequel était étendu le père malade, on obtient une interprétation des symptômes telle qu'aucun doute ne peut subsister quant à leur signification. On arrive ainsi à se former sur le rôle de la sexualité dans la vie psychique de cette jeune fille une idée qui diffère totalement de celle de son médecin.

55

Breuer disposait, pour le rétablissement de sa malade, d'un « rapport » suggestif des plus intenses, d'un rapport dans lequel nous pouvons voir précisément le prototype de ce que nous appelons « transfert ». J'ai de fortes raisons de croire qu'après avoir fait disparaître tous les symptômes, Breuer a dû se trouver en présence de nouveaux indices témoignant en faveur de la motivation sexuelle de ce transfert, mais que le caractère général de ce phénomène inattendu lui ayant échappé, il arrêta là son exploration comme devant un *untoward event*[18]. Il ne m'a fait aucune communication directe à ce sujet, mais il m'a fourni, à de nombreuses reprises, des points de repère qui suffisent à justifier cette supposition. Et lorsque j'ai adopté d'une manière définitive la conception relative au rôle essentiel que la sexualité joue dans le déterminisme des névroses, c'est de sa part que je me suis heurté aux premières réactions de cette mauvaise humeur et de cette réprobation qui, dans la suite, me sont devenues si familières, alors qu'à l'époque dont il s'agit j'étais loin de prévoir quelles me poursuivraient toute ma vie comme une fatalité.

BREUER ET CHARCOT AVAIENT-ILS RECONNU AVANT FREUD L'ÉTIOLOGIE SEXUELLE DE LA NÉVROSE ?

Le fait que le transfert sexuel, grossièrement nuancé, tendre ou hostile, s'observe au cours du traitement de la névrose, quelle qu'elle soit, sans qu'il soit désiré ou provoqué par l'une ou l'autre des deux parties en présence, m'est toujours apparu comme la preuve irréfutable de l'origine sexuelle des forces impulsives de la névrose. Cet argument n'a encore jamais obtenu toute l'attention qu'il mérite et n'a jamais été envisagé avec tout le sérieux qui convient, car si tel avait été le cas, l'opinion sur ce sujet serait, à l'heure actuelle, unanime. Quant à moi, je l'ai toujours considéré comme décisif, aussi (et plus souvent) décisif que tant d'autres données fournies par l'analyse.

Ce qui fut de nature à me consoler du mauvais accueil qui, même dans le cercle étroit de mes amis, fut réservé à ma conception de l'étiologie sexuelle des névroses (il ne tarda pas à se former alors un vide autour de ma personne), ce fut la conviction que je combattais pour une idée neuve et originale. Mais un jour, certains souvenirs vinrent troubler ma satisfaction, tout en me révélant certains détails très intéressants, concernant la manière dont s'effectue notre activité créatrice

18. Un événement malencontreux. (N.d.E.)

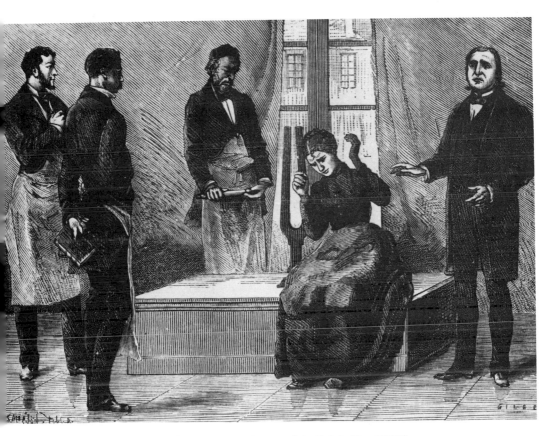

Charcot donnant une « leçon » à la Salpêtrière (1880)
(Bibliothèque de l'Académie Nationale de Médecine).

et relatifs à la nature de notre connaissance. L'idée dont j'avais assumé la responsabilité ne m'était nullement personnelle. Je la devais à trois personnes dont les opinions avaient droit à mon plus profond respect, à Breuer lui-même, à Charcot et au gynécologue de notre université, Chrobak, un de nos médecins viennois les plus éminents. Ces trois hommes m'avaient transmis une conception qu'à proprement parler ils ne possédaient pas. Deux d'entre eux contestaient cette transmission ; quant au troisième (le maître Charcot), il en aurait sans doute fait autant, s'il m'avait été donné de le revoir. Mais ces transmissions identiques que je m'étais assimilées sans les comprendre avaient sommeillé en moi pendant des années, pour se révéler un jour comme une conception originale, m'appartenant en propre.

Jeune médecin des hôpitaux, j'accompagnais un jour Breuer dans une promenade à travers la ville, lorsqu'il fut abordé par un monsieur

57

qui demanda instamment à lui parler. Je restai en arrière, et lorsque Breuer, la conversation terminée, vint me rejoindre, il m'apprit, dans sa manière amicalement instructive, que c'était le mari d'une malade qui venait de lui donner des nouvelles de celle-ci. La femme, ajouta-t-il, se comportait en société d'une manière tellement singulière qu'on avait jugé utile, la considérant comme nerveuse, de la confier à ses soins. Il s'agit toujours de *secrets d'alcôve*, fit-il en manière de conclusion. Étonné, je lui demandai ce qu'il voulait dire ; il m'expliqua alors de quoi il s'agissait au juste, en remplaçant le mot « alcôve » par les mots « lit conjugal », et en disant ne pas comprendre pourquoi la chose me paraissait si inouïe.

Y-a-t-il analogie entre ce que Freud nommait « névrose » et ce que les anciens appelaient « tempérament » ? (Les quatre Tempéraments, gravure du XVe siècle, Bibl. des Arts Décoratifs).

Quelques années plus tard, j'assistais à une réception de Charcot. Je me trouvais tout près du vénéré maître qui, justement, était en train de raconter à Brouardel un fait, sans doute très intéressant, de sa pratique. Je n'avais pas bien entendu le commencement, mais peu à peu le récit m'avait intéressé au point que j'étais devenu tout attention. Il s'agissait d'un jeune couple de lointains orientaux : la femme souffrait gravement, le mari était impuissant ou tout à fait maladroit. « Essayez donc, entendais-je Charcot répéter, je vous assure, vous y arriverez. » Brouardel, qui parlait moins haut, dut exprimer son étonnement que des symptômes comme ceux de la femme en question pussent se produire dans des circonstances pareilles. En effet, Charcot lui répliqua avec beaucoup de vivacité : « Mais, dans des cas pareils, c'est toujours la chose génitale, toujours... toujours... toujours. » Et ce disant il croisa les bras sur sa poitrine et se mit à sautiller avec sa vivacité habituelle. Je me rappelle être resté stupéfait pendant quelques instants et, revenu à moi, m'être posé la question : « Puisqu'il le sait, pourquoi ne le dit-il jamais ? »

SIGMUND FREUD[19]

---

19. « Contribution à l'histoire du mouvement psychanalytique », in *Cinq leçons sur la psychanalyse*, p. 74-78.

Je vois ce que c'est d'emblée : vous devez être névropathe.
Né...vropathe?... Mais non, mossieu ! Je suis née Pipelet !

Chapitre II

Le transfert :
premières approches

Si Breuer et Freud ont en commun rédigé la « Communication préliminaire » des Études sur l'hystérie, Freud a écrit seul le chapitre intitulé « Psychothérapie de l'hystérie ». Ses conceptions s'écartent, en des points fondamentaux, de celles de Breuer, et cette divergence théorique s'exprime avant tout par une divergence technique.

Freud a en effet observé que certains sujets résistent à l'hypnose, ce qui le conduit à abandonner la méthode cathartique pour lui substituer celle des associations libres[1]. Il découvre aussi, à partir de la résistance à l'hypnose, la résistance en général, c'est-à-dire le processus de défense s'opposant à la remémoration des représentations refoulées : aussi, du même coup, l'étiologie de la névrose est-elle centrée sur le conflit né d'une incompatibilité entre certains facteurs sexuels et le reste de la personnalité. Dès cet article, d'ailleurs, Freud tente de classifier les névroses, puisqu'il y précise : « Différents facteurs sexuels créaient différents facteurs cliniques de névroses. »

Nous verrons, dans un volume ultérieur consacré à la cure et dans lequel nous reproduirons d'autres extraits de ce travail, combien les vues que Freud exprime ici sur l'hystérie et les névroses en général se modifient pour se rapprocher de l'idée de névrose de défense. Il semble même que, s'il maintient la notion de traumatisme, c'est presque par fidélité à Breuer ; cette notion sera assez rapidement recouverte par celle de conflit.

Ce que nous souhaitons plutôt présenter au lecteur dans ce chapitre, ce sont les premières approches de la théorie du transfert. Dans cette étude, le transfert — les transferts, comme le dit alors Freud — est surtout considéré comme une gêne ou un obstacle. Le transfert est une fausse association, une mésalliance, un faux rapport, en quelque sorte

---

1. Cf. l'Identification : l'autre, c'est moi (chap. III, p. 62), dans la même collection.

◀ Cette caricature date des années 1880. Elle montre la vogue que connaissait alors la névrose et... son galvaudage.

une « erreur sur la personne ». Freud constate le fait et souligne que la confiance envers le médecin, qu'il appellera plus tard le transfert positif, est indispensable à la résolution du problème ; mais il ne discerne pas encore en quoi l'apparition, puis l'interprétation de ces « faux rapports » deviendront des outils indispensables au bon déroulement de la cure.

Nous reproduirons ensuite un fragment du cas de « Dora », publié en 1905, et dans lequel Freud revient sur la question du transfert, dont il parle encore au pluriel, comme dans les Études. *Cependant, il y montre que le transfert est un phénomène universel : « La cure, écrit-il, ne crée pas le transfert, elle ne fait que le démasquer. » L'existence d'un transfert négatif — celui des tendances hostiles — est décelée, bien que ni ce dernier, ni le transfert positif ne soient nommés comme tels. D'obstacle, le transfert est devenu le plus précieux auxiliaire de l'analyse, s'il est interprété au patient.*

Enfin, Freud note qu'il fut « surpris par le transfert » de Dora, la jeune fille reportant sur lui les affects qui s'attachaient à la personne de M. K., un ami de ses parents. Il impute au désir de vengeance de la jeune fille contre ce dernier — désir déplacé, transféré *sur le thérapeute — la rupture de la cure par la jeune fille. Il laisse entendre que lui-même n'a pas été en mesure de prévenir cette mise en action (cet acting out), qui s'est substituée à la remémoration et à l'élaboration psychiques, par une interprétation adéquate des émois transférentiels négatifs de sa patiente.*

En 1912, Freud rédige l'un de ses plus importants articles sur le sujet, intitulé « la Dynamique du transfert ». Bien que le mot n'y figure pas encore, c'est à la répétition que Freud fait en grande partie appel pour expliquer le phénomène. Chaque individu possède un cliché, un prototype de sa vie amoureuse, qui est amené à se reproduire dans la cure analytique, surtout lorsque le patient n'a pu, pour des raisons d'ordre essentiellement interne, pleinement développer ses émois libidinaux, qui sont dès lors, la plupart du temps, soit refoulés, soit vécus en fantasmes. Aussi bien le malade va-t-il se tourner avec espoir vers tout nouvel objet lui paraissant susceptible de satisfaire enfin, dans la réalité, son besoin d'amour. Le transfert est à la fois l'agent de la réussite de la cure et le facteur qui lui oppose la plus forte résistance.

C'est ce dernier point — la résistance de transfert — que Freud va tenter ici de cerner. On notera l'accent porté, dans cet article, sur le transfert négatif, dont il est injuste de dire, comme on le fait souvent, que son importance aurait été méconnue par Freud. Soulignons enfin que ces textes sont antérieurs à l'introduction de l'idée de névrose de transfert qu'il étudiera en 1914 dans son article « Remémorer, répéter,

*élaborer[2] ». La névrose de transfert est un produit de la cure elle-même,
à l'inverse du transfert qui s'exprime aussi bien hors de la cure. Elle
réédite la névrose du patient dans sa relation avec l'analyste, et de sa
résolution dépend celle de la névrose proprement dite. L'interprétation
de la névrose de transfert conduit à une totale appréhension de la
névrose infantile, masquée par l'évolution ultérieure.*

Dans notre « Communication préliminaire » nous déclarions avoir
découvert, en étudiant l'étiologie des symptômes hystériques, une
méthode thérapeutique ayant, à notre avis, une grande valeur pratique.
Nous fûmes d'abord extrêmement surpris *de constater que les divers
symptômes hystériques disparaissaient sans retour dès que nous réus-
sissions à évoquer et à mettre en pleine lumière le souvenir des incidents qui les avaient provoqués et en même temps l'affect concomitant.
Il fallait aussi que le malade décrivît, avec le plus de détails possible,
cet incident et qu'il donnât à l'affect une expression verbale.*
Nous cherchâmes ensuite à expliquer la façon dont agissait notre
procédé psychothérapique. *Il supprime l'action de la représentation
primitive non abréagie en permettant la liquidation, par expression
verbale, de l'affect concomitant. En ramenant la représentation dans le
conscient normal (par le moyen d'une hypnose légère), nous lui faisons
subir une correction associative ou encore nous la supprimons par suggestion médicale, de la même façon que pour l'amnésie, dans le somnambulisme.*

Bien que l'essentiel ait été dit sur ce sujet dans les cas déjà exposés,
il ne m'est pas possible d'éviter ici certaines répétitions et j'essaierai
maintenant de démontrer jusqu'où peut nous amener notre méthode,
quels sont ses avantages sur d'autres procédés, quelle technique elle
utilise et à quelles difficultés elle se heurte.

DES FACTEURS SEXUELS
À L'ORIGINE DES NÉVROSES

En ce qui me concerne, j'ai le droit de dire que je puis toujours soutenir les points de vue exposés dans la « Communication préliminaire ». Je reconnais toutefois que, n'ayant jamais cessé, au cours des
années écoulées depuis lors, de me préoccuper des questions qui y
furent abordées, de nouvelles opinions se sont imposées à mon esprit.

---

2. Nous aurons l'occasion de revenir sur cette notion dans *la Cure psychanalytique : sur le divan*, à
paraître dans la même collection.

J'ai été tout au moins amené à regrouper et à envisager différemment une partie des matériaux déjà connus. Il serait injuste d'attribuer à mon vénéré ami Joseph Breuer une trop lourde part de responsabilité dans cette évolution. C'est donc surtout en mon propre nom que je vais ajouter les considérations qui suivent.

Lorsque je tentai d'appliquer à un grand nombre d'hystériques hypnotisés la méthode thérapeutique de Breuer par détection et abréaction, je me heurtai à deux difficultés qui m'amenèrent, pour les résoudre, à modifier aussi bien ma technique que mes conceptions : 1° les sujets incontestablement hystériques et fort probablement soumis aux mêmes mécanismes ne sont pas tous hypnotisables ; 2° il m'a fallu déterminer ce qui caractérisait essentiellement l'hystérie et ce qui la différenciait des autres névroses.

Je décrirai plus tard la façon dont j'ai pu surmonter la première de ces difficultés et ce que celle-ci m'a appris. Commençons d'abord par exposer quelle attitude j'ai adoptée, dans la pratique quotidienne, à l'égard du second problème. Il est fort malaisé de se faire une opinion exacte d'un cas de névrose avant d'avoir soumis celui-ci à une analyse approfondie, qui ne peut être différente de celle utilisée par Breuer. Pourtant c'est avant même de connaître en détail le cas que l'on se voit obligé d'établir un diagnostic et de déterminer le traitement. Que faire alors sinon utiliser le procédé cathartique dans les cas probablement hystériques et présentant un ou plusieurs stigmates ? Parfois alors les résultats thérapeutiques, en dépit du diagnostic d'hystérie, restaient bien médiocres et l'analyse elle-même ne mettait rien d'important en lumière. D'autres fois, j'essayais de traiter par la méthode de Breuer des névrosés que nul certainement n'aurait tenus pour hystériques et sur lesquels néanmoins le procédé agissait et parfois même supprimait les symptômes. C'est ce qui m'arriva, par exemple, dans des cas d'idées obsédantes véritables, qui ne rappelaient l'hystérie par aucun trait. Ainsi le mécanisme révélé dans la « Communication préliminaire » ne pouvait être regardé comme un signe pathognomonique de l'hystérie ; cependant, il ne m'était pas possible, pour l'amour de ce mécanisme, de mettre tant d'autres névroses dans le même panier que l'hystérie. Un plan finit par surgir de tous mes doutes : je décidai de traiter, de la même façon que l'hystérie, toutes les autres névroses, de rechercher partout l'étiologie et le genre du mécanisme psychique. Ce furent les résultats de cette recherche qui déterminèrent et justifièrent finalement pour moi le diagnostic de l'hystérie.

En partant ainsi de la méthode de Breuer, j'arrivai à étudier d'une façon générale l'étiologie et le mécanisme des névroses. J'eus ensuite la chance d'aboutir, en un laps de temps relativement court, à des résultats appréciables. Je fus forcé de reconnaître que puisque l'on pouvait parler de *cause* dans l'acquisition d'une névrose, l'étiologie devait tenir à des facteurs *sexuels*. Je trouvai encore que, dans l'ensemble, différents facteurs sexuels créaient aussi différents tableaux cliniques de névroses. Dans la mesure où ce dernier fait se confirmerait, on pourrait donc essayer d'utiliser l'étiologie pour caractériser les névroses et établir, en ce qui les concerne, une stricte délimitation des tableaux cliniques. Au cas où les caractères étiologiques coïncideraient, de façon constante, avec certains caractères cliniques, cette manière de voir se trouverait justifiée.

UNE IMAGE SIMPLE
DE CERTAINES MALADIES

Je pus ainsi constater que la *neurasthénie* correspondait vraiment à un tableau clinique uniforme dans lequel, comme les analyses le montrent, aucun « mécanisme psychique » ne participe. La *névrose obsessionnelle* se distingue nettement de la neurasthénie. Dans ces névroses à idées obsessionnelles véritables on observe un mécanisme psychique compliqué, une étiologie semblable à celle de l'hystérie et une large possibilité de guérison par la psychothérapie. D'autre part, je constatai qu'il convenait sans hésiter de séparer de la neurasthénie un complexe de symptômes névrotiques à étiologie tout à fait différente et même au fond inverse, tandis que les éléments de ce complexe sont reliés par un de leurs caractères déjà reconnu par E. Hecker[3]. Il s'agit, en effet, soit de symptômes, soit d'équivalents ou de rudiments de manifestations d'angoisse. C'est pourquoi j'ai donné à ce complexe, distinct de la neurasthénie, le nom de *névrose d'angoisse*. J'ai dit de lui qu'il provenait d'une accumulation de tensions physiques, elles-mêmes d'origine sexuelle. Cette névrose, sans encore comporter de mécanisme psychique, agit toujours sur le psychisme, de telle sorte que l'attente anxieuse, les phobies, l'hyperesthésie à l'égard des douleurs, etc., font partie de ses manifestations habituelles. Cette névrose d'angoisse, telle que je la conçois, peut, en partie, se confondre avec la névrose décrite dans certains exposés à côté de l'hystérie et de la neurasthénie et dénommée « hypocondrie ». Toutefois, je ne considère aucune des descriptions faites jusqu'à ce jour comme exactes et je trouve qu'en n'attribuant au mot hypocondrie que le sens d'une « peur des maladies » on en limite fort la portée.

Après m'être ainsi formé de la neurasthénie, de la névrose

3. E. Hecker, *Zentralblatt für Nervenheilkunde*, décembre 1893.

d'angoisse, et des idées obsessionnelles, une image simple, je m'appliquai à comprendre ces cas banals de névrose que l'on considère comme des hystéries. Je me dis qu'il ne convenait pas de marquer une névrose du sceau de l'hystérie simplement parce que quelques traits de cette maladie résultaient du complexe des symptômes. Je m'expliquais fort bien cette habitude étant donné que l'hystérie est, de toutes les névroses connues, la plus ancienne, la mieux connue et la plus voyante. Mais c'était employer abusivement le mot hystérie que de porter au compte de cette maladie tant de traits de perversion et de dégénérescence. Dès que, dans un cas difficile d'anomalie psychique, l'on venait à découvrir quelque indice d'hystérie, une anesthésie, un accès caractéristique, la maladie dans son ensemble était considérée comme une « hystérie » et les cas les plus graves et les plus contradictoires se trouvaient réunis sous cette même étiquette. Ce diagnostic était de toute évidence inexact.

Je me propose d'examiner si les cas que j'ai décrits corroborent ma façon de concevoir l'autonomie clinique de l'hystérie. Anna O., la malade de Breuer, semble réfuter mon opinion et être affectée d'un trouble purement hystérique. Mais ce cas, si riche en renseignements pour la connaissance de l'hystérie, ne fut nullement considéré par son observateur sous l'angle de la névrose sexuelle et ne saurait, aujourd'hui, nous servir de démonstration. En commençant l'analyse de la deuxième malade, Mme Emmy v. N.[4], j'étais assez loin de donner comme support à l'hystérie une névrose sexuelle. A peine sorti de l'école de Charcot, je rougissais de la connexion entre l'hystérie et le thème de la sexualité, à peu près comme les patientes elles-mêmes le font en général. Quand je relis aujourd'hui les notes relatives à ce cas, j'y reconnais une névrose d'angoisse grave, avec attente anxieuse et phobies, névrose provenant d'une continence sexuelle et qui s'était combinée à une hystérie.

(Puis Freud décrit rapidement les différents cas figurant dans les Études, *afin de tenter d'isoler l'hystérie.)*

LA MÉTHODE CATHARTIQUE EXIGE LE CONCOURS DU PATIENT COMME L'INTÉRÊT DU MÉDECIN

Je vais maintenant aborder la question des difficultés et des inconvénients de notre thérapeutique pour le cas où les histoires de malades qui précèdent et les remarques sur la technique du procédé n'auraient

---

4. Non reproduite ici. Voir *Études sur l'hystérie*, P.U.F. (N.d.E.)

pas éclairé tout le monde. Je compte énumérer et esquisser plutôt que développer. Le procédé en question est fatiguant pour le médecin, lui prend un temps considérable et présuppose chez lui un grand intérêt pour les faits psychologiques et beaucoup de sympathie personnelle pour les malades qu'il traite. Je ne saurais m'imaginer étudiant, dans le détail, le mécanisme psychique d'une hystérie chez un sujet qui me semblerait méprisable et répugnant et qui, une fois mieux connu, s'avérerait incapable d'inspirer quelque sympathie humaine. Je pourrais, au contraire, soigner n'importe quel tabétique, n'importe quel rhumatisant, sans me soucier de sa personnalité. Quant aux malades, ce qu'on leur demande n'est pas peu non plus. Le procédé exige des sujets un certain degré d'intelligence au-dessous duquel il reste tout à fait inutilisable. Toute dose de débilité mentale en rend l'emploi extrêmement difficile. L'adhésion totale des patients, leur entière attention, mais surtout leur confiance sont indispensables, puisque l'analyse nous entraîne toujours vers les faits les plus secrets, les plus intimes. Bien des malades, parmi ceux auxquels le traitement se prêterait le mieux, échappent au médecin dès qu'ils ont le moindre soupçon de la voie où va les entraîner cette investigation. Pour ceux-là le médecin est demeuré un étranger. D'autres se décident à se livrer au médecin, à lui témoigner une confiance que l'on n'accorde généralement que par choix libre et sans qu'elle soit jamais exigible. Pour ces patients-là, il est presque inévitable que les rapports personnels avec leur médecin prennent, tout au moins pendant un certain temps, une importance capitale. Il semble même que cette influence exercée par le médecin soit la condition même de la solution du problème.

UNE « DIFFICULTÉ » DE LA CURE ANALYTIQUE : LES « FAUX RAPPORTS » OU TRANSFERTS

Il me reste enfin à traiter un sujet auquel incombe, dans la réalisation de cette analyse cathartique, un rôle important et gênant. Il peut parfois arriver que le procédé par pression[5] échoue et que, malgré toutes les assurances, toutes les insistances, aucune réminiscence ne surgisse. J'ajoutais que deux cas peuvent se présenter : 1) il n'y a vraiment rien à tirer de l'endroit où se fait l'investigation, ce que révèle d'ailleurs l'air parfaitement calme du malade, ou bien 2) le praticien se heurte à une résistance qu'il ne pourra vaincre qu'ultérieurement et se

---

5. Freud employait alors ce qu'il appelle l'« insistance » : il assurait au malade qu'il allait se rappeler la circonstance ayant déclenché le symptôme. Lorsque se rompait le fil des associations, il exerçait sur le front du patient une pression en lui affirmant que, tout le temps qu'elle durerait, un souvenir ou une image surgirait. (N.d.E.)

trouve devant une nouvelle assise dans laquelle il ne peut encore pénétrer. C'est à nouveau la physionomie contractée du patient, qui trahit une tension psychique. Mais un troisième cas peut aussi se présenter, un cas révélant également quelque obstacle, non intérieur mais extérieur cette fois. C'est ce qui se produit quand les relations du malade avec son médecin sont troublées et alors ce dernier se trouve devant le plus grand des obstacles à vaincre. Dans toute analyse importante, on peut cependant s'attendre à le rencontrer.

J'ai déjà fait allusion au rôle considérable que joue la personne du médecin dans la création des motifs servant à surmonter la puissance psychique des résistances. Dans bien des cas et principalement chez les femmes, et lorsqu'il s'agit d'expliquer des associations de pensées érotiques, la collaboration des patients devient un sacrifice personnel qu'il faut compenser par quelque succédané d'amour. Les efforts du médecin, son attitude de bienveillante patience doivent constituer des suffisants succédanés.

Dans les cas où les relations entre médecin et malade viennent à être troublées, la docilité de ce dernier cesse et lorsque le praticien tente de se renseigner sur l'idée pathogène qui va surgir, la prise de conscience par les patients des griefs qu'ils ont accumulés contre leur médecin s'oppose à leurs révélations. Pour autant que je sache, cette difficulté se présente surtout dans trois cas :

1° A cause d'un grief personnel, quand le malade se croit négligé, humilié ou offensé ou encore quand il a pris connaissance de propos défavorables sur son médecin ou sur la méthode de traitement. C'est le cas le moins grave ; il est facile de surmonter l'obstacle en le commentant et l'expliquant, encore que la susceptibilité et l'esprit soupçonneux des hystériques puissent, à l'occasion, se manifester dans des proportions inattendues ;

2° Quand la malade est saisie d'une crainte de trop s'attacher à son médecin, de perdre à l'égard de celui-ci son indépendance et même d'être sexuellement asservie à lui. Ce cas est plus grave parce que moins individuellement conditionné. La raison de cet obstacle tient à la nature même du traitement. La malade y trouve de nouveaux motifs de résistance et celle-ci se produit non seulement à l'occasion d'une certaine réminiscence, mais lors de chacune des tentatives thérapeutiques. Très fréquemment quand on utilise le procédé par pression, la malade se plaint de maux de tête. La plupart du temps, elle reste ignorante de la cause nouvelle de sa résistance et ne la révèle que par un symptôme hystérique nouveau. Le mal de tête traduit l'aversion de la malade à l'égard de toute influence qui s'exercerait sur elle ;

3° Quand la malade craint de reporter sur la personne du médecin les représentations pénibles nées du contenu de l'analyse. C'est là un fait constant dans certaines analyses. Le transfert au médecin se réalise par une *fausse association*. J'en donnerai ici un exemple. Chez l'une de mes patientes, un certain symptôme hystérique tirait son origine du désir éprouvé longtemps auparavant, mais aussitôt rejeté dans l'inconscient, de voir l'homme avec qui elle avait alors conversé, la serrer affectueusement dans ses bras et lui soustraire un baiser. Or il advient, à la fin d'une séance, qu'un désir semblable surgit chez la malade par rapport à ma personne ; elle en est épouvantée, passe une nuit blanche et, à la séance suivante où, cependant, elle ne refuse pas de se laisser traiter, le procédé reste entièrement inopérant. Après avoir appris de quelle difficulté il s'agissait et être parvenu à la surmonter, je puis reprendre le travail et voilà que le désir qui a tant effrayé la malade s'avère le plus proche des souvenirs pathogènes, celui même que faisait nécessairement prévoir l'enchaînement logique des faits. Les choses s'étaient déroulées de la façon suivante : le contenu du désir avait surgi dans le conscient de la malade, mais sans être accompagné du souvenir des circonstances accessoires capables de situer ce désir dans le passé. Le désir actuel se trouva rattaché, par une impulsion associative, à ma personne évidemment passée au premier plan des préoccupations de la malade. Dans cette *mésalliance*[6] — à laquelle je donne le nom de faux rapport — l'affect qui entre en jeu est identique à celui qui avait jadis incité ma patiente à repousser un désir interdit. Depuis que je sais cela, je puis, chaque fois que ma personne se trouve ainsi impliquée, postuler l'existence d'un transfert et d'un faux rapport.

SIGMUND FREUD[7]

LES TRANSFERTS SUR LE MÉDECIN : DES « ÉDITIONS REVUES ET CORRIGÉES » D'ANCIENS RAPPORTS

On peut dire que généralement la production de nouveaux symptômes cesse pendant la cure psychanalytique. Mais la productivité de la névrose n'est nullement éteinte, elle s'exerce en créant des états psychiques particuliers, pour la plupart inconscients, auxquels on peut donner le nom de *transferts*.

6. En français dans le texte.
7. *Études sur l'hystérie* (« Psychothérapie de l'hystérie »). p. 205-209. 213-214, 244-246.

Que sont ces *transferts* ? Ce sont de nouvelles éditions, des copies des tendances et des fantasmes qui doivent être éveillés et rendus conscients par les progrès de l'analyse, et dont le trait caractéristique est de remplacer une personne antérieurement connue par la personne du médecin. Autrement dit, un nombre considérable d'états psychiques antérieurs revivent, non pas comme états passés, mais comme rapports actuels avec la personne du médecin. Il y a des transferts qui ne diffèrent en rien de leur modèle quant à leur contenu, à l'exception de la personne remplacée. Ce sont donc, en se servant de la même métaphore, de simples rééditions stéréotypées, des réimpressions. D'autres transferts sont faits avec plus d'art, ils ont subi une atténuation de leur contenu, une *sublimation*, comme je dis, et sont même capables de devenir conscients en s'étayant sur une particularité réelle, habilement utilisée, de la personne du médecin ou des circonstances qui l'entourent. Ce sont alors des éditions revues et corrigées, et non plus des réimpressions.

Si l'on considère la théorie de la technique psychanalytique, on se rend compte que le transfert en découle nécessairement. Pratiquement du moins, on se rend à l'évidence qu'on ne peut éviter le transfert par aucun moyen et qu'il faut combattre cette nouvelle création de la maladie comme toutes les précédentes. Mais cette partie du travail est la plus difficile. L'interprétation des rêves, l'extraction d'idées et de souvenirs inconscients des associations du malade ainsi que les autres procédés de traduction sont faciles à apprendre ; c'est le malade lui-même qui en donne toujours le texte. Mais le transfert, par contre, doit être deviné sans le concours du malade, d'après de légers signes et sans pécher par arbitraire. Cependant, le transfert ne peut être évité, car il est utilisé à la formation de tous les obstacles qui rendent inaccessible le matériel, et parce que la sensation de conviction relative à la justesse des contextes reconstruits ne se produit chez le malade qu'une fois le transfert résolu.

On sera porté à considérer comme un grave inconvénient du procédé analytique, déjà incommode sans cela, le fait qu'il accroît le travail du médecin en créant une nouvelle sorte de phénomènes psychiques pathologiques. On sera peut-être même tenté d'en déduire que, par l'existence du transfert, la cure psychanalytique peut porter préjudice au malade. Ces deux considérations sont erronées. Le travail du médecin n'est pas accru par le transfert ; il peut, en effet, lui être indifférent, étant donné qu'il doit vaincre une certaine tendance du malade, que cette tendance se manifeste par rapport à lui, médecin ou par rapport à quelque autre personne. Et la cure n'impose pas non plus au malade, du fait du transfert, des efforts qu'il n'aurait pas eu à fournir.

Si des névroses guérissent aussi dans des maisons de santé où aucune méthode psychanalytique n'est employée, si l'on a pu dire que l'hystérie est guérie non par la méthode, mais par le médecin, si une sorte de dépendance aveugle et d'attachement perpétuel se manifeste d'ordinaire du malade au médecin qui l'a délivré de ses symptômes par la suggestion hypnotique, l'explication scientifique en réside dans les

Dora, héroïne d'une pièce de théâtre d'Hélène Cixous, mise en scène par Simone Benmussa (Théâtre d'Orsay, 1976).

transferts que le malade effectue régulièrement sur la personne du médecin. La cure psychanalytique ne crée pas le transfert, elle ne fait que le démasquer comme les autres phénomènes psychiques cachés. Ce qui différencie les autres cures de la psychanalyse ne se manifeste qu'en ceci : le malade, au cours des traitements, ne fait spontanément appel qu'à des transferts affectueux et amicaux en faveur de sa guérison ; là où c'est impossible, il se détache aussi vite que possible du médecin qui ne lui est pas « sympathique » et sans s'être laissé influencer par lui. Dans le traitement psychanalytique, par contre, et ceci en rapport avec une autre motivation, toutes les tendances, même les tendances hostiles, doivent être réveillées, utilisées pour l'analyse en étant rendues conscientes ; ainsi se détruit sans cesse à nouveau le transfert. Le transfert, destiné à être le plus grand obstacle à la psychanalyse, devient son plus puissant auxiliaire, si l'on réussit à le deviner chaque fois et à en traduire le sens au malade[8].

MAÎTRISER LE TRANSFERT : UNE NÉCESSITÉ POUR LE PSYCHANALYSTE

Il me fallait parler du transfert, car par ce facteur seulement peuvent s'expliquer les particularités de l'analyse de Dora. Ce qui en constitue la qualité et la rend propre à une première publication d'introduction à la psychanalyse, sa clarté particulière, est en rapport intime avec son grand défaut, qui fut la cause d'une interruption prématurée. Je ne réussis pas à me rendre à temps maître du transfert ; l'empressement avec lequel Dora mit à ma disposition une partie du matériel pathogène me fit oublier de prêter attention aux premiers signes du transfert qu'elle préparait au moyen d'une autre partie de ce même matériel, partie qui me restait inconnue. Au début, il apparaissait clairement que je remplaçais, dans son imagination, son père, ce qui se conçoit aisément, vu la différence d'âge entre elle et moi. Aussi me comparait-elle consciemment à lui, tâchait de s'assurer de façon inquiète si j'étais tout à fait sincère avec elle, car son père, disait-elle, « préférait toujours la cachotterie et les moyens détournés ». Lorsque survint le premier rêve,

8. (Note de 1923). L'on trouvera la suite de ce qui est dit ici à propos du transfert dans un article technique sur *Die Ubertragungsliebe* (« l'Amour de transfert »), 1915 (dans le volume x des *Ges. Werke*). Les « Remarques sur l'amour de transfert » ont d'abord paru dans l'*Internationale Zeitschrift für ärztliche Psychoanalyse,* vol. III (1915), puis dans la 4ᵉ série du *Recueil de petits essais sur les névroses,* ou ils sont réunis à deux travaux antérieurs : *Weitere Ratschläge zur Technik der Psychoanalyse* (« Nouveaux conseils sur la technique de la psychanalyse »), in *la Technique psychanalytique,* trad. Anne Berman, Presses universitaires de France, 1953. (N.d.T.)

dans lequel elle me prévenait qu'elle voulait abandonner le traitement comme, autrefois, la maison de M. K., j'aurais dû me mettre sur mes gardes et lui dire : « Vous venez de faire un transfert de M. K. sur moi. Avez-vous remarqué quoi que ce soit vous faisant penser de ma part à de mauvaises intentions analogues à celles de M. K., de façon directe ou de façon sublimée, ou bien avez-vous été frappée par quelque chose en moi, ou encore avez-vous entendu dire de moi des choses qui forcent votre inclination comme jadis pour M. K. ? » Son attention se serait alors portée sur quelque détail de nos relations, de ma personne ou de ma situation, qui eût masqué une chose analogue, mais bien plus importante, concernant M. K., et par la solution de ce transfert, l'analyse aurait trouvé accès à du matériel nouveau, sans doute constitué de souvenirs réels. Mais je négligeai ce premier avertissement, je me dis que j'avais encore largement le temps, puisqu'il ne se présentait pas d'autres signes de transfert et que le matériel de l'analyse n'était pas encore épuisé. Ainsi je fus surpris par le transfert et c'est à cause de ce facteur inconnu par lequel je lui rappelais M. K., qu'elle se vengea de moi, comme elle voulait se venger de lui ; et elle m'abandonna comme elle se croyait trompée et abandonnée par lui. Ainsi, elle *mit en action* une importante partie de ses souvenirs et de ses fantasmes, au lieu de la reproduire dans la cure.

SIGMUND FREUD[9]

LA FRUSTRATION LIBIDINALE REND LES NÉVROSÉS PLUS APTES AU TRANSFERT

N'oublions pas que tout individu, de par l'action concomitante d'une prédisposition naturelle et des faits survenus pendant son enfance, possède une manière d'être personnelle, déterminée, de vivre sa vie amoureuse, c'est-à-dire que sa façon d'aimer est soumise à certaines conditions, qu'il y satisfait certaines pulsions et qu'il se pose certains buts. On obtient ainsi une sorte de *cliché* (quelquefois plusieurs), cliché qui, au cours de l'existence, se répète plusieurs fois, se reproduit quand les circonstances extérieures et la nature des objets aimés accessibles le permettent et peuvent, dans une certaine mesure, être modifiés

9. *Cinq psychanalyses* (« Dora »), p. 86-89.

par des impressions ultérieures. L'expérience montre que, parmi les émois qui déterminent la vie amoureuse, une partie seulement parvient à son plein développement psychique ; cette partie, tournée vers la réalité, forme un des éléments de la personnalité consciente qui en peut disposer. Une autre partie de ces émois libidinaux a subi un arrêt de développement, se trouve maintenue éloignée de la personnalité consciente comme de la réalité et peut soit ne s'épanouir qu'en fantasmes, soit rester tout à fait enfouie dans l'inconscient, et dans ce dernier cas, être entièrement ignorée du conscient. Tout individu auquel la réalité n'apporte pas la satisfaction entière de son besoin d'amour se tourne inévitablement, avec un certain espoir libidinal, vers tout nouveau personnage qui entre dans sa vie et il est dès lors plus que probable que les deux parts de sa libido, celle qui est capable d'accéder au conscient et celle qui demeure inconsciente, vont jouer leur rôle dans cette attitude.

Il est ainsi tout à fait normal et compréhensible de voir l'investissement libidinal en état d'attente et tout prêt, comme il l'est chez ceux qui ne sont qu'imparfaitement satisfaits, à se porter sur la personne du médecin. Ainsi que nous le prévoyons, cet investissement va s'attacher à des prototypes, conformément à l'un des clichés déjà présents chez le sujet en question. Ou encore le patient intègre le médecin dans l'une des « séries psychiques » qu'il a déjà établies dans son psychisme. Tout concorde avec les relations réelles entre le patient et son médecin quand, suivant l'heureuse expression de Jung[10], c'est l'*imago* paternelle qui donne la mesure de cette intégration. Mais le transfert n'est pas lié à ce prototype et peut se réaliser aussi suivant les images maternelles, fraternelles, etc. Ce qui donne au transfert son aspect particulier, c'est le fait qu'il dépasse la mesure et s'écarte, de par son caractère même et son intensité, de ce qui serait normal, rationnel. Toutefois ces particularités deviennent compréhensibles si l'on songe qu'en pareil cas le transfert est dû non seulement aux idées et aux espoirs conscients du patient, mais aussi à tout ce qui a été réprimé et est devenu inconscient.

Il n'y aurait pas lieu d'épiloguer et de spéculer davantage sur les caractères du transfert si deux points n'y demeuraient obscurs, deux points particulièrement intéressants aux yeux de l'analyste. Il faut se demander d'abord pourquoi les névrosés développent, au cours de leur analyse, un transfert bien plus intense que d'autres sujets non analysés. En second lieu, nous en sommes encore à nous demander pourquoi, dans l'analyse, c'est le transfert qui oppose au traitement *la plus forte*

---

10. « Symbole und Wandlungen der Libido », *Jahrbuch für Psychoanalyse*, III.

des résistances, alors qu'ailleurs il doit être considéré comme l'agent même de l'action curative et de la réussite. Il nous arrive bien souvent de constater le fait suivant : quand les associations viennent à manquer[11], cet obstacle peut chaque fois être levé en assurant au patient qu'il se trouve actuellement sous l'empire d'une idée se rapportant à la personne du médecin ou à quelque chose qui concerne ce dernier. Une fois cette explication donnée, l'obstacle est surmonté ou, tout au moins, l'absence d'associations s'est transformée en un refus de parler.

LE TRANSFERT : AGENT
DE LA RÉUSSITE DE LA CURE...

Le fait que le plus efficace des facteurs de la réussite, le transfert, puisse devenir le plus puissant agent de la résistance semble, au premier abord, constituer un immense inconvénient méthodologique de la psychanalyse. Toutefois, en y regardant de plus près, on résout, tout au moins, le premier de ces deux problèmes. Il est faux que le transfert soit, dans une analyse, plus intense, plus excessif, qu'en dehors d'elle. Dans les établissements où les nerveux ne sont pas traités par les méthodes psychanalytiques, on observe des transferts revêtant les formes les plus étranges et les plus exaltées, allant parfois jusqu'à la sujétion la plus complète et ayant aussi un incontestable caractère érotique. Une subtile observatrice, Gabriele Reuter, a pu montrer, à une époque où l'analyse venait à peine de naître et dans un livre remarquable[12] plein de vues judicieuses sur la nature et la formation des névroses, que ces particularités du transfert ne sont pas imputables à la psychanalyse, mais bien à la névrose elle-même. En ce qui concerne le second problème, il n'a pas été résolu jusqu'à ce jour.

... MAIS AUSSI FACTEUR
DE RÉSISTANCE À LA CURE

Il est nécessaire d'étudier cette question de plus près et de voir pour quelle raison le transfert devient, dans l'analyse, une résistance. Considérons comment se présente, au cours d'une analyse, la situation

---

11. Je veux parler des associations qui ne se présentent réellement pas et non de celles que l'analysé tait par suite d'un simple sentiment de déplaisir.

12. *Aus guter Familie*, 1895.

Le sentiment d'insuffisance peut être l'un des motifs conduisant
le malade à consulter un psychanalyste.
(« Démons me ridiculisant », par James Ensor.
Musée des Arts, Philadelphie).

psychologique. Une condition invariable et inévitable du traitement des psychonévroses est ce que Jung a excellemment appelé l'*introversion* de la libido[13], ce qui revient à dire que la quantité de libido capable de devenir consciente et de se tourner vers la réalité est devenue moindre, tandis que la partie inconsciente et non tournée vers la réalité, bien qu'elle puisse sans doute encore, tout en étant inconsciente, alimenter les fantasmes du sujet, se trouve accrue d'autant. La

13. Bien que certaines affirmations de Jung donnent l'impression qu'il considérait cette introversion comme caractérisant la démence précoce et ne serait pas aussi observable dans d'autres névroses.

76

libido dont le sujet dispose s'étant toujours trouvée soumise à l'attraction des complexes inconscients (ou plus justement des éléments complexuels de l'inconscient), avait subi une régression parce que l'attirance de la réalité était devenue moindre. Pour la libérer, il faut faire cesser l'attraction de l'inconscient, c'est-à-dire lever le refoulement des pulsions inconscientes et de leurs dérivés. C'est ce qui explique le rôle énorme de la résistance qui, bien souvent, laisse persister la maladie, même une fois que la raison d'être du recul devant la réalité a disparu. L'analyse a donc à faire face aux résistances émanées de deux sources. La résistance suit pas à pas le traitement, et y imprime son empreinte sur toute idée, tout acte du patient qui représente un compromis entre les forces tendant vers la guérison et celles qui s'y opposent.

Étudions un complexe pathogène, parfois très apparent et parfois presque imperceptible, depuis sa manifestation dans le conscient jusque dans ses racines dans l'inconscient, nous parvenons bientôt dans une région où la résistance se fait si nettement sentir que l'association qui surgit alors en porte la marque et nous apparaît comme un compromis entre les exigences de cette résistance et celles du travail d'investigation. L'expérience montre que c'est ici que surgit le transfert. Lorsque quelque chose, parmi les éléments du complexe (dans le contenu de celui-ci), est susceptible de se reporter sur la personne du médecin, le transfert a lieu, fournit l'idée suivante et se manifeste sous la forme d'une résistance, d'un arrêt des associations, par exemple. De pareilles expériences nous enseignent que l'idée de transfert est parvenue, de préférence à toutes les autres associations possibles, à se glisser jusqu'au conscient *justement parce qu'elle satisfait la résistance.* Un fait de ce genre se reproduit un nombre incalculable de fois au cours d'une psychanalyse. Toutes les fois que l'on se rapproche d'un complexe pathogène, c'est d'abord la partie du complexe pouvant devenir transfert qui se trouve poussée vers le conscient et que le patient s'obstine à défendre avec la plus grande ténacité[14].

Une fois cette résistance vaincue, les autres éléments complexuels vont être moins difficiles à éliminer. Plus un traitement analytique dure longtemps et plus le patient se rend compte que les déformations du matériel pathogène ne peuvent, à elles seules, le préserver d'une mise en lumière, plus alors il s'obstine à faire usage du mode de déformation qui lui semble évidemment le plus avantageux : la déformation par le

---

14. Il ne faudrait pas conclure cependant à une importance pathogénique particulièrement grande de l'élément choisi en vue de la résistance de transfert. Quand, au cours d'une bataille, les combattants se disputent avec acharnement la possession de quelque petit clocher ou de quelque ferme, n'en déduisons pas que cette église est un sanctuaire national ni que cette ferme abrite les trésors de l'armée. La valeur des lieux peut n'être que tactique et n'exister que pour ce seul combat.

Le transfert, dessin de Georges Allary.

*Le transfert vu par Georges Allary dans
« Le Crapouillot » d'Octobre 1962.*

transfert. Ces incidents tendent tous à amener une situation dans laquelle tous les conflits sont portés sur le terrain du transfert.

C'est pourquoi, pendant les analyses, le transfert nous apparaît comme l'arme la plus puissante de la résistance et nous en concluons que l'intensité et la durée d'un transfert sont la conséquence et l'expression de la résistance. On explique, il est vrai, le mécanisme du transfert, par un état de complaisance de la libido demeurée sous l'influence des images infantiles, toutefois son rôle dans le processus de la cure ne peut s'expliquer qu'en mettant en lumière ses rapports avec la résistance.

D'où vient que le transfert se prête si bien au jeu de la résistance ? La réponse peut d'abord sembler facile. Il est clair que l'aveu d'un désir interdit devient particulièrement malaisé lorsqu'il doit être fait à la personne même qui en est l'objet. Une pareille obligation fait naître des situations à peine concevables dans la vie réelle et pourtant c'est justement là où le patient cherche à parvenir, quand il confond le praticien avec l'objet de ses émois affectifs. A y regarder de plus près, nous constatons que cet avantage apparent ne saurait fournir de solution au problème. D'autre part, une relation empreinte de tendre affection, de dévouement, peut aider le patient à surmonter toutes les difficultés de l'aveu. Il n'est pas rare de dire, en d'autres circonstances, dans la vie réelle : « Je n'ai pas honte de te parler, je puis tout te raconter. » Le transfert sur la personne de l'analyste pourrait aussi bien faciliter la confession et l'on ne comprend toujours pas pourquoi il soulève des difficultés.

DES SENTIMENTS TENDRES OU BIEN HOSTILES, MAIS TOUJOURS ÉROTIQUES ET REFOULÉS

La réponse à cette question si souvent posée ne saurait être dictée par la seule réflexion. C'est à l'expérience acquise en examinant, au cours du traitement, chaque cas particulier de résistance de transfert que nous la devrons. On finit par s'apercevoir qu'il est impossible de comprendre comment le transfert sert à la résistance tant qu'on n'envisage simplement que le « transfert ». Il faut, en effet, distinguer deux sortes de transferts, l'un « positif », l'autre « négatif », un transfert de sentiments tendres et un transfert de sentiments hostiles, et l'on se voit obligé de traiter séparément ces deux variétés de sentiments qui ont pour objet le médecin. Ensuite, dans le transfert positif, l'on distingue des sentiments amicaux ou tendres, capables de devenir conscients, et d'autres dont les prolongements se trouvent dans l'inconscient. En ce qui concerne ces derniers l'analyse prouve chaque fois qu'ils ont un fondement érotique ; nous en concluons ainsi que tous les rapports d'ordre sentimental utilisables dans la vie, tels que ceux où se marquent la sympathie, l'amitié, la confiance, etc., sont génétiquement apparentés à la sexualité et émanent, par effacement du but sexuel, de désirs vraiment sexuels, quelque innocents et dénués de sensualité qu'ils apparaissent à notre perception consciente. Originellement, nous n'avons connu que des objets sexuels ; la psychanalyse nous montre que des gens que nous croyons seulement respecter, estimer, peuvent, pour notre inconscient, continuer à être des objets sexuels.

Voici donc la solution de l'énigme : le transfert sur la personne de l'analyste ne joue le rôle d'une résistance que dans la mesure où il est un transfert négatif ou bien un transfert positif composé d'éléments érotiques refoulés. Lorsque nous « liquidons » le transfert en le rendant conscient, nous écartons simplement de la personne du médecin ces deux composantes de la relation affective ; l'élément inattaquable, capable de devenir conscient, demeure et devient, pour la psychanalyse, ce qu'il est pour toutes les autres méthodes thérapeutiques : le facteur du succès.

Le transfert négatif mériterait qu'on l'étudie plus à fond, mais ce n'est pas ici le lieu de le faire. Dans les formes curables des psychonévroses on le découvre, à côté du transfert tendre, souvent en même temps et ayant pour objet une seule et même personne. C'est à cet état de choses que Bleuler a donné le nom excellemment approprié d'*ambivalence*[15]. Une semblable ambivalence de sentiments semble, dans une certaine mesure, normale, mais, poussée à un degré trop élevé, elle est certainement l'apanage des névrosés. Dans la névrose obsessionnelle, une « scission précoce des paires contrastées » semble caractériser la vie instinctuelle et fournir l'une des conditions constitutionnelles du trouble morbide. C'est l'ambivalence de l'afflux des sentiments qui nous permet le mieux de comprendre l'aptitude des névrosés à mettre leurs transferts au service de la résistance. Lorsque la possibilité de transfert est devenue essentiellement négative, comme dans le cas des paranoïaques, il n'existe plus aucun moyen d'influencer ou de guérir les malades.

---

15. E. Bleuler, « Dementia Praccox oder Gruppe der Schizophrenien », in *Aschaffenburg's Handbuch der Psychiatrie*, 1911. Conférence sur l'ambivalence faite à Berne en 1910, publiée dans le *Zentralblatt für Psychoanalyse*, vol. I, p. 266. W. Stekel avait auparavant proposé le terme de « bipolarité » pour désigner le même phénomène.

LA LUTTE ENTRE LE MÉDECIN ET LE PATIENT SE DÉROULE SUR LE TERRAIN DU TRANSFERT

Au cours du dépistage de la libido échappée au contrôle du conscient, nous pénétrons dans le domaine de l'inconscient. Les réactions provoquées mettent en lumière certains caractères des processus inconscients, tels que l'étude des rêves nous a permis de les connaître. Les émois inconscients tendent à échapper à la remémoration voulue par le traitement, mais cherchent à se reproduire suivant le mépris du temps et la faculté d'hallucination propres à l'inconscient. Comme dans les rêves, le patient attribue à ce qui résulte de ses émois inconscients réveillés, un caractère d'actualité et de réalité. Il veut mettre en actes ses passions, sans tenir compte de la situation réelle. Or le médecin cherche à le contraindre à intégrer ces émois dans le traitement et dans l'histoire de sa vie, à les soumettre à la réflexion et à les apprécier selon leur réelle valeur psychique. Cette lutte entre le médecin et le patient, entre l'intellect et les forces instinctuelles, entre le discernement et le besoin de décharge se joue presque exclusivement dans les phénomènes du transfert. C'est sur ce terrain qu'il faut remporter la victoire dont le résultat se traduira par une guérison durable de la névrose. Avouons que rien n'est plus difficile en analyse que de vaincre les résistances, mais n'oublions pas que ce sont justement ces phénomènes-là qui nous rendent le service le plus précieux, en nous permettant de mettre en lumière les émois amoureux secrets et oubliés des patients et en conférant à ces émois un caractère d'actualité. Enfin, rappelons-nous que nul ne peut être tué *in absentia* ou *in effigie*.

SIGMUND FREUD[16]

16. *La Technique psychanalytique* (« la Dynamique du transfert »), p. 50-60.

Chapitre III

De la névrose d'angoisse aux névroses actuelles

Les textes que nous présentons dans ce chapitre sont centrés sur l'angoisse et, plus précisément, sur un type de névrose que Freud a très tôt isolée sous le nom de névrose d'angoisse. Dès sa correspondance avec Wilhelm Fliess, qui se poursuivit de 1887 à 1902, il essaie de cerner l'origine de l'angoisse, comme nous le verrons ci-dessous dans les manuscrits B et E, datant respectivement de 1893 et de 1894. L'année suivante, il rédige un travail intitulé « Qu'il est justifié de séparer de la neurasthénie un certain complexe symptomatique sous le nom de névrose d'angoisse », que nous découvrirons en second lieu. Freud tente d'y définir une entité nosologique dont le symptôme essentiel est l'angoisse. Il différencie cette affection de la maladie encore fort connue sous le nom de neurasthénie.

La névrose d'angoisse se caractérise par une angoisse permanente, une « attente anxieuse » ou une « angoisse flottante », susceptible de se fixer sur toutes sortes de représentations (entre autres, certaines formes d'hypocondrie, autrement dit des craintes à propos de la santé). Ce syndrome d'angoisse, cette association de symptômes, s'accompagne souvent de troubles somatiques (tachycardie, c'est-à-dire accélération désordonnée des battements du cœur, dyspnée, ou difficulté à respirer, céphalées diffuses, etc.). Parfois cette angoisse, qui parvient, nous l'avons dit, à se fixer de façon permanente sur une représentation, apparaît comme une phobie, sans toutefois que celle-ci puisse être mise en rapport avec un contenu refoulé.

Freud est tout naturellement amené à formuler des hypothèses sur l'étiologie de l'angoisse dans cette affection. Elle proviendrait, pour l'essentiel, d'une tension sexuelle résultant de l'impossibilité d'une décharge liée à des facteurs principalement externes : coït interrompu, continence forcée ou volontaire, etc. L'accumulation de l'excitation sexuelle somatique ne subirait pas d'élaboration psychique suffisante. Dans le manuscrit E communiqué à Fliess, Freud distingue l'excitation *psychique, présente dans l'hystérie et aboutissant à une conversion dans le soma, c'est-à-dire le corps, de l'excitation physique, présente dans la névrose d'angoisse, non déchargée psychiquement, et qui demeure donc dans le soma. Parfois, les deux processus se combinent pour donner alors une « névrose mixte » dans laquelle on trouve des mécanismes propres à la névrose d'angoisse, et d'autres à l'hystérie. Enfin, la névrose d'angoisse ne doit pas être confondue avec l'hystérie d'angoisse, synonyme de névrose phobique ou de phobie. Dans cette dernière, l'angoisse se rapporte à un objet précis, substitut de l'objet primitif dont l'identité reste inconsciente (cf. le cheval, objet de la phobie du petit Hans, l'un des cas célèbres analysés par Freud : le petit garçon avait déplacé sur l'animal les affects dirigés, en fait, vers son père).*

*Le terme de « névrose actuelle » apparaît sous la plume de Freud dans un article datant de 1898, consacré à « l'Étiologie sexuelle des névroses ». Névrose d'angoisse et neurasthénie deviennent des formes de névrose actuelle ; Freud y ajoute l'hypocondrie, comme nous le verrons dans l'extrait d'*Introduction à la psychanalyse, *publié en 1917, et que nous reproduisons à la fin de ce chapitre. Les névroses actuelles s'opposent aux psychonévroses. Elles sont consécutives à une absence de décharge de la tension sexuelle, ou à une décharge inappropriée. Elles trouvent leurs causes dans l'« actualité », comme l'indique leur nom, et non dans l'expérience infantile du malade. Les mécanismes des psychonévroses — symbolisation, déplacement, condensation — y font défaut.*

En somme, dans les névroses actuelles, l'accent est mis sur la stase libidinale, sur une accumulation énergétique liée à des facteurs externes ; en revanche, les psychonévroses dépendent de conflits psychiques ; lorsque la décharge de la tension sexuelle est entravée, c'est pour des raisons internes. Et l'on peut faire ici deux remarques :

1° Le concept de névrose actuelle s'est progressivement efface sans toutefois disparaître totalement ;

2° Il coïncide exactement avec la théorie générale des troubles mentaux élaborée par Wilhelm Reich, et qui se fonde sur un point de vue purement économique.

Les notions de névrose d'angoisse et de névrose actuelle, que nous découvrirons ici nous semblent avoir pour principal intérêt de bien montrer l'importance que revêtira de plus en plus en psychanalyse la notion de réalité psychique, c'est-à-dire de réalité interne. Et, d'autre part, de présenter les premières théories freudiennes sur l'angoisse, qui correspond, nous l'avons vu, à une tension physique accumulée, non élaborée psychiquement.

ÉTIOLOGIE DES NÉVROSES[1]

Manuscrit B

8-2-1893[2]

C'est à ton intention, cher Ami, que je relate tous ces faits pour la seconde fois. Cache ce manuscrit à ta jeune femme. [...]

NÉVROSES D'ANGOISSE. — Tout neurasthénique manque de confiance en lui-même, est dans une certaine mesure pessimiste et tend à se forger des idées antagonistes déprimantes[3]. Mais il faut se demander s'il ne conviendrait pas de considérer l'apparition de ces facteurs, surtout lorsque d'autres symptômes ne sont pas particulièrement développés, comme des cas spécifiques de « névrose d'angoisse », d'autant plus qu'on l'observe aussi fréquemment dans l'hystérie que dans la neurasthénie.

La névrose d'angoisse peut se manifester sous deux formes : *a l'état chronique* et par *accès d'angoisse*. Les deux formes sont souvent combinées et la crise d'angoisse n'apparaît jamais en dehors d'un symptôme permanent. Ces accès apparaissent le plus souvent dans les cas de névroses d'angoisse liés à l'hystérie, c'est-à-dire qu'ils se produisent surtout chez les femmes, alors que les symptômes chroniques affectent plus fréquemment les hommes.

Les symptômes chroniques sont : 1) l'anxiété relative au corps (hypocondrie) ; 2) l'anxiété relative aux fonctions physiques (agoraphobie, claustrophobie, vertiges de hauteurs) ; 3) l'anxiété à propos des décisions à prendre et de la mémoire, c'est-à-dire du fonctionnement psychique (folie du doute, ruminations mentales, etc.). J'ai toujours considéré tous ces symptômes comme équivalents. Il s'agit de déterminer : 1° dans quelle condition cet état s'instaure chez les sujets héréditairement prédisposés mais n'ayant subi aucun dommage sexuel ; 2° si chez les prédisposés de cette sorte un trouble sexuel quelconque peut le provoquer ; 3° si, dans la neurasthénie banale, il s'ajoute comme un facteur intensifiant. Une chose demeure certaine, c'est que cet état peut se produire, chez les hommes comme chez les femmes, dans le

---

1. Le premier manuscrit n'a pu être conservé. Dans une lettre datée du 5-1-1893, non publiée dans ce volume, Freud parle de ce second manuscrit dans les termes suivants : « Je refais mon histoire des névroses. » Les considérations sur la genèse de la neurasthénie chez l'homme et chez la femme contenues dans le manuscrit ont été ultérieurement remaniées dans le travail intitulé *Des motifs de séparer de la neurasthénie un certain syndrome de symptômes en tant que « névrose d'angoisse »*.

2. La date nous est donnée par l'oblitération du timbre.

3. [Voir à ce sujet « Un cas de traitement par l'hypnotisme couronné de succès » (Freud, 1892-1893, b).]

mariage, ce qui est imputable, durant la seconde période des poussées sexuelles, au coït interrompu. A mon avis, il n'est pas nécessaire qu'une prédisposition ait été créée par quelque neurasthénie antérieure. Toutefois, quand cette prédisposition est inexistante, la période de latence est plus longue. On trouve ici le même schéma causal que dans la neurasthénie.

Les cas, relativement plus rares, de névroses d'angoisse en dehors du mariage se rencontrent surtout chez les hommes qui, sentimentalement liés, pratiquent, par précaution, le coït interrompu. En pareil cas, ce procédé est plus nuisible encore qu'il ne l'est dans le mariage où le coït interrompu se trouve souvent compensé par des relations extra-conjugales normales.

La *dépression périodique* doit être considérée comme une troisième forme de névrose d'angoisse, comme une perturbation pouvant se prolonger pendant des semaines ou des mois. Elle se distingue, la plupart du temps, de la mélancolie vraie par son rapport, en apparence rationnel, avec quelque traumatisme psychique. Et pourtant ce dernier ne constitue qu'une cause déclenchante. De plus, cette dépression périodique est dépourvue de l'anesthésie psychique (sexuelle) qui caractérise la mélancolie.

J'ai réussi à ramener toute une série de cas semblables au coït interrompu.

D'ORIGINE SEXUELLE, LA NÉVROSE D'ANGOISSE EST-ELLE INCURABLE ?

CONCLUSIONS. — Il s'ensuit de ce qui précède que les névroses sont parfaitement évitables mais totalement incurables. La tâche du médecin est tout entière d'ordre prophylactique[4].

La première partie de cette tâche, celle qui consiste à prévenir les troubles sexuels de la première période, se confond avec la prophylaxie de la syphilis et de la blennorragie, dangers qui menacent tous ceux qui renoncent à la masturbation. Le seul autre système serait d'autoriser les libres rapports entre jeunes gens et jeunes filles de bonne famille, mais cela ne saurait advenir que si l'on disposait de méthodes anticonceptionnelles inoffensives. On se trouve ainsi devant l'alternative sui-

---

4. Freud n'a jamais soutenu ailleurs avec autant de netteté cette thèse. Dans les *Études sur l'hystérie*, il dit : « J'ose soutenir qu'elle [la méthode cathartique] est en principe, capable de supprimer n'importe quel symptôme hystérique tandis qu'elle reste totalement impuissante, comme on le constate aisément, devant les manifestations de la neurasthénie et qu'elle n'agit que rarement et par voie détournée sur les conséquences psychiques de la névrose d'angoisse. »

vante : masturbation avec neurasthénie chez les hommes et hystéro-
neurasthénie chez les femmes ou bien syphilis chez les hommes avec
hérédité syphilitique pour la génération suivante ou encore gonorrhée
chez les hommes et gonorrhée et stérilité chez les femmes.

Le traumatisme sexuel de la seconde période nous pose le même
problème, celui de la découverte d'une méthode anticonceptionnelle
inoffensive, puisque l'usage de la capote anglaise n'apporte aucune
sécurité réelle et ne saurait être toléré par aucun neurasthénique.

La continence sexuelle est-elle source d'angoisse ?

En l'absence de toute solution possible, la société semble condamnée à devenir victime de névroses incurables qui réduisent à son minimum la joie de vivre, détruisent les relations conjugales et entraînent, du fait de l'hérédité, la ruine de toute la génération à venir.

Bien affectueusement à toi,

ton
SIGM. FREUD.

COMMENT NAÎT L'ANGOISSE[5]

Manuscrit E.
Sans date (juin 1894 ?).

Tu as immédiatement mis le doigt sur la partie de mon plan dont je sens la faiblesse. Je ne puis dire à ce sujet que les choses suivantes :

Je me suis rapidement rendu compte que l'angoisse de mes névrosés était, en grande partie, imputable à la sexualité et j'ai en particulier observé de quelle façon le coït interrompu entraînait inévitablement chez la femme de l'angoisse névrotique. Au début, je m'engageai dans de fausses voies. Il me semblait que l'angoisse dont souffraient les malades n'était que la continuation de l'angoisse éprouvée pendant l'acte sexuel, donc en fait un *symptôme hystérique*. Il est vrai que les liens entre la névrose d'angoisse et l'hystérie sont suffisamment évidents. Il peut y avoir dans le coït interrompu deux motifs d'angoisse : chez la femme, une crainte de la conception, chez l'homme, la peur de rater son exploit. Mais l'expérience m'a appris que la névrose d'angoisse apparaît aussi là où ces deux facteurs sont absents et où les sujets n'avaient aucune raison de craindre la venue d'un enfant. Donc la névrose d'angoisse ne pouvait être le prolongement d'une angoisse remémorée d'ordre *hystérique*.

Une autre observation des plus importantes m'a permis d'établir le point suivant : la névrose d'angoisse atteint aussi souvent les femmes frigides que les autres. Le fait semble remarquable mais signifie seulement que la source de l'angoisse ne doit pas être recherchée dans les

---

5. Si nous avons ici inséré le manuscrit E, c'est à cause de son contenu qui semble concorder avec le reste. Une enveloppe timbrée portant la date du 6 6 1894 pourrait bien lui appartenir. Des parties très importantes de ce manuscrit concordent avec le premier travail de Freud sur la névrose d'angoisse (1895).

faits psychiques. Il faut donc qu'elle se trouve dans le domaine physique. C'est d'un facteur d'ordre physique que dépend, dans la sexualité, l'angoisse. Mais ce facteur, quel est-il ?

Pour résoudre cette question, je me suis attaché à recueillir tous les faits où l'anxiété me semblait avoir une cause sexuelle. Ils semblent au premier abord former une bien disparate collection :

1. Angoisse survenant chez des sujets *vierges* (lorsqu'ils ont fait quelque observation ou recueilli certains renseignements d'ordre sexuel ou qu'ils pressentent la vie sexuelle). C'est ce que confirment de nombreux exemples dans les deux sexes, mais surtout chez les femmes. Très souvent, on trouve un chaînon intermédiaire : une sensation dans les organes génitaux rappelant l'érection.

2. Angoisse chez les *sujets pratiquant volontairement la continence*, chez les prudes (type de névropathes). Il s'agit là d'hommes et de femmes tatillons, fanatiques de la propreté, qui ont horreur de tout ce qui concerne la sexualité. Ces gens ont tendance à transformer leur angoisse en phobies, en actes obsédants ou en folie du doute.

3. Angoisse des *gens continents par nécessité*, des femmes délaissées par leur mari ou insatisfaites par suite du manque de puissance de celui-ci. Cette forme de névrose d'angoisse peut certainement être acquise et est souvent, à cause de circonstances concomitantes, combinée à une neurasthénie.

4. Angoisse due au *coït interrompu* chez des femmes qui s'y adonnent habituellement ou, fait analogue, dont les maris souffrent d'éjaculation précoce, c'est-à-dire chez des personnes dont l'excitation physique reste insatisfaite.

5. Angoisse chez des hommes pratiquant le *coït interrompu* et surtout chez ceux qui, après de multiples excitations sexuelles, et malgré l'érection ne pratiquent pas le coït.

6. Angoisse des hommes qui s'astreignent au coït *au-delà de leur désir ou de leur force*.

7. Angoisse des hommes que *certaines circonstances obligent à rester continents* : jeunes hommes, par exemple, ayant épousé des femmes plus âgées qu'eux dont ils ont horreur, ou neurasthéniques, que leur occupation intellectuelle a détournés de la masturbation sans qu'ils aient trouvé, dans le coït, quelque compensation, hommes dont la puissance décline et qui s'abstiennent d'avoir des rapports avec leur femme à cause de sensations [désagréables] *post coitum*.

Dans les autres cas, le lien entre l'angoisse et la sexualité ne semblait pas aussi évident, bien qu'il fût possible de le mettre théoriquement en lumière.

ACCUMULATION DE TENSION SEXUELLE PHYSIQUE ET NÉVROSE D'ANGOISSE

Comment combiner tous ces cas individuels ? C'est le facteur de la continence qui y est le plus fréquent. Instruit par le fait que le *coït interrompu* engendre de l'angoisse même chez des frigides, on pourrait dire qu'il y a là *accumulation de tension sexuelle physique* et que cette accumulation est due à une décharge entravée. Ainsi la névrose d'angoisse, comme l'hystérie, est une névrose due à une excitation endiguée, ce qui explique la similitude des deux maladies. L'angoisse ne se manifestant nullement dans ce qui a été accumulé, on peut exprimer cet état de choses en disant qu'elle découle d'une *transformation* de la tension accumulée.

Ajoutons ici les informations simultanées que nous avons pu obtenir sur le mécanisme de la mélancolie. Il arrive très souvent que les mélancoliques soient des frigides. Ils ne ressentent pas le besoin du coït dont ils ne tirent aucune sensation, mais aspirent ardemment à l'amour sous sa forme psychique. Nous pourrions dire qu'ils éprouvent une grande tension érotique psychique ; lorsque cette dernière vient à s'accumuler sans qu'une décharge se réalise, la mélancolie fait son apparition. Il s'agirait donc, en ce cas, d'un pendant à la névrose d'angoisse.

Quand il y a accumulation de tension sexuelle *physique*, nous avons affaire à une névrose d'angoisse.

Quand il y a accumulation de tension sexuelle *psychique*, nous nous trouvons en présence d'une mélancolie.

Mais pourquoi cette accumulation de tension provoque-t-elle de l'angoisse ? Il conviendrait ici d'étudier le mécanisme normal de décharge d'une tension accumulée. Le second cas qui se présente à nous est celui d'une excitation *endogène*. La question de l'excitation exogène [premier cas] n'est pas aussi compliquée. La source d'excitation se trouve au-dehors et provoque dans le psychisme un surcroît de tension qui se décharge suivant sa quantité. Toute réaction capable de réduire de cette quantité l'excitation psychique est suffisante.

Les choses se passent différemment dans le cas d'une tension endogène dont la source se trouve au-dedans du corps du sujet (faim, soif ou pulsion sexuelle). Dans ce cas, seules les *réactions spécifiques* sont utiles, celles qui empêchent une production ultérieure d'excitation dans l'organe terminal intéressé, quelle que soit la somme d'efforts nécessaire pour y parvenir[6]. Il nous est permis de supposer que la tension endogène peut croître de façon continue ou discontinue mais qu'elle ne se

6. Ces vues sont exposées dans *l'Esquisse pour une psychologie scientifique*.

perçoit que lorsqu'elle atteint un certain *seuil*. Ce n'est qu'à partir de ce seuil qu'elle se trouve *psychiquement* utilisée en prenant contact avec certains groupes de représentations qui, ensuite, produisent l'action remédiante spécifique. Ainsi, une tension sexuelle physique, portée au-dessus d'un certain degré suscite de la libido psychique, qui alors prépare le coït, etc. Si la réaction spécifique ne se produit pas, la tension physico-psychique (l'affect sexuel) augmente à l'excès, mais bien qu'elle devienne gênante, rien ne suffit encore à motiver sa transformation. Toutefois, dans la névrose d'angoisse, une transformation se réalise, ce qui porte à croire que le déréglage s'est réalisé de la façon suivante : la tension physique accrue atteint le seuil qui permet de susciter un affect psychique, mais en pareil cas et pour une raison quelconque, la connexion psychique qui lui est offerte demeure insuffisante ; l'affect psychique ne peut se produire, parce que certaines conditions psychiques font partiellement défaut, d'ou transformation en angoisse de la tension qui n'a pas été psychiquement « liée[7] ».

Si l'on admet jusque-là cette théorie, il faut alors reconnaître qu'il y a dans la névrose d'angoisse une insuffisance d'affect sexuel, de *libido psychique*. C'est d'ailleurs ce que vient confirmer l'observation. Quand nous attirons l'attention de nos patientes sur cette question, elles ne manquent jamais de s'indigner et déclarent que, bien au contraire, elles ne ressentent plus aucun désir sexuel, etc. Les patientes reconnaissent avoir noté que, depuis l'apparition de leur angoisse, elles n'ont plus éprouvé de désirs sexuels.

Voyons maintenant si ce mécanisme se retrouve bien dans les cas énumérés plus haut :

1. ANGOISSE DES VIERGES. — Ici le champ de représentations où doit déboucher la tension physique n'existe pas encore ou est insuffisant ; en outre, il faut y ajouter un autre facteur, un rejet psychique de la sexualité qui constitue un résultat secondaire de l'éducation. L'hypothèse se trouve ici très bien confirmée.

2. ANGOISSE DES PRUDES. — Il y a défense, refus psychique total qui rend impossible toute élaboration de la tension sexuelle. C'est là qu'il faut ranger les obsessions banales. Nouvelle confirmation de l'hypothèse.

3. ANGOISSE DUE À UNE CONTINENCE FORCÉE. — Elle est, à vrai dire, identique à la précédente puisque, en pareil cas, les femmes, pour échapper à la tentation, opposent généralement un refus psychique. Ce rejet est ici occasionnel tandis que, dans le cas précédent, il est intrinsèque.

---

7. Voir au sujet de ce « lien » *l'Esquisse*. Et, pour l'explication du concept de « liaison », l'introduction au chapitre VI du présent ouvrage. (N.d.E.)

4. ANGOISSE DUE CHEZ LA FEMME AU COÏT INTERROMPU. — Le mécanisme est ici plus simple. Nous avons affaire à une excitation endogène qui ne s'est pas produite spontanément, mais qui vient du dehors et ne suffit pas à produire un affect psychique. Il se fait artificiellement une coupure entre l'acte physico-sexuel et son élaboration psychique. Quand ensuite la tension endogène s'accroît encore d'elle même, elle ne peut subir aucune élaboration et produit de l'angoisse.

Ainsi au *refus psychique* se substitue une *coupure psychique* et la tension endogène est remplacée par une tension provoquée.

5. ANGOISSE DUE CHEZ LES HOMMES AU COÏT INTERROMPU OU RÉSERVÉ. — Le cas du *coitus reservatus* est le plus clair. Le coït interrompu peut, dans une certaine mesure équivaloir à ce dernier. Nous avons ici encore affaire à une diversion psychique, étant donné que l'attention se porte ailleurs et se trouve détournée de l'élaboration d'une tension physique. Cette explication du coït interrompu a probablement besoin d'être plus approfondie.

6. ANGOISSE DÉCOULANT D'UNE PUISSANCE DIMINUÉE OU D'UNE LIBIDO INSUFFISANTE. — Si la transformation de la tension physique en angoisse n'est pas due à la sénilité, on l'explique en disant qu'elle est due à une impossibilité pour le sujet d'amasser assez de désir psychique pour réaliser son acte sexuel.

7. ANGOISSE ATTRIBUABLE AU DÉGOUT. NEURASTHÉNIQUES CHASTES. — Dans le premier cas, aucune explication n'est nécessaire. Dans le second cas, il peut s'agir d'une névrose d'angoisse à forme atténuée, puisque celle-ci ne se développe pleinement et normalement que chez des hommes puissants. Peut-être le système nerveux du neurasthénique ne tolère-t-il pas une accumulation de tension physique, puisque la masturbation implique l'accoutumance à un manque fréquent et total de tension.

ACCUMULATION DE TENSION SEXUELLE PSYCHIQUE ET HYSTÉRIE

Dans l'ensemble, ma théorie tient assez bien. La tension sexuelle se transforme en angoisse dans les cas où, tout en se produisant avec force, elle ne subit pas l'élaboration psychique qui la transformerait en affect, phénomène dû soit à un développement imparfait de la sexualité psychique, soit à une tentative de répression de cette dernière (c'est-à-dire à une défense), soit encore à une désagrégation, soit enfin à l'ins

UN DÉBUTANT, par Gyp

« Je me suis rapidement rendu compte que l'angoisse de mes névrosés
était, en grande partie, imputable à la sexualité... »

tauration d'un écart devenu habituel entre la sexualité physique et la sexualité psychique. Ajoutons encore à cela une accumulation de tension physique et le rôle joué par les obstacles qui empêchent une décharge vers le domaine psychique.

Mais pour quelle raison se produit-il justement de l'*angoisse* ? Celle-ci consiste en une sensation d'accumulation d'un autre stimulus endogène — le stimulus qui nous pousse à respirer et qui ignore toute autre élaboration psychique ; ainsi, l'angoisse peut correspondre à n'importe quelle tension physique accumulée.

De plus, en considérant de plus près les symptômes d'une névrose d'angoisse, nous y découvrons les fragments disjoints de la grande attaque d'angoisse : simple dyspnée, simples palpitations, simple sensation d'angoisse et combinaison de toutes ces manifestations. Une observation plus précise montre qu'il s'agit là des voies d'innervation qu'emprunte normalement une tension physico-sexuelle, même quand elle a subi une élaboration psychique. La dyspnée, les palpitations accompagnent le coït alors qu'elles ne sont généralement utilisées que comme moyens accessoires de décharges ; elles ne constituent ici, pour ainsi dire, que le seul débouché de l'excitation. Ainsi, dans la névrose d'angoisse, comme dans l'hystérie, il se produit une sorte de « conversion » (ce qui révèle une nouvelle similitude entre les deux maladies). Toutefois, dans l'hystérie c'est une excitation *psychique* qui emprunte une mauvaise voie en menant à des réactions somatiques. Dans la névrose d'angoisse, au contraire, c'est une tension *physique* qui ne peut réussir à se décharger psychiquement et qui continue, par conséquent, à demeurer dans le domaine physique. Les deux processus sont extrêmement souvent combinés.

Voilà où j'en suis arrivé aujourd'hui. Il reste bien des lacunes à combler, tout semble incomplet, et quelque chose y manque. Mais les fondements m'en semblent exacts. Naturellement, le travail ne saurait encore être publié. Suggestions, compléments, et même objections et éclaircissements seront accueillis avec la plus vive gratitude.

Bien cordialement à toi,

ton
SIGM. FREUD[8]

---

8. *La Naissance de la psychanalyse* (manuscrits B et E), p. 61, 64-66, 80-85.

CIRCONSTANCES D'APPARITION
ET ÉTIOLOGIE DE LA NÉVROSE D'ANGOISSE

Dans certains cas de névrose d'angoisse, aucune étiologie ne peut être découverte. Il est remarquable que, dans ces cas, la preuve d'une lourde tare héréditaire est rarement difficile à apporter.

Mais lorsqu'on est fondé à tenir cette névrose pour *acquise*, un examen soigneux et orienté en ce sens découvre comme facteurs étiologiques actifs une série de nuisances[9] et d'influences provenant de la *vie sexuelle*. Au premier abord celles-ci semblent être de natures diverses, mais on découvre facilement le caractère commun qui explique la similitude de leur action sur le système nerveux ; on les trouve soit de façon isolée, soit associées à d'autres nuisances *banales* auxquelles on peut attribuer une action adjuvante. Cette étiologie sexuelle de la névrose d'angoisse peut être démontrée dans l'immense majorité des cas, si bien que je me permets, *dans les limites de cette courte communication*, de laisser de côté les cas dont l'étiologie est douteuse ou d'autre nature.

LES SITUATIONS QUI ENGENDRENT
DE L'ANGOISSE

Pour une présentation plus précise des conditions étiologiques d'apparition de la névrose d'angoisse, il est souhaitable de considérer séparément les hommes et les femmes. Chez les individus du *sexe féminin* — en faisant ici abstraction de leur prédisposition — la névrose d'angoisse s'installe dans les cas suivants :

a) *Angoisse virginale* ou *angoisse des adolescentes*. Un certain nombre d'observations indubitables m'ont montré qu'une première rencontre avec le problème sexuel, une révélation plus ou moins soudaine de ce qui a été voilé jusqu'alors, par exemple par le spectacle d'un acte sexuel, une conversation ou des lectures, peuvent provoquer, chez des jeunes filles en voie de maturation, une névrose d'angoisse ; celle-ci est combinée, de façon presque typique, avec une hystérie.

b) *Angoisse des jeunes mariées*. Il n'est pas rare que de jeunes femmes qui sont restées anesthésiques pendant les premiers rapports, soient atteintes d'une névrose d'angoisse qui disparaît à nouveau une fois que l'anesthésie a fait place à une sensibilité normale. Mais comme la plupart des jeunes femmes ne tombent pas malades malgré une telle

---

9. *Schädlichkeit*. Nous avons employé le vieux vocable « nuisance » qui désigne tout facteur, action ou circonstance aux conséquences préjudiciables. (N.d.T.)

anesthésie des débuts, il faut, pour que survienne cette angoisse, que s'ajoutent d'autres conditions que j'indiquerai plus loin.

c) Angoisse des femmes dont les maris souffrent d'*éjaculation précoce*[10] ou d'une puissance sexuelle très diminuée ; et

d) dont les maris pratiquent le *coït interrompu* ou *réservé*. Ces cas vont ensemble car on peut facilement se convaincre, par l'analyse d'un grand nombre d'exemples, que le seul point important est de savoir si la femme parvient ou non à la satisfaction dans le coït. Dans le cas négatif, la condition est donnée pour que survienne la névrose d'angoisse. Par contre la femme est épargnée par la névrose lorsque l'homme atteint d'éjaculation précoce est capable aussitôt après de répéter le rapport avec un meilleur résultat. Le rapport réservé, au moyen d'un préservatif, ne comporte aucune nuisance pour la femme lorsqu'elle est très rapidement excitable et que l'homme est très puissant ; dans le cas contraire, cette sorte de précaution n'est pas moins nuisible que les autres. Le coït interrompu est presque régulièrement une nuisance ; mais, pour la femme, il n'en est une que si l'homme le pratique sans égards, c'est-à-dire interrompt le coït aussitôt qu'il est proche de l'éjaculation, sans se soucier du déroulement de l'excitation chez la femme. Au contraire, si l'homme attend la satisfaction de la *femme*, le coït a pour celle-ci la signification d'un rapport normal ; mais c'est alors l'homme qui est atteint de névrose d'angoisse. J'ai rassemblé et analysé un grand nombre d'observations d'où ressortent les affirmations ci-dessus.

e) Angoisse des *veuves* et des femmes *intentionnellement abstinentes*, qu'il n'est pas rare de trouver combinée, de façon typique, avec des obsessions.

f) Angoisse de l'*âge critique*[11], lors de la dernière grande augmentation du besoin sexuel.

Les cas *c)*, *d)* et *e)* comprennent les conditions les plus fréquentes et les plus indépendantes d'une disposition héréditaire pour que survienne la névrose d'angoisse dans le sexe féminin. C'est sur ces cas — guérissables, acquis — de névrose d'angoisse que je tenterai d'apporter la preuve que la nuisance sexuelle retrouvée constitue véritablement le facteur étiologique de la névrose. Mais auparavant je discuterai les conditions sexuelles de la névrose d'angoisse chez les *hommes*. Je constituerai les groupes suivants, qui trouvent dans l'ensemble leurs analogies chez la femme.

10. Ici et dans la suite, Freud emploie les termes latins, comme il est de tradition dans la médecine allemande : *Ejaculatio praecox, coitus interruptus, congressus reservatus.* (N.d.T.)

11. *Klimakterium.* (N.d.T.)

a) Angoisse des hommes *intentionnellement abstinents*, fréquemment combinée avec des symptômes de *défense* (obsessions, hystérie). Les motifs qui sont déterminants pour cette abstinence intentionnelle impliquent qu'un bon nombre de sujets héréditairement prédisposés, excentriques, etc., entrent dans cette catégorie.

b) Angoisse des hommes à l'excitation *frustrée* (pendant les fiançailles), des personnes qui (par peur des conséquences du rapport sexuel) se contentent de toucher ou de regarder la femme. Ce groupe de conditions (qui d'ailleurs peut être transféré sans changement à l'autre sexe — fiançailles, relations avec réserve sexuelle) donne les cas les plus purs de la névrose.

c) Angoisse des hommes qui pratiquent le *coït interrompu*. Comme on l'a déjà vu, le coït interrompu est nuisible pour la femme lorsqu'il est pratiqué sans considération pour sa satisfaction ; mais il devient nuisible pour l'homme lorsque celui-ci, pour atteindre la satisfaction de la femme, dirige volontairement le coït et retarde l'éjaculation. On peut ainsi comprendre que, dans un couple qui pratique le coït interrompu, seul *un* des partenaires tombe habituellement malade. Chez les hommes, d'ailleurs, le coït interrompu ne provoque que rarement une pure névrose d'angoisse, mais la plupart du temps un alliage de celle-ci avec la neurasthénie.

d) Angoisse des hommes à la *sénescence*[12]. Il est des hommes qui, comme les femmes, présentent un âge critique et font une névrose d'angoisse à l'époque où leur puissance diminue et où la libido augmente.

SIGMUND FREUD[13]

UNE VIE SEXUELLE NORMALE NE COMPORTE PAS DE NÉVROSE ACTUELLE

Dans les formes ordinaires des névroses dites *actuelles*, le rôle étiologique de la vie sexuelle constitue un fait brut, qui s'offre de lui-même à l'observation. Je me suis heurté à ce fait il y a plus de vingt ans lorsque je m'étais un jour demandé pourquoi on s'obstine à ne tenir aucun compte, au cours de l'examen des nerveux, de leur activité

---

12. *Im Senium* (N.d.T.)

13. *Névrose, psychose et perversion* (« Qu'il est justifié de séparer de la neurasthénie un certain complexe symptomatique sous le nom de névrose d'angoisse »), p. 23 à 26.

La harpe de David berçait-elle la neurasthénie du roi Saül ?
(Gravure de Lucas de Leyde, XVIᵉ siècle,
Bibliothèque des Arts Décoratifs).

sexuelle. J'ai alors sacrifié à ces recherches la sympathie dont je jouis-
sais auprès des malades, mais il ne m'a pas fallu beaucoup d'efforts
pour arriver à cette constatation que la vie sexuelle normale ne com
porte pas de névrose (de névrose actuelle, veux-je dire). Certes, cette
proposition fait trop bon marché des différences individuelles des hom
mes et elle souffre aussi de cette incertitude qui est inséparable du mot
« normal », mais, au point de vue de l'orientation en gros, elle garde
encore aujourd'hui toute sa valeur. J'ai pu alors établir des rapports
spécifiques entre certaines formes de nervosité et certains troubles
sexuels particuliers, et je suis convaincu que si je disposais des mêmes
matériaux, du même ensemble de malades, je ferais encore aujourd'hui
des observations identiques. Il m'a souvent été donné de constater
qu'un homme, qui se contentait d'une certaine satisfaction incomplète,
par exemple de l'onanisme manuel, était atteint d'une forme détermi
née de névrose actuelle, laquelle cédait promptement sa place à une
autre forme, lorsque le sujet adoptait un autre régime sexuel, mais tout
aussi peu recommandable. Il me fut ainsi possible de deviner un chan
gement dans le mode de satisfaction sexuelle d'après le changement de
l'état du malade. J'avais pris l'habitude de ne pas renoncer à mes sup
positions et à mes soupçons tant que que je n'avais pas réussi à vaincre
l'insincérité du malade et à lui arracher des aveux. Il est vrai que les
malades préféraient alors s'adresser à d'autres médecins qui mettaient
moins d'insistance à se renseigner sur leur vie sexuelle.

Il ne m'a pas non plus échappe alors que l'étiologie de l'état morbide
ne pouvait pas toujours être ramenée à la vie sexuelle. Si tel malade a
été directement affecté d'un trouble sexuel, chez tel autre ce trouble
n'est survenu qu'à la suite de pertes pécuniaires importantes ou d'une
grave maladie organique. L'explication de cette variété ne nous est
apparue que plus tard, lorsque nous avons commencé à entrevoir les
rapports réciproques jusqu'alors seulement soupçonnés, du Moi et de
la libido, et notre explication devenait de plus en plus satisfaisante à
mesure que les preuves de ces rapports devenaient plus nombreuses.
Une personne ne devient névrosée que lorsque son Moi a perdu l'apti
tude à réprimer sa libido d'une façon ou d'une autre. Plus le Moi est
fort, et plus il lui est facile de s'acquitter de cette tâche ; tout affaiblis
sement du Moi, quelle qu'en soit la cause, est suivi du même effet que
l'exagération des exigences de la libido et fraie par conséquent la voie à
l'affection névrotique. Il existe encore d'autres rapports plus intimes
entre le Moi et la libido ; mais comme ces rapports ne nous intéressent
pas ici, nous nous en occuperons plus tard. Ce qui reste pour nous
essentiel et instructif, c'est que dans tous les cas, et quel que soit le
mode de production de la maladie, les symptômes de la névrose sont
fournis par la libido, ce qui suppose une énorme dépense de celle-ci.

ASSEOIR SUR UNE BASE ORGANIQUE
L'ÉDIFICE THÉORIQUE
DE LA PSYCHANALYSE

Et maintenant, je dois attirer votre attention sur la différence fonda-mentale qui existe entre les névroses actuelles et les psychonévroses dont le premier groupe, les névroses de transfert, nous a tant occupés jusqu'à présent. Dans les deux cas, les symptômes découlent de la libido ; ils impliquent dans les deux cas une dépense anormale de celle-ci, sont dans les deux cas des satisfactions substitutives. Mais les symptômes des névroses actuelles, lourdeur de tête, sensation de dou-leur, irritation d'un organe, affaiblissement ou arrêt d'une fonction, n'ont aucun « sens », aucune signification psychique. Ces symptômes sont corporels, non seulement dans leurs manifestations (tel est égale-ment le cas des symptômes hystériques, par exemple), mais aussi quant aux processus qui les produisent et qui se déroulent sans la moindre participation de l'un quelconque de ces mécanismes psychiques com-pliqués que nous connaissons. Comment peuvent-ils, dans ces conditions, correspondre à des utilisations de la libido qui, nous l'avons vu, est une force psychique ? La réponse à cette question est on ne peut plus simple. Permettez-moi d'évoquer une des premières objec-tions qui a été adressée à la psychanalyse. On disait alors que la psy-chanalyse perd son temps à vouloir établir une théorie purement psy-chologique des phénomènes névrotiques, ce qui est un travail stérile, les théories psychologiques étant incapables de rendre compte d'une maladie. Mais en produisant cet argument, on oubliait volontiers que la fonction sexuelle n'est ni purement psychique ni purement somati-que. Elle exerce son influence à la fois sur la vie psychique et sur la vie corporelle. Si nous avons reconnu dans les symptômes des psychoné-vroses les manifestations psychiques des troubles sexuels, nous ne serons pas étonnés de trouver dans les névroses actuelles leurs effets somatiques directs.

La clinique médicale nous fournit une indication précieuse, à laquelle adhèrent d'ailleurs beaucoup d'auteurs, quant à la manière de concevoir les névroses actuelles. Celles-ci manifestent, notamment dans les détails de leur symptomatologie ainsi que par leur pouvoir d'agir sur tous les systèmes d'organes et sur toutes les fonctions, une analogie incontestable avec des états morbides occasionnés par l'action chro-nique de substances toxiques extérieures ou par la suppression brusque de cette action, c'est-à-dire avec les intoxications et les abstinences. La parenté entre ces deux groupes d'affections devient encore plus intime à la faveur d'états morbides que nous attribuons, comme c'est le cas de

« Le malade imaginaire » :
une description d'une « névrose actuelle » ?

la maladie de Basedow[14], à l'action de substances toxiques qui, au lieu d'être introduites dans le corps du dehors, se sont formées dans l'organisme lui-même. Ces analogies nous imposent, à mon avis, la conclusion que les névroses actuelles résultent de troubles du métabolisme des substances sexuelles, soit qu'il se produise plus de toxines que la personne n'en peut supporter, soit que certaines conditions internes ou même psychiques troublent l'utilisation adéquate de ces substances. La

14. Maladie résultant d'une hypersécrétion de la thyroïde. (N.d.E.)

sagesse populaire a toujours professé ces idées sur la nature du besoin sexuel en disant de l'amour qu'il est une « ivresse » produite par certaines boissons, ou filtres, auxquelles elle attribue d'ailleurs une origine exogène. Au demeurant, le terme « métabolisme sexuel » ou « chimisme de la sexualité » est pour nous un moule sans contenu ; nous ne savons rien sur ce sujet et ne pouvons même pas dire qu'il existe deux substances dont l'une serait « mâle », l'autre « femelle », ou si nous devons nous contenter d'admettre une seule toxine sexuelle qui serait alors la cause de toutes les excitations de la libido. L'édifice théorique de la psychanalyse, que nous avons créé, n'est en réalité qu'une superstructure que nous devons asseoir sur sa base organique. Mais cela ne nous est pas encore possible.

UN LIEN ENTRE LES NÉVROSES ACTUELLES ET LES PSYCHONÉVROSES : LA SEXUALITÉ

Vous êtes en droit de vous attendre à ce que nous portions aussi un certain intérêt aux névroses actuelles. Nous sommes d'ailleurs obligés de le faire, ne serait-ce qu'à cause des rapports cliniques étroits qu'elles présentent avec les psychonévroses. Aussi vous dirai-je que nous distinguons trois formes pures de névroses actuelles : la *neurasthénie,* la *névrose d'angoisse* et l'*hypocondrie.* Cette division n'a pas été sans soulever des objections. Les noms sont bien d'un usage courant, mais les choses qu'ils désignent sont indéterminées et incertaines. Il est même des médecins qui s'opposent à toute classification dans le monde chaotique des phénomènes névrotiques, à tout établissement d'unités cliniques, d'individualités morbides, et qui ne reconnaissent même pas la division en névroses actuelles et en psychonévroses. A mon avis, ces médecins vont trop loin et ne suivent pas le chemin qui mène au progrès. Parfois ces formes de névrose se présentent pures ; mais on les trouve plus souvent combinées entre elles ou avec une affection psychonévrotique. Mais cette dernière circonstance ne nous autorise pas à renoncer à leur division. Pensez seulement à la différence que la minéralogie établit entre minéraux et roches. Les minéraux sont décrits comme des individus, en raison sans doute de cette circonstance qu'ils se présentent souvent comme cristaux, nettement circonscrits et séparés de leur entourage. Les roches se composent d'amas de minéraux dont l'association, loin d'être accidentelle, et sans nul doute déterminée par les conditions de leur formation. En ce qui concerne la théorie des névroses, nous savons encore trop peu de choses relativement au point de départ du développement pour édifier sur ce sujet une théorie analogue à celle des roches. Mais nous sommes incontestablement dans le vrai lorsque nous commençons par isoler de la masse les entités cliniques que nous connaissons et qui, elles, peuvent être comparées aux minéraux.

Il existe, entre les symptômes des névroses actuelles et ceux des psychonévroses, une relation intéressante et qui fournit une contribution importante à la connaissance de la formation de symptômes dans ces dernières : le symptôme de la névrose actuelle constitue souvent le noyau et la phase préliminaire du symptôme psychonévrotique. On observe plus particulièrement cette relation entre la neurasthénie et la névrose de transfert appelée hystérie de conversion, entre la névrose d'angoisse et l'hystérie d'angoisse, mais aussi entre l'hypocondrie et les formes que nous désignerons sous le nom de paraphrénie (démence précoce et paranoïa). Prenons comme exemple le mal de tête ou les douleurs lombaires hystériques. L'analyse nous montre que, par la condensation et le déplacement, ces douleurs sont devenues une satisfaction substitutive pour toute une série de fantaisies ou de souvenirs libidineux. Mais il fut un temps où ces douleurs étaient réelles, où elles étaient un symptôme direct d'une intoxication sexuelle, l'expression corporelle d'une excitation libidineuse. Nous ne prétendons pas que tous les symptômes hystériques contiennent un noyau de ce genre ; il n'en reste pas moins que ce cas est particulièrement fréquent et que l'hystérie utilise de préférence, pour la formation de ses symptômes, toutes les influences, normales et pathologiques, que l'excitation libidineuse exerce sur le corps. Ils jouent alors le rôle de ces grains de sable qui ont recouvert de couches de nacre la coquille abritant l'animal. Les signes passagers de l'excitation sexuelle, ceux qui accompagnent l'acte sexuel, sont de même utilisés par la psychonévrose, comme les matériaux les plus commodes et les plus appropriés pour la formation de symptômes.

SIGMUND FREUD[15]

15. *Introduction à la psychanalyse*, p. 363-369.

« *Nous trouverons également significatif le fait que ce premier état d'angoisse est provoqué par la séparation qui s'opère entre la mère et l'enfant* » (*Gravure du début du* XIXe *siècle*).

Chapitre IV

La théorie de l'angoisse

Dans ce chapitre, nous allons découvrir comment s'élabore la théorie freudienne de l'angoisse à travers l'étude des névroses. On considère en général que la théorie de l'angoisse a subi un remaniement fondamental en 1926, date à laquelle Freud publie Inhibition, symptôme et angoisse. *Aussi donnons-nous ci-dessous l'extrait le plus significatif de cet ouvrage, dans lequel Freud discute ses premières vues sur la question pour leur en substituer de nouvelles.*

*Mais, avant cela, nous prendrons connaissance d'un autre extrait d'*Introduction à la psychanalyse, *écrit en 1917, et dans lequel Freud synthétise l'ensemble de ses conceptions initiales sur le problème de l'angoisse. Il y reprend en particulier ses idées sur la névrose d'angoisse en tant que névrose actuelle, dont l'affect de déplaisir — l'angoisse — naît de l'impossibilité de décharger l'excitation libidinale du fait de circonstances extérieures. Redisons-le : cette angoisse n'est pas psychiquement élaborée et ne s'enracine pas dans des conflits infantiles. Selon Freud, tout affect d'angoisse est calqué sur un prototype universel : l'angoisse de la naissance. Otto Rank, dans un ouvrage intitulé* le Traumatisme de la naissance[1] *(1924), a étendu ces vues à l'ensemble des troubles mentaux : pour lui, en effet, tous les conflits ultérieurs du sujet peuvent et doivent être ramenés à cet événement originel. Nous avons souligné qu'en revanche, pour Freud, cet événement reçoit après coup une coloration particulière provenant du conflit œdipien et de ce qui lui est inhérent : la crainte de castration. La menace de séparation d'avec le pénis donne en effet tout leur sens aux séparations antérieures, dont la séparation d'avec le corps de la mère au moment de la naissance. Cette discussion autour du complexe de castration et de l'angoisse est ici reprise dans* Inhibition, symptôme et angoisse.

---

1. Voir *la Castration : un fantasme originaire* (chap. IV), paru dans la même collection, et Otto Rank, *le Traumatisme de la naissance* (Payot).

*Dans l'extrait d'*Introduction à la psychanalyse *présenté ci-dessous, Freud va montrer de façon précise comment l'angoisse, flottante dans la névrose d'angoisse, devient une angoisse fixée dans les phobies. Freud y distingue les phobies non organisées et qui sont universellement répandues — telle la phobie des serpents, celle des araignées et celle de la solitude — des phobies névrotiques proprement dites, auxquelles il donne le nom d'hystéries d'angoisse pour les rapprocher des hystéries de conversion.*

Il aborde également le cas des névrosés obsessionnels, que l'angoisse semble épargner. Cependant l'angoisse les submerge lorsqu'ils ne peuvent exécuter leur cérémonial obsessionnel. Celui-ci a donc pour fonction de permettre au patient d'échapper à l'angoisse, l'acte obsédant — le symptôme — représentant un substitut de l'angoisse. Si, dans la névrose d'angoisse, l'angoisse provient d'une tension libidinale non assouvie, l'analyse de l'hystérie et des névroses obsessionnelles montre que l'angoisse y est liée, en dernière analyse, à des facteurs psychiques, d'où résulte également la non-satisfaction libidinale. C'est en effet le refoulement *qui empêche la libido de se décharger et qui la transforme en angoisse. Toutefois, comme nous venons de le voir dans la névrose obsessionnelle, l'acte obsédant — lorsqu'il n'est pas gêné dans son accomplissement — permet de faire taire l'angoisse. Freud inverse dans* Inhibition, symptôme et angoisse *les termes de sa proposition initiale : ce n'est plus « le refoulement qui crée l'angoisse », mais « l'angoisse qui crée le refoulement ».*

Soulignons encore ceci : on considère habituellement que la notion de signal d'angoisse[2] *apparaît en 1926 dans* Inhibition, symptôme et angoisse, *avec le remaniement de la théorie de l'angoisse. Cependant, neuf ans auparavant, dans* Introduction à la psychanalyse, *Freud parle déjà de l'angoisse comme d'un signal mettant le psychisme « en état de préparation ». Cette idée anticipe sur les vues qu'il exprimera en 1920, dans* Au-delà du principe de plaisir, *à propos des rêves de névrose traumatique[3] : lorsqu'il y a trauma, l'angoisse n'a pu se former pour jouer son rôle de signal ; ainsi, le psychisme est empêché de se préparer au danger. L'angoisse a en effet pour fonction, en cas de danger — vécu sur le plan de la réalité psychique —, de surinvestir les systèmes qui auront à recevoir l'excitation, créant ainsi une défense contre celle-ci. Cependant, six ans plus tard, dans* Inhibition, symptôme et angoisse, *Freud définira le Moi (différencié en tant qu'instance psy-*

---

2. Le signal d'angoisse, déclenché par le Moi devant un danger, a pour fonction d'éviter à ce dernier d'être submergé par des excitations auxquelles il ne pourrait faire face, en mobilisant des défenses. Le Moi agit, en quelque sorte, en envoyant un ballon-sonde pour mesurer le danger et l'anticiper.

3. Voir *les Rêves, voie royale de l'inconscient*, dans la même collection.

chique depuis 1923[4]*) comme le lieu de l'angoisse. Le signal d'angoisse intervient donc au cours du développement lorsque le Moi est suffisamment mature. Avant cela, l'angoisse est un phénomène « automatique », qui survient lorsque l'*infans*, le nourrisson, est encore en état de détresse*[5]*. En fait, Freud distingue dans ce texte une succession de formes d'angoisse, liées aux différentes étapes du développement :*

— *Dans un premier temps, l'appareil psychique du petit enfant, dépourvu d'un pare excitations suffisant, est incapable de maîtriser les excitations d'origine interne ou externe. Le Moi est à peine ébauché et l'angoisse revêt le caractère « automatique » et traumatique que nous venons de décrire.*

— *Comme, du fait de la prématuration humaine, l'enfant dépend d'autrui pour sa survie, il va bientôt connaître une seconde source d'angoisse : la perte d'amour ou la séparation d'avec ses objets (la mère). Nous avons vu le rôle que joue le sevrage dans cette forme d'angoisse*[6]*.*

— *Au moment de l'Œdipe (où, en principe, le Moi pleinement formé est le lieu de l'angoisse), la crainte de perdre le pénis est devenue la source d'angoisse fondamentale, qui donne, après coup, tout leur sens aux précédentes variétés d'angoisse.*

— *Enfin, la période post-œdipienne serait marquée par l'angoisse devant le Surmoi. Chez le névrosé, les anciennes sources d'angoisse restent actives et malgré le développement du Moi, il est à même d'être submergé par les excitations.*

Pour clore ce chapitre, nous découvrirons un extrait de la quatrième des Nouvelles Conférences sur la psychanalyse, *intitulée « l'Angoisse et la Vie instinctuelle ». Cette série de sept conférences fictives (Freud s'y adresse à un auditoire imaginaire) fut publiée le 6 décembre 1932, mais porte la date de 1933. Freud y retrace l'évolution de sa pensée depuis l'*Introduction à la psychanalyse, *quinze ans plus tôt.*

Il est certain que le problème de l'angoisse forme un point vers lequel convergent les questions les plus diverses et les plus importantes, une énigme dont la solution devrait projeter des flots de lumière sur toute notre vie psychique. Je ne dis pas que je vous en donnerai la solution complète, mais vous prévoyez sans doute que la psychanalyse

---

4. Voir *le Ça, le Moi, le Surmoi : la personnalité et ses instances*, dans la même collection.
5. Situation du nourrisson qui, en raison de son impuissance motrice, n'est pas encore capable de soulager les tensions internes nées de ses besoins (soif, faim...).
6. In volume II : *le Complexe de castration : un fantasme originaire*.

s'attaquera à ce problème, comme à tant d'autres, par des moyens différents de ceux dont se sert la médecine traditionnelle. Celle-ci porte son principal intérêt sur le point de savoir quel est le déterminisme anatomique de l'angoisse. Elle déclare qu'il s'agit d'une irritation du bulbe, et le malade apprend qu'il souffre d'une névrose du vague. Le bulbe, ou moelle allongée, est un objet très sérieux et très beau. Je me rappelle fort bien ce que son étude m'a coûté jadis de temps et de peine. Mais je dois avouer aujourd'hui qu'au point de vue de la compréhension psychologique de l'angoisse rien ne peut m'être plus indifférent que la connaissance du trajet nerveux suivi par les excitations qui émanent du bulbe.

Et, tout d'abord, on peut parler longtemps de l'angoisse sans songer à la nervosité en général. Vous me comprendrez sans autre explication si je désigne cette angoisse sous le nom d'angoisse *réelle,* par opposition à l'angoisse *névrotique.* Or, l'angoisse réelle nous apparaît comme quelque chose de très rationnel et compréhensible. Nous dirons qu'elle est une réaction à la perception d'un danger extérieur, c'est-à-dire d'une lésion attendue, prévue, qu'elle est associée au réflexe de la fuite et qu'on doit par conséquent la considérer comme une manifestation de l'instinct de conservation.

« L'HOMME SE DÉFEND CONTRE LA TERREUR PAR L'ANGOISSE »

Nous nous ferons peut-être une idée plus exacte de l'angoisse en analysant de plus près la situation qu'elle crée. Nous trouvons tout d'abord que le sujet est préparé au danger, ce qui se manifeste par une exaltation de l'attention sensorielle et de la tension motrice. Cet état d'attente et de préparation est incontestablement un état favorable, sans lequel le sujet se trouverait exposé à des conséquences graves. De cet état découlent, d'une part, l'action motrice : fuite d'abord et, à un degré supérieur, défense active ; d'autre part, ce que nous éprouvons comme un état d'angoisse. Plus le développement de l'angoisse est restreint, plus celle-ci n'apparaît que comme un appendice, un signal, et plus le processus qui consiste dans la transformation de l'état de préparation anxieuse en action, s'accomplit rapidement et rationnellement. C'est ainsi que, dans ce que nous appelons angoisse, l'état de préparation m'apparaît comme l'élément utile, tandis que le développement de l'angoisse me semble contraire au but.

Je laisse de côté la question de savoir si le langage courant désigne par les mots *angoisse, peur, terreur,* la même chose ou des choses diffé-

rentes. Il me semble que l'angoisse se rapporte à l'état et fait abstraction de l'objet, tandis que dans la peur l'attention se trouve précisément
concentrée sur l'objet. Le mot *terreur* me semble, en revanche, avoir
une signification toute spéciale, en désignant notamment l'action d'un
danger auquel on n'était pas préparé par un état d'angoisse préalable.
On peut dire que l'homme se défend contre la terreur par l'angoisse.

L'ANGOISSE DE LA NAISSANCE, PROTOTYPE DES ANGOISSES ULTÉRIEURES

En ce qui concerne l'état affectif caractérisé par l'angoisse, nous
croyons savoir quelle est l'impression reculée qu'il reproduit en la
répétant. Nous nous disons que ce ne peut être que la *naissance*, c'est-
à-dire l'acte dans lequel se trouvent réunies toutes les sensations de
peine, toutes les tendances de décharge et toutes les sensations corporelles dont l'ensemble est devenu comme le prototype de l'effet produit
par un danger grave et que nous avons depuis éprouvées à de multiples
reprises en tant qu'état d'angoisse. C'est l'augmentation énorme de
l'irritation consécutive à l'interruption du renouvellement du sang (de
la respiration interne) qui fut alors la cause de la sensation d'angoisse :
la première angoisse fut donc de nature toxique. Le mot *angoisse* (du
latin *angustiae,* étroitesse ; *Angst* en allemand) fait précisément ressortir la gêne, l'étroitesse de la respiration qui existait alors comme effet
de la situation réelle et qui se reproduit aujourd'hui régulièrement dans
l'état affectif. Nous trouverons également significatif le fait que ce premier état d'angoisse est provoqué par la séparation qui s'opère entre la
mère et l'enfant. Nous pensons naturellement que la prédisposition à la
répétition de ce premier état d'angoisse a été, à travers un nombre
incalculable de générations, à ce point incorporée à l'organisme que
nul individu ne peut échapper à cet état affectif, fût-il, comme le légen-
daire Macduff, « arraché des entrailles de sa mère », c'est-à-dire fût-il
venu au monde autrement que par la naissance naturelle. Nous ignorons quel a pu être le prototype de l'état d'angoisse chez des animaux
autres que les mammifères. C'est pourquoi nous ignorons également
l'ensemble des sensations qui, chez ces êtres, correspond à notre
angoisse.

Vous serez peut-être curieux d'apprendre comment on a pu arriver à
l'idée que c'est l'acte de la naissance qui constitue la source et le prototype de l'état affectif caractérisé par l'angoisse. L'idée est aussi peu spé-
culative que possible ; j'y suis plutôt arrivé en puisant dans la naïve
pensée du peuple. Un jour — il y a longtemps de cela ! — que nous
étions réunis, plusieurs jeunes médecins des hôpitaux, au restaurant

autour d'une table, l'assistant de la clinique obstétricale nous raconta un fait amusant qui s'était produit au cours du dernier examen de sages-femmes. Une candidate, à laquelle on avait demandé ce que signifie la présence de méconium dans les eaux pendant le travail d'accouchement, répondit sans hésiter : « que l'enfant éprouve de l'angoisse ». Cette réponse a fait rire les examinateurs qui ont refusé la candidate. Quant à moi, j'avais, dans mon for intérieur, pris parti pour celle-ci et commencé à soupçonner que la pauvre femme du peuple avait eu la juste intuition d'une relation importante.

L'« ATTENTE ANXIEUSE » DE MALHEURS À VENIR CARACTÉRISE LA NÉVROSE D'ANGOISSE

Pour passer à l'angoisse des nerveux, quelles sont les nouvelles manifestations et les nouveaux rapports qu'elle présente ? Il y a beaucoup à dire à ce sujet. Nous trouvons, en premier lieu, un état d'angoisse général, une angoisse pour ainsi dire flottante, prête à s'attacher au contenu de la première représentation susceptible de lui fournir un prétexte, influant sur les jugements, choisissant les attentes, épiant toutes les occasions pour se trouver une justification. Nous appelons cet état « angoisse d'attente » ou « attente anxieuse ». Les personnes tourmentées par cette angoisse prévoient toujours les plus terribles de toutes les éventualités, voient dans chaque événement accidentel le présage d'un malheur, penchent toujours pour le pire, lorsqu'il s'agit d'un fait ou événement incertain. La tendance à cette attente de malheur est un trait de caractère propre à beaucoup de personnes qui, à part cela, ne paraissent nullement malades ; on leur reproche leur humeur sombre, leur pessimisme ; mais l'angoisse d'attente existe régulièrement et à un degré bien prononcé dans une affection nerveuse à laquelle j'ai donné le nom de *névrose d'angoisse* et que je range parmi les névroses actuelles.

DES ANGOISSES « SANS APPEL » ASSOCIÉES AUX PHOBIES

Une autre forme de l'angoisse présente, au contraire de celle que je viens de décrire, des attaches plutôt psychiques et est associée à certains objets ou situations. C'est l'angoisse qui caractérise les si nombreuses et souvent si singulières « phobies ». L'éminent psychologue

« Cela ressemble à l'énumération des dix plaies d'Égypte.
Avec cette différence que les phobies sont beaucoup plus nombreuses »
(Gravure de Gustave Doré, Bibliothèque des Arts Décoratifs).

américain Stanley Hall s'est un jour donné la peine de nous présenter toute une série de ces phobies sous de pimpants noms grecs. Cela ressemble à l'énumération des dix plaies d'Égypte, avec cette différence que les phobies sont beaucoup plus nombreuses. Écoutez tout ce qui peut devenir objet ou contenu d'une phobie : obscurité, air libre, espaces découverts, chats, araignées, chenilles, serpents, souris, orage, pointes aiguës, sang, espaces clos, foules humaines, solitude, traversée de ponts, voyage sur mer ou en chemin de fer, etc., etc. Le premier essai d'orientation dans ce chaos laisse entrevoir la possibilité de distinguer trois groupes. Quelques-uns de ces objets ou situations redoutés ont quelque chose de sinistre, même pour nous autres normaux auxquels ils rappellent un danger ; c'est pourquoi ces phobies ne nous paraissent pas incompréhensibles, bien que nous leur trouvions une intensité exagérée. C'est ainsi que la plupart d'entre nous éprouvent un sentiment de répulsion à la vue d'un serpent. On peut même dire que la phobie des serpents est une phobie répandue dans l'humanité entière, et Ch. Darwin a décrit d'une façon impressionnante l'angoisse qu'il avait éprouvée à la vue d'un serpent qui se dirigeait sur lui, bien qu'il en fût protégé par un épais disque de verre. Dans un deuxième groupe nous rangeons les cas où il existe bien un rapport avec un danger, mais un danger que nous avons l'habitude de négliger et de ne pas faire entrer dans nos calculs. Nous savons que le voyage en chemin de fer comporte un risque d'accident de plus que si nous restons chez nous, à savoir le danger d'une collision ; nous savons également qu'un bateau peut couler et que nous pouvons ainsi mourir noyés, et cependant nous voyageons en chemin de fer et en bateau sans angoisse, sans penser à ces dangers. Il est également certain qu'on serait précipité à l'eau si le pont s'écroulait au moment où on le franchit, mais cela arrive si rarement qu'on ne tient aucun compte de ce danger possible. La solitude, à son tour, présente certains dangers et nous l'évitons dans certaines circonstances ; mais il ne s'ensuit pas que nous ne puissions sous aucun prétexte et dans quelque condition que ce soit supporter un moment de solitude. Tout cela s'applique également aux foules, aux espaces clos, à l'orage, etc. Ce qui nous paraît étrange dans ces phobies des névrosés, c'est moins leur contenu que leur intensité. L'angoisse causée par les phobies est tout simplement sans appel ! Et nous avons parfois l'impression que les névrosés n'éprouvent pas leur angoisse devant les mêmes objets et situations qui, dans certaines circonstances, peuvent également provoquer notre angoisse à nous, et auxquels ils donnent les mêmes noms.

L'HYSTÉRIE D'ANGOISSE OU PHOBIE :
UNE NÉVROSE TRÈS PROCHE
DE L'HYSTÉRIE DE CONVERSION

Il reste encore un troisième groupe de phobies, mais il s'agit de phobies qui échappent à notre compréhension. Quand nous voyons un homme mûr, robuste, éprouver de l'angoisse, lorsqu'il doit traverser une rue ou une place de sa ville natale dont il connaît tous les recoins, ou une femme en apparence bien portante éprouver une terreur insensée parce qu'un chat a frôlé le rebord de sa jupe ou qu'une souris s'est glissée à travers la pièce, comment pouvons-nous établir un rapport entre l'angoisse de l'un et de l'autre, d'une part, et le danger qui évidemment n'existe que pour le phobique, d'autre part ? Pour ce qui est des phobies ayant pour objets les animaux, il ne peut évidemment pas s'agir d'une exagération d'antipathies humaines générales, car nous avons la preuve du contraire dans le fait que de nombreuses personnes ne peuvent passer à côté d'un chat sans l'appeler et le caresser. La souris si redoutée des femmes a prêté son nom à une expression de tendresse de premier ordre : telle jeune fille, qui est charmée de s'entendre appeler « ma petite souris » par son fiancé, pousse un cri d'horreur lorsqu'elle aperçoit le gracieux petit animal de ce nom. En ce qui concerne les hommes ayant l'angoisse des rues et des places, nous ne trouvons pas d'autre moyen d'expliquer leur état qu'en disant qu'ils se conduisent comme des enfants. L'éducation inculque directement à l'enfant qu'il doit éviter comme dangereuses des situations de ce genre, et notre agoraphobe cesse en effet d'éprouver de l'angoisse lorsqu'il traverse la place accompagné de quelqu'un.

Les deux formes d'angoisse que nous venons de décrire, l'angoisse d'attente, libre de toute attache, et l'angoisse associée aux phobies, sont indépendantes l'une de l'autre. On ne peut pas dire que l'une représente une phase plus avancée que l'autre, et elles n'existent simultanément que d'une façon exceptionnelle et comme accidentelle. L'état d'angoisse générale le plus prononcé ne se manifeste pas fatalement par des phobies ; des personnes dont la vie est empoisonnée par de l'agoraphobie peuvent être totalement exemptes de l'angoisse d'attente, source de pessimisme. Il est prouvé que certaines phobies, phobie de l'espace, phobie du chemin de fer, etc., ne sont acquises qu'à l'âge mûr, tandis que d'autres, phobie de l'obscurité, phobie de l'orage, phobie des animaux, semblent avoir existé dès les premières années de la vie. Celles-là ont toute la signification de maladies graves ; celles-ci apparaissent comme des singularités, des lubies. Lorsqu'un sujet présente une phobie de ce dernier groupe, on est autorisé à soupçonner qu'il en

« Telle jeune fille, qui est charmée de s'entendre appeler
« ma petite souris » par son fiancé, pousse un cri d'horreur lorsqu'elle aperçoit
le gracieux petit animal de ce nom »
(Estampe japonaise, fin du XIXe siècle, Bibliothèque
des Arts Décoratifs).

a encore d'autres du même genre. Je dois ajouter que nous rangeons toutes ces phobies dans le cadre de l'*hystérie d'angoisse,* c'est-à-dire que nous les considérons comme une affection très proche de l'hystérie de conversion.

TOUTE ANGOISSE DOIT AVOIR UNE CAUSE

La troisième forme d'angoisse névrotique nous met en présence d'une énigme qui consiste en ce que nous perdons entièrement de vue les rapports existant entre l'angoisse et le danger menaçant. Dans l'hystérie, par exemple, cette angoisse accompagne les autres symptômes hystériques, ou encore elle peut se produire dans n'importe quelles conditions d'excitation ; de sorte que, nous attendant à une manifestation affective, nous sommes tout étonnés d'observer l'angoisse qui, elle, est la manifestation à laquelle nous nous attendions le moins. Enfin, l'angoisse peut encore se produire sans rapport avec des conditions quelconques, d'une façon aussi incompréhensible pour nous que pour le malade, comme un accès spontané et libre, sans qu'il puisse être question d'un danger ou d'un prétexte dont l'exagération aurait eu pour effet cet accès. Nous constatons, au cours de ces accès spontanés, que l'ensemble auquel nous donnons le nom d'état d'angoisse est susceptible de dissociation. L'ensemble de l'accès peut être remplacé par un symptôme unique, d'une grande intensité, tel que tremblement, vertige, palpitations, oppression, le sentiment général d'après lequel nous reconnaissons l'angoisse faisant défaut ou étant à peine marqué. Et cependant ces états que nous décrivons sous le nom d'« équivalents de l'angoisse » doivent être sous tous les rapports, cliniques et étiologiques, assimilés à l'angoisse.

Ici surgissent deux questions. Existe-t-il un lien quelconque entre l'angoisse névrotique, dans laquelle le danger ne joue aucun rôle ou ne joue qu'un rôle minime, et l'angoisse réelle qui est toujours et essentiellement une réaction à un danger ? Comment faut-il comprendre cette angoisse névrotique ? C'est que nous voudrions avant tout sauvegarder le principe : chaque fois qu'il y a angoisse, il doit y avoir quelque chose qui provoque cette angoisse.

UN RAPPORT CONFIRMÉ
PAR LES FAITS CLINIQUES
ENTRE LA LIBIDO ET L'ANGOISSE

L'observation clinique nous fournit un certain nombre d'éléments susceptibles de nous aider à comprendre l'angoisse névrotique. Je vais en discuter la signification devant vous.

a) Il n'est pas difficile d'établir que l'angoisse d'attente ou l'état d'angoisse général dépend dans une très grande mesure de certains processus de la vie sexuelle ou, plus exactement, de certaines applications de la libido. Le cas le plus simple et le plus instructif de ce genre nous est fourni par les personnes qui s'exposent à l'excitation dite fruste, c'est-à-dire chez lesquelles de violentes excitations sexuelles ne trouvent pas une dérivation suffisante, n'aboutissent pas à une fin satisfaisante. Tel est, par exemple, le cas des hommes pendant la durée des fiançailles, et des femmes dont les maris ne possèdent pas une puissance sexuelle normale ou abrègent ou font avorter par précaution l'acte sexuel. Dans ces circonstances, l'excitation libidineuse disparaît, pour céder la place à l'angoisse, sous la forme soit de l'angoisse d'attente, soit d'un accès ou d'un équivalent d'accès. L'interruption de l'acte sexuel par mesure de précaution, lorsqu'elle devient le régime sexuel normal, constitue chez les hommes, et surtout chez les femmes, une cause tellement fréquente de névrose d'angoisse que la pratique médicale nous ordonne, toutes les fois que nous nous trouvons en présence de cas de ce genre, de penser avant tout à cette étiologie. En procédant ainsi, on aura plus d'une fois l'occasion de constater que la névrose d'angoisse disparaît dès que le sujet renonce à la restriction sexuelle.

Autant que je sache, le rapport entre la restriction sexuelle et les états d'angoisse est reconnu même par des médecins étrangers à la psychanalyse. Mais je suppose qu'on essaiera d'intervertir le rapport, en admettant notamment qu'il s'agit de personnes qui pratiquent la restriction sexuelle parce qu'elles étaient d'avance prédisposées à l'angoisse. Cette manière de voir est démentie catégoriquement par l'attitude de la femme dont l'activité sexuelle est essentiellement de nature passive, c'est-à-dire subissant la direction de l'homme. Plus une femme a de tempérament, plus elle est portée aux rapports sexuels, plus elle est capable d'en retirer une satisfaction, et plus elle réagira à l'impuissance de l'homme et au *coitus interruptus* par des phénomènes d'angoisse, alors que ces phénomènes seront à peine apparents chez une femme atteinte d'anesthésie sexuelle ou peu libidineuse.

L'abstinence sexuelle, si chaudement préconisée de nos jours par des médecins, ne favorise naturellement la production d'états d'angoisse que dans les cas où la libido, qui ne trouve pas de dérivation satisfaisante, présente un certain degré d'intensité et n'a pas été pour la plus grande partie supprimée par la sublimation. La production de l'état morbide dépend toujours de facteurs quantitatifs. Mais alors même qu'on envisage non plus la maladie, mais le simple caractère de la personne, on reconnaît facilement que la restriction sexuelle est le fait de personnes ayant un caractère indécis, enclines au doute et à l'angoisse, alors que le caractère intrépide, courageux est le plus souvent incompatible avec la restriction sexuelle. Quelles que soient les modifications et les complications que les nombreuses influences de la vie civilisée puissent imprimer à ces rapports entre le caractère et la vie sexuelle, il existe entre l'un et l'autre une relation des plus étroites.

Je suis loin de vous avoir fait part de toutes les observations qui confirment cette relation génétique entre la libido et l'angoisse. Il y aurait encore à parler, à ce propos, du rôle que jouent, dans la production de maladies caractérisées par l'angoisse, certaines phases de la vie qui, telles que la puberté et la ménopause, favorisent incontestablement l'exaltation de la libido. Dans certains cas d'excitation, on peut encore observer directement une combinaison d'angoisse et de libido et la substitution finale de celle-là à celle-ci. De ces faits se dégage une conclusion double : on a notamment l'impression qu'il s'agit d'une accumulation de libido dont le cours normal est entravé et que les processus auxquels on assiste sont tous et uniquement de nature somatique. On ne voit pas tout d'abord comment l'angoisse naît de la libido ; on constate seulement que la libido est absente et que sa place est prise par l'angoisse.

L'ANGOISSE : UNE « MONNAIE D'ÉCHANGE » DES REPRÉSENTATIONS REFOULÉES

b) Une autre indication nous est fournie par l'analyse des psychonévroses, et plus spécialement de l'hystérie. Nous savons déjà que dans cette affection l'angoisse apparaît souvent à titre d'accompagnement des symptômes, mais on y observe aussi une angoisse indépendante des symptômes et se manifestant soit par crises, soit comme état permanent. Les malades ne savent pas dire pourquoi ils éprouvent de l'angoisse, et ils rattachent leur état, à la suite d'une élaboration secondaire facile à reconnaître, aux phobies les plus courantes : phobie de la mort, de la folie, d'une attaque d'apoplexie. Lorsqu'on analyse la situation qui a engendré soit l'angoisse, soit les symptômes accompagnés d'angoisse, il est généralement possible de découvrir le courant psychique normal qui n'a pas abouti et a été remplacé par le phénomène d'angoisse. Ou, pour nous exprimer autrement, nous reprenons le processus inconscient comme s'il n'avait pas subi de refoulement et comme s'il avait poursuivi son développement sans obstacles, jusqu'à parvenir à la conscience. Ce processus aurait été accompagné d'un certain état affectif, et nous sommes tout surpris de constater que cet état affectif qui accompagne l'évolution normale du processus se trouve dans tous les cas refoulé et remplacé par de l'angoisse, quelle que soit sa qualité propre. Aussi bien, lorsque nous nous trouvons en présence d'un état d'angoisse hystérique, nous sommes en droit de supposer que son complément inconscient est constitué soit par un sentiment de même nature — angoisse, honte, confusion —, soit par une excitation positivement libidineuse, soit enfin par un sentiment hostile et agressif, tel que la fureur ou la colère. L'angoisse constitue donc la monnaie courante contre laquelle sont échangées ou peuvent être échangées toutes les excitations affectives, lorsque leur contenu a été éliminé de la représentation et a subi un refoulement.

LE NÉVROSÉ OBSESSIONNEL SE DÉFEND DE L'ANGOISSE GRÂCE À SES « RITUELS »

c) Une troisième expérience nous est offerte par les malades aux actes obsédants, malades qui semblent d'une façon assez remarquable épargnés par l'angoisse. Lorsque nous essayons d'empêcher ces malades d'exécuter leurs actes obsédants, ablutions, cérémonial, etc., ou lorsqu'ils osent eux-mêmes renoncer à l'une quelconque de leurs obsessions, ils éprouvent une angoisse terrible qui les oblige à céder à l'obsession. Nous comprenons alors que l'angoisse n'était que dissimulée derrière l'acte obsédant et que celui-ci n'était accompli que comme un moyen de se soustraire à l'angoisse. C'est ainsi que dans la névrose obsessionnelle l'angoisse n'apparaît pas au-dehors, parce qu'elle est remplacée par les symptômes ; et si nous nous tournons vers l'hystérie, nous y retrouvons la même situation comme résultat du refoulement : soit une angoisse pure, soit une angoisse accompagnant les symptômes, soit enfin un ensemble de symptômes plus complet, sans angoisse. Il semble donc permis de dire d'une manière abstraite que les symptômes ne se forment que pour empêcher le développement de l'angoisse qui, sans cela, surviendrait inévitablement. Cette conception place l'angoisse au centre même de l'intérêt que nous portons aux problèmes se rattachant aux névroses.

Nos observations relatives à la névrose d'angoisse nous ont fourni cette conclusion que la déviation de la libido de son application normale, déviation qui engendre l'angoisse, constitue l'aboutissement de processus purement somatiques. L'analyse de l'hystérie et des névroses obsessionnelles nous a permis de compléter cette conclusion, car elle nous a montré que déviation et angoisse peuvent également résulter du refus d'intervention de facteurs psychiques. C'est tout ce que nous savons sur le mode de production de l'angoisse névrotique ; si cela semble encore assez vague, je ne vois pas pour le moment de chemin susceptible de nous conduire plus loin.

L'ANGOISSE DE L'ENFANT DEVANT CE QUI EST NOUVEAU POUR LUI

D'une solution encore plus difficile semble l'autre problème que nous nous étions proposé de résoudre, celui d'établir les liens existant entre l'angoisse névrotique, qui résulte d'une application anormale de la libido, et l'angoisse réelle qui correspond à une réaction à un danger. On pourrait croire qu'il s'agit là de choses tout à fait disparates, et pourtant nous n'avons aucun moyen permettant de distinguer dans notre sensation l'une de ces angoisses de l'autre.

Mais le lien cherché apparaît aussitôt si nous prenons en considération l'opposition que nous avons tant de fois affirmée entre le Moi et la libido. Ainsi que nous le savons, l'angoisse survient par réaction du Moi à un danger et constitue le signal qui annonce et précède la fuite ; et rien ne nous empêche d'admettre par analogie que dans l'angoisse névrotique le Moi cherche également à échapper par la fuite aux exigences de la libido, qu'il se comporte à l'égard de ce danger intérieur tout comme s'il s'agissait d'un danger extérieur. Cette manière de voir autoriserait la conclusion que, toutes les fois qu'il y a de l'angoisse, il y a aussi quelque chose qui est cause de l'angoisse. Mais l'analogie peut être poussée encore plus loin. De même que la tentative de fuir devant un danger extérieur aboutit à l'arrêt et à la prise de mesures de défense nécessaires, de même le développement de l'angoisse est interrompu par la formation des symptômes auxquels elle finit par céder la place.

La difficulté de comprendre ces rapports réciproques entre l'angoisse et les symptômes se trouve maintenant ailleurs. L'angoisse qui signifie une fuite du Moi devant la libido est cependant engendrée par celle-ci. Ce fait, qui ne saute pas aux yeux, est cependant réel ; aussi ne devons-nous pas oublier que la libido d'une personne fait partie de celle-ci et ne peut pas s'opposer à elle comme quelque chose d'extérieur. Ce qui reste encore obscur pour nous, c'est la dynamique topique du développement de l'angoisse, c'est la question de savoir quelles sont les énergies psychiques qui sont dépensées dans ces occasions et de quels systèmes psychiques ces énergies proviennent. Je ne puis vous promettre de réponses à ces questions, mais nous ne négligerons pas de suivre deux autres traces et, ce faisant, de demander de nouveau à l'observation directe et à la recherche analytique une confirmation de nos déductions spéculatives. Nous allons donc nous occuper de la production de l'angoisse chez l'enfant et de la provenance de l'angoisse névrotique, associée aux phobies.

L'état d'angoisse chez l'enfant est chose très fréquente, et il est souvent très difficile de dire s'il s'agit d'angoisse névrotique ou réelle. La valeur de la distinction que nous pourrions établir le cas échéant se trouverait infirmée par l'attitude même de l'enfant. D'un côté, en effet, nous ne trouvons nullement étonnant que l'enfant éprouve de l'angoisse en présence de nouvelles personnes, de nouvelles situations et de nouveaux objets, et nous expliquons sans peine cette réaction par sa faiblesse et son ignorance. Nous attribuons donc à l'enfant un fort penchant pour l'angoisse réelle et trouverions tout à fait naturel que l'on vienne nous dire que l'enfant a apporté cet état d'angoisse en venant au monde, à titre de prédisposition héréditaire. L'enfant ne ferait ainsi que reproduire l'attitude de l'homme primitif et du sauvage de nos jours qui, en raison de leur ignorance et du manque de moyens de défense, éprouvent de l'angoisse devant tout ce qui est nouveau, devant des choses qui nous sont aujourd'hui familières et ne nous inspirent plus la moindre angoisse. Et il serait tout à fait conforme à notre attente, que les phobies de l'enfant soient également, en partie du moins, les mêmes que celles que nous attribuons à ces phases primitives du développement humain.

UNE DISPOSITION NÉVROTIQUE
À L'ANGOISSE
QUI PEUT
SE MANIFESTER DÈS L'ENFANCE

Il ne doit pas nous échapper, d'autre part, que tous les enfants ne sont pas sujets à l'angoisse dans la même mesure, et que ceux d'entre eux qui manifestent une angoisse particulière en présence de toutes sortes d'objets et de situations sont précisément de futurs névrosés. La disposition névrotique se traduit donc aussi par un penchant accentué à l'angoisse réelle, l'état d'angoisse apparaît comme l'état primaire, et l'on arrive à la conclusion que l'enfant, et plus tard l'adulte, éprouvent de l'angoisse devant la hauteur de leur libido, et cela précisément parce qu'ils éprouvent de l'angoisse à propos de tout. Cette manière de voir équivaut à nier que l'angoisse naisse de la libido et, en examinant toutes les conditions de l'angoisse réelle, on arriverait logiquement à la conception d'après laquelle c'est la conscience de sa propre faiblesse et de son impuissance, de sa moindre valeur, selon la terminologie de A. Adler, qui serait la cause première de la névrose, lorsque cette conscience, loin de finir avec l'enfance, persiste jusque dans l'âge mûr.

Ce raisonnement semble tellement simple et séduisant qu'il mérite de retenir notre attention. Il n'aurait toutefois pour conséquence que de déplacer l'énigme de la nervosité. La persistance du sentiment de moindre valeur et, par conséquent, de la condition de l'angoisse et des symptômes apparaît dans cette conception comme une chose tellement certaine que c'est plutôt l'état que nous appelons santé qui, lorsqu'il se trouve réalisé par hasard, aurait besoin d'explication. Mais que nous révèle l'observation attentive de l'état anxieux des enfants ? Le petit enfant éprouve tout d'abord de l'angoisse en présence de personnes étrangères, les situations ne jouent sous ce rapport un rôle que par les personnes qu'elles impliquent et, quant aux objets, ils ne viennent, en tant que générateurs d'angoisse, qu'en dernier lieu. Mais l'enfant n'éprouve de l'angoisse devant des personnes étrangères qu'à cause des mauvaises intentions qu'il leur attribue et parce qu'il compare sa faiblesse avec leur force, dans laquelle il voit un danger pour son existence, sa sécurité, son euphorie. Eh bien, cet enfant méfiant, vivant dans la peur d'une menace d'agression répandue dans tout l'univers, constitue une construction théorique peu heureuse. Il est plus exact de dire que l'enfant s'effraie à la vue d'un nouveau visage parce qu'il est habitué à la vue de cette personne familière et aimée qu'est la mère. Il éprouve une déception et une tristesse qui se transforment en angoisse ; il s'agit donc d'une libido devenue inutilisable et qui, ne pouvant pas alors être maintenue en suspension, trouve sa dérivation dans l'angoisse. Et ce n'est certainement pas par hasard que dans cette situation caractéristique de l'angoisse infantile se trouve reproduite la condition qui est celle du premier état d'angoisse accompagnant l'acte de la naissance, à savoir la séparation de la mère.

Les premières phobies de situation qu'on observe chez l'enfant sont celles qui se rapportent à l'obscurité et à la solitude ; la première persiste souvent toute la vie durant et les deux ont en commun l'absence de la personne aimée, dispensatrice de soins, c'est-à-dire de la mère. Un enfant, anxieux de se trouver dans l'obscurité, s'adresse à sa tante qui se trouve dans une pièce voisine : « Tante, parle-moi ; j'ai peur. — A quoi cela te servirait-il, puisque tu ne me vois pas ? » A quoi l'enfant répond : « Il fait plus clair lorsque quelqu'un parle. » La tristesse qu'on éprouve dans l'obscurité se transforme ainsi en angoisse devant l'obscurité. Il n'est donc pas seulement inexact de dire que l'angoisse névrotique est un phénomène secondaire et un cas spécial de l'angoisse réelle : nous voyons, en outre, chez le jeune enfant, se comporter comme angoisse quelque chose qui a en commun avec l'angoisse névrotique un trait essentiel : la provenance d'une libido inemployée. Quant à la véritable angoisse réelle, l'enfant semble ne la posséder qu'à un degré peu prononcé. Dans toutes les situations qui peuvent devenir plus tard des conditions de phobies, qu'il se trouve sur des hauteurs, sur des passages étroits au-dessus de l'eau, en chemin de fer ou en bateau, l'enfant ne manifeste aucune angoisse, et il en manifeste d'autant moins qu'il est plus ignorant. Il eût été désirable qu'il ait reçu en héritage un plus grand nombre d'instincts tendant à la préservation de la vie ; la tâche des surveillants chargés de l'empêcher de s'exposer à des dangers successifs en serait grandement facilitée. Mais, en réalité, l'enfant commence par s'exagérer ses forces et se comporte sans éprouver d'angoisse, parce qu'il ignore le danger. Il court au bord de l'eau, il monte sur l'appui d'une fenêtre, il joue avec des objets tranchants et avec du feu, bref il fait tout ce qui peut être nuisible et causer des soucis à son entourage. Ce n'est qu'à force d'éducation qu'on finit par faire naître en lui l'angoisse réelle, car on ne peut vraiment pas lui permettre de s'instruire par l'expérience personnelle.

S'il y a des enfants qui ont subi l'influence de cette éducation par l'angoisse dans une mesure telle qu'ils finissent par trouver d'eux-mêmes des dangers dont on ne leur a pas parlé et contre lesquels on ne les a pas mis en garde, cela tient à ce que leur constitution comporte un besoin libidineux plus prononcé, ou qu'ils ont de bonne heure contracté de mauvaises habitudes en ce qui concerne la satisfaction libidineuse. Rien d'étonnant si beaucoup de ces enfants deviennent plus tard des nerveux, car, ainsi que nous le savons, ce qui facilite le plus la naissance d'une névrose, c'est l'incapacité de supporter pendant un temps plus ou moins long un refoulement un peu considérable de la libido. Remarquez bien que nous tenons compte ici du facteur constitutionnel, dont nous n'avons d'ailleurs jamais contesté l'importance. Nous nous élevons seulement contre la conception qui néglige tous les autres facteurs au profit du seul facteur constitutionnel et accorde à celui-ci la première place, même dans les cas où, d'après les données de l'observation et de l'analyse, il n'a rien à voir ou ne joue qu'un rôle plus que secondaire.

Permettez-moi donc de résumer ainsi les résultats que nous ont fournis les observations sur l'état d'angoisse chez les enfants : l'angoisse infantile, qui n'a presque rien de commun avec l'angoisse réelle, s'approche, au contraire, beaucoup de l'angoisse névrotique des adultes ; elle naît, comme celle-ci, d'une libido inemployée et, n'ayant pas d'objet sur lequel elle puisse concentrer son amour, elle le remplace par un objet extérieur ou par une situation.

DES SYSTÈMES DE DÉFENSE
CONTRE L'ANGOISSE ÉLABORÉS
PAR LA NÉVROSE

Et maintenant, vous ne serez sans doute pas fâchés de m'entendre dire que l'analyse n'a plus beaucoup de nouveau à nous apprendre concernant les *phobies*. Dans celles-ci, en effet, les choses se passent exactement comme dans l'angoisse infantile : une libido inemployée subit sans cesse une transformation en une apparente angoisse réelle et, de ce fait, le moindre danger extérieur devient une substitution pour les exigences de la libido. Cette concordance entre les phobies et l'angoisse infantile n'a rien qui doive nous surprendre, car les phobies infantiles sont non seulement le prototype des phobies plus tardives que nous faisons rentrer dans le cadre de l'« hystérie d'angoisse », mais encore la condition directe préalable et le prélude de celles-ci. Toute phobie hystérique remonte à une angoisse infantile et la continue, alors même qu'elle a un autre contenu et doit recevoir une autre dénomination. Les deux affections ne diffèrent entre elles qu'au point de vue du mécanisme. Chez l'adulte il ne suffit pas, pour que l'angoisse se transforme en libido, que celle-ci, en tant que désir ardent, reste momentanément inemployée. C'est que l'adulte a appris depuis longtemps à tenir sa libido en suspension ou à l'employer autrement. Mais lorsque la libido fait partie d'un mouvement psychique ayant subi le refoulement, on retrouve la même situation que chez l'enfant qui ne sait pas encore faire une distinction entre le conscient et l'inconscient, et cette régression vers la phobie infantile fournit à la libido un moyen commode de se transformer en angoisse. Nous avons, vous vous en souvenez, beaucoup parlé du refoulement, mais en ayant toujours en vue le sort de la représentation qui devait subir le refoulement, et cela naturellement parce qu'il se laisse plus facilement constater et exposer. Quant au sort de l'état affectif associé à la représentation refoulée, nous l'avions toujours laissé de côté, et c'est seulement maintenant que nous apprenons que le premier sort de cet état affectif consiste à subir la transformation en angoisse, quelle qu'aurait pu être sa qualité dans des conditions normales. Cette transformation de l'état affectif constitue la partie de beaucoup la plus importante du processus de refoulement. Il n'est pas très facile d'en parler, attendu que nous ne pouvons pas affirmer l'existence d'états affectifs inconscients de la même manière dont nous affirmons l'existence de représentations inconscientes. Qu'elle soit consciente ou inconsciente, une représentation reste toujours la même, à une seule différence près, et nous pouvons très bien dire ce qui correspond à une représentation inconsciente. Mais un état affectif est un processus de décharge et doit être jugé tout autrement qu'une représentation ; sans avoir analysé et élucidé à fond nos prémisses relatives aux processus psychiques, nous sommes dans l'impossibilité de dire ce qui dans l'inconscient correspond à l'état affectif. Aussi bien est-ce un travail que nous ne pouvons pas entreprendre ici. Mais nous voulons rester sous l'impression que nous avons acquise, à savoir que le développement de l'angoisse se rattache étroitement au système de l'inconscient.

J'ai dit que la transformation en angoisse ou, plus exactement, la décharge sous la forme d'angoisse, constitue le premier sort réservé à la libido qui subit le refoulement. Je dois ajouter que ce n'est ni son seul sort, ni son sort définitif. Au cours des névroses se déroulent des processus qui tendent à entraver ce développement de l'angoisse et qui y réussissent de différentes manières. Dans les phobies, par exemple, on distingue nettement deux phases du processus névrotique. La première est celle du refoulement de la libido et de sa transformation en angoisse, laquelle est rattachée à un danger extérieur. Pendant la deuxième phase sont établies toutes les précautions et assurances destinées à empêcher le contact avec ce danger, qui est traité comme un fait extérieur. Le refoulement correspond à une tentative de fuite du Moi devant la libido, éprouvée comme un danger. La phobie peut être considérée comme un retranchement contre le danger extérieur qui remplace maintenant la libido redoutée. La faiblesse du système de défense employé dans les phobies réside naturellement dans ce fait que la forteresse, inattaquable du dehors, ne l'est pas du dedans. La projection à l'extérieur du danger représenté par la libido ne peut jamais réussir d'une façon parfaite. C'est pourquoi il existe dans les autres névroses d'autres systèmes de défense contre le développement possible de l'angoisse. Il s'agit là d'un chapitre très intéressant de la psychologie des névroses ; nous ne pouvons malheureusement pas l'aborder ici, car cela nous conduirait trop loin, d'autant plus que pour le comprendre il faut posséder des connaissances spéciales très approfondies.

SIGMUND FREUD[7]

7. *Introduction à la psychanalyse* (« l'Angoisse »), p. 370-388.

TOUS LES ACCÈS D'ANGOISSE
NE SONT PAS RÉDUCTIBLES
À L'ANGOISSE DE LA NAISSANCE

Nous nous représentons volontiers le Moi comme impuissant en face du Ça, mais quand il se dresse contre un processus pulsionnel du Ça, il lui suffit de donner un *signal de déplaisir* pour parvenir à ses fins, grâce à l'aide de l'instance pratiquement toute-puissante du principe de plaisir. Considérons pour un instant cette situation d'une manière isolée : nous pouvons l'illustrer par une comparaison empruntée à une autre sphère. Dans un état, une certaine clique se défend contre une mesure dont la promulgation correspondrait aux aspirations de la masse ; cette minorité s'empare alors de la presse, l'emploie à travailler l'« opinion publique » souveraine et aboutit à ce que la décision envisagée ne soit pas prise.

Mais cette première réponse soulève de nouvelles questions. D'où provient l'énergie employée à produire le signal de déplaisir ? L'idée suivante peut ici nous indiquer la voie : la défense contre un processus interne indésirable pourrait se faire sur le modèle de la défense contre une excitation externe, le Moi empruntant le même chemin pour se défendre contre le danger interne et contre le danger externe. En cas de danger externe, l'organisme recourt à une tentative de fuite ; d'abord il retire à la perception de l'objet dangereux son investissement ; plus tard il s'aperçoit que le moyen le plus efficace consiste à exécuter des actions musculaires telles que la perception du danger, sans même être refusée, devient impossible, donc que le moyen le plus efficace est de se soustraire à la sphère du danger. C'est bien à une telle tentative de fuite qu'est assimilable le refoulement. Le Moi retire son investissement (préconscient) au représentant pulsionnel à refouler, et l'utilise à libérer le déplaisir (l'angoisse). Certes, le problème de savoir comment l'angoisse surgit lors du refoulement n'est pas simple ; néanmoins, on est fondé à se tenir fermement à l'idée que le Moi est réellement le lieu de l'angoisse, et à repousser la conception antérieure, selon laquelle l'énergie d'investissement de la motion refoulée serait automatiquement transformée en angoisse. Si je me suis jamais exprimé ainsi jadis, ce que je donnais là n'avait valeur que de description phénoménologique, non pas de représentation métapsychologique.

Une nouvelle question dérive de ce qui précède : comment est-il possible, du point de vue économique, qu'un simple processus de retrait et de décharge, comme celui qui s'effectue lors du retrait de l'investissement préconscient du Moi, puisse produire du déplaisir ou de l'angoisse, alors qu'ils ne peuvent, selon nos postulats, résulter que

*« Les contenus de l'angoisse y (être dévoré par le loup) sont des substituts,
obtenus par déformation, du contenu : être châtré par le père ».
(Imagerie du début du XIXe siècle).*

d'une augmentation d'investissement ? Je réponds que l'on ne doit pas
chercher à expliquer cette production du point de vue économique, que
l'angoisse n'est pas produite, lors du refoulement, comme une manifestation nouvelle chaque fois, mais reproduit, sous forme d'état d'affect,
une image mnésique préexistante. Mais si nous allons plus loin, et si
nous posons la question de l'origine de cette angoisse — comme des
affects en général — nous quittons le terrain proprement psychologique
pour le domaine voisin de la physiologie. Les états d'affect sont incor-
porés à la vie psychique à titre de sédiments d'événements traumatiques très anciens, rappelés dans des situations analogues comme symboles mnésiques. Je pense que je n'avais pas tort de les assimiler aux
accès hystériques, qui se manifestent plus tard et sont acquis individuellement, et de les considérer comme leurs prototypes dans le
domaine du normal. Chez l'homme et les êtres qui lui sont apparentés,

126

l'acte de la naissance, première expérience individuelle d'angoisse, semble avoir conféré à l'expression de l'affect d'angoisse des traits caractéristiques. Toutefois, nous ne devons pas surestimer cette relation ; et la reconnaître ne saurait nous amener à oublier qu'un symbole d'affect est une nécessité biologique pour la situation de danger, et que de toute façon il eût été créé. Je tiens aussi pour injustifié d'admettre que ce qui se passe dans la vie psychique lors de chaque accès d'angoisse, revienne à reproduire la situation de la naissance. Même, il n'est pas certain que les accès hystériques, qui sont bien à l'origine de telles reproductions d'un traumatisme, conservent de façon durable ce caractère.

L'ANGOISSE DE CASTRATION
CHEZ DEUX CÉLÈBRES PATIENTS DE FREUD :
LE PETIT HANS ET L'HOMME AUX LOUPS

Nous aboutissons à un résultat inattendu : dans l'un et l'autre cas, le moteur du refoulement est l'angoisse de castration ; les contenus de l'angoisse : être mordu par le cheval, et être dévoré par le loup sont des substituts, obtenus par déformation, du contenu, être châtré par le père. C'est à proprement parler ce contenu qui a subi le refoulement. Dans le cas du malade russe[8], il était l'expression d'un désir qui ne pouvait subsister devant la révolte de la virilité ; il était, chez Hans, l'expression d'une réaction transformant l'agression en son contraire. Mais l'affect d'angoisse, qui constitue l'essence de la phobie, n'a pas pour origine le processus de refoulement, ni les investissements libidinaux des motions refoulées, mais le refoulant lui-même ; l'angoisse de la phobie d'animaux est l'angoisse de castration, inchangée, angoisse devant un danger réel[9] par conséquent, devant un danger effectivement menaçant ou du moins jugé réel. Ici, c'est l'angoisse qui produit le refoulement et non pas, comme je l'ai pensé jadis, le refoulement qui produit l'angoisse.

---

8. C'est-à-dire l'Homme aux Loups (N.d.E.)

9. En allemand : *Realangst*. Ce terme est constamment opposé par Freud à *neurotische Angst* ou *Triebangst* et désigne l'angoisse devant un danger extérieur quel qu'il soit, c'est-à-dire non pulsionnel. La paraphrase à laquelle nous nous résignons se justifie par l'impossibilité de traduire *Realangst* par angoisse réelle (l'angoisse névrotique est tout aussi réelle) : par angoisse devant le réel ou du réel (beaucoup trop général et métaphysique pour un danger toujours précis) ; par angoisse-Réel ou-Réalité (sur le modèle de *Realich* traduit par Moi-Réalité), car le « réel » n'est pas ici une instance, la Réalité, mais encore une fois tel danger bien déterminé. (N.d.T.)

Il est parfaitement inutile de nier, même si cette pensée m'est désagréable, que j'aie plus d'une fois soutenu la thèse que par le refoulement le représentant pulsionnel se voyait déformé, déplacé, etc., tandis que la libido de la motion pulsionnelle était transformée en angoisse. L'examen des phobies, qui, mieux que tout autre, eût été à même de prouver cette thèse, loin de la confirmer, on vient de le voir, semble plutôt la contredire directement. L'angoisse des phobies d'animaux est l'angoisse de castration du Moi, celle de l'agoraphobie, que l'on a étudiée moins à fond, paraît être une angoisse de tentation, qui doit bien dériver génétiquement de l'angoisse de castration. La plupart des phobies renvoient, à ce que nous voyons aujourd'hui, à une telle angoisse du Moi, devant les revendications de la libido. La position d'angoisse du Moi y est toujours l'élément primaire et ce qui pousse au refoulement. Jamais l'angoisse ne naît de la libido refoulée. Si jadis je m'étais contenté de dire qu'après le refoulement, apparaît, en lieu et place de la manifestation de libido attendue, une certaine quantité d'angoisse, je n'aurais aujourd'hui rien à retirer. La description est correcte, et il existe bien une correspondance du genre de celle que j'alléguais entre la force de la motion à refouler et l'intensité de l'angoisse résultante. Mais, je l'avoue, je croyais donner plus qu'une pure description, j'admettais que j'avais décelé le processus métapsychologique d'une transformation directe de la libido en angoisse, ce qu'aujourd'hui je ne puis donc plus maintenir. Faut-il ajouter que j'étais alors bien en peine d'indiquer comment s'accomplit une telle transformation ?

UN PROBLÈME QUI DEMEURE PARTIELLEMENT INSOLUBLE

D'où en tout état de cause, tirais-je l'idée de cette transformation ? De l'étude des névroses actuelles ; en un temps où nous étions encore très loin de distinguer entre des processus dans le Moi et des processus dans le Ça, je découvrais que certaines pratiques sexuelles, telles que le coït interrompu, l'excitation frustrée, l'abstinence forcée donnaient naissance à des accès d'angoisse et à une propension générale à l'angoisse, dans tous les cas, par conséquent, où l'excitation sexuelle se trouvait inhibée, retenue ou détournée dans son cours vers la satisfaction. Étant donné que l'excitation sexuelle est l'expression de motions pulsionnelles libidinales, il ne semblait pas téméraire d'admettre que la libido se transforme en angoisse sous l'influence de telles perturbations. De fait, cette observation est encore valable aujourd'hui, et, d'un autre côté, on ne saurait nier que la libido des processus du Ça ne subisse, sous l'impulsion du refoulement, une perturbation ; peut-être est-il donc toujours exact d'affirmer que, lors du refoulement, de l'angoisse se forme à partir de l'investissement libidinal des motions pulsionnelles. Mais comment mettre cette conclusion en accord avec cette autre, d'après laquelle l'angoisse des phobies est une angoisse du Moi, apparaît dans le Moi, et ne provient pas du refoulement mais le suscite ? Voilà une contradiction qui ne paraît pas facile à résoudre. On parviendra difficilement à ramener les deux origines de l'angoisse à une seule. Nous pourrions nous y essayer en faisant l'hypothèse que le Moi, dans la situation du coït perturbé, de l'excitation interrompue, de l'abstinence, flaire des dangers auxquels il réagit par de l'angoisse, mais il n'y a rien à tirer de cette hypothèse. D'autre part, l'analyse des phobies que nous avons entreprise ne semble pas admettre de correction. *Non liquet !*

SIGMUND FREUD[10]

DE QUOI L'ANXIEUX A-T-IL PEUR ?

Nous disons de l'angoisse névrotique qu'elle se manifeste de trois manières différentes : d'abord en tant qu'anxiété générale, angoisse flottante, prête à s'attacher à toutes les représentations nouvelles capables de lui en fournir le prétexte : c'est là ce qu'on appelle l'anxiété d'attente comme, par exemple, dans la névrose d'angoisse typique. Ensuite, en tant qu'angoisse fortement liée à des représentations déterminées, comme dans ce que nous appelons les *phobies*. Toutefois, nous pouvons trouver un rapport avec quelque danger extérieur, mais la crainte du danger en question nous semble extrêmement exagérée. Enfin, en tant qu'angoisse hystérique ou accompagnant des névroses graves. Tantôt elle est liée à d'autres symptômes, tantôt elle se produit indépendamment, par accès, tantôt encore elle persiste longtemps et forme un état stable, mais jamais, en tous cas, elle ne paraît motivée par un danger extérieur. Nous nous posons ensuite deux questions : de quoi l'anxieux a-t-il peur ? Quel rapport y a-t-il entre l'angoisse et la peur réelle des dangers extérieurs ?

Nos recherches ne sont pas demeurées infructueuses et nous avons pu obtenir quelques résultats importants. En ce qui concerne l'attente anxieuse, l'expérience clinique nous a montré qu'elle est toujours liée

10. *Inhibition, symptôme et angoisse*, p. 8-10, 27-29.

au contenu libidinal dans la vie sexuelle. La cause la plus fréquente de la névrose d'angoisse est l'excitation fruste, l'excitation libidinale provoquée, qui n'est ni satisfaite, ni utilisée. L'anxiété apparaît alors à la place de cette libido détournée de sa fonction. Je crois pouvoir dire que la libido insatisfaite se transforme directement en angoisse. Cette opinion paraît être confirmée par certaines phobies très courantes chez les petits enfants. Beaucoup de ces phobies nous semblent tout à fait énigmatiques, d'autres, au contraire, telles que la crainte de la solitude, la peur des personnes étrangères, s'expliquent très bien. La solitude, le visage inconnu, éveillent chez l'enfant le désir de revoir les traits familiers de sa mère. Ne pouvant ni dominer cette excitation libidinale, ni la tenir en suspens, il la transforme en angoisse. Cette angoisse enfantine ne se range pas dans la catégorie des angoisses réelles, mais bien dans celle des angoisses névrotiques. Les phobies enfantines, tout comme l'attente anxieuse de la névrose d'angoisse, nous offrent l'exemple de la formation d'une peur névrotique par transformation directe de la libido. Nous allons maintenant apprendre à connaître un second mécanisme assez proche du premier.

LE REFOULEMENT, « GRAND RESPONSABLE DE L'ANGOISSE ET DES AUTRES NÉVROSES »

Disons d'abord que le grand responsable de l'angoisse et des autres névroses, c'est, d'après nous, le processus du refoulement. Nous pensons pouvoir mieux qu'autrefois décrire ce processus en étudiant séparément le sort de l'idée destinée à être refoulée et celui de la libido dont cette idée était chargée. L'idée à refouler peut être déformée au point de devenir méconnaissable, mais sa charge en affect, quelle qu'en soit la forme : agression ou amour, est infailliblement transformée en angoisse. Peu importe dès lors la raison pour laquelle la charge en libido est rendue inutilisable, que ce soit par suite de la faiblesse infantile du Moi, comme dans les phobies d'enfants, par suite de processus somatiques dans la vie sexuelle, comme dans la névrose d'angoisse, ou par suite de refoulement comme dans l'hystérie. Les deux mécanismes de la formation d'angoisse névrotique coïncident donc, pour ainsi dire. Au cours de ces rercherches, nous avons pu noter l'existence du rapport très important qui existe entre la production de l'angoisse et la formation du symptôme. On observe là une action réciproque, les deux phénomènes pouvant se remplacer mutuellement, se suppléer l'un l'autre. La maladie de l'agoraphobe, par exemple, débute par un accès d'angoisse dans la rue. Cet accès se renouvellerait à chaque sortie, mais la formation du symptôme, qu'on peut aussi considérer comme une inhibition, comme un rétrécissement fonctionnel du Moi, épargne l'accès d'angoisse. C'est l'inverse qu'on constate lorsqu'on tente d'intervenir dans la formation du symptôme, dans les actes obsédants, par exemple. Si l'on empêche le malade d'accomplir son cérémonial de lavage, il tombe dans le très pénible état d'anxiété dont évidemment son symptôme le préservait. A la vérité, il semble que la production d'angoisse ait précédé la formation du symptôme, comme si les symptômes avaient été créés pour empêcher l'apparition de l'état anxieux. Autre confirmation : les premières névroses de l'enfance sont des phobies, des états qui montrent avec évidence que la production initiale d'angoisse est arrêtée par la formation ultérieure du symptôme ; on a l'impression que rien ne saurait mieux que ces relations nous faire comprendre l'angoisse névrotique. En même temps, nous avons réussi à savoir de quoi l'on a peur dans l'angoisse névrotique et nous sommes ainsi parvenus à établir le rapport entre les angoisses névrotiques et les angoisses réelles. Ce qu'on redoute, c'est évidemment sa propre libido. La peur névrotique diffère donc par deux points de la peur réelle : d'abord parce que le danger est intérieur et ensuite parce que la peur névrotique ne devient pas consciente.

Dans les phobies, l'on observe nettement que le danger intérieur s'est transformé en danger extérieur et que, par conséquent, la peur névrotique s'est muée en une peur en apparence réelle. Admettons, pour la commodité d'une explication difficile à donner, qu'il s'agisse d'un agoraphobe tourmenté par la crainte des tentations. Certaines rencontres dans la rue peuvent réveiller ces tentations.

Le malade opère donc un déplacement dans sa phobie et s'inquiète d'une situation extérieure. Il pense certainement s'assurer ainsi une protection plus efficace. On peut échapper par la fuite au péril extérieur, mais c'est une entreprise malaisée que de chercher à fuir un danger intérieur.

Je terminais ma précédente conférence sur l'angoisse en avouant que les divers résultats de nos recherches, s'ils n'étaient pas contradictoires, ne concordaient cependant pas entièrement. L'angoisse est, en tant qu'état affectif, la reproduction d'un événement passé et périlleux ; elle reste au service de l'instinct de conservation et sert à signaler les nouveaux dangers. Elle provient aussi d'une libido devenue en quelque sorte inutilisable et se produit dans le processus du refoulement. Remplacée par le symptôme, elle lui reste cependant psychiquement liée... L'on sent bien qu'il manque ici quelque chose pour rassembler en un seul bloc tous ces morceaux épars.

C'EST L'ANGOISSE QUI CRÉE LE REFOULEMENT

Mesdames, Messieurs, la division de la personnalité psychique en Surmoi, Moi et Ça, telle que je vous l'ai décrite dans ma dernière conférence, nous a imposé une nouvelle orientation dans ce problème de l'angoisse. Nous avons admis que l'angoisse se produisait exclusivement dans le Moi et que seul le Moi était capable de créer et de ressentir l'angoisse : la position ainsi adoptée nous permet d'envisager la situation sous un angle nouveau. Et de fait, comment concevoir raisonnablement une « angoisse du Ça » ? Comment attribuer au Surmoi la possibilité de ressentir l'angoisse ? Par contre, nous sommes satisfaits de constater que les trois modalités principales de l'angoisse : l'angoisse réelle, l'angoisse névrotique et l'angoisse de conscience peuvent facilement être rapportées à ces trois dépendances du Moi : le monde extérieur, le Ça et le Surmoi. Cette nouvelle manière d'envisager les choses nous permet de saisir l'importance du rôle tenu par l'angoisse en tant que signal d'alarme, rôle qui n'était d'ailleurs pas ignoré de nous auparavant. Mais nous ne nous demandons plus avec autant d'intérêt de quoi est faite l'angoisse, et les relations entre l'angoisse réelle et l'angoisse névrotique sont éclaircies maintenant. Notons, de plus, que les cas dits compliqués semblent actuellement plus faciles à expliquer que les cas réputés simples.

Nous avons récemment étudié l'apparition de l'angoisse dans certaines phobies que nous imputons à l'hystérie d'angoisse. Les cas choisis étaient bien propres à montrer le refoulement typique des émois issus du complexe d'Œdipe. A notre avis, l'investissement libidinal de l'objet maternel avait été transformé en angoisse, puis, lié au substitut qu'est le père, s'était manifesté par le symptôme. Or, notre attente fut déçue : il m'est impossible de vous faire connaître ici tous les détails de notre étude ; sachez seulement qu'elle nous donna des résultats surprenants et contraires à ceux que nous escomptions. En effet, ce n'est pas le refoulement qui provoque l'angoisse, mais bien l'angoisse, apparue la première, qui provoque le refoulement ! Mais de quelle nature est donc cette angoisse ? Causée par un danger extérieur, elle est réelle. De fait, le garçonnet redoute les exigences de sa libido ; en l'occurence, il s'effraye de l'amour qu'il ressent pour sa mère. C'est donc bien d'une angoisse névrotique qu'il s'agit. Toutefois la menace intérieure perçue par le garçonnet n'est redoutée de celui-ci que parce qu'elle est susceptible d'évoquer un danger extérieur auquel il faut échapper par le renoncement à l'objet aimé. Dans tous les cas étudiés nous obtenons un résultat semblable. Avouons-le, nous ne nous attendions pas à voir le danger instinctuel intérieur conditionner et préparer le danger extérieur réel.

132

LE PETIT NAPOLÉON

Georges Allary
a illustré avec humour
l'onanisme du petit garçon,
et la réaction parentale
(« Le Crapouillot », Octobre 1962).

LA MENACE DE CASTRATION :
UN DANGER RÉEL, GÉNÉRATEUR D'ANGOISSE

Mais ce danger réel dont l'enfant se croit menacé à cause de l'amour qu'il ressent pour sa mère, quel est-il ? C'est la castration, la perte du membre. Vous m'objecterez naturellement qu'il ne s'agit pas là d'un danger réel. Nul ne songe à châtrer nos garçonnets quand ils sont, durant la phase œdipienne, amoureux de leur mère. Mais la chose est plus compliquée qu'elle ne le semble au premier abord. Il ne s'agit pas de savoir si la castration est réellement pratiquée ; ce qui nous intéresse, c'est que la menace vient du dehors et que l'enfant y croit, à juste titre d'ailleurs, car durant sa phase phallique, au moment de son onanisme précoce, on l'a souvent menacé de lui couper le membre et certaines allusions à ce châtiment ont dû, à coup sûr, se renforcer phylogénétiquement en lui. Nous croyons qu'aux époques primitives de l'humanité, la castration était vraiment pratiquée sur l'adolescent par un père jaloux et cruel. Chez certains peuples primitifs, la circoncision fait très souvent partie des rites de la virilité et tire certainement son origine de l'ancienne castration. Nous savons que notre avis sur ce point s'écarte de l'opinion générale, mais nous soutenons que la peur de la castration est l'un des moteurs les plus fréquents et les plus puissants du refoulement et par là de la formation des névroses. Notre conviction s'est nettement renforcée lorsqu'il nous a été donné d'analyser des individus chez lesquels on avait pratiqué non pas, bien entendu, la castration, mais la circoncision, soit dans un but thérapeutique, soit pour punir la masturbation. Ce fait n'est pas rare du tout dans la société anglo-américaine. Bien que nous ayons grande envie d'étudier plus à fond cette question, nous tenons à ne pas nous éloigner de notre sujet. La peur de la castration n'est assurément pas le seul motif du refoulement et n'existe pas chez les femmes, qui sont toutefois susceptibles d'avoir un complexe de castration. La peur de la castration est remplacée, dans l'autre sexe, par la crainte de perdre l'amour, continuation de la peur qu'éprouve le nourrisson en se voyant privé de sa mère. Vous le voyez, cette crainte correspond bien à un danger réel. Quand la mère est absente ou qu'elle prive l'enfant de son amour, cet enfant n'est plus sûr de voir ses besoins satisfaits, peut-être même est-il alors en proie à de très pénibles sentiments de tension. Il nous est bien permis de croire que cette peur n'est, somme toute, que la reproduction de la peur primitive subie lors de la naissance, première séparation d'avec la mère. En adoptant le raisonnement de Ferenczi, vous rangerez la peur de la castration dans la même catégo-

134

rie ; en effet, perdre le membre viril, c'est être incapable désormais de s'unir à nouveau, par l'acte sexuel, à sa mère ou à la remplaçante de celle-ci. Disons incidemment que le fantasme très fréquent du retour dans le sein maternel est un substitut de ce désir de coït. J'aurais là-dessus bien des choses intéressantes à vous apprendre, mais il ne m'est pas permis de dépasser les limites d'une simple introduction à la psychanalyse. Je me contenterai seulement de vous faire observer qu'ici les recherches psychologiques nous mènent jusqu'aux faits biologiques.

DES CRAINTES INFANTILES QUI PERSISTENT, EN SE TRANSFORMANT, CHEZ L'ADULTE

Otto Rank, à qui la psychanalyse est redevable de tant de belles études, a eu le mérite de faire ressortir nettement l'importance de la naissance, de la séparation d'avec la mère. Néanmoins nous rejetons tous, d'un commun accord, les conséquences qu'il tira de ce facteur au point de vue de la théorie des névroses et même de la thérapeutique psychanalytique. D'après lui, toutes les situations périlleuses ultérieures sont calquées sur cette première et terrible expérience : la naissance. En étudiant les situations périlleuses, nous constatons qu'à chaque période de l'évolution correspond une angoisse qui lui est propre ; le danger de l'abandon psychique coïncide avec le tout premier éveil du Moi, le danger de perdre l'objet (ou l'amour), avec le manque d'indépendance qui caractérise la première enfance, le danger de la castration, avec la phase phallique et enfin la peur du Surmoi qui, elle, occupe une place particulière, avec la période de latence. Les anciens motifs de crainte devraient disparaître au cours de l'évolution, puisque les situations périlleuses correspondantes ont perdu de leur valeur grâce au renforcement du Moi ; mais ce n'est pas tout à fait ainsi que les choses se passent dans la réalité. De nombreux individus ne parviennent jamais à maîtriser la peur de perdre l'amour, se sentir aimés étant pour eux un besoin insurmontable ; ils persistent donc à se comporter, à ce point de vue, comme des enfants. Normalement, la crainte du Surmoi ne cesse jamais, parce que la peur de la conscience s'avère indispensable au maintien des rapports sociaux. L'individu, en effet, dépend toujours d'une collectivité, sauf exceptions rares. Certaines parmi les situations périlleuses se maintiennent parfois jusqu'à des époques tardives, les causes de la peur étant opportunément modifiées. C'est ainsi que la peur de la castration peut apparaître sous le masque de la syphilophobie[11]. L'adulte ne redoute certes plus d'être châtré parce qu'il s'est abandonné aux voluptés sexuelles, mais, en revanche, il a appris qu'il risquait, en se livrant à ses instincts, d'attraper certaines maladies graves. Les personnes dites névrosées gardent incontestablement une attitude infantile devant le danger et ne parviennent pas à surmonter leurs craintes surannées. C'est là d'ailleurs un des traits saillants du caractère des névrosés ; mais le pourquoi de cet état de choses n'est pas facile à trouver.

Vous n'avez pas oublié, j'espère, que notre but est d'étudier les rapports existant entre l'angoisse et le refoulement. Deux faits nouveaux nous sont apparus : d'abord que l'angoisse crée le refoulement, à l'inverse de ce que nous supposions, et ensuite que la situation instinctuelle redoutée est provoquée, en fin de compte, par une situation extérieure dangereuse. Nous allons chercher maintenant de quelle manière se produit le refoulement sous l'influence de l'angoisse. Voici à mon avis comment les choses se passent : le Moi observe que la satisfaction d'une nouvelle exigence instinctuelle évoque l'une des situations périlleuses dont il a gardé le souvenir. Il lui est donc nécessaire de réprimer, d'étouffer, de rendre impuissant cet investissement pulsionnel. Nous savons que le Moi y parvient très bien quand il est fort et qu'il réussit à absorber dans son organisation la pulsion instinctuelle en question. Mais en cas de refoulement, cette pulsion appartient encore au Ça et le Moi, conscient de sa propre faiblesse, utilise alors une technique identique, en somme, à celle de la pensée normale. La pensée est une méthode d'essai pratiquée à l'aide de faibles quantités d'énergie ; elle rappelle le procédé d'un général qui, avant de donner à l'ensemble de ses troupes l'ordre d'avancer, déplace sur la carte du pays de petites figurines. Le Moi devance donc la satisfaction accordée à la pulsion instinctuelle inquiétante et permet aux sentiments de déplaisir de réapparaître au début de la situation périlleuse redoutée. Ainsi se déclenche l'automatisme du principe de plaisir-déplaisir qui réalise ensuite le refoulement de la pulsion instinctuelle dangereuse.

LES DIVERSES ATTITUDES
DU MOI FACE À L'ANGOISSE

Arrêtez, vous écrierez-vous, nous ne vous suivons plus ! Vous avez raison et pour que mes assertions vous paraissent plausibles, il faut que je les complète par d'autres détails. Tout d'abord, j'avoue avoir

---

11. Peur de contracter la syphilis. (N.d.E.)

tenté de traduire, dans le langage de notre pensée normale, un processus évidemment non conscient ou préconscient qui intéresse, sans
doute, les charges énergétiques d'un substratum indéfinissable. Cette
difficulté, impossible d'ailleurs à éviter, n'est pas insurmontable.
L'importance est de bien discerner ce qui se passe, au cours du refoulement, d'une part dans le Moi et d'autre part dans le Ça. Nous venons de
décrire le comportement du Moi qui se sert d'un investissement d'essai
et met en branle, par le signal de l'angoisse, l'automatisme plaisir-
déplaisir. Diverses réactions, parfois plus ou moins enchevêtrées, peuvent alors se produire : ou bien l'accès d'angoisse parvient à son plein
épanouissement et le Moi renonce alors à jouer dans l'émotion un rôle
quelconque, ou bien le Moi institue en lieu et place de l'investissement
expérimental un contre-investissement ; ce dernier s'associe à l'énergie
de l'émotion refoulée et peut, soit former le symptôme, soit, une fois
capté par le Moi, s'installer à demeure, en tant que formation réactionnelle, certaines dispositions se trouvant alors renforcées. Plus la production d'angoisse aura été réduite au rôle de simple signal, plus le
Moi devra utiliser de réactions de défense afin de lier psychiquement
ce qui a été refoulé et plus aussi le processus se rapprochera, sans
l'atteindre toutefois, de l'élaboration normale. Puisque nous voilà sur
ce chapitre, demeurons-y un moment encore. Il est certes difficile de
donner une définition de ce qu'on est convenu d'appeler *le caractère* ;
cependant vous avez pu voir par vous-mêmes que ce dernier est uniquement attribuable au Moi et nous avons appris à connaître quelques-
uns des facteurs qui le déterminent : en premier lieu, la transformation
de l'ancienne instance parentale en Surmoi, fait qui est bien le plus
important et le plus décisif de tous, plus tard l'identification aux
parents ou à d'autres personnes influentes, puis d'autres identifications
encore qui sont les résidus de relations objectales abandonnées. A tout
cela, ajoutons ces formations réactionnelles qui jouent toujours leur
rôle dans la formation du caractère et que le Moi acquiert par des
moyens plus normaux, d'abord dans ses refoulements et par la suite
quand il rejette les pulsions instinctuelles indésirables.

DANS LE ÇA,
LES PULSIONS REFOULÉES CONNAISSENT
DES DESTINS DIVERS

Revenons maintenant en arrière et occupons-nous du Ça. Que
devient la pulsion au cours du refoulement ? Voilà un problème bien
ardu. Quel est surtout le sort réservé à l'énergie, à la charge libidinale

de cet émoi et de quelle manière est-elle utilisée ? Nous crûmes long-temps, vous vous le rappelez, qu'elle était transformée en angoisse par suite même du refoulement. Nous n'osons plus l'affirmer aujourd'hui et, avec modestie, nous dirons que le sort réservé à cette énergie n'est pas toujours identique à lui-même. Sans doute subsiste-t-il un accord intime, à propos de la pulsion refoulée, entre les anciens processus dans le Moi et dans le Ça, accord qui devait nous être connu. En effet, après avoir mis en relief le rôle que joue dans le refoulement le principe de plaisir-déplaisir réveillé par le signal de l'angoisse, nous pouvons modifier nos conceptions. Ce principe régit souverainement les proces-sus dans le Ça et ne manque pas de provoquer, dans la pulsion instinc-tuelle en jeu, de très profondes modifications. Rien d'étonnant à ce que les effets produits par le refoulement soient très variables et aient une plus ou moins grande répercussion. En certains cas, la pulsion instinc-tuelle refoulée conserve sa charge libidinale et demeure intacte dans le Ça malgré la pression exercée par le Moi. D'autres fois, elle semble avoir subi une destruction totale, auquel cas sa libido paraît s'être engagée dans d'autres voies. Je supposai que tout se passait ainsi lors de la liquidation normale du complexe d'Œdipe qui, dans ces cas favo-rables, n'est pas seulement refoulé, mais aussi détruit dans le Ça. L'expérience clinique nous a montré, en outre, qu'il se produit fré-quemment, au lieu du refoulement habituel, une diminution de la libido, une régression de cette dernière vers un stade antérieur. Tout ceci ne peut naturellement s'accomplir que dans le Ça et seulement sous l'influence du conflit qu'a déclenché le signal d'alarme. C'est la névrose obsessionnelle qui offre le meilleur exemple de ce phénomène, car la régression libidinale et le refoulement y agissent de concert.

L'OBJET DE L'ANGOISSE EST TOUJOURS UN TRAUMATISME IMPOSSIBLE À ÉCARTER

Une remarque encore au sujet du problème de l'angoisse. La peur névrotique s'est, entre nos mains, transformée en peur réelle, en crainte de certains dangers extérieurs. Nous ne pouvons en rester là et sommes obligés de faire un pas, mais un pas en arrière. Nous nous demandons ce qui constitue vraiment le danger, la chose redoutée, dans la situa-tion alarmante en question. Ce n'est certainement pas la blessure : celle-ci, objectivement considérée, peut n'avoir aucune importance au point de vue psychique. Ce qui est à craindre, c'est plutôt la modifica-tion que cette blessure est capable de provoquer dans la vie psychique.

La naissance, par exemple, prototype à nos yeux de l'état d'angoisse, peut à peine être considérée en soi comme un préjudice, malgré le risque toujours possible d'une blessure. L'essentiel dans la naissance, comme dans toute situation périlleuse, est l'apparition dans le psychisme d'un état de grande tension ressenti comme un déplaisir et dont on ne peut se libérer par une décharge. Si nous qualifions de *traumatique* cet état où les efforts du principe de plaisir échouent, nous parvenons, en considérant la série angoisse névrotique — angoisse réelle — situation périlleuse, à la conclusion simple que voici : la chose redoutée, l'objet de l'angoisse, c'est toujours l'apparition d'un facteur traumatique qu'il est impossible d'écarter suivant la norme du principe de plaisir.

SIGMUND FREUD[12]

12. *Nouvelles Conférences sur la psychanalyse* (« l'Angoisse et la Vie instinctuelle »), p. 109-124.

Chapitre V

Du traumatisme sexuel
au conflit psychique

Pour Freud, l'abandon de la théorie de la séduction[1] a joué un rôle considérable dans la découverte de la psychanalyse proprement dite, et dans celle du complexe d'Œdipe en particulier. Durant la période au cours de laquelle la théorie psychanalytique est en gestation, Freud accorde en effet une grande importance à ce qu'il est convenu d'appeler la théorie de la séduction. En quoi consiste-t-elle ?

Freud avait remarqué que, chez la plupart des malades (hystériques) qu'il avait alors à traiter, survenaient des récits de séductions sexuelles qu'ils auraient eu autrefois à subir de la part d'un adulte. Ces scènes auraient eu pour conséquence un traumatisme dont l'effet aurait été différé : le malade aurait supporté tout à fait passivement et sans aucune excitation sexuelle la tentative de séduction à l'époque de la « première scène ». Une « deuxième scène » — ne présentant pas obligatoirement de coloration sexuelle —, à l'époque de la puberté, serait généralement venue évoquer la première et mobiliser une quantité d'excitations impossibles à maîtriser : ce serait là le « second temps » du traumatisme. Celui-ci surviendrait par conséquent après coup, en tant que « réminiscence » de la scène de séduction proprement dite. Le caractère pathogène du traumatisme proviendrait, dans cette perspective, du souvenir de la scène de séduction, et non de la séduction elle-même[2]. On voit ainsi que, si le traumatisme s'appuie sur un événement extérieur, il n'en comporte pas moins une référence à l'activité mentale du sujet et, donc, aux facteurs internes.

---

1. Nous avons déjà évoqué les raisons de cet abandon dans l'*Identification : l'autre, c'est moi* (chap. III, p. 61), paru dans la même collection.
2. Freud, « l'Étiologie de l'hystérie », 1896.

◀ *Les contes de fées qu'on raconte aux enfants sont loin d'être dépourvus de symboles sexuels (W. Crane, fin du XIXᵉ siècle, Bibliothèque des Arts Décoratifs).*

C'est dans une lettre en date du 21 septembre 1897, adressée à Fliess, que Freud reconnaît ne plus pouvoir continuer à admettre la théorie de la séduction : « Je ne crois plus à ma neurotica *» ; les accusations des hystériques concernant de prétendus actes pervers commis par leur père étaient en effet trop fréquentes. Dans la même lettre, que nous découvrirons en premier lieu, il note qu'il lui est impossible de distinguer la vérité de la « fiction investie d'affect » et remarque que le* fantasme *sexuel se joue toujours autour du thème des parents. Il mentionne en passant et comme par hasard* Hamlet. *Or, la lettre dans laquelle Freud annoncera à Fliess la découverte du complexe d'Œdipe sera écrite très exactement trois semaines plus tard[3]. Et, dans cette lettre, il se référera non seulement à* Œdipe roi, *la tragédie de Sophocle, mais également à* Hamlet...

Que reste-t-il en psychanalyse de la notion de traumatisme ? Le problème est complexe ; aussi, sans entrer ici dans les détails, nous aborderons l'entité nosologique appelée névrose traumatique en prenant pour exemple les névroses de guerre.

En 1920, dans Au-delà du principe de plaisir, *Freud remarque : « A la suite de graves commotions mécaniques, de catastrophes de chemin de fer et d'autres accidents impliquant un danger pour la vie, on voit survenir un état qui a été décrit depuis longtemps sous le nom de "névrose traumatique" »* — et, en note, il cite un ouvrage collectif publié un an auparavant en collaboration avec Ferenczi, Abraham, Simmel et Jones : ce sont les deux contributions d'Abraham et de Ferenczi que nous présentons ci-après.

« Jusqu'à ce jour, *précise Freud dans le même travail,* on n'a pas réussi à se faire une notion bien exacte tant des névroses de guerre que des névroses traumatiques du temps de paix. Ce qui, dans les névroses de guerre, semblait à la fois éclaircir et embrouiller la situation, c'était le fait que le même tableau morbide pouvait, à l'occasion, se produire en dehors de toute violence mécanique brutale. » *En ce qui concerne les rêves de malades ayant subi des traumatismes, rêves dans lesquels le patient* « se trouve constamment ramené à la situation constituée par l'accident », *nous avons dit[4] que l'une de leurs interprétations possibles était la suivante : ce type de rêve représenterait une tentative pour maîtriser le traumatisme vécu dans la réalité, sans que le signal d'angoisse préparant le psychisme au danger ait pu se déclencher. En fait, Freud finit par postuler l'existence d'une tendance « irrésistible » à la répétition, qu'il relie, en dernière analyse, à la pulsion de mort.* « Cela admis, ajoute-t-il, rien ne s'oppose à ce qu'on attribue à la pression exercée*

---

3. Voir *l'Œdipe : un complexe universel* (chap. I), dans la même collection.
4. Dans *Les Rêves, voie royale de l'inconscient* (chap. III), paru dans la même collection.

par cette tendance... les rêves du sujet atteint de névrose traumatique. »

Le concept de liaison, permet le mieux de comprendre, nous semble-t-il, ce que recouvre encore aujourd'hui le vocable de névrose traumatique. La répétition de l'expérience traumatique, soit agie, soit rêvée, fait apparaître qu'un système n'ayant pas été préalablement investi se trouve dans l'incapacité de lier psychiquement[5] une énergie trop brusquement mobilisée. La névrose traumatique se caractériserait donc par un état dans lequel il est impossible au Moi de maîtriser ou de lier les excitations. Si l'on se réfère à la dualité pulsionnelle Instinct de vie — Instinct de mort introduite précisément par Freud dans Au-delà du principe de plaisir, *la liaison serait en rapport étroit avec Éros[6], qui cherche à établir des unités toujours plus grandes, tandis que la déliaison serait, elle, en rapport avec Thanatos[7], dont le but est de désintégrer les ensembles, de briser les liens.*

Ainsi donc, la notion de névrose traumatique[8] nous conduit à nous interroger sur ce qui, dans la théorie psychanalytique, fait l'objet des plus nombreuses controverses et des plus vastes spéculations.

Dans l'extrait de « Contribution à l'histoire du mouvement psychanalytique » (1914) qui figure ensuite dans ce chapitre, on verra Freud retracer lui-même le chemin parcouru depuis la théorie traumatique de l'hystérie jusqu'à la découverte de la réalité psychique. Pour conclure, nous présentons un texte tiré de Ma vie et la psychanalyse, *dans lequel Freud, en 1925, synthétise l'évolution de sa pensée qui, dégagée de la théorie de la séduction, aboutit à centrer l'étiologie des névroses sur le conflit interne et, tout particulièrement, sur le complexe d'Œdipe.*

Sans vouloir reprendre ici l'ensemble des conceptions psychanalytiques sur l'Œdipe[9], rappelons que le complexe d'Œdipe est le « noyau central des névroses ». Il s'agit, de plus, d'un conflit universel, consubstantiel à la psyché humaine : « Rien n'a tant nui [à la psychanalyse] dans la faveur de ses contemporains, remarque Freud en 1926 dans Psychanalyse et médecine, *que le complexe d'Œdipe et l'élévation de celui-ci à la dignité d'une manière d'être généralement et fatalement humaine. »*

5. Rappelons que l'énergie est « libre » dans les processus primaires, c'est-à-dire dans l'un des deux modes de fonctionnement de l'appareil psychique. Freud dit de cette énergie libre qu'elle tend à se décharger sur le mode le plus direct et le plus court. En revanche, au niveau des processus secondaires, elle est « liée » : sa décharge est ajournée, détournée, maîtrisée. Voir *le Ça, le Moi, le Surmoi : la personnalité et ses instances* (chap. I), paru dans la même collection.

6. L'instinct de vie.

7. L'instinct de mort.

8. Dont Freud dira en 1926, dans *Inhibition, symptôme et angoisse*, qu'« il est vraisemblable que l'analyse des névroses traumatiques de guerre, terme qui d'ailleurs englobe des affections de natures très diverses, aurait montré que nombre d'entre elles ont avec les névroses actuelles des caractères communs ».

9. Voir *l'Œdipe et la Castration : un fantasme originaire*, tous deux parus dans la même collection.

Dr Sigmund FREUD,
chargé de cours de Neurologie
à l'Université.

21-9-1897.
IX, Berggasse 19.

Cher Wilhelm,

Me revoilà — nous sommes rentrés hier matin — dispos, de bonne humeur, appauvri, sans travail pour le moment et je t'écris dès notre réinstallation terminée[10]. Il faut que je te confie tout de suite le grand secret qui, au cours de ces derniers mois, s'est lentement révélé. Je ne crois plus à ma *neurotica,* ce qui saurait être compris sans explication ; tu avais toi-même trouvé plausible ce que je t'avais dit. Je vais donc commencer par le commencement et t'exposer la façon dont se sont présentés les motifs de ne plus y croire. Il y eut d'abord les déceptions répétées que je subis lors de mes tentatives pour pousser mes analyses jusqu'à leur véritable achèvement, la fuite des gens dont les cas semblaient le mieux se prêter à ce traitement, l'absence du succès total que j'escomptais et la possibilité de m'expliquer autrement, plus simplement, ces succès partiels, tout cela constituant un premier groupe de raisons. Puis, aussi, la surprise de constater que, dans chacun des cas, il fallait accuser le père de perversion..., la notion de la fréquence inattendue de l'hystérie où se retrouve chaque fois la même cause déterminante, alors qu'une telle généralisation des actes pervers commis envers des enfants semblait peu croyable[11]. (La perversion, en ce cas, devrait être infiniment plus fréquente que l'hystérie puisque cette maladie n'apparaît que lorsque les incidents se sont multipliés et qu'un facteur affaiblissant la défense est intervenu.) En troisième lieu, la conviction qu'il n'existe dans l'inconscient aucun « indice de réalité[12] », de telle sorte qu'il est impossible de distinguer l'une de l'autre la vérité et la fiction investie d'affect. (C'est pourquoi une solution reste possible, elle est fournie par le fait que le fantasme sexuel se joue toujours autour du thème des parents[13].) Quatrièmement, j'ai été amené à

---

10. A cause de la date inhabituellement tardive du retour de Freud après ses vacances.

11. Depuis plusieurs mois déjà Freud s'intéressait aux fantasmes infantiles, il étudiait leur fonction dynamique et avait acquis dans ce domaine des notions durables. Il approchait du complexe d'Œdipe où il découvrait les pulsions agressives de l'enfant contre ses parents, mais sans avoir nié encore la réalité de la scène de séduction. On peut facilement admettre que c'est l'auto-analyse de l'été qui lui a permis de faire le pas décisif, c'est-à-dire de rejeter l'hypothèse de la séduction.

12. Voir l'*Esquisse*, p. 382.

13. Un seul pas reste à faire pour arriver au complexe d'Œdipe.

constater que dans les psychoses les plus profondes, le souvenir inconscient ne jaillit pas, de sorte que le secret de l'incident de jeunesse, même dans les états les plus délirants, ne se révèle pas. Quand on constate que l'inconscient n'arrive jamais à vaincre la résistance du conscient, on cesse d'espérer que, pendant l'analyse, le processus inverse puisse se produire et aboutir à une domination complète de l'inconscient par le conscient.

Sous l'influence de ces considérations, j'étais prêt à renoncer à deux choses — à la totale liquidation d'une névrose et à la connaissance exacte de son étiologie dans l'enfance. Maintenant je ne sais plus où j'en suis, car je n'ai encore acquis de compréhension théorique ni du refoulement ni du jeu de forces qui s'y manifeste. Il semble douteux que des incidents survenus tardivement puissent susciter des fantasmes remontant à l'enfance. C'est pour cette raison que le facteur d'une prédisposition héréditaire semble regagner du terrain alors que je m'étais toujours efforcé de le refouler dans l'intérêt d'une explication des névroses.

Si j'étais déprimé, surmené, et que mes idées fussent brouillées, de semblables doutes pourraient être considérés comme des indices de faiblesse. Mais comme je me trouve justement dans l'état opposé, je dois les considérer comme résultant d'un honnête et efficace travail intellectuel et me sentir fier de pouvoir, après être allé aussi loin, exercer encore ma critique. Ces doutes constituent-ils seulement une simple étape sur la voie menant à une connaissance plus approfondie ?

Il est curieux aussi que je ne me sente nullement penaud, ce qui semblerait pourtant naturel. Évidemment, je n'irai pas raconter tout cela dans Gath, je ne l'annoncerai pas à Ascalon, dans le pays des Philistins — mais devant nous deux, je me sens victorieux plutôt que battu (à tort cependant)[14].

Quelle chance j'ai eu de recevoir juste maintenant ta lettre ! Elle me fournit l'occasion de te soumettre la proposition par laquelle je voulais terminer ma missive. Si, profitant de cette période de désœuvrement, je filais samedi soir à la gare du Nord-Ouest et que je sois dimanche à midi chez toi, il me serait possible de repartir la nuit suivante. Peux-tu

14. Dans une note datée de 1924 et ajoutée au chapitre intitulé « Étiologie spécifique de l'hystérie » dans *Autres remarques sur les neuropsychoses de défense* (1896), Freud écrit : « Ce chapitre comporte une erreur que j'ai depuis reconnue et corrigée. A cette époque je ne savais pas encore distinguer des souvenirs réels les fantasmes des analyses, relatifs à leurs années d'enfance. En conséquence, j'attribuais au facteur étiologique de la séduction une importance et un caractère général qu'il n'a pas. Après avoir réparé cette erreur, j'ai pu reconnaître les manifestations spontanées de la sexualité infantile et les ai décrites dans mes *Trois essais sur la théorie de la sexualité* (1905). Toutefois, il ne faut pas rejeter tout le texte en question. La séduction conserve toujours une certaine importance étiologique et je tiens encore aujourd'hui pour exactes certaines de mes opinions exprimées dans ce chapitre. »

consacrer cette journée à une idylle à deux, interrompue par une idylle à trois et à trois et demi ? Voilà ce que je voulais te demander. Mais peut-être attends-tu d'autres visites ou as-tu quelque chose d'urgent à faire ? Ou si j'étais obligé de regagner mon logis le même jour — ce qui n'en vaudrait pas la peine — pourrais-je prendre le train à la gare du Nord-Ouest dès le vendredi soir et passer un jour et demi avec toi, cela te conviendrait-il encore ? Je parle naturellement de cette semaine[15].

Je continue ma lettre par des variations sur les paroles d'Hamlet : *To be in readiness.* Garder sa sérénité, tout est là. J'aurais lieu de me sentir très mécontent. Une célébrité éternelle, la fortune assurée, l'indépendance totale, les voyages, la certitude d'éviter aux enfants tous les graves soucis qui ont accablé ma jeunesse, voilà quel était mon bel espoir. Tout dépendait de la réussite ou de l'échec de l'hystérie. Me voilà obligé de me tenir tranquille, de rester dans la médiocrité, de faire des économies, d'être harcelé par les soucis et alors une des histoires de mon anthologie[16] me revient à l'esprit : « Rébecca, ôte ta robe, tu n'es plus fiancée ! »

Quelques mots encore. Dans cet effondrement général, seule la psychologie demeure intacte. Le rêve conserve certainement sa valeur et j'attache toujours plus de prix à mes débuts dans la métapsychologie. Quel dommage, par exemple, que l'interprétation des rêves ne suffise pas à vous faire vivre !

Martha est revenue à Vienne avec moi. Minna et les enfants ne rentrent que la semaine prochaine. Leur santé a été parfaite...

Anticipant sur ta réponse, j'espère apprendre bientôt par moi-même comment vous allez tous et ce qui, en dehors de cela, se passe entre ciel et terre.

Très affectueusement à toi,

Sigm.

SIGMUND FREUD[17]

L'ABANDON DE LA THÉORIE DE LA SÉDUCTION : LES EXPLICATIONS DE FREUD

Sous l'influence de la théorie traumatique de l'hystérie qui se rattache à l'enseignement de Charcot, on n'était que trop disposé à attribuer une réalité et une signification étiologique aux récits dans

---

15. Freud partit pour Berlin et revint à Vienne le 29.
16. Une anthologie des histoires juives.
17. *La Naissance de la psychanalyse* (lettre n° 60), p. 190-193.

« J'avais rencontré ici, pour la première fois,
le complexe d'Œdipe, qui devait par la suite acquérir
une signification dominante... »
(Œdipe les yeux crevés, collection particulière, 1895).

lesquels les malades faisaient remonter leurs symptômes à des expériences sexuelles qu'ils avaient subies passivement au cours des premières années de leur enfance, autrement dit à ce que nous appellerions vulgairement le « détournement de mineurs ». Et lorsqu'on se vit obligé de renoncer à cette étiologie, à cause de son invraisemblance et de sa contradiction avec des faits solidements établis, on se trouva fort désemparé. L'analyse qui avait conduit à ces traumatismes sexuels infantiles aurait-elle donc suivi un chemin incorrect, puisque ces traumatismes se sont révélés dépourvus de tout fondement réel ? On ne savait à quel appui s'accrocher. J'aurais alors volontiers fait le sacrifice de tout le travail que j'avais accompli, comme l'avait fait mon vénéré prédécesseur Breuer à la suite de son indésirable découverte. Si je ne l'ai pas fait, ce fut sans doute parce que je n'avais pas le choix, que je ne pouvais m'engager dans aucune autre direction. Je me suis dit finalement qu'on n'avait pas le droit de se laisser décourager parce que les espoirs qu'on concevait ne s'étaient pas réalisés ; qu'il fallait plutôt soumettre à une révision ces espoirs eux-mêmes. Lorsque les hystériques rattachent leurs symptômes à des traumatismes inventés, le fait nouveau consiste précisément en ce qu'ils imaginent ces scènes, ce qui nous oblige à tenir compte de la réalité psychique, autant que de la pratique. Je ne tardai pas à en conclure que ces fantaisies étaient destinées à dissimuler l'activité auto-érotique de la première enfance, à l'entourer d'une certaine auréole, à l'élever à un niveau supérieur. Et, une fois cette constatation faite, je vis la vie sexuelle de l'enfant se dérouler devant moi dans toute son ampleur.

SIGMUND FREUD[18]

LA DÉCOUVERTE DU COMPLEXE D'ŒDIPE

Il me faut faire mention d'une erreur dans laquelle je tombai pendant quelque temps et qui aurait bientôt pu devenir fatale à tout mon labeur. Sous la pression de mon procédé technique d'alors, la plupart de mes patients reproduisaient des scènes de leur enfance, scènes dont la substance était la séduction par un adulte. Chez les patientes, le rôle de séducteur était presque toujours dévolu au père. J'ajoutais foi à ces informations, et ainsi je crus avoir découvert, dans ces séductions précoces de l'enfance, les sources de la névrose ultérieure. Quelques cas,

---

18. *Cinq leçons sur la psychanalyse* (« Contribution à l'histoire du mouvement psychanalytique »), p. 83-84.

où de telles relations au père, à l'oncle ou au frère aîné, s'étaient maintenues jusqu'à un âge dont les souvenirs sont certains, me fortifiaient dans ma foi. A quiconque secouera la tête avec méfiance devant une pareille crédulité je ne puis donner tout à fait tort, mais je veux mettre en avant que c'était alors le temps où je faisais exprès violence à ma critique, afin de demeurer impartial et réceptif en face des nombreuses nouveautés que m'apportait chaque jour. Quand je dus cependant reconnaître que ces scènes de séduction n'avaient jamais eu lieu, qu'elles n'étaient que des fantasmes imaginés par mes patients, imposés à eux peut-être par moi-même, je fus pendant quelque temps désemparé. Ma confiance en ma technique comme en ses résultats supporta un rude choc ; j'avais donc obtenu l'aveu de ces scènes par une voie technique que je tenais pour correcte et leur contenu était incontestablement en rapport avec les symptômes desquels mon investigation était partie. Lorsque je me fus repris, je tirai de mon expérience les conclusions justes : les symptômes névrotiques ne se reliaient pas directement à des événements réels, mais à des fantasmes de désir ; pour la névrose la réalité psychique avait plus d'importance que la matérielle. Je ne crois pas encore aujourd'hui avoir imposé, « suggéré » à mes patients ces fantasmes de séduction. J'avais rencontré ici, pour la première fois, le *complexe d'Œdipe,* qui devait par la suite acquérir une signification dominante, mais que sous un déguisement aussi fantastique je ne reconnaissais pas encore.

Sigmund Freud[19]

---

19. *Ma vie et la psychanalyse*, p. 43-44.

Chapitre VI

Qu'est-ce qu'un symptôme ?

La notion de conflit psychique implique l'existence, chez un sujet, de deux ou de plusieurs exigences internes contradictoires. Le conflit inconscient s'exprime sous forme de symptôme, qui est une manifestation du retour du refoulé. Ainsi que Freud l'expose en 1896, dans Nouvelles remarques sur les psychonévroses de défense, *le symptôme représente une formation de compromis entre des représentations refoulées et les défenses. Il est vrai que Freud parle essentiellement dans ce texte, à propos de sa théorie du compromis, de la névrose obsessionnelle. Cependant, la conception du symptôme, envisagée en tant que formation de compromis, va par la suite englober la totalité des symptômes.*

On se rappelle que, dans la « Communication préliminaire[1] », en 1892, et dans le cas d'Anna O., le symptôme était simplement envisagé en tant que substitut du souvenir oublié, *ce que Freud nomme un « symbole mnésique ». Le symptôme hystérique est alors conçu par lui comme un « monument commémoratif » de l'événement.*

Dans l'article « Obsessions et phobies[2] », dont on trouvera ici en premier lieu de larges extraits, on constatera que le symptôme — en tout cas, le symptôme dans la névrose obsessionnelle — est devenu le substitut d'« idées » que nous appellerions aujourd'hui fantasmes.

Nous avons eu l'occasion de voir[3] qu'il existait une analogie entre le rêve et les névroses, entre le rêve et le symptôme, comme Freud le développe en 1900 dans l'Interprétation des rêves. Le 3 janvier 1899, il écrit à Fliess : « Je ne te révélerai qu'une chose, c'est que le schéma du rêve peut avoir une utilisation très générale et que la clé de l'hystérie se

---

1. Voir *Refoulement, défenses et interdits* (chap. I), dans la même collection.
2. Directement écrit en français, ce qui explique certaines particularités du style.
3. In *les Rêves, voie royale de l'inconscient.*

◀ *Alors que la psychiatrie ne se préoccupe pas du contenu du symptôme, la psychanalyse, au contraire lui donne un sens et le rattache à la vie psychique du malade (Hallucination de l'ouïe, Bibliothèque de l'Ancienne Faculté de Médecine).*

trouve vraiment incluse dans le rêve... J'arriverai à décrire le processus psychique des rêves, de façon qu'y soit inclus le processus de forma-tion du symptôme hystérique[4]. » *Peu de temps après, le 19 février 1899, Freud expose très clairement à Fliess le caractère de compromis de la formation symptomatique :* « ... *Ma dernière généralisation tient bon et semble vouloir progresser à l'infini. Ce n'est pas seulement le rêve qui est une réalisation du désir, mais aussi l'accès hystérique... Puisque le rêve est maintenu loin de la réalité, il lui suffit d'être la réali-sation du désir d'une pensée refoulée. Mais le symptôme, lui, mêlé à la vie, doit être autre chose : la réalisation du désir de la pensée* refou-lante. *Un symptôme apparaît là où la pensée refoulée et la pensée refoulante peuvent coïncider dans une réalisation de désir[5].* »

*En 1916-1917, Freud écrit une série de conférences qui, réunies en volume, constitue la matière d'*Introduction à la psychanalyse. *Dans les extraits qui suivent, Freud montre que le symptôme obéit à deux maîtres,* « *les deux termes du conflit* » : *le désir sexuel et la défense contre celui-ci. Il peut paraître curieux, de nos jours, d'imaginer un temps où le symptôme était considéré comme l'expression d'une dégé-nérescence, par exemple... C'est à Breuer que Freud attribue le mérite d'avoir découvert, à travers l'observation du cas d'Anna O., que les symptômes possèdent un sens.*

Dans ce texte, on peut observer que si le symptôme reste bien, pour une part, une formation substitutive, réalisant symboliquement le désir insatisfait, il est avant tout le résultat d'un jeu de forces issu du conflit psychique. Ce qui s'ébauchait déjà dans les Nouvelles Remarques sur les psychonévroses de défense, *en 1896, s'affirme maintenant avec éclat. On mesurera ainsi l'évolution d'une pensée qui, partant de la notion d'expérience vécue — le symptôme comme substitut du sou-venir —, aboutit à celle de réalité interne — le conflit psychique.*

Ce symptôme réalisant, pour une part, le désir refoulé et se substi-tuant à lui, on comprend que sa levée ne soit ni une tâche aisée ni, sur-tout, une opération sans risques : sa disparition trop brutale provoque en effet un bouleversement de l'économie psychique dans son ensem-ble. C'est pour ces motifs que, dans la cure, le psychanalyste cherchera toujours à en déceler le sens, mais ne l'interprétera pas directement au patient : la modification technique depuis les Études sur l'hystérie, *comme on le voit, est d'importance.*

---

4. In *Naissance de la psychanalyse.* Lettre n° 101, p. 241 (P.U.F. éd.).
5. Idem. Lettre 105 p. 246.

Il faut distinguer : A) Les obsessions vraies ; B) Les phobies. La différence essentielle est la suivante :

Il y a dans toute obsession deux choses : 1° une idée qui s'impose au malade ; 2° un état émotif associé. Or, dans la classe des phobies, cet état émotif est toujours l'*angoisse*, pendant que dans les obsessions vraies ce peut être au même titre que l'anxiété un autre état émotif, comme le doute, le remords, la colère. Je tâcherai d'abord d'expliquer le mécanisme psychologique vraiment remarquable des obsessions vraies, qui est bien différent de celui des phobies.

ÉTAT ÉMOTIF ET IDÉES ASSOCIÉES DANS LES OBSESSIONS

Dans beaucoup d'obsessions vraies, il est bien évident que l'état émotif est la chose principale, puisque cet état persiste inaltéré pendant que l'idée associée est variée. Par exemple, la fille de l'observation I avait des remords, un peu en raison de tout, d'avoir volé, maltraité ses sœurs, fait de la fausse monnaie, etc. Les personnes qui doutent, doutent de beaucoup de choses à la fois ou successivement. C'est l'état émotif qui, dans ces cas, reste le même : l'idée change. En d'autres cas l'idée aussi semble fixée, comme chez la fille de l'observation IV, qui poursuivait d'une haine incompréhensible les servantes de la maison en changeant pourtant de personne.

Eh bien, une analyse psychologique scrupuleuse de ces cas montre que *l'état émotif, comme tel, est toujours justifié*. La fille I, qui a des remords, a de bonnes raisons ; les femmes de l'observation III, qui doutaient de leur résistance contre des tentations, savaient bien pour quoi ; la fille de l'observation IV, qui détestait les servantes, avait bien le droit de se plaindre, etc. Seulement, et c'est dans ces deux caractères que consiste l'empreinte pathologique : 1) *l'état émotif s'est éternisé ;* 2) l'idée associée *n'est plus l'idée juste, l'idée originale, en rapport avec l'étiologie de l'obsession, elle en est un remplaçant, une substitution.*

La preuve en est qu'on peut toujours trouver dans les antécédents du malade, *à l'origine de l'obsession*, l'idée originale, substituée. Les idées substituées ont des caractères communs, elles correspondent à des impressions vraiment pénibles de la vie sexuelle de l'individu que celui-ci s'est efforcé d'oublier. Il a réussi seulement à remplacer l'idée *inconciliable* par une autre idée mal appropriée à s'associer à l'état émotif, qui de son côté est resté le même. C'est cette mésalliance de l'état émotif et de l'idée associée qui rend compte du caractère d'absurdité propre aux obsessions. Je veux rapporter mes observations, et donner une tentative d'explication théorique comme conclusion.

QUELQUES EXEMPLES D'IDÉES OBSÉDANTES

Obs. I. — Une fille qui se faisait des *reproches*, qu'elle savait absurdes, d'avoir volé, fait de la fausse monnaie, de s'être conjurée, etc. selon sa lecture journalière.

Redressement de la substitution. — Elle se reprochait l'onanisme qu'elle pratiquait en secret sans pouvoir y renoncer.

Elle fut guérie par une observation scrupuleuse qui l'empêcha de se masturber.

Obs. II. — Jeune homme, étudiant en médecine, qui souffrait d'une obsession analogue. Il se reprochait toutes les actions immorales : d'avoir tué sa cousine, défloré sa sœur, incendié une maison, etc. Il en vint à la nécessité de se retourner dans la rue pour voir s'il n'avait pas encore tué le dernier passant.

Redressement de la substitution. — Il avait lu, dans un livre quasi médical, que l'onanisme, auquel il était sujet, abîmait la morale, et il s'en était ému.

Obs. III. — Plusieurs femmes qui se plaignaient de l'obsession de se jeter par la fenêtre, de blesser leurs enfants avec des couteaux, ciseaux, etc.

Redressement. — Obsessions de *tentations typiques*. C'étaient des femmes qui, pas du tout satisfaites dans le mariage, se débattaient contre les désirs et les idées voluptueuses qui les hantaient à la vue d'autres hommes.

Obs. IV. — Une fille qui, parfaitement saine d'esprit et très intelligente montrait une *haine incontrôlable contre les servantes de la maison*, qui s'était éveillée à l'occasion d'une servante effrontée, et s'était transmise depuis de fille en fille, jusqu'à rendre le ménage impossible. C'était un sentiment mêlé de haine et de dégoût. Elle donnait comme motif que les saletés de ces filles lui gâtaient son idée de l'amour.

Redressement. — Cette fille avait été témoin involontaire d'un rendez-vous amoureux de sa mère. Elle s'était caché le visage, bouché les oreilles et s'était donné la plus grande peine pour oublier la scène, qui la dégoûtait et l'aurait mise dans l'impossibilité de rester avec sa mère qu'elle aimait tendrement. Elle y réussit, mais la colère, de ce qu'on lui avait souillé l'image de l'amour, persista en elle, et à cet état émotif ne tarda pas à s'associer l'idée d'une personne pouvant remplacer la mère.

Obs. V. — Une jeune fille s'était presque complètement isolée en conséquence de la peur obsédante de l'incontinence des urines. Elle ne pouvait plus quitter sa chambre ou recevoir une visite sans avoir uriné nombre de fois.

Chez elle et en repos complet la peur n'existait pas.

Redressement. — C'était une obsession de *tentation* ou de *méfiance*. Elle ne se méfiait pas de sa vessie mais de sa résistance contre une impulsion amoureuse. L'origine de l'obsession le montrait bien. Une fois, au théâtre, elle avait senti à la vue d'un homme qui lui plaisait une envie amoureuse accompagnée (comme toujours dans la pollution spontanée des femmes) de l'envie d'uriner. Elle fut obligée à quitter le théâtre, et de ce moment elle était en proie à la peur d'avoir la même sensation, mais l'envie d'uriner s'était substituée à l'envie amoureuse. Elle guérit complètement.

Les observations énumérées, bien qu'elles montrent un degré variable de complexité, ont ceci de commun, qu'à l'idée originale (inconciliable) s'est substitué une autre idée, idée remplaçante. Dans les observations qui vont suivre maintenant, l'idée originale est aussi remplacée mais non par une autre idée ; elle se trouve remplacée par des actes ou impulsions qui ont servi à l'origine comme *soulagements* ou *procédés protecteurs*, et qui maintenant se trouvent en association grotesque avec un état émotif qui ne leur convient pas, mais qui est resté le même, et aussi justifié qu'à l'origine.

Obs. VI. — *Obsession d'arithmomanie*. Une femme avait contracté le besoin de compter toujours les planches du parquet, les marches de l'escalier, etc., ce qu'elle faisait dans un état d'angoisse ridicule.

Redressement. — Elle avait commencé à compter pour se distraire de ses idées obsédantes (de tentation). Elle y avait réussi, mais l'impulsion de compter s'était substituée à l'obsession primitive.

Obs. VII. — Obsession de *Grübelsucht* (folie de spéculation). Une femme souffrait d'attaques de cette obsession, qui ne cessaient qu'aux temps de maladie, pour faire place à des peurs hypochondriaques. Le sujet de l'attaque était ou une partie du corps ou une fonction, par exemple, la respiration : Pourquoi faut-il respirer ? Si je ne voulais pas respirer ? etc.

Redressement. — Tout d'abord elle avait souffert de la peur de devenir folle, phobie hypocondriaque assez commune chez les femmes non satisfaites par leur mari, comme elle l'était. Pour *s'assurer qu'elle n'allait pas devenir folle*, qu'elle jouissait encore de son intelligence, elle avait commencé à se poser des questions, à s'occuper de problèmes sérieux. Cela la tranquillisait d'abord, mais avec le temps cette habitude de la spéculation se substituait à la phobie. Depuis plus de quinze ans des périodes de peur (pathophobie) et de folie de spéculation alternaient chez elle.

Obs. VIII. — *Folie du doute*. Plusieurs cas, qui montraient les symptômes typiques de cette obsession, mais qui s'expliquaient bien simplement. Ces personnes avaient souffert ou souffraient encore d'obsessions diverses, et la conscience de ce que l'obsession les avait dérangées dans toutes leurs actions et interrompu maintes fois le cours de leurs pensées provoquait un doute légitime de la fidélité de leur mémoire. Chacun de nous verra chanceler son assurance et sera obligé de relire une lettre ou de refaire un compte si son attention a été distraite plusieurs fois pendant l'exécution de l'acte. Le doute est une conséquence bien logique de la présence des obsessions.

Obs. IX. — *Folie du doute (hésitation).* La fille de l'observation IV était devenue extrêmement lente dans toutes les actions de la vie ordinaire, particulièrement dans sa toilette. Il lui fallait des heures pour nouer les cordons de ses souliers ou pour se nettoyer les ongles des mains. Elle donnait comme explication qu'elle ne pouvait faire sa toilette ni pendant que les pensées obsédantes la préoccupaient, ni immédiatement après de sorte qu'elle s'était accoutumée à attendre un temps déterminé après chaque retour de l'idée obsédante.

Obs. X. — *Folie du doute, crainte des papiers.* Une jeune femme, qui avait souffert des scrupules après avoir écrit une lettre, et qui dans ce même temps ramassait tous les papiers qu'elle voyait, donnait comme explication l'aveu d'un amour que jadis elle ne voulait pas confesser.

A force de se répéter sans cesse le nom de son bien-aimé, elle fut saisie par la peur que ce nom se serait glissé sous sa plume, qu'elle l'aurait tracé sur quelque bout de papier dans une minute pensive[6].

Obs. XI. — *Mysophobie.* Une femme qui se lavait les mains cent fois par jour et ne touchait les loquets des portes que du coude.

Redressement. — C'était le cas de Lady Macbeth. Les lavages étaient symboliques et destinés à substituer la pureté physique à la pureté morale qu'elle regrettait avoir perdue. Elle se tourmentait de remords pour une infidélité conjugale dont elle avait décidé de chasser le souvenir. Elle se lavait aussi les parties génitales.

UNE DÉFENSE DU MOI
CONTRE UNE IDÉE QU'IL NE PEUT TOLÉRER

Quant à la théorie de cette substitution, je me contenterai de répondre à trois questions qui se posent ici :

1° *Comment cette substitution peut-elle se faire ?*

Il semble qu'elle est l'expression d'une disposition psychique spé-

---

6. Voir aussi la *chanson populaire allemande :*
Auf jedes weiße Blatt Papier möcht ich es schreiben :
Dein ist mein Herz und soll es ewig, ewig bleiben.

ciale. Au moins rencontre-t-on dans les obsessions assez souvent l'hérédité similaire, comme dans l'hystérie. Ainsi le malade de l'observation II me racontait que son père avait souffert de symptômes semblables. Il me fit connaître un jour un cousin germain avec obsessions et tic convulsif, et la fille de sa sœur âgée de onze ans, qui montrait déjà des obsessions (probablement de remords).

2° *Quel est le motif de cette substitution ?*

Je crois qu'on peut l'envisager comme un acte *de défense (Abwehr) du Moi contre l'idée inconciliable.* Parmi mes malades il y en a qui se rappellent l'effort de la volonté pour chasser l'idée ou le souvenir pénible du rayon de la conscience (voir les observations III, IV, XI). En d'autres cas cette expulsion de l'idée inconciliable s'est produite d'une manière inconsciente qui n'a pas laissé trace dans la mémoire des malades.

3° *Pourquoi l'état émotif associé à l'idée obsédante s'est-il perpétué, au lieu de s'évanouir comme les autres états de notre Moi ?*

On peut donner cette réponse en s'adressant à la théorie développée pour la genèse des symptômes hystériques par M. Breuer et moi[7]. Ici je veux seulement remarquer que, par le fait même de la substitution, la disparition de l'état émotif devient impossible.

CE QUI DISTINGUE LES PHOBIES DES OBSESSIONS EST LA PEUR

A ces deux groupes d'obsessions vraies s'ajoute la classe des « phobies », qu'il faut considérer maintenant. J'ai déjà mentionné la grande différence des obsessions et des phobies ; que dans les dernières l'état émotif est toujours l'anxiété, la peur. Je pourrais ajouter que les obsessions sont multiples et plus spécialisées, les phobies plutôt monotones et typiques.

Mais ce n'est pas une différence capitale.

On peut discerner aussi parmi les phobies deux groupes, caractérisés par l'objet de la peur : 1° phobies communes : peur exagérée des choses que tout le monde abhorre ou craint un peu, la nuit, la solitude, la mort, les maladies, les dangers en général, les serpents, etc. ; 2° phobies d'occasion, peur de conditions spéciales, qui n'inspirent pas de crainte à l'homme sain, par exemple l'agoraphobie et les autres phobies de la locomotion. Il est intéressant de noter que ces dernières phobies ne sont pas obsédantes comme les obsessions vraies et les

---

7. *Neurologisches Zentralblatt*, 1893, nᵒˢ 1 et 2.

phobies communes. L'état émotif ici ne paraît que dans ces conditions spéciales que le malade évite soigneusement.

Le mécanisme des phobies est tout à fait différent de celui des obsessions. Ce n'est plus le règne de la substitution. Ici on ne dévoile plus par l'analyse psychique une idée inconciliable, substituée. On ne trouve jamais autre chose que l'*état émotif, anxieux,* qui par une sorte d'élection a fait ressortir toutes les idées propres à devenir l'objet d'une phobie. Dans le cas de l'agoraphobie, etc., on rencontre souvent le *souvenir d'une attaque d'angoisse,* et en vérité ce que redoute le malade c'est l'événement d'une telle attaque dans les conditions spéciales où il croit ne pouvoir y échapper.

L'angoisse de cet état émotif, qui est au fond des phobies, n'est pas dérivé d'un souvenir quelconque ; on doit bien se demander quelle peut être la source de cette condition puissante du système nerveux.

Eh bien, j'espère pouvoir démontrer une autre fois qu'il y a lieu de constituer une névrose spéciale, la *névrose anxieuse,* de laquelle cet état émotif est le symptôme principal ; je donnerai l'énumération de ses symptômes variés, et j'insisterai en ce qu'il faut différencier cette névrose de la neurasthénie, avec laquelle elle est maintenant confondue. Ainsi *les phobies font partie de la névrose anxieuse,* et elles sont presque toujours accompagnées d'autres symptômes de la même série.

La névrose anxieuse est d'origine sexuelle, elle aussi, autant que je puis voir, mais elle ne se rattache pas à des idées tirées de la vie sexuelle : elle n'a pas de mécanisme psychique, à vrai dire. Son étiologie spécifique est l'accumulation de la tension génésique, provoquée par l'abstinence ou l'irritation génésique fruste[8](pour donner une formule générale pour l'effet du coït interrompu[9], de l'impuissance relative du mari, des excitations sans satisfaction des fiancés, de l'abstinence forcée, etc.).

C'est dans de telles conditions extrêmement fréquentes, principalement pour la femme dans la société actuelle, que se développe la névrose anxieuse, de laquelle les phobies sont une manifestation psychique.

Je ferai remarquer, comme conclusion, qu'il peut y avoir combinaison de phobie et d'obsession propre, et même que c'est un événement très fréquent. On peut trouver qu'il y avait au commencement de la maladie une phobie développée comme symptôme de la névrose anxieuse. L'idée qui constitue la phobie qui s'y trouve associée à la peur peut être remplacée par une autre idée ou plutôt par le *procédé*

---

8. Il est probable qu'il faut lire ici *frustrée.* (N.d. Jean Laplanche.)
9. Toutes les éditions avant 1952 donnent ici : *réservé.* (N.d. Jean Laplanche.)

protecteur qui semblait soulager la peur. L'observation VI[10] (folie de la spéculation) présente un bel exemple de cette catégorie, *phobie doublée d'une obsession vraie par substitution.*

SIGMUND FREUD[11]

UN CAS D'OBSESSION DÉCLENCHÉE PAR UNE LETTRE ANONYME

Un jeune officier en permission me prie de me charger du traitement de sa belle-mère qui, quoique vivant dans des conditions on ne peut plus heureuses, empoisonne son existence et l'existence de tous les siens par une idée absurde. Je me trouve en présence d'une dame âgée de cinquante-trois ans, bien conservée, d'un abord aimable et simple. Elle me raconte volontiers l'histoire suivante. Elle vit très heureuse à la campagne avec son mari qui dirige une grande usine. Elle n'a qu'à se louer des égards et prévenances que son mari a pour elle. Ils ont fait un mariage d'amour il y a trente ans et, depuis le jour du mariage, nulle discorde, aucun motif de jalousie ne sont venus troubler la paix du ménage. Ses deux enfants sont bien mariés et son mari, voulant remplir ses devoirs de chef de famille jusqu'au bout, ne consent pas encore à se retirer des affaires. Un fait incroyable, à elle-même incompréhensible, s'est produit il y a un an : elle n'hésita pas à ajouter foi à une lettre anonyme qui accusait son excellent mari de relations amoureuses avec une jeune fille. Depuis qu'elle a reçu cette lettre, son bonheur est brisé. Une enquête un peu serrée révéla qu'une femme de chambre, que cette dame admettait peut-être trop dans son intimité, poursuivait d'une haine féroce une autre jeune fille qui, étant de même extraction qu'elle, avait infiniment mieux réussi dans sa vie : au lieu de se faire domestique, elle avait fait des études qui lui avaient permis d'entrer à l'usine en qualité d'employée. La mobilisation ayant raréfié le personnel de l'usine, cette jeune fille avait fini par occuper une belle situation : elle était logée à l'usine même, ne fréquentait que des « messieurs » et tout le monde l'appelait « mademoiselle ». Jalouse de cette supériorité, la femme de chambre était prête à dire tout le mal possible de son ancienne compagne d'école. Un jour sa maîtresse lui parle d'un vieux monsieur qui était venu en visite et qu'on savait séparé de sa femme et vivant avec une maîtresse. Notre malade ignore ce qui la poussa, à ce

10. Lire : VII. (N.d. Jean Laplanche.)
11. *Névrose, psychose et perversion* (« Obsessions et phobies »), p. 40 à 45.

propos, à dire à sa femme de chambre qu'il n'y aurait pour elle rien de plus terrible que d'apprendre que son bon mari a une liaison. Le lendemain elle reçoit par la poste la lettre anonyme dans laquelle lui était annoncée, d'une écriture déformée, la fatale nouvelle. Elle soupçonna aussitôt que cette lettre était l'œuvre de sa méchante femme de chambre, car c'était précisément la jeune fille que celle-ci poursuivait de sa haine qui y était accusée d'être la maîtresse du mari. Mais bien que la patiente ne tardât pas à deviner l'intrigue et qu'elle eût assez d'expérience pour savoir combien sont peu dignes de foi ces lâches dénonciations, cette lettre ne l'en a pas moins profondément bouleversée. Elle eut une crise d'excitation terrible et envoya chercher son mari auquel elle adressa, dès son apparition, les plus amers reproches. Le mari accueillit l'accusation en riant et fit tout ce qu'il put pour calmer sa femme. Il fit venir le médecin de la famille et de l'usine qui joignit ses efforts aux siens. L'attitude ultérieure du mari et de la femme fut des plus naturelles : la femme de chambre fut renvoyée, mais la prétendue maîtresse resta en place. Depuis ce jour, la malade prétendait souvent qu'elle était calmée et ne croyait plus au contenu de la lettre anonyme. Mais son calme n'était jamais ni profond ni durable. Il lui suffisait d'entendre prononcer le nom de la jeune fille ou de rencontrer celle-ci dans la rue pour entrer dans une nouvelle crise de méfiance, de douleurs et de reproches.

Telle est l'histoire de cette brave dame. Il ne faut pas posséder une grande expérience psychiatrique pour comprendre que, contrairement à d'autres malades nerveux, elle était plutôt encline à atténuer son cas ou, comme nous le disons, à dissimuler, et qu'elle n'a jamais réussi à vaincre sa foi dans l'accusation formulée dans la lettre anonyme.

UNE IDÉE FIXE CONSCIENTE QUI DÉLIVRE D'UN REMORDS

J'espère pouvoir vous montrer que même dans un cas aussi difficilement accessible que celui qui nous occupe, la psychanalyse est capable de mettre au jour des faits propres à nous le rendre intelligible. Veuillez d'abord vous souvenir de ce détail insignifiant en apparence qu'à vrai dire la patiente a provoqué la lettre anonyme, point de départ de son obsession : n'a-t-elle pas notamment dit la veille à la jeune intrigante que son plus grand malheur serait d'apprendre que son mari a une maîtresse ? En disant cela, elle avait suggéré à la femme de chambre l'idée d'envoyer la lettre anonyme. L'obsession devient ainsi, dans une certaine mesure, indépendante de la lettre ; elle a dû exister antérieurement chez la malade, à l'état d'appréhension (ou de désir ?). Ajoutez à cela les quelques faits que j'ai pu dégager à la suite de deux heures d'analyse. La malade se montrait très peu disposée à obéir lorsque, son histoire racontée, je l'avais priée de me faire part d'autres idées et souvenirs pouvant s'y rattacher. Elle prétendait qu'elle n'avait plus rien a dire et, au bout de deux heures, il a fallu cesser l'expérience, la malade ayant déclaré qu'elle se sentait tout à fait bien et qu'elle était certaine d'être débarrassée de son idée morbide. Il va sans dire que cette declaration lui a été dictée par la crainte de me voir poursuivre l'analyse. Mais, au cours de ces deux heures, elle n'en a pas moins laisse échapper quelques remarques qui autorisèrent, qui imposèrent même une certaine interprétation projetant une vive lumière sur la genese de son obsession. Elle éprouvait elle-même un profond sentiment pour un jeune homme, pour ce gendre sur les instances duquel je m'étais rendu auprès d'elle. De ce sentiment, elle ne se rendait pas compte ; elle en etait à peine consciente : vu les liens de parenté qui l'unissaient a ce jeune homme, son affection amoureuse n'eut pas de peine à revêtir le masque d'une tendresse inoffensive. Or, nous possédons une experience suffisante de ces situations pour pouvoir pénétrer sans difficulte dans la vie psychique de cette honnête femme et excellente mere de cinquante-trois ans. L'affection qu'elle éprouvait était trop monstrueuse et impossible pour être consciente ; elle n'en persistait pas moins à l'état inconscient et exerçait ainsi une forte pression. Il lui fallait quelque chose pour la délivrer de cette pression, et elle dut son soulagement au mécanisme du déplacement qui joue si souvent un rôle dans la production de la jalousie obsédante. Une fois convaincue que si elle, vieille femme, était amoureuse d'un jeune homme, son mari, en revanche, avait pour maîtresse une jeune fille, elle se sentit délivree du remords que pouvait lui causer son infidélité. L'idée fixe de l'infidelité du mari devait agir comme un baume calmant appliqué sur une plaie brûlante. Inconsciente de son propre amour, elle avait une conscience obsédante, allant jusqu'à la manie, du reflet de cet amour, reflet dont elle retirait un si grand avantage. Tous les arguments qu'on pouvait opposer à son idée devaient rester sans effet, car ils étaient dirigés non contre le modèle, mais contre son image réfléchie, celui-là communiquant sa force à celle-ci et restant caché, inattaquable, dans l'inconscient.

Récapitulons les données que nous avons pu obtenir par ce bref et difficile effort psychanalytique. Elles nous permettront peut-être de comprendre ce cas morbide, à supposer naturellement que nous ayons procédé correctement, ce dont vous ne pouvez pas être juges ici. Première donnée : l'idée fixe n'est plus quelque chose d'absurde ni d'incompréhensible ; elle a un sens, elle est bien motivée, fait partie d'un événement affectif survenu dans la vie de la malade. Deuxieme donnée : cette idée fixe est un fait nécessaire, en tant que réaction contre un processus psychique inconscient que nous avons pu dégager d'après d'autres signes ; et c'est précisément au lien qui la rattache à ce processus psychique inconscient qu'elle doit son caractère obsédant, sa résistance à tous les arguments fournis par la logique et la réalité. Cette idée fixe est même quelque chose de bienvenu, une sorte de consolation. Troisième donnée : si la malade a fait la veille à la jeune intrigante la confidence que vous savez, il est incontestable qu'elle y a été poussée par le sentiment secret qu'elle éprouvait à l'égard de son gendre et qui forme comme l'arrière-fond de sa maladie. Ce cas présente ainsi, avec l'action symptomatique que nous avons analysée plus haut, des analogies importantes, car, ici comme là, nous avons réussi à dégager le sens ou l'intention de la manifestation psychique, ainsi que ses rapports avec un élément inconscient faisant partie de la situation.

LA SEXUALITÉ EN TOILE DE FOND

Il va sans dire que nous n'avons pas résolu toutes les questions se rattachant à notre cas. Celui-ci est plutôt hérissé de problèmes dont quelques-uns ne sont pas encore susceptibles de solution, tandis que d'autres n'ont pu être résolus, à cause des circonstances défavorables particulières à ce cas. Pourquoi, par exemple, cette femme, si heureuse en ménage, devient-elle amoureuse de son gendre et pourquoi la délivrance, qui aurait bien pu revêtir une autre forme quelconque, se produit-elle sous la forme d'un reflet, d'une projection sur son mari de son état à elle ? Ne croyez pas que ce soit là des questions oiseuses et malicieuses. Elles comportent des réponses en vue desquelles nous disposons déjà de nombreux éléments. Notre malade se trouve à l'âge critique qui comporte une exaltation subite et indésirée du besoin sexuel : ce fait pourrait, à la rigueur, suffire à lui seul à expliquer tout le reste. Mais il se peut encore que le bon et fidèle mari ne soit plus, depuis quelques années, en possession d'une puissance sexuelle en rapport avec le besoin de sa femme, mieux conservée. Nous savons par expérience que ces maris, dont la fidélité n'a d'ailleurs pas besoin d'autre explication, témoignent précisément à leurs femmes une tendresse particulière et se montrent d'une grande indulgence pour leurs troubles nerveux. De plus, il n'est pas du tout indifférent que l'amour morbide de cette dame se soit précisément porté sur le jeune mari de sa fille. Un fort attachement érotique à la fille, attachement qui peut être ramené, en dernière analyse, à la constitution sexuelle de la mère, trouve souvent le moyen de se maintenir à la faveur d'une pareille transformation. Dois-je vous rappeler, à ce propos, que les relations sexuelles

162

PRIAPE

*La malade dont parle Freud n'avait pas supporté l'échec sexuel
de son époux, et voulait le dissimuler par des actes compulsionnels.
(Culte de Priape, Dieu de la virilité,
Bibliothèque des Arts Décoratifs).*

entre belle-mère et gendre ont toujours été considérées comme particulièrement abjectes et étaient frappées chez les peuples primitifs d'interdictions *tabou* et de « flétrissures » rigoureuses[12] ? Aussi bien dans le sens positif que dans le sens négatif, ces relations dépassent souvent la mesure socialement désirable. Comme il ne m'a pas été possible de poursuivre l'analyse de ce cas pendant plus de deux heures, je ne saurais vous dire lequel de ces trois facteurs doit être incriminé chez la malade qui nous occupe ; sa névrose a pu être produite par l'action de l'un ou de deux d'entre eux, comme par celle de tous les trois réunis.

LE SOUVENIR OUBLIÉ D'UNE HONTE

Une dame âgée de trente ans environ, qui souffrait de phénomènes d'obsession très grave et que j'aurais peut-être réussi à soulager, sans un perfide accident qui a rendu vain tout mon travail (je vous en parlerai peut-être un jour), exécutait plusieurs fois par jour, entre beaucoup d'autres, l'action obsédante suivante, tout à fait remarquable. Elle se précipitait de sa chambre dans une autre pièce contiguë, s'y plaçait dans un endroit déterminé devant la table occupant le milieu de la pièce, sonnait sa femme de chambre, lui donnait un ordre quelconque ou la renvoyait purement et simplement et s'enfuyait de nouveau précipitamment dans sa chambre. Certes, ce symptôme morbide n'était pas grave, mais il était de nature à exciter la curiosité. L'explication a été obtenue de la façon la plus certaine et irréfutable, sans la moindre

12. Cf. *Totem et tabou*, Payot, Paris.

intervention du médecin. Je ne vois même pas comment j'aurais pu même soupçonner le sens de cette action obsédante, entrevoir la moindre possibilité de son interprétation. Toutes les fois que je demandais à la malade : « pourquoi le faites-vous ? » elle me répondait : « je n'en sais rien ». Mais un jour, après que j'eus réussi à vaincre chez elle un grave scrupule de conscience, elle trouva subitement l'explication et me raconta des faits se rattachant à cette action obsédante. Il y a plus de dix ans, elle avait épousé un homme beaucoup plus âgé qu'elle et qui, la nuit de noces, se montra impuissant. Il avait passé la nuit à courir de sa chambre dans celle de sa femme, pour renouveler la tentative, mais chaque fois sans succès. Le matin il dit, contrarié : « J'ai honte devant la femme de chambre qui va faire le lit. » Ceci dit, il saisit un flacon d'encre rouge, qui se trouvait par hasard dans la chambre, et en versa le contenu sur le drap de lit, mais pas à l'endroit précis où auraient dû se trouver les taches de sang. Je n'avais pas compris tout d'abord quel rapport il y avait entre ce souvenir et l'action obsédante de ma malade ; le passage répété d'une pièce dans une autre et l'apparition de la femme de chambre étaient les seuls faits qu'elle avait en commun avec l'événement réel. Alors la malade, m'amenant dans la deuxième chambre et me plaçant devant la table, me fit découvrir sur le tapis de celle-ci une grande tache rouge. Et elle m'expliqua qu'elle se mettait devant la table dans une position telle que la femme de chambre qu'elle appelait ne pût pas ne pas apercevoir la tache. Je n'eus plus alors de doute quant aux rapports étroits existant entre la scène de la nuit de noces et l'action obsédante actuelle. Mais ce cas comportait encore beaucoup d'autres enseignements.

Il est avant tout évident que la malade s'identifie avec son mari ; elle joue son rôle en imitant sa course d'une pièce à l'autre. Mais pour que l'identification soit complète, nous devons admettre qu'elle remplace le lit et le drap de lit par la table et le tapis de table. Ceci peut paraître arbitraire, mais ce n'est pas pour rien que nous avons étudié le symbolisme des rêves. Dans le rêve aussi on voit souvent une table qui doit être interprétée comme figurant un lit. Table et lit réunis figurent le mariage. Aussi l'un remplace-t-il facilement l'autre.

RÊVE ET ACTION OBSÉDANTE RÉALISENT TOUS DEUX UN DÉSIR

La preuve serait ainsi faite que l'action obsédante a un sens ; elle paraît être une représentation, une répétition de la scène significative que nous avons décrite plus haut. Mais rien ne nous oblige à nous en tenir à cette apparence ; en soumettant à un examen plus approfondi les rapports entre la scène et l'action obsédante, nous obtiendrons peut-être des renseignements sur des faits plus éloignés, sur l'intention de l'action. Le noyau de celle-ci consiste manifestement dans l'appel adressé à la femme de chambre dont le regard est attiré sur la tache, contrairement à l'observation du mari : « Nous devrions avoir honte devant la femme de chambre. » Jouant le rôle du mari, elle le représente donc comme n'ayant pas honte devant la femme de chambre, la tache se trouvait à la bonne place. Nous voyons donc que notre malade ne s'est pas contentée de reproduire la scène : elle l'a continuée et corrigée, elle l'a rendue réussie. Mais, ce faisant, elle corrige également un autre accident pénible de la fameuse nuit, accident qui avait rendu nécessaire le recours à l'encre rouge : l'impuissance du mari. L'action obsédante signifie donc : « Non, ce n'est pas vrai ; il n'avait pas à avoir honte ; il ne fut pas impuissant. » Tout comme dans un rêve, elle représente ce désir comme réalisé dans une action actuelle, elle obéit à la tendance consistant à élever son mari au-dessus de son échec de jadis.

A l'appui de ce que je viens de dire, je pourrais vous citer tout ce que je sais encore sur cette femme. Autrement dit : tout ce que nous savons sur son compte nous impose cette interprétation de son action obsédante, en elle-même inintelligible. Cette femme vit depuis des années séparée de son mari et lutte contre l'intention de demander une rupture légale du mariage. Mais il ne peut être question pour elle de se libérer de son mari ; elle se sent contrainte de lui rester fidèle, elle vit dans la retraite, afin de ne pas succomber à une tentation, elle excuse son mari et le grandit dans son imagination. Mieux que cela, le mystère le plus profond de sa maladie consiste en ce que par celle-ci elle protège son mari contre de méchants propos, justifie leur séparation dans l'espace et lui rend possible une existence séparée agréable. C'est ainsi que l'analyse d'une anodine action obsédante nous conduit directement jusqu'au noyau le plus caché d'un cas morbide et nous révèle en même temps une partie non négligeable du mystère de la névrose obsessionnelle.

UN CÉRÉMONIAL OBSESSIONNEL ACCOMPAGNANT LE COUCHER

Abordons notre deuxième exemple, d'un genre tout à fait différent, un échantillon d'une espèce très commune : un cérémonial accompagnant le coucher.

Il s'agit d'une belle jeune fille de dix-neuf ans, très douée, enfant unique de ses parents, auxquels elle est supérieure par son instruction et sa vivacité intellectuelle. Enfant, elle était d'un caractère sauvage et orgueilleux et était devenue, au cours des dernières années et sans aucune cause extérieure apparente, morbidement nerveuse. Elle se montre particulièrement irritée contre sa mère ; elle est mécontente, déprimée, portée à l'indécision et au doute et finit par avouer qu'elle ne peut plus traverser seule des places et des rues un peu larges. Il y a là un état morbide compliqué, qui comporte au moins deux diagnostics : celui d'agoraphobie et celui de névrose obsessionnelle. Nous ne nous y arrêterons pas longtemps : la seule chose qui nous intéresse dans le cas de cette malade, c'est son cérémonial du coucher qui est une source de souffrances pour ses parents.

Le cérémonial morbide comporte des conditions que nulle raison ne justifie, et d'autres qui sont nettement antirationnelles. Notre malade justifie les précautions qu'elle prend pour la nuit par cette raison que pour dormir elle a besoin de calme ; elle doit donc éliminer toutes les sources de bruit. Pour réaliser ce but, elle prend tous les soirs, avant le sommeil, les deux précautions suivantes : en premier lieu, elle arrête la grande pendule qui se trouve dans sa chambre et fait emporter toutes les autres pendules, sans même faire une exception pour sa petite montre-bracelet dans son écrin ; en deuxième lieu, elle réunit sur son bureau tous les pots à fleurs et vases, de telle sorte qu'aucun d'entre eux ne puisse, pendant la nuit, se casser en tombant et ainsi troubler son sommeil. Elle sait parfaitement bien que le besoin de repos ne justifie ces mesures qu'en apparence ; elle se rend compte que la petite montre-bracelet, laissée dans son écrin, ne saurait troubler son sommeil par son tic-tac, et nous savons tous par expérience que le tic-tac régulier et monotone d'une pendule, loin de troubler le sommeil, ne fait que le favoriser. Elle convient, en outre, que la crainte pour les pots à fleurs et les vases ne repose sur aucune vraisemblance. Les autres conditions du cérémonial n'ont rien à voir avec le besoin de repos. Au contraire : la malade exige, par exemple, que la porte qui sépare sa chambre de celle de ses parents reste entrouverte et, pour obtenir ce résultat, elle immobilise la porte ouverte à l'aide de divers objets, précaution susceptible d'engendrer des bruits qui, sans elle, pourraient être évités. Mais les précautions les plus importantes portent sur le lit même. L'oreiller qui se trouve à la tête du lit ne doit pas toucher au bois de lit. Le petit coussin de tête doit être disposé en losange sur le grand, et la malade place sa tête dans la direction du diamètre longitudinal de ce losange. L'édredon de plumes doit au préalable être secoué, de façon à ce que le côté correspondant aux pieds devienne plus épais que le côté opposé ; mais, cela fait, la malade ne tarde pas à défaire son travail et à aplatir cet épaississement.

LE TRAVAIL DE L'ANALYSE

Je vous fais grâce des autres détails, souvent très minutieux, de ce cérémonial ; ils ne nous apprendraient d'ailleurs rien de nouveau et nous entraîneraient trop loin du but que nous nous proposons. Mais sachez bien que tout cela ne s'accomplit pas aussi facilement et aussi simplement qu'on pourrait le croire. Il y a toujours la crainte que tout ne soit pas fait avec les soins nécessaires ; chaque acte doit être contrôlé, répété, le doute s'attaque tantôt à l'une, tantôt à une autre précaution, et tout ce travail dure une heure ou deux pendant lesquelles ni la jeune fille ni ses parents terrifiés ne peuvent s'endormir.

L'analyse de ces tracasseries n'a pas été aussi facile que celle de l'action obsédante de notre précédente malade. J'ai été obligé de guider la jeune fille et de lui proposer des projets d'interprétation qu'elle repoussait invariablement par un *non* catégorique ou qu'elle n'accueillait qu'avec un doute méprisant. Mais cette première réaction de négation fut suivie d'une période pendant laquelle elle était préoccupée elle-même par les possibilités qui lui étaient proposées, cherchant à faire surgir des idées se rapportant à ces possibilités, évoquant des souvenirs, reconstituant des ensembles, et elle a fini par accepter toutes nos interprétations, mais à la suite d'une élaboration personnelle. A mesure que ce travail s'accomplissait en elle, elle devenait de moins en moins méticuleuse dans l'exécution de ses actions obsédantes, et avant même la fin du traitement tout son cérémonial était abandonné.

DES SYMBOLES SEXUELS
SE RATTACHANT À L'OBSESSION

Notre malade commence peu à peu à comprendre que c'est à titre de symbole génital féminin qu'elle ne supportait pas, pendant la nuit, la présence de la pendule dans sa chambre. La pendule, dont nous connaissons encore d'autres interprétations symboliques, assume ce rôle de symbole génital féminin à cause de la périodicité de son fonctionnement qui s'accomplit à des intervalles égaux. Une femme peut souvent se vanter en disant que ses menstrues s'accomplissent avec la régularité d'une pendule. Mais ce que notre malade craignait surtout, c'était d'être troublée dans son sommeil par le tic-tac de la pendule. Ce tic-tac peut être considéré comme une représentation symbolique des battements du clitoris lors de l'excitation sexuelle. Elle était en effet souvent réveillée par cette sensation pénible, et c'est la crainte de l'érection qui lui avait fait écarter de son voisinage, pendant la nuit, toutes les pendules et montres en marche. Pots à fleurs et vases sont, comme tous les récipients, également des symboles féminins. Aussi la crainte de les exposer pendant la nuit à tomber et à se briser n'est-elle pas tout à fait dépourvue de sens. Vous connaissez tous cette coutume très répandue qui consiste à briser, pendant les fiançailles, un vase ou une assiette. Chacun des assistants s'en approprie un fragment, ce que nous devons considérer, en nous plaçant au point de vue d'une organisation matrimoniale prémonogamique, comme un renoncement aux droits que chacun pouvait ou croyait avoir sur la fiancée. A cette partie de son cérémonial se rattachaient, chez notre jeune fille, un souvenir et plusieurs idées. Étant enfant, elle tomba, pendant qu'elle avait à la main un vase en verre ou en terre, et se fit au doigt une blessure qui saigna abondamment. Devenue jeune fille et ayant eu connaissance des faits se rattachant aux relations sexuelles, elle fut obsédée par la crainte angoissante qu'elle pourrait ne pas saigner pendant sa nuit de noces, ce qui ferait naître dans l'esprit de son mari des doutes quant à sa virginité. Ses précautions contre le bris des vases constituent donc une sorte de protestation contre tout le complexe en rapport avec la virginité et l'hémorragie consécutive aux premiers rapports sexuels, une protestation aussi bien contre la crainte de saigner que contre la crainte opposée, celle de ne pas saigner. Quant aux précautions contre le bruit, auxquelles elle subordonnait ces mesures, elles n'avaient rien, ou à peu près rien, à voir avec celles-ci.

EMPÊCHER SES PARENTS D'AVOIR DES RAPPORTS SEXUELS

Elle révéla le sens central de son cérémonial un jour où elle eut la compréhension subite de la raison pour laquelle elle ne voulait pas que l'oreiller touchât au bois de lit : l'oreiller, disait-elle, est toujours femme, et la paroi verticale du lit est homme. Elle voulait ainsi, par une sorte d'action magique, pourrions-nous dire, séparer l'homme et la femme, c'est-à-dire empêcher ses parents d'avoir des rapports sexuels. Longtemps avant d'avoir établi son cérémonial, elle avait cherché à atteindre le même but d'une manière plus directe. Elle avait simulé la peur ou utilisé une peur réelle pour obtenir que la porte qui séparait la chambre à coucher des parents de la sienne fût laissée ouverte pendant la nuit. Et elle avait conservé cette mesure dans son cérémonial actuel. Elle s'offrait ainsi l'occasion d'épier les parents et, à force de vouloir profiter de cette occasion, elle s'était attiré une insomnie qui avait duré plusieurs mois. Non contente de troubler ainsi ses parents, elle venait de temps à autre s'installer dans leur lit, entre le père et la mère. Et c'est alors que l'« oreiller » et le « bois de lit » se trouvaient réellement séparés. Lorsqu'elle eut enfin grandi, au point de ne plus pouvoir coucher avec ses parents sans les gêner et sans être gênée elle-même, elle s'ingéniait encore à simuler la peur, afin d'obtenir que la mère lui cédât sa place auprès du père et vînt elle-même coucher dans le lit de sa fille. Cette situation fut certainement le point de départ de quelques inventions dont nous retrouvons la trace dans son cérémonial.

Si un oreiller est un symbole féminin, l'acte consistant à secouer l'édredon jusqu'à ce que toutes les plumes s'étant amassées dans sa partie inférieure y forment une boursouflure, avait également un sens : il signifiait rendre la femme enceinte ; mais notre malade ne tardait pas à dissiper cette grossesse, car elle avait vécu pendant des années dans la crainte que des rapports de ses parents ne naquît un nouvel enfant qui lui aurait fait concurrence. D'autre part, si le grand oreiller, symbole féminin, représentait la mère, le petit oreiller de tête ne pouvait représenter que la fille. Pourquoi ce dernier oreiller devait-il être disposé en losange, et pourquoi la tête de notre malade devait-elle être placée dans le sens de la ligne médiane de ce losange ? Parce que le losange représente la forme de l'appareil génital de la femme, lorsqu'il est ouvert. C'est donc elle-même qui jouait le rôle du mâle, sa tête remplaçant l'appareil sexuel masculin (*cf.* : « La décapitation comme représentation symbolique de la castration »).

L'analyse de ce cérémonial aurait pu nous fournir d'autres résultats encore si nous avions tenu exactement compte de tous les autres symptômes présentés par la malade. Mais ceci ne se rattachait pas au but que nous nous étions proposé. Contentez-vous de savoir que cette jeune fille éprouvait pour son père une attirance érotique dont les débuts remontaient à son enfance, et il faut peut-être voir dans ce fait la raison de son attitude peu amicale envers sa mère. C'est ainsi que l'analyse de ce symptôme nous a encore introduits dans la vie sexuelle de la malade, et nous trouverons ce fait de moins en moins étonnant, à mesure que nous apprendrons à mieux connaître le sens et l'intention des symptômes névrotiques.

LE REFOULEMENT, CONDITION PRÉALABLE DE LA FORMATION DES SYMPTÔMES

Une remarque à laquelle j'attacherais de l'importance serait celle que vous feriez en disant que l'organisation de l'appareil psychique, telle que je la postule ici[13] pour les besoins de ma cause, qui est celle de l'explication de symptômes névrotiques, doit, pour être valable avoir

---

13. Freud vient d'assimiler le système inconscient à une antichambre, à laquelle est attenant un salon : la conscience. Un gardien veille à l'entrée de l'antichambre. (N.d.E.)

une portée générale et nous rendre compte également de la fonction normale. Rien de plus exact. Je ne puis pour le moment donner à cette remarque la suite qu'elle comporte, mais notre intérêt pour la psychologie de la formation de symptômes ne peut qu'augmenter dans des proportions extraordinaires, si nous pouvons vraiment espérer obtenir, grâce à l'étude de ces conditions pathologiques, des informations sur le devenir psychique normal qui nous reste encore si caché.

Cet exposé que je viens de vous faire concernant les deux systemes, leurs rapports réciproques et les liens qui les rattachent à la conscience, ne vous rappelle-t-il donc rien ? Réfléchissez-y bien, et vous vous apercevrez que le gardien qui est en faction entre l'inconscient et le préconscient n'est que la personnification de la censure qui donne au rêve manifeste sa forme définitive. Les restes diurnes, sont les excitateurs du rêve, dans notre conception, des matériaux préconscients qui, ayant subi pendant la nuit l'influence de désirs inconscients et refoulés, s'associent à ces désirs et forment, avec leur collaboration et grâce à l'énergie dont ils sont doués, le rêve latent. Sous la domination du système inconscient, les matériaux préconscients subissent une élaboration consistant en une condensation et un déplacement qu'on n'observe qu'exceptionnellement dans la vie psychique normale, c'est-à-dire dans le système préconscient. Et nous caractérisons chacun des deux systèmes par le mode de travail qui s'y accomplit ; selon le rapport qu'il présentait avec la conscience, elle-même prolongement de la préconscience, on peut dire si tel phénomène donné fait partie de l'un ou de l'autre de ces deux systèmes. Or le rêve, d'après cette manière de voir, ne présente rien d'un phénomène pathologique : il peut survenir chez n'importe quel homme sain, dans les conditions qui caractérisent l'état de sommeil. Cette hypothèse sur la structure de l'appareil psychique, hypothèse qui englobe dans la-même explication la formation du rêve et celle des symptômes névrotiques, a toutes les chances d'être également valable pour la vie psychique normale.

Voici, jusqu'à nouvel ordre, comment il faut comprendre le refoulement. Celui-ci n'est qu'une condition préalable de la formation de symptômes. Nous savons que le symptôme vient se substituer à quelque chose dont le refoulement empêche l'extériorisation. Mais quand on sait ce qu'est le refoulement, on est encore loin de comprendre cette formation substitutive. A l'autre bout du problème, la constatation du refoulement soulève les questions suivantes : Quelles sont les tendances psychiques qui subissent le refoulement ? Quelles sont les forces qui imposent le refoulement ? A quels mobiles obéit-il ? Pour répondre à ces questions, nous ne disposons pour le moment que d'un seul élément. En examinant la résistance, nous apprenons qu'elle est un produit des forces du Moi, de propriétés connues et latentes de son caractère. Ce sont donc aussi ces forces et ces propriétés qui doivent avoir déterminé le refoulement ou, tout au moins, avoir contribué à le produire. Tout le reste nous est encore inconnu.

LE SYMPTÔME :
UNE SATISFACTION SUBSTITUTIVE

Vous vous rappelez sans doute que, dans ces deux cas[14], dont nous avions soumis les symptômes à un examen détaillé, l'analyse nous a fait pénétrer dans la vie sexuelle intime des malades. Dans le premier cas, en outre, nous avons reconnu d'une façon particulièrement nette l'intention ou la tendance des symptômes examinés ; il se peut que dans le deuxième cas cette intention ou tendance ait été masquée par quelque chose dont nous aurons l'occasion de parler plus loin. Or, tous les autres cas que nous soumettrions à l'analyse nous révéleraient exactement les mêmes détails que ceux constatés dans les deux cas en question. Dans tous les cas l'analyse introduirait dans les événements sexuels et nous révélerait des désirs sexuels des malades, et chaque fois nous aurions à constater que leurs symptômes sont au service de la même intention. Cette intention n'est autre que la satisfaction des désirs sexuels ; les symptômes servent à la satisfaction sexuelle du malade, ils se substituent à cette satisfaction lorsque le malade en est privé dans la vie normale.

Souvenez-vous de l'action obsessionnelle de notre première malade. La femme est privée de son mari qu'elle aime profondément et dont elle ne peut partager la vie à cause de ses défauts et de ses faiblesses. Elle doit lui rester fidèle, ne chercher à le remplacer par personne. Son symptôme obsessionnel lui procure ce à quoi elle aspire, relève son mari, nie, corrige ses faiblesses, en premier lieu son impuissance. Ce symptôme n'est au fond, tout comme un rêve, qu'une satisfaction d'un désir et, ce que le rêve n'est pas toujours, qu'une satisfaction d'un désir érotique. A propos de notre deuxième malade, vous avez pu au moins apprendre que son cérémonial avait pour but de s'opposer aux relations sexuelles des parents, afin de rendre impossible la naissance d'un nouvel enfant. Vous avez appris également que par ce cérémonial notre malade tendait au fond à se substituer à sa mère. Il s'agit donc ici, comme dans le premier cas, de suppression d'obstacles s'opposant à la satisfaction sexuelle et de réalisation de désirs érotiques. Quant à la

14. Freud parle ici de ceux de la dame âgée de trente ans et de la jeune fille de dix neuf ans. (N.d.E.)

complication à laquelle nous avons fait allusion, il en sera question dans un instant.

Afin de justifier les restrictions que j'aurai à apporter dans la suite à la généralité de mes propositions, j'attire votre attention sur le fait que tout ce que je dis ici concernant le refoulement, la formation et la signification des symptômes a été déduit de l'analyse de trois formes de névroses : l'hystérie d'angoisse, l'hystérie de conversion et la névrose obsessionnelle, et ne s'applique en premier lieu qu'à ces trois formes. Ces trois affections, que nous avons l'habitude de réunir dans le même groupe sous le nom générique de « névroses de transfert », circonscrivent également le domaine sur lequel peut s'exercer l'activité psychanalytique. Les autres névroses ont fait, de la part de la psychanalyse, l'objet d'études moins approfondies. En ce qui concerne un de leurs groupes, l'impossibilité de toute intervention thérapeutique a été la raison de sa mise de côté. Et puisque tout ce qui a été dit ici s'applique aux trois névroses de transfert, je me permets de rehausser la valeur des symptômes en vous faisant part d'un détail nouveau. Un examen comparé des causes occasionnelles de ces trois affections donne un résultat qui peut se résumer dans la formule suivante : les malades en question souffrent d'une *privation*, la réalité leur refusant la satisfaction de leurs désirs sexuels. Vous le voyez : l'accord est parfait entre ces deux résultats. La seule manière adéquate de comprendre les symptômes consiste à les considérer comme une satisfaction substitutive, destinée à remplacer celle qu'on se voit refuser dans la vie normale.

DES SYMPTÔMES À BUT SEXUEL « POSITIF » OU « NÉGATIF » SELON LA NÉVROSE

Certes, on peut encore opposer de nombreuses objections à la proposition que les symptômes névrotiques sont des symptômes substitutifs. Je vais m'occuper aujourd'hui de deux de ces objections. Si vous avez vous-mêmes soumis à l'examen psychanalytique un certain nombre de malades, vous me direz peut-être sur un ton de reproche : il y a toute une série de cas où votre proposition ne se vérifie pas ; dans ces cas, les symptômes semblent avoir une destination contraire, qui consiste à exclure ou à supprimer la satisfaction sexuelle. Je ne vais pas contester l'exactitude de votre interprétation. Dans la psychanalyse, les choses se révèlent souvent beaucoup plus compliquées que nous le voudrions. Si elles étaient simples, on n'aurait peut-être pas besoin de la psychanalyse pour les élucider. Certaines parties du cérémonial de notre deuxième malade laissent en effet apparaître ce caractère ascétique, hostile à la satisfaction sexuelle, par exemple lorsqu'elle écarte pendules et montres, acte magique par lequel elle pense s epar gner des érections nocturnes, ou lorsqu'elle veut empêcher la chute et le bris de vases, espérant par là préserver sa virginité. Dans d'autres cas de cérémonial précédant le coucher, que j'ai eu l'occasion d'analy ser, ce caractère négatif était beaucoup plus prononcé ; dans certains d'entre eux, tout le cérémonial se composait de mesures de preserva tion contre les souvenirs et les tentations sexuels. La psychanalyse nous a cependant déjà montré plus d'une fois qu'opposition n'est pas toujours contradiction. Nous pourrions élargir notre proposition, en disant que les symptômes ont pour but soit de procurer une satisfac tion sexuelle, soit de l'éluder ; le caractère positif, au sens de la satis faction, étant prédominant dans l'hystérie, le caractère négatif, asceti que, dominant dans la névrose obsessionnelle. Si les symptômes peuvent servir aussi bien à la satisfaction sexuelle qu'à son contraire, cette double destination ou cette bipolarité des symptômes s'explique parfaitement bien par un des rouages de leur mécanisme dont nous n'avons pas encore eu l'occasion de parler. Ils sont notamment, ainsi que nous le verrons, des effets de compromis, résultant de l'interférence de deux tendances opposées, et ils expriment aussi bien ce qui a été refoulé de ce qui a été la cause du refoulement et a ainsi contribué a leur production. La substitution peut se faire plus au profit de l'une de ces tendances que de l'autre ; elle se fait rarement au profit exclusif d'une seule. Dans l'hystérie, les deux intentions s'expriment le plus souvent par un seul et même symptôme ; dans la névrose obsession nelle il y a séparation entre les deux intentions : le symptôme, qui est a deux temps, se compose de deux actions s'accomplissant l'une après l'autre et s'annulant réciproquement.

Il nous sera moins facile de dissiper un autre doute. En passant en revue un certain nombre d'interprétations de symptômes, vous serez probablement tentés de dire que c'est abuser quelque peu que de vou loir les expliquer tous par la satisfaction substitutive des désirs sexuels. Vous ne tarderez pas à faire ressortir que ces symptômes n'offrent a la satisfaction aucun élément réel, qu'ils se bornent le plus souvent à rani mer une sensation ou à représenter une image fantaisiste appartenant a un complexe sexuel. Vous trouverez, en outre, que la prétendue satis faction sexuelle présente souvent un caractère puéril et indigne, se rap proche d'un acte masturbatoire ou rappelle ces pratiques malpropres qu'on défend déjà aux enfants et dont on cherche à les déshabituer. Et, par-dessus tout, vous manifesterez votre étonnement de voir qu'on considère comme une satisfaction sexuelle ce qui ne devrait être décrit que comme une satisfaction de désirs cruels ou affreux, voire de désirs contre nature. Sur ces derniers points, il nous sera impossible de nous mettre d'accord tant que nous n'aurons pas soumis à un examen approfondi la vie sexuelle de l'homme et tant que nous n'aurons pas défini ce qu'il est permis, sans risque d'erreur, de considérer comme *sexuel*.

LES MODES DE FORMATION DE SYMPTÔMES

Aux yeux du profane, ce sont les symptômes qui constitueraient l'essence de la maladie et la guérison consisterait pour lui dans la disparition des symptômes. Le médecin s'attache, au contraire, à distinguer entre symptômes et maladie et prétend que la disparition des symptômes est loin de signifier la guérison de la maladie. Mais ce qui reste de la maladie après la disparition des symptômes, c'est la faculté de former de nouveaux symptômes. Aussi allons-nous provisoirement adopter le point de vue du profane et admettre qu'analyser les symptômes équivaut à comprendre la maladie.

Les symptômes, et nous ne parlons naturellement ici que de symptômes psychiques (ou psychogènes) et de maladie psychique, sont, pour la vie considérée dans son ensemble, des actes nuisibles ou tout au moins inutiles, des actes qu'on accomplit avec aversion et qui sont accompagnés d'un sentiment pénible ou de souffrance. Leur principal dommage consiste dans l'effort psychique qu'exige leur exécution et dans celui dont on a besoin pour les combattre. Ces deux efforts, lorsqu'il s'agit d'une formation exagérée de symptômes, peuvent entraîner une diminution telle de l'énergie psychique disponible que la personne intéressée devient incapable de suffire aux tâches importantes de la vie. Comme cet effet constitue surtout une expression de la quantité d'énergie dépensée, vous concevez sans peine qu'« être malade » est une notion essentiellement pratique. Si, toutefois, vous plaçant à un point de vue théorique, vous faites abstraction de ces quantités, vous pouvez dire, sans crainte de démenti, que nous sommes tous malades, c'est-à-dire névrosés, attendu que les conditions qui président à la formation de symptômes existent également chez l'homme normal.

Pour ce qui est des symptômes névrotiques, nous savons déjà qu'ils sont l'effet d'un conflit qui s'élève au sujet d'un nouveau mode de satisfaction de la libido. Les deux forces qui s'étaient séparées se réunissent de nouveau dans le symptôme, se réconcilient pour ainsi dire à la faveur d'un compromis qui n'est autre que la formation de symptômes. C'est ce qui explique la capacité de résistance du symptôme : il est maintenu de deux côtés. Nous savons aussi que l'un des deux partenaires du conflit représente la libido insatisfaite, écartée de la réalité et obligée de chercher de nouveaux modes de satisfaction. Si la réalité se montre impitoyable, alors même que la libido est disposée à adopter un autre objet à la place de celui qui est refusé, celle-ci sera finalement obligée de s'engager dans la voie de la régression et de chercher sa satisfaction soit dans l'une des organisations déjà dépassées, soit dans l'un des objets antérieurement abandonnés. Ce qui attire la libido sur la voie de la régression, ce sont les fixations qu'elle a laissées à ces stades de son développement.

LE SYMPTÔME : UN HABILE COMPROMIS

Or, la voie de la régression se sépare nettement de celle de la névrose. Lorsque les régressions ne soulèvent aucune opposition du Moi, tout se passe sans névrose, et la libido obtient une satisfaction réelle, sinon toujours normale. Mais lorsque le Moi, qui a le contrôle non seulement de la conscience, mais encore des accès à l'innervation motrice, et, par conséquent, de la possibilité de réalisation des tendances psychiques, lorsque le Moi, disons-nous, n'accepte pas ces régressions, on se trouve en présence d'un conflit. La libido trouve la voie, pour ainsi dire, bloquée et doit essayer de s'échapper dans une direction où elle puisse dépenser sa réserve d'énergie d'après les exigences du principe du plaisir. Elle doit se séparer du Moi. Ce qui lui facilite sa besogne, ce sont les fixations qu'elle a laissées le long du chemin de son développement et contre lesquelles le Moi s'était chaque fois défendu à l'aide de refoulements. En occupant dans sa marche régressive ces positions refoulées, la libido se soustrait au Moi et à ses lois et renonce en même temps à toute l'éducation qu'elle a reçue sous son influence. Elle se laissait guider, tant qu'elle pouvait espérer une satisfaction ; mais sous la double pression de la privation extérieure et intérieure, elle devient insubordonnée et pense avec regret au bonheur du temps passé. Tel est son caractère, au fond invariable. Les représentations auxquelles la libido applique désormais son énergie font partie du système de l'inconscient et sont soumises aux processus qui s'accomplissent dans ce système, en premier lieu à la condensation et au déplacement. Nous nous trouvons ici en présence de la même situation que celle qui caractérise la formation de rêves. Nous savons que le rêve proprement dit, qui s'est formé dans l'inconscient à titre de réalisation d'un désir imaginaire inconscient, se heurte à une certaine activité (pré)consciente. Celle-ci impose au rêve inconscient sa censure à la suite de laquelle survient un compromis caractérisé par la formation d'un rêve manifeste. Or, il en est de même de la libido, dont l'objet, relégué dans l'inconscient, doit compter avec la force du Moi préconscient. L'opposition qui s'est élevée contre cet objet au sein du Moi

175

constitue pour la libido une sorte de « contre-attaque » dirigée contre sa nouvelle position et l'oblige à choisir un mode d'expression qui puisse devenir aussi celui du Moi. Ainsi naît le symptôme, qui est un produit considérablement déformé de la satisfaction inconsciente d'un désir libidineux, un produit équivoque, habilement choisi et possédant deux significations diamétralement opposées. Sur ce dernier point, il y a toutefois entre le rêve et le symptôme cette différence que, dans le premier, l'intention préconsciente vise seulement à préserver le sommeil, à ne rien admettre dans la conscience de ce qui soit susceptible de la troubler ; elle n'oppose pas au désir inconscient un *veto* tranché, elle ne lui crie pas : non ! Au contraire ! Lorsqu'elle a affaire au rêve, l'intention préconsciente doit être plus tolérante, car la situation de l'homme qui dort est moins menacée, l'état de sommeil formant une barrière qui supprime toute communication avec la réalité.

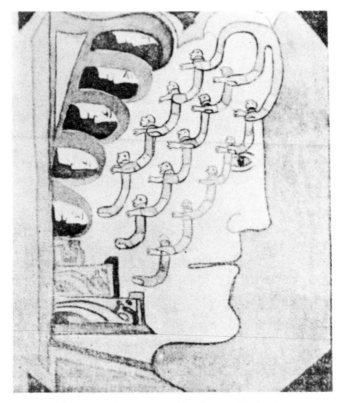

Le symptôme, comme le rêve ou le dessin
de ce psychotique, obéit aux lois
de la condensation et du déplacement.

LES ÉVÉNEMENTS
DE LA SEXUALITÉ INFANTILE :
DES POINTS D'APPUI POUR LA LIBIDO

Vous voyez ainsi que, si la libido peut échapper aux conditions créées par le conflit, elle le doit à l'existence de fixations. Par son retour aux fixations, la libido supprime l'effet des refoulements et obtient une dérivation ou une satisfaction, à la condition d'observer les clauses du compromis. Par ses détours à travers l'inconscient et les anciennes fixations, elle réussit enfin à se procurer une satisfaction réelle, bien qu'excessivement limitée et à peine reconnaissable. A propos de ce résultat final, je ferai deux remarques : en premier lieu, j'attire votre attention sur les liens étroits qui existent ici entre la libido et l'inconscient d'une part, la conscience et la réalité d'autre part, bien qu'au début ces deux couples ne soient rattachés entre eux par aucun lien ; en deuxième lieu, je tiens à vous prévenir, en vous priant de ne pas l'oublier, que tout ce que je viens de dire et tout ce que je dirai dans la suite se rapporte uniquement à la formation de symptômes dans la névrose hystérique.

Où la libido trouve-t-elle les fixations dont elle a besoin pour se frayer une voie à travers les refoulements ? Dans les activités et les événements de la sexualité infantile, dans les tendances partielles et les objets abandonnés et délaissés de l'enfance. C'est à tout cela que revient la libido. L'importance de l'enfance est double : d'une part, l'enfant manifeste pour la première fois des instincts et tendances qu'il apporte au monde à titre de dispositions innées et, d'autre part, il subit des influences extérieures, des événements accidentels qui éveillent à l'activité d'autres de ses instincts. Je crois que nous avons un droit incontestable à adopter cette division. La manifestation de dispositions innées ne soulève aucune objection critique, mais l'expérience analytique nous oblige précisément à admettre que des événements purement accidentels survenus dans l'enfance sont capables de laisser des points d'appui pour les fixations de la libido.

LA NÉVROSE DE L'ADULTE :
LA SUITE DIRECTE D'UNE
NÉVROSE INFANTILE

Arrêtons-nous maintenant à ce résultat de la recherche analytique qui nous montre la libido des névrosés liée aux événements de leur vie sexuelle infantile. De ce fait, ces événements semblent acquérir une importance vitale pour l'homme et jouer un très grand rôle dans l'éclosion de maladies nerveuses. Cette importance et ce rôle sont incontes-

Freud, le premier, a compris l'importance décisive
de l'enfance pour la formation de la personnalité.
(R.M. Eichler, 1900, Bibliothèque des Arts Décoratifs).

tablement très grands, tant qu'on ne tient compte que du travail théra-peutique. Mais si l'on fait abstraction de ce travail, on s'aperçoit facilement qu'on risque d'être victime d'un malentendu et de se faire de la vie une conception unilatérale, fondée trop exclusivement sur la situation névrotique. L'importance des événements infantiles se trouve diminuée par le fait que la libido, dans son mouvement régressif, ne vient s'y fixer qu'après avoir été chassée de ses positions plus avan-cées. La conclusion qui semble s'imposer dans ces conditions est que les événements infantiles dont il s'agit n'ont eu, à l'époque où ils se sont produits, aucune importance et qu'ils ne sont devenus importants que régressivement. Rappelez-vous que nous avons déjà adopté une attitude analogue à propos du *complexe d'Œdipe*.

Il ne nous sera pas difficile de prendre parti dans le cas particulier dont nous nous occupons. La remarque d'après laquelle la transforma-tion libidineuse et, par conséquent, le rôle pathogène des événements de la vie infantile sont dans une grande mesure renforcés par la régres-sion de la libido, est certainement justifiée, mais serait susceptible de nous induire en erreur si nous l'acceptions sans réserves. D'autres considérations doivent encore entrer en ligne de compte. En premier lieu, l'observation montre d'une manière indiscutable que les événe-ments de la vie infantile possèdent leur importance propre, laquelle apparaît d'ailleurs dès l'enfance. Il y a des névroses infantiles dans les-

178

quelles la régression dans le temps ne joue qu'un rôle insignifiant ou ne se produit pas du tout, l'affection éclatant immédiatement à la suite d'un événement traumatique. L'étude de ces névroses infantiles est faite pour nous préserver de plus d'un malentendu dangereux concernant les névroses des adultes, de même que l'étude des rêves infantiles nous avait mis sur la voie qui nous a conduits à la compréhension des rêves d'adultes. Or, les névroses infantiles sont très fréquentes, beaucoup plus fréquentes qu'on ne le croit. Elles passent souvent inaperçues, sont considérées comme des signes de méchanceté ou de mauvaise éducation, sont souvent réprimées par les autorités qui règnent sur la *nursery*, mais sont faciles à reconnaître après coup, par un examen rétrospectif. Elles se manifestent le plus souvent sous la forme d'une *hystérie d'angoisse*, et vous apprendrez à une autre occasion ce que cela signifie. Lorsqu'une névrose éclate à l'une des phases ultérieures de la vie, l'analyse révèle régulièrement qu'elle n'est que la suite directe d'une névrose infantile qui, à l'époque, ne s'est peut-être manifestée que sous un aspect voilé, à l'état d'ébauche.

En deuxième lieu, on est obligé de reconnaître que cette régression régulière de la libido vers la période infantile aurait de quoi nous étonner, s'il n'y avait dans cette période quelque chose qui exerce sur la libido une attraction particulière. La fixation, dont nous admettons l'existence sur certains points du trajet suivi par le développement, serait sans contenu si nous ne la concevions pas comme la cristallisation d'une certaine quantité d'énergie libidineuse. Il est des cas dans lesquels le seul facteur étiologique est constitué par les événements sexuels de l'enfance, d'origine sûrement traumatique et dont les effets, pour se manifester, n'exigent pas d'autres conditions que celles offertes par la constitution sexuelle moyenne et par son immaturité. Mais il est, en revanche, des cas où l'étiologie de la névrose doit être cherchée uniquement dans des conflits ultérieurs et où le rôle des impressions infantiles, révélé par l'analyse, apparaît comme un effet de la régression. Nous avons ainsi les extrêmes de l'« arrêt de développement » et de la « régression » et, entre ces deux extrêmes, tous les degrés de combinaison de ces deux facteurs.

RÉPÉTER LA SATISFACTION RESSENTIE DANS LA PRIME ENFANCE

Mais revenons aux symptômes. A la satisfaction dont on est privé, ils créent une substitution en faisant rétrograder la libido à des phases antérieures, ce qui comporte le retour aux objets ou à l'organisation qui ont caractérisé ces phases. Nous savions déjà que le névrosé est

179

attaché à un certain moment déterminé de son passé ; il s'agit d'une période dans laquelle sa libido n'était pas privée de satisfaction, d'une période où il était heureux. Il cherche dans son passé, jusqu'à ce qu'il trouve une pareille période, dût-il pour cela remonter jusqu'à sa toute première enfance, telle qu'il s'en souvient ou se la représente d'après des indices ultérieurs. Le symptôme reproduit d'une manière ou d'une autre cette satisfaction de la première enfance, satisfaction déformée par la censure qui naît du conflit, accompagnée généralement d'une sensation de souffrance et associée à des facteurs faisant partie de la prédisposition morbide. La satisfaction qui naît du symptôme est de nature bizarre. Nous faisons abstraction du fait que la personne intéressée éprouve cette satisfaction comme une souffrance et s'en plaint : cette transformation est l'effet du conflit psychique sous la pression duquel le symptôme a dû se former. Ce qui fut jadis pour l'individu une satisfaction, doit précisément aujourd'hui provoquer sa résistance ou son aversion.

Mais il est encore une autre raison pour laquelle les symptômes nous paraissent singuliers et, en tant que moyen de satisfaction libidineuse, incompréhensibles. Ils ne nous rappellent que ce dont nous attendons généralement et normalement une satisfaction. Ils font le plus souvent abstraction de l'objet et renoncent ainsi à tout rapport avec la réalité extérieure. Nous disons que c'est là une conséquence du renoncement au principe de réalité et du retour au principe de plaisir. Mais il y a là aussi un retour à une sorte d'auto-érotisme élargi, à celui qui avait procuré à la tendance sexuelle ses premières satisfactions. Les symptômes remplacent une modification du monde extérieur par une modification du corps, donc une action extérieure par une action intérieure, un acte par une adaptation, ce qui, au point de vue phylogénique, correspond encore à une régression tout à fait significative. Nous ne comprendrons bien tout cela qu'à l'occasion d'une nouvelle donnée que nous révéleront plus tard nos recherches analytiques sur la formation des symptômes. Rappelons-nous en outre qu'à la formation de symptômes coopèrent les mêmes processus de l'inconscient que ceux que nous voyons à l'œuvre lors de la formation de rêves, à savoir la condensation et le déplacement. Comme le rêve, le symptôme représente quelque chose comme étant réalisé, une satisfaction à la manière infantile, mais par une condensation poussée à l'extrême degré cette satisfaction peut être enfermée en une seule sensation ou innervation, et par un déplacement extrême elle peut être limitée à un seul petit détail de tout le complexe libidineux. Rien d'étonnant si nous éprouvons, nous aussi, une certaine difficulté à reconnaître dans le symptôme la satisfaction libidineuse soupçonnée et toujours confirmée.

*« Je vous rappellerai cependant que certains souvenirs d'enfance
que les hommes gardent toujours dans leur conscience,
en dehors et indépendamment de toute analyse,
peuvent également être faux, ou, du moins,
présenter un mélange de vrai et de faux ».
(C. Nanteuil, XIXe siècle).*

« DANS LE MONDE DES NÉVROSES, C'EST LA RÉALITÉ PSYCHIQUE QUI JOUE LE RÔLE DOMINANT »

Je viens de vous annoncer que vous alliez apprendre encore quelque chose de nouveau. Il s'agit en effet d'une chose non seulement nouvelle, mais encore étonnante et troublante. Vous savez que par l'analyse ayant pour point de départ les symptômes nous arrivons à la connaissance des événements de la vie infantile auxquels est fixée la libido et dont sont faits les symptômes. Or, l'étonnant c'est que ces scènes infantiles ne sont pas toujours vraies. Oui, le plus souvent elles ne sont pas vraies, et dans quelques cas elles sont même directement contraires à la vérité historique. Les événements infantiles, reconstitués ou évoqués par l'analyse, sont tantôt incontestablement faux, tantôt non moins incontestablement réels, et dans la plupart des cas ils sont un mélange de vrai et de faux. Les symptômes représentent donc tantôt des événements ayant réellement eu lieu et auxquels on doit reconnaître une influence sur la fixation de la libido, tantôt des fantaisies des malades auxquelles on ne peut reconnaître aucun rôle étiologique. Cette situation est de nature à nous mettre dans un très grand embarras. Je vous rappellerai cependant que certains souvenirs d'enfance que les hommes gardent toujours dans leur conscience, en dehors et indépendamment de toute analyse, peuvent également être faux ou du moins présenter un mélange de vrai ou de faux. Or, dans ces cas, la preuve de l'inexactitude est rarement difficile à faire, ce qui nous procure tout au moins la consolation de penser que l'embarras dont je viens de parler est le fait non de l'analyse, mais du malade.

Il suffit de réfléchir un peu pour comprendre ce qui nous trouble dans cette situation : c'est le mépris de la réalité, c'est le fait de ne tenir aucun compte de la différence qui existe entre la réalité et l'imagination. Nous sommes tentés d'en vouloir au malade, parce qu'il nous ennuie avec des histoires imaginaires. La réalité nous paraît séparée de l'imagination par un abîme infranchissable, et nous l'apprécions tout autrement. Tel est d'ailleurs aussi le point de vue du malade lorsqu'il pense normalement. Lorsqu'il nous produit les matériaux qui, dissimulés derrière les symptômes, révèlent des situations modelées sur les événements de la vie infantile et dont le noyau est formé par un désir qui cherche à se satisfaire, nous commençons toujours par nous demander s'il s'agit de choses réelles ou imaginaires. Plus tard, certains signes apparaissent qui nous permettent de résoudre cette question dans un sens ou dans un autre, et nous nous empressons de mettre le malade au courant de notre solution. Mais cette initiation du malade ne va pas sans difficultés. Si nous lui disons dès le début qu'il est en train de raconter des événements imaginaires avec lesquels il voile l'histoire de son enfance, comme les peuples substituent les légendes à l'histoire de leur passé oublié, nous constatons que son intérêt à poursuivre le récit baisse subitement, résultat que nous étions loin de désirer. Il veut, lui aussi, avoir l'expérience de choses réelles et se déclare plein de mépris pour les choses imaginaires. Mais si, pour mener notre travail à bonne fin, nous maintenons le malade dans la conviction que ce qu'il raconte représente les événements réels de son enfance, nous nous exposons à ce qu'il nous reproche plus tard notre erreur et se moque de notre prétendue crédulité. Il a de la peine à nous comprendre lorsque nous l'engageons à mettre sur le même plan la réalité et la fantaisie et à ne pas se préoccuper de savoir si les événements de sa vie infantile, que nous voulons élucider et tels qu'il nous les raconte, sont vrais ou faux. Il est pourtant évident que c'est là la seule attitude à recommander à l'égard de ces productions psychiques. C'est que ces productions sont, elles aussi, réelles dans un certain sens : il reste notamment le fait que c'est le malade qui a créé les événements imaginaires ; et, au point de vue de la névrose, ce fait n'est pas moins important que si le malade avait réellement vécu les événements dont il parle. Les fantaisies possèdent une réalité *psychique,* opposée à la réalité *matérielle,* et nous nous pénétrons peu à peu de cette vérité que, *dans le monde des névroses, c'est la réalité psychique qui joue le rôle dominant.*

SIGMUND FREUD[15]

15. *Introduction à la psychanalyse,* p. 230-236, 243-251, 277-282, 337-340, 341-347.

Chapitre VII

Refoulement et défenses
dans différentes névroses

A travers les extraits des trois cas qui figurent dans ce chapitre[1], nous allons découvrir succinctement comment opèrent le refoulement et les défenses dans différentes psychonévroses[2]. Par exemple, à propos du « Petit Hans », Freud montre que l'amour sexuel prenant pour objet la mère est refoulé, de même que l'agressivité à l'égard du père ; ce refoulement est facteur d'angoisse, car la libido est endiguée (non déchargée). Or, cette angoisse « flottante » doit se trouver un objet, c'est-à-dire qu'elle va se transformer en peur ; en l'occurrence, elle donne naissance à une phobie. Autrement dit, la phobie qui s'installe remplace une peur dont l'origine est inconnue en raison du refoulement par une peur portant sur un objet réel. Pour le petit Hans, c'est le cheval, substitut du père.

Chez le patient surnommé « l'Homme aux Rats », on voit le refoulement intervenir dans certains mécanismes propres à la névrose obsessionnelle. Freud étudie ainsi quelques actes compulsionnels présentés par le patient, qui constituent des symptômes et réalisent en deux temps deux tendances contradictoires ; dans le cas de l'Homme aux Rats, elles traduisent essentiellement un conflit entre l'amour et la haine. Le premier temps exprime la satisfaction de la tendance refoulée — ici, la haine ; le second annule cette réalisation ; or, l'annulation est un mécanisme de défense caractéristique de la névrose obsessionnelle. Notons aussi que l'ambivalence, qui constitue une marque de la névrose obsessionnelle, fait de l'amour et de la haine deux tendances contradictoires de force presque équivalente.

Dans les pages qui suivent, Freud étudie également le destin de l'affect chez l'obsédé. Chez celui-ci, indique-t-il, le refoulement diffère

1. Tirés des *Cinq psychanalyses*.
2. Pour le refoulement en général, voir *Refoulement, défenses et interdits*, paru dans la même collection.

◄ *On retrouve, dans le conte du charmeur de rats de Hamelin, l'équivalence enfants-rats présentée dans l'analyse de l'Homme aux Rats.*

du refoulement hystérique, particulièrement en ce qui concerne le facteur déclenchant de la névrose. Cependant, le refoulement lui retirant sa charge affective, la représentation de l'événement reste consciente, mais indifférente. En revanche, la charge affective peut se déplacer sur d'autres faits ou d'autres événements : un patient de Freud, un obsédé, avait déplacé sa culpabilité sur des faits anodins, n'en ressentant consciemment ainsi aucune pour des actes sexuels liés à la séduction de jeunes filles. Grâce au déplacement de l'affect, le patient pouvait de cette façon, sans culpabilité, continuer à jouir de certaines satisfactions sexuelles.

Le troisième extrait que nous reproduisons est celui de l'Homme aux Loups. A son sujet, Freud observe tout d'abord la présence d'un mécanisme de retournement en son contraire[3], qu'il avait précédemment décrit dans Pulsions et destins des pulsions, *en 1915. Le retournement du sadisme en masochisme consiste en une substitution de l'activité en passivité. Mais ce qui nous importe essentiellement ici, c'est la discussion qu'il mène à propos du refoulement aboutissant au triomphe de la virilité. Cette discussion — fort ancienne — porte sur le rôle de la bisexualité dans le refoulement ; Freud en vient à conclure que la virilité est acceptée par le Moi, tandis que la position féminine se heurte au narcissisme du sujet ; c'est pourquoi elle succombe au refoulement.*

Toutefois, le refoulement ne prend pas toujours le parti de la virilité contre la féminité. Ce qui, dans ce texte, nous semble intéressant à dégager pour notre propos est que Freud termine sur l'hypothèse suivante : le narcissisme attaché au pénis, mis en danger par l'attitude féminine à l'égard du père, n'est pas le motif fondamental du refoulement. On doit bien plutôt rechercher celui-ci dans le trop-plein d'excitations suscitées par l'homosexualité de l'Homme aux Loups — trop-plein d'excitations pour la maîtrise duquel les craintes narcissiques concernant la masculinité sont, en quelque sorte, appelées en renfort.

En somme, nous nous trouvons devant les effets traumatiques causés par un excès d'excitations. Un parallèle est à faire avec cette autre idée émise par Freud dans Inhibition, symptôme, angoisse *: le refoulement primaire serait lié à une tentative pour maîtriser un trop-plein d'excitations ayant traversé le pare-excitations[4].*

---

3. Qui n'est pas superposable à la formation réactionnelle, c'est-à-dire à un trait de caractère qui s'est formé par réaction vis-à-vis d'un désir refoulé.

4. « Terme employé par Freud dans le cadre d'un modèle psychophysiologique pour désigner une certaine fonction et l'appareil qui en est le support. La fonction consiste à protéger... l'organisme contre les excitations en provenance du monde extérieur qui, par leur intensité, risqueraient de le détruire. L'appareil est conçu comme une couche superficielle enveloppant l'organisme et filtrant les excitations » (J. Laplanche et J.-B. Pontalis, *Vocabulaire de la psychanalyse*, P.U.F.).

Le cas du petit Hans et celui de l'Homme aux Loups indiquent la place centrale qu'occupe le complexe de castration dans le développement de la névrose comme dans celui de l'angoisse.

L'angoisse correspond ainsi à une aspiration libidinale refoulée, mais elle n'est pas cette aspiration elle-même ; il faut tenir compte aussi du refoulement. Une aspiration se mue entièrement en satisfaction quand on lui procure l'objet qu'elle convoite ; une telle thérapeutique n'est plus efficace dans les cas d'angoisse ; l'angoisse persiste même s'il y a possibilité de satisfaire l'aspiration, l'angoisse n'est plus entièrement retransformable en libido ; la libido est maintenue par quelque chose en état de refoulement[5]. Les choses se montrèrent être telles chez Hans[6], à l'occasion de la promenade où sa mère l'accompagna. Il est avec sa mère et éprouve cependant de l'angoisse, c'est-à-dire une aspiration inassouvie vers elle. Il est vrai que l'angoisse est moindre, il se laisse en effet conduire à la promenade, tandis qu'il avait contraint la bonne à le ramener à la maison ; la rue n'est d'ailleurs pas un endroit propice à « faire câlin » ou à n'importe ce que pouvait désirer d'autre le petit amoureux. Mais l'angoisse a supporté l'épreuve et il faut maintenant qu'elle trouve un objet. C'est au cours de cette promenade qu'il exprime d'abord la peur d'être mordu par un cheval. D'où provient le matériel de cette phobie ? Sans doute de ces complexes, encore inconnus de nous, qui ont contribué au refoulement et maintiennent les aspirations libidinales envers la mère en état de refoulement.

LE CAS DE « L'HOMME AUX RATS » : DEUX TENDANCES CONTRADICTOIRES CHERCHANT À SE SATISFAIRE L'UNE APRÈS L'AUTRE

Chez cet amoureux, une lutte entre l'amour et la haine, éprouvés pour la même personne, fait rage ; et cette lutte s'exprime d'une façon plastique par un acte compulsionnel à symbolisme très significatif : il

---

5. Pour parler franc, cela est le critère même d'après lequel nous qualifions de normaux ou non de tels sentiments mêlés d'angoisse et de désir : nous les appelons « angoisse pathologique » à partir du moment où ils ne peuvent plus être résolus par l'obtention de l'objet convoité.
6. Un petit garçon de cinq ans dont Freud suivait le traitement par l'intermédiaire du père de l'enfant. *Cf. Cinq psychanalyses* (P.U.F.) et *la Castration : un fantasme originaire*, dans la même collection. (N.d.E.)

enlève la pierre du chemin de son amie mais annule ensuite ce geste d'amour, en la remettant à sa place, afin que la voiture s'y heurte et que son amie se blesse. Nous aurions tort de considérer que la seconde partie de cette compulsion fût inspirée par le sens critique du malade luttant contre ses actes morbides, signification que le malade voudrait lui attribuer. Ce geste, étant accompli compulsivement, trahit par là qu'il faisait aussi partie de l'action pathologique, mais qu'il fut déterminé par un motif contraire à celui qui provoqua la première partie de l'action compulsionnelle.

De tels actes compulsionnels, à deux temps, dont le premier temps est annulé par le second, sont des phénomènes caractéristiques de la névrose obsessionnelle. La pensée consciente du malade se méprend, bien entendu, sur le sens de ces compulsions et leur attribue des motifs secondaires, *elle les rationalise*[7]. Leur véritable signification réside dans le fait qu'elles expriment le conflit de deux tendances contradictoires et d'intensité presque égale, et qui sont, d'après mon expérience, toujours l'opposition entre l'amour et la haine. Ces actes compulsionnels à deux temps présentent un intérêt théorique particulier, car ils permettent de reconnaître un type nouveau de formation de symptômes. Au lieu de trouver, comme c'est le cas régulièrement dans l'hystérie, un compromis, une expression pour les deux contraires (tuant pour ainsi dire deux mouches d'un seul coup)[8], les deux tendances contradictoires trouvent ici à se satisfaire l'une après l'autre, non sans essayer, bien entendu, de créer entre les deux un lien logique, souvent en dépit de toute logique[9].

Le conflit entre l'amour et la haine se manifesta chez notre patient par d'autres signes encore. A l'époque où il redevint pieux, il inventa des prières qui, peu à peu, arrivèrent à durer une heure et demie car, à l'inverse de Balaam, il se glissait toujours dans ses formules pieuses des pensées qui les transformaient en leur contraire. Disait-il, par exemple : *Que Dieu le protège*, le malin lui soufflait immédiatement

---

7. Cf. E. Jones, « Rationalization in every-day life » (Rationalisation dans la vie quotidienne), *Journal of Abnormal Psychology*, 1908.

8. *Hysterische Phantasien und ihre Beziehung zur Bisexualität* (« Fantasmes hystériques et leur rapport avec la bisexualité »), vol. VII des *Ges. Werke*.

9. Un autre obsédé me conta un jour qu'en se promenant dans le parc de Schönbrunn, il avait heurté du pied une branche. Il la lança dans les buissons qui bordaient le chemin. En rentrant, il se mit à craindre que cette branche, dans sa nouvelle position, ne causât un accident à quelque promeneur qui prendrait le même chemin. Il sauta du tramway qui le ramenait, se précipita dans le parc, rechercha l'endroit en question et remit la branche dans sa position primitive. Et cependant, à tout autre qu'à ce malade, il eut été évident que la branche devait être plus dangereuse dans sa position primitive que dans les buissons. La seconde action, celle de remettre la branche sur le chemin, action exécutée de façon compulsionnelle, s'était parée, pour la pensée consciente, de mobiles altruistes empruntés à la première action, celle de jeter la branche dans le buisson.

un « ne »[10]. Un jour, lui vint alors l'idée de proférer des injures : il espérait que là aussi se glisserait une contradiction. Il s'agit de l'explosion de l'intention primitive refoulée par la prière. Dans sa détresse, notre patient supprima les prières et les remplaça par de brèves formules, composées de lettres et syllabes, initiales de diverses prières. Ces formules, il les disait si rapidement que rien ne pouvait s'y glisser.

Le patient me conta un jour un rêve qui représentait le même conflit dans son transfert sur le médecin : Ma mère est morte. Il veut venir me faire ses condoléances, mais craint d'avoir à cette occasion, *ce rire impertinent* qu'il avait eu à maintes reprises dans des occasions de ce genre. Il préfère laisser sa carte en y écrivant *p. c.* mais ces lettres se transforment, pendant qu'il écrit, en *p. f. (pour condoléances, pour féliciter)*[11].

UN EXEMPLE DE DÉPLACEMENT CHEZ UN MALADE ATTEINT DE NÉVROSE OBSESSIONNELLE

Un jour, notre patient mentionna en passant un événement dans lequel je pus reconnaître immédiatement la cause occasionnelle de sa maladie, ou du moins la cause occasionnelle récente de la crise actuelle de celle-ci, déclenchée six ans auparavant et qui durait encore. Le malade lui-même ignorait complètement qu'il venait de raconter un événement important. Il ne pouvait se rappeler avoir accordé quelque valeur à cet événement qu'il n'avait d'ailleurs jamais oublié. Cet état de choses réclame une mise au point théorique.

Dans l'hystérie, il est de règle que les causes occasionnelles récentes de la maladie soient oubliées tout comme les événements infantiles à l'aide desquels les événements récents convertissent leur énergie affective en symptômes. Là où un oubli complet est impossible, l'amnésie entame néanmoins les traumatismes récents, ou, pour le moins, les dépouille de leurs parties constituantes les plus importantes. Nous voyons, dans une pareille amnésie, la preuve d'un refoulement accompli. Il en est généralement autrement dans la névrose obsessionnelle. Les sources infantiles de la névrose peuvent avoir subi une amnésie, souvent incomplète ; par contre, les causes occasionnelles récentes de la névrose sont conservées dans la mémoire. Le refoulement s'est servi, dans ces cas, d'un mécanisme différent, au fond plus simple : au lieu de

10. A comparer avec les mécanismes analogues des pensées sacrilèges involontaires de certains croyants.

11. Ce rêve donne l'explication du rire compulsionnel si fréquent et apparemment si énigmatique qu'ont certaines personnes à l'occasion d'un décès.

*Dans l'hystérie, l'amnésie touche
les causes occasionnelles de la maladie.*

faire oublier le traumatisme, le refoulement l'a dépouillé de sa charge
affective, de sorte qu'il ne reste, dans le souvenir conscient, qu'un
contenu représentatif indifférent et apparemment sans importance. La
différence entre ces deux formes de refoulement réside dans le processus psychique caché derrière les phénomènes et que nous pouvons
reconstituer. Quant aux résultats de ces processus, ils sont presque les
mêmes, étant donné qu'un souvenir indifférent n'est évoqué que rarement et ne joue aucun rôle dans l'activité psychique consciente. Pour
distinguer ces deux formes du refoulement, nous ne pouvons nous servir pour le moment que de l'assertion même du patient : il a le sentiment d'avoir toujours su certains événements alors que d'autres, par
contre, étaient depuis longtemps oubliés[12].

12. Il faut admettre que les obsédés possèdent deux sortes de savoir et de connaissance, et on est
également en droit et de dire que l'obsédé « connaît » ses traumatismes et de prétendre qu'il ne les « connaît
pas ». Il les connaît, en ce sens qu'il ne les a pas oubliés, mais il ne les connaît pas, ne se rendant pas
compte de leur valeur. Il n'en est souvent pas autrement dans la vie courante. Les sommeliers qui servaient
Schopenhauer, dans l'auberge qu'il avait coutume de fréquenter, le « connaissaient » dans un certain sens,
à une époque où il était inconnu à Francfort comme ailleurs, mais ils ne le « connaissaient pas » dans le
sens que nous attachons aujourd'hui à la « connaissance » de Schopenhauer.

190

C'est pourquoi il arrive assez souvent que des obsédés, souffrant de remords et ayant rattaché leurs affects à de faux prétextes, font part en même temps au médecin des vraies causes de leurs remords, sans même soupçonner que ces remords ne sont que tenus à l'écart desdites causes. Ils disent même parfois avec étonnement, ou même avec vantardise, en racontant les événements qui sont les causes véritables de leurs remords : « Voilà qui ne me touche pas du tout. » Il en fut ainsi du premier cas de névrose obsessionnelle, voici de nombreuses années, qui me permit de comprendre cette maladie. Le patient en question, fonctionnaire, un scrupuleux, se signala à mon attention par le fait qu'il réglait toujours ses honoraires en billets propres et neufs (à cette époque, il n'y avait pas encore en Autriche de pièces d'argent). Un jour, je lui fis remarquer qu'on pouvait reconnaître un fonctionnaire aux billets neufs qu'il recevait de la caisse de l'État ; mais il répliqua que ces billets n'étaient nullement neufs, qu'il les faisait repasser à la maison. Car il se serait fait scrupule de donner à qui que ce fût des billets sales, couverts des microbes les plus dangereux et pouvant être nuisibles à qui les touchait. A cette époque, je pressentais déjà vaguement les rapports existant entre les névroses et la vie sexuelle, aussi osai-je, un autre jour, questionner mon patient à ce sujet. « Oh, dit-il, d'un ton léger, là tout est en ordre, je ne me prive guère. Dans bien des maisons bourgeoises je joue le rôle d'un vieil oncle, et j'en profite pour inviter de temps en temps une jeune fille de la maison à une partie de campagne. Je m'arrange alors pour manquer le dernier train et être obligé de passer la nuit à la campagne. Je prends alors deux chambres à l'hôtel, je suis très large ; mais lorsque la jeune fille est au lit, je viens chez elle et la masturbe. — Mais, ne craignez-vous pas, rétorquai-je, de lui nuire en touchant ses organes avec des mains sales ? Il se mit en colère : Nuire ? Mais comment cela peut-il nuire ? Cela n'a encore nui à aucune d'entre elles, et toutes se sont volontiers laissé faire ! Plusieurs d'entre elles sont mariées maintenant, et cela ne leur a pas nui ! » Il prit très mal ma remarque, et ne revint plus. Je ne pus m'expliquer le contraste entre ses scrupules concernant les billets de banque et son manque de scrupules à abuser des jeunes filles à lui confiées que par un *déplacement* de l'affect du remords. La tendance de ce déplacement était très claire : s'il avait laissé le remords rester là où il aurait dû être, il eût dû renoncer à une satisfaction sexuelle vers laquelle il était poussé probablement par de puissantes déterminantes infantiles. Il obtenait ainsi par ce déplacement un considérable *bénéfice de la maladie.*

LE REFOULEMENT PREND-IL TOUJOURS LE PARTI DE LA VIRILITÉ CONTRE LA FÉMINITÉ ? : LE CAS DE « L'HOMME AUX LOUPS »

L'organisation génitale qui avait été interrompue est rétablie d'un seul coup[13], mais le progrès réalisé dans le rêve ne peut être maintenu. Tout au contraire, un processus, que l'on ne peut rapprocher que d'un refoulement, amène une répudiation de cet élément nouveau et son remplacement par une phobie.

L'organisation sadique-anale se poursuit ainsi dans la phase, qui alors s'instaure, celle de la phobie des animaux, mais des phénomènes d'angoisse s'y adjoignent. L'enfant poursuit ses activités sadiques et masochiques, cependant il réagit par l'angoisse à une partie d'entre elles ; le retournement du sadisme en son contraire fait sans doute de nouveaux progrès.

L'analyse du rêve d'angoisse nous a montré que le refoulement se relie à la reconnaissance de la castration. L'élément nouveau est rejeté, parce que l'accepter coûterait à l'enfant son pénis. A regarder les choses de plus près, on voit à peu près ce qui suit : l'attitude homosexuelle au sens génital est ce qui se trouve refoulé, attitude qui s'était édifiée sous l'influence de la reconnaissance de la castration. Mais elle est à présent conservée dans l'inconscient, constituée en une stratification plus profonde et isolée. Le promoteur de ce refoulement semble être la masculinité narcissique du membre viril, qui entre en un conflit, préparé depuis longtemps, avec la passivité de l'objectif homosexuel. Le refoulement est ainsi un succès de la virilité.

A partir de ce point on pourrait être tenté de modifier une partie de la théorie psychanalytique. On croit en effet ici toucher du doigt qu'il s'agit d'un conflit entre les aspirations mâles et les aspirations femelles, donc de la bisexualité qui engendre le refoulement et la névrose. Cette conception, cependant, est incomplète. De ces deux aspirations sexuelles contraires, l'une est acceptée par le Moi, l'autre blesse les intérêts du narcissisme, c'est pourquoi celle-ci succombe au refoulement.

Ainsi, dans ce cas encore, c'est le Moi qui met le refoulement en œuvre, et ceci en faveur de l'une des deux tendances sexuelles. Dans d'autres cas, un tel conflit entre virilité et féminité n'existe pas ; il y a une seule aspiration sexuelle qui cherche à se faire accepter, mais qui, se heurtant à certaines forces du Moi, est en conséquence elle-même repoussée. Les conflits entre la sexualité et les tendances morales du

---

13. A un an et demi, l'Homme aux Loups avait observé un coït entre ses parents ; par l'entremise d'un rêve fait à quatre ans, le souvenir de cette scène avait été réactivé. (N.d.E.)

Moi sont bien plus fréquents que les conflits ayant lieu à l'intérieur de la sexualité elle-même. Un tel conflit moral fait défaut dans notre cas. Affirmer que la sexualité soit le mobile du refoulement serait une conception trop étroite ; dire qu'un conflit entre le Moi et les tendances sexuelles (la libido) le conditionne, voilà qui englobe tous les cas.

A la doctrine de la « protestation mâle », telle qu'Adler l'a édifiée, on peut opposer que le refoulement est loin de prendre toujours le parti de la virilité contre la féminité ; dans un grand nombre de cas, c'est la virilité qui doit se soumettre au refoulement par le Moi.

En outre, une estimation plus juste du processus du refoulement dans notre cas permettrait de contester que la virilité narcissique fut ici le seul mobile du refoulement. L'attitude homosexuelle qui s'établit au cours du rêve était d'une telle intensité que le Moi du petit garçon se trouva incapable de la maîtriser et s'en défendit par un processus de refoulement. La masculinité narcissique du membre viril, s'opposant à cette tendance, fut appelée à l'aide pour réaliser ce dessein. Je redirai, pour éviter des malentendus, que toutes les pulsions narcissiques partent du Moi et demeurent dans le Moi et que les refoulements sont dirigés contre des investissements libidinaux de l'objet.

SIGMUND FREUD[14]

---

14. *Cinq psychanalyses*, p. 108-109, 223-228, 410-411.

DEUXIÈME PARTIE

Les névroses
et leur classification

— Oui, monsieur le Directeur, depuis cinq ans je suis la victime d'une odieuse machination.
— Je sais bien !... votre « idée fixe » !

Dessin critique sur la psychiatrie paru dans « l'Assiette au Beurre ».

Chapitre I

Dora ou le destin d'une hystérique

Dans cette seconde partie, nous aborderons le problème de la classification des névroses, en laissant de côté les névroses actuelles et les névroses traumatiques, déjà traitées, pour nous attacher aux névroses proprement dites. Le mot « névrose » recouvre, nous l'avons vu précédemment, différentes sortes d'affections psychiques enracinées dans l'enfance de l'individu ; leurs symptômes traduisent de façon symbolique le conflit psychique. L'interprétation de ces symptômes permet d'en découvrir le sens ; ils représentent un compromis entre le désir et la défense.

Nous n'entrerons pas ici dans le détail des mécanismes qui spécifient les névroses par rapport aux psychoses[1]. Citons cependant la formule simple employée par Freud dans un article de 1924 précisément intitulé « Névrose et psychose » : La névrose serait le résultat d'un conflit entre le Moi et son Ça ; la psychose, elle, l'issue analogue d'un trouble équivalent dans les relations entre le Moi et le monde extérieur[2].

Après Jung, Freud a distingué les névroses de transfert des psychoses. Jung, puis Freud et Abraham considèrent en effet que, dans les psychoses, la libido se retire des objets pour venir investir le Moi du sujet. Dans la névrose, au contraire, la libido investit les objets du monde extérieur ou les objets fantasmatiques : aussi le névrosé présente-t-il une grande aptitude au transfert. Il a ainsi une certaine

1. Nous aborderons cette importante question dans *les Psychoses : la perte de la réalité,* à paraître dans la même collection. Notons que Freud a utilisé le terme de « psychonévrose » pour désigner les affections psychiques (psychoses et névroses) qui ont leur origine dans le conflit infantile, par opposition aux névroses actuelles. L'expression « psychonévrose de défense » a été employée par lui, essentiellement dans des articles de 1894 et 1896, pour mettre l'accent sur le conflit défensif, découvert dans l'hystérie et étendu aux névroses et aux psychoses : il l'abandonna au profit de celui de psychonévrose lorsqu'il reconnut la défense comme consubstantielle à toute psychonévrose.

2. C'est Freud qui souligne.

« faim » d'objets[3] *avec lesquels il reproduit ses conflits infantiles dans l'espoir de réaliser ses désirs autrefois frustrés et, tout particulièrement, le complexe d'Œdipe qu'il n'a pas résolu.*

L'individu dit « normal » possède lui aussi, il va sans dire, une aptitude au transfert, bien qu'en principe moins intense que celle du névrosé, dans la mesure où ses frustrations anciennes sont censées avoir été moins vives et mieux tolérées par lui. C'est à propos des « Types de déclenchement de la névrose » que Freud, en effet, parle de la frustration (Versagung), *désignant les obstacles tant extérieurs qu'intérieurs auxquels se heurte la libido dans sa recherche de satisfaction.*

L'infléchissement de la libido sur le Moi dans les psychoses conduit Freud à les appeler névroses narcissiques. *Elles s'opposent donc aux* névroses de transfert, *qui sont des névroses proprement dites. Le lien avec la réalité n'est pas coupé, à l'inverse de ce qui se produit dans les psychoses ; le Moi refuse une motion pulsionnelle issue du Ça, et s'en protège grâce au refoulement. Celui-ci, dans la névrose, subit un échec : le refoulé cherche à faire retour et finit par s'imposer au Moi grâce à cette formation de compromis qu'est le symptôme. Or, bien que le Moi ait généralement appelé le Surmoi en renfort pour l'aider dans son opération de refoulement, il n'en poursuit pas moins, ainsi perturbé, sa lutte — contre le symptôme cette fois : la névrose s'installe.*

Notons que Freud abandonnera en 1924 l'expression « névrose narcissique[4] *» qui recouvrait auparavant l'ensemble des psychoses ; désormais, elle ne désignera plus que la manie-mélancolie. On comprend que le mot « névrose », qualifiant des états dans lesquels il n'y a pas rupture avec la réalité, exclut du même coup les manifestations délirantes caractéristiques de la psychose.*

Ainsi, à l'intérieur des névroses, la psychanalyse distingue trois classes principales : l'hystérie de conversion, les phobies (ou hystéries d'angoisse) et la névrose obsessionnelle. En fait — nous aurons l'occasion d'y revenir —, l'entité appelée « névrose obsessionnelle », aujourd'hui partie intégrante de la nosographie[5] *psychiatrique classique, a été reconnue et délimitée par Freud dès 1896, dans un article intitulé « l'Hérédité et l'étiologie des névroses ». Avant lui, la psychiatrie englobait dans une même classe les obsessions et les phobies. De même, c'est à sa demande que Stekel introduisit le terme d'« hystérie d'angoisse » qui s'applique à la névrose centrée sur la phobie. Cette*

---

3. Nous en avions déjà parlé dans l'*Identification : l'autre, c'est Moi* (chap. I), paru dans la même collection.

4. Nous anticipons ainsi sur le volume spécifiquement consacré aux psychoses, à paraître dans la même collection.

5. C'est-à-dire de la description et de la classification systématique des affections mentales.

dénomination indique le lien de parenté de la névrose phobique avec l'hystérie de conversion.

Précisons-le tout de suite : les termes de « névrose » et de « caractère » sont en fait antinomiques ; certains psychanalystes récusent non l'entité nosologique décrite sous ce nom, mais bien sa dénomination. On peut en effet considérer que les traits de caractère décrits très tôt par Freud[1] s'opposent de façon absolue aux formations symptomatiques, typiques des névroses, dans la mesure où ils sont intégrés à l'ensemble de la personnalité, « conformes au Moi ou égosyntones », et où ils ne sont généralement pas vécus par le sujet comme gênants ou douloureux. En somme, le patient est rarement conscient de la pathologie de certains de ses comportements liés à des traits de caractère.

Ce sont généralement les plaintes de son entourage, l'échec de sa vie amoureuse ou professionnelle qui amènent le malade à consulter. De fait, les traits de caractère défendent le sujet à la fois contre ses pulsions et contre la formation de symptômes. Souvent, les « caractères névrotiques » comportent des mécanismes obsessionnels. Il serait en effet nécessaire d'envisager le rôle de la régression au stade sadique-anal comme prédominant dans les caractères névrotiques, ce qui confère à ces affections une rigidité qui en rend l'accès d'autant moins aisé et oblige à des aménagements techniques de la cure psychanalytique.

Il faut également noter que les caractères névrotiques recouvrent et colmatent, souvent difficilement — voire désespérément —, un noyau psychotique. Dans le texte qui suit, rédigé en 1953, Evelyne Kestengerg aborde tous ces problèmes dans une perspective à la fois théorique et clinique.

C'est par l'étude de l'hystérie de conversion qu'a commencé la psychanalyse, comme nous l'avons vu. L'hystérie de conversion se caractérise par l'inscription dans le soma du conflit psychique que symbolisent des symptômes étranges et multiples. Nous avons déjà évoqué la « boule » hystérique, les paralysies, les anesthésies. Il existe aussi des cécités et des surdités hystériques sans substrat organique. La « crise de nerfs », une propension à l'évanouissement, le théâtralisme et la dramatisation relèvent aussi d'une « manière d'être » hystérique. Elle nous renvoie l'écho atténué des grandes manifestations hystériques, dont l'opisthotonos ou cambrure du corps en arc de cercle.

L'originalité de la démarche freudienne consiste en ceci qu'elle a dégagé des mécanismes propres à l'hystérie, parmi lesquels

*l'identification[6], le refoulement[7], l'aptitude au transfert, etc. Récipro-
quement, l'observation et l'analyse des hystériques ont été déterminantes pour la découverte de l'inconscient.*

*Or, ces mécanismes, Freud les a précisément retrouvés chez certains
hommes — souffrant par conséquent d'hystérie — aussi bien que chez
les femmes. Le 15 octobre 1886, il présenta à la Société des médecins
un rapport intitulé « De l'hystérie masculine ». Reprenant la théorie de
Charcot, pour qui il n'existait aucun rapport nécessaire entre l'hystérie
et les organes génitaux féminins — ce que l'on pensait alors, « hystérie »
venant du grec* husterikos, *c'est-à-dire utérus —, Freud fut, selon ses
propres termes, « mal accueilli ». Meynert, sans doute le plus grand
anatomiste du cerveau de son temps, le mit au défi de trouver dans
Vienne tout entière un malade offrant les symptômes décrits par Charcot. A l'hôpital général, les médecins refusèrent de laisser partir les
patients atteints d'hystérie. Enfin, Freud parvint à découvrir un « cas
classique d'hémianesthésie hystérique chez un homme ». « Cette fois,
rapporte Jones dans sa biographie de Freud[8], [celui-ci] recueillit quelques applaudissements, mais il y avait, ce soir-là, tant de rapports à lire
que, faute de temps, aucune discussion ne put s'engager. » Freud ne
retourna jamais plus à la Société des médecins et, quarante ans plus
tard, ressentait encore de l'amertume au souvenir du traitement qui lui
avait été réservé.*

*Dans les premiers travaux de Freud sur l'hystérie, par exemple dans
son article de 1896 intitulé « Nouvelles Remarques sur les psychonévroses de défense », on le voit assigner à cette affection une étiologie
spécifique. Il y aurait toujours eu des traumatismes sexuels dans la
prime enfance, avant la puberté, et le contenu de ces traumas consisterait en une irritation effective des organes génitaux. Le trauma, passivement subi, aurait nécessité par conséquent une « passivité sexuelle en
des temps présexuels », qu'il s'agisse d'hommes ou de femmes. Cependant, le pourcentage plus important de cas d'hystérie chez les femmes
est précisément lié au fait que, dès l'enfance, celles-ci font l'objet
d'attaques sexuelles. D'autres phénomènes ont encore été isolés chez
les hystériques : la prédominance de certains fantasmes, bisexuels en
particulier, liés à la double identification dans la scène primitive[9], la
fixation aux objets incestueux sans régression temporelle en deçà de la*

6. Voir *l'Identification : l'autre, c'est Moi,* dans la même collection.
7. Voir *Refoulement, défenses et interdits, id.*
8. E. Jones, *la Vie et l'œuvre de Sigmund Freud,* t. I, p. 255 (P.U.F.).
9. Observation par l'enfant du coït entre les parents, transposée ensuite sur le plan fantasmatique. Voir *l'Identification : l'autre, c'est Moi* (p. 159-160), dans la même collection.

phase phallique-œdipienne[10], le « déplacement vers le haut » avec géni-talisation de la zone bucco-pharyngienne (par exemple, la toux de Dora traduisant des désirs inconscients de fellation)... Or, ce déplace-ment des investissements génitaux sur la zone orale pose un problème souvent débattu : l'hystérie implique-t-elle une véritable régression libi-dinale (temporelle), ou ne s'agit-il que d'une régression topique, au niveau des représentations déguisant les désirs génitaux en désirs oraux d'apparence plus « innocente » ? Par exemple, une hystérique rêve qu'elle absorbe des aliments pour lesquels elle éprouve un dégoût prononcé. D'un point de vue freudien, son rêve n'indique pas une régression libidinale à l'oralité : ses investissements demeurent génitaux ; seules régressent les représentations.

Cette question n'est pas sans rapport avec l'existence d'une hypothé-tique « psychose hystérique ». Peut-être aura-t-on remarqué, en effet, que Breuer parle souvent de psychose à propos d'Anna O.

Sans vouloir pousser plus avant cette discussion, remarquons cepen-dant que la plupart des tableaux cliniques ne sont pas « purs », et que les névroses évoluent : dans l'Homme aux Loups, *Freud fait apparaître non seulement les liens entre la névrose infantile et la névrose de l'adulte, mais aussi les phases successives de la névrose infantile elle-même. De plus, selon Freud, toutes les manifestations obsessionnelles ultérieures comporteraient un noyau hystérique. Ce qu'en revanche le texte ci-après va nous montrer, c'est qu'une névrose peut évoluer fâcheusement au cours de la vie adulte et se dégrader en troubles psy-chosomatiques et en traits de caractère : certaines potentialités psycho-somatiques de Dora sont déjà présentes dans la description même que donne Freud de son cas : dès l'âge de huit ans, la petite fille souffre d'une gêne respiratoire qui semble être d'origine asthmatique ; à douze ans apparaissent des migraines. Il faut en effet noter que l'asthme et la migraine sont des affections allergiques, de caractère psychosomati-que, et non des manifestations de l'hystérie de conversion.*

A la différence des conversions hystériques, les affections psychoso-matiques impliquent des lésions physiologiques ou, pour le moins, des modifications fonctionnelles. De surcroît, la maladie psychosomatique ne constitue pas l'expression symbolique d'un conflit. Elle n'est pas un langage. Freud signale en outre que « les symptômes principaux de l'état [de Dora] étaient de la dépression et des troubles du caractère ». Disons en passant que la dépression qui se manifeste dans la majeure partie des névroses ne doit être confondue ni avec la dépression psy-chotique, ni avec ce que l'on entend couramment par « dépression »

---

10. Voir *les Stades de la libido : de l'enfant à l'adulte,* dans la même collection.

Les névroses : l'homme et ses conflits

(« il a fait une dépression », « la dépression, maladie du siècle ») : celle-ci recouvre, en fait, aussi bien des affections névrotiques bénignes que des maladies psychotiques graves[11].

L'auteur du texte qui va suivre, Felix Deutsch, a été l'un des premiers médecins à examiner Freud et à déceler chez lui le cancer de la mâchoire qui l'emportera en 1939. Freud lui tint rancune de lui avoir dissimulé son diagnostic et ne se réconcilia vraiment avec lui qu'en 1925. En 1922, Felix Deutsch eut, dans les circonstances qu'il décrira ici, divers entretiens avec une malade âgée de quarante-deux ans. Dès leur première conversation, la malade lui révéla fièrement qu'elle était la « Dora » des Cinq psychanalyses.

Nous allons donc découvrir, dans cet article datant de 1957 et intitulé « Apostille au "fragment de l'analyse d'un cas d'hystérie" de Freud », quels furent le destin malheureux et le développement fâcheux des troubles multiples de celle qui reste l'un des cas les plus célèbres de toute l'histoire de la psychanalyse.

Ernest Jones, dans sa biographie de Freud, fait référence au cas bien connu de Dora[12] et à ses divers symptômes hystériques, aussi bien mentaux que somatiques ; après avoir rappelé qu'elle n'avait jamais terminé sa courte analyse de onze semaines, il ajoute qu'« elle est morte à New York il y a quelques années[13] ».

Si ce fait a retenu mon attention, c'est pour plusieurs raisons. De quoi était-elle morte ? Toute l'intuition de Freud avait-elle pu, de par la seule interprétation, si pénétrante soit-elle, de deux rêves, apporter vraiment une pleine lumière sur la personnalité de cette malheureuse jeune fille ? Et si Freud avait vu juste, est-ce que la vie même de Dora ne devait pas confirmer les hypothèses formulées quant aux raisons qu'elle pouvait avoir de tenir à ses symptômes de conversion ? Enfin, dernière question mais non la moindre, quelle lumière nouvelle avons-nous aujourd'hui pour tenter de comprendre ce « saut du mental dans le physiologique » ?

Ma curiosité toute particulière concernant la vie ultérieure de Dora aurait de toute façon rencontré, du vivant de Freud, l'obstacle insurmontable de son absolue discrétion. Il écrivait : « J'ai attendu plus de

11. Dans les Psychoses : la perte de la réalité, nous verrons en quoi la dépression névrotique se différencie de la dépression psychotique.
12. Freud, « Fragment of an Analysis of a Case of Hysteria ». Coll. Papers, III.
13. Ernest Jones, The Life and Work of Sigmund Freud, Londres, The Hogarth Press, vol. II, 1955, p. 289.

*« Les lavages de Lady Macbeth étaient symboliques
et destinés à substituer la pureté physique à la pureté morale
qu'elle regrettait d'avoir perdue ».*

quatre ans après la fin du traitement et j'ai retardé la publication jus
qu'à ce que je sois informé d'un changement tel, dans la vie de la
patiente, qu'il me permettait de supposer que les événements et les faits
psychologiques que j'allais relater ne pouvaient plus l'intéresser que
faiblement. Evidemment, je n'ai laissé apparaître aucun nom qui puisse
alerter l'attention d'un lecteur non médecin ; de plus, la publication
d'un cas dans un périodique purement scientifique et technique offre
une garantie contre ce genre de lecteurs en quelque sorte non autorisés.
Par contre, je ne peux pas éviter que la patiente elle-même ressente
quelque souffrance si sa propre histoire tombait accidentellement entre
ses mains. Mais elle n'y apprendrait rien qu'elle ne sache déjà et ne
pourrait que se demander qui, en dehors d'elle, serait à même de la
reconnaître dans ce récit. »

Vingt-quatre ans après le traitement de Dora par Freud se produisit
un événement qui leva, pour un autre analyste, et sans que Freud pût le
savoir, l'anonymat de ce cas.

Freud écrivit, dans une note de la postface au *Fragment de l'analyse
d'un cas d'hystérie* (1923) : « Le problème de la discrétion médicale qui
a fait l'objet de cette préface ne touche pas les autres histoires de cas
contenues dans ce volume ; car trois d'entre elles furent publiées avec
l'autorisation expresse des patients (ou plutôt, pour ce qui est du petit
Hans, avec celle de son père) alors que dans le quatrième cas (celui de
Schreber) le sujet de l'analyse ne fut pas à proprement parler sa per
sonne, mais bien un livre écrit par lui. Dans le cas de Dora, le secret
fut gardé jusqu'à cette année. Depuis longtemps j'étais sans nouvelles
d'elle, mais récemment j'ai appris qu'elle était retombée malade il y a
peu, pour d'autres causes, et avait confié à son médecin qu'elle avait
été analysée par moi quand elle était jeune fille. Cette révélation devait
facilement conduire mon collègue, bien informé, à l'identifier comme
la *Dora* de 1899. Un juge équitable ne saura retenir contre la thérapeu
tique analytique que le traitement de trois mois qu'elle reçut à cette
époque n'ait pu que la soulager de son conflit d'alors et ne réussît point
à la mettre à l'abri de maladies ultérieures. »

Freud, en accord avec le médecin consultant, ne dévoila pas son
nom, car, là encore, cela eut pu permettre d'identifier la patiente.
Maintenant que Dora n'est plus vivante, il est devenu possible de reve
ler, sans manquer à la discrétion qui protégeait son anonymat, pour
quoi la note de Jones sur la mort de Dora m'avait à ce point intéressé.
La raison en est que je suis le médecin qui relata à Freud, en 1922, sa
rencontre avec Dora. C'était peu après la présentation de mon travail
intitulé *Quelques réflexions sur la formation des symptômes de conver
sion*, lors du VIIe Congrès international de psychanalyse à Berlin, en

septembre 1922, le dernier auquel Freud devait assister. Faisant référence aux hypothèses que je formulais dans ce travail ainsi qu'à ce mystérieux « saut de la psyché vers le soma », je racontai à Freud comment, *volens nolens,* j'avais percé le secret.

VINGT-QUATRE ANS APRÈS, « DORA » REPARAÎT...

Vers la fin de l'automne 1922, un oto-rhino-laryngologiste me demanda mon opinion sur une de ses patientes, une femme mariée de quarante-deux ans, qui était alitée depuis quelque temps à la suite de symptômes prononcés du syndrome de Ménière : tintements, hypoacousie de l'oreille droite, étourdissements ainsi qu'insomnies dues à des bourdonnements ininterrompus dans cette même oreille. Comme l'examen de l'oreille interne et du système nerveux aussi bien que du système vasculaire ne révélait aucune lésion, il se demandait si un examen psychiatrique de la patiente, qui se comportait d'ailleurs « nerveusement », ne pourrait expliquer son état.

L'entretien commença en présence de son médecin. Son mari quitta la chambre après avoir écouté le début de ses plaintes, et ne revint pas. Elle entreprit une description détaillée de bruits insupportables dans l'oreille droite et d'étourdissements lorsqu'elle remuait la tête. Elle avait toujours souffert de migraines périodiques du côté droit. La patiente se lança alors dans une tirade sur l'indifférence de son mari devant ses souffrances, et sur le malheur ininterrompu de sa vie conjugale. Même son fils unique donnait maintenant des signes de désaffection à son égard. Il venait de sortir du collège, et se demandait s'il devait poursuivre ses études. Mais il sortait souvent jusqu'à une heure avancée de la nuit, et elle le soupçonnait de s'intéresser aux filles. Elle l'attendait toujours, l'oreille tendue, jusqu'à son retour à la maison. Elle en vint ainsi à parler de sa propre vie amoureuse, de ses frustrations et de sa frigidité. Une seconde grossesse lui était toujours apparue impossible à la seule pensée des douleurs de l'accouchement.

C'est avec ressentiment qu'elle exprima sa conviction de ce que son mari lui avait été infidèle ; elle avait songé au divorce mais n'avait jamais pu s'y résoudre. Puis, les larmes aux yeux, elle dénonça les exigences, la mesquinerie et l'égoïsme des hommes. Ces considérations la renvoyèrent à son passé. Elle évoqua avec beaucoup d'émotion combien elle avait toujours été proche de son frère, devenu par la suite leader d'un parti politique, et qui accourait encore aujourd'hui quand elle avait besoin de lui, tout à la différence de son père qui avait même été infidèle à sa mère. Elle reprochait aussi à son père une aventure avec une jeune femme mariée qui était une amie à elle, la patiente, et dont, jeune fille, elle s'était occupée des enfants. D'ailleurs, le mari de cette femme lui avait alors fait des avances qu'elle avait repoussées.

Cette histoire me sembla familière. Mon soupçon sur l'identité de la patiente fut vite confirmé. Entre-temps l'oto-rhino avait quitté la chambre ; la patiente se mit alors à bavarder avec coquetterie, s'enquérant de savoir si j'étais psychanalyste et si je connaissais le professeur Freud. Je lui retournai la question : le connaissait-elle et ne l'avait-il jamais traitée ? Comme si elle n'avait attendu que cette perche, elle s'empressa de me dire qu'elle était « Dora », ajoutant qu'elle n'avait, depuis son traitement chez Freud, vu aucun psychiatre. Il va sans dire que ma familiarité de l'œuvre de Freud créa alors un climat transférentiel éminemment favorable.

LES PLAINTES D'UNE PATIENTE « DIFFICILE »

De ce moment, elle oublia sa maladie et manifesta une immense fierté d'avoir fait l'objet d'un écrit aussi célèbre dans la littérature psychiatrique. Puis elle parla de la santé défaillante de son père qui semblait souvent ne pas avoir tous ses esprits. Sa mère, tuberculeuse, avait dû être hospitalisée récemment dans un sanatorium ; elle pensait que sa mère avait pu contracter cette maladie de son père, dont elle se souvenait qu'il en était atteint lorsqu'elle était petite. Apparemment elle ne gardait aucun souvenir de la syphilis de ce dernier, que Freud mentionne pourtant, et qu'il considérait en général comme une prédisposition constitutionnelle et comme « un facteur pertinent dans l'étiologie de la constitution névropathique chez les enfants ». Elle enchaîna sur le souci que lui causaient des rhumes occasionnels, des difficultés respiratoires ainsi que des quintes de toux matinales qu'elle attribuait d'ailleurs à l'excès de tabac depuis ces dernières années ; et comme pour minimiser la chose, elle ajouta que son frère avait aussi la même habitude.

Lorsque je lui demandai de se lever et de marcher dans la chambre, je constatai une légère claudication de la jambe droite ; elle ne put m'en donner l'explication ; c'est quelque chose qui remontait à son enfance, mais qui n'était pas toujours manifeste. Puis elle se mit à discuter l'interprétation que Freud avait faite de ses deux rêves et voulut connaître mon opinion.

Je m'aventurai à relier son syndrome de Ménière à sa relation à son fils dont elle guettait continuellement le retour de ses excursions nocturnes ; elle sembla l'accepter, et me demanda une autre consultation.

Lorsque je la revis, elle avait quitté le lit et déclara que ses « attaques » étaient passées. Les symptômes de Ménière avaient disparu. De nouveau, cependant, elle donna libre cours à une grande hostilité à l'égard de son mari, insistant sur le dégoût que lui inspirait la vie conjugale. Elle me décrivit des douleurs prémenstruelles ainsi que des pertes vaginales à la suite de ses règles. Puis elle m'entretint principalement de sa relation à sa mère, de son enfance malheureuse en raison de la propreté exagérée de cette dernière, de ses insupportables compulsions au lavage et de son manque d'affection pour elle. Le seul souci de sa mère avait été sa propre constipation dont maintenant la patiente souffrait elle-même. Enfin, elle fit état de la brillante carrière de son frère, mais se montra pessimiste quant à ce que son propre fils suivît ses traces. Lorsque je la quittai, elle me remercia avec effusion et promit de m'appeler si elle devait en sentir le besoin. Elle ne se manifesta jamais plus. Son frère me téléphona à plusieurs reprises, peu après mes rencontres avec sa sœur et m'exprima toute la satisfaction qu'il éprouvait devant ce prompt rétablissement. Il se montrait très préoccupé par ses longues souffrances, son désaccord non seulement avec son mari mais avec leur mère. Il admit qu'elle était d'un commerce difficile étant donné sa méfiance à l'égard des gens et sa façon de les monter les uns contre les autres. Il voulut venir me voir à mon bureau mais je n'acceptai pas, pour le bien de Dora.

LA CONVERSION HYSTÉRIQUE D'IDÉES EN SYMPTÔMES CORPORELS

Il est facile de comprendre qu'après cette expérience j'ai eu envie de comparer le tableau clinique de la patiente avec celui que Freud en avait tracé dans sa brève analyse, vingt-quatre ans plus tôt, alors qu'elle n'avait que dix-huit ans. Il est frappant de constater que le destin de Dora se déroula tel que Freud l'avait prédit. Il reconnaissait que « ... le traitement du cas et, conséquemment, sa perspective sur les évenements si complexes qui le constituaient étaient restés fragmentaires. Il y a donc plusieurs questions auxquelles je ne peux apporter de réponse ou plutôt pour lesquelles je ne puis m'appuyer que sur des indices et des hypothèses ». Ces considérations, cependant, n'affaiblissent en rien sa conception de base, à savoir, que « la plupart des symptômes hystériques à l'acmé de leur développement représentent une situation imaginée à la vie sexuelle ». Il est indiscutable que l'attitude de Dora à l'égard des rapports conjugaux, sa frigidité, son dégoût devant l'hétérosexualité viennent corroborer le concept freudien de déplacement qui est décrit en ces termes : « J'en arrive à retracer ainsi l'origine des sentiments de dégoût : ils semblent bien s'être constitués originellement en réaction à des *odeurs* (puis, par la suite, à la *vue*) d'excréments. Mais les organes génitaux peuvent agir comme tenant lieu des fonctions excrémentielles. »

Freud corrobora plus tard ce concept dans sa note à propos d'*Un cas de névrose obsessionnelle*, où il désigne le patient comme « un renifleur » (osphrésiophile) plus sensible aux perceptions olfactives que la moyenne des gens. Il ajoute que le patient « avait été sujet, dans son enfance, à de fortes propensions coprophiliques. C'est ainsi que son érotisme anal s'était déjà signalé[14] ».

Dans le cas de Dora, on peut se demander si certaines tendances à des perceptions *sensorielles* autres que l'*odorat*, le *goût* et la *vue* participèrent au processus de conversion. Il est certain que l'appareil auditif joua un rôle important dans l'éclosion du syndrome de Ménière. De fait, Freud émet l'hypothèse que la dyspnée de Dora ait pu être provoquée par l'attention qu'elle portait, enfant, aux bruits provenant de la chambre de ses parents, attenante à la sienne. Elle rééditait cette même façon de « tendre l'oreille » dans sa vigilance à entendre les pas de son fils rentrant à la maison le soir, à partir du moment où elle avait soupçonné son intérêt naissant pour les filles.

Pour ce qui est du sens du *toucher*, elle avait fait la preuve de son refoulement avec M. K. : quand il l'avait prise dans ses bras, elle avait réagi comme si elle ne remarquait en rien le contact de ses organes génitaux. Elle n'avait pu nier le contact de ses lèvres lorsqu'il l'avait embrassée, mais elle se *défendait* contre l'effet de ce baiser par le déni de sa propre excitation sexuelle ainsi que de sa perception du sexe de M. K., qu'elle repoussait avec dégoût.

Nous ne devons pas oublier qu'en 1894 c'est un type de *défense* que Freud désigne du nom de « conversion » alors qu'il élabore l'idée que « dans l'hystérie la pensée insupportable est rendue inoffensive par le transfert de la quantité d'excitation qui y est attachée à une forme d'expression corporelle[15] ». Plus tôt même, en collaboration avec Breuer, il formulait : « L'accroissement de la somme d'excitation emprunte des voies sensorielles et sa diminution, des voies motrices... Si cependant il ne se produit aucune réaction devant un trauma psychique, le souvenir de ce dernier reste lié à l'affect originel. » Cela reste vrai aujourd'hui.

---

14. Freud, « Notes upon a Case of Obsessional Neurosis », *Coll. Papers*, III, p. 382 (l'italique est de F.D.).

15. Freud, « The Defense Neuropsychoses », *Coll. Papers*, I, p. 63.

Y A-T-IL EU ÉCHEC DE LA PSYCHANALYSE DANS LE CAS DE DORA ?

Les années passent et Dora doit s'ingénier à protéger son Moi contre l'envahissement des sentiments de culpabilité. Nous la voyons tenter d'y échapper en s'identifiant à sa mère qui, atteinte d'une « psychose de la ménagère », se livrait à toutes sortes de rituels de propreté. Dora se met à lui ressembler, non seulement physiquement, mais aussi sous ce rapport. Elle et sa mère voient la saleté partout autour d'elles et jusqu'à l'intérieur d'elles-mêmes. Affligées toutes deux, déjà à l'époque du traitement par Freud, de pertes vaginales, elles le seront toujours au moment où je verrai Dora.

Tout aussi remarquable cette façon de traîner le pied observée par Freud chez la jeune fille et qui devait persister pendant vingt-cinq ans. « Ce type de symptôme, affirmait Freud, ne saurait survenir qu'à la condition de reproduire un prototype infantile. » Dora s'était un jour foulé ce pied-là en descendant l'escalier ; le pied avait enflé, on l'avait bandé et Dora dut garder le lit plusieurs semaines. On voit qu'un tel symptôme, s'il répond à l'exigence d'une expression somatique du déplaisir, peut être conservé toute une vie durant. Freud a toujours maintenu sa conception des lois biologiques et considéré le déplaisir « comme étant emmagasiné pour leur sauvegarde. La complaisance somatique, organiquement prédéterminée, pave la voie de décharge d'une excitation inconsciente ».

On ne saurait trop souligner le bien-fondé de la proposition de Freud selon laquelle « il semble beaucoup plus difficile de créer une nouvelle conversion que de former des frayages associatifs entre une pensée nouvelle, qui cherche la décharge, et une pensée ancienne qui n'en a plus besoin ». Est-ce dire que Dora, qui après vingt-cinq ans se révèle conforme à ce que Freud avait vu et prévu, n'a pu échapper à son destin ? C'est la conclusion fataliste, à laquelle on serait conduit, mais elle appelle des réserves. Freud[16] affirme lui-même qu'il n'a pas publié ce cas « pour établir sous son jour véritable la valeur de la thérapeutique analytique » et il ajoute que l'amélioration tout éphémère de Dora n'est pas imputable à la seule brièveté du traitement (trois mois à peine) ; Dora n'aurait pu, à vrai dire, profiter des découvertes ultérieures de Freud sur la névrose de transfert et l'élaboration secondaire, car sa brusque rupture fut « un acte de vengeance incontestable, qui en outre vint nourrir son dessein autodestructeur[17] ».

---

16. Freud, *Coll. Papers*, III, p. 138.
17. *Ibid.*, p. 131.

MALADIE ET MORT DE « DORA »

Plus de trente ans se sont écoulés depuis ma visite à Dora alitée. Sans la note du docteur Jones, sur son décès à New York, rien ne m'eut permis de recueillir d'autres données ; mais grâce à mon informateur j'ai pris connaissance de certains faits nouveaux et significatifs dans le destin de Dora ainsi que de sa famille, et je les relate ici.

Son fils l'emmena, de France, aux Etats-Unis. Contrairement à ce qu'elle redoutait, il fit une brillante carrière de musicien. Elle le harcela des mêmes revendications dont elle avait accablé son mari qui était mort d'une maladie coronarienne — ravagé par sa conduite quasi paranoïaque. Assez curieusement, et ce sont les mots de mon informateur, il avait préféré mourir plutôt que de divorcer. Voilà bien le seul type d'homme que Dora pouvait choisir comme mari ; n'avait-elle pas déclaré, sans équivoque, au temps de son analyse : « Les hommes sont si détestables que je préférerais encore ne pas me marier. Voilà ma vengeance. » Ainsi son mariage n'avait servi qu'à camoufler son dégoût des hommes.

Son mari et elle, tous deux amenés à quitter Vienne pendant la là elle avait été périodiquement soignée pour ces accès de migraines, de toux et d'enrouement que Freud avait interprétés lorsqu'elle avait toux et d'enrouement que Freud avait interprétés lorsqu'elle avait dix-huit ans.

Après la mort de son père, au début des années trente, elle commença à souffrir de palpitations cardiaques qu'on attribua au fait qu'elle fumait trop ; elle y réagit par des crises d'angoisse liées à la peur de mourir. Son entourage se trouva ainsi en état d'alerte permanente et elle en profita pour monter amis et parents les uns contre les autres. Son frère, grand fumeur également, mourut d'une affection coronarienne, longtemps après, à Paris où il s'était réfugié dans les circonstances les plus aventureuses. C'est là qu'il fut enterré avec les plus grands honneurs.

La mère de Dora mourut dans un sanatorium ; mon informateur m'apprit qu'elle avait déjà souffert de tuberculose dans sa jeunesse. Elle s'était tuée à la tâche compulsive et jamais achevée du nettoyage quotidien, que nul ne pouvait accomplir à sa satisfaction. Dora suivit ses traces, mais dirigea l'obsession vers son propre corps ; comme ses pertes vaginales persistaient, elle subit quelques interventions gynécologiques mineures. Sa constipation, cette impossibilité de « nettoyer ses intestins », lui fit problème jusqu'à la fin de sa vie ; habituée cependant qu'elle était à ses troubles intestinaux, elle les traita apparemment comme un symptôme familier jusqu'au moment où ils s'avérèrent plus graves qu'une simple conversion. Sa mort — d'un cancer du côlon diagnostiqué trop tard pour qu'une opération puisse réussir — survint comme une bénédiction pour ses proches. Elle avait été, ainsi que le formula mon informateur, « une des hystériques les plus rebutantes » qu'il ait jamais rencontrées.

Ce supplément d'information sur Dora n'est rien d'autre qu'une apostille à la postface de Freud. J'espère que sa présentation aujourd'hui suscitera la réévaluation de la théorie freudienne du processus de conversion : quel degré de validité peut-elle encore avoir pour nous et en quoi divergerait-elle de nos conceptions actuelles ?

FÉLIX DEUTSCH[18]

---

18. *Revue française de psychanalyse* (« Apostille au "Fragment de l'analyse d'un cas d'hysterie" de Freud »), p. 407-414.

Les personnes souffrant d'agoraphobie sont prises d'angoisses lorsqu'elles sortent seules dans la rue.

Chapitre II

Les phobies à travers l'agoraphobie

Freud aurait conseillé en 1908 à Stekel[1] d'introduire le terme d'« hystérie d'angoisse », qu'il préférait à celui, plus classique, de « phobie », pour désigner un certain type de névrose centrée sur la phobie, et dont il désirait souligner la parenté avec l'hystérie de conversion[2]. Rappelons-nous, en effet, que Freud avait démontré l'existence de certaines phobies presque universelles et que, de plus, des entités nosologiques autres que la névrose phobique proprement dite présentent elles aussi des symptômes phobiques.

C'est à partir de l'analyse du petit Hans, en 1905, qu'il isole la névrose phobique ; dégage également l'analogie entre certains de ses mécanismes et ceux de l'hystérie de conversion : dans les deux cas, le refoulement aboutit à une séparation de la représentation et de l'affect[3]. Mais si, dans l'hystérie de conversion, la libido est convertie en symptômes, dans l'hystérie d'angoisse, en revanche, elle est « libérée sous forme d'angoisse ». Le travail qui s'opère dans l'hystérie d'angoisse consiste à fixer la libido, devenue libre sous forme d'angoisse flottante, sur une phobie déterminée[4]. Autrement dit, l'hystérie d'angoisse tend vers la formation d'une phobie proprement dite. Les mécanismes propres à la névrose phobique sont le déplacement et l'évitement[5].

Le déplacement est précisément lié à la séparation entre l'affect et la représentation. L'affect — ici, l'angoisse — est déplacé sur un objet déterminé, qui devient l'objet phobique et qui se substitue à l'objet originel. C'est ainsi que, chez le petit Hans, le cheval a pris la place du

---

1. L'un de ses premiers disciples. Il entreprit une analyse avec Freud en 1901 et commença à pratiquer la psychanalyse deux ans plus tard, en 1903.

2. Cf. notre introduction au chapitre I de cette IIe partie.

3. Cf. notre introduction au chapitre VIII (Ire partie) du présent volume.

4. Cf. notre introduction au chapitre III (Ire partie) du présent volume.

5. Sans parler du refoulement commun, comme nous venons de le dire, à la névrose phobique et à l'hystérie de conversion.

père. Une fois constitué l'objet phobique, le malade, auparavant confronté à une angoisse panique résultant de son contact permanent avec le personnage qui est la cause inconsciente de son angoisse, peut éviter plus aisément l'objet sur lequel s'est déplacé sa phobie : il était en effet plus facile au petit Hans de fuir les chevaux que son père...

En somme, la possibilité d'éviter l'objet d'angoisse est précisément consécutive au déplacement : l'angoisse est ainsi plus étroitement circonscrite.

Pour illustrer la phobie, nous avons choisi de présenter ici des observations d'Hélène Deutsch, rédigées en 1928 et consacrées à des agoraphobies. Nous verrons comment l'auteur décrit, de façon claire et détaillée, les mécanismes de ces cas, ainsi que le rôle de l'objet contraphobique — c'est-à-dire de la personne qui doit accompagner le patient pour lui éviter l'angoisse.

En fait, l'agoraphobie pose, peut-être plus que tout autre symptôme phobique, des problèmes très complexes de diagnostic différentiel : un symptôme, aussi caractéristique soit-il, ne suffit pas à définir une structure. Ainsi, l'un des cas exposés par l'auteur est celui d'un agoraphobique dont certains symptômes sont typiquement conversionnels (l'arc de cercle) ; un autre cas d'agoraphobie se transformera aussi, en névrose obsessionnelle cette fois, avec régression à la phase sadique-anale de la libido.

Certaines agoraphobies sont très aisément curables lorsque les fixations incestueuses aux objets œdipiens sont prévalentes et lorsque la régression temporelle est absente. Au contraire, d'autres sont en relation avec de fortes fixations prégénitales et s'inscrivent même parfois dans des structures prépsychotiques. Elles sont alors réfractaires au traitement. Cette remarque clinique plaide en faveur d'une conception structurale de la phobie (et, du reste, de toutes les autres entités nosographiques) que le symptôme à lui seul ne suffit pas à délimiter. Ce fut d'ailleurs là un souci présent à la pensée de Freud, puisque — nous l'avons vu — il a toujours insisté sur la différence entre le symptôme phobique et la névrose phobique proprement dite, dont les mécanismes, les points de fixation et de régression corrélatifs au choix de la maladie sont toujours à prendre en compte : nous en reparlerons à propos de la névrose obsessionnelle.

Tous les cas dont je vais parler se conforment à un type précis de maladie. Ce sont des gens qui développent des états d'angoisse intense lorsqu'ils sont seuls dans la rue. Ils sont alors sujets à tous les phénomènes d'angoisse : tachycardie, tremblements et surtout le sentiment qu'ils vont s'effondrer et devoir affronter un désastre irréparable. Leur angoisse est une véritable angoisse de mourir et leur terreur phobique est : « Je vais mourir subitement. » Ils sont brusquement étreints par la pensée qu'ils vont succomber sur-le-champ à l'asthénie, la crise cardiaque, l'attaque d'apoplexie, ou autre catastrophe. L'angoisse est fréquemment centrée sur l'idée d'être écrasé, sur des accidents de chemins de fer ou de voiture, etc. Il est typique que ces états disparaissent complètement ou soient considérablement allégés lorsque le patient est accompagné par quelqu'un. Parfois le simple fait de voir sa maison au loin redonne au patient un sentiment de sécurité. Le compagnon doit généralement remplir certaines conditions, par exemple être lié étroitement au patient. De nombreux patients atteints d'agoraphobie insistent sur la compagnie d'une personne particulière. D'autres sont moins exigeants et sont satisfaits par quiconque est capable de leur prêter « assistance immédiate ». Certains patients fortunés ne sont heureux que lorsqu'ils ont leur médecin près d'eux avec la seringue hypodermique salvatrice.

Comme il semblait n'y avoir rien de très spécifique concernant le choix du compagnon, cet aspect de la question était négligé en faveur de l'affirmation du patient selon laquelle il s'agissait uniquement d'obtenir une aide en général. Mais, dans les trois cas dont je vais parler ici, le sens donné au compagnon semblait avoir de l'importance et jeter une certaine lumière sur l'essence même de cette forme de phobie.

ANGOISSE ET AGORAPHOBIE

Un de ces cas m'avait été confié il y a quelques années par un confrère quittant Vienne. La patiente était une jeune fille présentant des symptômes typiques d'agoraphobie. Chaque fois qu'elle sortait sans ses parents, elle était saisie d'une angoisse violente du type décrit ci-dessus. Son compagnon devait être son père ou sa mère. D'après elle, la première crise s'était produite en voyant s'effondrer dans la rue un homme en proie à une crise d'épilepsie. Elle fut désormais incapable de se remettre du choc de ce qu'elle avait vu, d'autant plus qu'elle entendait constamment parler de morts subites. Elle semblait être particulièrement malheureuse sous ce rapport, car elle rencontrait toujours des ambulances ou des enterrements et ces « expériences » lui faisaient chaque fois penser à nouveau à la possibilité de sa propre mort. Il est en effet remarquable de voir combien les gens atteints d'agoraphobie sont souvent étonnés par ces rencontres traumatisantes dues apparemment au hasard. Cela tient naturellement au fait qu'ils sont toujours à guetter ce genre de choses qui, pour d'autres, passent inaperçues, de sorte qu'ils sont capables de conserver l'impression qu'ils ont à cet égard une malchance particulière.

215

D'après l'histoire antérieure de notre patiente, je devrais mentionner qu'au moment où elle était tombée malade, c'est-à-dire environ un an avant le début du traitement, elle avait noué une liaison érotique avec un jeune homme — liaison sanctionnée par la morale bourgeoise de ses parents aussi longtemps qu'il s'agirait d'un « amour platonique ».

Le traitement avec le premier analyste avait considérablement amélioré son état. C'était manifestement un cas de « succès du transfert » dont le sens devint clair au cours de l'analyse. Le traitement bienfaisant et compréhensif qui servait dans la première partie de son analyse comme un substitut de gratification pour sa relation inconsciente avec son père lui avait permis de venir non accompagnée en analyse et d'aller et venir librement dans un large cercle autour de la maison de l'analyste. Le fantasme, dans le sens de l'amour accompli, qui mainte nant l'attachait à l'analyste, servait de protection contre l'angoisse et remplaçait le compagnon.

Peu après le départ de son premier analyste, le docteur X, un nouveau déplacement de l'angoisse intervint avec un contenu inattendu : quelque chose pourrait arriver au docteur X, au cours de son voyage, il pourrait par exemple avoir une crise cardiaque. Pendant un certain temps son angoisse au sujet du docteur X remplaça l'angoisse a son propre sujet. Mais ce ne fut que temporaire ; l'ancienne angoisse vis-a vis d'elle-même retrouva bientôt son importance première.

DÉSIR DE LA MORT DU PÈRE ET IDENTIFICATION MASOCHIQUE AVEC LA MÈRE

Quel était le facteur décisif dans l'agoraphobie de notre patiente ?

Je voudrais d'abord insister sur le fait que le départ de l'analyste était ressenti comme une déception amoureuse et appelait une réaction sadique qui était cependant niée et transformée en sollicitude angoissée. Son angoisse correspondait à une formation réactionnelle hystérique typique. Le fait que son angoisse était d'abord liée à sa propre personne puis à l'objet frustrant (l'analyste) permet de trouver une sorte de pont entre les deux.

L'analyse de la patiente était centrée sur deux expériences traumatisantes, la première dans la petite enfance, la seconde à la puberté. L'expérience infantile était d'avoir surpris le coït parental dont elle acquit l'impression que son père étranglait et torturait sa mère. L'expérience à la puberté était une attaque que son père avait eue en sortant d'un bain ; il était tombé en syncope, comme mort, et il avait dû être hospitalisé pendant un certain temps.

Tous les fantasmes pubertaires de la patiente faisaient revivre la situation d'écouter aux portes. Ils étaient de caractère féminin masochique et, en plus de leur contenu normal — viols, dégradation au rang de prostituée, etc. —, ils présentaient certains traits particulièrement violents : un fer chauffé au rouge était enfoncé dans ses organes génitaux, ou bien elle était enceinte et au cours du processus éclatait en morceaux.

Dans tous ces fantasmes masochiques nés du fait d'écouter aux portes, la patiente s'était identifiée à la mère. Le complexe d'Œdipe se termina avec la fixation de cette identification et du désir de mort contre sa mère, qui y était lié avec un caractère particulièrement agressif. La dernière expérience — l'attaque du père — qui eut lieu pendant les conflits de la puberté, avait ravivé les souvenirs de l'expérience infantile et les réactions contre le père jusque-là refoulées. Ces réactions culminaient dans un désir de mort dirigé contre le père. Le contenu de ce désir était : « Si tu ne m'aimes pas comme tu as aimé ma mère, alors meurs ! » Les convulsions du père et sa perte de connaissance étaient le lien d'association avec la scène primitive de l'enfance. Le désir de mort nié contre son père correspondait à la réactivation régressive du désir infantile de « châtrer » son père.

La première manifestation de sa névrose suivit une attaque sexuelle réelle de la part de son amant. Par conséquent, dans le premier cas, la protection de ses parents « dans la rue », c'est-à-dire hors de la maison, se rattachait à un danger fondé sur la réalité. Mais cela n'épuisait pas leur rôle en tant que compagnons. Car aussitôt que la patiente se trouvait dans la situation de tentation (c'est-à-dire en dehors de la protection du foyer), ses pulsions instinctuelles sinon bien refoulées étaient immédiatement mobilisées.

Comme nous l'avons déjà vu, ces pulsions avaient un caractère masochique défini. La relation infantile à la mère, maintenue par la fixation, à laquelle la patiente avait régressé, dépendait, comme nous le savons, d'une identification masochique avec la mère. Et cette identification avait pour but de retourner l'agression dirigée contre la mère, contre son propre Moi, constituant ainsi le plus grand danger pour le Moi.

PROTECTION DES PARENTS OU PROTECTION CONTRE LES PARENTS ?

Les tendances agressives dirigées contre le père frustrant s'étaient révélées d'une façon particulièrement claire dans la relation de transfert avec le docteur X. Mais l'amitié de l'analyste et l'espoir de son amour avaient modifié son agression et, en retour, cela semblait avoir

Les névroses : l'homme et ses conflits

libéré la patiente de son angoisse. Mais la frustration provoquée par son départ avait remobilisé toute l'attitude de vengeance sadique et avait donné à l'angoisse un contenu plus proche de son origine inconsciente. La forme de la mort à laquelle était condamné l'analyste correspondait exactement à l'impression que la patiente avait acquise de l'attaque de son père et aussi, notons-le, au destin qu'elle craignait pour elle-même dans son agoraphobie.

Le contenu tout entier bien refoulé n'était mobilisé que dans certaines conditions particulières. Quand ses parents n'étaient pas présents, la rue, qui était pour elle la « situation de tentation », en partie réelle et en partie symbolique, devenait l'une de ces conditions. Nous pouvons comprendre maintenant pourquoi l'angoisse en face des dangers intérieurs était diminuée quand elle emmenait ses parents avec elle. La protection apparente contre les dangers extérieurs de la rue n'était qu'une rationalisation évidente pour les dangers inconscients de sa vie intérieure. La présence des parents la protégeait non seulement de l'accomplissement des désirs sexuels interdits, mais aussi de l'agression contre les parents qui interdisaient, agression accrue dans la situation de tentation sexuelle et qui semblait être nettement compensée et modifiée par leur présence et leur tendre sollicitude. En même temps, le danger de mort que l'intensification de l'agression avait causé au Moi masochiquement identifié à la mère, avait diminué et l'angoisse en avait été allégée.

UN COMPAGNON DE ROUTE
QUI FAIT TAIRE
L'ANGOISSE DE MORT

La seconde patiente dont je vais parler était une femme de petite bourgeoisie, âgée d'environ quarante ans, mère de trois enfants et, jusque-là, pratiquement en bonne santé. La fille aînée, de dix sept ans, était élevée par la mère dans les règles strictes de la morale bourgeoise ; elle commençait à s'intéresser aux hommes, à l'amour, et à toutes les choses qui sont de la plus grande importance pour une jeune fille de son âge. La mère était bouleversée par cela, et quoiqu'elle se prétendît sympathisante, elle espionnait positivement sa fille, consumée de curiosité au sujet de sa vie amoureuse innocente et elle avait appris, en lisant son journal qu'elle avait trouvé « par hasard », qu'elle était en train de nouer une liaison avec un homme pour qui la mère éprouvait un certain intérêt.

C'était là le signal pour la névrose de la mère. Toute son activité fantasmatique consciente et inconsciente présentait une réactivation de sa puberté. Cette femme déjà d'un certain âge commença à avoir tous

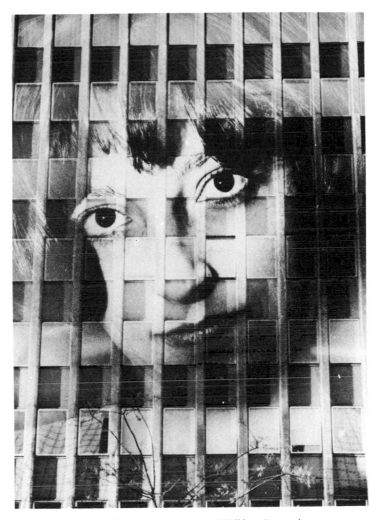

*Pour l'une des patientes d'Hélène Deutsch,
la rue « était une situation de tentation » ;
l'angoisse éprouvée contre ses dangers internes
était diminuée lorsque ses parents l'accompagnaient.*

ces fantasmes de défloration, de viols et de prostitution qui sont typi
ques de la puberté et qui représentaient tous des dangers qu'elle, la
mère aimante, aurait dû craindre pour sa fille. Dans toutes ces pulsions
de désirs interdits et déniés, la patiente s'était en effet identifiée à sa
fille. En même temps, la fille était devenue la rivale detestee contre qui
la réaction de vengeance tout entière de la patiente (une fois rattachee
à sa propre mère et maintenant à sa fille) était dirigee. Elle sentait
presque consciemment que sa fille se tenait entre elle et son bonheur.
comme sa mère l'avait fait autrefois dans son enfance. Elle avait cou
tume de dire que sa mère l'avait élevée très différemment des filles

« modernes ». Elle n'avait jamais le droit de sortir sans être accompagnée et toute sa vie amoureuse était strictement contrôlée. Elle répète maintenant cette même situation de contrôle dans son agoraphobie. Torturée par la terreur de la mort comme elle l'est, elle ne peut plus sortir seule. Le seul compagnon possible est sa fille, mais en réalité cette condition peut être rarement remplie et de ce fait elle se trouve plus ou moins confinée à la maison.

Il est assez facile de comprendre le sens de cette situation. La fille doit veiller à ce que sa mère ne succombe pas à ses pulsions instinctuelles, à savoir les pulsions dans lesquelles elle s'identifie à sa fille. En plus de ses autres dangers instinctuels, la patiente est exposée au désir agressif de mort contre sa rivale qui enrage contre le Moi du fait de l'identification qui s'est produite. Dans cette situation, la mère se trouve en même temps capable de surveiller sa fille qui est menacée par les dangers de sa sexualité naissante que la mère doit protéger, et aussi par les pulsions agressives inconscientes de la mère. Ainsi la fille, en tant qu'agent protecteur, a assumé le rôle du Surmoi, la protection qui interdit et qui menace, autrefois celui de la mère de la patiente. Nous avons ici un processus analogue à celui du premier cas : le compagnon devient le « protecteur protégé ». Le fait que l'objet de l'identification, contre lequel l'agression est dirigée, assume le rôle de compagnon protecteur et le joue comme un agent aimant et non menaçant, permet à l'angoisse de la mort de disparaître. Le processus d'identification, d'une part, et la menace de mort contre le Moi, de l'autre, sont tous deux transitoires par nature et liés à la situation de tentation représentée par le fait d'être hors de la maison. Il vaut la peine de noter que l'angoisse de la patiente était primitivement liée à une section particulière du chemin, un sentier le long d'une haie derrière laquelle elle avait souvent vu des hommes se soulager. Je mentionne cela parce que j'ai l'impression que des tendances exhibitionnistes jouent un rôle subsidiaire important dans la détermination de ces dangers de la rue. Mais je reviendrai sur ce point dans l'histoire de mon prochain cas.

UNE RIVALITÉ AVEC LA MÈRE

Dans l'histoire de ce troisième cas, nous avons affaire à une femme de vingt-sept ans, mariée depuis trois ans. Elle était la seconde de trois enfants. Dans sa première enfance, sa relation avec son frère de deux ans son aîné était une relation d'une jalousie particulière (envie du pénis) et sa relation avec sa sœur de deux ans plus jeune, celle d'une envie orale violente. Les deux relations étaient lourdement chargées d'agressivité et de culpabilité. Quand elle eut quatre ans et demi, son frère mourut d'une crise d'appendicite. Cette mort confirma en elle le sentiment de culpabilité le plus grave, d'autant plus grave en raison des événements décisifs qui y étaient rattachés. Le plus important de ceux-ci était la décision expérimentée du fait de sa mère, car au lieu de la gagner par la mort de son frère, elle la perdit. En effet, sa mère, consumée de chagrin, se retira de la famille, vécut dans une mansarde et mit ainsi sa fille dans une situation que certainement elle désirait mais qui néanmoins était dangereuse : car elle dormait maintenant dans le lit de son père et pouvait dans une grande mesure réaliser ses fantasmes œdipiens. Et quand la mère tenta au bout d'un an de reprendre la vie familiale, la petite fille présentait déjà les réactions névrotiques à ces incidents. D'autres difficultés névrotiques apparurent à la période de latence : peur du tonnerre et des tremblements de terre et autres petits symptômes de conversion que l'analyse révéla être des fantasmes de grossesse. Dans la période prépubertaire, elle avait entendu parler de femmes qui sont dehors la nuit et font quelque chose de « terrible », et par conséquent elle ne pouvait être persuadée de quitter la maison la nuit tombée. Les idées qu'elle se faisait de ces femmes s'alliaient à des fantasmes de dépréciation concernant sa mère et faisaient de la mère une prostituée.

Deux souvenirs de la période de latence jouaient un grand rôle dans l'analyse. Le premier était lié à une crise d'angoisse dans la rue en allant sur l'insistance de sa mère s'excuser auprès d'une dame dans le jardin de laquelle elle avait volé des fruits. Elle obéit rageusement à l'ordre de sa mère, mais fut incapable de l'exécuter car à mi-chemin elle fut prise de tachycardie et de tremblements. Elle admettait elle-même que cela représentait la haine refoulée contre les deux femmes.

Le deuxième souvenir était lié à une histoire appelée *le Guetteur dans la tour :* le phare est gardé par une femme qui y vit seule avec sa petite fille. Un jour la petite fille trouve sa mère morte sur le sol au sommet de la tour. Elle est morte subitement d'une crise cardiaque en accomplissant son devoir. La vaillante enfant prend froidement la place de sa mère et sauve héroïquement les bateaux en danger.

Après avoir lu cette histoire elle fut accablée par l'angoisse la plus vive : chaque fois que sa mère quittait la maison, elle guettait son retour à la fenêtre ou à la porte. La patiente s'expliquait de façon caractéristique : « Je ne sais pas si je me sentais vraiment angoissée à propos de moi-même ou de ma mère. » On peut deviner le contenu de cette angoisse par le contenu de l'histoire dans laquelle la petite fille prend la place de la mère. Mais chez la patiente la mort de la mère est la condition nécessaire à l'accomplissement d'un désir inconscient.

Le rôle que la patiente cherche à jouer dans son identification avec la mère est soumis à la même dépréciation et à la même humiliation de sa propre personne que celles qu'elle attribuait à sa mère. L'accomplissement de ces désirs inconscients ferait de la patiente une prostituée tout comme elle l'avait fait de sa mère dans ses fantasmes.

Vous vous souvenez de la situation infantile qui était certainement l'élément traumatisant de sa névrose. La petite fille avait été abandonnée par sa mère, un traumatisme dans le sens de la perte d'objet. La mère lui avait cédé la place près de son père, c'est-à-dire qu'elle l'exposait au danger de l'accomplissement de ses désirs inconscients culminant dans l'identification à la mère.

Quand la mère revint dans la famille, la petite fille était déjà fermement fixée dans la relation de rivalité ; mais il ne lui était possible de maintenir sa position qu'à une seule condition : si, comme dans le cas du guetteur de la tour, sa mère venait à mourir (l'analogie est renforcée par la scène dans les deux situations : mansarde — tour). Chaque fois que dans sa vie ultérieure la patiente se trouva dans des situations où ses tendances libidinales refoulées — chez elle aussi, de caractère masochique — pouvaient être réalisées, elle appelait sa mère auprès d'elle ; non seulement pour empêcher la réalisation de ses désirs, mais aussi pour que le désir de mort qui avait été dirigé contre la mère protectrice ou perturbante, ne se réalise pas contre elle-même. Le signal d'angoisse dans son agoraphobie se révélait dans l'analyse être l'ancien appel à sa mère.

LES CIRCONSTANCES D'APPARITION D'UNE AGORAPHOBIE

Revenons à l'histoire de son cas. Écolière, elle avait eu une amitié amoureuse avec un camarade d'école. A dix-huit ans, elle fit la connaissance de son futur mari qui fit sur elle une forte impression sexuelle et qui la demanda en mariage. Mais l'atmosphère domestique de son enfance était incroyablement sectaire. Après la mort de son fils, la mère avait adopté un ascétisme manifestement névrotique et son propre renoncement était accompagné d'une attitude morale extrêmement sévère qui interdisait rigoureusement tout ce qui était sexuel. La patiente se trouvait alors dans un conflit, car ses relations platoniques avec son premier ami, qui avaient été sanctionnées par la mère, étaient naturellement perturbées par ses sentiments pour son futur mari. On lui inculqua qu'il fallait rester fidèle à son premier amour « idéal ». La patiente se sentait incapable de prendre une décision dans un sens ou dans l'autre. Sa liaison avec son futur mari était nettement interdite, même extérieurement, car c'était un athée, alors que la mère était pieuse. Sur quoi le conflit prit un caractère névrotique et la patiente tenta de trouver une issue. Elle fut possédée par l'idée qu'en rompant avec le premier ami elle provoquerait sa mort, c'est-à-dire qu'elle désirait se débarasser de celui qui entravait ses désirs, comme elle avait désiré une fois se débarasser de sa mère. Elle subit la même opération dont son frère était mort (manifestement dans une tentative de se décharger préventivement du sentiment de culpabilité). De cette façon elle put prendre une décision : elle rompit avec son ami et se fiança joyeusement avec son futur mari. C'est alors que l'agoraphobie se déclara. Alors qu'un dimanche elle allait rendre visite à une amie de sa mère (la patiente habitait loin de chez elle), pour lui faire part de sa libération, elle fut soudain troublée par la pensée : « Que va-t-elle penser de mon comportement ? » Perdue dans ses pensées, elle s'engagea dans une rue assez calme où elle fut soudain envahie par l'angoisse : « Maintenant je vais m'effondrer sans force. » Incapable d'aller plus loin, elle envoya chercher l'amie à qui elle allait rendre visite et elle put terminer le trajet en sa compagnie.

Qu'était-il arrivé ? La rupture avec son premier ami avait lourdement pesé sur son sentiment de culpabilité et avait évoqué le souvenir de son frère mort. Mais par cette rupture elle avait rendu possible la gratification de ses désirs sexuels, tout comme la mort de son frère lui avait permis de dormir avec son père. Tous ses désirs prenaient maintenant un caractère infantile et étaient accompagnés d'interdits sévères. Comme alors, la mère retira son amour et la laissa seule face au danger. Et de même que dans la situation névrotique infantile elle avait l'habitude d'attendre sa mère, de même maintenant elle était incapable d'agir sans la protection de sa mère et sans la décharge de son sentiment meurtrier de culpabilité contre elle. D'où le fait qu'elle devait avoir cette amie, comme image de la mère, pour l'accompagner.

La névrose évolua en agoraphobie typique. Sur le conseil de ses médecins, elle se maria mais son état empira. Elle gagna une chose : c'est que son mari qu'elle torturait et qu'elle enchaînait par ses symptômes, pouvait agir comme accompagnateur. Bientôt le coït fut accompagné d'angoisse grave et de vaginite.

UNE INTENSE NÉVROSE DE TRANSFERT

Dans l'analyse elle développa une « névrose de transfert » sérieuse, qui me permit d'acquérir une compréhension profonde de sa maladie grâce à sa relation avec ma personne.

La première phase fut occupée par un « transfert négatif » : refus d'être guérie par moi et méfiance à l'égard de ma tolérance. Comment pouvais-je être une analyste quand je n'accordais à ma propre fille aucune liberté sexuelle ? Tel était le contenu de ses fantasmes. Chaque geste de ma part était construit comme un interdit et elle hésitait entre une opposition absolue et l'obéissance aveugle. Elle acceptait toujours mes interprétations sans discussion, mais il arrivait souvent, quand par exemple elle était sur le point de raconter un rêve particulièrement confirmatoire, qu'elle se mette à rire et soit incapable de s'arrêter pendant un quart d'heure. Il était clair que son acceptation apparente était accompagnée d'une méfiance dédaigneuse.

Quand par exemple je lui conseillai de voir une femme médecin, elle fut envahie d'un doute compulsif, sentit qu'elle devait obéir et pourtant ne put se décider à le faire. Un jour, je l'exhortai à venir à pied à mon cabinet de consultation au lieu de prendre un taxi comme elle le faisait habituellement. Néanmoins, elle prit un taxi en chemin, mais cette fois, contrairement à son habitude, elle fut prise dans le taxi d'une angoisse très violente, dont le contenu était qu'elle serait punie de mort pour avoir transgressé mon ordre. Dans l'escalier elle fut saisie du sentiment qu'il m'était arrivé quelque chose. Pendant cette séance d'analyse, elle fut pour la première fois prise d'une crise d'angoisse qui évolua progressivement en une crise hystérique tonique-clonique typique. Elle s'effondra par terre. A la fin de la crise, elle s'agenouilla devant moi et dit : « Pardonnez-moi. » Quand je lui demandai ce que je devais lui pardonner, elle dit : « Cette rage. » Elle avait compris d'elle-même que cette crise était une décharge de rage.

Elle partit ce jour-là libre de toute angoisse, pour la première fois depuis sept ans. Je dois dire que cette crise hystérique était la première qu'elle ait jamais eue.

Elle passa les quelques jours suivants pratiquement sans angoisse. C'était dû au fait qu'elle avait trouvé un rite axé sur ma personne. En marchant dans la rue, elle tentait de rester près de femmes chez qui elle trouvait une certaine ressemblance avec moi. Si la personne en question paraissait « délicate » elle l'évitait, car elle pourrait « s'effondrer ». Ou bien elle attendait près de ma maison pendant des heures, sans angoisse pendant ce temps. Elle utilisait une de mes cartes de visite comme une sorte de talisman, comme une partie de moi-même. De la même manière, elle investissait en un transfert partiel la logeuse que je lui avais recommandée. Elle sortait avec cette dame, quoique avec un certain sentiment de malaise, car elle craignait que la logeuse ne s'effondre dans la rue. Pour autant que son angoisse était concernée, le chemin pour venir chez moi était divisé en deux parties. La première partie était génératrice d'angoisse ; au milieu, il y avait un « trou » qui augmentait l'angoisse ; après cela, elle était sauve.

Avec le développement du transfert positif, il y avait une augmentation de l'angoisse, de peur que je refuse de la revoir si j'apprenais tout sur son compte. Puis elle produisit des fantasmes dans lesquels je faisais tout ce qu'il lui était interdit de faire. Elle fantasmait, par exemple, que j'avais de mystérieuses relations avec des hommes, que je me mettais nue devant mes patients et elle avoua un jour avec une résistance violente qu'elle pensait que je me masturbais pendant la séance d'analyse. Toutes ces accusations formaient le miroir de ses propres désirs fantasmés et établissaient une identité entre nous par une cause commune de culpabilité. Mais elle me voyait aussi sous un tout autre jour, comme une personne hypernormale et se châtiant elle-même, une

« Les mouvements qu'elle exécutait dans le rêve
étaient une répétition de l'arc de cercle typique qu'elle avait produit
pendant son attaque au cours de la séance d'analyse »
(Bibliothèque de l'Ancienne Faculté de Médecine).

image qui correspondait à son idéal du Moi ascétique. Le clivage de ma personne était l'équivalent de la double image qu'elle avait eue autrefois de sa mère ; elle s'était identifiée à cette double image, d'une part dans tous les actes sexuels interdits qu'elle avait imputés à sa mère, et, d'autre part, dans les interdits sévères de sa mère repris par son Surmoi. Même le désir de mort vindicatif contre moi était, comme le révéla l'analyse, le signe d'une révolte contre la mère et était ainsi transformé en une menace de mort contre son propre Moi.

LA PHOBIE SE TRANSFORME EN HYSTÉRIE OU EN NÉVROSE OBSESSIONNELLE

L'identification entre moi et la mère fut illustrée d'une manière particulièrement claire dans un rêve caractéristique :

La patiente est couchée sur un tréteau dur, les pieds vers l'âtre qui est une chose intermédiaire entre un poêle et un radiateur à gaz. Le tréteau est fait de deux chaises qui ont glissé, de sorte qu'une partie de son dos est dans le vide. Sur le sol, au-dessous de cette partie de son dos, se trouve une bougie allumée. Elle doit sans cesse se redresser pour ne pas se brûler. Le rêve est accompagné de tachycardie et d'angoisse.

Les associations de ce rêve ramenaient à cette situation de danger où elle s'était trouvée quand sa mère l'avait laissée dormir près de son père. Elle se souvenait que son père, manifestement un névrosé obsessionnel, avait l'habitude de regarder sous le lit avec une bougie avant de se coucher. Les mouvements qu'elle exécutait dans le rêve étaient une répétition de l'*arc de cercle* typique qu'elle avait produit pendant son attaque au cours de la séance d'analyse. L'âtre à ses pieds représentait un condensé entre le poêle de mon cabinet de consultation et le foyer de la cuisine à la maison. Sur la demande de sa mère elle y cuisait le petit déjeuner, et pendant cela elle avait la terreur des souris qui parfois se glissaient hors des trous au-dessous du foyer.

Des pulsions onanistes sont reconnaissables dans les mouvements du rêve et la culpabilité ressentie du fait de ces pulsions ainsi que des fantasmes au sujet du père, était attribuée à la mère qui l'avait mise dans ces situations, tout comme je l'avais fait récemment en rendant ses fantasmes conscients.

Dans un autre rêve, elle est couchée près de sa mère qui se masturbe. Elle tente de l'en empêcher et s'éveille dans un état d'angoisse. Ici, l'identification entre la rêveuse et sa mère d'une part, et, d'autre part, entre moi et la mère, devient claire quand nous nous rappelons l'acte masturbatoire qu'elle m'attribuait.

La tension d'angoisse dans ses rapports avec moi allant diminuant, la patiente fit appel à tout son courage pour confier ses fantasmes sexuels. Ils présentaient de bout en bout un caractère génital féminin, fortement masochique, et les fantasmes de naissance actifs et passifs qui y étaient liés avaient une très grande importance pour son agoraphobie. Les crises hystériques qu'elle produisait au cours de la séance d'analyse me permirent d'approfondir le contenu de cette agoraphobie.

Les crises se produisaient par exemple lorsqu'elle avait des rêves d'angoisse, ou qu'elles présentaient elles-mêmes le caractère d'un rêve et, la crise passée, la patiente était toujours capable de décrire le contenu des fantasmes qui l'avaient accompagnée. Ils s'avéraient des représentations de situations de naissance. Par exemple, elle rêve qu'elle est dans une cave obscure, poursuivie par une femme : elle est saisie de terreur, car elle ne peut trouver aucune issue. Brusquement, elle sent le sang couler d'un trou dans sa tête ; une ambulance arrive, l'emmène ; elle est sauvée.

Ses associations montraient sans l'ombre d'un doute que c'était une représentation de sa propre naissance.

Dans un autre rêve — en le racontant elle eut aussi une crise — elle se voit debout devant une fenêtre ; elle se demande pourquoi elle a peur de sauter par la fenêtre. Alors elle jette une petite poupée dans la rue et est immédiatement saisie d'un sentiment d'angoisse de mort. Les violentes convulsions de tout son corps pendant la crise étaient des tentatives pour éloigner cette angoisse. Ce rêve était aussi un exemple clair du symbole de la naissance.

La naissance progressive de la phobie en hystérie avec crises était particulièrement intéressante dans le cas de cette patiente. En même temps que ses rapports avec moi s'amélioraient et que la fonction destructive du Surmoi s'adoucissait, l'angoisse diminuait. Cependant, chaque fois que des pulsions liées à la mère étaient libérées dans l'analyse, la patiente faisait une crise d'hystérie, quoique ses crises fussent limitées de manière caractéristique à la séance d'analyse.

Ces crises représentaient des situations d'un caractère génital défini (masturbation, coït, naissance, accouchement). La patiente sentait qu'elle pouvait se permettre ces accès en ma présence, car quoiqu'ils fussent accompagnés d'une « sensation de mourir », elle savait qu'elle n'avait rien à craindre si j'étais là. Mais dehors, dans la rue, elle sentait que l'angoisse lui était nécessaire comme si elle agissait en tant que signal d'alarme en face du danger. Je crois que nous pouvons accepter l'interprétation de la patiente. Aussi longtemps que les tendances agressives de son Surmoi la menacent de mort, les pulsions de désir doivent être réprimées par des interdits sévères. Mais lorsque la tension

entre le Moi et le Surmoi (c'est-à-dire dans la situation analytique entre elle et moi) est diminuée, les forces permissives peuvent s'exprimer et la patiente peut se laisser aller dans la crise à la représentation symbolique de ses désirs instinctuels refoulés. Pour résumer, je crois que nous pouvons dire que par l'ajustement de ses tendances agressives dans l'analyse, la sévérité de son Surmoi était réduite, les tendances génitales pouvaient s'exprimer et au lieu de l'angoisse inhibitrice, la décharge motrice dans la crise d'hystérie était rendue possible.

Nous voyons dans ce cas la transformation d'une forme de névrose dans une autre, le changement de la phobie en hystérie avec crise. Et dans ce contexte, un autre cas dont l'hystérie d'angoisse s'est muée en névrose obsessionnelle.

La névrose obsessionnelle est habituellement capable d'obtenir une grande part d'absence d'angoisse par les formations de symptômes. Les pulsions obsessionnelles et leurs contre-investissements sont supprimés de la même manière du contenu primitif et toute la structure névrotique semblerait, de loin, être mieux organisée que dans ce cas. Cependant, le sentiment de la compulsion intérieure et l'angoisse de mettre à exécution la pulsion obsessionnellement urgente ont ici, de manière catégorique, un caractère névrotique obsessionnel. Comme nous l'avons vu, la régression à la phase sadique-anale était dans ce cas le motif de la transformation des symptômes.

Dans notre dernier cas d'agoraphobie, d'autre part, la transformation des symptômes se produisait comme un résultat de l'affaiblissement des tendances de haine et de la sévérité du Surmoi due aux conditions favorables du transfert.

LA PROJECTION D'UN DANGER INTÉRIEUR

Nous pouvons expliquer comme suit la relation de l'agoraphobie avec l'hystérie d'une part, et avec la névrose obsessionnelle d'autre part, à partir du matériel donné ci-dessus. Nous avons appris de Freud que la phobie, en vue de sa relation avec la phase génitale, doit être considérée comme une forme d'hystérie. A mon avis, nous avons affaire ici à des êtres chez qui le conflit ambivalent est plus aigu, les pulsions sadiques plus fortes qu'il n'est habituel dans la phase génitale. Le fait que la phase génitale a été atteinte et maintenue empêche pratiquement la formation de symptômes obsessionnels ; mais la phase sadique-anale est encore capable d'exercer une attraction qui peut provoquer une rechute régressive et produire une transformation de la névrose hystérique en une maladie obsessionnelle (comme dans le cas dont nous venons précisément de parler), ou bien une variation de symptômes.

◄ *Dans la phobie des animaux le malade choisit un animal approprié pour personnifier le danger. (Illustration de Gustave Doré pour la fable de La Fontaine : « Le Lion et le Rat », coll. part.)*

Dans certaines conditions, les pulsions refoulées seront mobilisées et la relation à l'objet tendrement aimé sera régressivement ramenée à l'identification antérieurement existante et fixée. Comme résultat de cette identification, les pulsions agressives mobilisées dans les mêmes conditions et qui sont dirigées contre cet objet identifié, sont tournées contre le Moi de façon à menacer son existence même.

Quand nous venons à discuter de la mélancolie, nous observons un processus similaire. Là, l'objet est introjecté et le Moi subit le destin de l'objet de par la pulsion de destruction : la menace de mort et sa réaction d'angoisse dans le Moi menacé. La différence est que dans l'agoraphobie l'identification se fait à un stade plus élevé du développement libidinal et qu'elle est ainsi temporaire et susceptible d'une adaptation. Elle ne se produit que dans certaines conditions et peut être éloignée par la présence de l'objet approbateur et aimant. Cela est également vrai de la tendance agressive qui, mettant le Moi en danger mortel, peut néanmoins être fructueusement adaptée par la présence et la protection de l'objet.

Je considère cette identification avec l'objet des tendances hostiles comme l'élément caractéristique de l'agoraphobie. Le sentiment de culpabilité peut être satisfait par le fait que dans le « retournement contre le Moi », ce dernier expérimente lui-même la menace de mort. Mais la tension entre le Moi et les agents menaçants dans le Surmoi ne sera relâchée que si la présence de l'objet protecteur confirme le fait que l'objet n'est pas en danger et n'a pas été déserté par le Moi.

Dans notre dernier cas, nous avons pu suivre dans le transfert la genèse de cette tension entre le Moi et le Surmoi. Elle tournait autour de deux identifications : l'une était liée à l'objet dégradé et les pulsions génératrices de danger constituaient le pont de l'identification. L'autre identification était liée à l'objet d'interdit sévère — la mère ascétique — dont la sévérité n'était cependant évoquée que par la situation de tentation dans la rue.

J'ai pu aussi observer des tendances exhibitionnistes contraignantes comme élément subsidiaire important. J'aimerais ajouter que ma dernière patiente était beaucoup plus exempte d'angoisse dans la rue quand elle fermait les yeux. Le fantasme actif et passif de la naissance avait une importance centrale, ce fantasme pour lequel le fait d'être éloigné de la maison et dans le monde avait une signification symbolique importante.

L'angoisse de l'accouchement en tant qu'élément du fantasme féminin-masochique est un héritage direct de l'angoisse de castration, et ce sont précisément les cas d'agoraphobie qui m'ont permis de voir clairement ce qui me paraît caractéristique dans l'évolution de la libido féminine en général. Le renoncement à l'envie du pénis est suivi par le vague désir d'une sorte de violation douloureuse, d'où le fait que le désir de castration et son successeur direct, le désir de défloration ou d'accouchement, acquièrent la même signification dans l'inconscient de la femme. L'angoisse de castration non dominée se transforme en angoisse névrotique de défloration ou d'accouchement. On peut suivre nettement ce processus de transformation dans l'analyse d'agoraphobies. J'ai, en outre, l'impression que le fantasme masochique féminin de la naissance joue également le même rôle chez les agoraphobes *masculins*.

Ces cas fournissent-ils une réponse complète à la question de savoir pourquoi l'angoisse ne se produit que dans la rue ? Je n'en sais rien. Bien entendu, il y a toujours une prédisposition à l'angoisse qui apparaît dans certaines conditions liées à la rue. Freud pensait que ces conditions se trouvaient d'une part dans la perte de la protection fournie par la maison et, d'autre part, dans les tentations de la rue. La tentation se produit là où la vie amoureuse est rabaissée à la prostitution par des facteurs régressifs ; cela est conditionné en particulier par les tendances masochiques qui étaient assez claires dans les cas dont j'ai parlé. La rue représente également un danger particulier pour les pulsions exhibitionnistes, qui étaient fortement représentées dans les cas que j'ai analysés.

Un autre facteur déterminant important était le fantasme actif et passif de la naissance. En outre, la signification fortement libidinale des jambes et de l'acte de marcher, sur laquelle Abraham (1913) a attiré l'attention, jouait certainement aussi un rôle.

Si nous comparons tous ces cas de phobie, nous verrons que leur terrain commun se trouve dans le fait que le danger intérieur est projeté à l'extérieur et rattaché à une situation ou à un objet particuliers. Dans la phobie animale, un animal approprié est choisi pour personnifier le danger et dans l'agoraphobie, c'est une partie de l'univers. Le Moi est ainsi capable de substituer un danger réel, donc évitable, à un danger inconscient, donc inévitable. En outre, par la réalisation de certaines conditions, le Moi peut obtenir l'absence d'angoisse. Dans le cas de la phobie animale, elles consistent en un simple évitement ; dans l'agoraphobie, c'est la présence de l'objet d'une agression écartée qui permet à l'agression de se rattacher à une pulsion libidinale et de réduire ainsi les dangers créateurs d'angoisse pour le Moi.

HÉLÈNE DEUTSCH[6]

6. *La Psychanalyse des névroses*, p. 89-104.

MIDAS' DAUGHTER TURNED TO GOLD

Chapitre III

La névrose obsessionnelle

C'est par rapport à l'hystérie que Freud a décrit les mécanismes propres à la névrose obsessionnelle, comme c'est par rapport à la sexualité masculine qu'il définit la sexualité féminine. Or, la plupart des hystériques sont des femmes, et la plupart des obsédés sont des hommes — fait qui n'a pas manqué d'attirer l'attention de Freud. Il s'est donc produit, dans le mouvement d'idées qui a conduit à la mise au point de la théorie psychanalytique telle que nous la connaissons aujourd'hui, une sorte de chassé-croisé qu'il n'était peut-être pas inutile de noter...

Lorsqu'en 1896 Freud rédige ses Nouvelles remarques sur les psychonévroses de défense, *il souligne que l'aptitude à la conversion est absente de la névrose obsessionnelle. Il suppose alors que, contrairement à ce qui existe dans l'hystérie, où il y a eu séduction passive, le futur obsédé a connu dans sa prime enfance des expériences sexuelles actives, agressives et pratiquées avec plaisir. En fait, le « substratum de symptômes hystériques » présent dans la névrose obsessionnelle est lié au fait que l'agression sexuelle précoce a été précédée d'une séduction passive exercée par un adulte. Deux expériences infantiles se seraient par conséquent succédées, l'une passive, l'autre active, chez le futur obsédé.*

En 1913, Ernest Jones rédige un article intitulé « Haine et érotisme anal dans la névrose obsessionnelle ». La même année, Freud reprend pour l'essentiel les conclusions de ce dernier dans « la Disposition à la névrose obsessionnelle[1] », qui porte, en sous-titre, « Une contribution au problème du choix de la névrose ». Il y conserve l'idée d'un double traumatisme, mais y insiste sur l'importance décisive, pour le choix de la maladie, de la fixation au stade sadique-anal et de la régression à ce stade à partir du stade œdipien génital.

---

1. Voir *les Stades de la libido : de l'enfant à l'adulte* (chap. IV), dans la même collection, et *Névrose, psychose et perversion* (P.U.F.).

◄ *Le roi Midas aimait à tel point l'or qu'il reçut la faveur de pouvoir changer en or tout ce qu'il touchait. Il fut puni de son désir par la transformation de sa fille en statue d'or. (Gravure de W. Crane, Bibliothèque des Arts Décoratifs).*

Cette étude est fondamentale pour expliquer le choix de la névrose - en fait, de toutes les névroses. Car le choix de la névrose, c'est à dire l'ensemble des processus aboutissant, chez un individu, à la constitution de telle névrose plutôt que de telle autre, y est étroitement rapporté aux stades de la libido et aux problèmes de la fixation et de la régression.

D'une façon générale, Freud a relié la névrose à la satisfaction qui en découle pour le sujet. Cela se rattache à ce que nous avons vu du bénéfice économique que représente le symptôme, ce bénéfice étant pour partie à l'origine de la résistance au traitement. Freud distingue le « bénéfice primaire » et le « bénéfice secondaire » de la maladie. Le bénéfice primaire est en relation avec la satisfaction procurée par le symptôme et par la « fuite dans la maladie ». Par « bénéfice secondaire », on entend les satisfactions que l'individu retire de sa maladie, en plus de celles résultant de la constitution même de celle-ci ; ainsi, dans le cas des névroses de guerre, ne plus retourner au front, obtenir une pension, etc. Il n'est pas toujours facile de délimiter bénéfice primaire et bénéfice secondaire : par exemple, la pression que le malade peut exercer du fait de sa névrose sur son entourage doit-elle être *considérée comme un bénéfice inhérent à la constitution même de sa maladie, ou comme un bénéfice venant s'y ajouter ? Rappelons ce qu'écrivait Félix Deutsch à propos de Dora dans un précédent chapitre : « Après la mort de son père, au début des années trente, elle commença à souffrir de palpitations cardiaques qu'on attribua au fait qu'elle fumait trop ; elle y réagit par des crises d'angoisse liées à la peur de mourir. Son entourage se trouva ainsi en état d'alerte perma*nente et elle en profita pour monter amis et parents les uns contre les autres. »

Si l'Homme aux Rats constitue le cas princeps *de névrose obsessionnelle analysé par Freud, son disciple Fénichel, dans les extraits qui vont suivre de son ouvrage didactique* la Théorie psychanalytique des névroses, *résume et synthétise pour nous les conceptions psychanalytiques des mécanismes propres à la névrose obsessionnelle.*

Le phénomène de compulsion est en fait une condensation des forces instinctuelles et contre-instinctuelles. Le tableau clinique manifeste révèle, plus ou moins selon les cas, le premier ou le second aspect. Le premier se manifeste dans les idées de meurtre ou d'inceste ; plus fréquemment les symptômes révèlent de façon certaine des ordres déformés du Surmoi ; la signification défensive ou punitive est mise, dans ce cas, davantage en valeur que dans la conversion. Le danger dont les

234

personnes tentent de se protéger est moins de l'espèce d'une perte d'amour ou d'une castration que d'une menace interne. La crainte principale se manifeste plutôt comme une espèce de peur de perdre l'estime de soi-même, et même comme un sentiment d'« annihilation » ; en d'autres termes les sentiments de culpabilité ont une importance plus décisive que le motif de la défense pathogène. Ceci est conforme au fait que les névroses obsessionnelles surviennent, chez les enfants, à une époque plus tardive que l'hystérie, en général pendant la période de latence.

Il est évident que dans certains cas les compulsions traduisent des ordres du Surmoi. Dans un cas de compulsion de lavage, un patient s'entendait commander « Va te laver », simple répétition d'un ordre souvent entendu dans son enfance. Il lui importait peu que cet ordre ne concerne alors que la propreté physique, le patient sentant que si ses parents avaient connu ses pensées sales ils lui auraient ordonné d'aller se laver. Ce commandement était maintenant utilisé comme défense contre de telles pensées.

Les compulsions ressenties comme des menaces sont de la même espèce. Un patient dans ce cas est obsédé par les sombres résultats que pourrait provoquer toute concession faite à la tentation. Par exemple : « Si tu fais cela ou oublies cela, tu mourras » ou « Si tu fais cela ou oublies cela, ton père mourra ». Il apparaît, par l'analyse de ces cas, que les actions devant être contenues ou évitées ont une signification instinctuelle répréhensible ; elles représentent en règle générale des tendances œdipiennes déformées, il est vrai, de façon caractéristique. Les menaces de punition impliquent que le danger (castration ou perte d'amour) est imaginé en liaison étroite avec les instincts défendus ou encore qu'elles représentent quelque active autopunition destinée à éloigner (ou à se substituer à) la castration ou à la perte d'amour.

La menace « Ou votre père mourra », à laquelle cette interprétation ne convient pas, peut être expliquée comme une soudaine prise de conscience du « signal d'angoisse ». Cela veut dire : « Ce que vous avez l'intention de faire n'est pas une chose dénuée de mal ; la vérité est que vous voulez tuer votre père et si vous cédez à la tentation, le meurtre de votre père en sera le résultat. »

Alors que certains symptômes obsédants constituent des modes déformés de percevoir les exigences instinctuelles et que d'autres expriment les menaces contre-instinctuelles du Surmoi, d'autres symptômes encore montrent la lutte entre ces deux modes. La plupart des symptômes du doute obsessif peuvent être couverts par la formule : « Puis-je être mauvais, ou dois-je être bon ? » Quelquefois, un symptôme présente deux phases, l'une représentant une impulsion répréhensible, l'autre la défense contre elle. L'*Homme aux Rats* de Freud par exemple, se sentait obligé d'enlever une pierre de la route, parce qu'elle aurait pu blesser quelqu'un, puis se sentait obligé de la reposer.

LE SYMPTÔME : UN COMPROMIS ENTRE LA PULSION REFOULÉE ET LE SURMOI

Quelquefois on peut observer, dans le cours d'une névrose obsessionnelle, la façon dont un symptôme peut changer de signification. Un symptôme qui exprimait la défense peut devenir de plus en plus une expression du retour de l'impulsion originelle.

Un patient pouvait dissiper l'angoisse qui apparaissait après la masturbation en tendant les muscles de ses jambes. Cette tension fut remplacée, par la suite, par un martèlement rythmique de la jambe, et encore plus tard par un autre acte masturbatoire. Un autre patient se sentait plein de remords après des exercices de gymnastique. L'analyse montra que ces exercices représentaient la masturbation. Alors, ce remords ruminé de façon obsessionnelle, lui fit penser finalement : « Masturbe-toi et mine-toi complètement » et il se sentait obligé de se masturber plusieurs fois sans éprouver le moindre plaisir.

Les patients obligés par leurs symptômes de vérifier continuellement s'ils ont, oui ou non, fermé le robinet à gaz, sont souvent obligés de ce fait de le rouvrir, précipitant ainsi le danger au lieu de le prévenir. Un autre patient passait tout son temps à ranger les objets qui se trouvaient sur sa bibliothèque de peur qu'ils ne tombent sur la tête de quelqu'un, leur donnant ainsi une réelle chance de tomber. Afin de protéger leurs proches contre leurs impulsions hostiles, de nombreux obsédés les gardent et les protègent contre des dangers imaginaires d'une façon si dévote qu'en réalité ils les tourmentent, exprimant leur hostilité en dépit d'eux-mêmes.

Le suprême degré d'un « retour du refoulé » se manifesta chez une patiente observée par Waterman ; elle souffrait d'une telle phobie de la saleté qu'elle restait au lit tout le jour lorsqu'elle avait le sentiment que ses vêtements ou sa chambre étaient sales. Sa peur de la saleté, qui l'empêchait de quitter son lit, faisait qu'il lui arrivait de souiller ce dernier.

236

Des pensées telles que : « Maintenant que tu t'es ruiné par l'exercice, tu seras traité comme tu le mérites, en te ruinant par la masturbation », indiquent comment expliquer le paradoxe apparaissant dans l'exigence instinctuelle vécue comme si elle était un ordre du Surmoi. Des symptômes de cette espèce représentent un compromis entre les pulsions refoulées et le Surmoi menaçant ; la pulsion s'exprime par le contenu idéique, le Surmoi par la forme de commandement déformant la pulsion originelle. Une masturbation compulsive dénuée d'agréments représente le maximum de cette espèce de condensation. Un acte apparemment sexuel est exécuté, non pour le plaisir sexuel, mais dans un but de punition et de suppression de la sexualité. Ceci représente fréquemment la fin d'un long développement : une compulsion, défense contre la masturbation, est remplacée par un retour du matériel refoulé, par une autre masturbation qui a maintenant un caractère compulsif et punitif. La punition de Midas, résultat d'un pseudo accomplissement de ses désirs est une réaction typique de l'obsession. Certains obsédés mettront fin occasionnellement à un état de doute et de discussions en se masturbant.

DES RITUELS DONT LES MALADES NE COMPRENNENT PAS LE SENS

Un développement similaire se rencontre souvent à propos des « équivalents masturbatoires ». Des compulsions du genre tappement, cérémonial de mouvements musculaires, rituels du toucher de certains objets, sont dirigés en premier lieu contre la masturbation, mais peuvent s'être transformés secondairement en équivalents masturbatoires ; le patient est parfois averti de façon vague de cette connexion et doit alors se punir de ce comportement dégoûtant. D'autres fois le patient ne soupçonne pas la signification du symptôme.

Les rituels compulsifs sont en général des équivalents caricaturaux de la masturbation. Quelquefois, un symptôme apparemment sans rapport avec la masturbation révèle ce rapport à l'analyse. Une patiente était obligée de compter jusqu'à cinq ou six chaque fois qu'elle tournait un robinet ou même quand elle passait devant un robinet. Elle était complètement dominée par l'envie d'un pénis, aussi pouvait-on s'attendre à ce qu'un symptôme en rapport avec un robinet d'eau fût aussi en rapport avec son envie d'un pénis. Elle se rappela, en fait, qu'une fois un de ses doigts s'étant infecté, sa mère l'avait effrayée, lui disant qu'il faudrait lui couper. Aussi le rituel peut être interprété comme suit : la vue du robinet (ou du pénis) forçait la patiente à se convaincre qu'elle n'avait pas quatre, mais cinq et même six doigts. Plus tard, il apparut que ce rituel avait un rapport étroit avec la masturbation. Elle avait eu l'habitude de se masturber avec un doigt et de laisser couler l'urine le long de ce doigt, comme s'il était un pénis.

Souvent, le complexe d'Œdipe peut être le centre des impulsions refoulées ; cela apparaît quelquefois même lors d'un examen superficiel, ce qui, du fait du refoulement, serait impossible dans l'hystérie.

Un patient, malheureusement pas analysé, se plaignait de deux types d'impulsions obsessives. Chaque fois qu'il voyait une femme, il était obliger de penser : « Je pourrais tuer cette femme » ; et chaque fois qu'il voyait des couteaux ou des ciseaux : « Je pourrais me couper le pénis. » La première de ces deux impulsions avait été exprimée à l'origine : « Je pourrais tuer ma mère » ; son extension aux autres femmes était déjà une déformation par généralisation. Le patient vivait une vie solitaire, et son unique issue sexuelle consistait en des rêves dans lesquels il se voyait étranglant ou tuant des femmes. Ainsi, son impulsion à tuer des femmes était une expression détournée de ses désirs incestueux. En éliminant cette déformation, on peut établir que ce patient souffrait de deux impulsions : attaquer sexuellement sa mère et se couper le pénis. Ces impulsions peuvent être comprises en tant que symptômes biphasiques : la première moitié présente la gratification du souhait œdipien, la deuxième la punition redoutée.

Des symptômes inintelligibles deviennent intelligibles lorsque leur histoire est étudiée. La forme originelle dans laquelle ils apparurent est plus près de la signification inconsciente. Un symptôme peut être une allusion à un événement du passé du patient ; cette allusion ne peut pas être comprise aussi longtemps que le contexte entier n'est pas connu.

Avant d'aller au lit, un patient était obligé de passer un long moment à ouvrir et à fermer sa fenêtre. Ce symptôme était d'abord apparu quand, adolescent, lui et son compagnon de chambre se battirent pour savoir si la fenêtre serait ouverte ou non. Ainsi, cette compulsion signifiait : « Lequel de nous gagnera ? Lequel de nous est le plus fort ? » Avec cette formule comme point de départ il devint clair, en dernière analyse, que le problème de ce patient était mobilisé par la tentation homosexuelle survenue du fait du partage de cette chambre avec son ami. La question réelle était de savoir s'il devait rentrer en compétition avec les hommes ou se résigner à subir leur loi d'une façon soumise et féministe. La névrose obsessionnelle de ce patient prenait racine dans ces faits.

LA RÉGRESSION DANS LA NÉVROSE OBSESSIONNELLE

L'exemple d'une expression ouverte de souhaits œdipiens, dans laquelle le patient ressentait les deux impulsions de tuer les femmes et de se couper le pénis, est typique de la façon par laquelle les désirs incestueux sont déformés dans la névrose obsessionnelle. Le patient parle de « tuer » sa mère quand il veut dire en fait « avoir des rapports sexuels » avec elle. Les rêves sexuels du patient étaient d'une nature sadique évidente. Il n'y avait pas ainsi seulement un attachement infantile à la mère, mais également une déformation spécifique de type sadique de cet attachement.

Des tendances ouvertes ou dissimulées à la cruauté, ou des formations réactionnelles contre elle, sont des composantes constantes de l'obsession. On y trouve, avec une constance égale, des impulsions érotiques anales et les défenses dirigées contre ces impulsions. Cette association constante de traits de cruauté et d'érotisme anal chez les obsédés, sur laquelle Jones attira le premier l'attention, fut ce qui convainquit Freud de la parenté étroite de ces deux types de phénomène, et de l'existence d'un stade d'organisation « sadique-anal » de la libido.

Les idées refoulées, dans l'hystérie, restent inaltérées dans l'inconscient et continuent à exercer, de là leur influence ; ce fait existe également dans l'obsession dans la mesure où le complexe d'Œdipe est à la base du symptôme compulsif, mais il apparaît en outre dans cette affection de très fortes tendances sadiques-anales tirant leur origine du stade précédent de développement libidinal, tendances régulièrement efficientes et combattues. L'orientation sadique-anale de l'obsédé peut, en règle générale, être aisément reconnue dans le tableau clinique, une fois l'attention attirée sur ce point. Les obsédés sont, en général, en butte à des conflits entre l'agressivité et la soumission, la cruauté et la gentillesse, la saleté et la propreté, l'ordre et le désordre. Ces conflits peuvent s'exprimer dans l'apparence extérieure et dans le comportement manifeste, alors qu'il est invariablement répondu aux questions concernant la vie sexuelle : « Aussi loin qu'on peut voir, tout est en ordre. » Les fonctions physiologiques semblent être en ordre, étant isolées de leur contenu psychologique ; la décharge physiologique de l'activité sexuelle du patient n'est pas une décharge adéquate à sa tension sexuelle, réellement exprimée dans ses idées sur la cruauté et la saleté. Quelquefois, l'orientation sadique-anale se révèle sous la forme de formations réactionnelles, telles que, par exemple, une bonté surcompensée, un sens exagéré de la justice ou de la propreté, une incapacité à la moindre agression, une méticulosité pour tout ce qui est en relation avec l'argent. Un mélange de formations réactionnelles et d'impulsions directes sadiques-anales peuvent donner une apparence contradictoire au comportement du patient. Le patient est simultané ment ordonné et désordonné, propre et sale, bon et cruel.

Un patient, non analysé, se plaignit à la première entrevue de présenter ce syndrome compulsif : il était obligé de regarder constamment derrière lui, craignant continuellement d'avoir omis quelque chose d'important. Les idées suivantes étaient prédominantes : il pouvait avoir oublié une pièce de monnaie dans un coin, blessé un insecte en marchant dessus ou un insecte tombé sur le dos pouvait avoir besoin d'aide. Le patient craignait tout autant de toucher les objets de peur de les détruire. Il n'avait aucune vocation, ses compulsions empêchant le moindre travail, mais il avait une passion : nettoyer les maisons. Il aimait rendre visite à ses voisins et nettoyer leur maison, juste pour s'amuser. Un autre symptôme fut encore décrit par ce patient : il était toujours préoccupé par l'état de ses vêtements. Il déclara également que la sexualité ne jouait qu'un faible rôle dans sa vie ; il avait des relations sexuelles deux ou trois fois par an, exclusivement avec des filles auxquelles il ne portait aucun intérêt. Plus tard, il mentionna qu'étant enfant il trouvait sa mère dégoûtante et était effrayé à l'idée de la toucher. Ceci n'était nullement justifié, sa mère étant une jolie et agréable personne.

Ce tableau clinique montrait l'orientation sadique-anale de la sexualité de ce patient, la peur incestueuse étant à la base de cette déformation.

LA PIERRE ANGULAIRE DE L'OBSESSION : UNE RÉGRESSION AU STADE SADIQUE-ANAL

L'orientation sadique-anale des obsédés devient naturellement en analyse encore plus claire. Tous les obsédés, a établi Freud, ont des rituels scatologiques secrets, qui sont en partie des jeux érotiques anaux et en partie des réactions contre ces jeux. W. C. Menninger a réuni les types les plus fréquents de rituels scatologiques. Les patients sont toujours en garde contre leurs tendances inconscientes anales mélangées à l'hostilité, par exemple contre la pulsion à jouer à des jeux sales avec leurs camarades.

Ainsi, Freud a établi que l'organisation instinctuelle des obsédés ressemble à celle des enfants dans la phase sadique-anale de leur développement. Cela semble contredire l'observation typique que les obsédés sont engagés dans une lutte défensive contre le complexe d'Œdipe, dont la crise maximale n'est pas atteinte avant la période phallique.

Une autre contradiction apparente réside dans le fait qu'en dépit du sadisme anal, beaucoup de compulsions sont étroitement en relation avec la masturbation.

L'explication de ces apparentes contradictions se trouve dans le concept de régression. On a l'impression que les impulsions sadiques anales croissent aux dépens du complexe d'Œdipe originellement phal lique. Les impulsions génitales œdipiennes décroissent en force pen dant que les impulsions sadiques-anales augmentent. Le patient tentant de refouler le complexe d'Œdipe, régresse en partie au niveau sadique-anal.

Cependant, l'obsédé n'est pas coprophile. Étant donné que ses impulsions sadiques anales sont également intolérables, ou parce qu'en régressant jusqu'à elles l'élément offensif du complexe d'Œdipe ne s'est pas complètement éliminé, le patient doit combattre à leur tour les impulsions sadiques-anales. L'interpolation de la régression fait de l'obsession une névrose plus compliquée que l'hystérie.

La théorie de Freud disant que la régression au stade sadique-anal forme la pierre angulaire de l'obsession peut expliquer bien des faits qui autrement, seraient contradictoires.

Il est maintenant compréhensible que les impulsions refoulées dans l'obsession soient composées de tendances œdipiennes phalliques et d'impulsions masturbatoires d'une part et qu'elles soient, néanmoins, de nature sadique-anale d'autre part. La défense a été, en premier, diri gée contre le complexe d'Œdipe phallique et l'a supplanté par le sadisme anal ; puis la défense a continué contre les impulsions anales.

ÉVITER L'ANGOISSE « ANALE » DE CASTRATION

L'analyse peut montrer, occasionnellement, un réel processus de régression pouvant ainsi prouver que l'obsession s'installe après lui.

Une fille souffrait de la peur obsessive qu'un serpent sorte de la toi lette et lui rentre dans l'anus. En analyse il apparut que cette peur s'était d'abord présentée sous une autre forme : elle craignait que ce serpent fût dans son lit. Pour la protéger de l'anxiété phallique, une régression s'était opérée ; la localisation de la peur fut transportée du lit à la toilette, des organes génitaux à l'anus.

Un garçon, pendant sa période de latence, fut pris d'une angoisse immense chaque fois qu'il était en érection. Il déclara qu'il avait peur de blesser son pénis. Il prit l'habitude de se masturber chaque fois qu'il avait une érection, dans le but de la faire cesser. Cette façon d'agir créa de nouvelles angoisses. Plus tard, il présenta le besoin urgent et fréquent d'uriner et de déféquer. Puis, après cela, se développa une névrose obsessionnelle intense. Il est évident qu'au début les impulsions génitales s'imposaient d'elles-mêmes en dépit de la crainte menaçante de castration, puis elles furent remplacées par des désirs prégénitaux ; la névrose obsessionnelle n'apparut qu'après la régression au stade anal.

Une preuve plus indirecte mais presque expérimentale de la régression sadique-anale dans l'obsession est fournie par les cas rares dans lesquels l'hystérie, après renonciation de la génitalité, est remplacée par une névrose obsessionnelle. Freud observa ce processus chez une femme qui, à cause de circonstances extérieures, cessa d'accorder la moindre valeur à sa vie génitale. On peut fréquemment observer un processus similaire après la ménopause, la régression étant provoquée alors par des facteurs organiques.

L'opération de régression peut être également prouvée dans les cas où son but défensif échoue. Quoique transférant son intérêt au domaine anal, le patient, dans de tels cas, ne réussit pas à éviter la peur de castration. Il développe, à la place, ce qu'on pourrait appeler une crainte anale de castration. Un tel patient peut arriver à ne pouvoir déféquer autrement qu'en petites quantités informes, essayant ainsi de « perdre un organe ». Le matériel traité par Freud sous le titre de l'équation symbolique fèces = pénis doit son origine, en partie, à cette régression.

Quelques-unes des craintes typiques en rapport avec les w.-c. chez les enfants et les obsédés, telles que crainte de tomber dans les toilettes ou d'être mangé par quelque monstre sorti de là, ou encore la crainte rationalisée d'y être infecté apparaissent, en analyse, comme des angoisses de castration. Un enfant, dont les craintes diverses pouvaient se ramener à la crainte de voir disparaître ses excréments, exprimait ainsi sa peur de voir son pénis disparaître en même temps, de la même façon.

Comme dans les peurs orales, le fait que les craintes anales couvrent des angoisses de castration ne contredit pas la nature autonome des craintes prégénitales. Cette déformation de l'angoisse de castration est régressive, formée par la remobilisation de vieilles angoisses prégénitales sur la perte des matières. Il est souvent très difficile de déterminer quelle fraction d'angoisse anale représente l'anxiété prégénitale originelle ; il est d'ailleurs possible qu'elle participe à l'angoisse de castration dès le début (les expériences prégénitales du sevrage, de la séparation des matières fécales, sont des avant-coureurs archaïques de la crainte de castration).

— Tiens, encore avec elle !... je croyais qu'elle l'avait lâché, depuis sa ruine ?
— Il s'était ruiné pour elle, il l'a épousée pour tout rattraper.

Certains couples d'obsédés fondent leur relation sur l'argent.

ÉROTISME ANAL ET BISEXUALITÉ

C'est toujours une source récurrente de surprise de voir apparaître en analyse, après la découverte d'un monde sadique-anal datant des premières années de la vie, un matériel réprimé encore plus vieux, d'orientation purement phallique, qui avait été disloqué par l'angoisse de castration. Il est important de ne pas se tromper en prenant ce matériel nouvellement apparu en référence avec des impulsions sadiques-anales, pour un ensemble de souvenirs datant du stade anal. Très souvent, il n'est pas d'origine, mais de nature régressive. Il vient après la phase phallique du complexe d'Œdipe et l'organisation prégénitale originelle date encore d'avant.

Le matériel clinique dans lequel les idées et le mode de comportement appropriés au niveau génital se trouvent entremêlés avec un matériel sadique-anal est abondant. Certains obsédés, par exemple, ne perçoivent la sexualité que sur un mode anal, comme une affaire de salle de bains ; d'autres considèrent ce sujet comme une affaire financière pouvant s'exprimer par des fantasmes de prostitution ou comme une matière de propriété. Un homme peut s'attacher surtout, pendant les relations sexuelles, à retenir l'éjaculation aussi longtemps que possible, quelquefois avec l'idée de faire durer le plaisir, d'autres fois avec l'idée de préserver le semen ; cette façon d'agir peut quelquefois être rationalisée, le patient pensant augmenter ainsi la jouissance de sa partenaire ; l'analyse montre qu'il fait, avec son semen, ce qu'il avait fait auparavant avec ses fèces. Toujours dans d'autres cas, la déformation sadique de la vie sexuelle entière est plus visible que la déformation anale. Pour certains obsédés, les relations sexuelles ont la signification d'un combat dans lequel un vainqueur castre une victime. Ne pas être la victime peut représenter tout l'intérêt sexuel du patient mâle de cette espèce (il semble d'ailleurs qu'il ne réussit jamais complètement à atteindre ce but) ; des patientes peuvent avoir le désir ardent de voir et de toucher des organes génitaux mâles ; dans ce souhait est contenu le désir dissimulé de les détruire.

L'effet immédiat de la régression est double : 1) le sadisme se combine avec l'hostilité œdipienne ressentie contre le parent du même sexe et impose de nouvelles tâches défensives au Moi ; 2) l'érotisme anal émergeant change le but sexuel et, de cette façon, le comportement de la personne. L'érotisme anal est toujours, comme il l'a été établi, de nature bisexuelle, l'anus pouvant être un organe actif dans sa fonction d'expulser et un organe creux, pouvant être stimulé par un objet pénétrant. Des hésitations entre l'attitude masculine originelle, maintenant renforcée et exagérée par la composante sadique-anale et l'attitude

244

féminine représentée par la composante passive de l'érotisme anal forment un conflit des plus typiques dans l'inconscient de l'obsédé mâle. L'attitude œdipienne phallique est inhibée par l'idée que sa satisfaction entraînerait la perte du pénis. La régression impose une attitude féminine, sans détruire complètement l'attitude masculine originelle.

L'importance accordée simultanément, dans l'éducation moderne, à l'indépendance et à la soumission, augmente le conflit entre les désirs passif-féminin et actif-masculin dans l'obsession. Une activité superficielle peut s'établir en réaction contre une plus profonde passivité, et vice versa. Une passivité réelle peut, de nombreuses façons, passer pour de l'activité. Un compromis normal de cette espèce est l'amour d'identification du garçon à son père ; en étant temporairement féminin envers lui, il obtient une promesse de participation future à sa masculinité. Cette « psychologie de l'élève » passif envers le maître, dans le but de devenir plus tard maître lui-même, est ouverte à quelques déformations pathologiques.

Le but des désirs féminins des obsédés n'est évidemment pas d'être castré, mais exprime plutôt le souhait de retenir quelque chose inséré dans le corps. L'idée que ce désir n'est pas en lui-même une protection de tout repos contre la castration, et que bien au contraire cette dernière peut être une condition préalable à sa satisfaction, provoque une angoisse intense et fournit en retour le motif à une défense plus serrée. C'était la situation de « l'Homme aux Loups » refoulant son complexe d'Œdipe inverti par peur de la castration. Sa peur d'être mangé par le loup exprimait à la fois ses désirs féminins envers son père et l'angoisse de castration en rapport avec ces désirs.

De cette façon, toute satisfaction sexuelle peut devenir si liée avec d'angoissantes idées de castration qu'elles deviennent inconcevables l'une sans l'autre. Le patient se comporte souvent comme s'il recherchait inconsciemment la castration, ce qu'il cherche réellement est quelque chose apportant une fin à l'angoisse prohibant son plaisir. La « castration » vraiment recherchée est soit une castration symbolique, un moindre mal prêt à être supporté par le patient afin d'éviter la castration complète, soit une anticipation active de ce qu'il voudrait vivre passivement. Après une manifestation symbolisant la castration, le patient, fréquemment, entreprend la démonstration contraire au moyen d'un rituel. De même que la bisexualité, l'ambivalence est une caractéristique de l'augmentation de l'érotisme anal. Une ambivalence marquée envers les relations objectales est typique des stades du développement prégénital libidinal, et elle reparaît avec l'abandon de l'organisation génitale. Pour autant que la fixation anale soit une précondition de la régression anale, les deux qualités associées avec cette dernière, l'ambivalence et la bisexualité, peuvent être considérées comme préconditions de la régression. Mais pour autant que la régression intensifie et rende persistante l'orientation sadique-anale, la bisexualité et l'ambivalence, attributs de cette orientation, sont des résultats de la régression.

Dans l'hystérie de conversion avec symptomatologie intestinale, la régression est limitée au choix de l'organe affecté, utilisé à exprimer des fantasmes génitaux. Il en est autrement dans l'obsession. Là, une régression complète au monde des désirs et des attitudes anaux prend place et change complètement le comportement. Fréquemment même, l'orientation olfactive caractéristique des enfants au stade anal et perdue chez les adultes normaux, réapparaît chez les obsédés. Souvent la régression ramène plus ou moins des traits narcissiques, la bisexualité augmentée permettant des fantasmes d'union sexuelle avec soi-même. Il existe des états de transition entre les névroses obsessionnelles et les psychoses maniaco-dépressives et les schizophrénies.

« Fréquemment même, l'orientation olfactive, caractéristique des enfants au stade anal et perdue chez les adultes normaux, réapparaît chez les obsédés ».

DES SYSTÈMES COMPULSIFS
DESTINÉS A SURMONTER L'ANGOISSE

L'ordre, mesure de protection contre les dangereuses exigences instinctuelles lors de la période érotique anale reprend cette fonction protectrice au cours d'une névrose obsessionnelle postérieure. L'obsédé menacé par la rébellion de ses exigences sensuelles et hostiles (déformées par la régression), se sent protégé aussi longtemps qu'il se comporte de façon ordonnée, en particulier en ce qui concerne l'argent et le temps. Cependant les pulsions sadiques-anales sabotent en général cet ordre, s'accrochant au « système » ; elles réapparaissent sous forme de désordre ou d'événements troublant le système, ou elles peuvent s'infiltrer dans le syndrome d'ordre lui même.

Lucille Dooley, dans un article intéressant, concernant l'ordre et les systèmes des obsédés en rapport avec le temps, montre que tout écart à cette routine signifie inconsciemment le meurtre et l'inceste. Beaucoup d'obsédés ont un vif intérêt pour toutes sortes d'emploi du temps. Ils peuvent même régler leur vie entière sur des emplois du temps systématisés. Aussi longtemps que les obsédés réussissent à régler leur vie sur des horaires, ils sont sûrs de ne pas commettre les péchés redoutés et aussi longtemps qu'ils savent à l'avance ce qu'ils feront, ils peuvent surmonter la crainte provoquée par leurs tendances à faire ce dont ils ont peur.

« L'orientation dans le temps » est une mesure de réassurance typique. Plus d'une peur de la mort a le sens d'une crainte d'un état dans lequel la conception usuelle du temps n'est plus valide. Lorsque l'orientation dans le temps devient plus difficile — crépuscules, longues nuits d'hiver et même les longs jours d'été —, les obsédés s'effraient. Cependant les peurs de cette espèce ont parfois pris racine simplement à l'occasion d'événements effrayants, ayant eu lieu pendant l'enfance, à ce même moment de la journée.

La compulsion, comme telle, est utilisée comme protection similaire ; elle garantit contre la menace venant d'une dangereuse spontanéité. Toute chose exécutée de façon compulsive l'est comme une routine, en accord avec un plan préarrangé, duquel les impulsions répréhensibles sont sensées être exclues. Aussi longtemps que les règles sont suivies, rien de mauvais ne peut arriver. L'obsédé est cependant conscient de l'existence de ses instincts. Il ne peut jamais parvenir à la certitude satisfaisante qu'il suit les règles, que ces règles sont aptes à englober toutes les possibilités, et qu'il les connaît toute suffisamment.

Les choses se compliquent lorsque la présence d'autres personnes, témoins nécessaires pour garantir la validité des exigences compulsives d'ordre et de règles précises, est devenue indispensable. Le patient se sent, non seulement obligé de s'astreindre lui-même à un ordre systématique, mais il requiert des autres la même conduite. Les autres, en règle générale, refusent de se soumettre à son système. Ceci augmente son hostilité et il essaie des moyens divers pour les y obliger ; il prend peur de l'hostilité exprimée dans ses tentatives et cette peur, en retour, augmente son besoin de règles précises ; un cercle vicieux est ainsi constitué. Les choses se compliquent encore plus lorsque les systèmes de plusieurs obsédés viennent à s'entrechoquer. Comme l'obsession a son origine dans une augmentation de l'érotisme anal, en partie déterminée par des facteurs constitutionnels, plusieurs cas d'obsession surviennent fréquemment dans la même famille. De sévères troubles familiaux peuvent se créer de cette façon.

EXCLURE TOUTE POSSIBILITÉ DE SURPRISE ET FORCER AUTRUI A L'APPROBATION

Il existe une névrose obsessionnelle faisant le pendant de la pseudologie. Certains patients estiment compatibles de grossières altérations de la réalité avec leur exactitude obsessive, et même avec un fanatisme obsessif pour la vérité ; ces falsifications, conformément à la tendance compulsive du déplacement au petit détail ne concernent que des petits détails peu importants. Les petites modifications réelles de la vérité en représentent de plus grandes ayant pour but d'obliger le monde à rentrer dans un système défini. Les faits sont supposés être non pas conformes à la réalité, mais tels qu'ils sont exigés par le système compulsif. La falsification exprime également l'envie de faire peser ce même système sur les autres : « Vous devez voir les choses non pas avec vos propres yeux, mais comme je vous le montre. » Une violence de cette espèce exercée sur le compagnon, peut satisfaire le sadisme et l'obstination anale de l'obsédé. Le but principal d'un tel comportement est cependant plus spécifique. Freud a comparé les souvenirs spontanés de la précoce enfance avec la création des mythes falsifiant l'histoire dans un sens de réalisations de désirs. Dans ces tentatives compulsives destinées à forcer l'acquiescement des témoins au système obsessif, la création de tels mythes peut être observée directement. L'adhérence des patients à leurs systèmes ne signifie nullement qu'ils soient capables de les maintenir ; une fois de plus ce qui a été refoulé fait son entrée dans la méthode de refoulement. De plus en plus le patient sent que ce système dans lequel il voudrait maintenir tout le monde a été violé ; il peut alors réagir en essayant d'augmenter la rigidité du système, mais il n'est jamais sûr que les exigences de son système soient entièrement remplies. L'isolation de choses représentant des tendances inconscientes, liées à l'origine l'une à l'autre, est exigée. C'est pourquoi ces patients voient une séparation du type « ou – ou bien » en fait de la relation « similaire à ».

Un obsédé joueur d'échec s'occupait pendant des heures à essayer de résoudre ce problème : devait-il utiliser plus de stratégie ou plus de tactique ? Il pensait à cela uniquement de façon abstraite, jamais dans une situation concrète ou au cours du jeu. Son idée « ou – ou bien » lui faisait en fait perdre chaque partie. Le doute réel prenait origine dans le doute inconscient : devait-il vaincre son adversaire ou se faire vaincre par lui, devait-il adopter une attitude virile ou féminine ?

La « compulsion névrotique à mettre des étiquettes » rapportée par Graber est en rapport avec ce mode de conduite. Les obsédés ont tendance à faire de fausses généralisations, à classer en toute hâte les idées en catégories s'excluant réciproquement, et, par la suite, à sombrer dans le doute quant à la nature et l'évaluation de ces catégories. « Je connais déjà à quelle catégorie ce phénomène appartient » signifie en général : « Ce n'est pas une tentation ou une punition, je n'ai pas de raisons de le craindre. » Plus un événement est surprenant, plus il est dangereux. La systématisation compulsive tend à exclure toute possibilité de surprise et de falsifier tout événement en « choses déjà connues ».

Ordonner l'inconnu dans des catégories connues est l'œuvre de la science. La systématisation compulsive, entreprise non dans le but de maîtriser la réalité, mais pour dénier et falsifier certains de ses aspects, est une caricature de la science.

L'obsédé est ambivalent ; il l'est même envers ses propres systèmes et règles. Quand il prend partie contre ses pulsions dangereuses, il a besoin de règles de systèmes pour le protéger. Quand il se tourne contre son Surmoi, il se tourne également contre ces systèmes et règles institués par le Surmoi. Il peut se rebeller ouvertement contre eux, ou il peut les ridiculiser en en montrant leur absurdité.

D'AUTRES MÉCANISMES DE DÉFENSE :
ISOLATION, ANNULATION
ET FORMATION RÉACTIONNELLE

L'altération typique du caractère des obsédés n'est pas toujours due directement à la régression. Elle est aussi causée par l'emploi d'autres mécanismes de défense : la formation réactionnelle, l'isolation et l'annulation. L'utilisation de ces mécanismes dépend également, il est vrai, de la régression pathognomonique, la formation réactionnelle, l'isolation et l'annulation étant beaucoup plus destinées à combattre des désirs prégénitaux, alors que le refoulement est un mécanisme plus en rapport avec la génitalité. Les formations réactionnelles sont pro fondément enracinées dans chaque personnalité obsédée. En combat tant une hostilité inconsciente, l'obsédé tend à être une personne agréable dans tous ses rapports et de façon générale. Ceci peut lui apporter une grande satisfaction narcissique rendant malheureusement difficile le traitement psychanalytique.

Les formations réactionnelles sont cependant rarement efficaces : l'esprit de l'obsédé reste occupé par la lutte perpétuelle entre la formation réactionnelle et l'impulsion originelle toujours effective.

Quelques exemples supplémentaires d'isolation typiques peuvent être donnés. Un patient présentant des doutes obsessifs, trouvait très difficile de se soumettre à la cure analytique, protestant violemment contre la règle fondamentale de l'association libre. Il apparut qu'il agissait ainsi afin de garder secrète l'existence d'une petite amie — non parce qu'il se refusait à en parler, mais parce qu'au cours de son traitement il avait parlé de masturbation, et il souhaitait que l'image de cette amie fût éloignée de tout ce qui pouvait avoir rapport avec la masturbation. Il sentait qu'il pourrait parler d'elle si, pendant la même séance, il était sûr de ne pas penser à la masturbation. Plus tard, il apparut combien cette isolation avait peu réussi ; un symptôme compulsif ressenti douloureusement par le patient et dissimulé à grand peine était l'obligation de penser « petite putain » chaque fois qu'il voyait cette jeune fille, ou qu'il entendait son nom. Ce symptôme provenait d'exigences instinctuelles incestueuses contre lesquelles le Moi se défendait. Ceci est un exemple de tentative infructueuse d'isoler la tendresse de la sensualité.

Il était intéressant d'observer comment le patient, qui avait des tendances aux réactions paranoïdes, combinait dans ses défenses contre l'instinct les mécanismes d'isolation et de projection. Une fois, pour démontrer l'absurdité de la psychanalyse, il déclara que l'association libre était un non-sens, les gens n'ayant que les pensées qu'ils désiraient, puisque la pensée « petite putain » n'était pas voulue par lui. Quelques jours plus tard il accusa l'analyste de sensualité et de vulgarité, de traiter son amie de petite putain, et de faire mauvais usage de sa confession en lui trouvant un comportement vil.

Quelquefois, les obsédés effectuent une remarquable isolation au moyen du mariage. Ils décident que leur vie conjugale n'a aucun rapport avec leur sexualité infantile. « Maintenant je suis marié, je n'ai plus à me tourmenter au sujet de la sexualité. » Ces mariages ne peuvent être heureux. Les patients érigent de sévères obsessions et compulsions dès que les désirs sexuels infantiles apparaissent dans le mariage, en dépit de l'isolation.

Il a été dit que le cas spécial le plus important d'isolation consiste dans l'isolation du contenu idéique de son investissement libidinal. Les cas typiques d'obsession apparaissent froids, abstraits et sans émotion ; en fait, leurs émotions peuvent trouver expression par quelque voie incongrue.

L'exemple d'une telle isolation est donné par un patient qui notait qu'il ne devait pas « oublier qu'il était en colère ».

Les difficultés présentées par les obsédés dans la pratique de la libre association pendant l'analyse, sont dues à leur penchant à l'isolation. Ils ne peuvent pas associer librement, étant toujours en garde pour ne pas relier entre elles des choses qui auparavant étaient en contact. Ils ne peuvent pas se laisser surprendre, soit par des sentiments, soit par des perceptions qui n'ont pas encore été classés en catégories. Cette façon de penser par classement en catégorie est une caricature de la pensée logique. Cette dernière est aussi basée sur l'isolation, mais l'isolation logique est au service de l'objectivité, l'isolation compulsive au service de la défense.

L'isolation, comme il l'a déjà été dit, est en rapport avec l'ancien tabou du toucher. De nombreux symptômes obsessionnels ont pour but de déterminer les objets qui peuvent ou ne peuvent pas être touchés. Les objets représentant les organes génitaux ou la saleté. Les choses « propres » ne peuvent communiquer avec les « sales ». Une application du tabou du toucher à la peur magique du changement d'une situation pour une autre est présente dans les fréquents rituels du seuil.

Fréquemment, l'isolation sépare les constituants d'un ensemble les uns des autres, alors que des personnes non obsédées n'auraient remarqué que l'ensemble et non les constituants. C'est pourquoi les obsédés ont fréquemment l'expérience de sommes et non d'unités, et bien des traits du caractère compulsif s'expriment exactement dans les termes « inhibition de l'expérience de la *Gestalt* ».

RÉPÉTITION ET « CHIFFRES FAVORIS »

Il existe encore la « répétition » en tant que forme d'annulation. L'idée contenue dans l'annulation est la nécessité de répétition d'une action dans un but différent. Ce qui a été fait avec une intention instinctuelle peut être refait sur l'instigation du Surmoi. Les instincts refoulés cependant, tentent de pénétrer également dans la répétition ; aussi, la répétition doit être répétée. En général, le nombre de répétitions augmente rapidement. Les « chiffres favoris », dont le choix peut avoir une raison inconsciente séparée, sont déterminés et règlent le nombre de répétitions nécessaires ; en dernier lieu, les répétitions peuvent être remplacées par le fait de compter.

Les chiffres favoris sont, en règle générale, toujours les mêmes. Ce ne sont que les mêmes chiffres qui peuvent donner la garantie que ni les instincts, ni le Surmoi l'emporteront. La plupart des compulsions « symétriques » ont la même signification.

On aurait tort cependant de croire que le compter « compulsif » est toujours ainsi motivé. Compter peut avoir des sens variés. Il représente fréquemment le compter des secondes, c'est-à-dire du temps. Le besoin de mesurer le temps peut avoir plusieurs déterminants. Quelquefois c'est un moyen de rendre une isolation certaine. Il peut être interdit de commencer une activité après une autre, et compter assure ainsi l'intervalle nécessaire. Les connexions de base entre le temps et l'érotisme anal ont déjà été mentionnées. La mesure du temps, à l'origine espace de temps entre deux défécations, peut être utilisée comme moyen de défense contre la tentation de la masturbation anale et peut éventuellement devenir un substitut de masturbation anale.

Le compter compulsif peut être également une défense contre des souhaits de meurtre ; en comptant on s'assure que rien ne manque. Mais la défense peut être envahie par l'impulsion, et le compter devenir, inconsciemment, un équivalent de tuer ; il peut être alors refoulé à son tour. Ceci est facilité par le fait que compter a, en lui-même, la signification de prise de possession, de maîtrise ; compter peut signifier « compter ses propres possessions ».

Un exemple simple du mécanisme de l'annulation est la compulsion névrotique fréquente du lavage. Le lavage est rendu nécessaire pour annuler une action sale antérieure (réelle ou imaginaire).

Cette action dégoûtante est, en règle générale, la masturbation ou, plus tard, une idée de possibilité éloignée de masturbation. La régression anale est responsable de la conception sale de la sexualité. La masturbation anale dans l'enfance était, de fait, trahie par des mains sales et malodorantes ; cette possibilité de trahison peut être évitée par le lavage. Occasionnellement, des obsédés peuvent faire disparaître tous leurs scrupules en se baignant et en changeant de vêtements, les mauvais sentiments étant conçus comme de la saleté pouvant être supprimée par le nettoyage. Le bain rituel, comme moyen de nettoyage des péchés, est aussi un procédé d'annulation. Il est probable que c'est pour cette raison que le cérémonial névrotique, durant la période de latence, est si souvent en rapport avec le lavage. Les enfants obstinés qui refusent la toilette, refusent, en réalité, l'abandon des impulsions instinctuelles plaisantes. Il est vrai cependant que les rituels en rapport avec le déshabillage et le coucher sont aussi prévalents pour une autre raison : cette occasion présente une tentative de se masturber.

UN EXEMPLE DE DÉPLACEMENT : LA « RUMINATION MENTALE »

Bien des symptômes typiques d'obsession luttent pour défaire des actions agressives, en général imaginaires. Cette intention est quelquefois manifeste, comme dans la fermeture compulsive des robinets à gaz, ou dans l'éloignement des pierres de la route ; quelquefois, l'intention de pénitence se révèle pendant l'analyse dans de nombreux symptômes. Il n'y a pas de frontière nette entre les symptômes de pénitence et les sublimations créatrices réalisées comme actions antagonistes de désirs sadiques infantiles.

L'usage de la régression, de formations réactionnelles, d'isolation et d'annulation, rend superflu l'emploi du mécanisme de défense du refoulement. Ceci répond à la question : comment se fait-il que, dans l'obsession, des impulsions offensives parviennent à la conscience ? L'impulsion consciente de tuer, par exemple, est, par l'isolation, tellement éloignée de l'impulsion motrice, qu'elle n'a aucune chance de se matérialiser et peut devenir consciente en toute tranquilité. C'est pourquoi, lorsque l'idée devient consciente, elle est dénudée de toute émotion. Le résultat de la rupture de la connexion originale est que la connaissance spontanée des événements pathogènes de l'enfance ne peut pas être utilisée directement par l'analyse. Aussi longtemps que les émotions correspondantes manquent, l'analyste ne sait pas plus que le patient quels souvenirs de l'enfance sont importants et en quoi réside leur importance ; même s'il en est averti, il ne peut en informer le patient avant que ce dernier n'ait surmonté sa résistance contre la vision de cette connexion.

Le manque de refoulement dans l'obsession est cependant tout rela tif. Les compulsions et les obsessions elles-mêmes peuvent entrepren dre un processus de refoulement secondaire. Quelquefois les patients ne peuvent pas expliquer en quoi consistent leurs compulsions, ces der nières ont des qualités vagues, incolores, embrumées, et il faut un cer tain temps de travail analytique pour dégager la compulsion du refou lement et la rendre compréhensible.

Quelquefois, les symptômes compulsifs sont secondairement refoulés, le patient ne les sentant plus appropriés à son système, c'est à-dire ne représentant plus uniquement des formes défensives, mais également des impulsions qui s'y sont introduites. En essayant d'approprier ses compulsions à son système, il falsifie et obscurcit leur contenu original. Ses propres compulsions, comme le monde entier, doivent s'adapter à son système qui est sa seule garantie de sécurité.

Le déplacement dans l'obsession est souvent un déplacement au petit détail. Bien des obsédés s'inquiètent de petites choses, apparem ment insignifiantes ; à l'analyse ces petites choses apparaissent comme étant de grosses choses. La plus connue est la « compulsion à penser » *(Gruebelzwang)* dans laquelle le patient est obligé de passer des heures à ruminer des pensées abstraites. Ce symptôme a son origine dans une tentative d'éviter des émotions répréhensibles par la fuite du monde des émotions dans celui des concepts intellectuels et des mots. Cette fuite échoue, les problèmes intellectuels dans lesquels le patient cherche une échappatoire à ses émotions acquérant, par un retour du refoulé, une valeur émotionnelle élevée.

LE DOUBLE FRONT
DU MOI DANS L'OBSESSION

Les mécanismes de défense caractéristiques de l'obsession ne tirent pas uniquement leur spécificité de leur nature mais également de leur utilisation. La prépondérance relative de la dépendance du Moi au Sur moi dans cette névrose rend compréhensible, non seulement l'obliga tion d'obéir au Surmoi en éloignant les exigences instinctuelles, mais également sa tentative de rébellion contre lui. Le Moi peut employer, contre le Surmoi, les mesures déjà employées contre les impulsions du Ça. Cette activité nécessite également une dépense continuelle d'énergie. Il a été mentionné que l'idée compulsive « Si vous faites ceci ou cela votre père mourra » est la prise de conscience d'un avertissement du Surmoi : « Si vous faites ceci ou cela, vous pouvez être tenté de tuer votre père. » Le Moi peut réagir à une telle menace par une contre menace. Lorsque « l'Homme aux Rats » eut sa première expérience sexuelle, il eut l'idée obsessive : « C'est splendide ! On tuerait son père pour ça. » En fait, le Moi se conduit avec le Surmoi comme il le fit naguère avec ses éducateurs : en obéissant ou en se rebellant, ou les deux à la fois. L'ambivalence du Moi envers le Surmoi est à l'origine des fréquents symptômes religieux de l'obsession.

Le conflit ambivalent avec le Surmoi peut être mieux observé quand il produit un comportement en deux temps : le patient se comporte alternativement comme s'il était un méchant garçon et tout de suite après comme un individu strictement discipliné.

Pour des raisons obsessives, un patient ne pouvait se brosser les dents. Après une certaine durée de ce comportement, il se frappait et se grondait. Un autre patient transportait toujours sur lui un carnet, sur lequel il mettait des marques pour indiquer les louanges ou le blâme mérités par sa conduite.

L'absurdité dans les rêves a la signification d'une intention moqueuse et malicieuse du rêveur. De façon similaire, l'absurdité de bien des pseudo-problèmes contenus dans la pensée obsessive indique une attitude moqueuse et malicieuse du patient envers son Surmoi, représenté souvent, durant l'analyse, par l'analyste. Ainsi, les absurdités du patient prolongent l'attitude de l'enfant ridiculisant son père.

Un patient, lors de la première consultation, demanda à l'analyste si le traitement le libérerait d'une pratique masturbatoire excessive. L'analyste répondit que la réussite de la cure arrangerait également cette question. Bien des mois plus tard, le patient rapporta cette pensée : « Je me demande comment l'analyse fera stopper ma masturbation, si je ne m'arrête pas moi-même » ; et il résolut de ne pas s'arrêter pour voir comment l'analyste ferait pour le faire arrêter sans effort de sa part.

UNE PSEUDO-MORALITÉ DU SURMOI CHEZ LES OBSÉDÉS

La régression au sadisme anal n'a pas seulement modifié le Moi, dont le sadisme et l'ambivalence sont alors dirigés contre le Surmoi aussi bien que contre des objets extérieurs ; elle a aussi modifié le Surmoi lui-même, devenu plus sadique et présentant des traits automatiques et archaïques, tels que l'accord, avec le principe du talion et l'obéissance à des règles magiques. Le sadisme du Surmoi, résultant de la régression, est augmenté par le refoulement des sentiments agressifs du Moi contre le monde extérieur. On peut supposer qu'une personne stricte avec elle-même et paisible, sait refouler son agressivité en raison de son attitude stricte ; en fait, le blocage de l'agression est primaire et la sévérité du Surmoi secondaire. Le sadisme non dirigé sur les objets est employé par le Surmoi dans son agression contre le Moi.

La moralité exigée par le Surmoi archaïque des obsédés est une pseudo-moralité, caractérisée par Alexander sous le nom de corruptibilité du Surmoi. Si le Moi fait une concession à une pulsion instinctuelle, il peut se soumettre par des demandes d'expiation ; quand il a expié, il peut utiliser cet acte expiatoire comme une licence lui permettant une nouvelle transgression ; le résultat est une alternance d'actes instinctuels et punitifs. Le besoin d'une stabilité relative entre les deux attitudes peut s'exprimer dans les compulsions symétriques magiques.

Les compulsions symétriques ont des formes multiples. Elles consistent toutes à éviter des troubles de l'« équilibre ». Tout ce qui peut arriver à la droite doit arriver à la gauche ; tout ce qui est fait en haut doit être fait en bas ; aucun compte ne doit s'arrêter à un chiffre impair, et ainsi de suite... Tout cela peut avoir une signification spéciale pour chaque individu, mais a toujours le but général du maintien de l'équilibre mental contre les impulsions refoulées ; tout mouvement instinctuel est annulé par le contre-mouvement symétrique.

Schilder a réuni des formes de compulsion de cette espèce, ayant leur origine dans des conflits mettant en jeu l'érotisme de l'équilibre et d'autres formes se manifestant en actions abstraites.

Pour comprendre la corruptibilité du Surmoi, on doit considérer la relation économique discutée par Rado sous le nom d'idéalisation. En se pliant aux exigences du Surmoi, le Moi gagne un plaisir narcissique pouvant entraîner avec lui une telle jouissance qu'il suspend temporairement ou affaiblit ses fonctions de juge objectif de la réalité et des impulsions.

256

L'idée que toute souffrance donne droit aux privilèges d'un plaisir compensateur, et qu'un Surmoi menaçant peut être apaisé et forcé à renouveler son pouvoir de protection aux moyens de souffrances volontaires est très archaïque. La même idée s'exprime dans les attitudes de sacrifice et de prières. Dans les deux pratiques, la sympathie de Dieu est achetée, et des punitions plus importantes évitées au moyen d'une acceptation active et volontaire d'un déplaisir, véritable « punition prophylactique ». Les attitudes extrêmes de ce genre sont ces actions pouvant être appelées « autocastration prophylactique ». Acheter la sympathie de Dieu peut tourner au chantage. Chez les névrosés dépressifs et impulsifs, on trouve bien des variations d'un tel chantage. Le cercle, acte-punition-nouvel acte, peut être ultimement tracé : faim-satiété-nouvelle faim.

La vacillation entre l'acte et la punition est fréquemment exprimée par le doute obsessif signifiant, en fait : « Suivrai-je les exigences du Ça, ou celles du Surmoi ? » Certaines névroses obsessionnelles sévères peuvent se terminer par des états dans lesquels le Moi, devenu un ballon ballotté par les impulsions contradictoires du Ça et du Surmoi, est éliminé complètement en tant qu'agent effectif.

En se défendant contre les exigences d'un Surmoi sadique, le Moi peut utiliser une rébellion contre sadique aussi bien qu'une soumission (pour regagner les bonnes grâces), ou les deux attitudes simultanément ou successivement. Le Moi semble vouloir prendre quelquefois sur lui-même des punitions, des actes d'expiation et même des tortures jusqu'à un degré étonnant. Ce « masochisme moral » apparaît comme complément du sadisme du Surmoi, et cette soumission peut se réaliser dans l'espoir d'en user comme une licence pour une liberté instinctuelle à venir.

UN SENTIMENT DE CULPABILITÉ QUI SE TRANSFORME EN ANGOISSE SOCIALE CHRONIQUE

Le « besoin de punition » du Moi est, en général, subordonné à un « besoin de pardon », la punition étant jugée nécessaire pour soulager la pression exercée par le Surmoi. Un tel besoin de punition de la part d'un Moi compulsif peut cependant se condenser avec des souhaits sexuels masochiques. Alors, comme l'a dit Freud, la moralité qui est sortie du complexe d'Œdipe a régressé et est redevenue le complexe d'Œdipe.

Un besoin de punition n'est, en général, qu'un symptôme d'un besoin plus général d'absolution ; ceci se voit clairement dans la tentative d'atteindre l'absolution en évitant la punition par l'utilisation d'objets extérieurs en tant que témoins dans le combat contre le Surmoi.

Un patient inventa une méthode de dispenses au moyen de scrupules et de craintes hypocondriaques. Après s'être masturbé, il allait voir un médecin, s'assurant ainsi qu'il était en bonne condition physique. L'analyse montra que le réconfort prodigué par le médecin représentait la renonciation du castrateur au droit de castrer ; la déclaration de santé représentait l'absolution désirée. Cette absolution mettait fin à la mauvaise conscience du patient et rendait tout autre moyen d'annulation inutile ; en particulier, le patient n'avait plus besoin de se punir.

La confiance dans les assurances d'autrui pour le maintien de l'estime de soi, détermine souvent le comportement social d'un obsédé. Le patient se sent soulagé en constatant que les autres personnes ne considèrent pas sa culpabilité comme bien grave, comme lui-même le fait ; cela revient à dire à son Surmoi : « Ce n'est pas si mauvais, après tout, puisqu'Untel et Untel ne me condamnent pas. » La peur du Surmoi est transformée par ce procédé en peur sociale. Cette reprojection du Surmoi est surtout exécutée par les personnes présentant des traits paranoïaques, néanmoins l'analyse de simples obsédés montre fréquemment également que leur angoisse sociale est une crainte d'échec de leur tentative d'alléger leur sévère sentiment de culpabilité. Le sentiment qu'ils sont néanmoins coupables peut se transformer en une crainte sociale chronique. Une personne qui est inconsciemment très agressive contre le monde extérieur a naturellement toute raison de craindre que ce monde extérieur ne l'aime pas.

Malgré que les conflits des obsédés soient enfouis plus profondément que ceux des hystériques, les obsédés essaient d'utiliser les objets pour résoudre ou soulager leurs conflits intérieurs. Les hystériques craignant la castration ou la perte d'amour vont essayer d'influencer leur entourage directement, afin de les dissuader d'agir dans ce sens ; l'obsédé craignant plus la perte de protection de son propre Surmoi, ayant peur d'être obligé de se mépriser lui-même, a besoin des autres personnes comme moyens indirects de soulagement. Peu importe ce qui est fait ou dit par les objets, tout est interprété soit en tant que pardon, soit en tant qu'accusations. Des tentatives variées, réelles ou magiques, sont exécutées dans le but d'influencer le témoignage des témoins.

Quelquefois le patient essaie simplement d'obtenir des objets des signes de sympathie, d'autres fois il attend les autres personnes qu'elles fassent ce que lui n'ose pas faire ou au contraire de ne pas faire ce que lui n'ose faire, la tentation pouvant être trop forte.

De l'avis de Freud la base inconsciente du concept de justice est : « Ce que je n'ai pas droit de faire, personne d'autre n'a droit de le faire. » Le besoin de justice est enraciné dans la tendance d'étendre une prohibition à tout le monde. Il existe une parenté entre la « justice » et la « symétrie ». Certains désirs de justice signifient simplement : « Il est bon que ce qui arrive à la droite arrive également à la gauche », et quelquefois le désir de symétrie signifie : « La symétrie est réussie si ce qui arrive à un enfant arrive également à ses frères et sœurs. »
Freud a établi que les personnes ayant pris le même objet comme Surmoi s'identifient les unes aux autres. En suivant Redl, nous pouvons ajouter : et les personnes utilisant le même témoin, unies dans une identification mutuelle, sont également ainsi.

UN CERCLE VICIEUX DE SOUFFRANCES TOUJOURS ÉLARGI, MAIS PEU DE CAS DE SUICIDES

Dans les cas extrêmes, le comportement du patient peut être, en dernière analyse, entièrement inauthentique ; quoi qu'il fasse, il le fait dans le but d'impressionner un auditoire ou un jury imaginaire.

Une dépendance ambivalente à un Surmoi sadique et la nécessité de se débarasser à tout prix de la tension insupportable de sentiments de culpabilité sont les causes les plus fréquentes de suicide. Aussi se pose-t-on la question : S'il est vrai que ces facteurs jouent un rôle dominant dans l'obsession, comment se fait-il que le suicide est si rare chez les obsédés ? Freud y donna la réponse suivante : Dans l'obsession, en contraste avec la dépression, la libido de l'individu n'est pas complètement investie dans le conflit du Moi avec le Surmoi ; une grande partie des relations objectales est préservée, et cela le préserve de la ruine ; il est même possible que la déformation régressive de ces relations objectales restantes, c'est-à-dire leur nature sadique, contribue à cet effet favorable : étant donné que l'obsédé réussit à exprimer réellement une certaine agression contre les objets, il n'a pas besoin d'en tourner beaucoup contre lui-même.

Néanmoins, les sentiments de culpabilité causent bien des souffrances aux obsédés. Les patients rentrent dans un cercle toujours grandissant : remords, pénitence, nouvelles transgressions, nouveaux remords. L'obsédé tend toujours à opérer de plus en plus de déplacements, d'agrandir sa symptomatologie (en analogie avec la façade phobique) et d'augmenter la signification instinctuelle des symptômes au prix de leur signification punitive.

Le besoin prévalent d'utiliser les objets pour trouver un soulagement du conflit, masquant tout sentiment direct envers les objets, n'est pas le seul facteur déformant la relation objectale des obsédés. Un second facteur est dû au simple fait que la régression sadique-anale prohibe le développement d'une relation objectale adulte, produisant une attitude incertaine, ambivalente envers les objets, conflits de bisexualité et de rétention des buts d'incorporation. Une troisième circonstance déformant la relation d'authenticité et de chaleur. Les investissements libidinaux attachés aux symptômes et aux substituts auto-érotiques sont absents quand le patient a affaire à des objets.

LA PENSÉE DANS LA NÉVROSE OBSESSIONNELLE

La régression au sadisme anal et le continuel conflit avec le Surmoi influencent les processus de la pensée des obsédés de façon caractéristique : la pensée devient imprégnée ou remplacée par les précurseurs archaïques de ce processus. Les fantasmes des obsédés, en contraste avec les rêveries visuelles des hystériques, sont verbaux et ressuscitent les attitudes archaïques qui accompagnent l'usage des premiers mots.

La fonction de jugement par anticipation du Moi est facilitée énormément par l'acquisition des mots. La création de cette réplique du monde réel rend possible à l'avance le calcul et l'action dans un monde modèle précédant l'exécution de l'action réelle. Les mots et les concepts verbaux sont les ombres des choses, construits dans le but d'ordonner, par des actions d'épreuves, le chaos des choses réelles. Le macrocosme des choses réelles de l'extérieur est réfléchi dans le microcosme des choses représentées à l'intérieur. Les choses représentées ont les caractéristiques de choses extérieures, mais manquent du caractère « sérieux » possédé par ces dernières et elles sont des « possessions », c'est-à-dire maîtrisées par le Moi ; elles tentent de doter les choses de la « qualité du Moi » dans le but d'en obtenir la maîtrise. Celui qui connaît le mot pour une chose maîtrise cette chose. Ce fait est le noyau de la « magie des noms » qui joue un rôle si important dans la magie en général. Il est représenté dans le vieux conte de fée de *Rumpelstilzchen*, dans lequel le démon perd son pouvoir une fois que son nom est connu.

Un patient connaissait plusieurs centaines de noms d'oiseaux ; lors qu'il était enfant, il craignait la cigogne, démon de la naissance et de la mort. Un enfant connaissait toutes les stations d'une ligne de chemin de fer ; l'analyse montra l'existence antérieure d'une phobie pour les trains, survenue plusieurs années auparavant. Un autre enfant avait une mémoire extraordinaire des noms de personnes, façon de maîtriser son angoisse sociale.

L'obsédé, craignant ses émotions, craint les choses éveillant ces émotions. Il fuit du macrocosme des choses au microcosme des mots. Craignant le monde, il essaie de reproduire le procédé par lequel, enfant, il avait appris à maîtriser les aspects effrayants du monde. Cependant, sous la pression des impulsions refoulées, la tentative échoue maintenant. Quand il essaie de fuir les choses pleines d'émo tion vers les mots sobres, le matériel refoulé réapparaît et les mots ne restent pas plus longtemps sobres mais deviennent surinvestis émotion nellement ; ils acquièrent ainsi la valeur émotionnelle que les choses ont pour les autres personnes.

Freud a souvent observé le pouvoir magique que les obsédés donnent aux noms ou aux mots, a l'instar de cette fée prononçant une formule magique. (Illustration hongroise de 1900).

She began to chant forth unearthly words.

Les premiers mots acquis dans l'enfance sont magiques et omnipotents, le microcosme, n'étant pas encore différencié suffisamment du macrocosme, en possède toujours toute la valeur émotionnelle.

La bénédiction et le juron sont des expressions de la qualité macrocosmique toujours effective des mots. Dans un développement plus avancé des facultés de penser et de parler, le monde gai, afin d'en faciliter la gestion, devient monotone. Seuls quelques termes et pensées irrationnelles restent gais tels que les rêveries et les mots obscènes. Dans l'obsession, le parler et le penser sont devenus les substituts des émotions en rapport avec la réalité ; ils reprennent ainsi leurs qualités originelles, se sexualisent et perdent toute valeur pratique. Les mots, une fois de plus, deviennent de puissantes bénédictions ou malédictions. Ils peuvent de nouveau tuer et ressusciter. Par une simple déclaration verbale, l'obsédé croit inconsciemment qu'il peut forcer la réalité dans la poursuite du but désiré. Étant donné que les mots et les pensées sont jugés capables de tels effets, ils sont dangereux. Un mot dit au hasard pourrait rendre efficaces les pulsions sadiques refoulées avec tant de soin. Les mots et les pensées doivent donc être maniés avec précaution, et si nécessaire refoulés et annulés. Leur mauvais usage appelle le même châtiment qu'une mauvaise action. Ils deviennent les substituts régressifs de l'action.

L'omnipotence des mots étant spécialement conservée dans les mots obscènes, ceux-ci ont gardé leur pouvoir magique, obligeant le parleur et l'auditeur à expérimenter les choses mentionnées comme si elles avaient été réellement perçues ; pour ces raisons, les mots sont souvent à la base des symptômes compulsifs. Une réticence embarrassée prévenant l'émission de mots obscènes (souvent troublée par une impulsion sacrilège à les prononcer dans les circonstances les plus embarrassantes) est une défense contre une impulsion spécifique à les dire. Cette impulsion pouvant apparaître comme une perversion est le plus souvent ressentie comme une compulsion. Elle est exécutée dans le but d'obliger l'auditeur à avoir, de façon magique, une expérience sexuelle. Ceci n'est pas l'expression d'un simple souhait sexuel, mais plutôt une tentative de combattre l'angoisse en rapport avec des idées sexuelles. Le facteur sadique dans ce besoin est certain, comme si les mots obscènes entraînaient un plaisir anal et le parler sexuel un gain libidinal oral.

La « coprolalie[2] » est une espèce de libido régressive jouant un grand rôle dans la symptomatologie de la névrose obsessionnelle.

---

2. Tendance compulsive à des expressions scatologiques. (N.D.É)

UN ASSERVISSEMENT A LA PENSÉE DONT L'OBSÉDÉ SE DÉFEND GRÂCE A DES MOTS « MAGIQUES »

La peur de l'omnipotence des pensées rend l'obsédé dépendant de sa façon de penser. Au lieu de maîtriser le monde au moyen de la pensée, il est asservi par sa pensée (compulsive) qui remplace sa sexualité incontrôlée.

La tendance à employer des mots « omnipotents » en tant que défense contre le danger explique le fait que les mesures défensives secondaires contre les symptômes compulsifs ont souvent la forme compulsive de la formule magique. La parenté entre la formule compulsive et la formule magique des primitifs a souvent été discutée.

Le tracas d'un patient pendant son traitement venait de l'idée obsédante de voir son analyste mourir pendant une séance ; il était donc obligé de se retourner fréquemment et de se rassurer en prononçant la formule sacramentelle : « Le docteur est assis, en vie derrière moi, à distance. » « A distance » le rassurait, ne violant pas le tabou du toucher.

Freud a montré que la croyance à l'omnipotence des pensées correspondait à un fait réel. Elles n'ont évidemment pas l'efficacité externe que leur prête l'obsédé, mais elles ont chez lui une puissance plus grande que chez les autres personnes. Les pensées compulsives ont vraiment un caractère obligatoire et cette qualité est leur pouvoir. Ce pouvoir est, pour une part un dérivatif de la force biologique des instincts et, pour une autre part, un dérivatif du pouvoir des exigences paternelles. Les obsédés, bien que dépendant de leurs compulsions, sont en fait non conscients de cette connexion. Ils sous-estiment réellement le pouvoir intérieur des pensées, aussi bien qu'ils en surestiment la force extérieure.

La retraite du sentiment de la pensée réussit, en règle générale, sous l'aspect suivant : la pensée compulsive est abstraite, isolée du monde réel des choses concrètes.

La pensée obsessionnelle n'est pas seulement abstraite, elle est générale, dirigée vers des systématisations et des mises en catégorie, elle est théorique au lieu d'être réelle. Les patients s'intéressent aux cartes géographiques, aux illustrations, plutôt qu'aux pays et aux choses.

Mais, sous un autre aspect, cette retraite échoue. Les clivages et les contradictions imprégnant la vie émotionnelle des obsédés sont déplacés sur des problèmes intellectuels sexualisés : il en résulte une rumination et un doute obsessif. Le doute est le conflit instinctuel déplacé au domaine intellectuel. Un patient, regardant la porte, était obligé de gaspiller tout son temps à ruminer autour de ce problème : « Quelle est la chose principale ? L'espace vide rempli par la porte, ou la porte remplissant l'espace vide ? » Ce problème « philosophique » couvrait un autre doute : « Quelle est la chose principale dans la sexualité : l'homme ou la femme ? » et ceci voulait dire : « Quelle est la chose principale en moi, l'homme ou la femme ? » Les contenus inconscients du doute obsessif peuvent être multiples, bien que les conflits multiples ne soient que des éditions de quelques questions générales, telles que : masculinité-féminité (bisexualité) ou haine-amour (ambivalence) et surtout Ça-Surmoi (exigences instinctuelles-exigences de la conscience).

La dernière formule est la plus décisive. La bisexualité et l'ambivalence ne sont pas des conflits en eux-mêmes ; ils ne le deviennent que lorsqu'ils sont témoins d'un conflit structural entre une exigence instinctuelle et une force opposante.

Certains doutes obsessifs sont de nature quelque peu plus simple. Par exemple ceux portant sur la validité du propre jugement ou des propres perceptions représentent le désir que ce qui est douteux ne soit pas vrai. Les faits douteux peuvent représenter la scène primitive ou la différence anatomique des sexes. La fréquence relative du doute obsessif en rapport avec des nouvelles de mort est avant tout une crainte de l'omnipotence de ses propres pensées : le patient essaie de nier le fait, pour réprimer l'idée que ce pourrait bien être de sa faute ; si le doute devient si torturant que le patient dit : « Merci, Seigneur » de soulagement à la confirmation de la nouvelle, la connexion psychologique est la suivante : si le doute était justifié et que l'idée de mort avait son origine dans une interprétation erronée de la nouvelle, la réalité des mauvaises pensées deviendrait certaine ; c'est pourquoi la confirmation de la nouvelle est accueillie avec soulagement par le patient ; elle annule le soupçon pesant sur lui d'avoir pensé de façon malicieuse à la mort de quelqu'un.

Une vue intérieure sur la nature du doute et de la rumination obsédante, fournit une simple règle technique : ne jamais discuter avec les obsédés de leur problème obsessif. En le faisant, l'analyste confirmerait au patient le mécanisme d'isolation. Aussi longtemps que les pensées du patient sont isolées de ses émotions, seule cette isolation peut être objet d'analyse et non le contenu qui a été isolé.

TOUTE-PUISSANCE DES IDÉES
CHEZ L'OBSÉDÉ

L'idée suivante est en rapport avec le déplacement de la pensée vers l'action. La pensée est préparatrice de l'action. Les personnes craignant l'action en augmentent la préparation. Les obsédés, de la même façon, pensent plus qu'ils n'agissent, préparant constamment le futur et ne vivant jamais le présent. Bien des symptômes compulsifs ont cette allure de préparation d'un futur qui ne sera jamais vécu. Le patient se comporte comme Tyll Eulenspiegel[3], se réjouissant, en montant, de la future descente, et s'attristant pendant la descente en pensant à la montée future. La principale cause de cette préparation exagérée est certainement la peur de la chose réelle. La tendance à la préparation exprime simultanément un plaisir anal à venir et une défécation reportée à plus tard par l'enfant, cette dernière ayant déjà une double signification : la lutte pour éviter une brusque perte de contrôle et l'obtention d'un plaisir érogène. Les parties sans importance vers lesquelles l'obsédé déplace l'importance d'un tout important représentent la préparation à l'action au lieu de l'action réelle.

L'obsédé, actif quant à la préparation, agit en accord avec la règle : le *statu quo* est préférable à toute chose nouvelle apportée par un changement. Le *statu quo* est un moindre mal.

La peur d'un changement quelconque des conditions présentes connues vers un état nouveau dangereux, incite le patient à se cramponner à ses symptômes. La névrose, toute inconfortable qu'elle puisse être, est bien connue et constitue un moindre mal, comparée aux possibilités que pourrait apporter un changement. Une telle attitude forme une résistance latente limitant les progrès du traitement. Pour le patient, la névrose est une vieille connaissance. Quelques formes de réactions thérapeutiques négatives à la cure analytique expriment une telle peur du changement.

La peur du changement peut être remplacée ou accompagnée de son opposé, la tendance au changement continuel. Le monde n'obéit pas, en fait, aux systèmes compulsifs des obsédés ; c'est pourquoi certains obsédés tendent continuellement à changer n'importe quoi, n'importe où, essayant d'amener le monde en accord avec leur système.

La croyance à l'omnipotence des pensées, les sentiments de culpabilité attachés à cette croyance, l'ordre utilisé dans le but de lutter contre ces sentiments de culpabilité, vont illustrer le cas suivant : Dans les

---

3. Personnage de la littérature néerlandaise, célèbre pour ses facéties. (N.D.É)

jours précédant la déclaration de guerre, un patient accrochait son manteau dans un placard. Soudain retentit le commandement compulsif : « Pends ce manteau avec plus de soin. » Il répondit, résistant : « Je suis trop fatigué. » Alors vint la réponse menaçante : « Si tu ne le fais pas, il y aura la guerre. » Il ne le fit pas.

Quelques jours plus tard, la guerre éclata. Le patient se souvint immédiatement de l'épisode du manteau. Il savait naturellement que ce n'était pas son manque de soin qui avait provoqué la guerre, mais il en avait l'impression. Quelque temps auparavant, il s'était convaincu qu'il mourrait pendant une guerre ; il ressentit cela comme une punition pour son manque de soin envers son manteau.

L'intérêt du patient pour la guerre avait une longue histoire. Enfant, il craignait son père tyrannique et refoulait son angoisse en effrayant son jeune frère. Il se comportait plutôt sadiquement envers ce jeune frère, en particulier en jouant à la guerre. Quand il fut adolescent, le jeune frère mourut de maladie. Le patient réagit à cette mort avec l'idée obsessive qu'il mourrait à la guerre. Cette idée obsessive exprimait l'idée inconsciente : « J'ai tué mon frère en jouant à la guerre, je dois m'attendre au talion et mourir à la guerre. »

Le père du patient était très ordonné. Pendre correctement le manteau signifiait obéissance au père. Des arguments tels que « Vous devez pendre ce manteau — Je suis trop fatigué » avaient souvent été échangés entre le père et le fils. Plus tard, l'ordre, obéissance au père, prit la valeur d'une protection contre le meurtre du père. « Le manque de soin », signifia « essayer de tuer au risque d'être tué ». Le jour de l'histoire du manteau, le patient avait subi une frustration professionnelle et était particulièrement en colère.

La connexion du « microcosme » des mots avec l'idée de « maîtrise des possessions » rend compréhensible que la sexualité attachée à la pensée prenne, à chaque sexualisation de cette dernière, un caractère anal. Pendant l'analyse les obsédés comparent, consciemment ou inconsciemment, la production ou la non-production d'association avec la production ou la non-production de fèces.

Une patiente, qui avait à parler souvent en public, montra l'équivalence certaine de ses mots, non avec les fèces, mais avec l'urine. En parlant, il lui arrivait souvent de perdre le contrôle des mots qui se déversaient de sa bouche. Quelquefois, ils s'arrêtaient brusquement, et elle ressentait une espèce de trac, ne sachant que dire et se sentant vidée de tout matériel. Mais elle inventa un truc pour surmonter cette inhibition : elle avait une bouteille d'eau sur son bureau et, après s'être

« remplie jusqu'en haut » d'eau, elle n'avait plus qu'à laisser ressortir les mots.

L'analyse peut aussi démontrer que des détails d'une nature beaucoup plus délicate de la manière de penser ou de parler sont des répétitions de détails correspondant à des habitudes de toilette enfantine. Les fantasmes d'omnipotence, qui sont en relation avec les pensées et les mots, apparaissent comme étant une répétition de la surestimation narcissique infantile des fonctions excrétoires.

Les manifestations névrotiques de la tête et de la voix sont souvent trouvées, en analyse, sous la dépendance de l'érotisme anal, ceci en accord avec la sexualisation anale des pensées et des mots.

Cette découverte n'est pas incompatible avec le fait que la pensée et la parole sont souvent utilisées comme symboles du pénis, et la capacité de parler ou de penser comme un signe de puissance. La concurrence de significations phallique et anale dans l'obsession est due à la régression.

Il est possible que la relation physiologique entre le volume sanguin de la tête et celui des organes abdominaux aide à l'établissement de la connexion inconsciente entre « pensées » et « fèces ».

Un obsédé souffrant de céphalées chroniques, se référait à ce symptôme en disant : « Mes nerfs me heurtent. » Il imaginait les nerfs comme des fils blancs ou rosâtres, idée acquise chez le dentiste à la vue d'un nerf dentaire. Une fois, il rêva de son « nerf vague », c'est-à-dire du nerf qui « errait ». Il l'associa avec un fil blanc qui aurait pu trouver son chemin vers sa tête venant d'en bas et qui devait maintenant tourner en rond dans sa tête et causer sa céphalée de cette façon. Cette idée était en rapport avec une expérience enfantine : il avait eu des vers intestinaux. Il supposait inconsciemment que ces vers produisaient maintenant des céphalées comme ils lui avaient provoqué des symptômes anaux, dans son enfance.

MAGIE ET SUPERSTITION DANS L'OBSESSION

La surévaluation de l'intellect fait que les obsédés développent leur intellect de façon remarquable. Cependant, cette haute intelligence a des traits archaïques et est pleine de magie et de superstition. Leur Moi présente un clivage : une partie est logique, l'autre superstitieuse. Le mécanisme de défense qu'est l'isolation, permet la possibilité d'un tel clivage.

267

La superstition des obsédés permit à Freud de montrer « les similitudes des vies mentales des primitifs et des névrosés ». Cette superstition est basée sur un narcissisme augmenté, lié avec un rétablissement régressif de la plus ou moins originelle omnipotence infantile. Les jeux obsessifs ayant pour objet cette omnipotence sont animés de sentiments contradictoires de dépendance et d'équivalents inconscients du « meurtre du père ».

Un patient tirait beaucoup de plaisir à jouer avec un petit bouquet de papier, changeant quelque peu de forme lorsqu'on l'agitait, comme un kaléidoscope. L'analyse montra qu'il jouait à « Dieu », créant magiquement des nouveaux mots. Un autre patient, dont le cérémonial se réalisait au moyen de son couvre-lit, avait l'habitude d'imaginer, étant enfant, être Dieu créant le monde. L'analyse montra que « créer le monde » voulait dire « créer des enfants » et qu'il jouait ainsi inconsciemment le rôle du père ayant des rapports sexuels avec sa mère. Cette « création du monde — rapports sexuels » était perçue cependant comme un acte anal, et la prétendue omnipotence était un produit de la surestimation infantile des fonctions excrétoires. Un autre patient, dont l'analyse avait aiguisé le sens de l'auto-observation, se surprit à penser combien il était étrange qu'il dût ouvrir une porte pour y passer. Il s'attendait réellement à ce que son souhait suffît pour que la porte s'ouvrît d'elle-même. Le rejet de cette idée par les niveaux supérieurs du Moi différencie une telle croyance d'un délire de grandeur.

LA NÉVROSE OBSESSIONNELLE EST-ELLE UNE « RELIGION PRIVÉE » ?

La plupart des religions patriarcales oscillent entre la soumission à une figure paternelle et la rébellion contre elle (soumission et rébellion étant sexualisées) chaque Dieu promettant, comme un Surmoi compulsif, la protection contre la soumission ; il existe bien des similitudes entre le tableau manifeste du cérémonial compulsif et du rituel religieux, similitudes dues à la ressemblance des conflits sous-jacents. C'est pourquoi Freud a appelé la névrose obsessionnelle une religion privée ; de même, le cérémonial des obsédés a été appelé rituel en raison de sa similitude aux rites religieux. Cependant, il existe également des différences d'origine entre les rites compulsifs et religieux, dont la discussion dépasse le cadre de ce chapitre.

La symptomatologie de l'obsession est pleine de superstitions magiques tels que les oracles compulsifs ou les sacrifices. Ces patients consultent les oracles, font des paris avec Dieu, craignent l'effet magique des mots des autres, agissent comme s'ils croyaient aux fantômes, aux démons et spécialement à un destin très malicieux, et sont également, en même temps, des personnes intelligentes complètement conscientes de l'absurdité de ces idées.

Consulter un oracle signifie, en principe, soit forcer la permission ou le pardon pour une action prohibée ordinairement, soit tenter de déplacer sur Dieu la responsabilité de choses dont on se sent coupable. L'oracle est demandé comme une permission divine pouvant agir comme un contrepoids à la conscience.

LE PROBLÈME DE L'ÉTIOLOGIE DIFFÉRENTIELLE

Le conflit de base de la névrose obsessionnelle est le même que celui de l'hystérie : la défense contre les tendances répréhensibles du complexe d'Œdipe. La prédominance de l'angoisse dans l'hystérie, pas plus que celle des sentiments de culpabilité dans l'obsession, ne constitue une différence de principe, puisque les sentiments de culpabilité sont présents dans l'hystérie et l'angoisse dans l'obsession.

La régression sadique-anale est pathognomonique[4] de l'obsession et détermine la formation des symptômes. Cette régression peut dépendre d'un des trois facteurs suivants, ou de leur combinaison : 1) les résidus de la phase sadique-anale du développement de la libido ; 2) l'organisation phallique ; et 3) la défense du Moi.

1. Ce qui reste de la phase sadique-anale originelle constitue probablement le facteur crucial. En général, plus la fixation à une phase est forte, plus facile est la régression. Sous l'influence de l'angoisse de castration, les personnes ayant une forte fixation à la phase sadique-anale régresseront à cette phase. Et les fixations peuvent être causées : *a)* par des facteurs constitutionnels ; l'hérédité dans la névrose obsessionnelle montre que l'augmentation constitutionnelle de l'érogénéité anale a son importance ; *b)* par des satisfactions exagérées ; *c)* par des frustrations exagérées ; *d)* par une alternance de satisfactions exagérées et de frustrations (plus les satisfactions ont été grandes, plus les frustrations postérieures seront traumatisantes) ; *e)* une concurrence de satisfactions instinctuelles avec des satisfactions de sécurité, c'est-à-dire avec la négation ou avec la réassurance de l'angoisse spécifique.

Les pulsions érotiques anales concordent, pendant l'enfance, avec l'éducation à la propreté ; la façon dont cette éducation est faite peut déterminer la fixation anale. L'éducation peut être trop précoce, trop

---

4. C'est-à-dire qu'elle suffit à elle seule à poser le diagnostic d'obsession. (N.D.É)

tardive, trop sévère, trop libidineuse. Si elle est faite trop tôt, le résultat typique est le refoulement de l'érotisme anal, caractérisé par une soumission et une obéissance superficielle et une profonde tendance à la rébellion ; si elle est faite trop tard, on peut s'attendre à la rébellion et à l'obstination ; la sévérité est cause de fixation par la frustration provoquée ; un comportement libidineux de la mère provoque la fixation par satisfaction ; cependant, cette satisfaction est toujours limitée, la mère excite l'enfant mais prohibe la satisfaction de l'excitation. Les laxatifs peuvent augmenter la tendance à la dépendance ; les lavements créent une excitation énorme accompagnée d'angoisse.

2. La faiblesse de l'organisation phallique peut provoquer la regression ; il est facile d'abandonner quelque chose de peu d'importance. Mais qu'est-ce qu'une organisation phallique faible ? Cette condition coïncide probablement cliniquement avec la précédente, plus les fixations prégénitales sont fortes, plus faible est l'organisation phallique. La régression paraît être également facilitée par une menace de castration survenue sur l'enfant de façon traumatique, c'est-à-dire par le brusque affaiblissement de la position phallique.

3. Le Moi spécialement apte à recourir à l'utilisation de la regression comme moyen de défense est fort sous un aspect et faible sous un autre. La fonction critique du Moi et le besoin de préparation à la pensée peuvent s'être développés particulièrement tôt, alors que la pensée est encore orientée de façon magique ; mais cette même nécessité pour le Moi défensif de commencer à fonctionner si tôt, fait que les méthodes employées sont archaïques et prématurées. Le Moi des obsédés peut être suffisamment fort pour renforcer ses protestations contre les instincts à une date très précoce, mais il est encore trop faible pour employer des méthodes plus mûres. En contraste, beaucoup de personnes enclines aux rêveries et qui développent plus tard des conversions, montrent une inhibition relative de leurs fonctions intellectuelles.

On peut se demander si toutes les névroses obsessionnelles sont reellement basées sur une régression. N'est-il pas possible que des troubles du développement durant la phase sadique-anale aient pu prévenir le développement d'un complexe d'Œdipe phallique ? Des cas de cette espèce surviennent. Ils ne représentent cependant pas la névrose obsessionnelle typique. La grande importance du complexe d'Œdipe, de l'angoisse de castration et de la masturbation dans la névrose obsessionnelle typique est bien établie. Les troubles du développement durant la phase sadique-anale, produisent plutôt des personnalités avec peu de symptômes compulsifs, mais avec un caractère similaire à celui des obsédés, mélangé à des traits infantiles généraux.

ÉVOLUTION DE LA NÉVROSE OBSESSIONNELLE

La névrose obsessionnelle chez l'adulte se présente sous deux for mes : les formes rares aiguës et les formes communes chroniques. Les cas aigus sont provoqués par des causes extérieures. Ces circonstances extérieures ne sont pas différentes de celles qui provoquent toute autre névrose ; ce sont des remobilisations de conflits sexuels infantiles refoulés ; des troubles d'un équilibre jusque-là maintenu entre les for ces refoulés et les forces refoulantes ; des augmentations soit absolues ou relatives de la force des impulsions refoulées ou des angoisses oppo sées. Pour provoquer une névrose obsessionnelle, ces faits doivent atteindre une personne prédisposée depuis l'enfance, c'est-à-dire une personne ayant effectué une régression au stade sadique-anal dans l'enfance. Cette régression peut, il est vrai, n'avoir embrassé qu'une faible partie de la libido, de façon telle que la génitalité ait pu être suffi samment préservée pour permettre à la puberté de se développer sans difficultés insurmontables ; néanmoins, les défenses infantiles ont pu, à un moment donné, choisir le chemin de la régression, sinon il ne pour rait être possible qu'un désappointement dans la vie postérieure, avec un nouveau flamboiement du complexe d'Œdipe, puisse créer une régression au niveau sadique-anal.

Le type chronique est beaucoup plus fréquent. Des névroses obses sionnelles de cette espèce continuent plus ou moins sans interruption depuis l'adolescence, quoique certaines circonstances extérieures parti culières puissent provoquer, de temps en temps, des exacerbations.

Les rituels compulsifs, succédant à de légers symptômes compulsifs contemporains du complexe d'Œdipe, apparaissent de façon plus defi nitive pendant la période de latence quand se développent les facultés intellectuelles. La sexualité qui émerge à la puberté suit un cours ana logue à celui poursuivi par la sexualité infantile et une autre regression au niveau sadique-anal se produit. Le Surmoi, avec qui les désirs sadi ques-anaux rentrent en conflit, est lui-même incapable d'échapper à la régression. Il devient sadique et s'exaspère contre les exigences instinc tuelles anales et sadiques, de la même façon qu'il le faisait auparavant contre les exigences génitales. Il s'exaspère également implacablement contre les restes phalliques du complexe d'Œdipe, qui ont persisté de concert avec les pulsions sadiques-anales. « Ainsi le conflit, dans la névrose obsessionnelle, est rendu plus aigu pour deux raisons : la défense est devenue plus intolérante, la chose à interdire plus insuppor table et tout cela sous l'influence d'un facteur, la régression de la libido » (Freud).

La lutte continuelle sur deux fronts et les ajustements que le Moi fait aux symptômes (conflits défensifs secondaires, contre-compulsions, formations réactionnelles nouvelles, tendances des symptômes à se développer de la défense vers la satisfaction) compliquent le développement postérieur. Les formations réactionnelles peuvent donner naissance à des gains narcissiques secondaires, tels que l'orgueil d'être particulièrement bon, noble, ou intelligent, et peuvent éveiller de sérieuses résistances au traitement analytique des obsédés.

Comme dans les phobies, il existe parmi les obsessions des cas stationnaires alors que d'autres évoluent progressivement. Dans ces derniers cas, ou bien il se produit des phases d'équilibre, avec une production ouverte d'angoisse et de dépression (ce qui peut être favorable pour l'analyse), ou alors il se produit une augmentation continuelle des symptômes compulsifs vers l'état final redouté de paralysie complète de la volonté consciente.

Un simple exemple de cette évolution dans la symptomatologie : un patient évitait obsessivement le nombre 3 pour sa signification sexuelle et castratrice. Il avait l'habitude de faire chaque chose 4 fois, pour être sûr de ne pas la faire 3. Un peu plus tard, il eut l'impression que 4 était bien près de 3, aussi par sécurité il employa le 5. Mais 5 est un chiffre impair, mauvais par conséquent, et il fut remplacé par 6. 6 était 2 fois 3, 7 était impair, alors ce fut 8. Et 8 resta le chiffre favori pendant des années.

Il n'est pas facile de dire ce qui peut déterminer l'évolution de la maladie soit vers un plafond, soit vers une progression continue.

Une complication pouvant se produire même dans les cas légers, est la rupture d'équilibre susmentionnée, maintenue jusque-là par des sacrifices propitiatoires, ou d'autres limitations compulsives du Moi.

Des événements bouleversants, imprévus par les systèmes du patient, peuvent faire éclater une rigidité compulsive. L'opposé d'une névrose traumatique est la cure traumatique d'un caractère compulsif.

Une telle occurence montre les connexions entre le symptôme compulsif et l'état originel névrotique actuel ou d'angoisse : l'angoisse est dissimulée secondairement par le développement du symptôme obsessif ou compulsif. Les rituels compulsifs qui remplacent les phobies précédentes démontrent encore plus clairement cet escamotage de l'anxiété. Il est cependant vrai que l'angoisse est toujours plus ou moins teintée de sentiments de culpabilité.

L'angoisse et les sentiments de culpabilité qui ont été couverts par les symptômes compulsifs font leur réapparition quand ces symptômes ont été analysés. Fréquemment, les patients étant habitués à dissimuler leur affect et à ne pas les reconnaître, ils apparaissent sous forme d'équivalents physiques ou de névroses actuelles.

UN PHÉNOMÈNE FONDAMENTAL : LA RÉGRESSION AU STADE SADIQUE-ANAL

En résumé, c'est le concept de régression au niveau sadique-anal de l'organisation libidinale qui explique les différences de la formation des symptômes de la névrose obsessionnelle avec ceux de l'hystérie. La confusion apparente résultant de la persistance de tendances phalliques associées au complexe d'Œdipe, tendances se révélant simultanément de nature sadique-anale, s'explique par le processus suivi par les mécanismes de défense : le complexe d'Œdipe est remplacé par le sadisme anal qui, à son tour, est combattu. Bien des différences sont dues au fait que, dans l'hystérie, le refoulement seul est utilisé comme mécanisme de défense, alors que, dans la névrose obsessionnelle, les formations réactionnelles, l'annulation, l'isolation et le superinvestissement libidinal du monde des concepts et des mots (cas spécial d'isolation) jouent leur rôle ; l'utilisation de tels mécanismes est due au fait que ce sont des impulsions anales et non génitales qui doivent être refoulées. L'utilisation de mécanismes de défense dissemblables explique également la différence du champ conscient des deux espèces de névrose. L'assaut tardif de l'obsession est en relation avec le facteur de régression. L'introjection des parents, entre temps, dans le Surmoi, explique à son tour les différences dans l'intériorisation, dans la prédominance du Surmoi, et dans la prédominance relative des punitions et des symptômes expiatoires sur les symptômes de satisfaction. En outre, la régression est également responsable de la sévérité particulière du Surmoi, ce dernier n'ayant pu échapper à la poussée régressive vers le sadisme. Le fait qu'à côté de la production de symptômes la maladie affecte la personnalité totale du patient à un point bien plus avancé que dans l'hystérie peut être aussi mis en relation avec le phénomène fondamental de régression.

Otto Fenichel[5]

5. *La Théorie psychanalytique des névroses*, p. 329-339, 346-367, 370-375.

*A l'encontre de Freud, Mélanie Klein pense que les névroses
n'ont pas leur origine dans le complexe d'Œdipe,
mais sont un recours contre des situations anxiogènes plus précoces.
(Œdipe et le Sphinx, gravure du XIXe siècle,
Bibliothèque des Arts Décoratifs).*

Chapitre IV

D'où vient la névrose ?

C'est en 1926 ; dans Inhibition, symptôme et angoisse, *que Freud pose cette question cruciale : « D'où vient la névrose ? Quelle est sa cause ultime, spécifique ? Après des dizaines d'années d'efforts, ce problème se dresse devant nous, psychanalystes, aussi entier qu'au départ. » Il fait alors ressortir trois facteurs essentiels : un facteur biologique, qui est l'état de détresse et de dépendance du petit de l'homme, lié à sa prématuration. De ce fait, l'influence du monde extérieur est renforcée. La distinction du Moi d'avec le Ça survient précocement. Les dangers du monde extérieur sont accrus, et la dépendance à l'égard de l'objet susceptible de protéger contre ces dangers et de prolonger ainsi la vie intra-utérine est pratiquement totale. C'est, dit Freud, « le facteur biologique qui est à l'origine des premières situations de danger et qui crée le besoin d'être aimé qui n'abandonnera plus l'être humain ».*

Le second facteur est d'ordre phylogénétique, et Freud fait ici allusion au mythe de la horde primitive, exposé dans Totem et tabou *en 1913[1]. D'après ce que Freud lui même appelle un « mythe scientifique », en effet, le père de la horde primitive châtrait ses fils et se réservait les femmes. La crainte de castration se serait transmise à travers les générations. Un jour, les frères s'unirent, tuèrent le père, puis, devant l'inanité de leur crime, éprouvèrent de la culpabilité et instaurèrent la morale et la religion. Au niveau individuel, l'angoisse de castration amène le déclin du complexe d'Œdipe, la formation du Surmoi et l'entrée dans la période de latence. Au moment de la puberté, les pulsions sexuelles sont à nouveau mobilisées ; non acceptées par le Moi, elles sont attirées par leurs prototypes infantiles et les suivent dans la voie du refoulement.*

---

1. Cf. *l'Œdipe : un complexe universel*, dans la même collection (1ᵉ partie).

Le troisième facteur est psychologique et réside dans une imperfection de notre appareil psychique, qui entraîne le Moi à traiter les motions pulsionnelles émanant du Ça comme s'il s'agissait de dangers externes. En raison de ses rapports intimes avec le Ça, le Moi ne peut se défendre qu'en restreignant sa propre organisation et en subissant la formation de symptômes. Dès lors, comme nous l'avons vu, la névrose s'installe. Et Freud conclut : « C'est à cela que se borne, je crois, ce que nous avons pu comprendre pour le moment de la nature et des causes des névroses. » Mais la réponse de Mélanie Klein à la question : D'où vient la névrose ? est différente.

Dans les introductions successives aux différents chapitres de cette partie, nous avons insisté sur le caractère souvent ténu de la limite entre la névrose et d'autres affections souvent plus graves. Ainsi, nous avons pu voir que Dora, qui présentait une hystérie de conversion, avait évolué vers des troubles psychosomatiques et des comportements caractériels, tandis qu'Anna O. avait posé le problème d'une hypothétique « psychose hystérique ». Les agoraphobies, avons-nous dit, plongent parfois leurs racines dans les couches prégénitales de la libido et s'inscrivent alors au sein de structures prépsychotiques où la régression — temporelle — de la libido risque de s'accompagner d'une régression du Moi. Nous avons précisé ailleurs[2] que la phobie de l'Homme aux Loups avait évolué vers un épisode psychotique et que l'ensemble du cas laissait entrevoir des troubles graves quant aux assises mêmes de l'identité sexuelle.

Les névroses obsessionnelles constituent elles-mêmes parfois la « couverture fragile » d'une psychose latente. Nous savons qu'Abraham avait constaté que les intervalles entre deux crises maniaco-dépressives étaient souvent occupés par des manifestations obsessionnelles[3]. Pour Mélanie Klein, tout enfant traverse des épisodes psychotiques lors des premières situations d'angoisse (position schizo-paranoïde, position dépressive).

Dans Inhibition, symptôme et angoisse *(1926), Freud compare la phobie de l'Homme aux Loups à celle du petit Hans, sans inscrire la première dans une structure prépsychotique. Il assigne à la peur d'être dévoré par le loup — substitut du père — le rôle d'une expression régressive du désir passif d'être comblé génitalement par le père. En somme, Freud y voit une régression topique et non une véritable régression libidinale (temporelle).*

---

2. Dans *la Castration : un fantasme originaire* (introduction au chapitre II), dans la même collection.
3. Cf. *les Stades de la libido : de l'enfant à l'adulte* (chap. V), *id.*

Pour Mélanie Klein, il s'agit bel et bien d'une projection, sur l'animal d'angoisse, des désirs sadiques-oraux (cannibaliques) qu'éprouve l'Homme aux Loups à l'égard du pénis paternel. L'Homme aux Loups selon Mélanie Klein, présenterait des traits paranoïdes liés à ses intenses pulsions destructrices, qui l'auraient amené à abandonner ses désirs œdipiens positifs et sa rivalité avec son père. C'est le sadisme de ses désirs archaïques qui le conduisit à refuser la réalité, à développer des traits obsessionnels et paranoïdes. La relation objectale de l'Homme aux Loups diffère de celle du petit Hans, beaucoup plus positive à l'égard de ses deux parents, du fait de la meilleure maîtrise et de la moindre violence de son sadisme primitif. Les phobies sont liées à l'oralité. La névrose obsessionnelle, liée au second stade anal, selon Abraham, « a pour but de guérir l'état psychotique qu'elle recouvre ». L'échec des mécanismes obsessionnels ouvre la voie à la paranoïa sous-jacente (premier stade anal d'Abraham).

Sans entrer plus avant dans la théorie kleinienne des névroses, dont le lecteur prendra connaissance ci-dessous, disons que celles-ci, dans la perspective de l'auteur, n'ont pas leur origine dans le complexe d'Œdipe et le complexe de castration (selon la conception de Freud), mais représentent avant tout des recours contre des situations anxiogènes précoces, de caractère psychotique. D'une certaine façon, il semble que la différence entre régression topique et régression temporelle tende, pour Melanie Klein, à s'effacer. La notion même de régression à un point de fixation, antérieur au conflit œdipien, semble être remplacée par celle d'une fuite en avant, plus ou moins réussie, devant des conflits archaïques. Rappelons cependant que l'apparition très précoce, selon elle, de l'Œdipe vient tempérer ces oppositions, non sans les obscurcir quelque peu en même temps.

Le complexe de castration y est, de fait, décentré[4]. Qu'il existe des « pseudo »-névroses phobiques ou des « pseudo »-névroses obsessionnelles qui sont des aménagements défensifs contre la psychose (dont nous verrons, dans le volume consacré aux psychoses, quelle est l'origine, selon Freud) ne fait cliniquement aucun doute. Faut-il pour autant considérer toutes les névroses comme destinées, avant tout, à permettre au Moi une plus ou moins heureuse gestion d'un noyau psychotique sous-jacent ? Ou faut-il plutôt mettre l'accent sur la névrose en tant qu'entité nosologique distincte, dont le noyau est le complexe d'Œdipe et dont l'organisation dépend des points de fixation et de régression (ce qui tend à rendre justice à l'importance de l'histoire prégénitale du patient) ? C'est précisément le défaut d'organisation de la

---

4. Voir *la Castration : un fantasme originaire,* dans la même collection.

névrose, la présence de multiples points de fixation, la virtualité d'une régression non seulement de la libido mais également du Moi, le polymorphisme des défenses qui signent la fragilité d'une structure et la présence proche d'un noyau psychotique. Convient-il encore, dans ces cas, de parler de névrose ? Ne faut-il pas évoquer ici une classe d'affections psychiques désignées comme « cas limites », qui tend, précisément, à souligner l'existence d'une catégorie de troubles psychiques différenciés en tant que névroses ?

Tels sont quelques-uns des éléments de la controverse entre « kleiniens » et « freudiens » que nous soumettons à la réflexion du lecteur.

La frustration orale amène l'enfant à chercher de nouvelles sources de satisfaction[5]. La fille se détourne de sa mère, et le pénis de son père devient pour elle l'objet d'une satisfaction qui est d'abord de nature orale, bien que les pulsions génitales soient déjà à l'œuvre[6]. Chez le petit garçon, on trouve la même attitude positive à l'égard du pénis paternel ; elle résulte du stade oral de succion et est due à l'assimilation du sein à un pénis[7]. Une fixation au pénis du père, selon une modalité propre au stade oral de succion, est, à mon avis, un facteur essentiel dans la genèse de la vraie homosexualité masculine[8]. Mais les sentiments de haine et d'angoisse à l'égard du père, engendrés par les pulsions œdipiennes naissantes, agissent d'ordinaire à l'encontre de cette fixation[9]. Quand le développement suit un cours favorable, les sentiments positifs à l'égard du pénis du père deviennent la base de bons rapports avec les hommes et permettent en même temps l'adoption d'une attitude franchement hétérosexuelle. Alors que des relations du type oral de succion avec le pénis du père peuvent, dans certaines

---

5. Dans son article « Notes on Oral Character-Formation » (1925), Edward Glover a signalé que la frustration est un facteur de stimulation pour le développement de l'individu.

6. Voir mes articles « The Psychological Principles of Infant Analysis » (1926) et « Early Stages of the Œdipus Conflict » (1928).

7. Dans son article « Nach dem Tode des Urvaters » (1923), Roheim suggère qu'après avoir dévoré son cadavre la horde primitive fit du père une mère nourricière. C'est ainsi, explique-t-il, que l'amour, dont l'objet exclusif avait été jusqu'ici la mère, put être transféré sur le père et qu'un élément positif modifia les rapports entièrement négatifs qui avaient existé entre les fils et leur père.

8. Voir Freud, *Kindheitserinnerung Leonardo da Vinci* (1910). Nous étudierons de plus près ces processus du développement au chapitre XII, en discutant de l'évolution sexuelle du garçon.

9. L'exemple suivant, d'observation directe, illustre le cours de ces changements du goût au dégoût. Un petit garçon, dans les mois qui suivirent le sevrage, montra une préférence alimentaire pour le poisson et un intérêt pour les poissons en général. A l'âge d'un an, il regardait avec un intérêt et un plaisir intenses et évidents sa mère tuer et préparer du poisson. Peu de temps après, il manifesta un dégoût marqué pour cet aliment, qui s'étendit à la simple vue, puis à une véritable phobie des poissons. L'expérience de nombreuses analyses de très jeunes enfants démontre que les attaques contre des poissons, des serpents, des lézards représentent des attaques contre le pénis du père. Ainsi pouvons-nous comprendre la conduite de cet enfant : en voyant sa mère tuer des poissons, il satisfaisait ses pulsions contre le pénis du père, ce qui eut pour conséquence de lui faire craindre son père ou, plus justement, le pénis de son père.

circonstances, conduire le garçon à l'homosexualité, elles constituent normalement, pour la fille, les signes avant-coureurs des pulsions hétérosexuelles et du conflit œdipien. Cette inclination de la fillette pour son père et, chez le garçon, le retour à la mère devenue objet d'amour génital donnent un nouvel objectif aux pulsions libidinales où le rôle des organes génitaux commence à se faire sentir.

LES PREMIÈRES SITUATIONS GÉNÉRATRICES D'ANGOISSE MODIFIÉES PAR LA LIBIDO ET PAR LES OBJETS

J'ai constaté que, pendant la période du développement denommée par moi phase d'exacerbation du sadisme, tous les stades prégénitaux, ainsi que le stade génital, sont coup sur coup investis ; c'est que la libido entre alors en lutte avec les tendances destructrices et consolide graduellement ses positions. Au nombre des facteurs qui sont d'une importance fondamentale pour la dynamique des processus psychiques, je suis d'avis de placer non seulement la *polarité,* mais aussi l'*interaction* des instincts de vie et de mort. Un lien indissoluble unit et, dans une large mesure, soumet la libido aux tendances destructives. Mais le cercle vicieux, dominé par l'instinct de mort, qui veut que l'agressivité engendre l'angoisse et que l'angoisse renforce l'agressivité, peut être brisé par la libido lorsqu'elle a acquis une force suffisante. Comme nous le savons, l'instinct de vie doit lutter de toutes ses forces, au cours des premiers stades du développement, afin de se maintenir en dépit de l'instinct de mort. Mais c'est précisément cette nécessité qui stimule l'épanouissement sexuel de l'enfant.

Les pulsions génitales de l'enfant demeurent longtemps masquées, et nous ne pouvons discerner clairement les fluctuations et l'enchevêtrement des diverses phases du développement qui résultent du conflit entre pulsions destructrices et pulsions libidinales. L'émergence des stades d'organisation, tels que nous les connaissons, ne correspond pas seulement, d'après moi, aux positions que la libido, dans sa lutte contre les tendances destructrices, a conquises et fortifiées ; comme ces deux instincts sont à la fois unis et opposés de manière indissoluble, elle dépend aussi de leur ajustement progressif.

Il est vrai que le jeune enfant ne laisse transparaître qu'une part relativement faible du sadisme terrible qui se révèle lorsqu'on analyse les couches les plus profondes de son psychisme. Mais en affirmant qu'au cours des stades les plus primitifs l'enfant traverse une période où ses tendances sadiques, issues de plusieurs sources, atteignent partout un point d'exacerbation, je me contente en somme de développer la théorie acceptée et bien établie d'après laquelle l'enfant passe d'un stade sadique-oral, ou cannibalisme, à un stade sadique-anal. Nous ne devons pas oublier que ces tendances cannibales elles-mêmes ne trouvent pas de moyen d'expression qui corresponde à leur portée psychologique ; l'enfant normal ne fournit que des indices assez faibles du besoin qu'il éprouve de détruire son objet et ne nous laisse voir que des émanations de fantasmes conçus sur ce thème. On comprend mieux que d'intenses pulsions sadiques dirigées contre des objets extérieurs s'expriment sous une forme aussi édulcorée, si l'on reconnaît que les fantasmes extravagants d'une période très précoce du développement ne deviennent jamais tant soit peu conscients. En outre, au moment où ces fantasmes surgissent, le Moi est à un stade fort primitif et les relations de l'enfant avec le réel subissent encore dans une large mesure l'influence de l'imagination. Il faut aussi tenir compte de l'infériorité physique de l'enfant par rapport à l'adulte et de sa dépendance d'origine biologique ; en effet, ses tendances destructrices se manifestent avec beaucoup plus de vigueur à l'égard des objets inanimés et des animaux de petite taille. Enfin, il se peut que les pulsions génitales, bien qu'encore dissimulées, exercent dès le début de la vie une influence modératrice sur les pulsions sadiques et contribuent à en diminuer la violence envers les objets extérieurs. Le jeune enfant entretient, semble-t-il, à côté de ses relations avec les objets réels, mais sur un autre plan, des relations avec des images fantasmatiques qui sont bonnes ou mauvaises à l'excès. D'ordinaire, ces deux catégories de relations objectales s'entremêlent et exercent l'une sur l'autre une influence toujours croissante. (C'est le processus que j'ai décrit comme étant une interaction entre la formation du Surmoi et les relations objectales.) Mais, dans le psychisme du tout petit enfant, il existe encore une séparation très nette entre les objets réels et les objets imaginaires ; sans doute est-ce là une des raisons pour lesquelles le sadisme et l'angoisse suscités par les objets réels ne se manifestent pas avec autant d'intensité que le caractère des fantasmes semblerait l'annoncer.

DES PROGRÈS DANS LA RÉALITÉ TANT INTÉRIEURE QU'EXTÉRIEURE

Nous savons, tout particulièrement depuis Abraham, que la nature des relations objectales et la formation du caractère dépendent étroitement de la prédominance des fixations soit au stade oral de succion soit au stade sado-oral. A mon avis, ce facteur joue un rôle tout aussi décisif dans la formation du Surmoi. Par suite de l'équivalence entre le sein et le pénis, l'introjection d'une mère bienveillante contribue à l'élaboration d'une imago paternelle également bienveillante[10]. De même, au cours de la formation du Surmoi, les fixations au stade oral de succion neutralisent les identifications terrifiantes produites par la suprématie des tendances sado-orales.

Avec la baisse des pulsions sadiques, les menaces du Surmoi perdent quelque peu de leur force et le Moi y répond autrement. Jusqu'ici, la peur que son Surmoi et ses objets inspiraient à l'enfant pendant les toutes premières phases de son existence provoquait, de la part du Moi, des réactions d'une égale violence. On dirait que le Moi cherche à se défendre du Surmoi, d'abord, pour employer le terme de Laforgue, en le scotomisant, puis en l'expulsant. A partir du moment où il tente de déjouer le Surmoi et de réduire la résistance que ce dernier oppose aux pulsions du Ça, on peut dire qu'il commence à tenir compte de la puissance du Surmoi[11]. Avec l'avènement du second stade anal, le Moi reconnaît encore plus clairement ce pouvoir et s'efforce de trouver un terrain d'entente avec le Surmoi, reconnaissant du même coup l'obligation de lui obéir.

A l'égard du Ça, le Moi change également d'attitude. A l'expulsion fait place, dans le second stade anal, la répression, ou plutôt le refoulement, au sens propre du terme[12]. En même temps, s'atténue sa haine de l'objet, car elle prend, dans une large mesure, sa source dans les sentiments autrefois dirigés contre le Ça et le Surmoi. L'accroissement des forces libidinales et la diminution parallèle des forces destructrices ont aussi pour effet de modérer les tendances sadiques primitives qui s'attachaient à l'objet. Le Moi semble alors redouter plus consciemment des représailles de la part de l'objet. En se soumettant à un Surmoi sévère et à ses interdictions, il reconnaît du même coup le pouvoir de l'objet. L'acceptation de la réalité extérieure dépend ainsi de l'acceptation de la réalité intrapsychique, d'autant que le Moi s'efforce de faire converger Surmoi et objet[13]. Une telle convergence marque une étape dans l'évolution de l'angoisse, et, avec l'aide des mécanismes de

10. Abraham écrit, dans *A Short Study of the Development of the Libido* (1924) : « Un autre aspect dont il faut tenir compte quant à la partie du corps qui a été introjectée, c'est que le pénis est régulièrement assimilé au sein de la femme et que d'autres parties du corps, comme le doigt, le pied, les poils, les selles et les fesses peuvent représenter secondairement ces deux organes » (p. 490).

11. Dans *Psychoanalyse der Gesamtpersönlichkeit* (1927), Alexander a signalé que le Ça, dans un certain sens, corrompt le Surmoi et que « cette entente » lui permet de réaliser des actes prohibés.

12. Dans *Hemmung, Symptom und Angst* (1926), Freud écrit : « Cependant, nous devons retenir, pour plus ample réflexion, la possibilité que le refoulement constitue un mécanisme spécialement relié à l'organisation génitale et que le Moi utilise d'autres moyens de défense contre la libido à différents niveaux de son organisation... »

13. Dans son article « Problem of the Acceptance of Unpleasant Ideas » (1926), Ferenczi remarque que la connaissance de la réalité extérieure va de pair avec celle de la réalité psychique.

projection et de déplacement, favorise le progrès des relations de l'individu avec la réalité. A ce moment, qu'Abraham situe au second stade anal et qu'il caractérise par le besoin d'établir la sécurité des objets, le Moi se défend contre l'angoisse surtout en cherchant à se concilier à la fois les objets du monde extérieur et ceux qui ont été intériorisés.

DES DÉFENSES DE PLUS EN PLUS EFFICACES CONTRE L'ANGOISSE

Cette modification dans le comportement à l'égard de l'objet peut se manifester de deux manières : ou bien l'enfant *se détourne* de l'objet, parce qu'il en redoute les dangers et qu'il veut le protéger contre ses propres pulsions sadiques, ou bien il *se tourne vers* l'objet avec encore plus de bienveillance. Ce type de relation objectale résulte d'un clivage de l'imago maternelle, qui se scinde en une bonne et une mauvaise imago. L'ambivalence de l'enfant envers son objet ne constitue pas seulement un progrès dans le développement de ses relations objectales ; c'est aussi un mécanisme qui joue un rôle de première importance dans la réduction de l'angoisse inspirée par la crainte du Surmoi. En effet, le Surmoi, une fois extériorisé, est réparti sur plusieurs objets ; certains d'entre eux représentent l'objet attaqué et par suite menaçant, tandis que d'autres, notamment la mère, tiennent lieu d'un personnage favorable et protecteur.

Au fur et à mesure que l'enfant approche du stade génital et que ses imagos introjectées acquièrent de la bienveillance, le comportement du Surmoi se transforme et les moyens mis en œuvre pour vaincre l'angoisse gagnent en efficacité. Lorsque les menaces, jusque-là inéluctables, du Surmoi s'affaiblissent et ne sont plus que des reproches et des remontrances, le Moi peut obtenir à leur encontre le soutien de ses relations positives. Il peut maintenant se servir, dans le but d'apaiser le Surmoi, de mécanismes réparateurs et de formations réactionnelles de pitié envers ses objets[14]. L'amour et la reconnaissance que lui témoignent ces objets et le monde extérieur sont alors considérés comme la preuve et la mesure de l'approbation du Surmoi. Sur ce point également, il faut tenir compte de la répartition des imagos, car le Moi, tout en se détournant de l'objet dangereux, cherche à réparer, grâce à l'objet bienveillant, les dommages imaginaires qu'il a causés.

LA FACULTÉ DE SUBLIMER

Le processus de sublimation peut désormais s'installer, car les tendances réparatrices à l'égard de l'objet constituent un mobile fonda-

---

14. Dans son article « Über das Mitleid » (1930), Jekels montre que la personne qui éprouve de la pitié traite l'objet comme elle voudrait être traitée par son propre Surmoi.

*Segantini a dû sublimer dans sa peinture toute son animosité
envers sa mère qui l'avait trop tôt quitté.*

mental à toutes les sublimations, même les plus précoces, telles que les manifestations tout à fait primitives du besoin ludique. Une condition préalable au développement des tendances réparatrices et des sublimations est l'affaiblissement de la pression exercée par le Surmoi et sa transformation en culpabilité. Les changements qualitatifs que commence à subir le Surmoi en raison de la force croissante des pulsions génitales et des relations objectales l'amènent à se comporter différemment à l'égard du Moi, qui devient alors apte à éprouver de véritables sentiments de culpabilité. Si toutefois de tels sentiments dépassent une certaine limite, le Moi en sera de nouveau affecté, mais sous forme d'angoisse[15]. Dans cette perspective, le manque de sens social chez certains individus, notamment chez les criminels et les soi-disant êtres « asociaux », serait dû non à une déficience, mais à une structure qualitative particulière du Surmoi[16].

ENTRE LE ÇA, LE MOI ET LE SURMOI, LES RAPPORTS DEVIENNENT PLUS POSITIFS

Pendant le premier stade anal, l'enfant, selon moi, se défend contre les imagos terrifiantes qu'il a introjectées au cours de la phase sado-orale. En expulsant son Surmoi, il fait, pour maîtriser son angoisse, une première tentative qui échoue parce que l'angoisse à surmonter est encore trop intense et que le mécanisme d'expulsion violente suscite sans cesse une nouvelle angoisse. L'angoisse qui n'a pu être dissipée par ce moyen l'incite à investir le niveau libidinal qui est juste au-dessus, soit le second stade anal et stimule ainsi tout son développement psychosexuel.

On admet que chez l'adulte le Surmoi et l'objet ne coïncident en aucune façon ; j'ai voulu montrer qu'ils ne le font pas davantage pendant l'enfance, à quelque période que ce soit. A mon avis, les efforts qu'accomplit le Moi, en raison de cette divergence, constituent un facteur fondamental de son développement[17]. L'équilibre mental est d'autant plus stable et l'issue des toutes premières situations anxiogènes heureuse, que cette différence diminue, c'est-à-dire que les imagos se rapprochent des objets réels avec l'avènement de la suprématie génitale et le dépassement graduel des imagos terrifiantes qui dominaient les stades antérieurs. A mesure que se renforcent les pulsions génitales, la répression du Ça par le Moi perd de sa rigueur, et le désaccord entre

---

15. Voir mon article « Infantile Anxiety-Situations Reflected in a Work of Art » (1929). Ella Sharpe a montré que, dans la sublimation, l'enfant projette ses parents introjectés sur un objet extérieur, lequel satisfait ses tendances sadiques et réparatrices, et auquel se rattachent ainsi ses sentiments de toute puissance magique (voir son article « Certain Aspects of Sublimation and Delusion », 1930).

16. Voir également la contribution de Jones à cette question : *Fear, Guilt and Hate* (1929).

17. Dans son article « Identifizierung » (1926), Fenichel exprime une opinion semblable.

ces deux instances s'aplanit. Ainsi les relations objectales de qualité plus positive qui s'instaurent au début du stade génital sont un autre indice de rapports satisfaisants entre le Surmoi et le Moi, entre le Moi et le Ça.

DES TRAITS PSYCHOTIQUES PASSAGERS CHEZ L'ENFANT SONT NORMAUX

Nous savons déjà que, dans les psychoses, les points de fixation se situent aux tout premiers stades du développement, et que la ligne de démarcation entre la psychose et la névrose est celle qui sépare les deux périodes du stade anal. Je suis portée à aller plus avant, et à considérer ces moments comme les sources non seulement des maladies plus tardives, mais aussi des perturbations qui marquent les débuts de la vie. Nous avons vu, dans le chapitre précédent, qu'à la phase d'exacerbation du sadisme, les situations anxiogènes excessives constituent un facteur étiologique fondamental des psychoses. Même les enfants normaux, d'après mon expérience, connaissent, dans les premiers stades de leur développement, des situations anxiogènes de caractère psychotique[18]. Si, pour des raisons extérieures ou intérieures, ces situations très précoces sont puissamment activées, l'enfant présentera des traits psychotiques[19], et, s'il est incapable de combattre, grâce à ses imagos secourables à ses objets réels, la pression exagérée de ses imagos terrifiantes, il sera exposé à des troubles qui seront à l'origine de maladies graves et de déviations du développement, ou qui ressembleront au comportement psychotique de l'adulte et, dans bien des cas, aboutiront avec le temps à une véritable psychose[20]. Des situations anxiogènes de ce type et d'une très grande intensité se produisent invariablement à une certaine période de l'enfance ; aussi tout enfant présente-t-il, à un moment ou à un autre, des symptômes psychotiques.

LA NÉVROSE CHEZ L'ENFANT

Ainsi, on retrouve régulièrement chez les enfants ce passage entre l'exubérance et l'accablement, qui est caractéristique des états dépressifs. On fait peu de cas du chagrin, pourtant si réel et si profond, qu'éprouve un enfant, précisément à cause de sa fréquence et de sa

---

18. Au chapitre suivant, nous étudierons plus en détail l'importance de ce facteur dans la formation du Moi et ses rapports avec la réalité.

19. Voir mon article « Personification in the Play of Children » (1929).

20. On se reportera aux cas d'Erna (chap. III), d'Egon (chap. IV) et d'Ilse (chap. V).

*Mélanie Klein a rapporté le caractère paranoïde de certaines
peurs des animaux qu'ont souvent les enfants seuls
dans le noir. (« Le chat noir », illustration de Beardsley
pour E. Poe, Bibliothèque des Arts Décoratifs).*

labilité. Mais j'ai appris par l'observation analytique que le chagrin et la dépression d'un enfant, même s'ils n'atteignent pas la même acuité que la mélancolie chez l'adulte, relèvent des mêmes causes et peuvent s'accompagner d'idées de suicide. Les accidents plus ou moins graves qui arrivent aux enfants, les coups et les blessures qu'ils se donnent, sont souvent, d'après mon expérience, de vraies tentatives de suicide, mais avec une insuffisance de moyens. Ils présentent aussi, à un degré variable, ce refus du réel, qui, dans une certaine limite, ne nous préoccupe pas, mais que nous interprétons, chez les adultes, comme un critère de psychose. Les traits paranoïdes s'observent plus difficilement en raison de la réserve et de la dissimulation qui en sont inséparables, et pourtant nous savons que les jeunes enfants se sentent assiégés et poursuivis par des figures fantastiques. J'ai constaté, dans des analyses de tout petits enfants, le caractère paranoïde de l'impression qu'ils avaient, étant seuls et surtout la nuit, d'être entourés de toutes sortes de persécuteurs, comme des sorciers, des sorcières, des démons, des animaux, et des formes fantastiques[21] ; l'angoisse qu'ils en éprouvaient était également de type paranoïde.

La névrose de l'enfant offre un tableau complexe, formé des divers traits et mécanismes psychotiques et névrotiques que nous trouvons chez l'adulte à l'état isolé et plus ou moins pur. Parfois, l'aspect de telle ou telle affection est plus nettement discernable ; souvent tout est obscurci du fait que les différents processus pathologiques et les défenses qu'ils mobilisent sont à l'œuvre ensemble et en même temps.

Dans *Inhibition, symptôme et angoisse* (1926), Freud déclare que « les premières phobies infantiles n'ont trouvé jusqu'ici aucune explication » et que « leur rapport avec les névroses manifestes et plus tardives de l'enfance n'est pas du tout éclairci » (p. 77). Je pense que ces premières phobies recèlent l'angoisse née au cours des premiers stades de la formation du Surmoi. Les toutes premières situations anxiogènes apparaissent vers l'âge de six mois, sous l'effet d'un accroissement du sadisme, et consistent en des craintes d'objets, tant extérieurs qu'introjectés, capables, dans leur violence, de dévorer, de couper et de castrer ; de telles peurs ne peuvent être suffisamment modifiées à un stade aussi précoce.

---

21. La croyance de l'enfant à des personnages imaginaires et secourables, tels que les fées ou le père Noël, l'aide à masquer et à vaincre sa peur de ses mauvaises imagos.

D'OÙ VIENNENT LES PHOBIES DES ANIMAUX ET LES DIFFICULTÉS ALIMENTAIRES ?

Les difficultés alimentaires des jeunes enfants sont aussi étroitement liées, d'après mon expérience, à leurs premières situations anxiogènes et ont invariablement une origine paranoïde. Durant la période cannibale, ils identifient tous les aliments à leurs objets, à l'image de leurs organes, de sorte que la nourriture tient lieu du pénis paternel et du sein maternel et est, au même titre, aimée, détestée et redoutée. Les liquides représentent du lait, des selles, de l'urine et du sperme ; les solides sont assimilés à des fèces et à d'autres matières corporelles. Ainsi, la nourriture peut-elle donner naissance à toutes ces craintes d'être empoisonné et détruit au-dedans que suscitent les objets intériorisés et les excréments, sous l'effet de situations anxiogènes primitives qui demeurent fortement agissantes.

Les zoophobies de l'enfance sont l'expression d'une angoisse de ce genre. Elles tirent leur origine d'un mécanisme caractéristique du premier stade anal, de l'expulsion du Surmoi terrifiant, et témoignent des moyens mis en œuvre pour surmonter la peur de ce Surmoi et du Ça. Dans un premier temps, ces deux instances sont rejetées dans le monde extérieur, et le Surmoi est assimilé à l'objet réel. La seconde étape nous est bien connue et consiste dans le déplacement sur un animal de la crainte inspirée par le vrai père. Il existe souvent une phase intermédiaire, au cours de laquelle l'enfant choisit comme objet de son angoisse dans le monde extérieur un animal assez doux, qui remplace les bêtes sauvages et féroces représentant le Surmoi et le Ça des stades primitifs de la formation du Moi. L'animal anxiogène s'attire non seulement la crainte, mais aussi l'admiration que l'enfant ressent à l'égard de son père ; on voit ainsi que la formation de l'idéal du Moi est engagée[22]. Les phobies d'animaux constituent déjà une modification à grande portée de la peur du Surmoi et leur genèse nous montre à quel point sont liés le Surmoi, les relations objectales et les zoophobies.

Freud écrit, dans *Inhibition, symptôme et angoisse* : « J'ai pensé autrefois qu'une phobie avait le caractère d'une projection, en ce sens qu'un danger interne, d'ordre instinctuel, était remplacé par un danger

---

22. Abraham m'a raconté l'histoire d'un tout petit enfant dont l'aversion pour un animal contenait déjà la peur d'être blâmé par ce dernier. Il avait offert un livre d'images à un enfant, âgé d'à peine un an et demi, de sa parenté. Abraham lui montrait les images et lisait le texte à haute voix. Sur l'une des pages, il y avait l'image d'un cochon qui disait à un enfant d'être propre. Les mots et l'image déplurent de toute évidence à l'enfant, qui voulut tourner la page immédiatement et, lorsque Abraham un peu plus tard revint à cette image, l'enfant refusa de la regarder. Par la suite, Abraham apprit que, quoique le livre plût beaucoup à l'enfant, il ne pouvait tolérer de voir la page où se trouvait le cochon. En guise de commentaire, Abraham ajouta : « Son Surmoi devait être, à ce moment-là, un cochon. »

perçu comme venant du dehors. C'est un avantage, car le sujet peut se protéger contre un danger extérieur en le fuyant ou en évitant de le percevoir, alors qu'aucune fuite ne peut être un recours contre un danger interne. Mais ce point de vue, sans être inexact, est trop superficiel. Après tout, une poussée instinctuelle ne constitue pas un danger en soi ; elle l'est seulement dans la mesure où elle entraîne un danger extérieur et réel, soit le danger de castration. En dernière analyse, une phobie ne consiste qu'en la substitution d'un danger extérieur à un autre » (p. 66, 67). Je croirais quand même qu'à la source des phobies se trouve un danger interne, lié à la crainte des instincts destructeurs et des parents introjectés. Décrivant les avantages des formations substitutives, Freud nous dit dans le même passage que « la crainte propre aux phobies est en fin de compte conditionnée. Elle n'est ressentie qu'au moment où l'objet redouté est perçu, et à juste titre, car c'est alors seulement que surgit la situation de danger. Il n'y a aucune raison de redouter la castration par un père qui n'est pas là. Mais on ne peut se débarasser d'un père, qui apparaît chaque fois qu'il le veut bien. Si toutefois l'enfant le remplace par un animal, il n'a qu'à éviter la vue, c'est-à-dire la présence de cet animal pour être délivré de tout danger et de toute angoisse ». L'avantage serait encore plus marqué si, grâce à une zoophobie, le Moi pouvait non seulement déplacer un objet extérieur par un autre, mais également projeter sur un objet extérieur un objet très redouté et inéluctable, parce qu'il a été intériorisé. Dans cette perspective, une zoophobie serait beaucoup plus qu'une crainte de castration par le père, déguisée en celle de se faire mordre par un cheval ou manger par un loup. La crainte d'être dévoré par le Surmoi, plus primitive que la peur de la castration, montrerait que la phobie est en fait une modification de l'angoisse propre aux stades les plus précoces du développement.

LE PETIT HANS : UNE NÉVROSE « NORMALE »

Pour illustrer ce que je veux dire, prenons deux cas célèbres de zoophobies, le petit Hans et l'Homme aux Loups. Freud a fait remarquer qu'en dépit de certaines ressemblances les deux phobies différaient Ainsi, la phobie du petit Hans fournit bien des indices d'un sentiment positif. L'animal anxiogène n'était pas en lui-même tellement terrible et n'était pas sans inspirer à l'enfant une certaine sympathie, puisqu'on le voit jouer au cheval avec son père juste avant l'apparition de la phobie. Il avait, à tout prendre, d'excellentes relations avec ses parents et son entourage, et son développement général indiquait qu'il avait dépassé la phase sado-anale et atteint

« L'animal anxiogène n'a pas ce caractère terrible en lui-même,
il n'est qu'un représentant de l'objet de trouble. »
(Gravure de 1534, Bibliothèque des Arts Décoratifs).

le stade génital. Sa zoophobie ne révélait que de rares traces de l'angoisse typique des premières étapes du développement, ou le Surmoi est assimilé à un animal sauvage et terrifiant et où la peur que suscite l'objet est proportionnellement intense. Dans l'ensemble, il avait, semble-t-il, fort bien surmonté et modifié cette angoisse primitive. Freud dit de lui : « Hans paraît avoir été un garçon normal, avec ce qu'on appelle un complexe d'Œdipe positif[23] », si bien que sa névrose infantile peut être considérée comme sans gravité, je dirais même « normale » ; aussi son angoisse céda-t-elle aisément à une brève période d'analyse.

UNE PEUR ÉCRASANTE
DU PÈRE CHEZ « L'HOMME AUX LOUPS »

La névrose du garçon de quatre ans qu'on a surnommé l'Homme aux Loups présente un tableau tout à fait différent. On ne peut décrire le développement de ce garçon comme étant normal. Pour citer de nouveau Freud, « ... ses relations avec l'objet sexuel féminin avaient été

23. *Hemmung, Symptom und Angst* (1926), p. 46.

290

perturbées par une séduction précoce. Sa passivité féminine était fortement accentuée, et l'analyse du rêve aux loups révèle peu d'agressivité voulue envers le père, mais démontre très clairement que le refoulement portait sur les sentiments tendres et passifs à son égard. Les facteurs mentionnés en premier lieu ont peut être joué un rôle pathogène, mais ils échappent à l'observation[24] ». L'analyse de cet enfant montra que l'idée d'être dévoré par le père était « l'expression, sous une forme régressive et dégradée, d'un désir passif et tendre à l'égard du père, visant à obtenir son amour sur un plan érotique génital[25] ». A la lumière de la discussion que nous venons de présenter, nous voyons dans cette idée bien plus qu'un désir de caractère tendre et passif, dégradé par la régression ; il s'agit avant tout d'un vestige d'un stade très précoce du développement[26]. Cette zoophobie ne serait pas uniquement un substitut déformé de la castration par le père, mais traduirait, selon mon hypothèse, une angoisse primitive et inchangée, persistant à côté de ses modifications ultérieures. Dans cette perspective, une crainte du père, agissant de l'intérieur, aurait beaucoup contribué à l'orientation du développement anormal de cet enfant. A la phase d'exacerbation du sadisme, déclenchée par les pulsions sado-orales, le désir d'introjecter le pénis du père et l'intense agressivité sado-orale engendrent des peurs de bêtes dangereuses et dévorantes, que l'enfant identifie au pénis du père. L'issue de ses efforts pour surmonter et modifier cette crainte du père dépend en partie de l'ampleur de ses tendances destructrices. L'Homme aux Loups ne réussit pas à dominer cette angoisse primitive. Sa peur du loup, qui tenait lieu de sa peur du père, montrait qu'il avait conservé au cours des années l'image de son père sous les traits d'un loup dévorant. Nous savons en effet qu'il retrouva cet animal dans ses imagos paternelles ultérieures et que tout son développement fut dominé par cette peur écrasante.[27].

J'accorde une importance capitale à cette énorme crainte du père dans la genèse de son complexe d'Œdipe inversé. En analysant plusieurs garçons névrosés, de quatre à cinq ans[28], gravement atteints et présentant des traits paranoïdes avec un très fort Œdipe inversé, j'ai acquis la conviction que ce type de développement était dans une large

24. *Ibid.*, p. 46.
25. *Ibid.*, p. 44.
26. Il me paraît important, d'un point de vue non seulement théorique, mais aussi thérapeutique, de déterminer si, à l'apparition de la névrose chez l'enfant, l'idée d'être dévoré ne reçoit qu'un investissement régressif ou si elle persiste telle quelle à côté de ses modifications ultérieures. Nous devons en effet nous intéresser moins au contenu de l'idée qu'à l'angoisse qui s'y rattache et nous n'arriverons à une véritable compréhension d'une angoisse de cette nature, sous ses aspects tant quantitatifs que qualitatifs, qu'en reconnaissant en elle une angoisse sous-jacente dans les névroses et spécifique dans les psychoses.
27. Voir Ruth Mack Brunswick. *A Supplement to Freud's History of an Obsessional Neurosis* (1928).
28. Mes analyses d'adultes ont corroboré ces observations.

mesure déterminé par une peur excessive du père, qui persistait dans les couches psychiques les plus profondes et qui avait son origine dans l'agressivité primitive d'une extrême violence dirigée contre lui. Avec un père aussi dangereux et dévorant, ces garçons ne pouvaient engager la lutte qui accompagne la situation œdipienne directe, et ils durent abandonner leur position hétérosexuelle. Je crois que l'attitude passive de l'Homme aux Loups envers son père remontait également à des situations anxiogènes de cet ordre ; la séduction par la sœur n'aurait fait que renforcer et confirmer une attitude déterminée par la peur du père.

UNE HOMOSEXUALITÉ ACCENTUÉE POUR LUTTER CONTRE LA PEUR PRIMITIVE DU PÈRE

On nous dit « qu'après le rêve décisif il avait été très méchant, qu'il avait cherché à ennuyer les gens et qu'il avait eu un comportement sadique » ; peu après, se manifesta une franche névrose obsessionnelle, dont l'analyse montra par la suite l'extrême gravité. Ces faits peuvent corroborer mon opinion : même à l'époque de la phobie du loup, il se débattait contre ses tendances hostiles[29]. Cette lutte restait chez lui profondément dissimulée, alors qu'elle s'étalait à nos yeux dans le cas du petit Hans ; j'explique cette différence par la manière beaucoup moins normale dont l'Homme aux Loups résolut une angoisse, ou un sadisme primaire, beaucoup plus intense. Hans ne présentait pas de traits obsessionnels, tandis que l'Homme aux Loups devint rapidement un grand obsédé typique ; cet élément concorde avec ce que je pense sur la nature extrêmement grave d'une névrose infantile à l'aspect obsessionnel trop prononcé et trop précoce[30].

Dans ces analyses de garçons sur lesquelles se fondent les conclusions que je viens d'exposer, j'ai pu remonter le cours de leur développement anormal jusqu'à un sadisme d'une force exceptionnelle ; en fait, il s'agit plutôt d'un sadisme qui avait mal évolué et qui, à un stade très primitif, était générateur d'un excès d'angoisse : d'où un refus très étendu de la réalité et la formation de traits obsesionnels et paranoïdes prononcés. Le renforcement des pulsions libidinales et homosexuelles qui se produisit chez ces garçons servait à écarter et à modifier la crainte qu'ils avaient ressentie si tôt envers le père. Cette façon de

---

29. Freud ne semble pas écarter la possibilité qu'une défense contre les pulsions sadiques ait pu jouer un rôle, même non manifeste, dans la structure de la maladie de l'Homme aux Loups.
30. Voir chapitre VI de *la Psychanalyse des enfants* (P.U.F.).

composer avec l'angoisse est, à mon sens, un facteur fondamental dans l'étiologie de l'homosexualité des paranoïaques[31] ; la paranoïa dont fut atteint par la suite l'Homme aux Loups confirme mon opinion .

LA NÉVROSE OBSESSIONNELLE RECOUVRE CHEZ L'ENFANT UN ÉTAT PSYCHOTIQUE

Dans *le Moi et le Ça* (1923), Freud, lorsqu'il aborde la vie amoureuse du paranoïaque, semble corroborer mon point de vue. « Il y a toutefois, dit-il, un autre mécanisme possible, que nous avons découvert par l'investigation analytique des processus responsables de la transformation qui se produit dans la paranoïa. Dès le début existe une attitude ambivalente, et le changement s'effectue grâce à un déplacement réactionnel de l'investissement, de sorte que l'énergie des pulsions érotiques sert à renforcer celle de l'agressivité » (p. 60). Dans la phobie de l'Homme aux loups on voit clairement, à mon avis, cette angoisse non modifiée qui appartient aux premiers stades du développement. Les relations objectales de cet enfant étaient loin d'avoir la qualité de celles du petit Hans. Enfin, ses positions génitales n'étaient pas assez affermies, et ses pulsions sado-anales trop fortes, comme l'indique l'apparition si précoce d'une aussi grave névrose obsessionnelle. Le petit Hans, semble-t-il, aurait davantage été à même de transformer en une imago moins dangereuse son menaçant et terrible Surmoi et de maîtriser son sadisme et son angoisse. Sa supériorité à cet égard se traduisit également dans ses relations objectales de qualité plus positive tant à l'égard de son père que de sa mère, dans la prédominance de l'attitude active et hétérosexuelle chez lui et dans l'accès à un stade génital satisfaisant dans son développement[33].

Résumons brièvement ce que nous avons vu sur l'évolution des phobies. Au stade oral de succion, dans la succion même, les premières situations anxiogènes se traduisent par certaines phobies. Le premier stade anal, avec ses zoophobies, comporte encore des objets très terrifiants. Au cours du stade suivant, et davantage encore avec le stade

31. Dans l'exposé que j'ai fait au chapitre III du même ouvrage d'un cas présentant des traits paranoïdes, j'ai tenté d'apporter une explication analogue au sujet de l'homosexualité féminine. Le lecteur peut également se reporter à l'analyse d'Egon (chapitre IV). Cette question est reprise au chapitre XII. Roheim (*Psycho-Analysis and the Folk-Tale*, 1922) arrive à la même conclusion à partir de ses recherches ethnologiques.

32. Voir Ruth Mack Brunswick, *op. cit.*

33. Dans *Hemmung, Symptom und Angst* (1926), p. 65, Freud dit : « Un cas comme celui du petit Hans ne nous permet pas de conclure. Il est vrai qu'ici le refoulement triomphe d'une pulsion agressive, mais seulement après l'établissement de l'organisation génitale. »

génital, ces objets anxiogènes subissent une importante transformation.

Ces changements sont liés, d'après moi, aux mécanismes qui soustendent la névrose obsessionnelle et qui commencent à fonctionner au second stade anal. La névrose obsessionnelle aurait pour but de guérir l'état psychotique qu'elle recouvre et les névroses infantiles comporteraient à la fois des mécanismes obsessionnels et des mécanismes propres à un stade antérieur du développement[34].

LE POINT DE DÉPART
DE LA NÉVROSE OBSESSIONNELLE :
LE STADE ANAL DE RÉTENTION

En soutenant que certains éléments de caractère obsessionnel jouent un rôle important dans le tableau clinique des névroses infantiles, il peut sembler à première vue que je ne suis pas d'accord avec l'opinion de Freud sur le point de départ de la névrose obsessionnelle. Je crois cependant qu'une explication satisfaisante est possible, tout au moins sur un point important. Il est exact que, d'après mes constatations, les origines de la névrose obsessionnelle se situent dans la première enfance ; les traits obsessionnels isolés qui surgissent à cette époque ne se structurent pas toutefois en une névrose obsessionnelle d'ordre nosographique avant la seconde enfance, soit au début de la période de latence. Selon la théorie courante, les fixations sado-anales n'interviennent que plus tard dans la névrose obsessionnelle, à la faveur d'une régression. J'estime que le véritable point de départ de la névrose obsessionnelle, soit le moment où se développent les symptômes et les mécanismes obsessionnels, se trouve à la phase du développement qui est dominée par le second stade anal. Il est vrai que ces premiers troubles obsessionnels diffèrent de la névrose obsessionnelle qui ne se déclare dans toute son ampleur qu'à une époque plus tardive ; on le comprendra si l'on retient que c'est seulement à la période de latence que le Moi, ayant acquis de la maturité et modifié ses rapports avec le réel, entreprend l'élaboration et la synthèse de ces éléments obsessionnels qui étaient en activité depuis la première enfance[35]. Dans le cadre

34. La névrose obsessionnelle n'est qu'un moyen de guérison parmi ceux qu'utilise le Moi afin de surmonter cette angoisse psychotique de la toute première enfance. Nous étudions une autre modalité dans le chapitre XII de *La Psychanalyse des enfants*.

35. Nous étudions plus en détail ces transformations au (chapitre X, *op. cit.*), dans lequel j'ai tenté de montrer qu'à la période de latence, la névrose obsessionnelle permet à l'enfant de répondre aux exigences du Moi, du Surmoi et du Ça, alors qu'à un âge plus jeune, lorsque le Moi n'a pas encore atteint sa maturité, il ne peut recourir à ce moyen pour dominer son angoisse.

de la névrose infantile, ces caractères obsessionnels se détachent avec moins de netteté que chez l'adulte pour une autre raison également : ils plus anciens qui ne sont pas encore liquidés et par les mécanismes de défense qui leur sont propres.

Néanmoins, comme je me suis efforcée de le montrer, même chez de très jeunes enfants on rencontre souvent des symptômes de nature franchement obsessionnelle, et il existe des névroses infantiles dont l'aspect le plus frappant est déjà celui d'une authentique névrose

anxiogènes primitives sont demeurées trop intenses et ont été insuffisamment modifiées.

L'OPINION DE FREUD SUR L'ORIGINE DE L'OBSESSION

En distinguant de la sorte la manifestation précoce de traits obsessionnels isolés de l'apparition plus tardive de véritables névroses obsessionnelles, j'espère avoir rendu mes vues personnelles sur la genèse de cette affection plus conformes à la théorie généralement admise. Dans *Inhibition, symptôme et angoisse*, Freud fait remonter « l'origine de la névrose obsessionnelle à la nécessité de se défendre contre les exigences libidinales résultant du complexe d'Œdipe ». Il ajoute que « l'organisation génitale de la libido est encore faible et incapable de résider adéquatement. La lutte défensive qu'entreprend alors le Moi a pour premier effet de faire reculer, dans son entier ou en partie, l'organisation génitale (du stade phallique) au stade sado-anal qui la précède. Tout ce qui surviendra par la suite est lié à cette régression » (p. 47). On peut aussi tenir pour une régression cette fluctuation, caractéristique des premières phases du développement, d'une position libidinale à une autre, avec l'abandon périodique, jusqu'à son affermissement et son établissement définitif, d'une position génitale déjà investie. Si, de plus, ce que je soutiens sur l'extrême précocité de la situation œdipienne est exact, la théorie que je viens d'exposer concernant les origines de la névrose obsessionnelle ne contredit sûrement pas l'opi

---

36. Voir chapitre VI, ainsi que le cas de Rita (chapitre III, *op. cit.*), qui, au début de son analyse, âgée de deux ans neuf mois, montrait déjà de nombreux symptômes obsessionnels marqués, dont les principaux étaient un cérémonial du coucher compliqué et un goût exagéré pour l'ordre et la propreté. Cet excès se traduisait dans un grand nombre d'habitudes qui révélaient l'orientation obsessionnelle de son caractère et de toute sa personnalité. De plus, il s'agissait déjà d'habitudes de longue date. Son cérémonial du coucher, par exemple, avait commencé dans le courant de sa deuxième année et s'était enrichi régulièrement depuis lors. Erna (chapitre III, *op. cit.*), qui vint me voir à l'âge de six ans, présentait certains symptômes obsessionnels qui remontaient également à la fin de la deuxième année. Dans ce cas très grave, la névrose montra très tôt de nombreuses similitudes avec une névrose obsessionnelle d'adulte.

nion citée plus haut de Freud et corroborerait même une de ses suggestions, qu'il n'a pas poussée très loin. « Il se peut, écrit-il, que la régression soit due à un facteur chronologique plutôt que constitutionnel et qu'elle soit rendue possible non par la faiblesse de l'organisation génitale de la libido, mais par un début prématuré de la lutte entreprise par le Moi à l'apogée du stade anal[37]. » Il s'élève contre cette hypothèse dans les termes suivants : « Sans être en mesure de me prononcer définitivement sur ce point, je dirai que l'observation analytique ne milite pas en faveur de cette hypothèse. Elle montrerait plutôt qu'un individu n'est sujet à une névrose obsessionnelle qu'après avoir atteint le stade phallique. D'ailleurs, cette maladie se manifeste plus tard que l'hystérie, soit au cours de la seconde enfance, après le début de la période de latence[38]... » Ces objections perdent de leur force si l'on admet avec moi que la névrose obsessionnelle a son point de départ dans la première enfance pour se manifester dans toute son ampleur au commencement de la période de latence.

LE SURMOI SÉVÈRE DES OBSÉDÉS EST CELUI DES PREMIERS STADES DU DÉVELOPPEMENT

Cette théorie sur la précocité des mécanismes obsessionnels, dont le fonctionnement débuterait vers la fin de la deuxième année, s'insère dans l'ensemble de ma doctrine, qui diverge encore ici de l'opinion orthodoxe. Je situe aux tout premiers stades du développement la formation du Surmoi, que le Moi de l'enfant ressent d'abord sous forme d'angoisse ; avec la terminaison graduelle de la phase sado-anale, le Surmoi devient également générateur de culpabilité. Dans la Première Partie de *La Psychanalyse des enfants*, j'ai exposé les faits sur lesquels j'ai édifié mon système ; je voudrais maintenant l'étayer d'arguments théoriques. Pour citer de nouveau Freud, « c'est la peur qu'éprouve le Moi à l'égard du Surmoi », écrit-il, « qui, de toute évidence, fournit ici » (dans la névrose obsessionnelle) « l'explication de toutes les formations réactionnelles ultérieures[39] ». On comprendra mieux, il me semble, la rigueur particulière du Surmoi dans cette névrose, en reconnaissant avec moi que la névrose obsessionnelle sert à modifier des situations anxiogènes primitives, et que le Surmoi sévère qui la caractérise n'est autre que le Surmoi terrifiant et inaltéré des premiers stades du développement.

37. *Hemmung, Symptom und Angst* (1926), p. 53.
38. *Op. cit.*
39. *Ibid.*, p. 69.

Les sentiments de culpabilité liés aux pulsions urétrales et sado-anales ont leur source, d'après mes constatations, dans les attaques imaginaires dont l'intérieur de la mère est l'objet à la phase d'exacerbation du sadisme[40]. Nous découvrons dans les analyses de jeunes enfants la peur de la mère cruelle qui exige restitution des selles et des enfants qui lui ont été volés. Ainsi la véritable mère, ou la nurse, lorsqu'elle impose des règles de propreté, devient-elle aussitôt pour l'enfant ce personnage terrible qui, dans son imagination effrayée, ne se contente pas d'insister pour qu'il lui rende ses selles mais songerait à les lui arracher de force. Une autre peur, encore plus effroyable, émane des imagos introjectées, dont le jeune enfant redoute des attaques aussi féroces à l'intérieur de son corps que ses fantasmes de destruction dirigés contre les objets du monde extérieur.

LE BESOIN DE SAVOIR CE QUI SE PASSE « A L'INTÉRIEUR » PARTICIPE À LA FORMATION DU CARACTÈRE OBSSESSIONNEL

Les excréments sont à cette époque identifiés à des substances dangereuses capables de brûler et d'empoisonner, à toutes sortes d'armes offensives ; c'est pourquoi l'enfant est alors terrorisé par ses propres excréments, comme s'ils devaient lui détruire l'intérieur du corps. L'équivalence sadique des excréments avec des substances destructrices, en plus des fantasmes d'agressions réalisées avec leur concours, amène en outre l'enfant à craindre d'être attaqué avec les mêmes moyens par ses objets tant extérieurs qu'intérieurs et à être terrorisé par les excréments et par toute saleté. Ces sources d'angoisse, d'autant plus redoutables qu'elles sont plus variées, constituent, d'après mon expérience, les causes les plus profondes des sentiments d'angoisse et de culpabilité liés à l'apprentissage de la propreté.

Les formations réactionnelles de dégoût, d'ordre et de propreté chez l'enfant remontent ainsi à l'angoisse, aux multiples origines, qui est engendrée par ses toutes premières situations de danger. Les senti-

40. L'opinion généralement admise associe par régression au dressage à la propreté le sentiment de culpabilité qui apparaît au stade génital ; elle ne tient pas compte toutefois de l'importance des sentiments de culpabilité en cause ni de leurs rapports étroits avec les tendances prégénitales. L'impression définitive laissée chez l'adulte par sa première éducation de la propreté et la manière dont celle-ci influence tout son développement ultérieur (ainsi qu'on le constate à maintes reprises dans les analyses d'adultes) indiquent l'existence d'une relation plus profonde et plus directe entre cet apprentissage et d'intenses sentiments de culpabilité. Dans *Psycho-Analysis of Sexual Habits* (1925), Ferenczi suggère l'existence d'une relation plus directe entre ces deux faits et peut-être d'une sorte de précurseur physiologique du Surmoi qu'il appelle « morale sphinctérienne ».

ments réactionnels de pitié sont particulièrement visibles, comme on sait, au début du second stade anal, qui amène une évolution dans les relations objectales. C'est aussi à ce moment, comme nous l'avons vu, que l'approbation venant de ses objets rassure l'enfant et le protège d'une destruction effectuée du dedans ou du dehors ; de leur restauration dépend sa propre intégrité corporelle[41]. L'angoisse des premières situations de danger me paraît intimement liée à l'éclosion des manifestations et des névroses obsessionnelles. Cette angoisse se rapportant à des blessures et à des destructions de toutes sortes à l'intérieur même du corps, c'est là également que doit s'accomplir la réparation. Mais l'enfant ne peut obtenir aucune certitude précise sur l'intérieur de son propre corps ou de celui de ses objets, ni sur le bien-fondé de sa crainte d'être blessé et attaqué au-dedans de lui-même, ni sur l'effet propitiatoire de ses pratiques obsessionnelles ; il n'en devient que plus anxieux et obsédé par le besoin de savoir. Il cherchera à maîtriser son angoisse, dont le caractère imaginaire défie tout examen critique, en se montrant pointilleux à l'excès, en s'attachant davantage à tout ce qui est réalité extérieure. On voit comment le doute qui naît de cette incertitude participe à la formation du caractère obsessionnel et aussi des tendances à la précision, à l'ordre, à l'accomplissement de certaines règles, de rituels[42].

L'angoisse issue des situations anxiogènes primitives se signale également par son intensité et ses nombreux aspects, dus à la multiplicité de ses sources. Le caractère des obsessions en porte la marque et les mécanismes de défense y puisent leur énergie. L'enfant se sent poussé à nettoyer et à rassembler de manière obsessionnelle tout ce qu'il a sali, brisé ou abîmé, à embellir et à restaurer l'objet endommagé par une variété de moyens qui s'accordent dans le détail avec ses divers fantasmes sadiques.

L'entourage de l'obsédé est souvent la victime de cette contrainte aussi bien que le malade. J'y verrais le résultat d'une projection à plusieurs aspects. Le névrosé cherche d'abord à se défaire de la compulsion intolérable dont il souffre, en traitant son objet comme son propre

---

41. A un ou deux endroits, Abraham corrobore cette conception, qui fait apparaître très tôt, dès la deuxième année, dans le développement du Moi, les formations réactionnelles et le sentiment de culpabilité. Il écrit, dans *Short Study of the Development of the Libido* (1924) : « Au cours du stade narcissique revêtant un but sexuel cannibalique, la première manifestation d'une inhibition instinctuelle se présente sous la forme d'angoisse morbide. Le processus qui aura raison des pulsions cannibaliques est intimement lié à un sentiment de culpabilité apparaissant comme un phénomène typique d'inhibition au cours du troisième stade » (p. 496).

42. Dans les *Notes upon a Case of Obsessional Neurosis* (1909), Freud fait l'observation suivante : « D'autre part, la compulsion est une tentative pour compenser le doute et corriger les conditions intolérables d'inhibition dont témoigne le doute » (p. 378).

Ça ou son Surmoi, et en reportant sur lui la contrainte de ces deux instances. De la sorte, il satisfait accessoirement son sadisme primaire par les sévices et la tyrannie qu'il exerce sur son objet. En second lieu, il détourne sur les objets du monde extérieur sa crainte d'être détruit ou attaqué par ses objets introjectés. Cette peur provoque en lui un besoin compulsif de contrôle et de domination sur ses imagos ; comme il ne parvient pas à réaliser ce souhait avec ses objets intériorisés, il les remplace par des objets extérieurs qu'il voudra se soumettre.

Si je ne me trompe pas en affirmant que l'ampleur et l'intensité des activités obsessionnelles et la gravité de la névrose dépendent des proportions et de la nature de l'angoisse que suscitent les premières situations anxiogènes, nous comprendrons mieux les liens étroits et connus qui rapprochent de la paranoïa les formes plus aiguës de la névrose obsessionnelle. D'après Abraham, la libido régresse, dans la paranoïa, au premier stade sado-anal. Mes propres observations m'inciteraient à aller plus avant. Au cours du premier stade sado-anal, l'enfant, sous l'effet de situations anxiogènes primitives assez puissantes, traverse des crises paranoïdes frustes, mais réelles, qui seront normalement surmontées au stade suivant, soit au second stade sado-anal. La gravité de la névrose obsessionnelle est en rapport avec l'importance des troubles de nature paranoïde qui l'ont juste précédée. L'échec des mécanismes obsessionnels ouvre la voie aux manifestations paranoïdes sous-jacentes, et même à une franche psychose paranoïaque.

DES PRATIQUES OBSESSIONNELLES OBSERVÉES CHEZ LES ENFANTS

Nous savons de quelle angoisse s'accompagne la répression des pratiques obsessionnelles ; c'est la preuve qu'elles sont destinées à vaincre l'angoisse. En admettant que l'angoisse dominée de cette façon provient des situations anxiogènes les plus primitives et qu'elle atteint son paroxysme dans la peur qu'éprouve l'enfant de voir détruire de toutes sortes de manières son propre corps et celui de ses objets, nous parviendrons, me semble-t-il, à une compréhension meilleure et plus profonde de bien des actes de type obsessionnel. La compulsion à accumuler des objets et à s'en démunir devient d'autant plus claire à nos yeux que nous pouvons mieux identifier l'angoisse et la culpabilité qui sont à la base de tout échange au niveau anal. Cette compulsion à prendre, puis à rendre, s'exprime sous les formes les plus diverses dans l'analyse par le jeu, et apparaît, avec des manifestations d'angoisse et de culpabilité, par réaction contre des fantasmes de vol et de destruction. Des enfants, par exemple, transporteront en entier ou en partie le contenu d'une boîte dans une autre, ils y rangeront soigneusement chacun des objets, pour les conserver avec toutes les marques de l'angoisse, et, s'ils ont l'âge voulu, iront jusqu'à les compter un a un. Ce contenu est très varié et comprend des allumettes brûlées (l'enfant se donnera souvent la peine de les frotter pour en détacher la cendre), des découpages, des crayons, des cubes de construction, des bouts de ficelle, et une multitude d'objets. C'est là tout ce que l'enfant a pris dans l'intérieur de sa mère : le pénis du père, les enfants, des selles, de l'urine, du lait, et le reste. Il peut agir de même avec des blocs de papier, en arrachant les feuilles qu'il mettra ensuite dans un endroit sûr. En raison de son angoisse qui augmente, il ne lui suffit pas toujours de remettre ce qu'il a symboliquement pris dans l'intérieur de sa mère, pour satisfaire son besoin compulsif de donner, ou, plutôt, de restaurer. Il est sans cesse contraint de rendre, sous des formes diverses, plus qu'il n'a pris, mais ses pulsions sadiques primitives réussissent quand même à percer dans ses efforts de réparation, à côté de ses tendances réactionnelles.

Ainsi, à cette phase de son analyse, un de mes petits malades, John, âgé de cinq ans, qui était un enfant très névrosé, se mit à avoir la manie de compter ; ce symptôme avait peu attiré l'attention, comme c'est assez courant à son âge. Au cours de son analyse, il notait soigneusement sur la feuille de papier la position de ses petits personnages et de ses autres jouets avant de les placer sur une autre feuille. Non content de savoir exactement où ils avaient été posés afin de les remettre sans se tromper au même endroit, il ne cessait de les compter pour s'assurer du nombre d'objets (des selles, le pénis du père et les enfants), qu'il avait pris à sa mère et qu'il lui fallait rendre. Ce faisant, il me traitait de femme sotte et méchante, et disait : « Il est *impossible* d'enlever treize de dix, ou sept de deux. » Cette peur d'avoir à rendre plus qu'on ne possède est caractéristique des enfants ; elle s'explique à la fois par la différence de taille entre eux et les adultes, et par les proportions que prend leur sentiment de culpabilité. Ils se croient incapables de rendre, avec leur petit corps, tout ce qu'ils ont pris à celui de leur mère, si énorme à leurs yeux en comparaison du leur ; le poids de leur culpabilité, qui leur reproche sans cesse de voler et de détruire leur mère ou leurs parents, renforce leur conviction de ne pouvoir jamais rendre assez. L'impression, qu'ils ont très tôt, de « ne pas savoir », alimente encore leur angoisse. Je voudrais revenir sur ce sujet plus loin.

300

UNE ANGOISSE ACCRUE
PEUT PROVOQUER UNE RÉGRESSION
A UN STADE ANTÉRIEUR DU DÉVELOPPEMENT

Il arrive très souvent que les productions infantiles à thème de « restitution » soient interrompues par un besoin d'aller à la selle. Un autre de mes petits malades, du même âge que John, devait aller parfois à la toilette à quatre ou cinq reprises pendant sa séance, à la même phase de son analyse. Quand il revenait, il se mettait à compter de façon obsessionnelle, afin de se convaincre, en atteignant des nombres élevés, qu'il avait de quoi rendre ce qu'il avait dérobé. L'accumulation de biens, une activité sado anale qui semble motivée par le plaisir d'amasser pour amasser, prend dans ce contexte un tout autre sens. Dans les analyses d'adultes, je me suis également rendu compte qu'en désirant avoir à sa disposition des sommes d'argent pour parer à l'imprévu, on veut en fait s'armer contre une attaque éventuelle de la mère qu'on a volée, afin d'être en mesure de lui rendre ce qui lui a été enlevé. (Dans plusieurs cas, la mère de ces malades était décédée depuis de nombreuses années.) La peur d'être dépouillé du contenu de leur corps les oblige à accumuler sans cesse plus d'argent de manière à ne jamais manquer de « réserves » disponibles. Par exemple, lorsque John eut convenu avec moi que c'était sa crainte de ne pouvoir rendre à sa mère tous les excréments et les enfants dérobés, qui le forçait à tout couper en morceaux et à voler, il me fournit d'autres raisons de son incapacité à restituer en entier ce qu'il avait pris. Il me dit que ses selles avaient fondu entre-temps, qu'enfin il n'avait cessé de les donner et que même s'il en formait de nouvelles sans arrêt, il ne parviendrait jamais à en faire assez. D'ailleurs, il ignorait si ses excréments seraient « assez bons ». Ce doute portait d'abord sur la valeur de ses selles, qui devait être égale à ce qu'il avait pris à sa mère — d'où, soit dit en passant, le soin qu'il mettait à choisir formes et couleurs dans les scènes de restitution. Mais, à un niveau plus profond, « assez bons » signifiait inoffensifs, non toxiques[43]. D'autre part, sa fréquente constipation se rattachait au besoin d'amasser ses selles et de les garder en lui, de manière à n'être jamais vide. Toutes ces tendances contradictoires, j'en ai mentionné seulement quelques-unes, provoquaient chez lui une très vive angoisse. Chaque fois que grandissait sa peur de ne pouvoir produire des selles avec la qualité ou la quantité voulues, ou encore de ne pouvoir réparer ce qu'il avait abîmé, ses tendances destructrices primaires

---

43. Dans : *Fear, Guilt and Hate* (1929), Ernest Jones observe que le mot « innocent » veut dire « qui ne fait pas mal », de sorte qu'être innocent signifie ne pas faire de mal.

retrouvaient toute leur virulence, son besoin de détruire devenait insatiable, et il se mettait à déchirer, à couper en morceaux et à brûler ce qu'il avait fabriqué quand prédominaient ses tendances réactionnelles, comme la boîte qu'il avait collée et remplie, représentant sa mère, ou le papier sur lequel il avait dessiné un plan de ville. Son comportement faisait alors ressortir dans toute son étendue la signification sadique primitive de l'acte d'uriner et de déféquer. Il déchirait du papier, le coupait en morceaux, le brûlait, il mouillait des objets avec de l'eau, les souillait avec de la cendre, les barbouillait avec un crayon — toujours dans le même but de destruction. Mouiller et salir avaient le sens de fondre, de noyer ou d'empoisonner. Des boulettes de papier mouillé, par exemple, figuraient des projectiles empoisonnés particulièrement dangereux à cause du mélange d'urine et de selles dont ils étaient faits. Les divers détails de ses productions montraient que la signification sadique attachée aux actes d'uriner et de déféquer était à la source de son sentiment de culpabilité et du besoin de réparation qui se traduisait par ses mécanismes obsessionnels.

Le fait qu'un surcroît d'angoisse amène une régression aux mécanismes de défense de stades plus anciens met en lumière le rôle décisif du Surmoi écrasant de la phase initiale du développement. La pression exercée par ce Surmoi primitif renforce les fixations sadiques de l'enfant et l'oblige à répéter de manière incessante et compulsive ses premiers actes destructeurs. Sa crainte de ne pouvoir remettre les choses en état ranime une peur encore plus profonde, celle d'être livré à la vengeance des objets qu'il a tués dans son imagination et qui ne cessent de le harceler. Il utilise alors des mécanismes de défense qui appartiennent aux stades antérieurs : quand on ne peut apaiser ou satisfaire quelqu'un, il faut le supprimer. Le Moi faible de l'enfant est incapable d'arriver à un compromis avec un Surmoi aussi brutal et menaçant ; c'est seulement plus tard que son angoisse prend aussi la forme d'un sentiment de culpabilité et qu'elle suscite l'action des mécanismes obsessionnels. On découvre avec étonnement qu'à cette phase de son analyse, l'enfant, en obéissant à ses fantasmes sadiques sous l'empire d'une angoisse intense, trouve son plus grand plaisir à la dominer.

LES PRATIQUES MAGIQUES : UNE DÉFENSE CONTRE LES SOUHAITS DE MORT

A chaque poussée d'angoisse chez l'enfant, son désir de posséder fait place à un désir de pouvoir restituer, en raison du besoin qu'il éprouve d'être en état d'affronter les menaces de son Surmoi et de ses objets. Ce désir toutefois ne saurait être satisfait que si l'angoisse et le conflit ne dépassent pas certaines limites ; aussi voyons-nous l'enfant très névrosé inlassablement soumis à la compulsion de prendre pour être à même de donner. (Ce facteur psychologique est présent dans tous les troubles fonctionnels de l'intestin, ainsi que dans un grand nombre d'affections somatiques.) Réciproquement, avec la baisse de l'angoisse, les tendances réactionnelles perdent leur caractère violent et compulsif, irrégulier et instable, pour se faire sentir avec plus de modération et de continuité, et devenir en même temps moins susceptibles d'être troublées par les pulsions destructrices. Il apparaît alors de plus en plus clairement que l'enfant subordonne sa propre restauration à celle de ses objets. Les forces destructrices n'ont certes pas cessé complètement d'agir, mais elles n'ont plus leur violence de naguère et peuvent mieux se plier aux exigences du Surmoi. Et tout en participant aux formations réactionnelles, dans le second des deux moments successifs dont se compose l'acte obsessionnel, elles se laissent plus facilement diriger par le Surmoi et le Moi et deviennent libres de poursuivre des buts approuvés par ces instances.

On n'ignore pas le lien étroit qui rattache les actes obsessionnels à la « toute-puissance de la pensée ». Freud a fait ressortir le caractère essentiellement magique de certaines pratiques de type obsessionnel chez les primitifs. « Si ce ne sont pas des actes de magie, écrit-il, ce sont tout au moins des actes de contre-magie, destinés à prévenir le malheur, dont l'attente marque habituellement le début de la névrose. » Il ajoute : « Les formules propitiatoires de la névrose obsessionnelle ont leur pendant dans les incantations. On observe, dans la genèse des actes obsessionnels, qu'ils commencent par être une sorte de sorcellerie dirigée contre des désirs maléfiques et tenue à l'écart de toute contagion sexuelle, pour se substituer à la fin aux activités sexuelles interdites qu'elles essayent d'imiter fidèlement[44]. » Nous verrons donc dans les actes obsessionnels de contre-sorcellerie, outre des activités sexuelles, une protection contre les mauvais désirs, plus précisément contre les souhaits de mort[45].

Nous devrions retrouver ces éléments, réunis pour une action de défense, dans les fantasmes et les actes qui ont d'abord éveillé un sentiment de culpabilité et ainsi provoqué cette action défensive. Un semblable mélange de magie, de souhaits maléfiques et d'activités sexuelles, existe, à mon avis, dans une situation décrite au chapitre

44. *Totem und Tabu* (1912), p. 108.
45. Décrivant le malade obsessionnel, Freud écrit dans *Totem und Tabu* (1912) : « Cependant, son sentiment de culpabilité est justifié, car il est fondé sur la présence, dans l'inconscient de l'obsédé, d'intenses et fréquents désirs de mort à l'égard de ses semblables » (p. 145).

précédent, dans la masturbation chez le petit enfant. Je montrais que les fantasmes masturbatoires dont s'accompagnent les débuts du conflit œdipien sont, comme ce conflit même, entièrement dominés par les pulsions sadiques. Ces fantasmes se centrent sur le coït des parents et se rapportent à des attaques sadiques dirigées contre eux ; c'est ainsi qu'ils deviennent une des sources les plus profondes de la culpabilité dans l'enfance. J'en concluais que si la masturbation, et en général toute activité sexuelle, revêt pour l'enfant cet aspect de mal et d'interdiction, c'est à cause de la culpabilité qu'il ressent à l'égard des pulsions destructrices dont ses parents sont l'objet, et que par conséquent la culpabilité de l'enfant ne se rattache pas à sa libido incestueuse, mais à ses tendances destructrices[46].

SENTIMENT DE TOUTE PUISSANCE INFANTILE ET CONFIANCE EN SOI

La phase du développement où je situe le point de départ du conflit œdipien et des fantasmes masturbatoires de caractère sadique qui l'entourent, est celle du narcissisme, dans laquelle, pour citer Freud, « les actions psychiques sont très valorisées, et, à notre point de vue, surestimées[47] ». A cette époque, et c'est là une de ses particularités, l'enfant éprouve, à l'égard de ses fonctions vésicales et intestinales d'évacuation, un sentiment de toute-puissance qu'il applique par extension à ses pensées[48]. Il ne peut donc que se sentir coupable de toutes ses attaques imaginaires contre ses parents. Cet excès même de culpabilité, qui découle de la foi en la toute-puissance des excréments et des pensées, constitue précisément, à mes yeux, l'un des facteurs qui poussent névrosés et primitifs à conserver leur sentiment originel de toute-puissance ou à y régresser. Quand leur culpabilité déclenche des actes obsessionnels en guise de défense, ils se servent de leur culpabilité dans un but de réparation, mais ils doivent alors la subir sous une forme

46. Au chapitre I de *La Psychanalyse des enfants*, j'ai signalé déjà le lien existant entre mes propres idées sur ce sujet et certaines des conclusions auxquelles Freud est arrivé dans on ouvrage *Civilization and its Discontents* (1930) : « C'est donc en fait uniquement l'agressivité qui, ayant été supprimée, est assumée par le Surmoi et se transforme en sentiment de culpabilité. Je suis persuadé que de nombreux processus s'expliqueront plus simplement et plus clairement si les découvertes de la psychanalyse réduisent aux pulsions agressives l'origine du sentiment de culpabilité » (p. 131). Et encore : « Il semble maintenant possible de formuler la proposition suivante : lorsqu'une tendance instinctuelle est refoulée, ses éléments libidinaux se transforment en symptômes et ses composantes agressives en sentiment de culpabilité » (p. 132).

47. *Totem und Tabu* (1912), p. 110.

48. Ferenczi a attiré l'attention, dans son travail *Stages in the Development of a Sense of Reality* (1913), sur la relation entre les fonctions anales et la toute-puissance de la parole et du geste. Voir également Abraham, *The Narcissistic Evaluation of Excretory Processes in Dreams and Neurosis* (1920).

compulsive et excessive, leurs réparations étant obligatoirement sous le même signe de la toute-puissance que leurs destructions.

« Il est difficile, a dit Freud, de savoir si ces premiers actes obsessionnels et propitiatoires sont soumis au principe de la ressemblance ou du contraste, car dans la structure de la névrose ils sont le plus souvent déformés, par le déplacement, en une bagatelle, en une action par elle-même tout à fait insignifiante[49]. » Les analyses de jeunes enfants ne laissent subsister aucun doute à ce sujet ; elles démontrent· que les mécanismes de réparation, leur nature et leur intensité s'expliquent finalement, et dans chaque détail, par ce principe de ressemblance, ou de contraste. Si avec les fantasmes sadiques persistent de très forts sentiments primitifs de toute-puissance, l'enfant n'en aura qu'une plus grande foi dans la toute-puissance créatrice qui doit l'aider dans ses tentatives de réparation. On voit très clairement, dans les analyses d'enfants et d'adultes, à quel point ce facteur favorise ou inhibe un comportement constructif et réactionnel de ce genre. Leur sentiment de toute-puissance à l'égard de leurs aptitudes réparatrices n'est en aucune façon comparable à celui qu'ils éprouvent à l'égard de leurs aptitudes destructrices ; rappelons-nous que les formations réactionnelles se dessinent à une phase du développement du Moi et des relations objectales où l'enfant a acquis une connaissance plus exacte de la réalité. Ainsi, lorsqu'il faut à l'individu, pour ses besoins de réparation, un sentiment excessif de sa toute-puissance, est il entravé dès le début par son manque de confiance dans ses capacités réparatrices[50].

LE « BESOIN DE SAVOIR » DE L'ENFANT CONCERNE PRIMITIVEMENT LA MÈRE

J'ai constaté chez certains de mes analysés qu'un facteur supplémentaire aggravait l'effet de cette disposition entre les potentialités destructrices et réparatrices. Quand le sadisme primaire du malade et son sentiment de toute-puissance avaient atteint dans les premières années de sa vie une intensité excessive, ses tendances réactionnelles s'en trouvaient également renforcées ; ses fantasmes de réparation émanaient alors de fantasmes mégalomaniaques. Dans son imagination d'enfant, les ravages causés par lui avaient quelque chose de gigantesque et d'unique en leur genre ; il lui fallait donc réparer de façon

---

49. *Totem und Tabu* (1912), p. 108.

50. Dans une discussion portant sur ce thème, M.-N. Searl a fait remarquer que la tendance réparatrice de l'enfant est inhibée par ses premières expériences, car s'il est facile de casser des choses, il est extrêmement difficile de les réparer. Une telle évidence des faits doit contribuer, je pense, a accroître ses doutes sur ses pouvoirs créateurs.

identique. Cette impossibilité suffirait déjà à mettre en échec la réalisation de ses tendances constructives, quoique, je le mentionne en passant, deux de ces malades eussent des talents artistiques et créateurs remarquables. Ses fantasmes mégalomaniaques n'empêchent pas ce type de malade de n'être nullement sûr de pouvoir disposer de la toute-puissance qu'il lui faudra déployer pour accomplir des réparations d'une telle étendue. Il tentera donc de nier sa toute-puissance jusque dans ses actes de destruction, mais chaque fois qu'elle lui sert dans un sens positif, il obtient par le fait même la preuve qu'elle s'est auparavant exercée dans le sens contraire ; il devra par conséquent éviter de l'utiliser tant qu'il ne sera pas tout à fait persuadé du parfait équilibre des manifestations opposées de sa toute-puissance. L'attitude du « tout ou rien », qui découle du conflit de ces tendances, avait gravement compromis, chez les deux adultes auxquels j'ai fait allusion, leur capacité de travail, et chez quelques-uns de mes petits malades, le processus de sublimation.

Ce mécanisme ne semble pas spécifiquement obsessionnel. Je l'ai observé chez des malades qui présentaient un tableau clinique complexe, différent d'une pure névrose obsessionnelle. Grâce à un mécanisme, si important dans cette maladie, du « déplacement sur des vétilles », l'obsédé se contente de réalisations assez pauvres pour se convaincre de sa toute-puissance et de sa capacité de réparation intégrale. Les doutes qu'il peut entretenir sur ce point[51] l'incitent, dans son cas, à répéter ses actes de manière obsessionnelle.

Les pulsions « épistémophiliques » et sadiques sont étroitement unies ; c'est là un fait bien connu. « On a souvent l'impression, écrit Freud, que le désir de savoir, en particulier, peut se substituer réellement au sadisme, dans la névrose obsessionnelle[52]. » D'après mes constatations, ce lien s'établit à un moment très précoce de la formation du Moi, au cours de la phase d'exacerbation du sadisme. A cette époque, les besoins épistémophiliques sont activés par le conflit œdipien naissant, et sont tout d'abord au service des tendances sado-orales. Leur premier objet semble être l'intérieur du corps de la mère, que l'enfant considère, pour commencer, comme une source de satisfaction orale, puis comme l'endroit où s'effectue le coït des parents et où se trouvent le pénis du père et les enfants. Tout en voulant pénétrer par la force dans le corps de la mère pour s'emparer de son contenu et le détruire, il souhaiterait également savoir ce qui s'y passe et de quoi cela peut avoir l'air. Les

---

51. Dans *Notes upon a Case of Obsessional Neurosis* (1909). Freud explique le doute chez l'obsédé comme un « doute qui porte sur son amour même. [...] Celui qui doute de son propre amour pourra douter, ou plutôt, *ne pourra* faire autrement que de douter de n'importe quoi » (p. 376).
52. *The Predisposition to Obsessional Neurosis* (1924).

désirs de connaître l'intérieur de la mère et d'y pénétrer par effraction sont assimilés l'un à l'autre, se renforcent mutuellement et deviennent interchangeables. Ainsi se forment les liens qui unissent aux pulsions sadiques, rendues à leur apogée, les besoins épistémophiliques naissants ; on comprend qu'ils soient si intimement rapprochés et que ces derniers suscitent des sentiments de culpabilité[53].

LA CONNAISSANCE : UN MOYEN
DE LUTTE CONTRE L'ANGOISSE

Nous voyons le jeune enfant accablé par une foule de questions et de problèmes qu'il se pose sans que son intelligence soit encore apte à les résoudre. Son reproche typique est qu'on ne répond pas à ses questions, et il en fait grief surtout à sa mère, qui ne satisfait pas davantage son besoin de savoir qu'elle n'a satisfait ses besoins de nature orale. Ce reproche joue un rôle important dans le développement aussi bien du caractère que des tendances épistémophiliques. L'accusation remonte à des temps reculés, qui ont précédé l'acquisition du langage, car ce grief est souvent associé à un autre, qui se rapporte à cette période et dans lequel il se plaint de ne pouvoir comprendre ce que disent les grandes personnes ou les mots qu'elles emploient. Ces griefs, soit isolés soit réunis, sont extraordinairement chargés d'affect ; en cours d'analyse, l'enfant parle alors de manière à ne pas être compris, tout en reproduisant la rage qu'il ressentit pour la première fois à l'époque préverbale de son développement[54] : il devient incapable de formuler verbalement ses questions ou de comprendre une explication verbale. Mais ces questions, en partie du moins, sont toujours demeurées inconscientes. Les troubles importants des tendances épistémophiliques remontent à la déception inévitable qui en accompagne les manifestations originelles aux premières phases de la formation du Moi[55].

Nous avons vu que ce sont d'abord les pulsions sadiques dont l'intérieur de la mère est l'objet qui activent le besoin épistémophilique, mais l'angoisse qu'elles ne manquent pas de susciter renforce et intensifie de nouveau ce besoin. La peur qu'éprouve l'enfant à l'égard des dangers qu'il se représente dans l'intérieur de sa mère, au dedans de lui-même et dans ses objets introjectés, le pousse encore davantage à découvrir ce que recèlent l'intérieur de sa mère et son propre corps. La

---

53. Cf. Abraham, *Psycho-Analytical Studies on Character Formation* (1925).
54. Ainsi agissait Rita, âgée de deux ans neuf mois, pendant son analyse (voir chapitre II).
55. L'hostilité ressentie vis-à-vis des gens qui parlent une autre langue et la difficulté d'apprendre une langue étrangère me semblent dériver de ces premières déceptions des pulsions épistémophiliques.

connaissance devient alors un moyen de maitriser l'angoisse, et le besoin de savoir, un facteur essentiel dans la croissance et l'inhibition des tendances épistémophiliques. L'angoisse en accélère ou en retarde le développement comme pour la libido. Nous avons eu l'occasion, dans *La Psychanalyse des enfants,* de discuter quelques cas graves de la pathologie de ce besoin[56], et nous nous sommes rendu compte de la terreur qui s'empare de l'enfant lorsqu'il prend connaissance des effroyables destructions fantasmatiques perpétrées par lui dans l'intérieur de sa mère et de représailles non moins terribles qu'il s'est ainsi attirées. L'ensemble de ses désirs de savoir s'en trouve profondément affecté, de sorte que sa curiosité, si intense et si peu satisfaite, qui portait primitivement sur la forme, les dimensions et le nombre des pénis paternels, des excréments et des enfants contenus dans la mère, se transforme en un besoin compulsif de mesurer, d'additionner et d'énumérer.

Avec le renforcement des pulsions libidinales et l'atténuation des tendances destructrices, il se produit des changements qualitatifs dans le Surmoi, qui se manifeste de plus en plus à l'égard du Moi par des remontrances. Avec la diminution de l'angoisse, les mécanismes de réparation, ayant perdu de leur caractère obsessionnel gagnent en efficacité, et, dans le comportement de l'enfant, se dégagent avec plus de clarté des réactions d'un niveau spécifiquement génital. L'avènement du stade génital traduirait donc le triomphe ultime des éléments positifs dans les interactions qui, à mon sens, dominent tout le développement primitif de l'enfant et qui concernent les rapports réciproques de la projection et de l'introjection, des relations objectales et de la formation du Surmoi.

MÉLANIE KLEIN[57]

56. Voir les cas d'Erna (chapitre III), de Kenneth (chapitre IV) et d'Isle (chapitre V).
57. *La Psychanalyse des enfants* (« les Rapports entre la névrose obsessionnelle et les premiers stades de la formation du Surmoi »), p. 163-190.

BIBLIOGRAPHIE*

Liste des abréviations :

— *RFPsa : Revue française de psychanalyse.*
— *The Psychoanal. Quaterly : The Psychoanalytic Quarterly.*
— *Int. Univ. Press : International University Press.*
— *Int. J. of Psa : International Journal of Psychoanalysis.*
   JAPA : Journal of American Psychoanalytic Association.

ABRAHAM (G.), « le Corps, dépressif et déprimé », *RFPsa*, 1977, vol. XLI.
ABRAHAM (K.), « les Différences psychosexuelles entre l'hystérie et la démence précoce », *Œuvres complètes*, Payot, 1965, t. I, A, chap. III (1908) ; « les Relations psychologiques entre la sexualité et l'alcoolisme », *ibid.*, chap. IV (1908) ; « Mariage entre personnes apparentées et psychologie des névroses », *ibid.*, chap. V (1909) ; « les États oniriques hystériques », *ibid.*, chap. VII (1910) ; « le Cérémonial compliqué de certaines névrosées », *ibid.*, chap. X (1912) ; « Quelques remarques sur le rôle de grands-parents dans la psychologie des névrosés », *ibid.*, chap. XIV (1913) ; « Limitations et modifications du voyeurisme chez les névrosés », *Œuvres complètes*, t. II, chap. I (1913) ; « Effets "suggestifs" des médicaments dans les états névrotiques », *ibid.*, chap. II (1914) ; « A propos de l'exogamie névrotique. Contribution à l'étude comparée de la vie psychique des névrosés et des primitifs », *ibid.*, chap. III (1914) ; « Une forme particulière de résistance névrotique à la méthode psychanalytique », *ibid.*, chap. VII (1919) ; « les Névroses du dimanche », *ibid.*, chap. VIII (1919) ; « la Valorisation narcissique des excrétions dans le rêve et la névrose », *ibid.*, t. II, A, chap. X (1920) ; « Sauvetage et meurtre du père dans les fantasmes névrotiques », *ibid.*, chap. XVII (1922) ; « Mélancolie et névrose obsessionnelle : deux étapes de la phase sadique-anale », *Œuvres complètes*, t. II, (1924).
ADLER (A.), « On the organic bases of neuroses », *Minutes of the Vienna psychoanalytic society*, 1906-1908, vol. I ; « Sadism in life and neurosis-discussion », *ibid.* ; « The Oneness of the neuroses », *ibid.*, 1908-1910, vol. II ; *le Sens de la vie — Étude de psychologie individuelle comparée*, Payot, 1968 ; *les Névroses. Commentaires, observations et présentation des cas*, Paris, Aubier-Montaigne, coll. « la Chair et l'Esprit », 1969.

---

* Sauf en ce qui concerne les articles de Freud, on trouvera les références des extraits reproduits dans cet ouvrage à la section « origine des textes ».

Les névroses : l'homme et ses conflits

AIGRISSE (G.), *Psychothérapie analytique. Huit cas*, Paris, P.U.F., 1967.

AJURIA GUERRA (J. DE), « les Organisations névrotiques chez l'enfant », *Manuel de Psychiatrie de l'enfant*, Paris, Masson, 1970.

ALBY (J.), « Névroses de caractère et caractères névrotiques », *Encéphale*, 1958, vol. XLVII.

ALEXANDER (F.), « Neurosis and the whole personality », *Int. J. of Psa*, 1926, vol. VII ; *The psychoanalysis of the total personality. The application of Freud's theory of the ego to the neuroses*, New York, Mc Grath publishing Company, 1970.

ALEXANDER (J. M.) et ISAACS (K. S.), « Obéissance à la réalité : contribution à la théorie psychanalytique de la dépression », *RFPsa*, 1963, vol. XXVII.

ALLENDY (R. F.), « les Névroses », *Esprit nouveau*, 1924 ;

LAFORGUE (R.), *la Psychanalyse et les Névroses*, Payot, 1951

AMADO-LÉVY-VALENSY (E.), « Névroses et psychoses comme savoir actualisé », *le Dialogue psychanalytique*, Paris, P.U.F., 1972.

ANTHONY (E. J.) et BENEDEK (T.), *Depression and human existence*, Main Selection, 1976.

ARLOW (J.), « Conflit, régression et formation des symptômes », *RFPsa*, 1963, vol. XXVII.

AZOULAY (J.), « les États dépressifs », *Perspectives psychiatriques, 1963, vol. III*.

BADEL (D. W.), « Transitional and prepsychotic symptoms in depression », *Bull. of Philadel. Assoc. Psycho-anal.*, 1965, vol. XV.

BALINT (M.), « Incidence et évaluation des symptômes névrotiques », *le Médecin, son malade et la maladie*, Paris, Payot, 1966.

BARANDE (R.), « Aperçu clinique de la dépression névrotique », *Perspectives psychiatriques*, 1963 ; « les États dépressifs », *Perspectives psychiatriques*, 1963, vol. III.

BARAT (L.), « la Nature des maladies mentales et les méthodes psychoanalytiques », *J. Psycho-norm. et path.*, 1914, vol. XI.

BASTIDE (R.), « le Névrosé, l'Enfant et le Primitif », *Sociologie et psychanalyse*, Paris, P.U.F., 2ᵉ éd., 1972.

BECACHE (S.), « le Noir et le Rouge. Essai sur la dépression féminine », *RFPsa*, 1977, vol. XLI.

BECK (A.), *Depressive neurosis*, American handbook of psychiatry, 1974.

BEGOIN (J.), « Quelques remarques à propos de la structure de la sexualité dans la dépression », *RFPsa*, 1976, vol. XL.

BENEDEK (Th.), « Superego and depression », *in* LOEWENSTEIN (R. M.), NEWMAN (L. M.), SCHUR (M.), SOLNIT (A. J.), *Psychoanalysis − a general psychology*, 1966.

BENO (N.), « la Névrose dite réactionnelle », *RFPsa*, 1951, vol. XV, n° 3.

BERGERET (J.), « les États limites », *RFPsa*, 1970, vol. XXXIV ; *la Dépression et les états limites. Points de vue théorique, clinique et thérapeutique*, Payot, 1975 ; « Dépressivité et dépression. Dans le cadre de l'économie dépressive », *RFPsa*, 1976, vol. XL.

BERGERET (J.) et CALLIER (J.), « A propos de deux cas d'agoraphobie chez l'homme », *RFPsa*, 1969, vol. XXXIII.

BERGLER (E.), *The basic neurosis. Oral regression and psychic masochism*, Grune and Stratton, 1949 ; « les Neuf points de base de chaque névrose », *RFPsa*, 1960, vol. XXIV ; *la Névrose de base*, Payot, 1963.

BONNAFE (L.), EY (H.), FOLLIN (S.), LACAN (J.), ROUART (J.), « Problème de la psychogenèse des névroses et des psychoses », *Évolution psychiatrique*, 1951, vol. II.

Bouvet (M.), « Importance de l'aspect homosexuel du transfert dans le traitement de quatre cas de névrose obsessionnelle masculine », *RFPsa*, 1948, vol. XII ; « le Moi dans la névrose obsessionnelle », *RFPsa*, 1953, vol. XVII ; « Dépersonnalisation et relation d'objet », *RFPsa*, 1960, vol. XXIV ; « la Clinique psychanalytique – la relation d'objet », *RFPsa*, 1960, vol. XXIV.

Burger (M.), « l'Organisation orale chez une hystérique cleptomane », *RFPsa*, 1962, vol. XXVI.

Burrow (T.), « Character and the neuroses », *The Psychoanalytic Review*, 1913-1914, vol. I, n° 2.

Bychowski (G.), « Structure des dépressions chroniques et latentes », *RFPsa*, 1961, vol. XXV.

Codet (H.) et Laforgue (R.), « la Sexualité dans les névroses », *Évolution psychiatrique*, 1925, vol. I.

Covello (L.) et Covello (A.), « Épilepsie et névroses », *Épilepsie, symptôme ou maladie*, Paris, Hachette, 1971

Creasey (H. M.), « Psychoanalysis and its relation to the neurosis », *The Psychoanalytic Review*, 1921, vol. VIII.

Decobert (S.), « Étude clinique d'un cas d'agoraphobie », *RFPsa*, 1969, vol. XXXIII.

Deutsch (H.), *Neuroses and character types clinical psychoanalytic studies*, New York, Int. Univ. Press, 1965.

Diatkine (R.) et Favreau (J.), « le Caractère névrotique », *RFPsa*, 1956, vol. XX, p. 151-201.

Dolto (F.), « Éclaircissement sur la théorie freudienne des instances de la psyché au cours de l'évolution de la sexualité, en relation à l'Œdipe. Névrose et psychose », *le Cas Dominique*, Paris, Seuil, coll. « Points », 1971.

Dreyfus-Moreau, « Étude structurale de deux cas de névrose concentrationnaire », *Évolution psychiatrique*, 1952, vol. II.

Dujarier (L.), « A propos du traitement des maniaco-dépressifs », *RFPsa*, 1972, vol. XXXVI.

Hey (H.), « Contribution à l'étude des relations des crises de mélancolie et des crises de dépression névrotiques », *Évolution psychiatrique*, 1955, vol. III ;

Henric (E.), « Hérédité et névroses », *Évolution psychiatrique*, 1959, vol. II.

Fain (M.), « Contribution à l'étude des variations de la symptomatologie », *RFPsa*, 1962, vol. XXVI.

Fairbairn (R. D.), « A revised psychopathology of the psychoses and neuroses », *Int. J. of Psa*, 1941, vol. XXII ; « The repression anal and the return of bad objets with special reference to the "war neuroses", *Psychoanal. studies of the pers.*, 1952 ; « The war neuroses, their nature and significance », *ibid.*

Fenichel (O.), « Outline of clinical psychoanalysis », *The Psychoanal. Quarterly*, 1932, vol. I ; « Hysterien und Zwangsneurosen », *The Psychoanalytic Review*, 1932, vol. XIX ; « Neurotic acting out », *The Collected Papers of Otto Fenichel*, New York, Norton, 1954.

Ferenczi (S.), « les Névroses à la lumière de l'enseignement de Freud et de la psychanalyse », *Œuvres complètes*, t. I, chap. II (1908 ; « Des psychonévroses », *ibid.*, chap. V (1909) ; « l'Alcool et les névroses », *ibid.*, chap. XIV (1911) ; « le Développement du sens de réalité et ses stades », *Œuvres complètes*, t. II (1913) ; « Deux types de névroses de guerre », *ibid.* (1916) ; « Difficultés techniques d'analyse d'hystérie », *Œuvres complètes*, t. III, chap. I (1919) ; « Phénomènes de matérialisation hystérique », *ibid.*, chap. V (1919) ; « Psychanalyse d'un cas d'hypocondrie hystérique », *ibid.*, chap. VII (1919) : « Pour comprendre les psychonévroses du retour d'âge », *ibid.*, chap. xvii (1921) ; « la Psychanalyse et les troubles mentaux de la paralysie générale », *ibid.*, chap. xviii (1922) ; « Matérialisation dans le globus hystérique », *ibid.*, chap. xxvii (1923) ; « les Névroses d'organe et leur traitement », *ibid.*, chap. xlvi (1926).

Freeman (L.), *l'Histoire d'Anna O.*, Paris, P.U.F., coll. « Perspectives critiques ».

Freeman (Th.), « Aspects of defence in neurosis and psychosis », *Int. J. of Psa*, 1959, vol. XL.

Freud (A.), *le Moi et les mécanismes de défense*, P.U.F. ; « Problems of infantile neurosis : a discussion », *Psychoanalytic study of the child*, 1954, vol. IX.

Freud (S.), *les Psychonévroses de défense*, 1894 ; *Études sur l'hystérie*, 1893-1895, Paris, P.U.F., 1967 ; « Qu'il est justifié de séparer de la neurasthénie un certain complexe symptomatique sous le nom de "névrose d'angoisse", 1895, *Névrose, psychose et perversion*, Paris, P.U.F., 1973 ; « Nouvelles remarques sur les psychonévroses de défense », 1896, *Névrose, psychose et perversion*, Paris, P.U.F., 1973 ; « l'Hérédité et l'Étiologie des névroses », 1896, *Névrose, psychose et perversion*, Paris, P.U.F., 1973 ; *la Naissance de la psychanalyse*, Paris, P.U.F., 1969 ; « Fragment d'une analyse (Dora) », 1901-1905, *Cinq psychanalyses*, Paris, P.U.F., 1973 ; « les Fantasmes hystériques et leur relation à la bisexualité », 1908, *Névrose, psychose et perversion*, Paris, P.U.F., 1973 ; « Caractère et érotisme anal », 1908, *Névrose, psychose et perversion*, Paris, P.U.F., 1973 ; « Considérations générales sur l'attaque hystérique », 1909, *Névrose, psychose et perversion*, Paris, P.U.F., 1973 ; « Remarques sur un cas de névrose obsessionnelle (l'Homme aux rats »), 1909, *Cinq psychanalyses*, Paris, P.U.F., 1973 ; « Sur les types d'entrée dans la névrose », 1912, *Névrose, psychose et perversion*, Paris, P.U.F., 1973 ; « la Dynamique du transfert », 1912, *la Technique psychanalytique*, Paris, P.U.F., 1970 ; « la Disposition à la névrose obsessionnelle », 1913, *Névrose, psychose et perversion*, Paris, P.U.F., 1973 ; « Contribution à l'histoire du mouvement psychanalytique », *Cinq leçons sur la psychanalyse*, Petite Bibliothèque Payot, 1973 ; « Extrait de l'histoire d'une névrose infantile (l'Homme aux loups »), 1914-1916, *Cinq psychanalyses*, Paris, P.U.F., 1973 ; *Introduction à la psychanalyse*, 1921, Payot, 1961 ; *Ma vie et la psychanalyse*, 1924-1925, Gallimard, coll. « Idées », 1972. *Nouvelles conférences sur la psychanalyse*, 1933, Gallimard, coll. « Idées », 1971.

Geahchan (D. J.), « Haine et identification négative dans l'hystérie », *RFPsa*, 1973, vol. XXXVII.

Gehl (R.), « Dépression et claustrophobie », *RFPsa*, 1965, vol. XXIX.

Gendrot (J. A.) et Racamier (P. C.), « Névrose d'angoisse », *EMC Psychiatrie*, t. II, 1955.

Gero (G.), « The construction of depression », *Int. J. of Psa*, 1936, vol. XVII.

Gillespie (M.), « The psychoneuroses », *J. Ment. Sci.*, 1944, vol. XC.

Glover (E.), « The neurotic character », *On the early development of mind*, Imago pub. C., 1956 ; « The etiology of alcoholism », *ibid.* ; « A developmental study of the obsessional neuroses », *ibid.*

Green (A.), « Névrose obsessionnelle et hystérie ; leurs relations chez Freud et depuis », *RFPsa*, 1964, vol. XXVIII.

Greenacre (Th.), « Problems of infantile neurosis : a discussion », *Psychoanalytic study of the child*, vol. IX.

Grinberg (L.), « Rapports entre les mécanismes obsessionnels et certains troubles du Soi », *RFPsa*, 1967, vol. XXXI.

Grunberger (B.), Étude sur la dépression », *RFPsa*, 1965, vol. XXIX ; « En marge de "l'Homme aux Rats" », *RFPsa*, 1967, vol. XXXI ; « Conflit oral et hystérie », *RFPsa*, 1955.

GUILLAUMIN (J.), « l'Énergie et les structures dans l'expérience dépressive. Le rôle du préconscient », *RFPsa*, 1976, vol. XL.

HAYNAL (A.), « le Sens du désespoir », *RFPsa*, 1977, vol. XLI.

HELD (R.), « De la singularité de la structure obsessionnelle aux nécessités techniques impliquées par cette singularité », *RFPsa*, 1961, vol. XXV.

HOLLANDE (C.), « l'Humeur dépressive comme défense contre la dépression », *RFPsa*, 1976, vol. XL.

HORNEY (K.), « What is neurosis » ? *American Journal of Sociology*, 1939, vol. XLV, p. 426-432.

JANET (P.), *les Obsessions et la psychasthénie*, Paris, Alcan, 1903 ; *les Névroses*, Flammarion, 1909, 397 p. : « Qu'est-ce qu'une névrose ? » *Rev. scient.*, 1909, vol. XI, p. 129-138 ; *Névroses et idées fixes*, Paris, Alcan, 1924.

JONES (E.), « Des rapports entre la névrose d'angoisse et l'hystérie d'angoisse », *Traité théorique et pratique de psychanalyse*, Payot, 1925, chap. XXVII ; « Étude analytique d'un cas de névrose obsessionnelle », *ibid.*, chap. XXIX ; « Hate and anal erotism in the obsessional neurosis », *Int. Zeitschrift Psychoanalyse*, 1913 ; « Treatment of the neuroses », *The Psychoanalytic Review*, 1920, vol. VIII.

JOSEPH (B.), « Angoisse persécutoire chez un garçon de quatre ans », *RFPsa*, 1967, vol. XXXI.

JUNG (C. G.), « la Névrose et l'autorégulation psychologique », *la Guérison psychologique*, Genève, librairie de l'Université, Georg et Cie., 1970 ; « The etiology of the neuroses », *in* « The theory of psychoanalysis », *The Psychoanalytic Review*, 1913-1914, vol. I.

KELMAN (H.), « Psychoanalysis and the study of etiology : a definition of terms », *in* NAGLER (S. H.) et MERIN (J.), *The etiology of neuroses*, Sci. and Behav. Books, 1966.

KEMPF (E. J.), « Fundamental factors in the psychopathology and psychotherapy of malignant disorganization neuroses », *Medical Record*, 1937, vol. CXLVI.

KERSENBERG (J. S.), « Rythme et organisation dans le développement obsessionnel compulsif », *RFPsa*, 1967, vol. XXXI.

KESTENBERG (E.), « Contribution à l'étude des névroses de caractère », *RFPsa*, 1953, vol. XVII ; « Problèmes posés par la fin de traitements psychoanalytiques dans les névroses de caractère », *RFPsa*, 1966, vol. XXX.

KHAN (M. R.), « la Névrose infantile comme organisation du faux soi », *le Soi caché*, Paris, Gallimard, 1976.

KLEIN (M.), « Une névrose obsessionnelle chez une fillette de six ans », *la Psychanalyse des enfants*, 1932, Paris, P.U.F., 1975, chap. III ; « la Névrose chez l'enfant », *ibid.*, chap. VI ; « Sur la théorie de l'angoisse et de la culpabilité », *Développements de la psychanalyse*, 1948, Paris, P.U.F., 1976.

KUBIE (L. S.), « The neurosis wears a mask », *in* MAC IVER (R. M.), *Moments of personal discovery*, Inst. for religions and social studies, 1952.

LAFORGUE (R.), « The mechanisms of isolation in neurosis and their relation to schizophrenia », *Int. J. of Psa*, 1929, vol. X ; « De l'aspect psychosomatique des névroses », *Réflexions psychanalytiques*, Genève, éd. du Mont-Blanc, 1965.

LAMPL DE GROOT (J.), « Formation de symptômes et formation du caractère », *RFPsa*, 1963, vol. XXVII.

LAPLANCHE (J.), « Première théorie de l'angoisse : à propos de la névrose actuelle », *Bulletin de psychologie*, 1970-1971, vol. XXIV, n° 5-6.

LAPLASSOTTE (F.), « Sexualité et névrose avant Freud : une mise au point », *Psychanalyse à l'université*, 1978, vol. III, n° 10.

LEBOVICI (S.) et DIATKINE (R.), « Contribution à la théorie de la technique en psychanalyse infantile à la compréhension des névroses de caractère », *RFPsa*, 1966, vol. XXX.

et BRAUNSCHWEIG (D.), « A propos de la névrose infantile », *la Psychiatrie de l'enfant*, 1967, vol. X.

LECHAT (F.), « Névrose et religiosité », *RFPsa*, 1950, vol. XIV ; « Jamais deux sans trois (Considérations sur l'angoisse et sur les comportements névrotiques) », *RFPsa*, 1953, vol. XVII.

LECLAIRE (S.), « Observation : Philon ou l'obsessionnel & son désir », *Démasquer le réel*, Paris, Seuil, 1971.

LEUBA (J.), « la Pensée magique chez le névrosé », *RFPsa*, 1934, vol. VII.

LIBERMAN (D.), « Critères d'interprétation pour des patients à traits obsessionnels, *RFPsa*, 1967, vol. XXXI.

LOEWALD (H. W.), « The problem of defence and the neurotic interpretation of reality », *Int. J. of Psa*, 1952, vol. XXXIII ; « The transference neurosis ; comments on the concept and the phenomenon », *J.A.P.A.*, 1971, vol. XIX, n° 1.

LOEWENSTEIN (R. M.), « la Conception psychanalytique des névroses », *Évolution psychiatrique*, 1930.

LUBTCHANSKY (J.), « le Point de vue économique dans l'hystérie à partir de la notion de traumatisme dans l'œuvre de Freud », *RFPsa*, 1973, vol. XXXVII.

LUQUET (C. J.), « la Structure obsessionnelle », *RFPsa*, 1961, vol. XXV ; « Organisation objectale du Moi dépressif », *RFPsa*, 1976, vol. XL.

MC KERROW (J.C.), « Neuroses », *British J. of Med. Psychology*, 1924, vol. IV.

MALLET (J.), « la Dépression névrotique », *Évolution psychiatrique*, 1955, vol. III, p. 483-501.

MARTIN (A. R.), « The body's participation in neurotic conflicts », *Am. J. of Psychiatry*, 1948, vol. VIII ; « Emphasis on the healthy aspects of the patient in psychoanalysis : a round table discussion », *Am. J. of Psychiatry*, 1966, vol. XXVIII.

MARTY (P.), FAIN (M.), DE M'UZAN (M.) et DAVID (Ch.), « le Cas Dora et le point de vue psychosomatique », *RFPsa*, 1968, vol. XXXII.

MARTY (P.) et FAIN (M.), « la Dépression essentielle », *RFPsa*, 1968, vol. XXXII.

MASSERMAN (J. H.), « Neurosis and alcohol », *Am. J. of Psychiatry*, 1944, vol. CI ; « The neuroses progress », *Neurology and psychiatry*, 1948, vol. III.

et MURRIN (F. H.), « The neuroses », *ibid.*, 1950, vol. V, chap. XXVI.

et TOURLENTES (T.), « The neuroses », *ibid.*, 1951, vol. VI, chap. XXV.

et BACON (G. A.), « The neuroses », *ibid.*, 1952, vol. VII.

et DUSHKIN (M. A.), « The neuroses », *ibid.*, 1953, vol. VIII.

BERKWITS (G.) et PAUNCZ (A.), « The neuroses », *ibid.*, 1954, vol. IX.

et PAUNCZ (A.), « The neuroses », *ibid.*, 1955, vol. X.

PAUNCZ (A.) et NATHAN (R.), « The neuroses », *ibid.*, 1956, vol. XI.

ALAN (B.) et KLOTZ (M.), « The neuroses », *ibid.*, 1957, vol. XII.

PAUNCZ (A.), SCHER (J.) et NORTON (A.), « The neuroses », *ibid.*, 1958, vol. XIII.

PAUNCZ (A.) et SCHMITT (J. O.), « The neuroses », *ibid.*, 1960, vol. XV.

PAUNCZ (A.) et PARKS (F. M.), « The neuroses », *ibid.*, 1961, vol. XVI.

KAGAN (I. N.) et PAUNCZ (A.), « The neuroses », *ibid.*, 1962, vol. XVII.

KOSTRUBALA (T.) et STERN (J. J.), « The neuroses », *ibid.*, 1963, vol. XVIII.

KOSTRUBALA (T.) et FARKAS (M. E.), « The neuroses », *ibid.*, 1964, vol. XIX.

KOSTRUBALA (T.) et D. W. SOLD (D. D.), « The neuroses », *ibid.*, 1965, vol. XX.

SMALL (S. R.), FAI (L. L.) et KAPPLIS (H. C.), « The neuroses », *ibid.*, 1967, vol. XXII.

et WIGDAHL (L. C.), « The neuroses », *ibid.*, 1968, vol. XXIII.

et BORELLI (N.), « The neuroses », *ibid.*, 1969, vol. XXIV.

MENNINGER (W. C.), « Neuropsychiatry and the general practitioner », *J. Michigan State Medic. Soc.,* 1944, vol. XLIII.

MIJOLLA (A. DE) et SHENTOUB (S. A.), *Pour une psychanalyse de l'alcoolisme,* Payot ; « Élise dans la voiture », *RFPsa,* 1969, vol. XXXIII.

MORGENTHALER (F.), « Régression fonctionnelle du Moi et problèmes techniques dans l'analyse des névroses obsessionnelles », *RFPsa,* 1967, vol. XXXI.

MOSS (R. E.), « The neuroses : their diagnosis and treatment », *Med. Clinics North America,* septembre 1950, p. 1487-1497.

M'UZAN (M. DE), « transfert et névrose de transfert : en relisant "analyse terminée et analyse interminable", *RFPsa,* 1968, vol. XXXII ; « Transferts et névrose de transfert », *De l'art à la mort,* Paris, Gallimard, 1977.

NACHT (S.), « Cause et mécanismes des déformations névrotiques du Moi », *RFPsa,* 1958, vol. XXII ; « la Névrose de transfert et son maniement technique », *ibid.* ; « Problèmes techniques de la cure des névroses obsessionnelles », *RFPsa,* 1961, vol. XXV ; « Particularité technique du traitement des phobiques », *RFPsa,* 1964, vol. XXVIII.

NAGERA (H.), *les Troubles de la petite enfance,* P.U.F., 1969.

OCKER (G.), *Die Neurosen,* Berlin, Sicker, 1949, 63 pages.

ODIER (C.), « la Névrose obsessionnelle ou Distinction analytique et nosographique de la phobie et de l'hystérie », *RFPsa,* 1927, vol. I.

PARCHEMINEY (G.), « De l'idée de régression dans le problème de la genèse des symptômes névrotiques », *RFPsa,* 1933, vol. VI.

PASCHE (F.), « la Névrose narcissique », *RFPsa,* 1955, vol. XIX ; « Régression, perversion, névrose », *RFPsa,* 1962, vol. XXVI ; « De la dépression », *RFPsa,* 1963, vol. XXVII ; « Genèse et dépression », *RFPsa,* 1976, vol. XL.

PECK (M. W.), « Neurotic illness from the viewpoint of psychanalysis », *Medical Record,* 1939, vol. CXLIX.

PERROTTI (N.), « Aperçus théoriques de la dépersonnalisation », *RFPsa,* 1960, vol. XXIV.

PETO (A.), « The fragmentizing function of the Ego in transference neurosis », *Int. J. of Psa,* 1961, vol. XLII.

RAMZY, « Facteurs et traits de la névrose compulsive dans l'enfance », *RFPsa,* 1967, vol. XXXI.

RANK (O.), « Perversion and neurosis », *Int. J. of Psa,* 1923, vol. IV ; « la Reproduction névrotique », *le Traumatisme de la naissance. Influence de la vie prénatale sur l'évolution de la vie psychique individuelle et collective,* Paris, Payot, 1968.

REBOUL (J.), « Une tache d'encre. Sexualité féminine et névrose obsessionnelle », *la Psychanalyse,* 1864, vol. VII.

REHDER (H.), *Konversion und Reversion klinischer Neurosen,* Cologne, Arzte Verlag, 1953.

REICH (W.), « Phobie infantile et formation du caractère », *l'Analyse caractérielle,* Payot, 1971 ; « Quelques formes caractérielles bien définies », *ibid.* ; « le Caractère masochiste », *ibid.*

REIK (Th.), *Variations psychanalytiques sur un thème de Gustav Mahler,* Payot, 1972.

RENARD (M.), « la Conception freudienne de la névrose narcissique », *RFPsa,* 1955.

RITVO (S.), « Corrélation entre une névrose infantile et une névrose à l'âge adulte », *RFPsa,* 1967, vol. XXXI.

ROSENBERG (E.), « A clinical contribution to the psychopathology of the war neuroses », *Int. J. of Psa,* 1943, vol. XXIV.

ROSENFELD (H. A.), « Note sur le facteur précipitant », *RFPsa,* 1961, vol. XXV ; « le

Besoin d'acting out durant l'analyse chez les patients névrosés et psychotiques »,
Bulletin de l'Association psychanalytique de France, avril 1969, nᵒ 5.

ROUART (J.), « les Névroses : généralités », *Encyclop. Méd. Chirurg.*, 1955, vol. II.

RUDDICK (B.), « Agoraphobia », *Int. J. of Psa*, 1961, vol. XLII.

SAFOUAN (M.), *Études sur l'Œdipe*, Paris, Seuil, 1974, chap. V.

SARLIN (C. N.), « The dissection of a neurotic personality », *Mental hygiene*, 1940, vol. XXIV.

SCHLUMBERGER (M.) et CHASSEGUET-SMIRGEL (J.), « le Rêve et la névrose : le symptôme névrotique et son analogie avec le rêve », *la Théorie psychanalytique.*

SCHULTZ (J. H.), *Grundfragen der Neurosenlehre : Aufbau und Sinn-Bild ; Propädeutik einer medizinischer Psychologie*, Stuttgart, G. Thieme, 1955.

SCHUR (M.), « la Stratification du danger et son influence sur la formation des symptômes », *RFPsa*, 1966, vol. XXX.

SCOTT (W. C.), « Dépression, confusion et polyvalence », *RFPsa*, 1961, vol. XXV.

SOULE (M.), « Une observation d'agoraphobie "pour raisons de famille" », *RFPsa*, 1969, vol. XXXIII.

SPERLING (M.), « les Phobies scolaires », *RFPsa*, 1972, vol. XXXVI.

VICHON (J.), *les Névroses*, Paris, Maloine, 1932.

WINTER (H.), « Facteurs préœdipiens dans la genèse de la névrose hystérique », *RFPsa*, 1966, vol. XXX.

WISDOM (J.), « A methodological approach to the problem of hysteria », *Int. J. of Psa*, 1961, vol. XLII.

ZETZEL (E.), « 1965 : "Notes supplémentaires sur un cas de névrose obsessionnelle" : Freud 1909 », *RFPsa*, 1967, vol. XXXI.

La bibliographie a été réunie par Éliane ZENATTI.

ORIGINE DES ILLUSTRATIONS

La documentation iconographique a été réunie par ANNE VAN EISZNER.

JEAN-LOUP CHARMET : 10, 13, 23, 31, 34, 43, 54, 57, 60, 76, 78, 82, 87, 93, 98, 104, 107, 111, 114, 126, 133, 140, 147, 150, 163, 178, 181, 184, 196, 203, 219, 225, 228, 232, 243, 246, 261, 274, 283, 286, 290.

JEAN GROB : 19, 176.

STUDIO DES GRANDS-AUGUSTINS : 190.

ROGER VIOLLET : 71.

ORIGINE DES TEXTES

Les Éditions TCHOU remercient les Éditeurs qui leur ont permis la reproduction de textes de leur fonds :

PRÉFACE
Professeur Daniel WIDLÖCHER

PREMIÈRE PARTIE
A la découverte des névroses

317

V. *Du traumatisme sexuel au conflit psychique.*
S. FREUD : *Naissance de la psychanalyse* (lettre n° 69 du 21 septembre 1897), p. 190 à 193, Presses universitaires de France, coll. « Bibliothèque de psychanalyse » ; *Cinq leçons sur la psychanalyse* (« Contribution à l'histoire du mouvement psychanalytique », 1914), p. 83-84, Payot, coll. « Petite Bibliothèque Payot » ; *Ma vie et la psychanalyse* (1924-1925), p. 43-44, Gallimard, coll. « Idées ».

VI. *Qu'est-ce qu'un symptôme ?*
S. FREUD : *Névrose, psychose et perversion* (« Obsessions et phobies », 1895), p. 40-45, Presses universitaires de France, coll. « Bibliothèque de psychanalyse » ; *Introduction à la psychanalyse* (1915-1917), p. 230-236, 243-251, 277-282, 337-340, 341-347, Payot, coll. « Petite Bibliothèque Payot ».

VII. *Refoulement et défenses dans différentes névroses.*
S. FREUD : *Cinq psychanalyses* (« Analyse d'une phobie d'un petit garçon de cinq ans [le petit Hans] », 1909), p. 108-109 ; « Remarques sur un cas de névrose obsessionnelle [l'Homme aux Rats] », 1909, p. 223-228 ; « Extrait de l'histoire d'une névrose infantile [l'Homme aux Loups] », 1914-1918, p. 410-411), Presses universitaires de France, coll. « Bibliothèque de psychanalyse ».

DEUXIÈME PARTIE
Les névroses et leur classification

I. *Dora ou le destin d'une hystérique.*
F. DEUTSCH : « Apostille au "Fragment de l'analyse d'un cas d'hystérie" de Freud » (1957), *Revue Française de psychanalyse*, t. XXXVII, mai 1973, p. 404-414. Avec l'aimable autorisation d'Hélène Deutsch, des directeurs de la revue et de ses diffuseurs, les Presses universitaire de France.

II. *Les Phobies à travers l'agoraphobie.*
H. DEUTSCH : *la Psychanalyse des névroses* (« Agoraphobie »), 1928, p. 89-99 et 101 à 104, Payot, coll. « Science de l'Homme ».

III. *La Névrose obsessionnelle.*
O. FENICHEL : *la Théorie psychanalytique des névroses* (« Obsessions et compulsions »), p. 329-339, 346-367, 370-375, Presses universitaires de France, coll. « Bibliothèque de psychanalyse ».

IV. *D'où vient la névrose ?*
M. KLEIN : *la Psychanalyse des enfants* (« les Rapports entre la névrose obsessionnelle et les premiers stades de la formation du Surmoi », 1932), p. 163-190, Presses universitaires de France, coll. « Bibliothèque de psychanalyse ».